ALSO BY ELIZABETH ABBOTT

Haiti: The Duvaliers and Their Legacy

A
History
of Celibacy

Elizabeth Abbott

DA CAPO PRESS

Excerpts from *The Body and Society* by Peter Brown, © 1988 Columbia University Press, are reprinted with the permission of the publisher.
Excerpts from *Church Fathers, Independent Virgins* by Joyce E. Salisbury, Verso London 1991, are reprinted with the permission of the publisher.
Excerpts from Ovid, "Amores," in Diane J. Raynor and William W. Batshaw (Eds.), *Latin Lyric and Elegiac Poetry: An Anthology of New Translations*, Garland Publishing 1995, are reprinted with the permission of the publisher.
Excerpts from *Untold Sisters: Hispanic Nuns in their Own Works*, Electa Arenal and Stacey Schau (Eds.) (translated by Amanda Powell), University of New Mexico Press 1989, are reprinted by permission of Electa Arenal.
Excerpts from *Three Plays by Aristophanes*, translated by Jeffrey Henderson, Routledge 1996, are reprinted with the permission of Taylor & Francis/Routledge, Inc.

Designed by Erich Hobbing
Set in Adobe Garamond

Cataloging-in-Publication data for this book is available from the Library of Congress.

ISBN 0–306–81041–7

First Da Capo Press edition 2001
Reprinted by arrangement with Scribner, an imprint of Simon & Schuster.
Originally published in Canada by HarperCollins Publishers, Ltd.

Published by Da Capo Press
A Member of the Perseus Books Group
http://www.dacapopress.com

Da Capo Press books are available at special discounts for bulk purchases in the U.S. by corporations, institutions, and other organizations. For more information, please contact the Special Markets Department at the Perseus Books Group, 11 Cambridge Center, Cambridge, MA 02142, or call (617) 252-5298.

1 2 3 4 5 6 7 8 9 10——04 03 02 01

To Yves Pierre-Louis
For his gift of precious friendship
Through the best of times and the worst of times

CONTENTS

Contents

Contents

Contents

Contents

Contents

AUTHOR'S NOTE

Two technical matters, my footnote and bibliographical systems, should be explained. To clarify, and to avoid the forest of footnotes that cluttered earlier drafts, I have provided footnotes that include all the main sources for each section. Afterward, only direct quotations or concepts are referenced.

Because of the vast range of topics covered in this book, I eliminated a general bibliography and instead included bibliographical references in the footnotes. This makes it much easier to locate source material by subject.

Considering Celibacy

Two incidents inspired me to launch a wide-ranging exploration of celibacy. The first, and most significant, was the 1990 revelation, trumpeted in the international media, that a number of the avowedly celibate Christian Brothers of Mount Cashel Orphanage in Newfoundland were actually practicing pedophiles who preyed, with hands, tongues, penises, straps, and chains, on the foundlings entrusted to their care. The second was a friend's whispered confidence that a certain husband of our acquaintance tolerated his wife's infidelity because he was chaste, startling news that was my introduction to the New Celibacy.

I began my research assuming I knew what celibacy was: abstinence from sexual intercourse, usually self-proclaimed. I also thought that, as a long-term commitment, it was unnatural. In fact, my initial working title was "Celebrating the Unnatural: The Story of Celibacy," and among my friends, it was nicknamed "The Dry Season."

This tittering stage of the project was short-lived. Soon into the research that would ultimately consume me for over six years, I was struck by the narrowness of my Christianity-oriented perspective and my simplistic definition. Throughout the world and the ages, celibacy has been a key element of human existence. In all its various forms, it has shaped religious lives, as well as the lives of laity, and its embrace has included the very young and the very old. It has haunted widows and prisoners, and conditioned athletes and shamans. It has pulsated throughout classical poetry and camp literature, throughout canon and civil law.

Everywhere I looked, celibacy loomed. It resonated in the mellifluous sopranos of Italy's operatic castrati, in the agonized shrieks of little girls kept housebound and pure by foot-binding, and of little boys made more useful by castration. It wafted up from dingy harems and from sun-kissed Incan temples. It permeated ancient history, from the celibate shift workers of the Oracle of Delphi and the virginal trio of Athena, Artemis, and Hestia, the

Greek world's greatest goddesses, to Rome's majestic vestal virgins. It echoed in Hamlet's ringing "Get thee to a nunnery!" urging Ophelia to accept the fate of so many other unwanted, unwillingly cloistered women.

Celibacy paraded through history under a legion of names. It was Joan of Arc, Elizabeth I of England, Florence Nightingale. It was Mahatma Gandhi and his curious brahmacharya experiments, the naked nights he spent with nubile young women, testing his chastity. It was the ranting disharmony of *The Kreutzer Sonata,* as Leo Tolstoy pounded out his message of celibacy. It was Leonardo da Vinci, fearful of a second accusation of sexual impropriety, Sir Isaac Newton mourning his lover's defection, Lewis Carroll looking but not daring to touch a procession of young Alices in Wonderland.

Celibacy is also writ large in the world's medical literature, monopolizing large sections of textbooks and the wisdom of most cultures. Therein are elaborated a wealth of semen-centered perspectives and philosophies, and detailed instructions about regimens that help conserve the precious, protein-rich ejaculate.

Celibacy abounds as well in symbols. Most typical Western kitchens harbor the shades of the intense, celibate social movement that sought to encourage semen-focused celibacy and quench the embers of sensuality: which one of us hasn't at one time enjoyed cornflakes and Graham flour, designed by the chaste John Harvey Kellogg and Sylvester Graham to cool ardor and promote bland healthfulness? Who does not use clothespins, brooms, or buzz saws, the inventive sublimations of chaste Shakers? Who has not given the greeting "Peace," another venerable relic of committed, Father Divine–inspired chastity?

On today's school grounds and campuses, celibacy also marches under the banners of students pledged to the proposition that True Love Waits. Celibacy announces itself among the graying population of self-proclaimed reborn virgins. It peeps out through the gaunt boniness of anorexic women dedicated to mastering their bodies, and in the chaste handshakes of gay men who have forsworn the deadly risks of AIDS-haunted sex.

Celibacy, I quickly understood, was a staggering panorama of reality, involving humanity everywhere and always. As I expanded the parameters of my research, I altered and refined my working definition, scrapped the title and underlying hypothesis that assumed celibacy was unnatural, and began to listen closely to what my data could tell me.

My second, tongue-in-cheek working title, "The Kama Sutra of Celibacy," hit closer to the mark, but was too ambitious: the more I read, the more I realized my lifetime would be too short to produce a survey of celibacy as comprehensive as the collected wisdom of the Kama Sutra is about sexual expression. A much more feasible goal was to identify, interpret, and describe as many experiments in celibacy as I could. This notion eventually shaped this book.

I also drafted a definition of celibacy that discarded the rigidly pedantic and unhelpful distinctions between celibacy, chastity, and virginity, all of which I used as key words in my research. Despite dry, dictionary distinctions, they are, in the context of this book, synonymous. Risking tedium, I cite Webster's dictionary. Chastity as it relates to sexuality is "abstention from unlawful sexual activity: said especially of women. Sexual continence; celibacy or virginity." Celibacy is "the state of being unmarried, especially that of a person under a vow." Virginity, the most unambiguous, is "the state of maidenhood, chastity, spinsterhood."

Of course, chastity once described faithful marriage partners as well as virgins, but that concept has receded into historical usage. I follow today's common usage, in which the words *chastity* and *celibacy* are interchangeable, and virginity is as Webster defines it. Celibacy or chastity is abstaining from sexual relations, intentionally or under duress, temporarily or for indefinite periods. This definition is both simple and generous in scope, and descriptive rather than analytical. It is also the most useful and moral tool I could devise to explore the fascinating, inspiring, troubling, complex, and sometimes bizarre lifestyles of celibate men and women the world over, throughout recorded history.

As my research accumulated, major themes and truths began to emerge. I began to perceive patterns in humankind's celibacy experiments. Slowly, tentatively, I devised categories into which, eventually, my material obligingly and comfortably fell. Not unexpectedly, sex-negative, celibacy-obsessed Christianity dominates the first part of *A History of Celibacy*, though its pagan and Jewish Essene antecedents marked important passages along the celibate path, and other religions, notably Hinduism, have devised unique experiments based on their own very different understandings of celibacy.

But celibacy is at Christianity's core, the story of a divine infant miraculously born to a human, virgin mother. The issues that consumed the religion's earliest converts and proselytizers were the nature, process, and meaning of his birth. Mary became a controversial and much debated figure. The Christian fixation on celibacy, from its condemnatory preoccupation with lustful Eve to its ideological sterilization of chaste Mary and, in the Catholic Church, its rejection of married priests, has endured for twenty centuries, embraced hundreds and millions of people, and imbued Western civilization with its ideals and ideology.

Through the lens of Christian celibacy, I saw women seize on this new doctrine as a tool to emancipate themselves from the drudgery of marriage and childbearing. Determinedly celibate, they transformed themselves into independent people who traveled extensively, studied at a time when education was a male preserve, wrote, preached, and directed their own lives, frequently in the chaste company of like-spirited women or men.

The first of these, the feisty and courageous Desert Mothers, were contemporary with St. Paul. The chaste zealot Thecla braved hostile crowds, a burning stake, lions, bears, bulls, and an infuriated husband rather than submit again to intercourse. Later, medieval Beguines dedicated to apostolic life, but impatient with the constraints and control of convents, lived with their parents or in Beguine communities. Every day they left these havens to mingle with the poor they had pledged themselves to serve, protected from the dangers of mainstream society only by their sworn celibacy. Other enterprising religious, cloistered and uncloistered, embraced celibacy as part of their strategy to achieve sainthood. St. Catherine of Siena and her namesake, Kateri Tekakwitha, the first Iroquois saint, were among the more spectacular. Ambitious, well-born abbesses controlled convents and created near-independent fiefdoms, havens of scholarship and learning. A married laywoman, the scatterbrained but driven Margery Kempe, struggled with sexuality until she achieved chastity in her marriage, essential to her quest for posthumous beatification.

Male religious, on the other hand, perceived the celibacy demanded of them as a continual battle against relentless lust, temptation, and the unbidden indignity of nocturnal emissions. The earnestly self-absorbed St. Augustine's heartfelt prayer, "Give me chastity, but do not give it yet," encapsulates their dilemma. Chastity brought them far fewer rewards than it did women, because as men, they were already socially empowered. As a painful consequence, they experienced celibacy more as a hunger to be starved, flagellated, or beaten into submission.

Two of the most successful uncloistered celibate experiments were North American and working class: Mother Ann Lee's Shakers in the eighteenth and nineteenth centuries, followed by Father Divine's Peace movement in the nineteenth and twentieth centuries. Both adopted celibacy as the cornerstone of their religious communities, and their strict adherence to it enabled each of them to slice through the boundaries that so limited women and black people and kept white and black neatly segregated. Shakerism instituted egalitarian structures and accepted female leadership, black as well as white. Father Divine, the black son of freed slaves, presided over men and women, white and black, and even married a white Canadian who remained as virginal as he was. Mother Ann's and Father Divine's shared vision and their successful experiments in chaste communities proved the power of celibacy over some of the most entrenched norms of their societies. Most notably, it defused racial tensions over sex, an enormous achievement.

Apart from its universal religious dimensions, another recurring theme in celibacy is the power of semen. The urgency of conserving this vital fluid or "life force" has led thinkers as disparate as Greek doctors, Hindu sages, athletics coaches, and moral reformers to proselytize for the celibate ideal with its promise that vigor, energy, and intellectuality will be retained along with the precious hoard of semen. French writer Honoré de Balzac put it most succinctly when he groaned in postcoital *tristesse,* "There goes another novel!"

Celibacy is also a pervasive theme in attaining a state conducive to communicating with spirits—shamans and vodoun priests and priestesses must practice short-term abstinence during their apprenticeship and as a tool of their trade. This celibacy heightens their awareness and sensitivity and conciliates the gods jealous of devotees' relationships with others, mortal or divine.

The more crucial mission of the vestal virgins, guarding Rome's sacred fire, the nation's symbolic core, demanded that these women commit to at least thirty years of virginity and perform the duties with undivided loyalty, devotion, and attention. The Incas, who had a similar system, required perpetual virginity of their *acllas,* the priestesses who tended the sun god and who, because they were usually chosen from among conquered peoples, were essential players in the imperial policy of postconquest reconciliation.

Celibacy took another form altogether when it was used by nonreligious (but not necessarily unreligious) women to defy the "natural" order their world decreed for them—subservience, servility, and submission. Joan of Arc and a Crow Indian, Woman Chief, traded womanly ways, including sex, for lives as warrior chiefs. Nineteenth-century British women glorified spinsterhood, lived in independent solitude, and forged careers: Florence Nightingale, resisting relentless family pressure, spurned suitors and marriage for virginity and a mission to transform the shameful and lowly occupation of nursing into one of the world's noblest professions. In Albania and India, rural women (who might in today's Western society be labeled transsexuals) swore perpetual celibacy, donned men's clothes and lifestyles, and became farmers. Elizabeth I of England preserved her chastity through a lifetime of passion and flirtation and, despite councillors constantly pressing her to marry for the sake of the nation, established herself as one of England's most outstanding monarchs.

Celibacy has other benign, though less dramatic, forms. It is used to prevent conception and to encourage fertility for subsequent pregnancies in lactating women. In some societies, aging women publicly adopt it, signaling an end to their ability or willingness to endure the burdens of more childbearing.

However, celibacy is not always so uplifting. Most notably, the great value most societies place on bridal virginity gives this dimension of celibacy a decidedly ugly side. Girls' tiny feet are no longer bound, and chastity belts are rusty museum curiosities, but female genital mutilation (FGM) and Middle Eastern "honor killings," the most flagrant examples, paint an ongoing scenario of bloody despair. Even now, six thousand little girls a day fall victim to FGM, and honor killings continue to snuff out young lives, all in the name of sexual purity.

Of course, this ferociously monitored premarital virginity is almost exclusively a bridal trademark. Most men, except Aztec and Enga bachelors, need not be virgin bridegrooms. This inequality stems from the double standard, the very different rules that govern sexuality in men and in women. This double standard is so deeply entrenched and widespread that, for centuries, it has encouraged and justified the existence of large-scale prostitution—in the name of celibacy. St. Augustine, always able to identify with libertine males, summarized the argument this way: "Remove prostitutes from human affairs, and you would pollute the world with lust." He and other influential moralists, religious and civil, have defended harlotry as an essential outlet for the randy males it diverts from seducing the more suitable virgins they will later marry and with whom they will procreate. The classic proof of this double standard was the late-nineteenth-century crusading journalist William Stead's purchase of an adolescent virgin he later sold to a brothel, just to prove how easily it could be done.

Often celibacy is imposed on unwilling subjects, both male and female: prisoners; nineteenth-century schoolteachers in Russia and Canada; millions of Chinese herded into work camps in the most repressive days of Maoist China; unloved Arab wives doomed to crowded marriages with husbands who love and bed newer favorites; millions of Chinese bachelors condemned to celibate existences because the nation's "one child per family" policy provoked mass destruction of unvalued female fetuses and infants and created today's massive gender imbalance.

Throughout history, celibacy was imposed on certain males even more brutally by surgery: castration, or excision of male genitals. Eunuchs were created for various purposes. They often served in harems, where the frustrated women could not be supervised by genitally intact men. In the Byzantine and Ottoman empires, they also filled top administrative and military posts, controlling millions of dollars and the destinies of entire peoples. A prime qualification for such plum jobs was the inability to procreate; unlike uncastrated men, who had families of their own, eunuchs could be trusted not to intrigue on behalf of the sons they would never have.

As opera mania swept Europe in the eighteenth century, the mutilating knife found different victims: young boys it transformed into the most mellifluous sopranos who have ever graced the operatic stage. The price these beardless, rotund, and ever resentful and angry castrati consequently paid was permanent sexual inadequacy, but in the frenzied search for musical perfection, that counted for naught. Elsewhere, in India and Pakistan, men still voluntarily go under the knife to become *hijras*, entertainers who traditionally take vows of chastity, describe themselves as neither men nor women, and live together in celibate communities.

Women, too, have been victims of drastic forms of celibacy. The most egregious was the hungry and hopeless life forced on Hindu widows, even tiny girls married as toddlers to husbands they never lived with. The sole alternative to this hellish existence was an early and fiery death, often involuntary, as sons and other male relatives pushed the widow onto her husband's funeral pyre.

Celibacy also has much softer variations, for instance when it is practiced by people uneasy about expressing their unconventional sexuality—gay men such as Leonardo da Vinci, pedophiles such as Lewis Carroll, eccentrics such as John Ruskin, and brokenhearted lovers such as Sir Isaac Newton. Celibacy can be a healing tool for victims of sexual abuse and rape, allowing them time and space to confront the issues that sexuality evokes for them. Today, in the time of AIDS, some people adopt celibacy as a tool of physical survival, just as it was, for example, in Europe's syphilis-riddled sixteenth century. When sex suddenly presents itself as a death's head, celibacy can seem like a guardian angel.

Physical conditions causing impotence also produce unwilling celibates. The extensive lead in Rome's vaunted aqueducts, so progressive as technology and so destructive to male sexual powers, drove even the great Ovid (among other poets) into wry lyricism about his despair at a penis that was "as limp as yesterday's lettuce." Anorexia, which mostly afflicts females, has precisely the same effect—it saps the strength from emaciated bodies so sexual energy drains away. But unlike Ovid, Karen Carpenter and her gaunt comrades are no distraught observers of their failed sexuality. Their breasts and bottoms are not all that have disappeared—so, too, has all sexual desire.

Celibacy's ubiquitous presence in human life is reflected in literature, and not just the Roman "impotence genre." Milton, Tolstoy, and Virginia Woolf all wrote about it. So did John Irving, whose Garp's mother had only one (albeit fruitful) lapse from celibacy. Even vampires, whose love is bloodred, are chaste.

Over the centuries, experiments in celibacy have lost none of their fascination. In addition to our ever-younger sexually active children are increasingly proud and vocal Power Virgins, card-carrying members of True Love Waits and other pro-chastity youth movements. As part of my research, I sent away for their introductory package. It included a stylishly decorated T-shirt I sometimes wear bicycling, wondering if any passersby have noticed its unusual message.

In fact, interest in celibacy is not confined to the junior generation. Even in middle or old age, men and women are increasingly turning to celibacy as a means of achieving personal autonomy, spirituality, and connections with God, nature, and each other. Some declare themselves reborn virgins, an apparent oxymoron solemnly sanctioned two millennia ago by Christian theologians responding to contemporary pleas that the Church recognize and dignify such a status. Other people praise the richness celibacy has given their relationships, including marriages. Like chaste husbands and wives in the first centuries of Christianity, like St. Francis of Assisi and his beloved companion, St. Clare, these men and women find peace and fulfillment in nonsexual commitment that thrives free of possessiveness or jealousy.

At the heart of this movement toward celibacy is the ideal of choice without stigma, and each individual's right to empower and enrich his own life. The new celibacy assumes new attitudes and new ways of perceiving and judging, so that gays and lesbians are gaining mainstream recognition, men and women can cohabit chastely, and married coupledom is no longer heralded as the only acceptable form of life.

Years into researching and drafting this history of celibacy, I myself espoused celibacy—this despite decades as an avowed anticelibate who used to quip (and sometimes believe) I had invented sex. It happened that, several years after clawing myself out from under the debris of a collapsed marriage and assuming a new life in an unfamiliar city, I was not involved in a sexual relationship. But after vicariously experiencing—*celebrating* is a better word—the sense of liberation so many other women have derived from voluntary celibacy, I embraced it as a conscious choice. From then on, I have no longer seen myself as merely uninvolved with a man. After reevaluating my life and its priorities, including the need for deep emotional connections, I have chosen a way of life that, to a satisfying degree, incorporates my personal principles at its wellspring.

I was profoundly impressed and influenced by some of those people whose experiments in celibacy figure in this history, the courageous women who braved the harsh and desolate desert to devote their lives to God, the proud, purposeful, and powerful vestal virgins, the maverick Native American warrior Woman Chief, and the rebellious Florence Nightingale, though their lifestyles and problems were remote from mine. More particularly, I was intensely moved by accounts of women and men driven by individual missions—art, literature, science—who opted for celibacy to forestall relationships that would consume the time and energy they longed to direct to their work. Much as I once reveled in sexual indulgence, I realized that at this stage of my life, I value even more the independence and serenity chaste solitude brings me. I welcome my freedom from the jealousy and possessiveness that characterized the most passionate of my relationships, and I am immensely and perpetually relieved that someone else's domestic demands no longer dominate my daily agenda.

I also cherish the unexpected outpouring of confidences that mention of this history of celibacy has elicited, from friends and acquaintances who had never before disclosed details of their intimate lives. Even never-met Internet and phone-only pals have responded spontaneously to even the briefest mention of my current undertaking, amazing me with the frankness and the humor that color the stories of their own, almost always deliberate, celibacy. The bonds formed between us are an unforeseen reward of my own public venture into chastity. Their revelations, sparked by my own, are part of the final chapter in this history of celibacy.

CHAPTER 1

Divine Pagan Celibacy

In ancient Greece, premarital chastity was such an essential requirement in brides that young women were thrust into marriage just after puberty to eliminate any possibility of a sexual lapse. But among the pantheon of deities, three intense, powerful, and ambitious goddesses maintained lifelong vigilance over their virginity. Hestia personified modesty and domesticity. Athena and Artemis, however, parlayed celibacy into independent lifestyles otherwise permitted only to men. For them, celibacy was a mighty instrument that liberated them from traditional roles. It was, indeed, their only means of escape from the drudgery and subordination to husband, father, or brothers that awaited all other Greek females. (In the Roman pantheon, Hestia, Athena, and Artemis were worshiped as Vesta, Minerva, and Diana.)

GREEK MYTHS

ATHENA, ARTEMIS, AND HESTIA

Eons after they stormed and stalked, loved and hated, avenged and persecuted each other and the mortals who revered, feared, respected, and honored them, the Olympian deities of ancient Greece are still towering presences. They insinuate themselves into our literature and dominate our metaphors. They are reference points for philosophy, mathematics, medicine, and religion. For the early Christians, who shared the heritage of the Greco-Roman world, the pantheon of gods and goddesses was blasphemous heresy and fundamental error, all the more dangerous for being the intellectual and cultural framework they were struggling to reform and defy.

The pantheon had a dozen major players, divided equally between gods and goddesses. None of the gods was in the least bit chaste: Zeus (Jupiter), the leader; Apollo, the sun god, and also the god of beauty, youth, poetry, music, prophecy, and archery; Ares (Mars), the god of war; Hermes (Mercury), the messenger and thief; Poseidon (Neptune), the god of the sea; and Hephaestus (Vulcan), god of metal crafts. All were hot-blooded males who ranged the earth and sky seducing, raping, and impregnating. Celestial celibacy, like its earthly counterpart, was left to goddesses.

The three chief goddesses—Athena (Minerva), goddess of war, wisdom, and crafts; Artemis (Diana), goddess of hunting and animals; and Hestia (Vesta), goddess of the hearth—were all dedicated virgins and alone had the power to withstand Aphrodite (Venus), the goddess of love and sexual desire. A fourth goddess, Hera (Juno), Zeus' wife and patroness of marriage, was a semivirgin, a chaste wife who annually renewed her virginity by bathing in the cleansing waters of a spring called Canathus.

Zeus' first wife was the wise Metis. When she became pregnant, other deities beguiled Zeus with doomsaying to the effect that if Metis lived, she might produce a son so mighty he would supplant his father as king of both gods and men. Zeus was taken in by these scaremongers and decided to eradicate Metis by swallowing her whole, right down into his belly. Soon he was tormented with a headache so agonizing that a sympathetic god, either Hephaestus, Prometheus, or Hermes, took an ax and split open his head to relieve the pain. Out of Zeus' forehead sprang the goddess Athena, fully formed.

And what a goddess! Athena had a remote, standoffish kind of beauty, piercing eyes, and a no-nonsense costume: a golden helmet, enormous spear, and fluttering shield. Her role as a maiden warrior expert in strategy and discipline constantly compelled her to intervene in the war between the Greeks and the Trojans. She rode or strode onto battlefields and with warlike shrieks and hand-to-hand combat rallied Greek soldiers and petrified Trojans. Athena was a deadly fighter, and her temple, the pure, cold, white-marble edifice known, as Athena herself was, as the Parthenon or Virgin, dominated Athens.

Like all Greek deities, Athena was far from perfect. Once, jousting with her friend Pallas, she and the other woman quarreled. As Pallas raised her arm to slug Athena, the goddess rashly charged and killed her assailant, then bitterly repented her hastiness. In another instance of moral imperfection, she was so ragingly jealous of Arachne's exquisite tapestry that she smashed up her face with the boxwood shuttle of the loom, provoking Arachne to hang herself. Athena revived her, but as a spider, endlessly spinning its trailing web.

Athena had a range of skills that make her difficult to classify, other than as a Renaissance woman. She was revered for her wisdom in political and domestic matters. She could break horses and was a skilled trainer. She was knowledgeable about ships and chariots and invented the flute. (She tossed it out, however, when she realized that playing it distorted her lovely features.) She was also the patroness of all arts and crafts.

Athena's virginity, so integral to her existence, was inviolable. She might be vain, jealous, petty, and vindictive, but never for a second could she permit the breach of her personal fortress.

> No mother gave me birth.
> I honor the male, in all things but marriage.
> Yes, with all my heart I am my Father's child,

exclaims Athena, the "Child sprung full-blown from Olympian Zeus, / never bred in the darkness of the womb." When her brother Hephaestus sexually assaulted her as she stood in his forge, ordering new weapons, she furiously repelled him and he ejaculated onto her thigh. Athena scraped the loathsome semen onto the ground near Athens, fertilized Mother Earth, and a child, Erichthonius, was born. Suddenly the bellicose goddess softened and agreed to raise the child herself. She was an implacable soldier who would defend her virginity with her life, but in response to a mewling infant, she who was motherless became the epitome of motherliness.

Athena was also extremely conscious that her nakedness made her sexually vulnerable. Her gleaming body was the last image the prophet Teiresias ever saw, for after he inadvertently came across her as she bathed outdoors in a spring, she blinded him. (Later, she compensated for this by granting him the gift of prophecy or inward sight.)

These incidents, and others when she repulsed all those who longed to marry her, had everything to do with the value she placed on chastity and did not mean she disliked men. To the contrary, she preferred them to women and assisted several heroes. She also maintained peaceful and affectionate relations with her father, Zeus.

Athena led a wondrously adventurous life. She was fearless, brave, and cunning as a warrior; subtle, wise, and witty as a counselor; ambitious, temperamental, and impetuous with rivals, especially women. She denied her sexuality like the soldier she was, with physical violence, but melted into tenderness at the sight of a baby. Above all else, she charted her own course.

Artemis, daughter of Zeus and Leto, had much in common with her half-sister Athena, including the virginity she had longed for since she was a toddler. As she sat cradled on her father Zeus' knee, a surge of affection infused him, and on the spur of the moment he asked her to tell him what gifts he should give her.

"Give me to keep my maidenhood, Father, forever," Artemis replied instantly.

> And give me arrows and a bow . . . and . . . a tunic with
> embroidered border reaching to the knee, that I may

slay wild beasts. And give me sixty daughters of
Oceanus for my choir—all nine years old, all maidens
yet ungirdled; and give me for handmaidens twenty
nymphs of Amnisus who shall tend well my buskins, and,
when I shoot no more at lynx or stag, shall tend my
swift hounds. And give to me all mountains . . . for
seldom is it that Artemis goes down to the town.

Almost as an ironic afterthought, she added that women in labor would
constantly call upon her, because her mother's feat in delivering her painlessly
had prompted the Fates to designate her patroness of childbirth.

Artemis' articulate and ready list of desires was not the whimsy of your
average three-year-old. From the beginning she was as independent and self-
directed as Athena. The life she had mapped out for herself was aggressively
virginal. The first clue was in her demand for scores of innocent girls as companions. Unlike Athena, Artemis was a watchful and wary virgin, and she
demanded celibacy from her followers. She also inspired it—the Amazons,
for instance, who both worshiped and resembled her, were archers and disdained men's company.

Artemis was ruthless to men unable to adapt to her rigid rules. The best
example of this is her destruction of Orion for an attempted rape. (Her treatment of the tragic Hippolytus, son of the Amazon Hippolyte, was immortalized in Euripides' tragedy *Hippolytus,* described below.) When the giant Tityus
tried to rape her mother, she and Apollo, her brother, conspired to murder him.

Nor did Artemis extend compassion to women. When her favorite
maiden, Callisto, began to swell in pregnancy after Zeus seduced her, Artemis
cruelly transformed her into a bear and set her pack of hounds on it. Only
Zeus' intervention—plucking Callisto up into the heavens—foiled Artemis'
plans for the maiden's bloody death.

Artemis' relations with women focused primarily on their life cycles of menstruation, loss of virginity, childbirth, and death. All involve pain and bleeding,
the price Artemis forces women to pay if they abandon her world of virginity.
As patroness of childbirth she exacted even more, the great pain of labor.

Artemis' other major occupation was to roam the forests and mountains
with wild beasts, shunning the company of men. However, when hunters
arrived, she sided with them against the animals. Her beauty, elusiveness, and
mystery drove the river god, Alpheius, to fall in love with her and track her
throughout Greece. Finally Artemis forced him to abandon his hopeless quest;
she and all her nymphs plastered white mud on their faces so Alpheius could
not distinguish among them and retreated to the sound of mocking laughter.

A much worse fate befell a young man named Actaeon, who was propped against a rock when he noticed Artemis bathing in a nearby stream. Had he fled before she noticed him, he might have lived. As it was, she was so infuriated that he might brag about the sight of her nakedness that she transformed him into a stag. His own hounds instantly tore him apart and devoured him.

Unlike the gregarious Athena, Artemis preferred a more solitary existence, though she was always accompanied by her troop of nymphs. She had antagonistic relationships with young women as well as men, prompting her stepmother Hera to jeer, "Zeus has made you a lion / among women, and given you leave to kill any at your pleasure." She forced Agamemnon to sacrifice his firstborn, Iphigenia, in return for favorable winds for his naval expedition against Troy. With Apollo, her twin, she killed all twelve children of the mortal Niobe, who had boasted she had more children than Artemis' mother, the goddess Leto.

Artemis' strident chastity, her manly occupation of hunting, her raging pride, and the brutality of her vengeance stamped her as independent and as strong-willed as Athena. She was seen as an implacable deity who, since childhood, had shrugged off womanly pursuits and frailties. Her virginity was as virulent as her wrath and recast Zeus' little girl into a towering divinity devoid of most feminine qualities.

The only chaste goddess who is a paragon of Greek womanly values is Zeus' sister Hestia. Like good Greek women, Hestia stayed at home, keeping the fires burning on Mount Olympus. Her life was routine and unexciting—no wars, conflicts, or adventures—but she was worshiped daily throughout Greece as the deity in charge of the heartland of Greek life, the family hearth.

Hestia's only deviance from dull predictability was her rejection of suitors such as Poseidon and Apollo. Homer tells her story lovingly:

> She was completely unwilling to marry, and stubbornly refused. Touching the head of aegis-bearing Zeus, she, that shining goddess, swore a great oath which truly has been fulfilled that she would be a virgin forever. Zeus gave her a high honor instead of marriage, and she holds a place in the middle of the house and the richest share. In all the temples of the gods she has a portion of honor, and among mortals she holds first place among the goddesses.

Ironically, Hestia became the goddess of family life and values by forswearing the very process by which families are created.

Athena, Artemis, and Hestia were an immensely powerful trio whose virginity permitted them a latitude unthinkable in the unchaste. Athena and Artemis ventured into the male preserves of war and hunting, and with their great physical strength reinforced by weaponry, skill, determination, and courage, they dominated their worlds. Athena oversaw the cities, Artemis the countryside, and Hestia ubiquitous home life.

The parallels and distinctions between the goddesses and real Greek women are obvious. Virginity was essential in a bride though not in her groom, but lifelong celibacy was seldom perceived as a good thing. Hestia's bachelorhood is the most intriguing, and probably Greeks understood it as being not in defiance of women's traditional role but necessary to preserve the stability of their world and the gods'. Married women always transferred to their husband's hearth, so the only way Hestia could remain at home in Mount Olympus was to renounce marriage.

Athena and Artemis paid the price of their sexuality, so enjoyed by their male counterparts, for the enormous privilege of leading manlike lives. They had to forgo marriage and motherhood, the only acceptable lot of human women, and they also determinedly resisted rape, the common fate of the women the male gods fancied.

To real women, the goddesses' freedom from sexual passion and, above all, from the men inspiring it made them trustworthy, fitting creatures to marvel at and worship. Celibacy for real women brought no rewards except drudgery and the snide comments of the brothers or fathers obliged to feed them. If, however, they had any illusions about emulating Athena or Artemis, Socrates' advice on the subject of how to treat unmarried women would have set them straight: set them to work like slaves, the wise man declared. The hopelessness of their own condition must have painted the magnificent independence of the goddesses' freewheeling lives yet more indelibly. For real Greek women, the lesson that virginity equals independence remained an affair of the gods.

MYTHICAL VIRGINS

Greek mythology also displayed a fascination with virgins, sometimes associated with deities, sometimes only with other mortals. These included virgin huntresses, fleeing virgins transformed, raped virgins, prophetesses and priestesses, sacrificial virgins, and even three of that most unusual commodity, male virgins. Most of these stories dealt with the trials of maintaining chastity against the devious intrigues of libidinous gods who devoted themselves to seducing virgins and bedding unwilling beauties.

Atalanta's is the most spectacular story. Abandoned at birth by her father, she was saved and suckled by a bear, then raised by hunters. Not surprisingly, Atalanta was the quintessential tomboy. She was a huntress, an excellent markswoman, and an athlete who routinely triumphed over male competitors, even in wrestling. She was also a beautiful virgin as determinedly chaste as Artemis and once even shot to death two centaurs who tried to rape her.

Atalanta's fame spread until it reached her father, who despite having abandoned her, exercised his paternal right to order her to marry. Atalanta had no choice but to agree, but on the stipulation that suitors had to compete with her in a footrace. She would marry the first man to beat her and kill all losers. So lovely was she that many young men risked and, of course, lost their lives sprinting against her, though they ran naked and she was hampered by her clothes and sometimes weapons.

One cunning young man connived with Aphrodite to outwit Atalanta because he could not outrun her. As they sped along, he threw down Aphrodite's gift—three golden apples—and Atalanta slowed down to retrieve them, giving him the edge he needed to win. That was the end of Atalanta the virgin, who was forthwith married and deflowered. But so amorous was the newlywed groom that he made love to Atalanta in a temple, thereby defiling Aphrodite. Aphrodite was ragingly angry and transformed the young couple into lions.

Daphne, also a huntress, managed to preserve her virginity, though at enormous cost. Daphne, wearing a headband to control her mane of hair, loved hunting deep in the forest. When her father asked her to marry and give him grandchildren, she implored him, "Allow me, dearest Father, always to be a virgin."

Nonetheless, a king's son fell in love with her and disguised himself as a woman to insinuate himself into her company. But Apollo, who was also attracted to Daphne, was jealous, and he put the notion of bathing into the huntresses' minds. The young man refused to doff his clothes so the women stripped him, and when Daphne saw his genitals, she killed him.

The other Daphne myth has Apollo and Eros vying for her attention. In revenge for an unkind remark, Eros shot both Apollo and Daphne with arrows that rendered Daphne impervious to any lover but caused Apollo to burn with desire for her. "Yet consider who loves you," Apollo urged her. "I am not a mountain peasant; I am not an uncouth shepherd who watches here his flocks and herds." Unmoved, Daphne fled his relentless stalking, her clothes clinging to her body and her hair streaming behind her. Apollo pounded along, his breath panting on her neck.

"Help me, Father," she cried to the river god. "Change me and destroy my beauty, which has proved too attractive!" Instantly her wish was granted. Her limbs hardened and bark covered her breasts, her hair turned into leaves, and her lovely face became the top of the laurel tree. She had lost her humanity, but her virginity was forever intact.

Nemesis' flight from her admirer Zeus contains multiple metamorphoses— she jumped into the water and became a fish, he followed as a beaver; she vaulted onto the shore as a beast, he became a faster one; she soared into the sky as a wild goose, he mounted her as a swan. Her virginity was gone, and the egg she laid became Helen of Troy.

Greek gods were a lustful lot, and many of the rapes they committed used the ploy of transformation. Zeus turned himself into a bull to transport Europa far out to sea, then became an eagle so he could deflower her. Apollo did the same to seduce Dryope, becoming a tortoise she petted, then a snake that raped her. Poseidon did one better. He assumed the guise of the river god his victim Alcidice was in love with and assaulted her in the ocean.

One of the three mythical male virgins was Narcissus, so handsome that both men and women lusted after him. He spurned them all, until one bitter nymph appealed to either Nemesis or Artemis, who doomed Narcissus to gazing at his reflection in the water. As he stared, Narcissus fell deeper and deeper in love with himself, until his passion for himself consumed his body, and he died and became the narcissus flower.

These myths are remarkable for their soap opera–like ingenuity, twisting plots, and endless repetitions of the same theme—a god's sexual attraction to a virgin, the virgin's plight in repulsing his advances, and the denouement, almost always some sort of defeat for the virgin. These were not uplifting stories but rather the bemused record of divine and human interaction in that most primal of realms, the sensual. The gods were the last to value chastity and hounded the virgins they hoped to seduce. The virgins fought valiantly, but usually unsuccessfully, so that this chapter of mythology is littered with fallen virgins done in by the gods' superior tactics and weapons.

GREEK LITERATURE

HIPPOLYTUS OPPOSES LOVE

The myth of the steadfast virgin Hippolytus, immortalized in Euripides' tragedy, underscores the Greeks' perspective on love. They did not see it, as the Christians later would, as an ignoble consequence of concupiscence to be combated by individual resolve but rather as the direct outcome of Aphrodite's caprice or will. Only three divinities were immune to it, the virgins Athena, Artemis, and Hestia. Hippolytus' tragedy was that he resisted Aphrodite, for as Plato commented, "No one should oppose Love, and to get on the wrong side of gods is to oppose Love."

Hippolytus was a young hunter devoted to Artemis, though as Euripides had him remind us, "I greet her from afar: my life is clean." As Aphrodite complains, he

> . . . spurns my spell and seeks no woman's kiss.
> But great Apollo's sister, Artemis,
> He holds of all most high, gives love and praise.

Hippolytus' chastity was anomalous in a man, for virginity was a female quality, but his deceased mother was Antiope, a queen of the Amazons, warrior women who sliced off one breast to better accommodate their bows and who forswore men when they joined this all-female military corps. Hippolytus shared the Amazon regard for chastity and disgust for female lust and raged:

> O God, why hast Thou made this gleaming snare,
> Woman, to dog us on the happy earth?
> . . . Woe upon you, woe!
> How can I too much hate you, while the ill
> Ye work upon the world grows deadlier still?
> Too much? Make woman pure, and wild Love tame,
> Or let me cry forever on their shame!

Hippolytus' story is both simple and Byzantine. Aphrodite decided to punish him for his strict commitment to celibacy, and his stiff-necked refusal to love. With typical Olympian degeneracy, she employed his stepmother, Phaedra, as her instrument of retribution—she made Phaedra fall profoundly in love with her husband's son.

Poor Phaedra was an honorable woman, and the passion that clutched her heart consumed her so that she could neither eat nor speak about why she was slowly sickening.

Finally Phaedra's old nurse, terrified that her mistress will die, worms out her guilty secret. The nurse then attempts to intercede with Hippolytus, with disastrous consequences. Instead of mellowing, he savagely attacks Phaedra, humiliating her so deeply that she commits suicide. However, before dying, she leaves an incriminating message for Theseus, her husband, accusing Hippolytus of rape.

The grieving widower has no reason not to believe his wife's last words and lashes out bitterly at the son he thinks has betrayed him. Over and over, Hippolytus denies it—"Dost see / This sunlight and this earth? I swear to thee / There dwellest not in these one man—deny / All that thou wilt!—more pure of sin than I. . . . No woman's flesh / Hath e'er this body touched."

But Theseus blunders on and invokes a curse so that Hippolytus' horses are startled by a bull rising from the sea, causing an accident that fatally injures him. Having rejected the yoke of marriage, Hippolytus is killed by the yoke of his horses—a nice Aphrodite touch. Just before Hippolytus passes away, Artemis appears and tells Theseus, "One Spirit there is, whom we / That know the joy of white virginity / Most hate in heaven. / She sent her fire to run / in Phaedra's veins, so that she loved thy son."

Hippolytus' dying words were to curse the gods—"Ah me! / Would that a mortal's curse could reach to God!" Artemis comforts him by promising vengeance, and she also grants her acolyte a cult in which virginal maidens cut their hair in worship. Hippolytus dies, triumphing over Aphrodite in maintaining his chastity and in enlisting Artemis to avenge his untimely death.

What lessons did Euripides' vast and enthusiastic audiences take from Hippolytus? They needed no background prompting about either Aphrodite or about love, and they had no reason to share Hippolytus' adamant defense of his chastity, most unusual in a man, and undeniably peculiar. They might have understood his motivation—to honor the powerful Artemis—but they understood equally well that he had brought Aphrodite's wrath down onto his head and surely appreciated the fine points of her vengeance. Love and lust were inextricably linked. The Greeks made no sharply honed distinctions between them and labeled them in one breath as love, subject to Aphrodite's command.

Only Nurse interpreted love sensitively, when she made the ageless observation that "I know / How love should be a lightsome thing / Not rooted in the deep o' the heart. . . . Why do I love thee so [Phaedra]? O fool, / O fool, the heart that bleeds for twain." For the rest, love is throbbing loins, chastity is for young women, and a celibate young hunter is bound to endure merciless retribution for so arrogantly defying a powerful goddess.

LYSISTRATA'S ULTIMATUM

Aristophanes' comedy *Lysistrata* approaches celibacy from an entirely different optic, that of ordinary mortal women exasperated that, after two decades, the Peloponnesian War between Athens and Sparta raged on. The popular play exposes the raucous, ordinary side of Greek life, where Greek women, summoned by the Athenian Lysistrata, uncharacteristically take control of a political-military situation by organizing a sexual strike against their husbands.

"Hand in hand we'll rescue Greece," Lysistrata announces to a delegation of women from Athens, Sparta, and other enemy states, proposing as weapons "our fancy little dresses, our perfumes and our slippers, our rouge and our see-through underwear! If we sat around at home all made up, and walked past them wearing only our see-through underwear and with our pubes plucked in a neat triangle, and our husbands got hard and hankered to ball us, but we didn't go near them and kept away, they'd sue for peace, and pretty quick, you can count on that."

But the women are aghast. "Count me out; let the war drag on," says Kalonike. "I'm even ready to walk through fire; that rather than give up cock."

"Oh, what a low and horny race we are," Lysistrata laments. "No wonder men write tragedies about us."

Finally Lampito, a Spartan, says in her fractured Greek, "By Twain Gods, is difficult for females to sleep alone without the hard-on. But anyway, I assent; is need for peace."

And so Lysistrata's plan to occupy the Acropolis and wait it out there was put into action. There the women collectively swear an oath:

> No man of any kind, lover or husband, shall approach me with a hard-on. At home in celibacy shall I pass my life wearing a party dress and makeup so that my husband will get as hot as a volcano for me but never willingly shall I surrender to my husband.

But the waiting is long, the women edgy. Finally, in Lysistrata's words, "We need to fuck!" Her allies, wavering, try to sneak home. Lysistrata prevails and locks them inside, coercing them into solidarity with her plan to use their bodies as weapons to force a decision in the political-military arena where women otherwise have no say at all. Celibacy, therefore, becomes as empowering as it is difficult.

The men, too, are suffering. "I've got terrible spasms and cramps," moans one deprived husband.

> Now what shall I do? Whom shall I screw?
> I'm cheated of the sexiest girl I knew!
> How will I raise and rear this orphaned cock?
> . . . I need to rent a practical nurse!

Sparta's military delegates are no better, arriving with huge, visible erections they attempt to explain away—"Is Spartan walking stick." Finally they admit the truth, and also admit to the Athenians that Spartan men now "walk around town bent over, like men carrying oil lamp in wind."

Lysistrata's strategy soon succeeds. The men are so desperate for sex that after a mere six sexless days, they negotiate an honorable peace. As the Athenian ambassador expresses it, they all reach the same urgent decision, "namely, to fuck." In the play at least, the Peloponnesian War was over. Celibacy, Aristophanes and his applauding audiences agreed, was unthinkable in Greek marriages.

They were right. Virginity was for maidens only, and men and gods devoted considerable energy to seduction, though punishments as severe as death were meted out to offenders. With the exception of certain philosophers and their followers, the concept of celibacy in marriage was risible, as comic writer Aristophanes well knew. Indeed, some, usually wealthy, married men slept with not only their wives but also prostitutes, slaves, and young boys. Aristophanes ignored these outlets for the sake of the plot and also because ordinary Greeks—the laborer, artisan, and fisherman who attended his dramatic productions—seldom wanted or could afford these alternatives.

What made the celibacy twist particularly funny was that it was women who initiated it. In ancient Greece, women were reputedly the lascivious ones, incapable of controlling their sexual appetites unless rigidly restrained, continually monitored, confined to women's quarters, and married off as soon as they were pubescent. Men, on the other hand, believed they could apply their vaunted self-discipline to lust as to everything else. Zeus and Hera once argued about this and decided to submit the question to the seer Teiresias, whose past included bouts of being both male and female. Women, Teiresias ruled, experience nine-tenths of the pleasure of sexual intercourse, leaving a mere 10 percent for their male partners. To his audiences, Aristophanes' reversal of gender roles was wickedly clever. Lusty wives resorting to celibacy? What an imagination that Aristophanes had!

From beginning to end, the dialogue reinforces the sacrifice the women are making. Their talk is lewd, and they refer continually to sex and their bodies. Puns about sexual positions, lovers, and what today we call sexual toys are also rife. Penetration from behind, anally or vaginally, was a position of preference, so part of the women's celibacy pledge included, "I won't crouch down like a lioness on a cheese grater." In Greek homes, many household utensils had handles in the form of crouching animals, daily reminders of the female sexual position. And one woman complained that, for some time, "I haven't even seen a six-inch dildo, which might have been a consolation, however small." We all know Greek women are fiendishly lusty, Aristophanes was saying, which made his story of celibacy even more preposterous. Virginity was one thing, but celibacy was quite another.

CLASSICAL RITUALS

THESMOPHORIA

Greek matrons could only contemplate celibacy from afar, in their goddesses and mythical heroines. Yet once a year, the Thesmophoria, an annual religious festival of central importance to the participating city-states, liberated them from sexual relations with their husbands by imposing celibacy, albeit for just three days. The Thesmophoria was held each autumn in Athens and a few other cities, just before the sowing season, in honor of Demeter, goddess of agriculture. It was directed by two female officials and was probably confined to upperclass women. Men were strictly excluded, and the celebrants observed their three-day celibacy with a host of symbolic crutches that gave the Thesmophoria a unique character in the male-dominated, unchaste Greek city-states.

In Athens, the Thesmophoria was held on Pnyx Hill, otherwise the gathering place for (only male) citizens to congregate in democratic assembly. On the first day, the Way Up, the women traipsed up in a procession, carrying sacred objects. Once in the Thesmophorion, an open space, they set up rows of primitive shelters for themselves. When they sat or slept, it was on litters of willow, the chaste tree, reputed to calm the sexual appetite. They wore no makeup or jewelry, and only plain, unembroidered gowns.

Day two was the Fast, abstinence upon abstinence. Their breath and phlegm were so musty from fasting that the air in the Thesmophorion stank, another guarantee of sexual abstinence. This fast day reenacted both a mythical goddess's grief at losing her daughter and also the olden days before agriculture.

Day three was the joyous Bearer of Beautiful Offspring, when the women celebrated the fertility they stimulated by their temporary celibacy. They made sacrifices and they feasted. Probably this was also when the Bailers went to work. Prior to the festival, these women, purified by three days of sexual abstinence, had buried piglets and dough models of snakes and male genitalia. Later, during the Thesmophoria, the Bailers would dig up and retrieve the decomposed remains. These were laid on altars, then mixed with the ritually planted seed corn that encouraged the coming season's fertility.

The Thesmophoria was unique in several ways. Matrons alone were admitted, not virgins. It was the only festival requiring laywomen to be celibate both as they prepared for it and as they participated in it. Men were actively chased away, and the women repeated a gory myth about an ancient Thesmophoria where women with blood-streaked faces and swords castrated King Battus, whom they had caught spying on them. A real man, Aristomenes of Messenia, once did sneak up too close, and the women captured him, using sacrificial knives, roasting spits, and torches as weapons.

Another unique feature of the Thesmophoria was that all its celebrants were known as *melissai*—bees—because of a mythical collaboration between a goddess and Melisseus, king of the bees. The Greeks greatly admired the bee's chaste, hardworking lifestyle and the way it abominates adultery, which it punishes by attacking the adulterer or flying away. During the Thesmophoria, the matrons become *melissai*, sexually abstinent maiden-bees.

Given Greek women's subordinate status in society, the Thesmophoria was an extraordinary three-day release, freeing matrons to leave their homes and chores to mingle together, deliberately unappealing with their rancid breath and unkempt appearance, fiercely driving off curious males, expressing themselves in men's coarse, forbidden idiom, like the fictional women of Lysistrata. The importance of the festival overruled the notion that unsecluded, unguarded women are naturally whorish and emotional. The *melissai* were both unsecluded and unguarded, yet through unaccustomed celibacy and communion with other women, they performed crucial fertility rituals the men dared not neglect. Put another way, by matrons using this temporary celibacy to escape their daily grind, their husbands' authority, and the rigid constraints of their existences, the women reaffirmed among themselves their relevance to society. Finally, the oblations made and the corn seed planted, they exited from their brief camaraderie and slipped back inside the gates to the servitude of their separate quarters. Their ritual escape into celibacy for the sake of agricultural fertility was over for another year.

CULT OF ISIS

Ancient Roman matrons, whose religion was so similar to the Greeks', enjoyed a festival reminiscent of but much shorter than the Thesmophoria. A more sustained, sometimes permanent Greco-Roman foray into celibacy involved the religious cult of Isis. Isis was a gentle Egyptian goddess who, transplanted to Hellenistic Rome, found tremendous support among those drawn to her sphere of the spiritual and physical aspects of love. Isis routinely appeared to people in their dreams, summoning them to her rite.

In the Isiac cult in Egypt, some women served as priestesses, and in Greece as secondary priestesses. Far fewer women than men were permitted into the cult societies, but temple and other inscriptions show that in Athens and Rome, major cult centers, more women were initiates than anywhere else, and Isis attracted more of them than any domestic religion. In Greece, two light-bearers and two dream interpreters were also women.

Isis' cult had a particularly large number of lay devotees, divided into three levels: the simplest believers; the devotees who served in a strong cult headed by a priest; and those whose functions were so high people often confused or equated them with priests. Very rarely, a woman served in the highest level.

Isis was a relatively chaste goddess, and early Christian Fathers such as Clement and Tertullian praised her chaste devotees and priestesses. Her cult tended toward the ascetic, with no sexual symbols in evidence. Hair was shorn and linen garments were modestly cut. The ritual processions and prayers, and their accoutrements of water, incense, and musical instruments, were all austere.

Cultists were celibate, men as well as women, a rarity in the classical world. But this abstinence was short-term—ten days was the usual length. Female devotees were required to observe this ten-day fast from sex before initiation and thereafter at specified periods. The Isis of Hellenistic romances protected the chastity of separated lovers, and women fleeing sexual assault found a safe house in her temple.

Very devout women abandoned their marital sex lives, becoming what Tertullian styled "widows." They refused any further physical contact with their husbands, sometimes even providing new wives to replace themselves. Some avoided contact with men to the extent that they refused to kiss even their sons.

Literature reveals how faithfully Isiac cultists observed the requisite celibacy. In Apuleius' ancient novel, the Isis book, an initiate speaks about "how extremely hard were the rules of chastity and abstinence." Ovid, deprived of his mistress's favors, complained, "Does any think this is a goddess to joy in the tears of lovers, and to see fit worship in the torments of lying apart?" And sardonically, to Isis, "Because lying apart was sad for thee, O golden goddess, must I now suffer thus on thy holy days?"

The plaintive tone of so many poets with the same lament is ironic testimony to the strength of Isis' hold on her devotees, in particular women who risked their husband's or lover's anger to fulfill the sacred demand for celibacy. During these ten-day periods, the women ritually purified themselves and conscientiously slept alone, on clean linen. The goddess's province of spiritual and physical love was her great appeal, and when she imposed a condition of cyclical celibacy, her devotees accepted her wisdom in the matter and gracefully obeyed. They did so at the cost of upsetting their men by withholding their bodies for longer than most other deities demanded, in a society that did not value celibacy. It was a small token of independence, and the kindness and goodness of their chaste goddess made the sacrifice worthwhile.

Oracle of Delphi

Celibacy was also essential in women employed by male gods as their earthly voices. Apollo, for example, demanded that those through whom he revealed his oracles be sexually pure, so that he had sole entry into their bodies. In the ancient world, oracles were highly valued deities who, through their priests and priestesses, counseled legions of citizens on crucial questions, from the unsure suitor's "Should I marry this girl?" to the prudent diplomat's "Should my city-state declare war?" The most popular was the oracle of Apollo's sanctuary at Delphi. On the seventh day of each month, the oracle was open for questions. A priestess, called a Pythia, responded after falling into a trance during which Apollo spoke through her in what seemed to be gibberish but which priestly interpreters then deciphered, usually in dactylic hexametered verses, for the waiting supplicant. During busy periods, three Pythias held oracular consultations in shifts.

The Pythia's prophetic prop was a bowl set in a humble tripod, an everyday cooking utensil. Before she answered, she inspected a goat, afterward sacrificed, to see if its limbs all trembled just as hers would when Apollo possessed her. Among other rituals, she also purified herself in the sacred water of the Castalian spring.

At one time, each Pythia had been a young virgin, but after a client seduced one of them, the rules were changed and the Pythia were peasant women at least fifty years old, although in memory of the long-ago despoiled virgin, a Pythia dressed in girlish, asexual dress. They became strict celibates when they took up their prestigious positions and left any husband behind when they moved into the sanctuary. The Pythia's chastity was essential. Apollo could not enter a body bound up with sexual pleasure with another mortal, so settling on older, postsexual women was a good strategy. This was also an instance where celibacy for mature women was both respected and valued, an anomaly in the ancient world.

Special Virgins

Certain Greco-Roman cults required virgin priestesses, so a few young women were propelled into religious rather than marital service. For them, long-term or even perpetual celibacy was mandatory. Just as much as unmarried maidens, they had to remain undefiled or face horrendous consequences.

The custom of virgin priestesses remained until the Christian era. Throughout the Roman empire, temples had hierodules, virgins dedicated to serve their god as his bride. The hierodules at the temple of Diana (Artemis) at Ephesus were, like the vestal virgins, perpetual virgins. Other gods required their priestesses to be chaste for specified periods, seldom forever, and the same was true for priests. At Thebes, Zeus' young, virginal brides were chosen for their physical perfection and high rank. When they reached puberty, they observed a period of ritual mourning for Zeus, their first, divine husband. Afterward, they were married off to suitable humans.

In all cases, virginity was a ritual requirement and implied no notion about ascetic ideals and corrupt flesh. Pagan religions rarely required long-term celibacy, and society frowned on it. Usually, temporary abstinence was sufficient, though rare examples of lifelong celibacy exist. Usually, priestesses could graduate to marriage; as we will see, even the vestals had this option, after thirty years in office.

Ironically, virginity could also cause the virgin's death. In times of greatest crisis, a devastating flood or plague, for instance, the most dazzling offering was an undefiled maiden, ritually sacrificed to the appropriate god. Macaria, Heracles' virgin daughter, nobly sacrificed herself to ensure a military victory. Metioche and Menippe did likewise, after Apollo's oracle declared that two virgins were required to end a famine and drought that gripped their city. They did the deed themselves, with the shuttles of their loom.

Most virgins, however, were forced into the sacrificial role. King Demophon, for instance, decreed that each year, one virgin had to be slain to stave off a plague that he had been warned about by an oracle. He selected the victim by lottery, always carefully omitting his own daughters' name. When Mastusius, a citizen, questioned the fairness of this arrangement, Demophon immediately chose Mastusius' daughter as that year's tribute. In retaliation, Mastusius killed all Demophon's daughters and served their father wine mixed with their blood. Legend does not tell us how Demophon proceeded with his next year's immolation.

For Greek girls, these stories must have reinforced their sense that virginity defined their value, instilling at least slight alarm that they would be either raped or selected as a human sacrifice.

VESTAL VIRGINS

By far the best known of antiquity's virgins were the vestals, in whose perpetual chastity the highest authorities of state and all of civil society entrusted the security of Rome. In return for this overwhelming responsibility, the six vestals lived deeply satisfying lives as revered and powerful women of such exalted status that, alone of Roman women, they enjoyed the same legal rights as men.

The vestals harked back to Hestia/Vesta, one of antiquity's trio of virgin goddesses. In Rome as in Greece, Vesta was the supreme guardian of the home and sacred hearth, and every Roman household centered around its hearth fire, sacred to Vesta. The ritual of throwing a salt cake onto the fire was a daily reminder that Vesta was at the heart of the family's spiritual life and physical welfare.

Vesta was also publicly worshiped in the Aedes Vestae, a round building shaped like a primitive chieftain's home. This temple housed Rome's national treasure, its official fire of state, essential to the well-being and successful functioning of the entire nation. All Romans knew that if the fire was ever extinguished, even the outcome of battles would be adversely affected.

The life-or-death responsibility of tending this fire fell to the vestal virgins, Rome's only pagan version of nuns. The vestals' origins are uncertain. The Romans, however, believed that Romulus, Rome's founder, was the offspring of Rhea Silvia, a vestal virgin impregnated by Mars, the god of war. The first vestals were probably kings' daughters, charged to mind the tribal fire. This would explain their annual rite of solemnly warning the *rex sacrorum*—king of sacrifices—"Vigilasne rex? Vigila!" "Are you watchful, king? Be watchful!" as the daughters of long-ago kings had once done.

Its immense prestige and low turnover made the order of vestal virgins as desirable as it was exclusive. Novices were admitted after a complicated election process held, on average, once every five years. Eligibility was rigid: candidates had to be patrician girls between the ages of six and ten, physically perfect and mentally sound, whose mother and father were both alive.

In the first round, the Pontifex Maximum, chief priest of the city, eliminated all but twenty girls. Immediately, each had an equal chance, for the future vestal virgin was then chosen by lot. What excitement there must have been among twenty pairs of parents and the relatives, if not the small contenders themselves. The climax came when the Pontifex Maximum identified the winner by taking her hand and addressing her with the ritual words "Te, amata, capio!" "My beloved, I take possession of you," the formula for admission into the order.

The new vestal virgin instantaneously became a new person. She was no longer a member of her blood family, even for purposes of inheritance. She was released from her father's control (patria potestas), granted legal independence, and given a substantial dowry. Then she was taken to the Atrium Vestae, a spacious house adjacent to the temple of Vesta, usually the only home she would know for the rest of her life.

At the Atrium Vestae, the little vestal would meet her five colleagues. Did she realize that, from then on, these women would be her only intimates? Was she already missing her parents, her brothers and sisters, her home? And when, under the vigilant eyes of the senior virgin, the Virgo Vestalis Maxima, the youngster's long hair was shorn, did her lips quaver and her eyes overflow with tears?

This haircut was not all; the little vestal also had to surrender her clothes, to be dressed entirely in white: a long, sleeveless gown girdled at the waist, with a loose robe draped over it, and a diadem-like headband with ornamental ribbons. In this garb, her cropped hair covered, she lisped her vow of celibacy: she swore she would preserve her virginity for at least thirty years. Doubtless she did not grasp yet the implications of this, but when she had completed her three decades—the first spent learning, the second practicing what she had learned, and the third teaching it to neophytes—she could resign as a vestal and resume the civilian life she had been plucked from in childhood. She could even marry, although in reality, after thirty years of privilege and power, few cared to relinquish their splendid lives for marriage. Most of those who did were rumored to be miserable.

Before her election, the vestal's parents had surely impressed on her the gravity of her pledge and the draconian consequences of violating it. But at age six or eight, she could scarcely comprehend what this sacred celibacy actually was. It would be years later, as her body ripened, when she would have to battle her surging sexuality or risk being buried alive in the Campus Sceleratus—the Field of Crime.

Meanwhile, the unresistingly celibate vestal's primary duty was to tend the sacred fire in the Temple of Vesta. For at least eight hours a day, teams of two vestals watched it zealously. Even so, the fire occasionally went out. The repercussions were severe. The chief priest would identify and punish the culprit, taking her to a dark place, stripping her naked from behind a curtain, then scourging her.

The severity of her punishment matched the crime the vestal had committed, for those cold ashes had been no ordinary fire but a symbol of the life and religion of the state. Its extinction, except in the chief priest's annual Ides of March relighting ceremony, spread consternation and terror throughout Rome. The responsibility for ensuring this didn't happen was the chief mission of Rome's six most exalted women.

The Romans prized female chastity—virginity in vestals and maidens, fidelity in matrons—with the same intensity they did fire, and they expected virtuous women to die rather than surrender it. The logical extension of this collective obsession was to demand, on pain of death, thirty chaste years from the women charged with the sacred fire. The vestal virgins' celibacy was the principal guarantee of their purity and incorruptibility, qualities essential in those charged with such weighty state duties.

In fact, most vestals honored their vows, and their virtue earned them universal respect and many privileges. They could testify in court without taking an oath and were entrusted with sacred relics and valuable documents. Lictors, the official escorts of magistrates, accompanied them everywhere. Jostling a vestal was a capital offense. Vestals might even pardon any criminal who chanced upon them in the street. No wonder so many parents jockeyed to place their little daughters in the order.

But what was the reality of daily life in the Atrium Vestae? Until puberty, and the temptations of raging hormones, the vestals' lives were satisfying and secure. Apart from tending the fire, they had to fetch water from a sacred spring and carry it on their heads back to the Atrium or the temple. They baked Vesta's salt cakes and mopped the floors of her temple. They also baked sacrificial cakes for religious holidays, first pounding the grain into flour. They guarded the October equus, the blood and ashes of calves sacrificed before they were born. The vestals were always busy, and until puberty, their lives were structured and pleasant.

In adulthood, however, the inevitable sometimes happened. Vestal virgins fell in love, and an imprudent few succumbed to their passion and took lovers.

They ran a terrible risk, for those detected were condemned to die. Theirs was a special death, designed to acknowledge their status. Too holy to execute, the unchaste vestal was dressed in a shroud, placed in a closed litter, and carried like a corpse through funereally silent crowds of mourners. Her destination was a small, underground room at the Campus Sceleratus, near the Colline Gate, where either starvation or asphyxiation would kill her. This death cell contained a bit of bread, water, oil, and milk so the Romans could say they had not starved the errant vestal to death. The victim descended a ladder and was sealed alone into her tomb. Elsewhere, and in a public place, her lover was beaten to death.

Not all disgraced vestals went quietly. Beautiful and fashionable, saucily made up and elaborately coiffed, Claudia Quinta was haughty and sharp-tongued. She was also courageous, and when she was charged with breaking her vows of chastity, she supplicated the goddess's image: "They say I am not chaste. If you condemn me, I will acknowledge guilt, and pay for it with my life. But if I am free of blame, demonstrate my innocence. You are chaste; follow my chaste hands."

Fortunately for Claudia, Vesta's statue appeared to move, and the vestal virgin was exonerated. Vestal Tuccia, accused not merely of breaking her vows of chastity but also of incest, proved her innocence by performing a miracle. She scooped water into a sieve and carried it across the city without losing a drop.

Vestal virgins faced a far greater danger than sexual impropriety: the risk that reversals in either politics or war would be blamed on their having broken their sacred oath of celibacy. Chief Vestal Cornelia, for one, was certainly the victim of such machinations. And in 216 B.C., Roman leaders did not attribute the disastrous military defeat at Cannae to battlefield errors but to sexual misconduct among the vestal virgins. In consequence, two vestals ended their probably virginal lives in the suffocating blackness of the Campus Sceleratus. Of the ten documented cases of vestal virgins being entombed alive, most were celibate scapegoats of misfortune.

It was not unknown for powerful Romans to instigate trumped-up charges simply to create a vacancy in the Atrium Vestae for their own daughter. With only six spaces available, a convenient execution appealed to the unscrupulous as a way of speeding up openings. And in 215, the Emperor Caracalla destroyed a trio of vestals. First, he seduced one of them. Afterward, he arranged for his victim and two of her colleagues to be buried alive in the Campus Sceleratus.

Despite such injustices, happily infrequent, the vestal virgins survived for centuries. Indeed, the order was so powerful, and so feared, that in 394, after defeating Eugenius and triumphantly entering Rome, the militantly Christian emperor Theodosius the Great disbanded the six vestals and abolished their holy order.

The power and continuity of the vestal virgins symbolize the importance of virginity in Roman society. Their treatment as privileged and respected religious figures made their lives so enviable that few retired after their thirty years of service. Their celibate state brought them too many rewards to throw it over for a sexual, civilian life. The vestal virgins, it is fair to say, enjoyed supremely satisfying conditions equaled only by the *aclla*s of the ancient Incan empire.

PAGAN AND JEWISH ASCETICISM
THE INFLUENCE OF GREEK PHILOSOPHY

The Greco-Roman world of antiquity demanded virginity of all unmarried women, and so did many of its deities. Most priestesses who served chaste goddesses such as Athena or Vesta, or jealous gods such as Apollo, were virgins. Those few who had formerly been married had to observe strict celibacy. But as the centuries passed, philosophies developed that, through the very different avenue of asceticism, would inspire a mini-movement toward an ideal that highlighted celibacy and inspired Pythagoras, Plato, and other philosophers and thinkers.

Pythagoras was a sixth-century B.C. philosopher who created a religious movement that melded Orphic doctrine with Indian and Persian beliefs. The Orphic religion was not widely practiced, but it appealed to intellectuals, who responded to its dogmatic absolutes, including the promise of eternal life to the ritually and physically pure. To further his goal of the moral regeneration of society, Pythagoras founded a celibate brotherhood that, stripped of its economic and political dimensions, survived for centuries as a religious cult.

Pythagoras' commune members, including women accepted on equal terms with men, had to surrender their possessions into the collective pot, for he taught that "friends have all things in common" and "friendship is equality." He divided lifetimes into four twenty-year seasons corresponding to spring, summer, fall, and winter: twenty years a boy, twenty years a youth, twenty years a young man, twenty years an old man. For the first segment of their studies, his disciples had to listen to Pythagoras speaking from behind a cover so they could never even glimpse him. After five years of this, he permitted them into his house where he conversed with them in person.

Pythagoras preached of a world divided into opposing principles: the inferior Unlimited Breath, which included darkness, even numbers, and femaleness, and the superior Limit, meaning light, odd numbers, and maleness. The superior soul was trapped inside the inferior body alongside the Furies of wicked passions. To release and thereby save their imprisoned souls, people had to observe taboos, in particular against the debasement of sexual intercourse.

However, Pythagoras counseled celibacy only during the hot and dry summer, and if possible the spring and fall. Wintertime sex was less desiccating, and therefore more acceptable, though like all the pleasures of love, still harmful to health. To a man eager to know when he should have sex with a woman, Pythagoras replied, "When you want to lose what strength you have."

Pythagoras also stressed that any sexual activity should not begin before a man's twentieth birthday, and he praised the stringency of Greek rules against making love in a temple with a woman who was either someone's sister, mother, or daughter—in other words, any woman at all. The only sex he tolerated was for the express purpose of procreating children, and then only between husband and wife.

Plato refined and transmitted many Pythagorean ideas into his own immeasurably influential philosophy. He, too, was a dualist and saw the soul as morally superior to the body, which impeded it in its execution of higher goals. Depending on its expression, he saw love as sacred and elevating or profane and degrading. Sexual intercourse was the lowest form of all, plunging humans into bestiality. What was required to surmount these lower forms of love was virtuous living, defined by austerities compatible with Pythagoreanism, in particular sexual continence.

In Plato's *Republic,* a jovial man asked Sophocles the poet a crude question about his sexuality: "How about your service of Aphrodite, Sophocles—is your natural force still unabated?" To which Sophocles replied, "Hush, man, most gladly have I escaped this thing you talk of, as if I had run away from a raging and savage beast of a master."

Centuries after Plato elaborated his concept of Ideas versus Matter, Christian theologians immersed in Platonic thought would laud him as a Christian before Christ was even born. Ideas were so pure, immutable, ubiquitous, and unceasing that they corresponded to deities, while Matter was clearly mortal humankind in all its filth and sorrow.

Stoicism had similar teachings about sexuality. It was not despicable in itself, only when immoderate passion and lust propelled people into performing it. As a procreative act within marriage, it was tolerable. The Roman Seneca wrote, "[A] wise man ought to love his wife with judgment, not affection. Let him control his impulses and not be borne headlong into copulation. Nothing is fouler than to love a wife like an adulteress." Stoics guided themselves by the watchwords of nature, virtue, decorum, and moderation, manifested in ascetic lives that attracted many adherents.

Over the centuries, a growing number of ascetics made considerable impact on the lifestyle that normally included uninhibited sexual access to female slaves, homosexual affairs between men and young boys, widespread prostitution, and the institution of semipermanent courtesans known as hetaerae. (Arranged marriages, tight control over women, especially of the higher classes, and terrible penalties for seducing virgins were also features of the society.) Chastity, often mentioned in the same breath with abstemiousness, endurance, and energy, was more and more widely practiced. By the time Christianity came onto the horizon, chastity had implanted itself into a world already fertilized with sexual asceticism.

THE ESSENES PREPARE FOR ARMAGEDDON

At the same time that pagan asceticism was intensifying, an apocalyptic and ascetic Jewish cult developed. The Essenes, priestly and messianic, claimed descent from Moses' brother Aaron. They scrupulously obeyed the Law of Moses, observed the Sabbath and the religious calendar, and practiced ritual purity. They believed in the End of Days and the concept of the Chosen People. Here, however, they parted ways with other Jews. They saw themselves as "Israel that walks in the way of perfection," "true Israel," and so they excluded themselves from mainstream Jewry as the Chosen People. (Unlike the Pharisees and the second century B.C. Hasidim, self-named "the Congregation of the Pious," the Essenes called themselves the Jewish people.)

The Essenes' antagonistic relations with other groups precipitated their flight into the wilderness, where they established mostly male monastic communities governed by their unique doctrine. They were celibate and did not marry. They held no slaves, either because of their egalitarianism or because they did not want Gentiles, the only slaves available, in their midst. (They hated Gentiles and, unlike other Jews, considered them hell-bound. However, a more moderate, open Essene group in Damascus did hold slaves.) They rejected many other Jewish rituals, but made offerings to Jerusalem and sacrificed among themselves.

Essene life was austere and frugal. Twice daily, the priests prepared monotonous, one-course meals accompanied by bread, which the community consumed in utter silence. Flavius Josephus, who spent some time living with the Essenes, described their routine. After hours of work, they gathered together, donned white loincloths, and bathed in cold water. This ablution performed, they quietly sat down and awaited their repast. The baker brought them loaves of bread, and the cook added a single plate heaped with a single kind of food. The rule was that no one could taste anything until grace had been said, and so before and after they ate, they praised God for his bounty. Afterward, they shucked off their white garments and returned to work again until suppertime.

The Essenes wore their clothes and their shoes till they disintegrated. They affected a rugged appearance and refrained from grooming themselves with oil, as others did. They bathed ritually before each meal and after relieving themselves, an ablution they performed while modestly covering their nakedness with an apron. They defecated only at a distance from the settlement, digging a hole, covering themselves as they squatted, then burying the feces with earth. On the Sabbath, natural urges were forbidden.

Contemporary witnesses marveled at Essene celibacy—strict, total, unseasonal—but the presence of female skeletons in the Qumran excavations proves a few women were present. It may be that a few wives accompanied their husbands into the settlement but lived there in chastity. One scholar, David Flusser, interprets certain of the Dead Sea Scrolls, the recently discovered Essene literature, as implying that an Essene man could marry, after age twenty, "when he knew what to do," and that such marriages were strictly to propagate the race. Perhaps this was true at the beginning, but other scholars claim all the Essenes were strict celibates.

Essene asceticism evolved from a maturing theology that painted a world of the Sons of Light and the Sons of Darkness, the latter doomed to destruction, the former predetermined by God. Increasingly, the Essenes saw people as evil and flesh as the locus of that evil—hence their loathing of sexuality, even of normal bodily functions. But unlike Plato, they did not understand man as a duality of warring mind and matter. They saw instead two kinds of humans, the corporal or the unredeemed, and the elect, namely themselves.

If this description of the rituals and doctrine of the Essene sect rings oddly familiar, it may be because, in so many dimensions, it harks forward to Christianity. The flight into monasticism in the wilderness; the cumbersome style of bathing, so that even the bather could not observe his own body; the meagerness of the simple meals and their silent consumption; the forced surrender of all private property; the sense of vocation; the quiet sureness of purpose; even the accumulation of riches; and above all the celibacy—soon enough, all these would be features of Christianity and its cloisters.

The publicity showered on the Essenes through the writings of several distinguished writers, including Josephus, who bore personal witness to their proceedings, familiarized them to many early Christians. As these new religionists set about organizing themselves, they would draw heavily on Platonic concepts of duality, on Essene experiences, procedures, and canons, and above all, on Essene-style celibacy. Here was the religious, philosophical, and social soil into which fledgling Christianity, unarguably the world's most extensive and long-lived experiment in celibate living, would be sown and take root.

CHAPTER 2

Early Christianity

ORIGINS

A TALE OF TWO WOMEN

Two thousand years ago, a thoughtful and righteous carpenter discovered the young woman he was betrothed to was pregnant. This was not the usual dilemma of overeager young lovers, who in such a situation would have to resort to a tiny bag of pig's blood to fake the marks of a torn hymen on the pristine linen sheet of their marriage bed. This pregnancy spelled big trouble, at least for Mary, the mother-to-be. How could she explain it to Joseph, her betrothed, or even to herself? The terrifying truth was that she and Joseph had never made love.

Many men, probably most, would have reacted furiously at this humiliation. Betrothals were as binding as marriage, so despite Mary's predicament, Joseph could not simply leave her. They could only be separated by divorce.

Mary and Joseph must have talked and talked. Mary must have pleaded, begged him to believe that she did not know how this had happened, that she had never betrayed him with another man. Joseph must have argued that nobody makes a baby alone and her explanations made no sense. However, her tearful misery must have moved him. Joseph decided to take the high road and "dismiss her quietly," rather than subject her to the suffering that would follow his repudiating her in front of witnesses.

Still tormented by the magnitude of his situation, Joseph fell asleep considering his options. A dream began, and in it the angel of the Lord appeared to him and said, "Joseph, son of David, do not be afraid to take Mary as your wife, for the child conceived in her is from the Holy Spirit." The angel even revealed the gender and name of the infant: a boy, whom Joseph was to name Jesus, a form of Joshua meaning "God is with us." Jesus, the angel added before retiring from Joseph's dream, would "save his people from their sins."

As Joseph lay sleeping, Mary's protests were entirely vindicated. When he woke up, no doubt elated and also shaken, Joseph must have confided the nocturnal revelations to a vastly relieved and astounded Mary. There was no more talk of sending her away. Instead, Joseph "took her as his wife," though they refrained from sexual relations at least until after the baby was born.

All went according to plan until the final hours of Mary's pregnancy. Because of an imperial decree enacting a mass registration of citizens, Joseph and his bride had to travel to Bethlehem, Joseph's ancestral city, rather than await their baby's birth at home in Nazareth. Worse, an influx of other out-of-towners had packed the local inn, and in the end, Joseph could find no better lodgings than a stable. There, amid the curious donkeys and other animals, Mary delivered her child. It was as the prophet Isaiah had predicted: "Look, the virgin shall conceive and bear a son, and they shall name him Emmanuel, which means, 'God is with us.' "

Years passed. Jesus grew and began to preach. When he was thirty-three, and a radical populist mocked by the establishment as King of the Jews, the chief priests, scribes, and elders gathered at the high priest's palace and plotted to kill him. The murder would take place right after Passover.

The plotters had power and money on their side. They bribed Jesus' disciple, Judas Iscariot, to double-cross his leader, offering him the enormous sum of thirty pieces of silver. They did not, however, take Jesus by surprise. "You know that after two days the Passover is coming, and the Son of Man will be handed over to be crucified," he advised his horrified disciples. Crucified he was, his agony compounded by the indignity of a crown of thorns and nakedness, as Roman soldiers ripped off and kept his clothes in keeping with the tradition of the crucifixion military detail.

Jesus died at last, but did not stay dead. On the third day, his gouged body revived, and for a brief time he again walked the face of this earth. He spent his final moments with his eleven surviving disciples, Judas Iscariot having hanged himself in feverish repentance. "Go therefore and make disciples of all the nations," Jesus urged, "baptizing them in the name of the Father and of the Son and of the Holy Spirit, and teaching them to obey everything that I have commanded you. And remember, I am with you always, to the end of the age." Then, as his disciples watched in amazement, he ascended into heaven.

This divine son of a virgin mother had lived and died, consumed by a mission to found a new proselytizing religion that eventually became Christianity. His death and the miracles surrounding it led the earliest Christians to conclude that an apocalypse was at hand. Why, given the end of the world, produce children? Better remain celibate and focus on spiritual purification.

As we have seen, the Greek and Roman world Jesus inherited was not without its virgins and proponents of celibacy. But Athena's miraculous springing forth from Zeus' head, the vestal virgins, ascetic philosophers urging sexual abstinence, or even the self-isolated Essenes were quite different from the Christian fixation on widespread celibacy with its concomitant zeal to proselytize.

From the outset, Christianity was sex-negative. Jesus' pronouncements on divorce, for instance, prompted his disciples to wonder if they were not better off to remain unmarried. Jesus' response has reverberated through the ages:

> For there are eunuchs who have been so from birth, and there are eunuchs who have been made eunuchs by others, and there are eunuchs who have made themselves eunuchs for the sake of the kingdom of heaven. Let anyone accept this who can.

The disciples, and a legion of believers who followed, accepted it. Metaphorical eunuchism or strict celibacy became one of their religion's greatest and most rigorous features. A few, including Origen, a third-century Church Father, interpreted Jesus' words so literally that they castrated themselves.

For Christianity's first four centuries, the Church Fathers—Ambrose, Jerome, Tertullian, Cyprian, and Augustine—wrestled with the theological and practical implications of Jesus' holy eunuchs. Ought Christians to marry at all? And if they did, ought they to indulge in sexual relations? The concept of celibate marriage became very real. The Apostle Paul's famous stricture— "It is better to marry than to burn"—reflects Christianity's negative view both of men's weakness in the face of tempting women and also the relative merit of marriage; on balance, it is preferable to its searing alternatives.

As the Fathers analyzed the Scriptures, Jesus' own indifference to familial blood ties reinforced their conviction that celibate childlessness is no tragedy but rather a sign of holiness. Once, as Jesus stood talking to his followers, someone noticed that his mother, Mary, and his brothers, James, Joses, Simon, and Judas, wished to have a word with him outside. But Jesus paid them no attention. "Who are my mother and my brothers?" he demanded. Then he stretched out his arms toward his disciples and thundered, "Here are my mother and my brothers! Whoever does the will of God is my brother and sister and mother."

A number of themes emerged over the years: the virtue of virginity, or the reborn virginity of celibacy; the primacy of God's community of believers rather than human families in society; and increasingly, the carnal, lustful, seductive nature of women. Like the early Greek philosophers, most Church Fathers were bachelors and held similar, harsh views of any sexual activity, within or without marriage. Even Tertullian, who was married, condemned sexuality as "illicit" and referred to women's vaginas as the "Gateway to the Devil."

Reams of pages and vats of ink later, the Fathers had isolated the culprit responsible for humanity's aggravated sexuality, and with collective venom, they pinned the blame on Eve. St. Paul in particular painted her with his misogynous brush. Slowly, the theology of prelapsarianism developed, the lapse, of course, referring to Adam and Eve in the Garden of Eden, at the moment they indulged in the sweet meat of the divinely forbidden apple. As Mary, mother of Jesus, was deified and decarnalized, Eve became the focus of the sin of the world. The essential plot of Christianity's Tale of Two Women was beginning to develop.

In Genesis, Adam is God's first man and Eve his helpmeet, created from Adam's rib after God had anesthetized him so he would feel no pain from the operation. In the Garden of Eden, the naked man and his woman, bone of his bones, flesh of his flesh, had free rein to taste and enjoy everything. Only the Tree of the Knowledge of Good and Evil was strictly off-limits: "You shall not eat of the fruit of the tree in the middle of the garden, nor shall you touch it, or you shall die," God warned them.

The serpent-cum-Devil, however, convinced Eve otherwise. How could she die when, by tasting the tree and comprehending the nature of good and evil, she would herself become godlike? Eve was convinced and just as easily persuaded Adam to join her in sampling a tasty morsel. He nibbled and provoked the Fall of Man.

God's punishment was swift and made mockery of the Devil's assurances. Even the serpent was condemned, to a cursed life on its belly. Eve's lot, and hence that of all women, would be great pain and sorrow, and subservience to her husband: "I will greatly increase your pangs in childbearing; in pain you shall bring forth children, yet your desire shall be for your husband, and he shall rule over you."

Adam's sentence was Everyman's: no more easy labor in the Garden of Eden from which he and Eve were banished, but hard, sweaty, thankless toil amid thorns and thistles. Much more severe was the end of eternal life and the return of Adam's and Eve's bodies to the ground, for "you are dust, and to dust you shall return." Because he had heeded Eve's words and defied God's commandment, the first man and all who followed would die. The serpent/Devil, not God, had lied, and the wages of sin were, indeed, death.

MARTYRDOM TOUGHENS THE NEW RELIGION

The Church Fathers were not a static group of academics stooped endlessly over their Bibles. They were administrators as well as theologians, building the Church as they guided it through tremendous danger, preaching to the converted and proselytizing among pagans and Jews. For its first four centuries, Christians faced waves of often deadly persecutions. In the third century,

Emperor Diocletian was their worst oppressor, persecuting and torturing them. Some of the accusations against them were slanderous nonsense: they murdered babies, practiced cannibalism via their Eucharist, indulged in incest, dimmed the church lights as a prelude to group sex, caused famines, disasters, and drought. "No rain, because of the Christians" became a Roman cliché. Other charges were at least true: they did deny Rome's divinities, refused to eat sacrificial meat, and revered celibacy.

Wealthy and well-born virginal Christians were special targets. Envious pagans could falsely incriminate substantial property owners in the hopes of benefiting. Christian girls were also targeted and, before execution, sent to a brothel for defloration. In his brilliant and comprehensive *Pagans and Christians,* Robin Lane Fox speculates that the campaign against Christians targeted old people, women, children, and on at least one occasion, the disabled. With such vulnerable victims as scapegoats, the authorities had little trouble enforcing their anti-Christian decrees.

The persecutions ebbed and flowed, with Decius (249–51) and Diocletian (284–305) their most notorious instigators. Brutality was common, and prisons bulged with Christian men, women, and children, often crammed together in horrendous conditions. Banishment was another punishment, or forced labor in mines and quarries, heads half-shorn, the victims wary of their captors' whips.

The Romans chose February 23, 303, a pagan festival, to post the first of four edicts that formalized the persecution. It ordered the destruction of all Christian churches, outlawed their services, stripped Christians of all rank and privilege, and excluded them from the law courts. Within hours, cooperative pagans demolished a Christian building, the beginning of widespread devastation.

Most dramatic of all were the executions, wildly exaggerated in number but nonetheless atrocious. Gruesome tortures often preceded public massacre in the great arenas. Jeering, bloodthirsty pagans jammed inside to gawk as naked virgins and Christians of all other stripes, notably elderly men, women, and children, were forced into the pits to be torn apart by starved wild lions, gored by bulls, speared by gladiators, decapitated, or burned at the stake.

Christians endured these horrors in myriad ways. Pagan onlookers were often perplexed and disturbed that many victims offered no resistance, even welcoming their death as a passage to paradise. Martyrdom was a magnificent catapult to that heavenly place. It canceled out all sin and elevated one to angel status. Doomed Christian prisoners waited for death dreaming of their glorious rewards. Some almost longed for the torments they would overcome. "When torn by all instruments of cruelty," a jailed band of them wrote Bishop Cyprian, "[we aspire] not to shudder at our own blood, streaming forth. . . . We feel, in our Lord's words, 'torches' put under us to kindle our faith."

Other prisoners, however, decided to spend their final hours sinning as lavishly as possible, since all would soon be forgiven; "Eat, drink, and make love, for tomorrow we die" was their motto. First they confessed, then abandoned themselves to heavy partying, including sex with visiting Christian women.

The vast majority of Christians, however, either lapsed into paganism, bribed officials and ransomed prisoners, bought or forged certificates of paganism, or took to the hills. After all, as reported in the Gospel of Matthew, Christ himself had urged the persecuted to flee. Many bishops followed this advice, leaving frightened congregations to "lapse" or to disintegrate into factions squabbling about how to save themselves. Then, in 313, it was all over. The Emperor Constantine signed the Edict of Milan, which granted Christians the right to their religion and restored their confiscated property. The persecutions were effectively ended.

Martyrdom, however, prevailed in Christian lore if not in reality. Legendary physical bravery and spiritual fortitude comforted and encouraged the masses of Christians who feared persecution even when times were calm. Heroes and heroines arose from the charred ashes of men, women, and children sacrificed by enraged, jealous pagans powerless to force them to recant or turn their backs on the one true God.

This, then, was part of the Fathers' operational background. Quite apart from the Church's internal challenges, the Fathers led an often illegal, defiant, fractious, proselytizing, theologically arrogant, and exclusive upstart religion. Throughout, the intensity of their faith sustained them.

THE SECOND COMING

Each Father pored over the Scriptures, prayed earnestly for enlightenment, debated and corresponded with other religious thinkers. Each also drew upon his personal experiences. Frequently these included bitter struggles against sexual temptation that transformed these men, almost all bachelors, into misogynists who mistrusted women as much as they feared them. Jerome, for instance, recalled, "[In the desert] where I had no companions but scorpions and wild beasts, I often found myself amid bevies of girls. My face was pale and my frame chilled with fasting; yet my mind was burning with desire, and the fire of lust leapt bubbling up before me when my flesh was as good as dead."

In attempting to construct a sophisticated belief system grounded in scriptural authority, Jerome and other Fathers interpreted the characters and histories of Eve and Mary as life lessons in sexuality and related questions of the human condition. This did not make for a theology sympathetic to women.

The Fathers accepted a division between the carnal or sexual and the spiritual, but they understood as well that people could keep their bodies either holy or polluted, temples consecrated to God or brothels dedicated to sinful lust. They also pointed directly to Adam and Eve and concluded that, because they had been innocent virgins before the Fall, their (hence mankind's) original sin must have been marriage and the sexuality it evoked. Jerome encapsulated this in his usual indelicate fashion: "There is no greater calamity connected with [marital] captivity than to be the victim of another's lust." Tertullian, who so despised marriage, especially his own, that he later joined the brutally antisex Montanist sect, declared, "It is laws which seem to make the difference between marriage and fornication; through diversity of illicitness, not through the nature of the thing itself."

To the Fathers, the world was split into good and evil, spirit and flesh, and marriage vows or not, sex was evil. "The body is meant not for fornication but for the Lord, and the Lord for the body," Paul preached. ". . . But because of cases of sexual immorality, each man should have his own wife, and each woman her own husband. . . . This I say by way of concession, not of command. I wish that all were as I myself am," he added grandly. Adam and Eve had created the carnal bond of marriage, which before the Fall had been spiritual and pure—in fact, angels were asexual—and righteous Christians who earned entry into paradise "shall not perform the functions of sex," Jerome said.

The road to angelic existence was clear: virginity, or if this message was too late, celibacy. "While you remain chaste and virgins you are equal to the angels of God," enthused Cyprian, the first African bishop, who would be martyred in 258. Ambrose concurred: "For chastity has made even angels. He who has preserved it is an angel; he who has lost it, a devil." Until the Second Coming transformed mankind into angels "of no sex" who would therefore never perform "the functions of sex," perfect chastity was a Christian's only proper way of life.

This united front of aggressive antisexuality and pro-celibacy produced outpourings of how-to-avoid-temptation writings that cast women as devilishly cunning temptresses. Even during the greeting ritual at church services, men ought to wrap their hands in their robes to dull the feeling of women's seductive touch. Jerome warned against succumbing to the "sickly taste" of married women who, "pressing their teeth together, now keeping their lips wide apart, speak with a lisp, and purposely clip their words . . . in what I call adultery of the tongue."

The sight and scent of a woman were equally tantalizing, but virginity had a different fragrance: "The smell of your right hand will be musty to you, and your limbs will be redolent with the odor of the resurrection; your fingers will exude myrrh," Ambrose informed virgins.

This identification of men with spirituality and goodness, women with carnality and evil, was a major common denominator in Fatherly thought. Jerome summed it up well: "It is not the harlot, or the adulteress who is spoken of, but woman's love in general is accused of ever being insatiable; put it out, it bursts into flame; give it plenty, it is again in need; it enervates a man's mind, and engrosses all thought except for the passion which it feeds."

Paul, who was obsessed by the need for women to veil themselves, recalled the ominous story of angels who lost control of themselves and fell head over heels in love with mortal women. The fallen angels impregnated these temptresses—in Paul's interpretation, the women were seductresses who victimized the poor angels—with offspring so evil that God retaliated by deluging their world with the Flood.

Women seduced even without trying, simply by being what they were: carnal beings, daughters of Eve. The wondrous exception, of course, was undefiled, virginal Mary. However, even this did not stop Jerome from commenting on how disgusting Jesus' infancy must have been: "[to be in the womb] for nine months growing larger, the sickness, the delivery, the blood, the swaddling clothes. Picture to yourself the infant in the enveloping membranes." Not, Jerome clearly felt, a pretty picture.

Early Christianity's major thrust was its preoccupation with sexuality, and with virginity and celibacy in particular. The reverence for chastity was not new, recalling a legacy of asceticism, from Essene communalism to major Greek thinkers. In scholar Morton S. Eslin's words, "Christianity did not make the world ascetic; rather the world in which Christianity found itself strove to make Christianity ascetic."

The emphasis on asceticism among Pythagoreans, Platonists, Stoics, and other philosophical schools was the source of inspiration and confirmation for the early Church Fathers' ideas. In the second century, for example, Justin Martyr loved repeating that Plato was a Christian long before Jesus ever appeared.

Christian celibacy, however, did much more than imitate Greek philosophers or renegade Jewish ascetics. Instead, it offered believers nothing less than freedom from the chains of the tyrannical Present Age. As John Chrysostom wrote, virginity revealed that "the things of the resurrection stand at the door." Though Christ's birth, crucifixion, and resurrection had ended the Present Age, the faithful had little sense of this great change; they lived, struggled, and suffered in their daily lives as they always had. "How can you possibly think that you are freed from the Ruler of this age, when even his flies still crawl all over you?" demanded Tertullian. How could the struggling, insect-ridden Christian announce to the world that the Present Age was indeed over?

Something tangible was needed. Christian thinkers searching for a solution found it in the ascetic practices and philosophies around them and formulated their own notion of sexual renunciation. In a world where individuals seemingly had little control over how their lives unfolded, the human body seemed the one place they could exercise free choice. At the same time, the sexual urge, like the instinct to eat or to sleep, was regarded as irreversible, unstoppable, and indispensable. The Greeks even called the penis "the necessity." So if Christians could harness their sexual urges and maintain lives built on chastity and a new way of living, they would be living proof of the end of an age. As historian Peter Brown has argued, sexuality was an ideal locus for radical change precisely because it was an innate drive or a process. This meant that renouncing and overcoming it was the perfect emblem for the blessed New Age.

From this perspective, the significance of the body was that it was a bridge between the individual self and society. Adam and Eve had exercised free choice and indulged in sex, thereby provoking the Fall and postlapsarian society, the Devil-driven Present Age. Human renunciation of sex could smash it down to re-create the exalted state of the pristine Garden of Eden.

Translated, this meant that married Christians, unlike the frankly sexual pagan newlyweds, went to bed "to avoid fornication" rather than to propagate society's citizenry. Christians also eschewed the customary public nudity of the baths. In the great church of Antioch, they constructed high railings to separate men and women. The Christian sexual revolution elevated male and female virgins to moral and cultural superiority. And Church leaders were usually celibate.

Contemporary pagans, Jews, and Zoroastrians were astounded at Christian celibacy and its implications of genetic suicide. "For you have received a curse, and have multiplied barrenness," Jews told Aphraat, a fourth-century bishop. For Jews as for other non-Christians, virginity was a treasure to be bestowed and, in the bestowing, lost. Christians, however, countered that as the Second Coming was on the horizon, they had no need to populate the earth. Later, after the Second Coming failed to materialize, they were comforted by the notion that their chastity was preparing their souls for a triumphal admission into paradise.

As Christianity matured, its devotees strove for lifelong celibacy in the face of intense social pressures to marry and procreate. Celibates lived the lives of angels and built around themselves another, unsecular society of believers no longer bound by the familiar blood ties of family and kinship. The Fathers understood the compulsion for children and family as well as sex, but Gregory of Nyssa and John Chrysostom, for example, argued that this was simply a response to the terrifying notion of death that had accompanied the Fall.

Moreover, because each individual had free choice about reserving his body for Christian celibacy or giving it to mainstream society, alternative communities eventually sprang up for those choosing the former: convents, nunneries, and a celibate upper clergy. Christianity also developed striking and satisfying rituals of participation, transformation, and promotion. Baptism, for example, delivered believers into angelhood; the Holy Eucharist transported them into an intimacy with God.

Early Christianity's ongoing theological debate about virginity sought to clarify how humans related to each other, and whether their bodies belonged to society or to themselves, to manage as they chose. Against the backdrop of their highly stratified world, even the poorest Christians were offered the virginity of their bodies as vehicles to carry them to an angelic life, with access to the holiest of holies, the one God.

The same theological debate, in its refinements of the Virgin Mary's story, also underscored the fundamental paradoxes of its own notions of virginity. As Christ, God had united with humanity through a woman's womb and suckled at her breasts. But how could hers be a fleshly human womb? God could not have devised such a filthy entry, and so her womb must have been virginal.

The maturing religion made harsh demands on its followers, particularly the renunciation of their sexuality, but it rewarded in even greater proportion. Faithful Christians, poor as well as rich, women as well as men, could wrest control of their bodies from society and dedicate them to godly celibacy, an empowering act that raised them up to the company of angels. And through the intercessions of Mary, the greatest virgin of all, they were permitted to know God.

Hail Mary? The Progressive Virginities of the Holy Mother

Christianity's obsession with chastity has blazed at meltdown intensity ever since Christ's birth to his virgin mother. This obsession targets all Christians, and though it focuses especially on women and religious, it embraces even married believers. Its deadly logic is unleavened by the demographic concern that celibate Christians cannot reproduce themselves, as incredulous Jewish and Muslim critics have pointed out. But the most warped and humorless debates focus on Mary, Christ's mother, culminating in a series of dogmas that, over the centuries, have relentlessly cleansed Mary of the earthiness and humanity she exudes in the Bible. She has metamorphosed from a virgin impregnated by the Holy Ghost to a still-virgin even after delivery, to an ever-virgin throughout her marriage, to an unearthly virgin immaculately conceived in her own mother's womb. The theological stranglehold on Mary's virginity, of course, has ensured that virginity in general never loses its fascination as a topic for Christian thinkers.

It took over eighteen centuries to formulate the creed about Mary that the

Roman Catholic Church still subscribes to. Most other Christian denominations are uncomfortable with any but the earliest versions. Interestingly, their official fixations with virginity are in almost direct ratio to the level of their belief in Mary's virginity.

The Gospel of Luke is the scriptural core of Mary's story, but includes later items such as Mary's habit of joining the apostles and Jesus' other followers in the "upper room" at Jerusalem. Luke's verses, a very few other New Testament sources, and Isaiah's "Look, the virgin shall conceive and bear a son, and they shall name him Emmanuel, which means, 'God is with us' " are the documentary evidence that convinced the Church Fathers of Mary's virginity and therefore of Christ's virgin birth.

Flimsy and incomplete though the sources are, Mary's story has been endlessly rewritten, edited, fact-checked, fact-fabricated, amplified, and commentated upon. Mariology, the Church teachings about Mary, expanded early on into a serious discipline that has devoured the scholarly lifetimes of celibate theologians. As they restructured her story, they stuffed libraries, confusing as they clarified, obfuscating as they rationalized. Then, in 1854, Pope Pius IX delivered the final edition, swaddled in the solemnity and pomp of ecclesiastical authority as an ex cathedra proclamation.

During the second century, Christian thinkers turned their thoughts to Mary and, by extension, to Joseph. The premise that Christ had been born of a virgin mother impregnated by the Holy Spirit was unremarkable—Zeus and other gods had routinely done this. But with the ascetic impulse that first permeated, then dominated, early Christianity, the idea of God hungering after Mary's youthful beauty, plotting and executing her seduction, struck a discordant note. God was no randy seducer—lust was the Devil's domain.

How, then, had the conception happened? Origen and other Church Fathers proposed several methods: through the words of an angel; through Mary's ear; through the mystical breath of the Holy Spirit (St. Ambrose's favorite). Sacred art was more imaginative: semen oozing from God's mouth down a tube ending up Mary's skirt; a dove instead of a tube; the Angel Gabriel inserting the seed into Mary's ear.

The Apostles' Creed, developed at the end of the fourth century and actually formalized in the eighth, had the Holy Ghost implanting the Child fully formed rather than as a seed nourished by Mary's body. By the seventeenth century, Francisco Suarez, Mary's first systematic theologian, laid it down that Mary had neither lost her virginity delivering Christ nor experienced womanly erotic sensations. This is the basic history of *virginitas ante partum*.

Obviously, many people could not and did not believe any of this, either as the doctrine was being hammered out or after it had been. They searched their hearts and could believe only that Christ was the blood son of Mary and

Joseph. Non-Christians respectful of Christianity—Muslims, for example—to this day revere Christ as a flesh-and-blood prophet. Alternately, some Christians believed he was not human at all but was a divinity who had simply appeared on earth as an adult. As early as the second century, however, these views were becoming dangerously heretical.

Believers, on the other hand, supported the virginal conception by referring to the apocryphal Book of James. Here, Mary had taken a vow of chastity that Joseph respected. Also, she was only engaged, not yet married—she had to be still a virgin.

The virginal conception was relatively palatable compared to the virgin birth, *virginitas in partu*. Now Mary remained virginal even after Christ's birth. The primary source for this was, once again, the apocryphal Book of James. In this version, the midwife who assisted in Christ's birth met Salomé and exclaimed, "A virgin has given birth, which nature never permits." Salomé was properly disbelieving. "As sure as the Lord, my God, lives, until I place my finger inside and examine her condition, I shall not believe that a virgin has given birth," she declared.

Salomé went directly to Mary and prepared her for the examination. But as she stuck her finger into the vagina, Salomé screamed with pain and instantly withdrew it. "I have tempted the living God," she cried. "See, my hand is consumed by fire and is falling off." She prayed and repented, and God promptly forgave her. Through her, the proof that Mary had somehow delivered Christ with her hymen intact became established fact.

This new doctrine was too far-fetched for some Church Fathers—Origen and Tertullian, for example—to swallow. However, its proponents slowly began to hold sway, and the *virginitas in partu* became dogma. Toward the end of the fourth century, the Churchman Jovian argued the point with Pope Siricius, the virulent celibate, insisting that Christ's birth had ended Mary's virginity by breaking her hymen. The pope was so furious at this apostasy that he excommunicated Jovian. It was official: Mary had given birth without losing her virginity.

Even this was not enough. Now single-minded ascetics demanded her virginity be extended in perpetuity. Pope Siricius explained why this must be so: "Jesus would not have chosen birth from a virgin, had he been forced to look upon her as so unrestrained as to let that womb, from which the body of the Lord was fashioned, that hall of the eternal king, be stained by the presence of male seed."

However, several serious obstacles to this thesis existed. Matthew refers clearly to a time before Mary and Joseph made love and mentions that Jesus was Mary's firstborn son, suggesting that others followed. Another Gospel informs us that James, Joses, Simon, and Judas were his four brothers. How, then, could Mary have remained a perpetual virgin? Tertullian, among others, contended she did not and Jesus' siblings were, indeed, his siblings.

Nonsense, said many other theologians. Christ's brothers were actually half brothers, Joseph's sons by a previous marriage. What previous marriage? Suddenly the fledgling Mariologists aged the kindly, upright young carpenter into a kindly, stooped old man who had already had four sons with his first, presumably deceased wife.

This was not acceptable to Jerome, however. What about poor Joseph? "He who was worthy to be called the father of the Lord, remained a virgin." How dare his colleagues delete Joseph from the list of approved virgins! It was "godless, apocryphal daydreaming" to suggest that an unchaste Joseph would have been good enough for the virginal Mary. Those pesky brothers, Jerome explained, were "brethren in point of kinship" only, "not by nature." Meaning? Cousins, of course. James, Joses, Simon, and Judas were Christ's cousins.

Mary had become a lifelong virgin, who had birthed without interference to her hymen, and was married to Joseph, another lifelong virgin. The Mariologists couldn't stop there. What about Mary's own birth from Anne's sperm-contaminated womb? But it wasn't; Origen argued that "my Savior Jesus entered into this world without defilement; in his mother he was not impure, he entered into a body that remained intact." How was that? Because Mary was so spiritually pure that she effectively had no body, and Anne and Joachim had conceived her without feeling the slightest lust. Ergo, Mary's conception had been immaculate—and the doctrine of the Immaculate Conception was born.

Twelfth-century England refined the Immaculate Conception. Anselm of Canterbury wrote that "it was fitting that she be clothed with a purity so splendid that none greater under God could be conceived." Eadmer, also of Canterbury, honed this to its current status: Mary's conception in Anne's womb was pure and devoid of lust. In 1854, Pope Pius IX proclaimed this as dogma: Mary's conception was "preserved immune from all stain of original sin."

Today, the catechism of the Catholic Church reiterates Mary's Immaculate Conception and cites Pius IX as above. It affirms Mary's virginity when Christ was conceived "by the Holy Spirit without human seed." And though Mary as the Ever-Virgin is an integral part of the Catholic liturgy, St. Augustine is invoked for an all-embracing definition. Mary "remained a virgin in conceiving her Son, a virgin in giving birth to him, a virgin in carrying him, a virgin in nursing him at her breast, always a virgin." In 1964, however, the Second Vatican Council decided against proclaiming Mary's virginity during and after birth as an article of faith. Too many Catholics were tormented by doubts about it.

Mariology differs absolutely from the hagiography that so lyrically painted portraits of Mary of Egypt, St. Bridget of Sweden, and hundreds of other holy women. They all, even Catherine of Siena, had lusts and bodies to deny, and they all erred, sinned, repented, and were forgiven. Mary, on the other hand, was angelically sexless, like Eve before the Fall, and no human woman could ever emulate her. Nonetheless, in thrusting Mary forward as a godly creature, the Mariologists provided women with a comforting figure they could turn to, who would intercede for them with God. Mortal women also related strongly to Mary's mothering qualities, accentuated through the Middle Ages and expressed in sacred paintings of her tenderly breast-feeding the infant Jesus.

Seen from another angle, Mary was so utterly, blamelessly unsexual that her virginity was an object of veneration only. It suggested nothing about celibacy, about its issues, temptations, or rewards. Hers was a special case, never replicated. Mary was, in sum, almost accusingly virginal, a reproach to women who could not even remotely approximate her purity. Nor did her elevation to the highest realm of divinity improve women's status. If anything, in many women it fostered a revulsion to marriage.

Nonetheless, Mariology had enormous significance for Christian celibacy, because as it matured and intensified, it cast its shadow on discussions of human virginity and celibacy and on the essential nature of women. In early Christianity, for example, Church Fathers pondered deeply the question "Are virgins still women?" The answer was usually a qualified no, at least in the case of dead, deified virgins who could not suddenly stumble from the path of righteous lustlessness and prove that, at heart, they were just weak women. Young, living women had to prove themselves far more strictly, if possible by living alone and enduring the most defeminizing, desexualizing austerities, in particular fasting to bony, bloodless emaciation.

A fundamental sadness underlies Mariology, the study of a simple heroine who left no diaries or personal testimonies. The great paradox of the virginalization of Mary is that its authors were celibate men who mistrusted and disliked women. Their hatred for the usual occupations of her gender—marriage, childbirth, and motherhood—transformed Mary into a Queen of the World, unrecognizable as a woman or even a human. More disturbing still was how their fundamental misogyny washed out over the Christian world, seeping into other doctrines. The most obviously affected was celibacy, based as it was on a notion of women as evil, weak-willed, lustful seductresses.

Despite the Mariologists' immense power, they were unable to halt the development of a persistent tendency among freethinking Christian women to reject this orthodoxy in favor of an assertive and liberating celibacy. These Church Mothers, Beguines, ambitious abbesses and nuns, and chaste wives were celibates who had their own mission: a devout, holy, deeply religious self-purification. From this flowed consequential benefits—liberation from husbands in particular and men in general; access to prohibited professions and scholarship and knowledge; recognition as holy women; self-actualization and direction. Their personal crusades were too unstoppable for even the Mariologists to vanquish them in the name of the everlasting Virgin, Mary, Queen of the World.

ENCRATITES AND GNOSTICS BOYCOTT THE WOMB

In the early centuries of the Church, the Fathers' basic ideas about women, men, sexuality, and celibacy should be contextualized: they were not the only Christian thinkers, merely the most powerful. Two other major sects were the Encratites and the Gnostics, both virulently antisex celibates, whose premises deeply influenced the evolution of the mainstream Christian concept of celibacy.

The Encratites, who were especially strong in Syria, derived their name from the Greek *enkrateia*—continence—their overriding principle. They labeled marriage a "polluted and foul way of life" and beseeched future spouses to forgo the "filthy intercourse" that their leading theologian, Tatian, credited the Devil with inventing. Virginity, on the other hand, was perfection incarnate.

The Encratite preoccupation with celibacy stemmed from Tatian's interpretation of the famous events in the Garden, where the Fall had played out as a sexual tragedy. Then Adam and Eve had been chaste, nonanimal beings, each "married" to the Holy Spirit. They knew God just as the angels did and were destined to live forever. But, lured by the serpent who taught Eve its bestial ways, they forsook this pure life for sexual relations with one another.

The consequences were apocalyptic: a descent from bestial behavior into bestiality itself, then death. "And marriage followed the woman, and reproduction followed marriage, and death followed reproduction." More eloquently, "For that which befalleth the sons of man befalleth beasts: as the one dieth, so dieth the other; yea, they have all one breath: so that a man has no preeminence above a beast: for all is vanity."

In that one coupling, Adam and Eve had undone mankind's union with God. To reclaim it, therefore, each individual had to renounce sexual intercourse—in effect, to boycott the womb, "for it is ordained that everyone should correct his own fall," a promise of hope in an otherwise gloomy moral scenario. Virgins were blessed with original celibacy, but married people had only to embrace celibacy after baptism and they, too, entered into a state of holiness.

Encratite baptism was designed as a desexualizing ritual. Men and women stripped off their clothes and walked naked into the baptismal pool. This cold immersion nullified the heat of their fiery birth, and the Holy Spirit entered the water and enveloped the bare flesh in a robe of glory. Thus garbed, the baptized adults stood around the pool as sexually innocent as children.

In Encratite tradition, Judas Thomas was Christ's "twin," and his valiant earthly struggles against the demons of the Present Age were recorded in the Acts of Judas Thomas.

Boycotting the womb was the Encratite declaration of war against bestial sexuality and the Devil-designed Present Age, where poor people went hungry while kings squandered fortunes on elaborate palaces. Boycotting the womb also liberated women from lifelong enslavement. Encratites saw the virgin's wedding veil as a symbol of sexual shame to come and the dismantling of the lavish wedding tent as the corruption of bondage to the body, sexuality, childbirth, and child-rearing. As Judas Thomas taught, "marriage passeth away with much contempt, Jesus alone abideth."

Once committed to celibacy, however, men and women could peacefully assemble together, live as couples, and congregate in communities that seem like precursors to American Shaker havens. These communities flourished in the mountains of Syria and Asia Minor, sustained by converts and orphaned children. Jesus, the Second Adam, was succeeding in his mission to redeem mankind from its sin of sexuality, dating from when the First Adam disobeyed God and did as Eve coaxed him.

The Gnostics—*gnosis* means "true knowledge" in Greek—were another immensely influential Christian sect. One of the leaders, Marcion, so abhorred sexuality that he denied Jesus' birth from a woman and portrayed him instead as a fully formed man who had floated down from the heavens. Marcion was celibate and forbade his followers to marry. He granted Christian rites such as baptism and the Eucharist only to virgins, widows, and husbands and wives who consented to "repudiate the fruit of their marriage."

Marcion based his teachings on the Gospel according to the Egyptians, in which Jesus replied to Salomé's query about how long human death will last: "As long as you women bear children." Another Gnostic gospel had Jesus saying about a woman, "I will lead her that I may make her male, so that she may become a living spirit like you males. For every woman who makes herself male shall enter the kingdom of heaven."

This signified, the Gnostics thought, that unsteady Eve would disappear back into Adam's hard, clean rib. "Enter through the rib whence you came and hide yourself from the beasts," they urged her. Secrete yourself away from all knowledge of sexuality, for sexual desire undermines the soul's longing to reunite with God. Sex was "the unclean rubbing that is from the fearful fire that came from the fleshly part," but ceasing to indulge in it was not enough. Overcoming sexual desire was necessary to achieve the resurrection of the self.

One young Christian learned this lesson the hard way. To rid himself of his unruly sexual organ, he took a sickle and sliced it off, saying, "There you have the pattern and cause of all this!" But the Encratite apostle John did not congratulate him for castrating himself, for the danger lay elsewhere, in "the unseen springs through which every shameful emotion is stirred up and comes to light."

For Gnostics who managed to subdue their desire and experience their soul's union with God, life was an oasis of physical and spiritual serenity in a hard, unjust world. This was doubly true for women, who sat alongside men at the feet of Gnostic teachers, indifferent to their flesh, thirsting for true knowledge, raised by faith to the unique status of equality with Gnostic men.

So startling was the contrast between mainstream and Gnostic treatment of women that almost every Gnostic teacher faced charges of sexual malfeasance. No wonder—Gnostic acceptance of redeemed women as on a par with men had no parallel in Judaism, standard Christianity, or paganism. Rabbis, for instance, warned that teaching the Torah to a daughter was teaching her immorality. For Gnostics, the spiritual salvation of baptism and wisdom was their legacy to posterity, not the production of children. Like the Encratites, boycotting the womb was the fertile path back to the godly paradise Adam and Eve had forfeited by their Fall in the Garden of Eden. When women responded, boycotting their own wombs, forgoing childbearing, Gnostics recognized their spiritual redemption and ushered them into the study groups and fellowship traditionally reserved to males. The cruel physical world dissolved in the warm glow of their Gnosticism, the true knowledge that divested the ways of the world—marriage, love, parenthood—of all significance and reassured them that their "unity of perfect thought" was, indeed, God's community on earth.

Give Me Chastity . . . but Not Yet

Augustine's youthful plea—"Lord, give me chastity and continence, but not yet"—is perhaps the Christian world's most famous prayer. Since he uttered it, it has resonated down through the centuries and made Augustine a soul mate in human love, confusion, and good intentions. Which one of us has not, at least once, translated his appeal into his own life, if not with chastity, then with other cherished sins?

Augustine was a privileged, educated young man whose long life, 354 to 430, covered some of Christianity's most interesting transformations and movements, including the fourth-century monastic revolution. He himself, as a brilliant and devout Catholic, arguably the greatest of the Church

Fathers, was enormously influential in shaping orthodox theology, especially on the subject of celibacy.

For at least a decade, celibacy was very little on Augustine's mind. He was intensely religious and belonged to the Manichean Christian sect, later regarded as heretical. Mani, its founder, had lived and died—by crucifixion—in southern Babylonia from 216 to 277. His religion drew from Gnosticism, Christianity, Zoroastrianism, and Greek philosophy, had a hierarchy and apostles, and was inspired by the doctrine contained in the seven books of Mani.

Manicheanism was dualistic, contrasting a Prince of Darkness with a God of Light. In this contest between light and dark, good and evil, the body of the Manichean was no more than a prison, created by demons, which trapped the good light within. The great Manichean goal was to liberate that imprisoned light. The only way to achieve this was through celibacy, which would prevent the creation of new prisons, and other ascetic practices, which would release trapped light.

For eleven years Augustine had followed Manicheanism as an Auditor or "hearer" of the truth, all the while longing to become one of the Elect. Membership in the Elect, the elite group of the religion, required celibacy, since procreation, because it trapped light inside, was evil. The Elect also had to renounce private property and trade and follow a strict vegetarian regime, releasing light by eating bread, vegetables, or seeded fruit.

Augustine, however, remained outside the Elect pale. Like his fellow Auditors, he was considered morally good though spiritually inferior to the Elect. This was because Auditors were flawed by their inability to relinquish such worldly preoccupations as the pursuit of money, property, meat-eating, and marriage, or—as in Augustine's case—concubinage. In the Manichean worldview, everyone else—the non-Elect and non-Auditor—was hopelessly hedonistic, evil, and doomed.

Augustine's great moral dilemma was that he could not forgo sex. For eleven years as an Auditor, he struggled to qualify as an Elect, but celibacy was the stumbling block. Augustine was obsessed by sex and, throughout this period, lived with a concubine, the mother of his son, Adeodatus.

Since childhood, Augustine had been tormented by lust. He could even pinpoint the first time this had happened. His father had taken him to a public bath, where he had had an erection. The young Augustine was deeply embarrassed. Not so his father, who delighted in "the signs of active virility coming to life." In stark contrast, his mother, Monica, was distraught about the incident. So was Augustine, and it stuck forever in his impressionable mind.

Despite his striving to join the Elect, Augustine lived in open sin. At the same time, he agonized about the lustfulness he despised yet could not bring himself to renounce. Hence his frequent, prayerful cries.

Monica was another source of acute pressure. Though she accepted her son's concubine and her grandson Adeodatus, she pushed Augustine to convert to Christianity and to marry. Gradually, and unwillingly, Augustine decided marriage would, indeed, be the best outlet for his carnal desires; he would rather marry than burn. Unhappily, his concubine was not a candidate—she was probably of an inferior social rank. Augustine, though drenched in her tears and scalded by her reproaches (or so we may suppose), shipped her off, though he kept Adeodatus, whom death soon also swept away. With his concubine out of the way, Augustine became betrothed to a girl so young he had to wait to marry her, which meant she was under the minimum legal age of twelve, far closer in age to Adeodatus than to Augustine.

But Augustine soon discovered he could not contain his lust until his child fiancée grew up. Instead of fighting his recalcitrant penis, he again took a mistress. As he would later reiterate time and again, "The law in our members fights with the law of our mind."

Augustine's member was sufficiently undisciplined that he developed a loathing of erections, "that bestial movement . . . modesty would have to struggle" against. Passion, he wrote, is that which "rises up against the soul's decision in disorderly and ugly movement." Vulgar erections were, Augustine believed, why men and women had to conceal their lust under an apron of fig leaves after the Fall. Women, too, are stirred by sexual feelings, he admitted, but he believed the main benefit in shrouding their nakedness was to prevent it from arousing men.

During the interregnum between mistress and marriage, Augustine had an epiphany in the form of this passage from Romans: "Not in rioting and drunkenness, not in chambering and wantonness, not in strife and envying; but put ye on the Lord Jesus Christ, and make not provision for the flesh, to fulfill the lusts thereof."

Galvanized, he took these words as a summons to renounce sexuality. At last his mother got her way, but only partially. Her son converted to Christianity but rejected marriage. "You converted me to yourself," Augustine later addressed himself to Christ, "so that I no longer desired a wife or placed any hope in this world." The former libertine had become a lifelong celibate. Adeodatus was the only grandchild Augustine would give his mother.

Like many neophytes, Augustine flung himself fervently into the new religion. He was especially adamant about celibacy, the touchstone of his conversion. He hated coitus with all the passion of the newly converted celibate and remarked that he knew nothing that more wrenched "the manly mind down from the heights than a woman's caresses and that joining of bodies without which one cannot have a wife."

But unrequited, uninvited lust still racked him. At night his dreams betrayed him with sexual visions, and his tormented body responded so that he woke to find that, during the night, he had unknowingly ejaculated. This primal lust tortured Augustine and, in combination with his Manichean background, shaped his sternly lust-condemnatory theology.

Over his long life, Augustine distilled his thoughts about sex and celibacy in a number of books, most still widely studied today. He wrote that sexual intercourse was evil if it was corrupted by desire, and his experiences suggested it was always so corrupted, even in old age. His chagrin at the irrepressibility of lust seeps through his discovery that an acquaintance, "a man eighty-four years of age who, after living religiously and in continence with a religious wife for twenty-five years, bought himself a Lyristria [lyre girl] to satisfy his lust."

Augustine located sexuality at the core of each human being, and he interpreted it as the echo of mankind's original sin, Adam and Eve in the Garden, disobeying God. Through the prism of sexuality he saw reflected lust, man's fundamental flaw. Hateful erections were its mark, and even miserable wet dreams—every man's—testified to it. Unlike the earlier Fathers, Augustine did not localize lust in women.

Furthermore, decades of ministering had taught him the sad lesson that his ideal of marital celibacy could never be imposed. Husbandly fidelity and abstinence from sex during Lent were the most he could expect from married Catholics. However, though the natural urge to marry was a God-given good, sexual lust, manifested by erections, was demonic and had to be countered with chastity.

> Your flesh is like your wife. . . . Love it, rebuke it; let it be formed into one bond of body and soul, one bond of married concord. . . . Learn now to master what you will receive as a united whole. Let it now go short, so that it will then enjoy abundance.

Christians should not, however, plunge zestily into providing children for society, but should "descend with a certain sadness" into sexual intercourse, which could never be the pure, passionless coupling that had existed before the Fall. In any case, married people tended to see themselves as mothers and fathers more than women and men, which alleviated lust.

Marital sex had another moral advantage: it drained each partner's lust so that neither strayed into infidelity. Unlike his theological predecessors, Augustine rated women's sexuality, indeed their very nature, as far weaker than men's, making celibacy easier for them but requiring their subordination as a logical outcome.

Yet despite his compassionate, realistic views on marital sex, Augustine's spiritual and intellectual commitment to, and understanding of, celibacy impelled him to endorse it. "The evil of carnal concupiscence is so great that it is better to refrain from using it than to use it well," he wrote. Nor did he advocate ascetic regimens such as fasting to conquer it. What really mattered was humility, and bending always to God's will.

Women, in Augustine's opinion, could not even choose chastity; unless God called them to it, they ought to assume their female responsibilities. Not for them the joys of shucking off the burdens of marriage and the bearing and raising of children. But virgins by vocation could live in chaste communality, modestly veiled, enjoying each other's friendship and pure love. Obedience was the key, for unlike other Fathers, Augustine taught that "greater, indeed, is the good of obedience than the good of continence."

To the end of his long life, the man who had implored God to grant him delayed chastity urged it upon fellow Christians who had not had the benefit of his own decades of prior self-gratification. Probably because of his own highly charged erotic drive, Augustine minimized women's role as temptresses, though he did not translate this into any sort of reprieve from the rigors of marriage and child-rearing, except for those few virgins exempted by God from their gender's usual calling. At least a few of these latter were to prove pious Christian thorns in the side of the Church Fathers, who watched, askance, as the women seized on sexual abstinence as a tool of personal liberation as much as it was an expression of their obedience to God's will.

UNCONVENTIONAL VIRGINS
Church Mothers

For many women, Christianity was a powerful, all-consuming religion that demanded much and delivered in equal proportion. They embraced it with gusto and modeled their lives on its principles, emphasizing what suited their natures. For some, extreme asceticism—self-flagellation and fasting to the point of starvation—was the path to salvation. For others, it was self-appointed, solitary service to God, freed from the constraints of marriage and household supervision, of pregnancy and child-rearing.

Not surprisingly, the Church Fathers worried about unconventional virgins. Tertullian's persistent instructions that virgins should wear veils was in response to those who went about unveiled; Jerome's concerns about their traveling and mingling with men stemmed from the number of virgins doing just that; and Augustine's stricture against unholy pride was directed against chaste maidens openly proud of their independence.

Stories about outstanding virgins astounded, impressed, influenced, and outraged the Christian world. Whether true, wildly embellished, or entirely fictional, these women's stories survived for centuries and inspired countless others with their examples of courageous and confident devotion to celibate, godly ways of life.

The story of Constantina, daughter of a Christian emperor, is actually a fable that has inspired legions of Christians. Curiously, it portrays Constantina as diametrically opposite to the flesh and blood—and bloody—Constantina. But it is the good Constantina who endures, not the brutal, conniving woman known to historians. Here, then, is her legend.

Though Constantina's father was Constantine the Great, her noble lineage did not protect her from the scourge of childhood leprosy. Shy and sickly from her dread affliction, Constantina was taken to Rome, perhaps by her Christian grandmother Helen, to the shrine of St. Agnes, the virgin who had been martyred in 304 under Diocletian's terror. During Agnes' trial, the prosecutor had mocked her Christianity and warned that, before her execution, he would confine her to a bordello so she would not die a virgin. Prior to being raped, Agnes was stripped and displayed to a throng of spectators, one of whom was struck blind as he goggled at her nakedness. Nonplussed, the governor voided the order for her defilement and had her decapitated instead.

Miraculously, St. Agnes visited Constantina and instructed her to be constant and have faith in Jesus Christ, who was the son of God and a healer. Then, at St. Agnes' tomb, Constantina was cured. Profoundly affected, she vowed to be "constant" and committed her virginity to Jesus. She also convinced her father to honor St. Agnes with a church.

Emperor Constantine, however, clearly did not comprehend the scope of his daughter's pledge. His gratitude to St. Agnes must have been enormous, for she had healed his little daughter. However, he still considered Constantina a marriageable young woman whose betrothal he could arrange for his political purposes. Within the Roman cultural context, this was entirely reasonable. The daughters of high-ranking families were important to their fathers, who expected nothing less than irreproachable moral conduct and total obedience from their beloved girls. Even as married women, they were supposed to seek protection and support from their fathers rather than their husbands.

Roman custom came into play over Christianity when the widowed Gallicanus, a powerful general, asked Constantine's permission to marry Constantina. For the emperor it was an excellent match that would ally him with a military strongman who might, in other circumstances, try to challenge or overthrow him. Gallicanus was also a good and popular man, and so Constantine finalized the engagement to Constantina.

But how could Constantina, a sworn virgin, marry anyone? With atypical, undaughterly rebelliousness, she argued her case with Constantine. And, from her point of view, why not? "In truth, virgins have so much rank in their soul that they may withstand imperial order," she said with pious defiance.

Surprisingly, Constantine conceded her position and asked her advice on how to solve the dilemma. Constantina produced an instant solution: she sent her faithful servants, John and Paul, to witness to Gallicanus, and she brought his little daughters Attica and Artemia to the palace where she lived in a community of 120 virgins. The plan was to convert these children, who would then plead the cause of Christian virginity to their father.

Attica and Artemia could withstand Constantina's proselytizing bombardments for only so long. After twenty-one debates with their stepmother-not-to-be, they capitulated and became Christian virgins. One of the perks of this unusual state was the right to flout social norms in favor of Christian values, while demanding the highest status because of their sexual virtue.

Gallicanus, too, out on the martial trail, was transformed. The enemy was crushing his legions and Roman tribunes were surrendering. John and Paul, Constantina's emissaries, sprang into action, preaching Christianity until the desperate general promised to accept it. At that instant, a gigantic young man appeared, shouldering a cross and leading soldiers who turned Gallicanus' defeat into splendid victory. So thankful was Gallicanus that when he returned to Rome, he no longer attended the temple. His new place of worship was the Christian church. And, of course, he gracefully accepted—indeed, agreed with—Constantina's firm decision to remain an unmarried virgin.

(The real Constantina married her Christian father's general Hannibalianus and, as the queen of this king of kings, ruled with him in Pontus. After Emperor Constantine died, however, Constantina's brother had Hannibalianus killed and remarried his sister to their cousin Gallus, who became caesar in 351, but was assassinated two years later. Constantina, his widow, died soon after, her legacy a reputation as a cold-blooded and power-hungry conspirator.)

The legend of Constantina has several messages, but the principal one is defiance. Christian women may—indeed, should—opt for virginity, which will automatically elevate them socially beyond the pale of even their father's authority. And though Constantina was an emperor's daughter, Christian women of any rank, even the humblest, could follow her example and vault upward to outrank even the highest of earthly leaders. Then, as chaste paragons, they could opt out of almost all womanly responsibilities.

The legend's longevity is testimony to its appeal. Of course, the tiny coincidences of myth and history helped: both Constantinas were really buried in the tomb of St. Agnes, whose basilica their emperor father actually constructed. Constantina's force of character and bold disregard of social conventions and lines of authority were, ultimately, exceedingly attractive to

Christian women who hoped they, too, could liberate themselves through devout virginity.

Our second Church Mother, Mary of Egypt, was a virgin of the reborn variety and one of the best-loved heroines of morality literature, a prostitute redeemed by Christianity into the highest level of holiness. In Rome, where women had few political rights, prostitutes were either slaves or freedwomen without social standing and were rarely Roman born. They worked in brothels or were kept by hoteliers, bakers, or restaurateurs to entertain customers. Others freelanced, sauntering the streets in search of customers. Some hustled in cemeteries and moonlighted as professional mourners. The lowest of the low, the *diabolariae* or twopennies, worked the baths, street corners, alleys, the usual grungy venues.

Once prostituted, a woman could never reclaim the status accorded decent women. The law forbade Roman men to marry even repentant, retired prostitutes, who were considered eternally dishonored. For their entire lifetimes, all prostitutes were forced to distinguish themselves from their chaste sisters by appearing in the street in togas, strictly men's wear, instead of the *stolica* or stole.

Perhaps the flamboyance of Mary's profession and the irreversibility of its stigma contributed to the great popularity of her legend. It endured for centuries, translated into several languages, and was recorded in both prose and poetry.

Mary's story begins when she was twelve years old. She abandoned her parents and went off to live in Alexandria, where, she told the ascetic monk Zosimas, "for seventeen years I sold my body, not to accumulate riches but just to live a luxurious life. I abandoned myself to drinking, sleeplessness, and lived a defiled life with laughter, ardor, and friends."

In sophisticated and cosmopolitan Alexandria, Mary the harlot would have driven through the streets unveiled, her hair streaming behind her, brightly dyed to highlight its free flow. She would have oiled it to shiny sleekness and parted it to cascade down in waves, fastening the coils with finely wrought metal barrettes, nets, and tiaras.

Mary's wardrobe would have been gaily colored to match or to contrast with her startling hair. She would have worn metal bracelets, necklaces, rings, anklets, hairpins, brooches, and buckles, all decorated with precious or semiprecious stones. Her earrings, two or three per ear, might have been pearl. She might also have favored slender, long, golden chains that coursed over her breasts and sides.

She certainly bathed often and, like other Egyptian women, shaved off or plucked out all her bodily hair. She would have oiled and perfumed her body and made herself up with concealing rouge to enhance her natural beauty or disguise the ravages her dissolute lifestyle had etched into her careless face.

After a decade of dissipated living, Mary was struck by a procession of Christian pilgrims from Libya about to set sail for Jerusalem. Could she join them? she inquired. Certainly, they replied, but she had to pay her own passage across. Mary had no money, having frittered it all away on various extravagances, but she saw that as no problem. Take my body instead of money, she suggested, and someone—the lecherous captain? randy sailors? surely not a pilgrim!—must have accepted her offer, for she was permitted onto the ship and landed with the troop in Jerusalem.

Mary and the others marched in the procession of the Cross to the church, but a mysterious force barred her from following them inside. Try as she might, she could not enter the sanctuary. At last, her egregious sins had caught up with her. Mary sank down to the ground and wept, heartbroken at her depraved way of life. Something stirred and she looked upward. Her namesake, the Virgin Mary, gazed down. Sinful Mary implored pure Mary for forgiveness and repented heartily of her sins. Suddenly she found she could walk through the doorway into the church.

After she had worshiped inside, Mary heard a disembodied voice intone, "If you cross the Jordan, you will find rest." With God as her guide, Mary set out on her journey. A godly man gave her three coins and she bought three loaves of bread. Then, shedding copious tears of repentance, she crossed the river Jordan and set out alone into the desert.

Forty years later, the kindly monk Zosimas found her there. He saw a figure in the distance, naked and burnt black by the relentless sun, covered only by a mass of hair that resembled white wool. Zosimas began to pursue this odd person, who moved swiftly away from him. When he finally won the chase, the creature astonished him by saying, "Father Zosimas, why do you chase me? Forgive me for not turning toward you, for I am a woman nude. Lend me your cloak so I may turn toward you and accept your prayers."

Who and what was this wraith? And how had she known his name? Zosimas slipped out of his cloak and handed it to her. Then, standing there in the glare of the desert sun, they debated about who should first bless the other, each crediting the other with superior holiness. Zosimas won the argument. "I see, O Mother, that you are full of the holy spirit, knowing my name and priestly office when you've never seen me. You are proven great by your works. I join with you through God in first accepting a benediction from you."

And so Mary, the high-living-harlot-turned-ascetic-hermit, was judged holier than the peaceable old monk. Her conversation with Zosimas turned on her struggles with the flesh. For her first seventeen years in the desert, she had been plagued by memories of her debauched but agreeable past life. Tears and prayer had finally triumphed, and she had ever since subsisted on her initial three loaves of bread and wrapped her body in God's word. She did not read the Scriptures, but merely gloried in the knowledge of God's word. Zosimas, overcome by the "miracles without number" she had performed, prostrated himself before her.

A year later, following her instructions, Zosimas returned with the Holy Host of the Eucharist. Mary was waiting on the other side of the Jordan, and seeing him arrive, she walked straight across the water to where he stood. He marveled at this new miracle, then administered the Holy Communion. Spiritually purified, Mary bid him farewell and marched back across the Jordan.

The next year at the same time, Zosimas came back and found Mary dead. In the sand around her corpse was this message: "Father Zosimas, bury Mary in this place, and return her to the earth. Pray for me to the Lord at whose command I left this earth on the second day of April."

Sobbing, Zosimas scrabbled at the hard ground with his bare hands but could not dredge out a hollow. Suddenly he noticed a big lion. "The holy woman wants me to bury her body," he told the ferocious animal. "But I am too old to dig and I don't have a shovel." So with its huge claws the lion dug Mary's grave, and Zosimas laid her gently into it, once again covering her nakedness with his own cloak.

Back at his monastery, Zosimas recounted his amazing story. His fellow monks rejoiced and began an annual celebration of the holy woman. Zosimas, who lived to be one hundred, never tired of repeating the wondrous tale. Over the centuries, it was told and retold, and countless Christians took its mysteries straight into their hearts.

Mary's story, like Constantina's, was both spiritually uplifting and thrillingly subversive. As a slip of a girl, Mary had sinned. She had deserted her family and headed straight for wicked, delightful Alexandria. As a runaway, she had chosen the world's oldest, most iniquitous profession. Worse, she had reveled in her degenerate life, the orgies of food, wine, and sex, the gorgeous clothes and sparkling jewels, the glorious, hennaed hair gleaming with olive oil. She was as prodigal of her money as of her body, spending, wasting, never saving, existing from orgasm to orgasm, hers and those of her stream of paying clients. No redeeming question of seduction or force—for seventeen years, Mary was the happiest of hookers, carefree, profligate, spendthrift, hedonistic. If ever there was a prodigal daughter, Mary was she.

And so God saw it. Through the intervention of the best Mary, He rescued this worst Mary and gently, kindly, urged her onto the path of righteousness. From a life of silks and perfume, pomegranates and wine—all enjoyed with her many friends—gregarious, fun-loving Mary plunged—alone!—into the hostile desert, with only three loaves of bread between her and starvation.

The privations that lurked there were almost, but not quite, unimaginable: blistering days, freezing nights, scarce water, flying pests and biting insects, wild animals, evil nomads. Her clothes shredded and fell away, exposing her now chaste body. She munched on the crumbs of her dry, hard bread and quenched her parched tongue with the juice of desert herbage. But though she soon stilled her bodily needs, her carnal appetite remained ferocious. Each year of sated lust required a year of ascetic penitence to obliterate, and so for her first seventeen years, Mary was tormented not only by sexual temptation but also by visions of the food and drink she had consumed during her seventeen years of harlotry. A year for a year—and finally, she was purified.

At the end, what nobility and purpose, what confident holiness! For Mary the Chaste Hermit was as independent as Mary the Rollicking Whore, enduring harsh nature and loneliness without even the Scriptures to comfort her. She needed nothing, so abundant were her internal resources and her devotion to God. The poorest of the poor, Mary had the richest soul of all.

The last in our tales of Christian virgins is that of Helia, another woman who existed entirely in the imagination of her literary creator, Theodora, wife of Lucinius, who corresponded with Church Father Jerome and embellished Helia's story with anecdotes from Jerome's writings. Theodora and Lucinius were wealthy Spaniards obsessed with leading ascetic lives. So certain were they that the Churchmen had the key to asceticism that, Jerome said, in 398 Lucinius "sent six copyists . . . to copy for him all that I have ever dictated from my youth until the present time." However, Lucinius died soon after, leaving the perusal of Jerome's opuses to Theodora, who probably borrowed from them to create her own best-selling hagiography, which focused on her preoccupation with sexual renunciation.

Like Theodora, Helia was the beautiful daughter of the Christian metropolitan bishop of Epiro, a member of the Spanish nobility. As a young girl with deep religious leanings, Helia vowed "not to be subject to the curse of Eve, but rather to participate in the blessings of Mary." She would never marry a mortal man, she decided. Instead, she would be the bride of Christ.

Helia set about preparing herself by strict fasts and interminable prayer, though she prudently concealed her intentions from her family. A priest, however, became aware of Helia's vocation and connived to provide sacred books she could study in secret. At last, her mother must have noticed that Helia was too thin, too secretive, too withdrawn from worldly concerns. She began to snoop and perhaps caught Helia with the illicit books or overheard a fervent prayer for eternal virginity. Whichever it was, she confronted Helia, who revealed her unnatural plans for her future.

Helia's mother was frantic. But she was a dignified woman who handled her problem in style. She and Helia had a classic little chat that, as Theodora reported it, filled two books and fourteen folio pages. The issue: Should Helia be obliged to marry or should her family tolerate her desire to remain chaste?

The argument raged. Women's roles should be defined by men's achievements, her mother contended. Not mine, Helia countered. I am not interested in helping a man achieve spiritual perfection. I want to achieve it myself, by myself. Finally, the dismayed mother conceded defeat and took her case to court, hauling her stubborn daughter in front of a blustering, bullying judge and demanding he grant permission to have Helia "seized as a wife." How, the mother must have wondered grimly, could she lose this round against her recalcitrant daughter?

Helia's interrogation was a hellish experience, a public spectacle "watched by the world of angels and men." In a "terrifying" voice, the judge opened fire. But Helia was no cringing coward, and she steadfastly argued and defended her position. Despite his authority and belligerence, the judge fared no better than Helia's mother. The girl simply would not waver.

Helia's arguments were mainly Jerome's, with convenient extrapolations, interpretations, and of course, omissions. Her distillation of ideas constituted an early Christian feminist defense of virginity and spoke to Christian (and soul-searching pagan) women with a clear, articulate voice.

Helia (Jerome) delved into the Old Testament for examples of holy, celibate, mainly male bachelors—the best known being Joshua, Elijah, and Gideon—and New Testament virgins—Christ the Virgin Savior himself, John the Baptist, the apostles John and Paul. "[Before Christ's birth] sterility was bad, now sterility is blessed," Helia declared. Then she related this to female virginity: "When she accepts a spouse, a woman is called away from the house of God; a virgin remains joined with Christ. Marriage is in Adam; virginity is in Christ. Marriage is death; virginity grants salvation. Marriage is pain; virginity is benediction." Directly plagiarizing Jerome, Helia went on, "For marriage fills the earth; but heaven is filled with virginity."

Helia also endorsed the Church Fathers' hierarchy of virtuous women: virgins are in first place, with widows and wives trailing behind. Helia wanted to be in first place. Furthermore, since she had already promised herself to Christ as his bride, marriage to a mortal man would be tantamount to adultery.

Despite the power of Helia's exposition, the debate—for that was what it was—ended inconclusively. "No woman may be saved unless it is by bearing children. Either do what Scripture says, or be judged a violator of sacred laws," said the judge in a thunderous finale. Never, Helia retorted, still utterly committed to the perpetual chastity of marriage to Christ.

Constantina, Mary of Egypt, and Helia were women who never existed in the flesh yet, paradoxically, merit the title of Church Mothers, a term that pays tribute to their profound influence on the millions of women (and some men) who idolized them. As heroines of medieval hagiography, the "pop fiction" of the Middle Ages, their exploits and ultimate triumphs dazzled readers, who took away from each life a lesson about faith, individual independence, commitment, sacrifice, and glorious, godly rewards.

For centuries, these Church Mothers dominated hagiography, even after scholars unmasked them as figments of various imaginations. The very sparseness of their stories—merely outlines of a few key episodes—endeared them to women, who reinvented them in their minds and in literature. Each writer paints them according to her own fancies and projects her own assumptions onto their characters. She reads meanings from her own life into every skimpy phrase the women spoke and embroiders their joys and vicissitudes with the threads that adorn hers. In a mystical sense, she transforms Constantina, Mary, and Helia into personal acquaintances.

The imperial Constantina and the noble Helia represent families and society we know—conventional, ordered, affluent, comfortable. Mary's underworld, on the other hand, is obscene, chaotic, opulent, and unstable, a gilded treadmill leading from one night to another. Despite their differences, the women are drawn together in faith—strong, willful, independent women choosing virginity and defending that decision against beloved parents and suspicious society alike. Mary's reborn virginity was just as consequential—it cost her the only trade she knew, her sole livelihood since she was twelve years old.

Real-life Christian women could well relate to such practical problems. If they were converts from pagan families, their deviation from orthodox paganism was contentious enough. When Perpetua's pagan father pleaded with her to renounce Christianity, he wept but also "threw himself at me to tear my eyes out." The destruction of family relations must have been one of the most unbearable consequences of conversion from paganism.

More than one recently converted maiden provoked even greater distress by pledging herself to eternal celibacy. Unless a virgin had personal means, how was she to live? Waged work was out of the question, for pagan society had no truck with bachelor women other than priestesses and refused all dealings with traveling women or those attempting to work without benefit of family associations. Christian virgins had it marginally easier if their parents accepted their decision and agreed to support them.

On the other hand, the Church itself had a motive, quite apart from theology, to encourage virgins to remain celibate forever and devote themselves to religion. By the third century, congregations were heavily female. This had financial implications. True, poor virgins either remained relentlessly poor or became a drain on the increasingly prosperous Church. But rich virgins and celibate widows who inherited property were a commodity not to be sniffed at, because they often willed their worldly goods to the Church. "By idealizing virginity and frowning on second marriage," Robin Lane Fox concludes, "the Church was to become a force without equal in the race for inheritance."

Who can say how many virgins and widows were so struck by Constantina, Mary, or Helia that they, too, pledged perpetual celibacy? What is certain is that, for centuries, the threesome drew women into their lives, and their impassioned defenses of virginity and celibacy stirred, moved, and ofttimes convinced and converted. The women recast the misogynist, bachelor world of the Church Fathers into a splendid, challenging one where virgins were honorable and could also be powerful, and where God's love empowered the humblest woman (which none of them remotely approximated). Mary was also living refutation of Jerome's Fatherly assertion that even God could not restore a fallen virgin. He could, indeed.

The trio went further than vindicating virginity. They used it as their tool to carve out unorthodox lives, with independence the common theme. Constantina was a master of Byzantine pro-celibacy intrigue. Helia was as sophistical a bush lawyer as any Jesuit. And Mary, naked in the desert, continued outrageous in her sanctity. All were self-directed and confident, highly respected and successful in their endeavors. Celibacy, of course, made it all possible.

FEMALE TRANSVESTITE MONKS

Other, real Christian women had adventures every bit as spectacular as those of the Church Mothers as they, too, pursued lives of chaste independence. Among the most sensational were a duo of transvestite monks who successfully challenged their world and wrested from it the right to independence and personal satisfaction otherwise reserved for men.

Castissima was the cherished only child of a wealthy and pious Christian couple. By the time she was a teenager, the entire city of Alexandria raved about her remarkable wisdom, devotion to learning, and spectacular beauty. Her future was assured as high-ranking families competed to secure her as a bride for one of their sons. Eventually, the most powerful family in all Alexandria reached a settlement with her father, Paphnutius. Gifts were exchanged, and the lovely Castissima was officially betrothed.

Before the wedding, when Castissima was eighteen, Paphnutius took her to spend three days at a monastery. Entranced, the lovely young woman listened as the abbot spoke about virginity, purity, and the fear of God. Blessed are all who live in this place, she thought. They are like angels who praise God without ceasing. And after death they will be worthy of eternal life.

Castissima was transformed. She forgot her joy at her impending marriage and longed instead to live as the monks did, celibate and devout. But surely Paphnutius, despite his piety, would never agree to it! Castissima pondered her problem and soon confided it to a visiting monk. "No, my daughter, do not give your body up into corruption, nor surrender your beauty to shameful passion," the monk replied. Become instead a bride of Christ. "Run and hide; join a monastery and there you will be saved."

Castissima's trembling hands crept up to her wondrous tresses, symbol of her sexuality and gender. She would have them chopped off, she decided, as a first gesture of self-abnegation. "I do not wish to be shaved by a layman, but by a servant of God" was her only stipulation. Her monkish accomplice persuaded an old recluse to crop her hair. He also provided her with a penitent's garment, suitable for a cloister.

But Castissima, shorn and plain-garbed, was distraught. Fleeing to a convent seemed futile, for when Paphnutius returned home and found her gone, he would mount an unrelenting search for her in all the women's communities. Eventually, he would locate her and force her to marry her fiancé. But her mission was to shun marriage and live a righteous life of chastity and dedication to God. At all costs, she had to remain hidden from her father.

"I will put myself in a monastery of men in the disguise of a eunuch," she decided. "No one will suspect me." And so that evening, the bald and determined Castissima, in men's clothes and carrying the large sum of five hundred solidi, presented herself at the monastery. "Brother," she lied to the porter, "please go and tell the abbot that a certain eunuch from the palace is at the door and wants to speak to him."

The abbot accepted both her story and her money and admitted her into the monastery as Emerald, her alias. As simply as that, Castissima walked through the cloister gate and became a man—a mutilated one, to be sure, for only a eunuch could have such a radiantly beautiful face. Indeed, "Satan made many to stumble at his beauty," and soon the abbot had to segregate her. Castissima, aka Emerald, was undismayed. She retreated to her isolated cell and plunged into her new life with the unshakable confidence of the true zealot. She remained indifferent to the presence of scores of males. What mattered was maintaining her virginity and devoting herself to the glory of God.

Paphnutius, however, was in despair. Finding his daughter gone, he searched, as Castissima had predicted he would. Indeed, all Alexandria searched for her. Finally, Paphnutius sought divine intervention through his friend the abbot. All the monks prayed fervently for a revelation from above, but Castissima prayed even harder. Despite her "brothers'" prayers and vigils, she succeeded in keeping her whereabouts hidden.

Finally, to solace his grieving friend, the abbot introduced him to the reclusive young eunuch. Fasting and other austerities had so altered Emerald's appearance that Paphnutius failed to recognize her. He was tremendously struck by her piety and wisdom and developed a close relationship with her that endured until death. "How much have I profited from this man," he raved to the abbot. "God knows how my soul has been captured by his love, as if he had been my own daughter."

Thirty-eight years passed, and Emerald, now fifty-six years old, lay dying. Thanks to the chastity she so treasured, she had spent most of her life as a man, a man of God, buried in the bowels of a monastery. Her beauty had faded and she looked the part she played, an ascetic and devout eunuch committed to God's service. Paphnutius, now a very old man, came to see her, entreating her to intercede with God to reveal the fate of his long-lost daughter Castissima.

Emerald, in her death throes, had no more need of subterfuge. "My father," she whispered, "end your grief for Castissima your daughter. I am she." As a shocked Paphnutius stared at her wasted body, Castissima died.

Burial preparations confirmed that Emerald was no eunuch but a woman. At the funeral, her chaste body performed another miracle: its touch cured a monk's blind eye. Castissima's initial deceptions—lying her way into the monastery, deceiving her father, even shaving her head in defiance of both biblical and canon law—were forgotten. What counted was the godliness of her life, even though she had lived it as a man. Like other transvestite monks, Castissima chose celibacy as her personal goal and transvestism as a strategy to obtain it: disguising her gender, and therefore her identity, so she could travel her earthly path as she wished. She was an eager, untroubled celibate whose transvestism liberated her and fueled the spirituality that sustained her and, through sainthood, earned her the eternal life she craved.

Pelagia of Antioch was an even more remarkable celibate transvestite, a courtesan so spectacularly beautiful her clients showered her with fabulous gifts. One day, as the saintly Bishop Nonnus of Edessa stood preaching in the courtyard of the basilica of the Blessed Julian the Martyr, Pelagia rode by, flanked by a throng of haughty servants tricked out in golden girdles and jewelry. Even her donkey was adorned with tiny bells that tinkled at every step. Pelagia herself was resplendent in luxurious clothes and bejeweled with bracelets, anklets, rings, and ropes of gold necklaces inlaid with pearls and precious stones. She left her head uncovered and draped a scarf around her shoulders. The fragrance of her perfume and cosmetics was so powerful it assaulted the staring clerics' senses.

But it was Pelagia's beauty that mesmerized them and induced Bishop Nonnus to weep so bitterly that even the hair shirt he always wore next to his skin was sodden with his tears. When he could speak, Nonnus raved about Pelagia's astounding loveliness and the hours she must have spent in her boudoir, applying her elaborate makeup and costume: "She will have looked at her face in the mirror with the greatest attention, making sure there is not the slightest speck of dirt on it . . . all this in order to lead astray and lure her lovers after her—lovers today, but gone tomorrow. . . . For she, a creature of dust and ashes, has employed the utmost zeal in trying to please Satan." The assembled clerics were deeply moved as Nonnus continued to moralize about Pelagia, and to implore God to save her.

Later, officiating at Antioch's largest church, Nonnus' sermon was so eloquent and moving that the floor was wet with his congregation's tears. Many were shed by Pelagia, whom God had inspired to attend church, a most unusual occurrence. This was the first time the notion of sin had ever occurred to her, and she was profoundly affected. The other worshipers, moved by her evident emotion, marveled in whispers about how Bishop Nonnus had just converted their city's sinful playgirl from her evil ways.

After the service, Pelagia sent two menservants with a letter to Bishop Nonnus, requesting an audience. He agreed, but on condition they not meet alone. He was, he cautioned, a mere man and susceptible to temptation. At the church, the site of their rendezvous, and in full sight of the clergymen Nonnus had summoned as chaperons, she flung herself at his feet and begged him to baptize her as a Christian.

"I am a prostitute, a disgusting stone upon which many people have tripped up and gone to perdition. I am Satan's evil snare: he set me and through me he has caught many people for destruction. I am a ravenous vulture . . . a sly she-wolf . . . a deep ditch of mire," she groaned, prostrating herself on the muddy ground. All spectators but Nonnus were reduced to tears at the dramatic spectacle, but he insisted Pelagia conform to church law, which required prostitutes to find godparents before they could be baptized.

Pelagia, impetuous and tempestuous, was not to be thwarted. "You will have to answer for me to God if you do not baptize me now," she cried out, adding for good measure a curse worthy of a camel driver: "You will become a stranger to your holy altar and deny your God if you don't make me a bride of Christ this very day."

Nonnus was convinced, and soon the bishop of Antioch arrived for the ceremony. The harlot popularly known as Marganito, the Syriac word for the pearls she wore in such abundance, was christened Pelagia, her birth name. Just as everyone sat down to table for a celebratory meal, the Devil pounded at the door and shouted recriminations at Nonnus for stealing away his prize.

Renounce Satan, Nonnus instructed Pelagia, anointing her with oil. She did so, and sure enough, the Evil One disappeared. During the eight days of her baptismal ritual, he often reappeared, offering her jewels and riches to return to his service and moaning that she had jilted him. In response, she inventoried all her belongings and donated them to Nonnus, her mentor and spiritual guide. Worldly possessions would no longer matter. She intended to wed her newly chaste person to Jesus as his bride, and nothing could deter her.

On the eighth day, instead of doffing her white baptismal robe for the dress of a Christian woman, Pelagia pressed a hair shirt against her tender flesh, covered it with Bishop Nonnus' tunic and cloak, and slid away into the night. Her metamorphosis was complete. She had, in less than a fortnight, renounced the Devil and her sinful profession. She had reclaimed her birth name and her chastity and traded harlotry for spirituality, silken robes for a hair shirt. Alone, she set out into the world as a man.

Pelagia became Pelagios, a eunuch monk who swiftly became famous as a holy man. She lived in a cell on the Mount of Olives, a thin, gaunt, and hollow-eyed ascetic whose fasting and penances eradicated all her beauty. As Pelagios the eunuch, Pelagia transcended gender and adopted celibacy as the means to spiritual purification. The wildly successful courtesan became a wildly successful ascetic, impervious to even the Devil's entreaties. Only after her death a few years later did her skeletal body reveal to the astonished monks preparing it for burial that Pelagios the eunuch was a woman. Pelagia, later sainted, was one of several transvestite holy women whose celibacy permitted them to experience the spiritual life of the holiest man.

Thousands more transvestite monks undoubtedly infiltrated religious communities. Many sought refuge from abusive or unwanted husbands and fiancés, and as we have seen, hiding out in a male community was an ideal sanctuary, with castration a convenient explanation for their physical femininity. Others bluffed their way inside monasteries so they could shed the constraints of womanhood for the relative freedom of life as a male. Of course, all these women shared a commitment to celibacy that bordered on the obsessional. They were devoutly religious, either born or converted to the exciting and demanding Christian faith, and so the cloister appealed to them as a combination of what they loved: celibacy and dedication to God. Otherwise, they would have done what other, adventurous transvestite women did: join armies or professions in their search for freer personal existences.

The other main group of transvestites who wormed their way into monasteries and elsewhere were the noncelibate lovers in pursuit of beloved, shakily celibate, or uncelibate monks. The most famous of these is Pope Joan, who bedeviled the Catholic Church for hundreds of years until, in the sixteenth century, Church authorities and scholars relegated her to the realm of the apocryphal.

As John Anglicus, Joan supposedly served as pope in the ninth century, after her career as a monk earned her a reputation for great erudition. She had disguised herself as a monk, however, so she could secretly meet with a male monk with whom she had fallen in love. At the time of her installation, so the story goes, Joan, aka John Anglicus, was pregnant by another lover. During a papal procession, she suddenly squatted down in the street and delivered a child. The story has two endings. Either John/Joan and her son died soon after, or he grew up to become Pope Adrian III.

The legend has a hoary subplot. Because of Joan/John's duplicity, the story continues, all subsequent popes have had to sit bare-bottomed on a papal "testing seat," strategically pierced so a deacon can verify that new popes are indeed men rather than women or eunuchs. However, as a fifteenth-century prefect of the Vatican Library sensibly concluded, the real function of the perforated chairs, which did exist, was simply to allow the dignitary enthroned on one to answer inconvenient calls of nature.

The transvestite saints were outstanding women among legions of other fake-male monks, revered by their church though they flouted canon and biblical law and duped abbots and fellow monks. Their main objective was to maintain a celibate life in safety, so the attraction of celibate religious communities was paramount. But except for Castissima, whose father would have hunted her down, they could have joined women's communities. Instead, they dared to defy their societies and families and braved all-male cloisters.

As monks, these cross-dressing women renounced not merely their female gender but sexuality itself. Their craving for celibacy was so powerful that they satisfied it by suppressing their femininity. In all cases, theirs was the celibacy of religious fanaticism. These women had agendas that extended far beyond merely safeguarding themselves from men and marriage. They needed to commit themselves, body and soul, to the service of God and to do so with the greatest possible intensity. They undertook the most rigorous austerities, enduring privations so severe their health was ruined and their appearance entirely altered. Often they devised these punishing penances themselves.

Unlike so many male monks, none of the transvestites complained of difficulty in observing their vows of celibacy. Celibacy was, after all, what first drove them into the monasteries, celibacy rooted in religious zeal. Once ensconced as monks, they would have risked everything by indulging in a sexual encounter. Celibacy was, in other words, both end and means to that end.

Other than celibacy, the adoption of male garb and identity had rewards that intelligent and intense women such as Castissima and Pelagia must have greatly appreciated. As men, they shucked off not merely womanly obligations but also their inferior status. The lowliest monk was nonetheless a man and, as such, permitted freedoms and a measure of respect no woman could dream of. For these women, life as celibate monks was also empowering, and they wrested from it respect and reverence usually reserved for males. Their celibacy was the most delicious of all: transformative and liberating, and the instrument of its own success.

BEARDED FEMALE SAINTS

Another breed of celibate male impersonators were the bearded female saints. Uncumber was the daughter—one of a set of septuplets or even nontuplets—of a Christian mother and a pagan father, the latter a ruler of Portugal. Uncumber, also known as Wilgefortis, longed to remain a virgin and dedicate her life to God, but her father ignored her wishes and arranged her betrothal to the king of Sicily.

Uncumber pleaded unsuccessfully with her strong-willed father. Then she turned to God and pleaded to Him, too, for deliverance. God granted her prayer by disfiguring her with a long, drooping mustache and a curly, silken beard. Despite this, Uncumber's irate father simply hid his suddenly hirsute daughter under a veil. In retaliation, Uncumber tugged it open so her Sicilian fiancé could see her. He gasped and promptly canceled the wedding. Her father, infuriated by this scotching of his plans, had Uncumber crucified. She died on the cross, a martyr to the virginity God had helped her preserve, her soft facial tresses the means of her salvation.

Two other bearded saints are Galla, a widow determined to resist remarriage, and Paula of Avila, a virgin who so loathed her suitor that she ran away from him and begged Jesus to maim her. He complied, for she immediately sprouted a thick, uglifying beard, which so transformed her that her admirer did not recognize her.

The bearded saints are unique in that they were all delivered from sexual relations with men by the sudden appearance of unattractive masculine facial growth. In each case, they were powerless to defend their chastity and turned in desperation to God, who provided them with the tool they needed. It is intriguing that Saint Uncumber became the patron saint of women who wished to "unencumber" themselves from their husbands (and the etymological source for that verb). Uncumber's plight echoed their own despair and hopelessness, and far from scoffing at her fate—beardedness and crucifixion—they sympathized and plied her with offerings of oats to encourage her to intercede with God to aid them in their antimarital struggles.

Some, perhaps many, of these unhappily married women may merely have hated their individual husbands. Others were undoubtedly like Uncumber, forced into unwelcome marriage when they longed instead for a life of devout celibacy and good works. They saw Uncumber's mutilation—and Galla's and Paula's—as convenient weapons employed on the side of chastity.

CELIBACY OUT IN THE DESERT

The Desert Fathers' New Alphabet of the Heart

In ancient Egypt, the desert was a metaphor for the brutishness of life in the famished and toiling Near East. It pressed, in all its feral wildness, against the edge of villages and cities. Even Alexandria, that loveliest and most cultured of cities, was only fifty kilometers from its lawless, untamed desolation.

The desert was a terrible place—this was, in part, its great appeal. Even today, its vast solitude terrifies villagers, who fear cackling hyenas and demons and can seldom be induced to spend the night there.

You can look at the desert that way, as a menacing world held at bay. But you can also see it as so many of the early Christians did, as a realm of freedom, whose boundaries defined the outer reaches of the treacherous world of civilization. A man, or a woman such as Mary of Egypt, could go there and take his or her chances with nomads, hunger, and cold, the only company a questing soul and, when it could be achieved, God's presence.

The desert had always framed the horizon of twenty-year-old Anthony, whose wealthy father's farm lay on the outskirts of a village in the Fayum. Eventually, the desert would become Anthony's refuge from the world he had renounced by giving all his possessions to the municipal senate and establishing his sister as a "dedicated virgin." But at first, he must have stared out toward it as he brooded with his terrible problem—sexual desire the Devil urged him to satisfy. So frantically did Anthony try to resist the Satanic One's diabolical scheming that even passersby could tell he was tormented by an internal struggle.

At first, Anthony sought only solitude and silence to pore over the Scriptures and pray for knowledge of Christ. He found this at a slight distance from the village, where it was quiet and he could meditate without hearing other people going by.

Yet the full fury of sexual longing continued to consume the young man, sabotaging his hopes for a calm, ascetic existence. "The demons' traps are evil thoughts," he later reported. He fought the demons pitchfork for pitchfork, toughening his body by robbing it of sleep, any little comfort, even sustenance. He ate only bread and salt, once a day or every two or four days, and drank water. This ascetic regime, however, did not banish "the itch of youth"—in other words, "the demon of fornication."

Battling as hard as he could, Anthony immured himself in a tomb, weaving baskets to earn money, his sole human contact one friend's occasional visit to provision him. For over fifteen years he persisted, only to conclude, "He who wishes to live in solitude in the desert is delivered from three conflicts:

hearing, speech, and sight; there is only one conflict for him and that is with fornication."

(Hieronymus Bosch's famous painting *The Temptations of Saint Anthony* portrays a faintly haloed, fully garbed Anthony kneeling prayerfully on a rock, staring apprehensively at hideous creatures, many bearing spears, and a naked woman bending over crudely, exposing her backside to Anthony as she peers at him from between her knees. All around are horrifying brutes, naked women and a humpback, obscene goblins and evil tempters, whilst an anxious monk, one of Anthony's few supports, clutches a Bible.)

From the eerie, still world of his crypt, Anthony moved on to an abandoned fortress. Twenty years later, in 305, he decided to seek disciples from among wandering Christian ascetics who had also escaped from the temporal world, fleeing its merciless demands and rigidity, its persecutions, indebtedness, even vindictive and dangerous coreligionists. With his acolytes, Anthony struck out for the eastern desert, where the only humans were nomads, and settled into a cave on Mount Kolzim. He lived in this simple hermitage on the Mountain of Saint Anthony till his death in 356.

Anthony is famed as the Desert Father who founded monasticism, but in his days as a "renouncer," he was part of a trend. Renouncers roamed Egypt's towns and villages, then claimed the desert as their domain. Another Desert Father, Amun of Nitria, was a celibate who had, early on in his marriage, persuaded his wife to renounce sexual relations. After eighteen years of chaste wedlock, Amun's wife convinced him to go out into the desert. "It is inappropriate that you should hide such virtue as yours," she argued. A flattering argument, and off into the desert Amun went, where his spirituality attracted a flock of renouncers. Later, they moved farther into the desert, at Kellia carving "the Cells" out of the basins between the dunes. Each man dug his own well of brackish desert water and created a cluster of minuscule oases.

But the Cells were still too close to civilization, with all its pain and temptation. A full day and night's trek farther was Scetis, now Wadi Natrun, remote but better watered by springs edging a nitrate-rich marshland. By 400, it was home to thousands of Desert Fathers. Anthony, Amun, and their disciples had transformed the desert into a little city.

Freed from the entanglements and vicissitudes of society, the Desert Fathers faced two towering adversaries: the Devil's temptations and daunting nature. Their prime purpose was to use God's gift of free choice to redeem their sinfulness and achieve again "the perfect life," corrupted by the Fall. Jerome, a Desert Father in his youth, loved to recall his experiences. He would sit alone, "limbs stuck inside an ugly sackcloth . . . skin black as an Ethiopian's," fighting off sleep. When it overpowered him, his bare bones ground into the earth. His dietary regimen was pitiful: cold water and meager amounts of uncooked food.

Yet these terrible privations, undertaken to assuage his fear of hell, could not banish Jerome's unbidden lust, and as he sat feverish and starving in the desert, he saw dancing girls twirling all around him. He was "more dead than alive," he exclaimed, but still his "burning lust continued to boil."

Life in the desert took on its own rhythms, with crises, solutions, and guidelines. Eventually, desert monastic John Cassian and others devised complex rules about how to succeed in this way of life. The foremost problem, as in the life left behind, was food and water, both obtaining it and then, even more difficult, rationing it so that consumption was more fasting than eating. Finding food was indelibly etched in these men's psyches, for Egypt was a ravenous land always menaced by the specter of starvation. The Nile was a food basket, the desert an empty trough. For this reason, the popular imagination applauded even more heartily than their conquest of sexual lust the Fathers' victories against hunger and the belly. Fasting replicated Adam's most irresistible temptation, but the outcome was quite different, for unlike the fruit-eating First Man, the Fathers conquered it.

The Fathers gathered their desert's slim offerings: bulbs, roots, plants, berries. They drew water from near and far. For fifteen years, one hermit lived twenty-six kilometers from a spring. Moses the Ethiopian, a deeply penitent ex-criminal, probably a murderer, traipsed all night between sources to fill his fellow Fathers' water jars.

Ordinary meals might consist of two loaves of bread, salt, and diverse roots or wild herbs, scarcely enough to sustain adult men despite their sedentary lifestyles spent in weaving baskets or other monotonous tasks, meditating, gathering foodstuffs and water, and above all, praying.

Cassian endorsed the two-loaf daily-meal plan as a six-month path to sexual chastity. Historian Aline Rousselle agrees, after comparing it with a U.S. wartime experiment on malnutrition on male sexuality. Thirty-two men knowingly reduced their food intake from 1,700 to 1,400 calories daily and maintained this level for six months. By then, their sexuality had shrunk as much as their bellies: no more sexual desire, dreams, aggressions, or nocturnal ejaculations. Ergo, Cassian was probably right. Starve the belly, nourish chastity.

Among the Fathers, Devil-driven lust was the mightiest enemy, and asceticism, notably food deprivation combined with too little sleep, was the mightiest weapon to combat it. Conjuring up erotic visions of women was not the only manifestation of sexual sinning. Masturbation was an obvious one, and for many, so were wet dreams. As one Father warned, monks had to "transcend the laws of nature" by mortifying the flesh and thereby preventing too much semen from accumulating. The trick was extended fasting. Otherwise, erotic impulses would arise. However, not everyone considered wet dreams sinful. A few thinkers argued that they occurred without imagined stimuli, unconsciously, and were therefore natural.

Both ascetics and medical men believed sperm was the consequence of an overabundance of food, the antidote to which was fasting or drying out the body. The drier the body, the better for the soul. Drying foods were lentils, salted olives, figs, grapes and prunes, grilled salt, salted fish, brine and vinegar, leeks and roasted chickpeas. Meals ought to be raw and cold to counter the bodily heat that led to sensuality. A surfeit of liquid was also a problem, for in swelling the bladder, it stimulated the other organs. Again, less was better.

And so the Father, scrabbling for sustenance, had to store in his primitive cell the foodstuff his spiritual goals also forced him to ration. In a corner was his stack of dried, stale loaves, tasteless, nourishing, his reward for much hard handiwork. And hungry as he always was, that humble bread must ofttimes have been as tempting as his fantasies of naked, beckoning women.

It sometimes happened that years and years of subduing the flesh and carnal instincts—fasting, praying, eating, keeping vigil—drove Fathers into breakdowns known as adiaphoria. They would escape their tiny cells and tramp across the wasteland, grubbing for grassy herbs, chomping and sucking and devouring them, staving off the perpetual pangs of hunger and the relentless grind and slow pace of their solitary lives. This state of adiaphoria, in fact, troubled the Fathers even more than eroticism, even the sexual lapses they sometimes observed in others or could not prevent in themselves.

Women sometimes appeared in the desert—nomads; bands of women seeking a glimpse of a hermetic brother, father, husband; families fleeing debtors; adventurous courtesans who had money riding on their ability to seduce a Father. But harlots were overkill. For some hermits, the mere sight of a woman after twenty womanless years sabotaged their moral courage so they despaired of ever loving only God.

A few did more than fantasize. One young girl was seduced by the riverside, in the reeds, when several Fathers succumbed to a folie à deux and decided they had to have sex. Another ailing and aged man left his fellow Fathers to spare them the burden of his care. They warned him against temptation, but he assured them his body was dead. In the village, however, it revived, and he impregnated his kind hosts' daughter. Later, she gave him their baby to care for back in the desert. In fact, so many Fathers lapsed with available women that they became easy scapegoats for unwanted pregnancies. Such accusations, sometimes false, often true, became so common that the Fathers stopped trading with the peasant laborers whose women were both temptresses and victims.

Lust was a miserable companion and a worse foe. One old monk, Pachon, confided to a newcomer that forty years in the desert had not cured his, and that not a single night between the ages of fifty and seventy had been devoid of lewd thoughts. Another old man also admitted to "the same feelings of revolt and the same storms," also daily.

Most Fathers endured the anguish of lustful thoughts and longings but resisted them, even to the point of self-mutilation and mortification. Some went to extraordinary lengths to preserve their celibacy. Ammonius seared his flesh with a flame-red iron to dispel his carnal passions. Old Pachon braved a hyenas' den, expecting death, and placed an asp next to his genitals. Evagrius, who was in love with a noblewoman, froze desire by submerging himself in an icy well. A Father obsessed by memories of a beautiful woman devised the most gruesome lust preventative of all. After someone informed him the woman had died, he located her corpse and dunked his cape in her putrefying flesh. This cape he carefully preserved, so its stench would quash his fixation on her loveliness. He died, aged fifty-four, lust-free for three years.

General rules were more helpful: do nothing to risk evoking women's images, avoiding even Scriptures that mention them; keep perfect silence and do not speak of or to them; do not meet anyone's eyes so that you will not notice if a woman should happen past you. A monk who slipped to one side of the trail as some nuns walked by was reproached by their superior: "If you were a perfect monk, you would not have looked at us and you would not have seen that we were women."

Women were, however, a rare commodity in the desert. Young boys were much commoner, and so many Fathers succumbed to their charms that many of the Sayings, the Fathers' collective wisdom, railed against cohabiting with children. But some sons arrived with their fathers, while others were entrusted to them as youngsters. "When you see young children, take up your sheepskins, and go away," advised one wise Father. Said another, "Do not bring young boys here. Four churches in Scetis are deserted because of boys."

The most obvious source of temptation was each other, and Fathers resisted as best they could, shielded by their solitary lifestyles. Few, however, abandoned their vocation because of a lapse, homosexual or otherwise. They repented, sought counsel from other, older anchorites, and renewed their attempts to achieve a perfect life.

For centuries, the pitiless desert was a metaphorical reflection of the Fathers' battle for chastity. They hunkered down in its inhospitable crannies, famished, endlessly fasting, tempted by the food they thought would heighten their already throbbing senses, much of their lives devoted to prayer and contemplation of their every sinful thought. The remedy provoked the ailment, or so it must have seemed, as they accused, tried, and judged themselves guilty of lustfulness, the dreaded enemy of the celibacy they strove so painfully to achieve.

This celibacy was a complicated, merciless condition that required mind, soul, and body to cooperate. John Cassian elaborated the six stages in the crawl toward mastering it. First stage: upon awakening, the monk is not "smitten by carnal impulse." Second stage: he does not dwell on "voluptuous thoughts" that sneak into his mind. Third stage: he can survey the outside world, including women, without lustful feelings. Fourth stage: he is unaware of any physical movement. Fifth stage: discourses or readings dealing with procreation evoke no thought of sexual pleasure but instead the idea of an activity that is performed calmly and purely, so he is as unmoved by it as by "thinking about bricklaying or some other trade." Sixth stage: even sleep is untroubled by visions of seductive women.

This logical progression in the stages of celibacy is a measure of how the Fathers approached their calling. It contrasts strikingly with Constantina, Mary of Egypt, and Helia, and legions of the real women who emulated them, for whom celibacy was easier to endure and maintain. Unlike the men, their fight was not so much against the bodies they were quite comfortable with but against tremendous social and family pressures, and against food, which preoccupied them much as sex preoccupied male celibates. The Fathers' bodies—in particular their loins—were their own worst enemies, more exacting and treacherous than the hungry desert. Sexual desire was a very real, immediate thing, their gauge to assess the state of their souls—which led back to the desert.

The spiritual quest and emphasis on the body transformed the elemental desert into the generator of what Peter Brown labels "a new culture," a rejection of the urban intellectuality that focused on the Scriptures, weighing the exact meaning and significance of every word, every turn of phrase. The Fathers changed perspectives, so that what mattered were "movements of the heart" and the Devil's infinitely subtle tactics and trickeries in manipulating it. It was, in Brown's elegant phrase, "rightly hailed as the greatest and the most peculiar achievement of the Old Men of Egypt: it amounted to nothing less than the discovery of a new alphabet of the heart." In this alphabet, sexuality—measured by celibacy both progressive and lapsed—was a symbol of the heart of fallen man.

St. Simeon's Chastity at Sixty Feet High

A few fanatical holy men were consumed by the urge to commune with God through such outlandishly severe hardships that they dismissed the asceticism of the desert and the monasteries as too paltry for their requirements. For these men, celibacy was easy, so brutal were their austerities. St. Simeon the Stylite, born at the end of the fourth century, was the most illustrious.

Simeon was a Syrian shepherd's son who wandered into a church, where he was converted to Christianity and had a vision that called him to the religious life. He joined other ascetics, then entered the monastery at Teleda. Its strict regime did not satisfy Simeon, a sweet-tempered, enduring man whose humility failed him only in his ambition to be the most abstemious of all. His most drastic attempt at this nearly killed him, precisely the result he had intended. He wrapped a rope all around his body, binding himself inside it like a corpse. Somehow he managed to pull it so tight, his flesh putrefied and worms crawled over it in a giant feast. As they ate him alive, Simeon must have rejoiced, for he wished to die in this martyrly fashion. Presumably his brother monks intervened, forcibly releasing him and cleansing his wounds, because after this incident, the abbot and the entire community requested him to leave.

Simeon left but did not go far. He built a small, domed hut on a nearby hill and remained there for three years. Then he lived in the open air, inside a circle of stones. His next abode was a pillar, on which he stood and prayed continuously. Two pillars later, he had reached his summit: a pillar sixty feet high, topped with a six-foot-square platform with an enclosure. There Simeon stood, exposed to the blazing sun, the driving rain, and the freezing winds, until he died in 459, over seventy years old.

Simeon's object in standing perpetually on a pillar, an unknown Christian austerity, was to dedicate his life to prayer by uniting his body and soul. He did this by totally suppressing his carnality. Even to himself, Simeon must have been a worshipful metaphor of the phrase "standing before the Lord." In the harsh, hungry fifth-century Byzantine world, Simeon drew the pain and the hunger, the fear and the sorrow, within his own body. With Simeon at its apex, the pillar became an altar and its lonely inhabitant the incense wafting upward to heaven.

Sixty feet beneath, needy supplicants gathered, until Simeon's pillar, conveniently located on a major commercial route, became a pilgrimage center. People poured in from all over, even Spain, Britain, France, and Italy. One of Simeon's contemporary hagiographers described the throngs as "a human sea into which rivers from all sides debouched."

Simeon's devotees, however, had to be male, for he barred women from gathering around his pillar, despite the sixty-foot buffer. He refused to see even his own mother and communicated with women only through male messengers. This was consistent with male domination and also with ascetic terror of the concupiscent powers of Eve's daughters. So though celibacy was guaranteed by Simeon's solitary vigil in the air, he protected himself by banishing all temptation.

Simeon's minimal needs were met by his followers, while he ministered to their greatest. He had an eclectic agenda: sickness and pain, infertility, sinfulness, social issues, natural disasters. By the thousands, male pilgrims hiked miles along a dusty path, then trekked up the mountainside for a chance to climb up the ladder and consult the saintly man who performed miracles.

These consultations had to be scheduled, for Simeon had a rigid timetable. He prayed from sunset to 3 P.M., when he delivered a divine teaching. Only then was he free to listen, counsel, and heal. He intervened in tax disputes; assisted guild workers, cucumber farmers, and choirboys; healed the sick; converted pagans; and averted plagues, famines, and other calamities. In his hagiographer's words, "He can be seen sitting in judgement and handing down proper and just sentences." As his reputation spread, he became an important diplomat, advocating for the poor, negotiating between the emperor and the defiant bedouin tribes, and soothing ecclesiastical squabbles. During debates on the extent and nature of Mary's virginity, Church Fathers even sought Simeon's chaste opinion.

Simeon's saintliness radiated so far that others were inspired to emulate him. Daniel, a Mesopotamian monk, ascended to the platform and was transformed by Simeon's radiant holiness and by his promise that Daniel would have his tunic after he died. Daniel left and stood for the next thirty-three years at the edge of Constantinople, until he died at age eighty-four. Until the late nineteenth century, Eastern Stylites such as Daniel modeled themselves on Simeon and stood for lifetimes on pillars, worshiping God.

Simeon's extreme (and at first glance, bizarre) asceticism appealed to generations of desperate pilgrims and religious. It symbolized apostolic simplicity frozen forever, a pure minute for a lifetime, a square pulpit for a world, perfect deprivation for serial austerities. The wild, unkempt, and radiant soul who stood, arms outstretched like a human crucifix, was the final solution to the yearnings in the hearts of those who beheld him. The little-educated shepherd's son who corresponded with emperors and chastised tax collectors, averted droughts and reconciled feuding families, had endured harsh life for the privilege, figuratively as well as literally, of hovering close to the chaste, unsexed, hallowed angels he longed to join.

MARRYING "THE TRUE MAN"

The great Egyptian desert was vast enough to shelter the few desperate or determined women who also sought to commune with God in the hushed silence of its rugged terrain. Like the legendary Mary of Egypt, who spent over forty years in the desert, some were hermits. Others made connections with austerely run monasteries and lived close by in mud huts they had fashioned for themselves in the style of their Fatherly confreres.

These *ammas*—Mothers—faced the same challenges: hunger, fear, doubt, and lust, probably in that order. Mary of Egypt's life was fabricated from tales of dozens of real *ammas*, and her struggle to achieve indifference to perpetual hunger reflects the way the real *ammas* recounted their experiences to the scholars and spiritual seekers who tracked them down or simply encountered them on the peripheries of the Old Men's settlements.

Early Christians revered these holy women who suppressed the womanliness that, besides nurturing and loving, tempted men to repeat Adam's sin and taste taboo treats. What counted was not these women's strong-mindedness, personal ambition, or independence, though without these, how would they have survived in the desert? Their lack of womanliness, the shabbiness of their unadorned garments, their ascetic gauntness, their otherworldly sexlessness that transcended celibacy—these, and of course their dedication to God, were what early Christian Fathers and chroniclers revered.

Febronia and Alexandra were Christian virgins celebrated for devotion to virginity so extreme, they isolated themselves from all contact with temptable men. Febronia was a Syrian nun reared since infancy in a convent near Nisibis. The sisters there were famous for their learning and wisdom, but Febronia was exceptionally talented. She was also famous for the diligence of her asceticism and was also praised for having never seen or been seen by a man. For this reason particularly, Febronia's name was cherished in the convent as well as the city proper.

During the persecutions in 302, vindictive pagans discovered and jailed this hidden treasure. They were excited by the challenge of conducting her mostly sexual interrogation-by-torture in public, savoring her agonies by extending them so she did not die at once but lingered for a satisfyingly long time. Finally, uttering pious words, Febronia left this world without recanting. The legion of women who mourned her death included pagans, for all women lamented the tragedy of her death and her violation at the hands of men. They had not seen Febronia as the convent's captive but as a free spirit dedicated to education, contemplation, and friendship. Despite life confined within her convent's walls, her seclusion from damaging men was seen as a privilege, and her existence as a blessed one.

Alexandra, on the other hand, personified the phrase "living death," self-imposed. Her story began with a young man who had developed an unrequited fixation on her. His problem, surely? Not to Alexandra. To avoid scandalizing a soul created in God's image, she entombed herself alive so that the lusting young man would neither suffer nor feel she had rejected him.

And there she stayed, sealed away from human eyes, provisioned through a tiny window, busying herself with household tasks leavened by spiritual reflections. From the first flush of dawn until the early morning she prayed as she spun flax. For the rest of the time she mentally reviewed holy men—patriarchs, prophets, Christ's disciples, and martyrs. Then she munched her crusts of bread and waited patiently and hopefully for the hour of her death.

"How virtuous!" everyone exclaimed, including Melania, the educated, independent, wealthy, and newly chaste Christian evangelist who came across Alexandra in her travels and recorded her story. But did no one—Melania, Alexandra's parents or brothers, even the servant or friend who ventured into the burial ground with her modest supplies—attempt to persuade her that she should come home?

Probably not, because, as similar stories illustrate, her contemporaries considered men to be victims of women's wiles and so applauded Alexandra's solution as admirably correct rather than—as we might consider it today—neurotically self-effacing.

Febronia and Alexandra were revered in Christianity's early centuries because they embodied qualities the Church Fathers, chroniclers, and hagiographers esteemed: submission, altruism, seclusion. They also divested themselves of the trappings of femininity and adopted male values—Febronia, an ascetic, manless, intellectual religiosity. Alexandra went further, sacrificing her life to a religiously inspired, altruistic zeal to save lustful young men by removing the object of temptation—herself.

This latter is crucial. When early Christianity urged its women to pledge perpetual virginity, it had a more compelling motive than their spiritual righteousness. What was also at stake was the shaky spiritual righteousness of Christian males, who would otherwise succumb to mortal temptation in the face of the burning female eroticism that had so fatally tempted males ever since Adam. The solution, obviously, was female chastity, though it required enormous personal sacrifices from all women, including childlessness. The reward for this was proportionately high: great respect from the Church and society and possible sanctification.

Except for St. Augustine, whose heavy personal baggage included his decades-long indulgence in sexual liaisons, the Church Fathers believed women were lustier than men. From this premise (shared by most cultures from the Aztec to the Chinese), it followed that a woman who successfully repressed her innately lascivious nature was holy indeed. Furthermore, her steadfast celibacy protected men from temptation, making female virgins literally God-sent. Second best were born-again virgins, who had married or whored but were determined never to stoop to carnality again. Febronia and Alexandra were venerated not merely as virgins but as so adamantly virginal that they withdrew entirely from society.

The problem with all this was that few women, no matter how religiously inclined, cared to live in isolation such as Febronia or, especially, Alexandra.

The ideal was an active, independent life of devotion and service out in the world. Take, for instance, the apostle Paul's disciple Thecla, who is probably fictional and modeled on St. Macrina, the sister of the two saints Gregory and Basil. Thecla was deeply religious, educated, articulate, and independent, the product of a family of comfortable circumstances. Such women manifested their faith their own way, often in quite public venues. Thecla was already betrothed when she first heard Paul preach. She found his comments about celibacy so spellbinding that, for three days, she sat in a window, motionless and without eating, listening to him. Her mother was so anxious about her daughter that she sent for Thamyris, her fiancé. But instead of hearing him out, Thecla broke off their engagement, an act with enormous social repercussions, since annulling a betrothal was tantamount to divorce. Thamyris was furious and so jealous of Paul that he persuaded the city leaders and the Roman governor to imprison him.

Thecla, obsessed with Paul, bribed a jail guard and followed him into the prison. When the Roman citizens heard about this, they forced the authorities to act. Paul was flogged and exiled from Rome. Thecla was condemned to death by burning, but God directed the roaring flames away from her and sent a rain-filled cloud to burst over her funeral pyre, extinguishing the fire. Thecla stepped away from this close call with death to catch up with Paul, who had been released from prison and had resumed his missionary work.

Thecla insisted on traveling about the country with Paul. She cut her hair and implored him to allow her to disguise herself in boy's clothing, a request which Paul found repellent but reluctantly permitted. Thecla became an evangelist herself. However, despite her good works and resolute celibacy, she was unable to convince him to baptize her. Meanwhile, Alexander, a civic leader, fell in love with her; as Paul had warned her, "Thou are comely." Alexander asked Paul if he could buy her, but Paul denied even knowing her. Alexander forced himself on Thecla, who rejected him violently and in public. Humiliated, he dragged her before the governor. Thecla's intransigence landed her once again in prison and earned her another death sentence, this time in a contest with a savage beast in the arena.

In preparation for his encounter with Thecla, her lion executioner had been starved for days. In the arena, he lunged, no doubt salivating in anticipation of her tender, maidenly flesh. But Thecla did a curious thing: she leaned over and, in Ambrose's words, "offered her vital parts to the fierce lion." He stopped dead, amazed to see she was a virgin. Then he dropped to the ground and licked her feet, unable to "injure the sacred body of a virgin." Other beasts were brought in, but more miraculous phenomena rescued Thecla. Saved again, she baptized herself, committing her soul to God. The Romans, dumbfounded by this extraordinary spectacle, freed her, and she struck out again, proselytizing and gathering around her a group of Christian virgins who looked to her as an *amma*.

Thecla's independent and interesting lifestyle was much more appealing to many Christian women than the self-effacing virgins touted by the Church Fathers. Thecla argued, notably with her adored Paul, and generally did whatever she wanted. She rejected men's advances, even honorable proposals of marriage, and she trekked alongside Paul, a free spirit impatient with the constraints of a woman's life. The Church Fathers certainly admired her, but felt strongly that women of her indomitable will needed reining in. They emphasized her valor in defending her virginity, and her asceticism, but women took away another lesson: Thecla's enormous personal strength, determination, independence, and ambition.

By the fourth century, the Council of Elvira devised a public "pact of virginity" in which a bishop would ceremoniously veil a woman's head and intone, "I wish to present you . . . as a chaste virgin to Christ." The veiled virgin would respond, "The king hath brought me into his chambers," and her companions would add, "The king's daughter is all glorious within." The designated virgin was now categorized, and the Church dictated her lifestyle: sequestered, locked into her room praying and serving Christ. And why not? Was she not married to him? "Do not seek the Bridegroom in the streets," Jerome warned, "stay home with [Him]."

The Fathers meant staying home literally—no more going to market or weddings or public events or celebrations, even visits to anyone but other official virgins, certainly not "the daughters of a strange land." She could, however, attend church, but only under a veil. After all, Jerome reminded them, "Jesus is jealous. He does not choose that your face should be seen of others."

The next logical thought—and the Fathers thought it—was that these Brides of Christ should not live alone. The Fathers pointed to the excesses of male hermits and concluded, "If all this is true of men, how much more does it apply to women, whose fickle and vacillating minds, if left to their own devices, soon degenerate." Ergo, they invented a spiritual community of virgins all married to Jesus, "the true Man," under the guidance of a spiritual elder.

An ascetic lifestyle was also prescribed, with daily fasting, meager meals of bland, unseasoned vegetables and mild herbs accompanied by water, never wine. The object, Jerome wrote, was to create a virginal community of "women pale and thin with fasting." Dirty, smelly, too, for bathing was an immodest, stimulating activity no decent virgin should indulge in. Anyway, "a deliberate squalor . . . makes haste to spoil her natural good looks," and the sooner spoiled, the better—another temptress less.

A virgin would also observe almost total silence—the Fathers found chattering virgins loathsome. "Your mouth should neither open easily nor respond to every commonplace address," Ambrose instructed. "Speak to Christ alone. . . . For in truth in much speaking there is abundance of sin."

Property and riches were also forbidden; the Church would administer them for Christ's work. Having divested herself of her worldly possessions, the impoverished, veiled, greasy-haired, odoriferous virgin would study Scriptures and Church Fathers and pray, at least six times daily. During her leisure time, she could spin, weave, or wind yarn. Above all, she must banish impurities from her mind, for "virginity may be lost even by a thought," Ambrose wrote, and it was possible to be physically intact but spiritually uncelibate. "O virgin," Ambrose summed it up, "let the love, not of the body, but of the word come to you. Off with eye cosmetics and other follies of artificial beauty. . . . Your ears . . . were not made to carry heavy loads or to suffer wounds [but] to listen to what is profitable."

Virgins could also strengthen their resolve by recalling the horrors of marital life, the agonies of childbirth, the irascibility of husbands, and the grief when children died.

Difficult though this style of virginity was, the conscientious virgin could expect an important payoff. "Immaculately your faith will be born and your piety exposed; that in your uterus you will receive the Holy Spirit and bring forth the spirit of God," Ambrose predicted. An excellent reward for an arduous and tedious venture.

This tableau is, of course, one-dimensional, depicting only the Church Fathers' guidelines and rationale for Christian women to achieve virginity. Another perspective is to consider the implications of disobedience or disagreement. One virgin charged with unchastity was hauled before her bishop and forced to submit to a midwife's intrusive examination of her genitals. Another more critical flaw in the Fathers' portrayal of virginity was that so many Christian women disagreed with some of its premises—for instance, that sensuality was bad. They did not accept or fear the evil the Fathers saw in womanly bodies; to the contrary, they celebrated the God-given senses. "We need to seek how to please God in our bodily members [as well as spiritually]," Constantina declared, then lovingly inventoried the carnal senses, describing rapturously how delightful each was. God designed and created bodies, she reasoned, and so the senses innate to them must be good, and God must intend them to be well used and never abused.

Constantina's equanimity about—indeed, her reverence for—the wonders of touch, sight, sound, and smell was shared by other Christian virgins. So was her indifference to the Fatherly strictures about staying home alone. These women valued celibacy and never questioned its spiritual power, but they could and did challenge much else. They understood the burdens marriage and childbirth would bring and rejoiced that the virginity that liberated them also made them spiritually superior. But they interpreted that superiority as meaning freedom as well, to travel, to teach, to preach, to speak out in public, to minister to willing acolytes.

Many women and men as well swore perpetual celibacy and then set up family-style housekeeping together. They maintained strictest chastity, lived according to the dictates of Christian asceticism, but also observed traditional divisions of labor. As one male celibate explained, he enjoyed this arrangement. His female partner cared for his belongings, prepared his food and set the table, made his bed, lit the fire, and even washed his feet. Bishops frowned on this modus vivendi and ordered participants to do penance for their sinfulness, but it was common during Christianity's first four centuries, and even bishops entered into it.

Individual freedom for female virgins was, however, probably celibacy's most tangible reward. Melania the Younger is a case in point. Melania was the one who encountered Alexandra and recorded her story, but unlike the Church Fathers, she was relatively unaffected by the other woman's simplicity, isolation, and meekness. Melania's neutrality is understandable: she, too, had once adopted, then abandoned, a life of solitary asceticism.

Alexandra and Melania were a study in contrasts. While the virginal Alexandra martyred herself inside a tomb, the confident, resourceful, privileged, and formerly wealthy Melania wore her celibacy like armor against danger. First she browbeat her unwilling husband, Pinian, to swear a mutual oath of chastity. Her strategy was brutally simple: she stopped bathing. Pinian, however, desperate for a son, persisted. Melania capitulated, bore two children, who both died, then resumed her campaign for celibacy. By the time she succeeded, she had reversed the power structure of their marriage, dictating Pinian's clothing and even where he lived—away from her. First came her foray into isolated deprivation. Then, with a band of like-minded virgins, she began to travel.

Melania's adventures included several miracles. She personally intervened and saved a woman from a butchering surgeon attempting to cut a dead fetus from her womb. Then, in a pointedly antipatriarchal vein, she praised childbirth as divinely created and blessed the vaginas that gave birth to saints, apostles, and other holy people.

Melania cured two women suffering from a curious oral paralysis described as demonic in origin and not real lockjaw. These miracles may be metaphors for Melania's rescuing women from the asceticism of Church Fathers. Deprivation and silence taken too far, she might well have been saying, render virgins feeble, mute, and impotent.

Melania established a women's community and exhorted the sisters to be obedient to each other. With this she dismissed hierarchical authority and stressed mutual respect and consideration. She also laid down community house rules much milder than the Fathers'. Instead of their orthodox self-denigration and abstemiousness, she demanded excellence and simplicity. The Fathers' vaunted silence, for instance, was not part of her vocabulary. From dawn to dusk, her community resonated not with serene stillness but with her animated voice discussing theology with her enthusiastic virgins.

Though Melania gave up the intimacies of marriage, her passionate friendships were legendary. She was, for instance, inseparably close to Empress Eudocia, with whom she shared a powerful spiritual bond. She also lived in harmonious company with scores of women devoted, as she was, to the pursuit of righteous knowledge.

Melania's brand of asceticism was relatively mild. Unlike the Fathers, she did not require rigorous fasting, which she considered only a minor virtue. She diligently divested herself of her enormous personal fortune and, with more effort, gave up the lavish clothes, jewels, and elaborate hairstyle appropriate to a high-ranking married woman. Her new clothes expressed her new vocation, her changed marital status, and her emancipation from male authority. Even her funereal garments proclaimed her personal status to the world.

Melania is an outstanding example of the celibates enshrined in hagiographic Lives, a shining model for centuries of Christian women. Legions of women sat mesmerized as her hagiography was solemnly read aloud to them. It did not escape their notice that, for her and her virgins, celibacy was a liberating lifestyle. It exempted them from womanly tedium and toil and granted them excitement, freedom to travel wherever they wished, the luxury of scholarship and debate, and a secure, simple life among women who celebrated each other's friendship. Melania's miracles proved as well that God favored her, hence her postmortem glorification in Christian literature. And Melania herself directed every step she took along the path to saintliness, accepting what she wished to, but rejecting even received wisdom if it clashed with her own analyses.

CHAPTER 3

Later Christianity

CELIBACY AND CLERICS

MEDIEVAL EASTERN MONASTERIES

Some fathers lived alone, insisting that only solitude could properly test them and also preserve them from temptation. The great majority, however, congregated in small bands under the spiritual guidance of such holy men as Anthony the hermit and Pachomius the cenobite or monk, the founders of Christian monasticism.

Life in a desert community, no matter how small and haphazardly organized, centered on the spiritual authority of an *abba* (abbot) or Old Man. The father, wrestling with his demons, could only hope to elude them if he opened his heart to the Old Man. "For nothing displeases the demon of fornication more than to reveal his works, and nothing gives him greater pleasure than to keep one's thoughts to oneself," explained an ancient Christian authority.

Origen, the great Christian thinker famous for castrating himself to make himself a eunuch for the Kingdom of Heaven, as well as for his spellbinding teaching and profound writing in Scripture, philosophy, and ethics, had first articulated this idea. It came to be understood that the heart was where the body and the soul converged, the point at which the subconscious was linked with the conscious and the supraconscious, and the human with the divine.

Christian monasticism was the revolutionary movement that ultimately queried the very existence of nonmonastic life: Could true Christians exist outside the chaste, austere, and otherworldly precincts of these "great, walled-in monasteries . . . in clusters of cells built into the sandy plateau of Egypt like ancient grave-houses, on the tops of mountains, perched on columns, walled up in the nooks and crannies of the cities . . . huddled in grottoes carved into the cliffs and in the fairy-tale rock formation of great ravines"?

Could the outside world, with its sinful distractions, rampant corruption, and errant rulers, tolerate citizens loyal and accountable only to their God?

Should all Christians renounce the world and flee to monasteries? Or should a new order—Christianitas—prevail, in which Christianity would take the offensive and transform the world into one colossal monastery, headed by a universal abbot to whom everyone had to pledge obedience?

Of course, monasticism fostered Christianitas, its logical theological extension, which developed from mature reflections on the nature and working of monasteries. It was not the fathers wandering up and down the Egyptian desert or tucked away in caves, sand dunes, mountainside huts, and other hermitages who inspired monasteries. That honor goes to the cenobites, who were drawn to a spiritual leader and settled in close proximity to him. These early Christian pioneer Desert Fathers in their improvised cells became known as monks—*monachos*—from the Greek word *monos,* one who lives alone, though they were quite different from the later fathers, who belonged to more structured establishments.

"To save souls you must bring them together," the great monk Pachomius declared. Pachomius had a great gift: with his searing gaze, he could penetrate to the inner depths of a Christian's heart. When that heart was pure, Pachomius could see "the Invisible God . . . as in a mirror." To achieve that purity in the collectivity he deemed necessary, Pachomius founded what we now consider the first Christian monastery at Tabennisi.

There, Pachomius had over thirty houses, each lodging forty monks. A legion of rules governed their conduct. Celibacy was the key precept, and many of Pachomius' rules were designed to safeguard it. The monastic silence served to nip deepening, intermonk relationships in the bud, as well as to promote self-reflection and ambulatory prayer. Other rules quite clearly related to Pachomius' concerns about celibacy, for away from women, some men turned to each other.

In his *Precepts,* Pachomius spelled out correct, chaste brotherly behavior. First of all, monks must not tempt each other. They should, therefore, observe the following niceties: covering their knees when sitting together; remembering not to hike their tunics too high when bending over doing laundry; keeping eyes lowered and avoiding direct glances at other brothers, at work and even during the silent meals; never borrowing from or lending to each other; never doing or requesting a brotherly favor; never performing such intimacies as removing a thorn from another monk's foot or bathing or oiling one another; never contriving to be alone with another brother, either in a cell, on sleeping mats on the terraces, in a boat, or riding donkey-back; never talking to each other in the dark; never holding hands; always maintaining an arm's-length distance between each other; abstaining from joining in the games and laughter of children raised in the monastery; never locking the cell door; and always knocking before entering a cell.

These rules had nothing to do with the ascetic regime that underlay the monastery's existence. They dealt specifically with the causes of erotic temptations and sexual lapses. Pachomius was determined that in his godly establishment, celibacy would reign, at all costs.

The ascetic regimen was also strict, though not as severe as among the fathers. Fasting was the daily habit, with a recommended single, simple meal. Bread, with salt, was the main staple. Monks who could not wait it out till the setting sun summoned them to the day's repast were permitted to eat twice, the first time in early afternoon. However, they did not receive more rations. The usual amount was merely divided into two portions.

The timing of the evening meal permitted the brothers to sleep without the cramps that otherwise attacked their shrunken, rumbling stomachs. In wintertime, Pachomius ate only every third day. This near-starvation diet, of course, was a principal tool in the struggle to maintain sexual chastity by dampening all sexual desires.

Another *abba*, Dioscorus of Thebaid, justified extreme asceticism with a rhetorical question that resonates today. "A monk must have nothing whatever to do with the sensual appetites," he instructed. "Otherwise how would he differ from men living in the world?" In fact, hungry monks were not substantially hungrier than their nonreligious compatriots. Villagers and farmers probably ate comparably, at least in terms of calories. When wellborn novices sat down to their first meal in a monastery, the shock to their systems was considerable, whereas those from humbler circumstances often found the fare tolerably generous. A former senator who lamented his new regime to a shepherd was told that the portions sounded ampler, and the quality finer, than anything in his listener's experience. In a stratified society where rich and poor lived wildly disparate lives, the senator-and-shepherd syndrome was common, so much so that monks came to suspect that economic hardship rather than religious vocation or idealism drove newcomers to seek admission to the monasteries. Some monasteries even initiated probationary periods to eliminate such applicants.

Despite the minimalist lifestyle, the rigid regulations, and the spiritual challenges of the monastery, monks still had terrible trouble subduing their sexuality. So many resorted to molesting novices that it was said, "With wine and boys around, the monks have no need of the Devil to tempt them." Female donkeys were other favorite targets of monkish lust.

WESTERN MONASTERIES

In the West, the Egyptian monastic experiment was monitored with increasing interest, despite the lowly origins of most Egyptian monks. Ironically, these ascetics were living answers to the question that nobles and intellectuals in the West eagerly posed to their physicians: Can one achieve permanent celibacy, and if so, how? Accounts of the monks' lives became popular. Scholars did fieldwork, living with and observing Egyptian monks. They collected and published sayings of the fathers, which readers fell upon and cherished for their great truths.

By the end of the fifth century, the West had transplanted and modified this Eastern, desert-based asceticism so that in the sixth century, monasteries also appeared there. Like their Eastern counterparts, these, too, had rules. St. Benedict's Rule, seventy-three chapters long, made Benedict Western monasticism's patriarch.

Benedict's ideal monastery was a single edifice with an elected abbot, whose brothers renounced all private property and swore perpetual poverty, chastity, and obedience to the rules of their community. But unlike the Eastern retreats, Benedict's was the training ground for Christian soldiers. "We must create a *scola* [unit of the militia] for the Lord's service," he wrote.

Benedict's goal, "to form a school of divine servitude in which . . . nothing too heavy or rigorous will be established," effectively eliminated what Westerners considered excessive Eastern asceticism. (Centuries later, Benedictines maintained this anti-ascetic bias as they countered criticisms that their comfortable monasteries clashed with the apostolic poverty monks were supposed to vow. Surely not, they argued. How could a monk in today's world of secure Christendom be expected to tolerate the privations of the era of pagan persecutions?)

Despite its apparent similarities—celibacy, silence, humility, and obedience—the Benedictine version of monasticism was radically different from its anti-Church, Eastern cousin. Benedict accommodated to his century and to European conditions and moved the focus away from the individual heart and body as a barometer of spirituality. Instead, monasteries allied to the Church and the papacy increased, consolidated, and enjoyed their real estate and other temporal holdings. Before long, many had degenerated into cesspits of political intrigue, money-mongering, and power-brokering, and— antithetical to the core reason for monasticism—libertine venues for sexual scandals on a breathtakingly vast scale.

Comparison with the Eastern monasteries, where monks sometimes succumbed to temptation with village women, handsome boys, and each other, is impossible. There, monks agonized over their lapses, repented, and tried again. In the West, these incidents became so commonplace they could not be considered lapses but ways of life for entire communities. Some monasteries installed lay rather than religious abbots, and these men transplanted their entire households to live among the monks: wives, children, soldiers, hunting dogs. Not surprisingly, given this intrusive worldliness and sexual flamboyance, monks emulated their superiors' examples, bad as well as good. At one time the monks of Italy's Farfa abbey openly recognized their concubines. In France, the monks of Trosly were nearly all married, and each monk of St. Gildas at Ruits abbey "supported himself and his concubines, as well as his sons and daughters," reported abbey official Peter Abelard. Abelard himself was castrated by agents of Canon Fulbert of Notre Dame, the powerful cleric whose niece Héloise Abelard tutored, seduced, impregnated, and later married.

Homosexuality was also rampant in these sexually permissive cloisters where celibacy was a flickering light at best, an extinguished wick at worst. Benedict's Rule had attempted to forestall it by forbidding obvious temptations. Two monks were never to sleep in one bed. Lights were to be kept burning the night long, and the monks had to sleep fully clothed. Bathing, involving as it did the allure of the naked body, was discouraged and was permitted only as a complicated procedure in which concealing garments were never removed all at the same time, so that various body parts were never exposed, even to their owner, in one enticing expanse of moistly glistening flesh.

(Centuries later, Italian seminaries employed the "purity paddle," a wooden paddle shaped like a small oar that was used to tuck shirts into trousers. This minimized the tantalizing proximity twixt hand and genitals, because the paddle did the actual tucking in and kept fingers as far away as possible from the unmentionable, untouchable, unseeable, but ever-so-sensitive nether region.)

Among monks, Bernard of Clairvaux was (apocryphally) singled out as the exception to the rule: he was celibate and immune to the attractions of his own sex, as this story reveals. A Burgundian marquis implored Bernard to heal his ailing son. The monk requested everyone to leave him alone with the boy, then stretched out on top of him. The point of this oft-repeated story is not the boy's miraculous cure, but that Bernard performed this feat without an erection. "He was indeed the most unhappy of monks," tittered the satirical poet Walter Mapes, "for I have never heard of a monk who had lain on top of a boy and who did not immediately *rise* after him."

A large part of the problem was that too many monasteries forgot the primacy of their religious focus. Wealth, sometimes great wealth, stole into their collectivities, preoccupying and seducing them. They became major landowners with vast agricultural capacity and a committed, unpaid workforce. Monks and their relatives from wealthier families, along with other, devout Christians, willed the monasteries fortunes and more property. The holdings remained intact, protected from division between two or more legatees, as secular possessions were. Abbots of these empires had to be saints—and a few were—to resist the pull of power and the lure of luxury their positions offered. And once a monastery's Old Man sacrificed spirituality and wisdom for savoir faire and cynicism, his monks' souls went unprotected from the Devil's best efforts.

In 813, a synod of bishops convened at Tours and deplored the degeneracy of most monasteries. Throughout Christendom, reformers attempted to halt the decay. King Louis the Pious imposed Benedict's Rule on establishments within the Frankish Empire, but after his death, his sons' internecine warfare swiftly secularized them. This was typical; the monasteries had become huge, wealthy corporations without temporal protection, so feudal nobles and kings preyed on, attacked, terrorized, dismantled, and robbed them.

From the eighth century onward, monasteries were forced into feudal civic and military relationships with kings and ruling nobles. Abbots became their vassals and assumed political, judicial, and military responsibilities. One Norman duke could always count on his nine allied monasteries to provide forty knights for his incessant warmongering. German abbots were particularly enthusiastic about their military obligations. In 981, for example, they supplied hundreds more knights to Otto II's army than his lay vassals contributed.

On the political and diplomatic level, abbots and monks were their monarchs' most trusted—hence powerful—advisers: Alcuin the monk with Charlemagne; Benedict of Aniane with Louis the Pious; the abbot of Fulda with Germany's Henry IV; Archbishop Lanfranc of Canterbury and his successor, the abbot of Bec, St. Anselm, with William the Conqueror, then with his son Henry I.

The truth was, alliances with temporal powers became essential if the monasteries were to survive. Perhaps they ought not to have, for in surviving by compromise rather than unenviable asceticism, they were transmogrified into travesties of what monasteries had once been. They even began to own churches, evidence of how they now accommodated to the Church, whose scrambling conformities and squabblings they had originally escaped by running away to the desert.

The tortuous historical development of monasteries and the Church piloted Christian monks away from the celibate ideal and lifestyle. Reform of the sorry and chaotic mess that was medieval monasticism led back to it. In 1073, the Benedictine monk Hildebrand became Pope Gregory VII and unleashed his own burning agenda on his extended flock: perfect celibacy for all Christians.

Hildebrand/Gregory came from the monastery of Cluny, where the Benedictine Rule was severely enforced. Cluny was entirely under papal, not secular, authority, and Cluniacs taught Christianity should mean that, instead of monks renouncing the world, all Christians should adopt monastic ideals. This pristine notion, in the midst of uncontrolled hedonism, appealed to so many that satellite Cluniac monasteries rooted and grew, and Cluny quickly became the most important religious institution in the West.

Cluny's spectacular success led to the familiar scenario of vast landholdings and properties. The more its ascetic, apostolic mission attracted people, the more removed from apostolic asceticism it grew. Disgust at this living contradiction inspired Gregorian Reform, which harked back to Cluny's initial purity and conformity to the Benedictine Rule. Gregorians also advanced the model of a church of the saints with strictly celibate clergymen.

The eleventh century's Gregorian Reform was revolutionary, perhaps as much so as the sixteenth century's Protestant, the eighteenth century's liberal, and the twentieth century's communist revolutions. Gregorian Reform aimed, quite simply, to smash the old order and replace it with a new order of papal supremacy, liberating Christendom from secular rulers and placing it squarely under papal domination. This new order—Christianitas—was Gregory VII's vision of an ascetic, renunciatory, monastic Christian world with a papal abbot at its helm.

Five decades of struggle, agitation, repression, and crisis settled the question: Gregorian Reform failed. Instead, the purest religious withdrew into other, Cistercian monasteries much like the ancient Egyptian ones, refuges from the secular world. The stern, irascible, temptation-proof Bernard of Clairvaux was among these purists, though he was never able to resist proselytizing for Gregory's Christianitas new world order. In his reflective moments, however, Bernard realized how incongruous it must seem to everyone but his pure-souled fellows.

> What else do worldlings think we are doing but playing about when we flee what they most desire on earth, and what they flee, we desire? We are like jesters and tumblers who, with heads down and feet in the air, draw all eyes to themselves. . . . Ours is a joyous game, decent, grave, and admirable, delighting the gaze of those who watch from heaven.

Joyous or not, the Gregorians lost the game. Christianitas died, but not the principle of celibacy, which survived not merely in Cistercian monasteries and those of other persuasions but also in the world. Many laypeople celebrated and adopted it. Others who felt they could not were solaced by the Church's teaching that sex within marriage was acceptable, if it was strictly for procreation.

Centuries after monasticism was corrupted by the riches and the slack values of the world, monasteries were again returning to the asceticism that originally assisted monks who strove to achieve both carnal and spiritual celibacy.

Martin Luther on Nocturnal Emissions

In a sixteenth-century German monastery, the prior attempted to force a rigid rule of celibacy on his monks. Sexual activity of any sort was strictly prohibited, and he interpreted this to mean even involuntary nocturnal emissions. The monks tried their utmost to quash all provocative thoughts and fantasies, yet many nights, the dreaded dreams crept into their slumbering unconsciousnesses.

Each morning that they awoke to discover moist evidence of the previous night's sinfulness sticky on their thighs, the brothers dutifully refused to celebrate mass. They did this out of deepest conscience, to comply with their order's regulations on the subject.

But the matter reached crisis proportions when an unusually large number of masses were scheduled and so many monks had to absent themselves that the public was apprised of the situation and, worse, of what had caused it. The prior was deeply embarrassed and hastily changed directions. He "conceded that anybody at all could and should celebrate Mass, even if he had had nocturnal pollutions."

This affair of the wet dreams made a deep impression on Brother Martin Luther. He reflected on their nature and ultimately concluded that unprovoked emissions were natural and therefore acceptable, but that those stimulated by conscious effort were sinful, except in marriage. It also led him to ponder other aspects of sexuality. From nocturnal emissions he extrapolated to sex itself, declaring that depriving the body of a natural, God-ordained function was dangerous. Slowly and radically, his views on celibacy became diametrically opposed to received Catholic wisdom.

Celibacy One, Lust Zero

Even with monastic cells swarming with scoundrels and scandals, religious authorities thought Irish holy man Scuthin was acting outrageously. Could what they heard be true, that Scuthin took two voluptuous maidens into his bed each night? They sent Brendan the Navigator to investigate.

At bedtime, two lovely young women appeared at Brendan's lodgings. Upon entering the room where Brendan lay in bed, the duo crawled into bed and snuggled up against him, assuring him that this is what they did every night with Scuthin.

Brendan lay sleepless, tossing and turning restlessly, tormented by lust. After a while the women spoke out, complaining about Brendan's obvious problem. Their usual bedmate never responded at all, they said, though sometimes he had to resort to jumping into a tub of cold water. Brendan was astonished and realized the injustice of accusing Scuthin of sexual impropriety.

Later, Brendan met the man he had been sent to spy on. Scuthin explained how he slept with the full-breasted temptresses to challenge himself, so that—shades of the Great Old Man Barsanuphius—the lust he conquered would be all the greater. Brendan was totally won over, and he and Scuthin became good friends.

Centuries later, Scuthin and Brendan were made saints. In a reckless age going out of control, Scuthin was a righteous man who nightly tested his sexuality and, by the same token, his spirituality. Twentieth-century India's Mahatma Gandhi would have understood—his brahmacharya experiments were a sophisticated Hindu version of Scuthin's Christian ones.

To Wed or Not to Wed

Quite unlike all other religious, cloistered or out in the world, for whom celibacy was a nonnegotiable absolute, uncloistered priests spent centuries wrestling with the issue. These men were radically different from both Desert Fathers and monks, who were seekers after spirituality and for whom celibacy was an ongoing test of their commitment. These men devoted their entire lives to their own salvation.

But until the arrival of the Kingdom of Heaven, what about everyone else's soul? Who would teach, guide, scold, punish, and condemn sinning humanity? For the vast majority of humankind, priests were needed.

But what kind of priests? Ascetic celibates like the monks? Or spiritually inclined people with a sense of mission and a desire to serve? The first Christian clergy were not highly trained professionals. They were men—only men—who lived and worked alongside their coreligionists and functioned like everyone else. This included marrying, and for the first centuries of Christianity, clergymen married, made love to their wives, and produced children.

Lifetime celibacy was, as we have seen, a primarily Christian preoccupation. Most pagans and Jews considered it peculiar and unnatural, detrimental to society, and fatal to the species. The law required pagan priests to marry, and most Jewish religious leaders did so voluntarily, though they abstained from sexual relations before and during certain festivals and ritual events, such as sacrificing at the altar. But as the struggling cult of Christianity swelled in number, its leaders began to argue that a permanently celibate priesthood should be established.

It was never a popular notion, especially among married priests and, one must presume, their wives. To this day, clerical celibacy is the most divisive, difficult, and draining issue in the Roman Catholic Church, the only Christian denomination to demand it. In a later chapter, we will see how Catholic priests and nuns continue to trickle away from the dwindling religious communities that could once count on a seemingly endless stream of young people, whether called by God or forced by their families, into celibate service.

Meanwhile, the first concerted calls to impose clerical celibacy began in the fourth century. By 250, some clergymen were celibate by conviction, reinforced by the occasional canon that endorsed/recommended/demanded celibacy. However, large numbers were married and fully intended to stay married.

This sentiment was forcefully expressed by Synesius, bishop of Ptolemaïs. God, the law, and "the sacred hand of Bishop Theophilus" had given him a wife, he declared, and he had no intention of leaving her or of having clandestine relations with her, which would make a mockery of marriage. In any case, he expected to father numerous children with her. In other words, Bishop Synesius categorically refused to stoop to the subterfuge of so many of his colleagues: skirt the issue, protect their jobs, swear false vows of celibacy, then contrive, in unpriestly stealth, to creep into her bed at night and pray— if they dared—that no children would arrive to give the lie to the supposedly chaste marital arrangement.

The battle to impose celibacy on clergymen lasted over one thousand years and ended in victory in the thirteenth century. It was a downhill fight, targeting first the highest prelates and gradually, slowly, lowering the sights of the cannon downward until even the humblest priest was included in its scope.

The celibacy issue also helped perpetuate the rent in the Church, with the Western clergy triumphantly celibate, at least in theory, and the Eastern clergy unabashedly uncelibate, in theory as well as in fact. But until the thirteenth century, even among disunited Western clerics and policy-makers, celibacy was primarily a monkish thing.

What really matters in this story is not so much the details of its development—intermittent religious edicts, blatant defiance, compromise, retreat, renewed attack, sullen acceptance, furtive noncompliance—but the doctrinal basis for imposing it and the social context in which it happened. We already know the climax of the tale of the Church's great rift: the Protestant Reformation, and integral to it, former monk Martin Luther's vitriolic offensive against clerical celibacy. "Nothing," Luther thundered, "sounds worse to my ears than the words 'nun,' 'monk' and 'priest.'"

But what underlay the mammoth battle over clerical celibacy? Foremost was the conviction that celibacy was a fundamental component of "good" Christianity. The Church Fathers strongly influenced this perception, reaching a wide, receptive audience through their writings, their preaching, and their teaching. They set personal examples as well, for most were unmarried celibates. In our survey of their theology, we saw how they evoked the Scriptures as proof of their arguments, quoting the words of the apostles and of Christ, and the Old Testament tale of Adam and Eve, as irrefutable evidence.

A watershed was reached when Christian emperor Constantine issued his 313 edict legitimizing Christianity. By then, the Fathers had inadvertently captured the popular imagination, and their asceticism and fixation on purest celibacy fascinated and influenced many. The monastic movement that evolved from their humble little settlements also revolutionized Christian— and some pagan—thought. So did Augustine of Hippo's famous teachings, and the *Confessions,* which struck straight into so many sinful hearts. For women and some men, the heroic virgins Constantina and Helia, and the ex-harlot, born-again virgin Mary of Egypt, inspired fanatical devotion to celibacy as an ideal central to Christianity.

One major consequence of all these theological, spiritual, and political contortions was that, increasingly, lay Christians adopted celibacy, so that a core of many communities lived as spiritually pure a life as the Fathers or St. Augustine could have wished. Often, they put professional religious to shame, and during the periods of widespread "lapsing" and apostasy in monasteries and women's cloisters, these chaste and committed Christians shone— metaphorically, at least—with the pristine glow of a guiding star.

This was the loose tapestry upon which Christian officialdom embroidered with squirmy, lopsided stitches the wavering lines of their policy on clerical celibacy. For the first few centuries of the new religion, the main thrust of policy-making consisted of intermittent rulings that bestowed exalted religious status on the clergy. Then, in 305, the synod of Elvira published a canon prohibiting all clerics, from bishops down to deacons, from having sexual relations or children with their wives. The penalty for flouting this canon was defrocking.

Of the eighty-one canons ratified at Elvira, almost half, including the one cited above, concerned sex, meting out stricter penalties for sexual truancy than for heresy and other grave sins. So many clergymen were married that these celibacy crusaders outlawed marital sex but did not dare ban marriage itself. Nonetheless, theirs was a shattering pronouncement. For the tiniest infraction, clergy and laymen risked eternal exclusion from the Holy Eucharist.

Elvira was a draconian edict and, given the realities of the day, rash, foolish, and unenforceable. No wonder that two decades later, at Nicaea, a Church council reversed it. Paphnutius, the Egyptian martyr who had preferred to be blinded in one eye rather than renounce his Christian beliefs, argued strongly against clerical celibacy on the grounds that it was too difficult for most men. In any case, he said, marriage was a respectable form of life. Paphnutius swayed many by the force of his reasoning and also of his character. He was personally celibate, so he spoke purely on principle. Other synods and councils confirmed this marriage-tolerant attitude. In 345, a ruling at Gangra censured worshipers who declined a sacrament because it was dispensed by a married priest.

But the great ideals of celibacy and celibate monasticism had set in motion an irreversible groundswell for clerical celibacy. After all, argued the pro-celibacy churchmen, how were clergymen to distinguish themselves from ordinary mortals if they engaged in this basest of activities? Furthermore, the opinion gained currency that caring for a wife and children was a major distraction when a priest should be focusing on his ministry and exemplary spirituality.

The growing wealth of monasteries, other cloisters, and the Church in general was another important reason to implant clerical celibacy. Bachelors leave no heirs, so would not be tempted to divvy up the property they administered, which would pass intact to the next generation of monks and churchmen. (As we will see, a similar line of reasoning in Persia about administrative and military leaders, and in China about guardians of harems, produced the bizarre social category of unalterably mutilated eunuchs.)

From 370 onward, papal dicta banned clerics from indulging in sexual relations. These dicta were widely considered unenforceable, and most married priests continued to sleep with their wives. However, clerics did interpret the papal decrees as a ban against a clergyman's right to marry after he was ordained. They also suspected that unmarried candidates would be favored in the Church, and that celibacy would be a good career move.

Over the years, the celibacy campaign pressed on. In 401, priests at Carthage were required to swear an oath of celibacy, the first-ever instance of this. Churchwide, a priest's private life was now—theoretically—heavily monitored. His wife had to be virginal at the time of marriage and remain so forever. She could not share his bedroom, much less his bed. Instead, she passed her nights elsewhere, with a chaperone, while he lay with other clerics. Should her husband die, the widowed virgin was not permitted to have another go at marriage. A later edict went further: married clergymen had to leave their wives at their ordination.

And so it went, edicts, rulings, papal decrees, a plethora of sometimes contradictory and usually petty decisions leading inexorably to a policy, in the Western but never the Eastern Church, of clerical celibacy from top to bottom. The policy varied from time to time and place to place, and often the impact was negligible. By 400, however, sexual abstinence had been imposed on all major clerics in the Western Church. By 450, the net had extended to include even the lowly position of subdeacon. Despite official decrees, however, the campaign to enforce clerical celibacy encountered persistent opposition. In 483 and again in 535, it was seriously undermined by two embarrassing papal elections—Popes Felix II and Agapitus I were both the sons of priests.

Theology, ascetic monasticism, practical and property considerations, dominated the push for clerical celibacy, but other factors also surfaced. As the Church consolidated and grew, for instance, it offered daily mass. How could it be administerd by officials who, just hours before, had writhed in contorted, lustful, and sinful sexual ecstasy with their wives?

In fact, this was a routine occurrence, as reality clashed daily with policy. Consider not the highborn clerics with access to fortunes but the lowly priests who constituted the greatest part of the clerical corpus. Material life in the postclassical West was so brutishly difficult that, while it also drove some unreligious men into ostensibly celibate monasteries as havens from hunger, it drove some sincere priests to marry as a form of economic survival. Alongside the children they would produce, wives could cultivate the parish landholdings and in other ways arrange to feed and clothe their priest husbands. More ambitious priests contrived to marry women with dowries, property, or small businesses, even if the latter consumed so much of the couple's time that the business of religion was secondary to the exigencies of commerce.

In other words, a perusal of the Western Church's decrees and ordinances would give the false impression that celibacy was a well-established feature in its clerics. Of course, it might also give rise to a certain suspicion that all was not well. Take, for example, the following list of penances: Clerics who sinned carnally would be imprisoned and allowed only bread and water. An ordained priest would be flogged until he bled, suffer other punishment at the bishop's discretion, and serve two years in jail. Clerks or monks, however, were treated more leniently—three bouts of flogging followed by various penances performed during a one-year term in prison. Worse was in store for the wives and children—they were to be sold into slavery.

Severe and scary, but applied only in the breach. How could it be otherwise in a Church where an eighth-century high official—in this case, the man later canonized as St. Boniface—was reduced to begging the pope for permission to treat as sinners deacons steeped since childhood in sinful carnality and other filthy behavior, and who, as deacons, shamed their holy office by sleeping with four or five concubines?

Pope Zachary's answer was a model of compromise: if said clerics were adulterous or had more than one wife, Boniface should bar them from performing priestly duties. Clearly, it was too difficult to function as if the complex of strict rules, notably about celibacy, were actually operational.

Boniface, of course, and other highly placed ecclesiastical celibates despaired of the discrepancy between ideal and actual, and their correspondence tended to highlight their problems with clergymen who behaved outrageously rather than their quieter and more obedient brethren. Congregations, too, gossiped freely and judged harshly, suspecting all priests on the basis of the rogues and scoundrels among them.

Another favorite pastime was tattling about shameful activities in the hope that authority would crack down on the offender. Telling tales—*denunciation* was the current phrase—was not only an unreliable source of information but many bishops actively discouraged it as markedly detrimental to both the cleric denounced and also to his denouncer.

Some tattling, of course, was justified, particularly when priests and bishops fathered children. The great fear, entirely vindicated by subsequent events, was that the clerics would then use Church property as a personal legacy to provide for their sons and daughters. Expecting them to live with their wives "as if they were not wives" assumed as well that they would manage their church's possessions as if they were men who had no possessions, which was literally the case. Informing on priests and bishops who flouted Church policy with even a single infant was not motivated by personal spite but by a grave concern for the material future of the Christian community.

An objective overall assessment of clerical celibacy is difficult. We lack sufficiently credible sources, and the celibate life is by nature private and seldom documented. Estimates of how widespread it was vary wildly, but Peter Brown, a highly respected authority on the early Church, suggests that by late in the sixth century, few priests had wives and the same was true for the bishops, most of them former monks who had left ascetic cloisters to take up administrative positions in the cities. That said, so many legitimately documented examples of widespread, flagrant violations exist that it is equally clear that, though celibacy was becoming the norm from the highest ecclesiastical levels down to the lower clergy, egregiously uncelibate clerical lifestyles continued to challenge the official policy.

By the tenth century, for instance, rural priests in particular, some urban priests, and even a few bishops lived in marriages demonstrably sexual through their repeated production of children. The *focaria* or priest's mistress was a stock character in medieval fiction.

Until Gregorian Reform in the eleventh century, married clergy continued to function. Most claimed to be celibate and perhaps were. Civil law recognized their unions as legitimate, but canon law defined their wives as "concubines" and their children as "bastards," legally barred from inheriting property. Furthermore, their sons were barred from the priesthood.

These restrictions were easily circumvented. Sons and daughters were introduced as nephews and nieces and raised with the priest and his wife. Alternatively, if a "bastard" son felt called to the priesthood, a bishop could, subject to the pope's approval, grant a dispensation to permit it. As late as 1398, for instance, one dispensation for fifty illegitimate males included ten sons of clergymen.

Gregorian Reform lowered the boom on these easy subversions of clerical celibacy, and the eleventh and twelfth centuries resounded with bitter battles between sexually active clergy and doctrinally celibate Churchmen. Defiantly uncelibate clergymen were harassed and some lost their jobs, while the covertly uncelibate must have exercised discretion. Undoubtedly the Reform convinced more clergymen to adopt celibacy and attracted more ascetic-minded men and women into service and cloisters. Ultimately, it was sabotaged by the notorious disobedience of lustful priests, bishops, even popes, and also a chorus of dissent openly challenging celibacy as a valid form of life even for clerics.

Individual violation of this newly compulsory celibacy was extraordinary, even at the highest levels. Pope John XIII committed adultery and incest. In 1171, the abbot-elect of St. Augustine at Canterbury fathered seventeen children in a single village, but this was a puny production compared to a twelfth-century bishop of Liège who was unseated because he had sired sixty-five. The most ludicrous, later-century case was Pope Innocent VIII, a proud father who publicly acknowledged his brood of "bastards" and was then forgiven because he had been honest.

Celibacy was also a key issue in the next great reformation, Martin Luther's, which sliced like a jagged knife through ailing Catholicism, cauterizing the Church's wounds and severing the flailing limbs that had, as they matured, bruised and gouged their host body's face and torso. The operation gave birth to a reformed Catholic Church and the new rite of Protestantism. It gave incisive answers—two quite opposed ones—to the question of clerical celibacy, so that a Protestant perspective validated the spiritual capacity of clergymen who wished to be married, while a Catholic lens reaffirmed the sacred nature of clerical celibacy.

By October 31, 1517, when he nailed his ninety-five theses to the wall of the Palest Church in Wittenberg, Martin Luther had clarified his thinking about celibacy. It was, he concluded, theologically wrongheaded, because it had been conceived as a self-imposed chore performed in the hope of currying divine favor. But the Christian God could not be cajoled by such paltry and ignoble maneuvers. God granted salvation for faith alone, and so compulsory celibacy, which Luther regarded as an attempt at a good work, was morally irrelevant to both God and the coerced celibate.

Luther was by no means an anticelibate; he believed strongly that God bestowed the gift of celibacy on some people. "This is Christ's way," he wrote in explanation of celibacy. When the apostles concluded that celibacy was so virtuous that men should not marry, Christ reminded them that not everyone could accept this precept. Christ's will was, Luther declared, that only a certain few should pledge themselves to celibacy. Everyone else was divinely mandated to follow the road more traveled. Luther himself married an ex-nun, Katharina von Bora, and lavishly praised the marital state for its many blessings, especially children.

Luther's views on celibacy, like St. Augustine's and the earliest Church

Fathers', have had a profound doctrinal effect on Christian life. Because of their misogyny, Luther and John Calvin, another major Protestant theologian, both considered celibacy superior to marriage, but only justified in those to whom God had granted it. This meant, they agreed, that celibacy should never be imposed nor pledged rashly by people, lay or religious, unable to fulfill their commitment. "You lucky man," Luther enthused to a priest who had just married, "that you have by an honorable marriage conquered that unclear celibacy which is reprehensible because it causes either a constant burning or unclean pollutions."

The Reformation was a great cleansing that liberated thousands of religious from unwilling celibacy and legitimized the unions of the previously uncelibate. The Counter-Reformation, however, Catholicism's self-healing, reaffirmed clerical celibacy with a vigor and confidence hitherto unthinkable. The renewed Catholic Church was smaller and stronger, no longer plagued by festering dissension among its clerics and the consequent contempt of its faithful. The rot was excised. Purchased indulgences could no longer substitute for penance. Church policy could no longer be flouted or even challenged. Strict clerical celibacy was now a major distinction between Roman Catholic and Protestant rites, and under no circumstances could it be set aside. Centuries would elapse—close to five, to be precise—before clerics would once again launch a concerted attack against the perpetual celibacy imposed on them as a condition of their commitment to a life in God's service.

APOSTOLIC WOMEN

In the early Renaissance, when Europe was awash in religious fervor, devout Christian women anxiously sought outlets to manifest their spirituality. An obvious choice was to enter a cloister. Some monasteries had double cloisters, one for men, the other for women, an arrangement that had originated in the need for spiritual guidance, economic assistance, and defense against attack. Abbesses began to head some nunneries as early as 514, but unlike the earlier cloisters, which accepted the direction of each individual abbot as the word of God, these abbesses followed either the severe rule of Columbanus (d. 615) or of St. Benedict.

But many women needed different outlets for their spiritual enthusiasm. They longed to live as Christ and his apostles had, chaste and poor, devoted to serving even their humblest fellow mortals. And they wanted to move freely among these people, living in their midst, rather than be shut away from them in cloistered convents. From the collective longings of these apostolic women sprang the great religious movement known as Beguinage.

BEGIN THE BEGUINE

Beguinage's exact origins and evolution cannot be as precisely dated or documented as those of other institutions, but historians generally agree it emerged in the twelfth century. Beguines (whose name was probably a corruption of *Albigensians,* the heretics that certain orthodox Churchmen suspected these women of supporting) are easier to describe than define. They were groups of women who dedicated themselves to chastity and poverty, pooled their possessions, and formed spiritual or residential communes. Often they lived together, but some continued to live at home with their families. They acknowledged no formal rule and established no network with sister organizations. They worked and worshiped together and devoted themselves to the apostolic service of others. Sometimes they accepted men into their communities.

We like to identify movements' founders—Pachomius, for example, is the name associated with monasticism. For Beguinage, the most commonly mentioned names are Lambert le Bègue and Marie d'Oignies, both of Belgium, where the first Beguines sprung up. Lambert is usually credited with founding the first Beguinage in Liège, for gentlewomen wishing to live chaste, austere, and charitable lives.

Marie, the best known of the earliest Beguines, was born in 1176 to moneyed parents. Fourteen years later, she was married. However, she and her husband afterward pledged chastity and set off together to serve at a lazaretto, a lepers' colony. After a while, Marie grew restless. She longed for a more austere, spiritual life. At some point, she disposed of her personal wealth. She left the lazaretto and joined an unaffiliated Augustinian order that admitted women as well as men. This first Beguinage suited Marie well, and she remained there until her death in 1213.

In the depth of her piety, Marie was in the forefront of holy women; even though unassociated with a formal cloister, she had fewer restraints on her behavior. Marie was renowned for her rapturous encounters with God, her adoration of the Eucharist, and an asceticism so intense it included such mortifications as hacking off a piece of her flesh. Her commitment to chastity, coupled with her rejection of marriage (though she was actually married), also had a great impact. Additionally, her pursuit of apostolic poverty, personal humility, and zealous volunteering among lepers, the outcasts of society, raised her to the highest pinnacles of holiness. Women attracted to these qualities were fortunate Marie had an excellent biographer whose stirring account of her exceptional life—including her bouts of uncontrollable weeping—spread her fame far beyond Belgium.

Belgium was the birthplace of this apostolic women's movement, which spread along North Europe's trade routes and became particularly strong in Cologne. Unlike nuns, who were usually from wellborn families, Beguines were a social mix, with upper-class women predominating at first but gradually embracing so many of the working class that by the end of the thirteenth century, the Beguinages gained a reputation as refuges for the poor.

Beguinage was quite different from monasticism and other cloistered organizations whose initiates swore formal vows: chastity, poverty, and obedience. Beguines, too, cherished these precepts, but rather than pledging to them, they observed them. As one approving Belgian bishop observed, Beguines chose to be eternally celibate rather than vow eternal celibacy. They obeyed instead of swearing obedience, and they considered it more prudent to live frugally and philanthropically endow their personal fortunes rather than unloading all their properties and possessions. In fact the Beguine movement's four pillars—as opposed to oaths—were celibacy, poverty, humility, and charity, the latter executed in indefatigable service to the poor.

What magnet induced women to become Beguines? Undoubtedly a combination of factors, headed by a fervent desire to express their religious devotion by following the apostolic path of chastity and poverty. Certainly their preservation of celibacy was what motivated nobles and royalty to endow Beguinages. But like the apostles, Beguines did not hide themselves away in cloisters. They lived fearlessly and piously in the world, alongside those they served: the poor, the ill, the orphaned, society's unfortunates. So amorphous was the movement that some Beguines continued to live with their parents while others moved into communal houses or communities. Some earned their living in mainstream society, plying whatever skills they had for women's wages. Some Beguines begged. A few enjoyed substantial incomes from personal fortunes.

Beguines were neither secular nor religious, except in their piety, which equaled that of any cloistered nun. Their professions of chastity and obedience were temporary and they continually renewed them. Theirs was a voluntary way of life, without the coercion associated with formal cloisters. The possibility of returning to worldly ways always existed, alleviating pressure on a Beguine to suffer guilt if she changed her way of life. She had free choice and did not find herself trapped in a life to which she was no longer committed.

Belgian Beguines wore simple garments in plain colors, unadorned except for a penitent rope of gray-brown, undyed wool. They were poor, by birth or choice, and wanted to live with the poor they served. They inhabited the world and, unlike cloistered religious, were not forced to sever emotional ties to their blood relatives.

Four external factors profoundly influenced the Beguine movement:

demography, celibacy, the nature of marriage, and Church politics. During this period of the Middle Ages, wars and crusades helped unbalance the gender ratio so that many women had no hope of ever marrying. On top of this, celibacy, both voluntary and imposed, removed yet more men from the marriage field. Apostolically inspired chastity and spiritual purity drew some men to the monasteries. Rigid guild rules that banned married apprentices forced large numbers of workingmen into unwanted celibacy. Demographics, therefore, consigned enormous numbers of women to singleness.

In parts of France and Spain, the Albigensians played on this, harping on their hatred of marriage and the sanctity of celibacy to lure women into their movement. This explains, in part, why Beguines—voluntary bachelor women—were initially suspected of subscribing to the Albigensian heresy. The Albigensians taught that marriage and its sexual intercourse prevented salvation and that parents, who had by definition already fornicated, were doomed souls. Albigensianism must have influenced at least some women to look elsewhere than unlikely marriage for a satisfying life.

In fact, many women needed no prodding to consider abstaining from marriage. Living, as most did, in cramped quarters with no privacy from their families, they observed their parents' marriages firsthand and understood well what lay in store for them. Centuries earlier, Ambrose had discouraged women from abandoning their virginal state with his succinct reminder of what marriage would bring: "pregnancy, the crying of infants, the torture caused by a rival, the cares of household management." Women who married were often the most melancholy mourners of the virginity they had surrendered and the most fervent advocates for the celibacy that would restore a modicum of serenity and control to their frenetic lives.

Church politics tolled the death knell of Beguinage by attempting to regulate it. Ecclesiastical authorities were distressed by the phenomenon of unregulated communities of women springing up in urban centers throughout Northern Europe. These women worked, taught, spoke out, read the Scriptures, and selected their own spiritual guides, all without even consulting male Church officials. What were they if not uncloistered nuns?

The Church, in total agreement, clamped down on these voluntary celibates and in 1312 ordered them into cloisters. The reason for this order? Dogmatically simple, though circularly and sophistically argued: Church officials could not believe such celibate free agents as the Beguines could manage to survive chastely in the wicked world and so they must be locked up. Furthermore, the private or informal vows of sexual purity they had previously sworn were now forbidden—they were directed to swear formal oaths. Then these formally avowed celibates had to be cloistered lest they face temptation, weaken, and renege on their vows.

The Church had some initial difficulty controlling all the Beguines, who were purposely scattered, uncentralized, and unassociated. But one by one, unable to withstand the Churchly onslaught, the Beguinages capitulated, retreated behind walls, formalized their arrangements, and submitted to the ecclesiastical authorities.

By the fourteenth century, Church control had tightened and radically altered the nature of Beguinages. Everything from habits to entrance requirements to rites and daily rituals was prescribed. This ran counter to the essence of Beguinage, where voluntarism, informality, family ties, and life among the poor were cornerstones. Nurses, teachers, and social workers were driven off the streets and into cloisters, away from their clientele and, indeed, their raison d'être. They could no longer teach adults, only children, and behind cloister walls, and they were not allowed to produce marketable goods. One by one, their orders folded or were transformed beyond recognition, their pursuit of apostolic life smashed by the exigencies of a rigid, ambitious, domineering Church hierarchy. In the tradition of the early Fathers, who wrote that "sin came from a woman, but salvation through a virgin," these men revered virgins but hated women.

The standardization and control of Beguinage, a female invention, cost women dearly. It had provided an outlet for the explosion of piety that, among Beguines, translated into a passionate desire to imitate Christ's life, to live chastely, as he had, among the poor, sharing their misery and their hunger, all the while ministering to them. Ultimately, the Church smashed what may have been the world's most significant movement ever derived from women's collective urges to lead productive, charitable, independent, and celibate lives. But for over a century, Beguine-style celibacy had empowered women at the same time as it enabled them to serve multitudes of their needy compatriots. Beguines survived the rigors of the street and were admirably faithful to their vows of chastity, but they could not survive the wrathful jealousy of the autocratic Church, which, in the name of holy chastity, snatched these apostolic angels of mercy away from their needy clients and locked them away in cloisters.

WOMEN OUT OF THIS WORLD

A surge of yearning for the purity of apostolic life swept early Renaissance Europe. The Beguines were its most visible interpreters, but other women acted out the same drama. They lived at home with their parents, self-confined to a cell or a room. They survived outside, alone or with kindred spirits, usually engaged in social work. In Milan such women were called *umiliati,* the humble, in Spain *beatas,* the holy. The *beatas* took informal vows of chastity, claimed immunity from sexual passion, and dedicated themselves to charity and visionary piety. A number found their way into convents or, like Catherine of Siena, into Dominican or Franciscan tertiary orders.

In the sixteenth century, Angela Merici established a noncloistered women's order, the Company of St. Ursula, the legendary British saint martyred, with her eleven thousand virgin companions, as she rode to her wedding. Angela's choice of St. Ursula was significant; virginity was the cornerstone of her Company, and social work, teaching, and nursing its mission. Novices required their parents' permission and had to be at least twelve, the minimum legal age for women to marry. Angela directed novices to preserve their virginity, which she considered an angelic quality.

The young women continued to live at home, "consecrated virgins" devoted to prayer and the social service that drove them to dedicate their lives to the poor. Not all women had suitable family situations, and these Angela placed in decent families where they earned their keep as housekeepers or governesses. Twice monthly, the "daughters" assembled, first at the Hospital for Incurables, later in their own edifice, where they consulted with the "mothers"—older, wiser spiritual guides.

Angela designed the Company as a community where rich and poor were indistinguishable, and unlike most convents, she willingly received poor "sisters." She ensured in as many ways as she could that no distinctions would be made, and the women wore only the plainest garments that proclaimed to the world their poverty, modesty, and simplicity. In fact, Angela conceived of her Company as an alternative to convents and specified nonclaustration as one of its essential features.

Thanks to Angela's public relations and, after her death in 1540, the massive efforts of her secretary and confidant, the priest Gabriele Cozzano, St. Ursula's was exempted from the forced claustration of Beguinages and other religious societies. Surprisingly, Angela's saintly reputation and Cozzano's arguments prevailed. The primitive Church had had neither cloisters nor convents, so the Company of St. Ursula was simply replicating its historical past.

The Company of St. Ursula survived until 1810, its sisters grateful that the Church granted them permission to maintain their chastity in the world of their blood relatives, neighbors, and the struggling poor they were dedicated to serving.

Mary Ward, Who Was "But a Woman"

The Church was not so lenient with England's Mary Ward, a Poor Clare sister and an erudite and visionary educator. In 1609, Mary founded a Euro-

pean network of schools modeled on the Jesuit college at St. Omer. All the
teachers in these schools were laywomen, members of the Institute of the
Blessed Virgin Mary. The Institute established itself in several European cities
and by 1631 counted a membership of three hundred. Some of its schools
had hundreds of students, and several allowed poor children to attend day
school free of charge.

"It seems that the female sex should and can . . . undertake something
more than ordinary," Mary wrote. "We also desire . . . to devote ourselves
according to our slender capacity to the performance of those works of Christian
charity toward our neighbor that cannot be undertaken in convents."

Girls as well as boys studied religion, Latin, Greek, French, local languages,
and mathematics. Girls learned needlepoint and music and, with the
boys, participated in drama productions in Latin. This curriculum reflected
Mary's views on women. Though she conceded male expertise in heading
families and the Church, she was convinced women could do "all other
things."

> Wherein are we so inferior to other creatures that they should term us "but
> women"? For what think you of this word, "but women"? but as if we were in
> all things inferior to some other creature which I suppose to be a man! Which
> I dare to be bold to say is a lie.

Some of the other things Mary thought women could do were to live
chastely and devoutly outside a cloister, elect their own "mother general,"
conduct business in modest clothes rather than a strict habit, and mix with
each other and mainstream society.

These were dangerous viewpoints, and the Church attacked both the Institute
of the Blessed Virgin Mary and the other, defiantly earthbound, Mary. In
1631, it invoked the Bull of Suppression and suppressed—killed—the Institute
by expelling its three hundred teaching sisters back to England. Worse
was in store for Mary Ward; she was denounced as a heretic and jailed for a
short spell in a Munich convent.

Her Church's treatment of Mary Ward was a lesson to all devout and celibate
women. If they were also independent, strong-minded, ambitious, and
visionary, their virtue was suspect—witness the fate of the chaste Beguines.
Their motives, too, were questioned, their social contributions disregarded,
their success scorned, their community dismembered or imprisoned in cloisters.
Ironically, cloisters often produced the very consequences the Church so
feared but that the uncloistered sisters had rigorously avoided. As we will see
when we consider the fate of unwillingly cloistered women, the shotgun
celibacy aimed directly at them was often the first target of those who rebelled
against their condition.

BRIDES OF CHRIST

Devout women dedicated to chastity, spirituality, and service to God and their fellow man were not all suited to the apostolic lives of Beguines and other sisters. For some, asceticism was a magnetic attraction because, carried to extremes and combined with proofs of divine favor, it could lead to sainthood. For the religious celibate who was exceedingly ambitious, this spiritual route had infinitely more appeal than that of compliant motherhood in an obedient marriage.

Some determined women indulged in marathon bouts of asceticism, fasting to starvation, mortifying their flesh, depriving their senses, even devising humiliations so repulsive that they could be assured few could replicate them. No Beguine or ordinary nun would dream of drinking cancerous pus or the wash water of rotting, leprous limbs.

Achieving sainthood was a serious business. Only 3,276 people who died from the beginning of Christianity to 1500 became saints, with only 87 successful candidates from 1350 to 1500. On the plus side for women, in that same period the male-to-female ratio of saints went from five to one to about two and a half to one. From 1350 to 1500—and this statistic is the most pertinent here—laywomen saints overtook males, though the greater number of clerical males gave male saints a clear lead over women in orders. For aspiring female saints, this was the most promising era ever.

Sainthood was that era's great challenge, akin to aspiring to the Olympics or a Nobel Prize today. For women severely limited in vocations other than drudging labor or motherhood, the stretch to being the very best practitioner of religion was appealing, especially to highly intelligent perfectionists such as Catherine of Siena, whose brief, bursting life won her the eternity of sainthood.

Catherine of Siena

Catherine was born Caterina Benincasa in 1347, the twenty-second of the twenty-five children of Lapa Piacenti and her husband, Giacomo, an enterprising dyer. She was also the twin sister of the ailing infant Giovanna, whom Lapa sent out to a wet nurse while she breast-fed the sturdier Catherine at home. Giovanna soon died, while Catherine fattened on her mother's milk. For a whole year Lapa nursed her, longer than any of her other children, until she again conceived and ceased to lactate.

The year Catherine was weaned, 1348, the bubonic plague struck Italy full force. Her family was spared, but the terror and panic that prevailed affected everyone. Did Catherine suffer especially? Probably not, though she was always sensitive about Lapa's constant reminders that she was a special child, chosen to live while Giovanna died. As a youngster, she fasted normally for a devout little girl. She enjoyed her childhood, laughing and playing, often outside. By the age of five, she would genuflect and say a Hail Mary on each step of the staircase up to her bedroom. She hero-worshiped Euphrosyne, a legendary virgin who escaped marriage by disguising herself as a man and entering a monastery.

At six or seven, Catherine had a vision of Jesus and several saints. For years, she meditated on what this might mean. She and her little friends started a sort of club in which they flagellated themselves with knotted ropes. Catherine's role in instigating this was an indication of the depth of her religiosity, but in that pious age, it caused little comment.

When Catherine was an adolescent, Lapa began to tutor her in the ways of impending womanhood. She had to scrub her face, apply makeup, dye her hair blond, and curl it. All this, of course, was in preparation for her inevitable marriage. Then, at fourteen, Catherine envisioned a mystical marriage to Christ, a glorious ceremony attended by the Virgin Mary, John the Evangelist, Saints Paul and Dominic, and even King David, who carried the Psalter. Jesus was his own ring-bearer and tenderly slipped the pearl-and-diamond-studded gold ring onto her finger. "Now I betroth you to me in a faith that will survive from this hour forward forever immutable, until the glorious heavenly marriage, in perfect conjunction with me in the second eternal wedding," he intoned, "when face-to-face you will be allowed to see me and enjoy me." Overwhelmed, the new, fourteen-year-old Bride of Christ instantly pledged her virginity to her husband.

At fifteen, Catherine's world was shattered. Her idolized older sister Bonaventura died in childbirth. Soon after, so did Giovanna, the sister named for Catherine's dead twin. She blamed herself—once again, she had been chosen to live while others died. Her religious convictions shifted from devout to obsessive. Then began the asceticism that would kill her when she, like Christ, was thirty-three. One manifestation was that she ceased eating anything but bread, uncooked vegetables, and water. Meanwhile, Lapa and Giacomo focused their attention onto their sole surviving daughter, all the others having died. Catherine's mission, as they saw it, was to contract a marriage that would help consolidate the family business. What better choice than Bonaventura's widower?

Catherine disliked her brother-in-law, a coarse and ribald man, and loathed the idea of marriage. Defiantly, she invoked her pledge of virginity and mystical marriage to Christ. Furious struggles with her parents only strengthened her determination to resist wedding a mortal man. She found an ally, a sympathetic priest who suggested she prove her sincerity by lopping off her blond hair. Enthusiastically, Catherine hacked it off, so her plain face was unadorned.

Her family was livid. "Vilest girl, you cut off your hair, but do you think perhaps that you are not going to do what we wish?" her mother taunted. "Your hair will grow back and even if your heart should break, you will be forced to take a husband."

The family took away Catherine's privileges. Her most serious loss was the bedroom that had permitted hours of secret flagellation, nightly vigils, intense prayer and meditation. Now she had to share her brothers' bedroom and, until she came to her senses, do the family's domestic chores.

Catherine accepted this calmly and served her family as if it were Christ's, pretending her parents were Mary and Joseph, the clamorous horde of her male siblings the holy apostles. This visualization enabled her to continue her devotions unimpeded. After several months, she made a startling announcement. I shall never marry, she said, and you are wasting your time trying to force me to do so. "There is no way I intend to accommodate you. I must obey God and not men."

"God watch over you, sweet daughter," Giacomo finally uttered. "Do as you please and as the Holy Spirit instructs you."

Lapa restored the private bedroom, where Catherine imposed harsher austerities than ever before. She flagellated herself three times daily, one and a half hours each session, and tortured her flesh with an iron chain bound tightly around her hips. She spoke only to confess, slept only half an hour every second night, and that on a short, wooden board. She gave up bread and soon lost half her body weight.

"Daughter, I see you already dead," Lapa wailed, her anguish at Catherine's deterioration driving her close to madness. "Without a doubt you will kill yourself. Woe is me! Who has robbed me of my daughter?"

But Catherine still had years before she starved herself to death, and she resolved to spend them as a sister in a Dominican tertiary order. Members of third orders make promises that echo the vows of the full-fledged sisters, but they remain uncloistered and not subject to the strict regimen of a convent community. But they are religious and not secular and by their vocation renounce any possibility of marriage.

Poor Lapa! She carted Catherine off to a spa in the forlorn hope the healing waters would cure her. Instead the inventive girl managed to sneak into a forbidden part of the pool and scald herself with the boiling sulfuric water that, diluted and cooled, healed everyone else.

Back in Siena, Catherine nagged until Lapa finally agreed to take her to the sisters. To Lapa's delight, they refused Catherine—a too young virgin who might easily stray from the path of chaste righteousness would be an "inopportune" novice, and they preferred mature widows. Catherine was devastated. She developed a high fever and disfiguring boils. Lapa was terrified, and Catherine, manipulative as ever, seized the opportunity to renew her demand for admission to the Sisters of Penance. Otherwise, she threatened, God and St. Dominic, who wanted her for their holy work, would make sure something drastic happened to her.

Lapa raced to the convent and begged, this time sincerely, with her whole heart. The sisters listened, then warned her that if Catherine was too pretty, she might provoke some kind of sexual scandal. But Catherine was not pretty at all, and for once Lapa was thankful. Come and see for yourselves, she implored the nuns. A jury of wise, widowed sisters accompanied the frantic mother back to her daughter's bedside, where they judged Catherine suitably plain and devout. They relented and accepted her. In days, Catherine recovered and donned the white-and-black habit.

Catherine might never have met the higher standards at a convent, the repository for well-bred women, but her more modest birth had nothing to do with her decision to join a third order. She did not wish to be cloistered and subject to the discipline of an overseeing mother superior. This was not because she feared the rigors of religious community life. To the contrary, the regimen she had in store for herself was so radical she must have guessed no convent would have tolerated it. Uncloistered, she was free to execute her most fanatical ideas.

Now Catherine went all out in subduing what little flesh still hung on her bony frame. She relied mainly on the Holy Host for sustenance and usually swallowed only cold water and chewed bitter herbs, rarely food. Food literally sickened her, convulsing her shriveled stomach and causing her such pain that, as her confessor wrote, "anything she ingested needed to exit by the same way it entered." Catherine's chew-and-spit technique sometimes failed and a morsel—for instance a single bean—descended into her stomach. Then she vomited back up whatever she had eaten. She was unable to do this at will, however, and so developed the agonizing habit of inserting stalks of fennel and other plants into her stomach to cause the necessary spasms. (The great St. Teresa of Avila used an olive twig for the same purpose.)

Today, Catherine would be hospitalized and force-fed, though she would almost certainly still die. In the fourteenth century, she was widely criticized, slandered as a secret eater and condemned as a witch. At the same time, her confessors and acolytes "understood" and revered her as a holy woman obedient to God's command, however mysterious.

One day, tending a wretched and bitter woman dying of breast cancer, Catherine was revolted by the stench of the rotting flesh. So great was her revulsion that she saw it as a moral dilemma she had to resolve. Hunger and lust were long gone, but how, she wondered, could she conquer even this sort of bodily sensation? In answer, she ladled a cupful of the reeking pus and gulped it all down.

That night, Christ appeared to her. When he showed her his gouged side, Catherine was consumed by her longing to place her lips on the sacred wound. God did not let Catherine off scot-free—His consoling succor cost her an acute chronic pain in her breast. However, from then on she no longer needed food because she could not digest it.

No hint of sexual scandal tainted her, despite, or because of, the constant presence of her confessor, Father Raymond of Capua, personally selected by the pope to monitor and guide her. Catherine never wanted to marry, and a young woman of her social standing would scarcely think of sex in any other context. Lapa's eternal pregnancies, Bonaventura's death in childbirth, and the death of so many siblings must also have affected Catherine's view of marriage—sex could kill much faster than starvation, and with no benefits whatsoever for the victim. As well, Catherine's holy anorexia eliminated any stray twinges of sexuality, transforming her into a eunuch for the Kingdom of Heaven, a purposefully impotent celibate who joyfully sacrificed sex for the glorious rewards of the infinitely better next world.

Not only did Catherine's extravagant asceticism kill any sexual desire in her famished body, it very nearly killed her outright. Several times her weakened heart temporarily stopped beating. Once when this happened, she imagined that she saw Christ save her life by exchanging his own sacred heart for hers. She later exulted that He had often scooped her body up from the earth and she had felt her soul in perfect union with God's. Any eroticism remaining in her ravaged body was surrendered, in sublime sublimation, to Christ.

Catherine's burning ambition was to preach as a man would, and she so defeminized herself that she actually succeeded. God had primed her, assuring her it was as easy for Him to create angels as insects. With an energy incredible in one so malnourished, she flung herself into lobbying for her causes: peace and reform in the Church, the pope's return to Rome, and a crusade against the Muslims.

Catherine was a dynamic and fearless speaker and lobbyist, lecturing and scolding leaders on every level—religious, municipal, and state—about needed reforms. She even chided the pope—Babbo or Daddy, she called him—urging him to end churchly inequities or else resign and let someone else do the job. Catherine's reputation grew until she was internationally renowned as a political and ecclesiastical authority, arguably Italy's leading fourteenth-century statesman.

Catherine was not merely a high-profile public figure. She had her private work as well, as "mamma" to the disciples she called "sons," as nurse to dying patients in public hospitals, and as spiritual mentor to prisoners awaiting execution. As one of them was dispatched and died murmuring, "Jesus, Catherine," she stood so close, his blood spattered onto her robe. Later, she rejoiced that his soul was at rest and could not bear to wash off his fragrant blood.

Catherine maintained her lethal regimen until, at thirty-three, she was ready for glorious death and union with her Husband, who had also died at thirty-three. She had known for years she would die and had planned and longed for the moment as the consummation of her personal mission. Her terrible austerities had lifted her above mortal experience, so that she was rarely gripped by carnal hunger for food and even less for sex. She managed a fine balance between anesthetizing her senses and almost, but not quite, extinguishing them. She wished to time her death precisely and linger on in life until she could die at the same age as Christ her Husband.

After she died of starvation, Catherine's admirers set out on canonization for her almost at once. She had achieved what she had striven for—to be the holiest of holy women, to live as a Bride of Christ in strict chastity, to deny her body physical sustenance, and to scourge it into submission to her fiery will.

Intelligent, resourceful, courageous, outrageous, and driven, Catherine was the quintessence of a successful Bride of Christ. The competition was stiff. Colomba da Rieti so mutilated herself with spiked chains bound across her hips and breasts, already scraped raw and blistered from her hair shirts, that a gang of would-be rapists who stripped her were too awed to consummate the deed. Angela of Foligno quaffed water in which she had just bathed a leper's putrefying flesh. And Bridget of Sweden, whom Christ had wed after her human husband's death, equaled and in fact cooperated with Catherine as a diplomat, reproached her king, and nagged the pope. Ultimately, Bridget gained her own particular goal: the Bridgettine order of nuns, a feminist fantasy, directed by a woman and regulated by a simple, Spartan, and sensible rule.

These women and their contemporaries were the stars of the Middle Ages. Through superhuman effort and careful strategy, they achieved success, power, and influence unimaginable to most women irredeemably destined for marriage and motherhood. In most cases, the common denominators were extreme asceticism and celibacy glorified through mystical marriages with Christ. From the thirteenth to the seventeenth centuries, 30 percent of Italian holy women indulged in near-starvation regimens. Their emaciated, sexless bodies ensured their earthly chastity, while they sublimated any lingering eroticism in fantastic visions of union—physical as well as spiritual—with Christ their husband. Their celibacy, so arduously preserved, was the essential precondition on which all of these triumphantly ascetic women built their stunningly successful careers.

HILDEGARD OF BINGEN
FROWNS ON FASTING

An exception to the rule of exaggerated asceticism was Hildegard of Bingen, known as the Sibyl of the Rhine, the Dear Abby of the twelfth century. The aristocratic, devout, brilliant, scholarly, curious, and compassionate abbess of a women's Benedictine monastic community, Hildegard supervised her sisters and wrote prodigiously. She kept up a voluminous personal correspondence and published major works on visions, medical science, natural history, and the lives of several saints. She was also musical, and her output of liturgical music was the Middle Ages' greatest and most distinctive.

Like Catherine of Siena and Bridget of Sweden a century and a half later, this "poor little figure of a woman," as she disparaged herself, was exceedingly influential with people on all levels of society: monks, bishops, and popes, emperors, queens, and kings. She castigated the Holy Roman Emperor Frederick Barbarossa as a madman because he backed schismatic popes, and she cursed an order of monks as sons of the Devil because of a financial dispute. Much of her teaching was couched in visions, so God, not Hildegard, was responsible for their content.

Hildegard's forthright advice in letters included a gentle reproof to the saintly but excessively ascetic Elisabeth of Schongau. Her advice, imparted as a description of a vision, was too late, for Elisabeth subsequently died. Bodies are like fields, Hildegard wrote, and just as unseasonable downpours or neglect will ruin their crops, so excessive strain will ruin a human being.

"That pitch-black bird, the Devil," she added, preys on sinners and people plagued by erotic desires by urging them to "trample your body underfoot through sorrows, tears, and strivings without moderation." His diabolic suggestion is that this will expiate sin. In fact, Hildegard warned, all that happens is that the zealous ascetic weakens, sickens, and loses her zest for life, including for her holy spiritual mission, which is precisely what the Devil intended. This was, of course, the crisis point Elisabeth had already reached, and one wonders if, even at the last moment, Hildegard's hard-hitting warning stirred the dying woman.

What a provocative view of unrestrained asceticism! And Hildegard, who heartily endorsed only one deprivation—celibacy—had more bad news. The victims of these galloping austerities were guilty of the sin of pride and thought they were better than other good people. Exactly so, but the great ascetics such as Catherine of Siena either did not read Hildegard or they disregarded her advice as applying, perhaps, to privileged, highly educated intellectuals whose minds and pens were sufficiently overpowering to win sainthood.

For women less endowed, the exhibitionist practice of self-inflicted bodily abuse seemed the best possible course of action.

The most spectacular of all New World Brides of Christ was the Iroquois maiden Tekakwitha, venerated centuries after her death as a Roman Catholic saint and as a mesmerizingly tragic heroine by Leonard Cohen in his novel *Beautiful Losers*. In 1656, Tekakwitha was born at Ossernenon (Auriesville, New York), to a Mohawk subchieftain and his wife, an Algonquin Christian captured from a neighboring village. When she was four, a smallpox epidemic decimated her village and infected her whole family. Her parents and little brother died. Tekakwitha recovered, but the disease ravaged her, disfiguring her face and permanently damaging her eyesight.

The orphaned child went to live with her aunt and her uncle, traditionalists who resisted the current wave of Christian proselytizing. They taught Tekakwitha Mohawk values and customs, brought her with them on the annual hunt, and prepared her for life as a Mohawk woman. She gathered firewood, cultivated the cornfields, and decked herself in native finery.

When Tekakwitha was ten, French soldiers defeated the Iroquois, who were forced by the subsequent peace treaty to open up their lands to Jesuit missionaries. A year later, three Jesuit fathers arrived in Tekakwitha's village. Despite her uncle's hatred of these enemy emissaries, his position as village chief required him to greet them. Dutifully, he did so and, for the three days of their visit, instructed his young niece to assist them. Later, one of these Jesuits returned and focused on the Mohawks' Huron and Algonquin captives, who, like Tekakwitha's deceased mother, were often Christian converts.

Did Tekakwitha remember her mother's faith? Did her traditionalist family reproach her about it? Was she intrigued or inspired by the Jesuit newcomers? Was her fascination with Christianity a long-standing phenomenon that merely surfaced later, when puberty propelled her into the adult world of human choice?

Whatever the origins of her conversion, Tekakwitha revealed it when she reached puberty, after her family set about arranging her marriage. This was standard Mohawk procedure, for a husband would hunt and provide his wife with meat and contribute to her longhouse. But Tekakwitha refused to consider marriage and did not relent even when, according to a Jesuit account, her angry relatives punished her with extreme violence.

The family crisis intensified. On one side was the industrious, virtuous, pox-riddled Tekakwitha, on the other, the relatives who had harbored her after her parents' deaths. Yet she continued to defy them, challenging even her chieftain uncle. And what had he done, except attempt to ensure her future by finding a young Mohawk brave willing to wed his homely, squinting niece?

Yet the teenaged Tekakwitha had another, entirely different agenda. She was ineluctably drawn to her mother's religion and already "burned with an intense desire to embrace the Christian faith." She had learned about Christianity in the village, from captive Indian women. At Jesuit father Lamberville's invitation, she attended his catechism classes and became his star pupil. When he inquired among her people about her moral character, he concluded that "she had none of the vices of the girls of her age." Indeed, she led "a life so pure as if to be a tacit reproach of their [the Iroquois'] deprivations."

On Easter 1676, Father Lamberville baptized the twenty-year-old Tekakwitha, now called Kateri or Catherine. This was a startling exception to the policy of withholding baptism to Indians until the moment of death or until the Jesuits were certain no relapse was likely. "One sees savages fall back almost right after their baptism—because they do not have enough courage to scorn public opinion that is the only law of these people there," a Jesuit explained.

The pressures on Kateri were especially severe. The shamans ridiculed her, the villagers accused her of witchcraft and hounded her, and her own aunt denounced her as a wanton seductress. "Catherine, in whom you value virtue so much, is even so a hypocrite who deceives you," her aunt informed Father Lamberville. "She has, in my presence, enticed my husband to sin."

Father Lamberville had judged correctly—Kateri did not regress. But the battle lines had been drawn, and in the middle stood Kateri, a symbol of Jesuit victory over the chief and his villagers' way of life. Finally, Lamberville advised his protégée to flee to the St. François Xavier Mission near Montreal. She took his advice, and when her uncle was away parleying with Dutch traders, she escaped.

At the mission, Kateri became deeply attached to two other young Indian converts, the widowed Marie-Thérésa Tegaiguenta and Marie Skarichions. The trio dreamed of establishing their own nunnery, but after the mission's chief priest discouraged them, they committed themselves to each other and to modeling their lives on the hospital nuns who had once cared for Marie in Quebec. Poverty, chastity, and obedience—to the teachings of the Church they had so fanatically accepted—were the obvious ideals. But, under the influence of an elderly convert, Kateri was obsessed as well with Christian repentance in its goriest manifestations.

Seventeenth-century penances—fasting, abstinence, flagellation, self-torture—appealed to Kateri as a means of sharing Christ's agonies. They also paralleled the real life of her namesake, St. Catherine of Siena, who was the subject of so much Jesuit sermonizing. At Kateri's urging, the trio of friends constructed a shrine in the woods and crept out there to do penance. In this secret place she scourged her friends and was herself scourged. She thrust coals and burning cinders between her toes and branded her feet as the Mohawks marked their captives. She walked barefoot in ice and snow, slept for three nights on a bed of thorns, and when she ate, mixed ashes into her food. Kateri also fasted strenuously, though like all other residents of the mission, she had to do her share of the daily work.

Finally, Kateri's mortifications became so extravagant that Marie-Thérésa feared for her life. Deeply concerned, she confided in a Jesuit, Father Cholenec. Her extraordinary tale surprised him, and he ordered the women to moderate their activities.

Kateri had other issues to deal with, including the recurrent marriage issue. Her adopted sister, whom she lodged with, and Anastasie Tegonhatsiongo, her spiritual counselor, were pressuring her to marry. As before, Kateri refused. This time, though, she had a counterproposal: she wished to consecrate her virginity to Christ.

Christ or a Mohawk as husband: even Father Cholenec, to whom Kateri's mentors appealed, did not find this an easy choice. Mission life was hard, a constant struggle to find enough food and to survive brutal winters, disease, and military hostilities. For an Indian woman living far from any protection her family could provide, a human husband was a major asset. Father Cholenec advised Kateri to think carefully about her decision.

"I have deliberated enough," Kateri replied. "I have consecrated myself entirely to Jesus, son of Mary, I have chosen Him for husband and He alone will take me for wife."

Kateri's determination and single-mindedness convinced Father Cholenec and other mission priests. In 1679, on the Feast of the Annunciation, they presided over a ceremony in which she pledged perpetual virginity and gave herself to Christ as his wife. In the eyes of the Roman Catholic Church, Kateri Tekakwitha had become the first Iroquois sacred virgin.

This commitment to lifelong, virginal celibacy was anomalous in seventeenth-century Iroquoian society. Virginity existed as a concept, though without the reverence devout Catholicism attached to it. Iroquois legends told of a society of virgins, but this was a long-ago phenomenon and Indian women were not tempted to replicate it.

Celibacy, too, was an honored tradition, an essential preparation for successful hunts or battles. But it was for men, not women, and it was purely strategic and short-term. As a permanent condition—for example the Jesuits' lifestyle—it was considered peculiar. When these men tried to impose celibacy on the natives they lived among, Iroquois reaction ranged from puzzled incredulity to ridicule and anger.

In Kateri Tekakwitha's era, Church-ordained virginity had more than religious connotations. In the turbulence of French-Indian relations, Kateri's purposeful and publicly sworn celibacy had dual meanings and consequences. It was her personal declaration of ownership of her body and soul, which she withheld from her native community and offered instead to the foreign god. It was also a significant victory for the Jesuit intruders, who boasted in letters to French supporters how sharply Kateri's celibacy deviated from the usual Iroquoian sexual indulgence. From both Jesuit and Iroquois perspectives, Kateri's vow of perpetual virginity made the score Jesuits one, Iroquois nothing.

The Iroquois did not gracefully accept Kateri's defection. Some even reported that her celibacy was a sham, and that she slipped off into the woods for sexual trysts with a married man. In fact, these sylvan excursions were to her shrine, where she could indulge privately in her most punishing mortifications.

The Jesuits, on the other hand, had an important stake in her success. It had taken them little time to recognize her as a unique personality, immensely strong and committed, but also deeply impressionable and malleable. Now they could document how well they had taught her and could point to her frail, abused, but virginal body as evidence of their successful proselytizing.ˋ

The Jesuits were less enthusiastic about Kateri's excruciating penances, which provoked as much curiosity and concern as praise. But they were intent on changing Indian sexual customs and replacing traditional family structures with French-style patriarchy. However, in a classic case of the means justifying the ends, the Jesuits overlooked Kateri's persistent defiance of her relatives, male as well as female. Her perpetual virginity and mystic marriage to Christ so thoroughly vindicated their teachings that they were loath to criticize how she achieved them. The Jesuits also either ignored, or failed to comprehend, the extent to which Kateri's virginity was as much symbol as object of her independence. Had she responded to them as disobediently as she did to her family, they might have interpreted her insistence on chastity with less sympathy.

Kateri the Virgin spent the final year of her life as she had since arriving at the mission. She flung herself into the rituals of Catholicism, taking special comfort from the Holy Eucharist. She continued her mortifications, expiating on behalf of her martyred husband, Jesus, the horrible sins committed by her Indian people.

Then in February 1780, Kateri began to suffer stomach pains so severe she suspected death was near. For two months she endured them, always refusing to curtail the practices that so debilitated her. By the time she lay dying, she was so weakened she could not move from her lodge. Normally, Indians were carried—literally on their deathbeds—to the Jesuits for last rites. For the Iroquois virgin, however, Father Cholenec made a special exception. He packed up his ritual accoutrements and, for the last time, heard the confession and gave the absolution that would ease her into the next world. "Jesus, I love you," Kateri uttered, and died.

It is tempting to wonder how deeply the Jesuits grieved Kateri Tekakwitha's passing. In death, safe from the scandalmongers and angry relatives who had plagued her in life, she was their best weapon in their holy war for Indian allegiance. Alive, she might somehow have embarrassed them, perhaps by false accusations of apostasy when she sneaked off into the woods or, in freezing midwinter, stripped off all her clothes to stand penitently in front of a cross in the cemetery.

Worse, she might eventually have challenged the Jesuits, as she had her family. Empowered by her asceticism, her celibacy, and the glory of her marriage to Jesus, she might well have stood her ground against them as her namesake, Catherine of Siena, did even with the pope. All it would have taken, after all, was a disputed principle she was passionate about. Fortunately for the Jesuits, she died too soon for such an issue to arise.

Instead, her name quickly assumed an authority the living Kateri had never enjoyed. In remembrance, the Iroquois emulated her chastity, or so Jesuit father Cholenec reported. "Married people separated through mutual consent, many young widows vowed themselves to perpetual continence; others made the same promise in the case that their husbands died before them and they held to this promise."

Saintliness swiftly followed, with Kateri appearing in visions, interceding for supplicants, and performing miracles through the power of her dust and other relics. In 1943, Pope Pius XII declared Kateri, now known as the Lily of the Mohawks, venerable. In 1980, Pope John Paul II took the final step and canonized her. In lieu of miracles, the twenty-four-year-old bride of Christ had achieved the highest ranking in the Roman Catholic Church on the basis of her remarkable commitment to celibacy, reinforced by physical austerities so extreme they probably killed her. Reflecting on her real life, it is easy to imagine that, at last, Kateri Tekakwitha would have felt herself vindicated in choosing the un-Iroquois path of perpetual virginity.

Ironically, there is no reason to suppose that, like Catherine of Siena, Margery Kempe, or scores of other holy women, Kateri Tekakwitha was aiming for sainthood. Instead, she seized on Christianity and its emphasis on chastity, which immediately pitted her against her family and tribal values. They expected her to marry; she adamantly refused, empowered by her burning faith to defy her entire village. Sadly, the very priests who encouraged her rebellion and used her as a human battering ram in their battle for Indian souls denied Kateri entrance into a convent, her greatest desire. Instead, she had to resort to a mock cloister, dangerous in its uncontrolled penances, the wildness of the surrounding forest, and her own feverishly unbridled spirit.

When she died, a starved and tortured young virgin, she was a martyr to Jesuit Indian policy as much as to the intensity of her own devotion to Christian ideals, in particular the celibacy that so enraged her Iroquois people. Unlike the Virgin Mary, a real woman deformed by centuries of theology, Kateri Tekakwitha was a real woman deformed by her own fanatic interpretation of Christian doctrine, her identification with St. Catherine of Siena, and the manipulations of her spiritual counselors. These priests were well-intentioned but ultimately content to see Kateri as a convenient symbol of the sexual chastity they so regretted was lacking in all the other Iroquois.

COMMITTED SISTERS

Women religious viewed the issue of celibacy from vastly different perspectives. Most male clerics took holy orders by choice or were resigned to their family's decision to provide a son as priest or monk. A great many women, however, were consigned to convents, and to celibacy, without consultation and against their will. These women responded in a variety of ways, from meek obedience or sullen acquiescence to bitter defiance or open rebellion.

But for the women summoned to their vocation by God rather than by parsimonious, impoverished, or otherwise coerced or coercing parents, the compulsory vow of celibacy was seldom a privation. For them, it was an instrument of faith, and of personal independence.

CONVENTS OF JOY

Like Catherine of Siena and a host of other holy women who consecrated themselves to God, the committed religious unhesitatingly pledged eternal chastity. The moral pressure to preserve their virginity was particularly strong, for virginity was a perennial obsession of religious thinkers and writers. The thirteenth-century *Hali Meidenhad*—Holy Maidenhead, in modern English—was a vitriolically antisex, antimarriage essay addressed to young virgins in the hopes of keeping them that way. The maidenhead was "a virtue above all virtues, and to Christ the most acceptable of all." Even marital sex was impure, loathsome, and bestial, an "indecent burning of the flesh . . . [and] shameless coition, that fullness of stinking ordure and uncomely deed." It was, in fact, merely "a bed for the sick, to catch [in their fall] the unstrong, who cannot stand in the high hill, and so near to heaven, as the virtue of maidenhood." In case this was unclear, the author commanded his virginal reader: "Break not thou that seal that sealeth you together!"

For the determinedly marriage-minded or the wretchedly married, *Hali Meidenhad*'s description of marriage must have struck a terrifying note, for it surpasses even Leo Tolstoy's *The Kreutzer Sonata* in its scalding condemnation of marriage. The rare happy wife or husband, the author declares, must worry that the other will die. Most, however, hate each other, and the housewife is a miserable drudge who, when her despised mate is home, "his looking on thee makes thee aghast; his loathsome mirth and his rude behavior fill thee with horror." On top of this he mocks her, beats her, and pummels her as if she were his slave.

Of course, sex with this beast is mandatory. The next stage of the marital purgatory is pregnancy, when the wife's face turns "green as grass," her eyes dark-rimmed and her head a throbbing ache. Her mouth tastes bitter and she throws up everything that enters her nauseous stomach. A more unappealing description of pregnancy and morning sickness may never have been penned and undoubtedly left a powerful impression on the women who read it.

Much other popular literature also focused on the theme of defending virginity, and the widely read lives of various female saints were inspiringly dramatic. Like the ordinary folks in *Hali Meidenhad,* saintly virgins had violent encounters, though with wicked rulers, savage beasts, and spiteful soldiers rather than their own horrible husbands. *Hali Meidenhad* was strong stuff, but though exaggerated, reflected the actual lot of countless husbands and wives. In homes where little activity could be concealed from family members, shocked readers must have recognized their parents' marriage, their mother's excruciating and life-threatening birthings, their father's foul temper and heavy whip-hand.

During this period, even the daughters of wealthy families had to share the crowded women's quarters, where they could still not escape male relatives and servants. They could never be alone, and for those who craved solitude, life was nightmarishly public. Women were barred from some rooms and often had to sit on cushions, not chairs. They owned nothing, including themselves. They could not travel alone, study, question authority. They could not teach or nurse, manage or administer. They controlled no aspect of their life, including their future. Given this reality, *Hali Meidenhad*'s bleak portrayal of marriage and childbearing must have jolted many young women into serious consideration of their options, including the virginal alternative its author pressed them to adopt.

With no romantic view of marriage to seduce them, women attracted to spirituality easily slipped into thinking about, then longing for, life in a convent. Chastity was almost always an overriding attraction, because their pledge meant they renounced their sinful lust and their traditional role as wife and mother in return for Christ's approval and society's admiration and respect. "You sing a new song," rhapsodized a leading fifteenth-century French theologian. "You will be singled out and crowned with a divine crown in paradise. . . . You are queen of the earth and heaven by the ardent song of contemplation."

This virginity was not merely abstention from sex. It had an all-embracing mystical quality as well, lyrically described by a sixteenth-century Spanish writer: "The virginity of the body is nought worth except the mind be pure withal, and if that, nothing to be more clean, nothing more pleasant to God and herself to be the follower of the most holy Mother of our Lord."

Virginity was unequivocally endorsed by the Church and guaranteed an angelic afterlife. It also eliminated the need for nasty marriage and messy childbirth and the grief of dying children. But you could not expect to practice perpetual virginity at home, for parents would insist on marrying you off. If you were lucky, they packed you off to a convent where chastity was the cardinal virtue.

In a suitable, serious cloister, the sky was both literally and figuratively the limit for a determinedly devout virgin. The spiritual rewards were mystical union with Christ, a place in paradise, possibly sainthood if virginity was accompanied by enough other accomplishments. The outside world, too, offered respect and prestige, and for the exceptional religious, such as Catherine of Siena, Bridget of Sweden, and Hildegard of Bingen, power and influence on great affairs of state. The convent gave European women more freedom to develop and express themselves than any other institution, including the family. Those inclined to leadership could fulfill their vocation within the confines of the cloister, though they were barred from the secular outlets open to their brothers.

Within the convent, an aspiring nun could seek the education denied her outside—in general, only women destined for the cloister could expect an education. Those with scholarly yearnings could satisfy them, whereas in worldly society, erudite women were rare and often scoffed at as aberrant. Cloisters offered instruction, access to archives and libraries, correspondence with learned theologians. (Fanatical clerics discouraged these activities, but some sympathetic father confessors were encouraging, and the cleverest nuns circumvented the obstacles.)

The convent was also a legitimate way of fleeing the complications and confusions of family life and substituting passionate, intimate relationships with other nuns. Best of all, the convent offered a nun that elusive commodity—solitude—in the form of a room or cell of her own. That cell would be tiny, but it would contain all that she needed: a desk and a chair, a crucifix, a bed. It would be hers alone, and for hours at a time she could pray or meditate or think or read and write to her soul's content. In sum, a devout woman wedded to Christ and her virginity could expect convent life to propel her up avenues blocked at every turn in secular life. However, this was the idealized view of convent life. The reality was a convent mainly inhabited by spiritually unsuited women who had entered for want of anything else to do. They regarded nunhood as a career and accepted it because they had no other. Their parents or guardians had endowed the convent with the requisite sum, and now they had a lifetime to while away. "The majority of people are not moved . . . by the Evangelical conviction," lamented one nun. Into this less than hallowed realm crept the ardently chaste novice. No wonder that from each nun's perspective, her convent was an entirely different thing—"a career, a vocation, a prison, a refuge; to its different inmates the medieval nunnery was all these things."

The smattering of nuns divinely called to their vocation usually stood out from the rest and often rose to positions of authority that enabled them to shape the moral climate of their convent. Sometimes they had understanding parents who dutifully, even enthusiastically, cooperated in furthering their daughters' career choice by providing the essential dowry. Some women, however, arrived in the convent only after terrific battles with their families.

Widows were a major source of dedicated nuns. Many treated the convent as a peaceful retirement home, but others had longed for it throughout marriages imposed on them by strict parents. The German holy woman Dorothy of Montau was married at sixteen to a man who might have been the model for the husband described in *Hali Meidenhad*. After they had nine children, he died, and Dorothy fled to a walled-in cell in a cathedral.

Angela of Foligno was, spiritually speaking, the merriest widow and mourner of all. Her mother, whom she considered a great obstacle in her life, died. Soon after, her husband and all her children passed away as well. Angela felt "great consolation" at their deaths, which she had prayed for, and in her own chillingly honest words, "I thought that from then on, after God had done these things for me, that my heart would always be within God's heart, and God's heart always within mine."

For women of deep and abiding faith, the impetus to take these vows began with liberating celibacy. Apostolic poverty, humility, and obedience had their own rewards as well. For committed nuns, explained an Anglo-Saxon abbess, the tranquillity and routine of the cloister freed women rather than constrained them. This was not, however, what the male ecclesiastical authorities had in mind, and slowly and surely Church edicts tightened control over the nuns' little worlds. They did away with the double monasteries, where abbesses had ruled the women's community. In 1215, they forbade the creation of any new women's orders and legislated further restrictions on convents. Official Church misogyny dictated that chaste women dedicated to the Kingdom of Heaven should live under male authority, in exile from the world. This meant nuns with a vocation for service, for example teaching or healing, had to draw clients inside the convent walls rather than expose themselves to tempting secular life on the streets.

The view from inside the cloister, of course, reflected the daily trials, tests, and triumphs of the dedicated nun. The larger, analytical perspective was limited to a few of the most insightful intellectuals, and of course to a plethora of historians fortified by centuries of hindsight. Happily, that elusive, niggling everyday life was captured for eternity in the poems and plays of one exceedingly witty and talented abbess, Spain's Marcela de San Félix, illegitimate daughter of the great playwright and writer Lope de Vega, whose works have been a towering presence in Spanish literature since the end of the sixteenth century.

Convent dwellers were not spared the annoyances of uncloistered existence, and Marcela noted their poverty, "the mighty hordes of lice, bedbugs, and fleas," and the endless bickering of women confined together in perpetuity: the tensions, hypochondria, raging tempers, bossiness, rivalries, disloyalties. The competition to outdo each other in asceticism, always a major drama, provoked more strain:

> So many pains, such deprivations,
> you find in everything, it seems
> that this sad world must end.
> All are weeping, everyone sobs.
> Only Sister Juana's cheered,
> because she sees her sufferings
> already canonized.

Marcela's ironic comments about food are especially telling, for in convent life food dominated its inmates' thoughts. Whereas lust tormented monks and priests, food haunted nuns and was infinitely harder to conquer than sensual appetite. All fasted, but many were immoderate and starved themselves, so that the thin, pale virgins of the Church Fathers' fantasy were actually gaunt, yellow anorectics whose emaciated bodies did not menstruate or feel or inspire the least sexual desire.

So drastically did some nuns reduce their intake that they reveled in the puny wafer and bead of wine of the daily Eucharist. This morsel replaced the delights of eating, and swallowing it was a flagrantly sensual act, ingesting the body of Christ their Husband, to whom they had surrendered their entire beings. Some confessors exercised their powers by denying their spiritual charges the right to almost daily Communion, depriving nuns of the "sweet pleasures" of communing with Christ and reinforcing their own moral authority.

But the rewards for these committed women far outweighed their privations. Like Marcela, their greatest solace was in their uninterrupted relationship with God, which the blissful (though bug-ridden) solitude of the convent invited and nurtured. These nuns saw the world within their convent's four walls as a sanctuary and a hallowed place where God manifested His mercy to them. Even when, during the Reformation, outsiders smashed down their doors to "liberate" them, these devout women refused to leave the place where God had called on them to serve Him.

Unwilling Nuns

Medieval convents were great establishments that housed—or warehoused—a significant percentage of Europe's patrician women. In sixteenth-century Florence, for instance, half the city's elite daughters were cloistered. In mid-seventeenth-century Venice, 3 percent of the entire population—three thousand women—were nuns, almost all from wealthy families. Why were so many privileged women shut up inside these religious institutions? After all, affluence and status are not the usual incentives for celibacy, poverty, and obedience, the pledges at the spiritual core of every convent.

Religious conviction inspired many of the nuns, but other forces drove thousands of unwilling girls and women into taking the veil. Weep, struggle, and protest though they might, relegating them to a nunnery was the era's conventional solution to their families' problems.

A family's fortune could be dissipated by inheritances split between too many sisters or squandered on too many dowries, but with birth control, infanticide, and adoption considered unacceptable remedies, nunneries were an excellent alternative. One unwilling nun wailed in a folk song:

> My mother wished me to become a nun
> To fatten the dowry of my sister
> And I to obey my Mama
> Cut my hair and became one.

Inconvenient bastard daughters also cost money and created problems, but as nuns, they disappeared forever. When spinsters and widows likewise dug into the family purses, once again the convent was an obvious answer.

The dowry required of a novice was much smaller than a husband would demand, and once it was paid, the inconvenient woman became a lifelong charge on her convent, not on her relatives.

A father's bad investments, addictive gambling, unwise political alliances, or personal extravagances might also drive him to rid himself of surplus female relatives by donating them, along with a small bequest, to the service of God. Girls in line for inheritances were also sometimes shunted off into cloisters because in the eyes of the law, a nun was dead, and a dead daughter could make no claims on her father's estate. Kings, too, shut up rebels' wives and daughters in convents, biblically justified punishment for their fathers' sins.

Occasionally, one of these little girls escaped. Margaret de Prestiwych was only eight when she was coerced into a convent, where for years she remained defiant, refusing to profess her vows. Hauled shrieking into the chapel, she roared her dissent, but the presiding monk declared her duly pledged. Finally she sneaked out into the world, married, and had children. She then successfully appealed to the Church for release from her vows. Margaret's case is the classic exception to the rule of heiresses forever imprisoned in convents.

Parents also disposed of disabled, deformed, deaf and dumb girls by placing them in nunneries. Sometimes the abbesses or prioresses were loath to accept them, especially the mentally retarded or insane, but financial considerations won some over, so a nun without the least comprehension of what she was pledging gave her solemn oath of chastity, poverty, and obedience. A popular poem observed sadly:

> Now earth to earth in convent walls
> To earth in churchyard sod.
> I was not good enough for man,
> And so am given to God.

Civil unrest and wars, danger and insecurity, also sent thousands of women inside the safety of convent walls. Even girls as young as five and six were cloistered, with nine being the average age in Italy. A fifteenth-century Venetian law bemoaned the legion of noble girls "imprisoned in monasteries with just tears and complaints," and the *chansons de nonne,* songs about reluctant nuns, was a favorite theme of medieval poetry. For these women, a parent's peremptory "Get thee to a nunnery" condemned them to a life sentence in a wretched prison.

SHOTGUN CELIBACY

Madre Marcela was somewhat of an exception in her commitment to convent life. Until well into the eighteenth century, nunneries were dumping grounds for inconvenient women, and their lives within the dour convent interior were at best tolerably dull and hollow, at worst savagely unhappy or recklessly rebellious. Madre Marcela understood this only too well and warned in poetry against being forcibly confined to cloisters:

> For the physical cell
> should serve as a case
> to hold the inward cell,
> Where the dear Husband sleeps.
>
> For if spirit is lacking
> and there is no prayer in the soul
> rather than a holy Sister
> one will be but a woman enclosed.

Enclosed in what? To the unwilling, convents were monstrous prisons in which time served was eked out in minuscule rations, crushing tedium, terrible loneliness, and countless small cruelties. Enforced celibacy increased their angst, for they had to cope simultaneously with the sexuality they could never express or satisfy and the knowledge that marriage and family life were permanently closed to them. Release or escape were seldom options. Most endured in despairing silence, but a few left written testimonies to their desperation. Through a character in her drama, *Love of Virtue,* Florentine nun Beatrice del Sera groaned that "I, poor and alone in the rock [convent], put my hopes in the good of my future life."

Arcangela Tarabotti, trapped in her Venetian convent of Santa Anna for thirty-two years until her death, poured out her rage on paper. Her magnum opus, *Simplicity Betrayed,* is a scathing attack on fathers who imprison their daughters in nunneries to prevent the erosion or division of the family fortune or to indulge in sinful luxuries. Your heartlessness, she lambasted them, is greater than Nero's or Diocletian's because, unlike these heartless fathers, they only "cruelly murdered and tormented the bodies of the holy martyrs" but did not torment their souls. Worst of all was the betrayal. These men watched delightedly as their tender little girls lisped their first words, gamboled gracefully, sang joyously like baby songbirds. Then, "guileful, weaving the web of deception, they think of nothing but to force them from sight as soon as possible and bury them, as if they were dead, in cloisters, for the rest of their lives, bound by indissoluble knots."

Convent life was contrary to nature, Arcangela charged. This gentle little girl was forced to cut her long tresses, symbol of her freedom. She was stripped of her winsome gowns and hidden in a drab habit. She was forced to obey the convent rule; eat, pray, meditate when told; cast her eyes downward, hold her tongue; suppress her every emotion, even her longing for her vanished home life. And this way of life was interminable, a sentence from which no appeal was possible. "There is an inscription over the gate of hell: 'Abandon all hope, you who enter'; on the gate of monasteries, the same should appear. Rather, it would be more painfully appropriate to include an inscription for the dying: 'The torments of death surround me. The torments of hell surround me.'"

Why not kill all but one male baby per family? Arcangela suggested bitterly. At least their innocent souls would fly straight to heaven. But nuns kidnapped and entombed alive will plunge downward into fiery depths to seek out their anguished fathers, for whom looking at their daughters' accusing faces will be infinitely worse than all hell's other torments.

Your motive for abusing your daughter, Arcangela charged, for thrusting her into a convent and a life for which she has no vocation, is simply to cheat her out of her inheritance, so you can give it to someone else you prefer. Arcangela's indictment was no exaggeration. One English father consigned his unwanted daughters to a European convent where they languished, miserable and lonely. Cut off from home, they wrote letters pleading for continued contact and love. Certainly not, their father responded. One message each year was perfectly satisfactory.

These cloistered children, even infants, were routinely trained in nunly ways and, at sixteen or younger, professed their vows. Some did so willingly, or at least not unwillingly, but many mouthed the words on pain of beatings or worse, or because they had no alternative. In strict convents, obedience was hammered home. Penalties were degrading and brutal—stepping on a nun's face, hauling her across the floor, spitting at her, ostracizing her, depriving her of food, humiliating her. Saint Douceline whipped a seven-year-old bloody and threatened her with death because she had glanced at some convent workmen. Escapees were usually caught and disciplined, severely beaten, shut up for years, sometimes shackled, forced to fast on bread and water, sentenced to silence or to lowly ranks in the choir or chapel.

Maud of Terrington was a runaway who was caught after years of sinful living. She was barred from ever leaving the convent, confined to solitude except during choir, beaten daily, humiliated, twice weekly deprived normal meals and shoes, and never permitted any contact or mail with the outside world. Maud's treatment was particularly harsh, but transgressing against the complicated and habitual mechanics and rituals of an alien way of life never went unpunished.

Chastity was the fundament of the nun's vocation, the most crucial of her vows, with the farthest-reaching consequences. For committed nuns, it was not particularly difficult to honor. For unwilling nuns, as with monks and priests, it was immensely difficult. A dedicated nun approached the issue of her chastity from several perspectives, shoring up her resolve by recalling its spiritual meaning and rewards, her sacred obligations as Christ's Bride, and the hellish sinfulness of wavering. To help her, she sublimated her erotic sensations into a sublime adoration of Christ; mysticism and sexuality melded into rushes of frenzied outpourings, trances, or fits of weeping or screaming, all solemnly recognized by the highest ecclesiastical authority as manifestations of divine possession. The voluntary nun also starved her body into submission, killing its natural flows and cycles.

But the unwilling nun was, by definition, reluctant to surrender her woman's essence just to satisfy this unwelcome requirement. As a wellborn laywoman, she would almost certainly have grasped and accepted the need for premarital virginity. But as a nun forced into an unwelcome world in which marriage was forbidden, she could not even comfort herself with the knowledge that her chastity would ensure her eligibility for a future good marriage. From this sad perspective, what had she to lose, having already lost everything?

Even the tools available to willing nuns made no sense to their incarcerated sister: The meals were stingy enough, so why deprive herself further? Why relinquish the tiny pleasure of a feast-day candy? Why scourge herself when life was whiplash enough? And why obey a domineering mother superior whose stony heart felt no mercy for the wretchedness of her bitter, frightened, and despairing captive?

Though the majority of nuns likely remained chaste, a significant minority faltered and fell. In strict convents, this was rarer and trickier, but when abbesses themselves had been pressed into the cloister, they sometimes ran hopelessly dissolute convents. A seventeenth-century English abbess allegedly had twelve children, and a prioress dowried her daughter by selling off her convent's possessions. The double monasteries were notorious for sexual liaisons. Bishops routinely issued edicts barring the free intercourse—in all senses—between the male and female sides.

The nuns of some slackly regulated convents had servants, ate lavish meals, adapted their habits to current fashion, carried pet lapdogs, strolled outside, or drove into the city. They received men in unsupervised visits, had sexual relations, connived at elopements. Critics charged that any man could walk into a convent and that the nuns also came and went as they wished.

The worst excesses were in Venice, where nunneries were often little more than whorehouses. In the fourteenth century, legal action was taken against thirty-three convents that tolerated, sometimes even facilitated, fornication between nuns and their gentlemen callers. The Benedictine Sant'Angelo di Contorta convent was the most outrageous, though its nuns were drawn from the Venetian elite. The nuns, and two abbesses, did not even bother with discretion but enjoyed sex at picnics and—putting Madre Marcela's vaunted solitude to a more mundane use—in their cells. Babies were conceived and born, lovers quarreled, and jealousy abounded. The pope shut down Sant'Angelo in 1474, but it was just one of many egregiously misbehaving religious institutions.

Another bordello-like convent was England's Cannington, in Somerset, small and poor, but peopled by daughters of the finest families. One culprit was Maud Pelham, a reluctant nun, the other Hugh Willynge, a chaplain "as hot . . . and lecherous as a sparrow." Not only did Maud engage in feverish sex, she was infuriated when reproached. "Turning like a virago upon the prioress and the other sisters who abhor the aforesaid things . . . she threatens to do manly execution upon them with knives and other weapons."

Certain English nuns were so free, they indulged in gadfly social lives, enjoying feasts, visits to and from friends, minstrel shows. Sexually active nuns took the initiative in their affairs, for though some Anglo-Saxon kings specifically selected mistresses from convents and chaplains preyed on their charges, English laymen were more reticent. Nuns arranged rendezvous within and without the convent and sometimes shucked off the habit for secular life with their beloved. In sixteenth-, seventeenth-, and eighteenth-century France and Italy, young playboys haunted the convents, seeking nubile nuns as lovers.

The record of documented sexual transgressions and pregnancies—5 percent in some contemporary investigations of English convents, which undoubtedly missed many affairs and which, in French, German, and Latin convents, would have been much higher—is an impressive indictment of enforced celibacy. Not surprisingly, when unwilling nuns predominated or were governed by unwilling abbesses, an overtone of worldliness and sexuality tinged the moral tone of the entire establishment. The wonder is that so many unwilling nuns in strict, watchful cloisters found the courage to break that most basic of vows at the risk of humiliation, beatings, and shame.

Cheek by cowl with sisters who agonized over the symbolism of dreams or the implications of quickened breath at devilishly tempting images, unwilling nuns understood only the hot tingling of their yearning loins. Their despair and rebellion at their lot, their contempt for their captors, their craving for sensual affection and for sex, children and normalcy, betrayed their false vows. They nurtured sexual oases in their sterile desert, schemed, intrigued, and plotted, and risked hellfire for the present solace of fiery joy.

An Unwilling Nun's Love Cut Short

In the twelfth century, at the request of Archbishop Henry of York, who probably knew her family, a wellborn, four-year-old girl was thrust into the nunnery of Watton, in Yorkshire, England. Despite her surroundings, she developed into a flighty and flirtatious young woman without the least vocation for religion. Even professing her vows had no impact on her character. A handsome young day laborer she encountered in the convent set her heart beating faster. She glanced, he responded; they communicated by sighs and signs and arranged a meeting at night, when the man signaled her by tossing a stone onto the wall or roof of her building.

The plan went off without a hitch; "she went out a virgin of Christ, and she soon returned an adulteress." The lovers met as often as they could, but after a time, the other nuns grew suspicious of the nightly hail of stones. They confabulated and reached a terrible conclusion. They caught their sinning sister, beat her and shackled her legs, locked her into a cell, and tore the chaste veil from her head. They starved her, allowing her only bread and water. They refrained from worse torments only because she was both pregnant and remorseful.

Finally, the nun of Watton talked, revealing the identity and the whereabouts of her fled lover. The vengeful nuns sent monks from a nearby monastery to hunt him down. Using the ruse of disguising one of the brothers as a veiled nun, they captured their quarry. The nuns applauded and requested that the young man be brought to the convent for questioning. But the interrogation was actually torture, with the prisoner pinioned on the ground. His pregnant lover was pushed in and the nuns thrust a tool into her hands. Then they forced her, "unwilling, to cut off the virus with her own hands." One of the spectators at this brutal castration snatched up the severed organs and stuffed them, "befouled with blood," into the sinner's mouth.

Exit the young eunuch. The horrified nun was tossed back into her cell, where she continued to curse Archbishop Henry, who then appeared to her in a dream. Why do you curse me? he demanded. Because you forced me into this evil convent, she replied. Confess your sins and pray, he said, and I will handle your problem.

The next night, two angels assisted at the birth of her twins, whom they took away. The Watton nuns inspected the errant nun and accused her of killing her baby. However, neither her body nor her cell revealed the least evidence of childbirth. More curiously, her fetters had fallen off. The nuns consulted their spiritual adviser, who perceived divine intervention. "What God hath made clean, do not call common," he wrote, "and what He has absolved, thou should not bind." The nun had been forgiven and blessed, and the chaos and division within her convent healed.

Interpreted according to the mores of the time, the castration of the young man was a normal punishment for violating a nun, much gentler than previous centuries' hanging or beheading. The new twist on the affair was the nun's forced participation in his mutilation, including choking him with the bloodied organs.

From today's perspective, the story is a bitter condemnation of forcing children into convents and the religious life. The nun of Watton had no religious vocation or proclivity for moral issues, and she fell in love with the handsomest of the men visible in her constricted world. The inevitable happened, and she was caught, condemned, and confined to a cell. Analyzing her predicament, she daily cursed the bishop who had first entrusted her to the vindictive nuns. The rest of the story is clouded in legend, a medieval solution to a troubling question.

The nun's curse is the crux of the story. As a toddler, she had been sequestered in a convent, then coerced into professing vows she did not believe. When she followed her rebellious heart and loins and embarked on her disastrous love affair, she was brutalized into betraying, then ruining, her lover, a savage punishment for scorning a chastity she had never valued.

The other nuns' violence was sadistic sublimation and suggests more a collective mania or folie à deux than a love of celibacy. The persecuted nun had never loved it. She was merely a woman trapped in a way of life that held no appeal for her. When she damned Archbishop Henry for burying her in a convent shuddering under the weight of the celibacy preached by the other nuns, she must have still felt the blood of her lover's genitals on her fingers.

SECULAR CELIBATES AND AGAPE LOVE

The obsession with sex, which ranged from obliterating even thoughts of sexuality and revering virginity to elevating celibacy to the most sacred of vows, was too much at the fundament of Christian theology to ignore married people. Increasingly, the early Christian Fathers were plagued by the knowledge that, sometimes, even the most virtuous of married Christians fornicated.

Many solutions presented themselves. That elusive, one-strike-and-you're-out virginity was redefined: after seven years of penitent celibacy, a mother (by definition a sexual being) could once again become a virgin. Old men or spiritual counselors put to earnest young men the question formerly relevant only to their sisters: Are you a virgin?

Gradually, the Church demanded temporary abstinence on specific occasions: during Lent, on Sunday, if possible Saturday night or any night before attending mass or celebrating the Eucharist, and during the wife's menstrual period. Even abbreviated celibacy purified the soul and cleared the channel of communication between the celibate and God. Additionally, the belief was current that abstaining during menses and holy days eliminated the possibility of conceiving lepers, epileptics, and other "tainted" offspring.

The Fathers targeted the wedding night as well, a time of guaranteed coitus. Celebrate with chastity, they urged, the first night for sure and, if possible, the following three or four as well. By the Middle Ages, many dioceses required impatient bridegrooms to pay a fee to an ecclesiastical authority for the right to disregard this stricture. (This is probably where the myth of the jus primae noctis, and later the droit du seigneur, originated, from the Church's—and later the seigneur's or feudal lord's—assumption of this novel, trick-or-treat, moneymaking scheme.)

Later, the celibacy requirements were expanded. Husbands and wives had to abstain three times each year, for forty-day stretches, which amounted to about one-third of the time. Increasingly Christians began to observe these strictures. A noticeable decline in the birth rate resulted, as well as a consolidation of property in fewer hands. One beneficiary of the latter phenomenon was the Church, which naturally appreciated this development. Deep in its administrative heartland, certain wizard financial officers deduced that secular celibacy equaled ecclesiastical wealth, a formula to be cherished.

The next logical stage, of course, was extending the rule of celibacy to infinity—this became known as spiritual marriage. Christian asceticism oiled this process, which was accompanied by increasingly vicious attacks on women as temptresses and daughters of Eve whose very natures were lustful and evil. Other couples, unmarried, renounced eros and lived chastely in agape love, pure and godly. Ironically, lust-ridden clergymen attacked these unions: impossible, they thundered, that a man and woman share a home, even a bed, without fornicating.

They were wrong. Chaste marriages and agape relationships existed, and some worked well. The classic one was Mary and Joseph's, for as the dogma surrounding the Virgin Mary's virginity matured, she not only conceived Jesus without sex but she also delivered him without tearing her hymen, and subsequently never had either sex or other children. (This despite the clear scriptural identification of four of Jesus' brothers by Mary.)

The Mary-Joseph model had served well for struggling Christian couples such as the wealthy senator Paulinus of Nola, whose chaste marriage greatly impressed St. Augustine. Paulinus married at age forty, fathered a son who died in infancy, then gave up his possessions, adopted celibacy, and retired, with his obedient wife, Therasia, to a family retreat.

Even bishops recognized that mutual agreement was essential if a celibate marriage was not to lead to sexual "misdemeanors." When one partner, usually the wife, simply withheld her body, the bishops blamed her for the ensuing "adultery, fornication, and domestic strife." Basil of Ancyra, however, spelled out how unwilling wives could cope with their husbands' sexual advances: they could render themselves spiritually absent from the unpleasant event, a form of devastating mockery that often caused their true Husband, Jesus Christ, to strike their earthly mate with a flaccid penis and impotence.

Throughout Christendom and the ages, Augustine's sanction of agape love in marriage held much appeal. Some spouses disliked or abhorred sex or feared unending pregnancies. Others cherished spirituality above all else and wished to live a pure life, undefiled by the bestial urges of eroticism. The famous chaste marriage of John and Margery Kempe was inspired by a combination of these factors, and especially by the medieval Margery's burning ambition to achieve sainthood. Thanks to the intimately detailed autobiography the illiterate Margery dictated to two long-suffering scribes at the end of her life, the Kempes' marital saga is literally an open book.

Several years after Margery Burnham married John Kempe in 1393, God appeared to her and demanded that she desist from sexual relations. Margery attempted to obey, but John delighted in his pretty, wealthy, and exuberant wife and fathered fourteen children with her before he reluctantly agreed to a chaste marriage. Margery happily donned the white robes of the chaste widow, though Church authorities had forbidden her to do so. She burned with ambition to become a saint like Bridget of Sweden and eagerly set out on pilgrimages that would prove her piety. She also wrestled with terrible temptations, namely lust for two young men. Fortunately for her soul, they both repelled her advances. One even told her he would prefer to be chopped into pieces and stewed rather than sleep with her.

Toward the end of her life, Margery had to suspend her pursuit of saintliness to nurse John, incontinent and filthy, through his final illness. Then she took up kissing lepers and other worthy activities and hired two scribes to chronicle her life story. Alas for Margery, the manuscript they produced never served a future hagiographer. However, as the record of a chaste marriage, her autobiography has survived as a classic.

Multitudes of men and women have been attracted to monasticism as a way of dedicating their entire lives to their religious ideals. Within these cloisters they strive for spiritual growth and depth, union with their God, communion with their saints, and in general, to shun worldliness. Celibacy is, as we have seen, an integral part of the monastic system, exalted as an absolute good and exacted as an essential instrument for achieving spiritual purity. It is seldom, however, what motivates people to enter cloisters. They merely accept it, even embrace it, as an essential component of their determined pursuit of godliness.

Occasionally, however, celibacy by and of itself is one of the bedrock principles that inspires religious movements. Often, devotees forsake mainstream society for celibate communal life. The Essenes were one such group. More recently, various Christian sects including the Shakers, Peace Mission angels, Koreshan Unity, and Sanctificationist Commonwealth have celebrated celibacy as the cornerstone of their belief systems. These groups concur wholeheartedly with the orthodox Christian theological premise that sex is the root of evil, but they draw quite contrary conclusions about what this means. Not for them the corrosive, postlapsarian vision of a bifurcated humanity, Eve's seductive daughters forever tempting Adam's weak sons. Instead, these sectarians zero in on the evils of sexual intercourse, glorify celibacy as redemptive, and develop cogent doctrines with feminist values at their core.

The Shaker United Society of Believers and Father Divine's communal heavens, later renamed the Peace Mission, were the most stable of these intriguing sects. They also bequeathed to the world unforgettable symbols of their struggle to devise a strictly celibate world: the common clothespin, the buzz saw, and the popular greeting "Peace!"

The Shakers

Mother Ann Lee, the founder of American Shakerism, was born in 1736 into the misery and degradation of Manchester, England. After eight years of joyless, unschooled childhood, the delicate little girl joined the ranks of child laborers in the textile mills.

Ann's world was typical of her class and time: harsh and hungry, a cesspit of open toilets and crammed bedrooms. By night she lay sleepless beside her copulating parents and, by day, hounded her mother to refuse her father's advances. Early on, she developed a lifelong revulsion to sex. This was not unusual—in her world, children routinely observed adults engaged in sex and the grim realities of childbirth. They had no illusions about either one, and girls in particular were often disgusted by and frightened of what lay in store for them.

Though Ann developed into a lovely young woman admired by many men, she remained implacably virginal. Her interests were spiritual, not sensual. In her twenties, she converted to the Shaking Quakers, a breakaway Quaker sect led by charismatic preacher Mother Jane Wardley. Services included frenzied shouting, shaking, and dancing, an ecstasy of worship Ann found utterly satisfying and that surely neutralized her repressed sexual tensions.

However, against her repeated pleas, her father forced Ann into marriage—and its dreaded conjugal duties—with blacksmith Abraham Stanley. Three babies arrived and quickly died, the fate of half of Manchester's children. But after her fourth child, six-year-old Elizabeth, succumbed, Ann was tormented by grief and guilt. After a marathon of self-recrimination, she concluded the root of her personal tragedy, and indeed of all human depravity, was sex.

Her mentor, Mother Jane Wardley, agreed. "James and I lodge together but we do not touch each other any more than two babes," she confided. Sexless marriage, and between such estimable spouses! This revelation rebuilt Ann's shattered psyche. It also inspired her to avoid her own marriage bed, "as if it had been made of embers."

Stanley protested vehemently and enlisted Anglican priests, who hectored Ann with St. Paul's command: "Wives, submit yourselves to your own husbands, as unto the Lord."

Ann countered gospel with gospel. Hadn't Paul also observed, "He that is unmarried careth for the things that belong to the Lord, how he may please the Lord: But he that is married careth for things that are of the world, how he may please his wife."

Despite Stanley's passion for his beautiful, blue-eyed, chestnut-haired wife—"he would have been willing to pass through a flaming fire for my sake, if I would only live in the flesh with him," she said—Ann's commitment to celibacy was unshakable. Reluctantly, rather than lose her, Stanley accepted both celibacy and Shakerism.

Ann, for her part, was reborn. Freed of the sexual obligation she found so repellent, she became a preacher so articulate, witty, and convincing that she converted even her father and two brothers. But patriarchal England was hostile to women preachers, even more so to heretical ones. Persecution, including imprisonment, began. In one brutal dungeon, Ann had a vision. Adam and Eve were in the Garden of Eden, fornicating, whereupon God flung them out of his sight. This was, Ann believed, a divine revelation. Sex had caused humankind's alienation from God. Celibacy, therefore, was essential for spiritual rebirth.

Ann's version of the Fall differed radically from the Church's. God had punished Adam and Eve equally, so their sexual longings, not Eve's special wickedness, were at the crux of His fury. Ann wasted no hatred on womankind but spent it all on that great evil, sex.

Ann's apocalyptic dreams and ordeals forged her into an unstoppable crusader. Men and women flocked to her meetings, where sinners expiated their sins—including "the most hidden abominations"—by elaborating them in graphic detail, rather like a verbal peep show. But this sensational format only lured the curious. It was Ann's startling message—celibacy, even after marriage—that converted people.

Women had their own special reasons to welcome celibacy. With no effective birth control except abstinence, they equated sex with childbearing as much as with pleasure, and many dreaded it. Childbirth could be agonizing and often fatal: mortality rates for mothers and newborns were sky-high. Women delivered squatting over filthy birthing stools or straw, and postpartum puerperal fever killed them in droves. Poor nutrition deformed pelvic bones so that babies were trapped in misshapen birth canals. Midwives used hooks to extract them, often in chunks. Those children who survived into adulthood faced only the same bleak poverty their parents could never escape.

Abstinence was a woman's main defense against these prospects, but husbands, churches, and society would not tolerate it. Mother Ann's style of celibacy was different. It was a form of devotion, a duty to God, a conscious renunciation of odious carnal indulgence. It bestowed on the believer the moral authority to resist opposition, including irate husbands. Slowly, the number of Shakers grew.

As Ann's fame increased, so did the hatred of civil authorities. They imprisoned her time and again and did little to prevent enraged citizens from chasing, kicking, and stoning her. Ann's suffering simply strengthened her faith and honed her theology. Once, Jesus appeared to her and revealed that she, Mother Ann, was Himself made flesh. Afterward, her pronouncements became more outrageous. "I am married to the Lord Jesus Christ," she said, rejoicing. "He is my head and my husband, and I have no other."

For centuries, nuns had made this kind of claim, but Ann Lee was married, which gave a completely different twist to the notion. Whereas the nuns were often amorous brides awaiting the final, spiritual consummation, Mother Ann saw her marriage to Christ as evidence of her own greatly exalted status as a person entrusted with divine truths and wisdom.

In consequence, the Shaker spiritual hierarchy was expanded to include a mother and a father in the Godhead, with Mother Ann and Christ as fleshly incarnations. As well, earthly women were equal to earthly males, so Shaker eldresses and deaconesses officiated alongside elders and deacons. Shaker celibacy was not only its own reward but also the precursor of other, tangible offices and honors.

Mother Ann's feminist egalitarianism was too challenging for mainstream society to tolerate. By 1774, she concluded her sect would fare better in the New World. There, righteous colonists were rebelling against English oppression and religious freedom flourished. That summer, she and eight faithful set sail and established New Lebanon, a commune near Albany, New York, where American converts soon joined them.

*   *   *

From the outset, Mother Ann designed Shaker society so that even its physical plant reflected the celibacy at its ideological core. Men and women lived in segregated quarters and were never alone. At religious services, they sat apart.

But Mother Ann was too wise to suppose that forced separation could, by itself, forestall all lapses in conduct. Lust, she knew all too well, was a powerful force: her husband, Abraham, for one, had lusted after her for years. In fact, his unquenchable longing for a carnal relationship was one of the first things she dealt with in America. Somehow, she managed to convince him that never, never would she relent about sex, and her grieving husband finally walked out, leaving his wife alone in her splendid celibacy.

Perhaps because she had been forced so often to contend with her importuning husband, Mother Ann proved a genius at devising ways to channel and sublimate sensuality. Shaker clothes—serviceable, dull, and unrevealing—were an ever-present weapon against arousing sexual interest. American neighbors scoffed at the women in particular, whom Artemus Ward famously described as "a solum female, lookin somewhat like a last year's beanpole stuck into a long meal bag . . . unnatural, onreasonable and dismal. . . . You mope away your lives here in single retchidness."

For socializing, the Shakers enjoyed thrice-weekly "union meetings" where men and women sat face-to-face, talking or reading or singing. They released their tensions by speaking in tongues: we can only guess what steamy yearnings were dissipated in the babel.

The mightiest form of sublimation is probably dance, as today's True Love Waits movement is well aware, and this was where the Shakers were spectacular, dancing, as David had "with all his might before the Ark of the Lord" to celebrate his killing of Goliath. Shakers danced with rhythmic and ecstatic frenzy, swirling and stamping and singing like creatures possessed, "swiftly passing and repassing each other like clouds agitated by a mighty wind." Upstretched hands shook away sin and evil; upturned palms grasped for blessings; torsos sagged and fainted. One refrain went:

> Oh ho! I will have it,
> I will bow and bend to get it,
> I'll be reeling, turning, twisting,
> Shake out all the starch and stiff'ning!

This mass sublimation worked, for the danced-out Shakers were acquiescent celibates. No great sexual scandals ever surfaced, though hostile neighbors and apostate Shakers in custody battles over children still with Shaker parents accused the Shakers of every sort of licentiousness. However, no evidence ever substantiated these charges. Sexual sublimation, orchestrated into daily life, made celibacy joyous for many believers, tolerable for those with aching loins. It helped that Mother Ann, usually gentle and compassionate, was vitriolic about any lapses. "You are a filthy whore," Mother Ann told one woman at first sight.

The force of Mother Ann's antisexual fury was central to Shakerism. So, ironically, was her penchant for immoderate language. In most respects, Shakers practiced an austere minimalism, but in self-expression, she and her flock were wildly fanciful. Their metaphor for accepting celibacy, for instance—submitting to "the circumcising knife"—is both powerful and telling.

Shaker literature, too, showcases visions rather than parables from daily life. Drearily garbed Shakeresses—*hijab,* American-style?—dreamed of heavenly beings "clad in garments of rich changeable colors, glossy, like silk, while some were enveloped in soft, fleecelike drapery, as white as snow . . . some were decorated with diamonds, stars, pearls, and other precious gems," which never, of course, adorned a Shaker neck, hand, or earlobe.

However, sublimation through dance and imagery was not enough to sustain a functional celibate community, and Mother Ann hit upon the same time-tested methods many institutions, notably cloisters, rely on to wean followers away from "the world" and to ensure their undivided loyalty. She and the Shakers abolished, indeed excoriated, the very heart of orthodox society: the traditional family.

> Of all the relations that ever I see
> My old fleshly kindred are furthest from me,
> So bad and ugly, so hateful they feel
> To see them and hate them increases my zeal.
> O how ugly they look!
> How ugly they look!
> How nasty they feel!
>
> —SHAKER HYMN

> I'll leave the world behind, I will
> Their filthy carnal lives
> Their husbands and their wives
> I'll leave them all behind I will.
>
> —SHAKER HYMN

Divested of spouses, the Shakers communed as brothers and sisters. For the unhappily married, this abrupt annulment of marriage vows must have seemed God-sent. The happily married and the unmarried also accepted it as a privation essential to salvation. Celibacy was not enough: even loyalty between celibate spouses threatened the tightly knit Shaker community.

Shaker celibacy's redefinition of human society extended to children. Parents had to relinquish them to the Children's Order, to be reared communally with adopted orphans. A lapsed Shaker later charged that "no pity, in their acts or measures, was ever shown to social or earthly ties."

Mother Ann made sure, however, never to leave dangerous voids, and so in place of severed blood ties, Shakers belonged to spiritual families, thirty to one hundred and fifty siblings strong, parented by two elders and eldresses. These authorities wielded great power. They heard compulsory confessions, inspected mail, and separated infatuated men and women. They punished all lapses by public taunts and ostracism and, without locking up their charges, kept them safe from contaminating influences. They also reinforced the reality of Shakerism's gender equality, an enormous reward for Shakeresses who might have wrestled with celibacy.

Other rewards for both genders came later, as the industrious, motivated, and organized Shakers flourished. Initially, though, life was difficult and the pioneer Shakers were as poor as they had been in "the world." The dismemberment of their families, the social and economic communism, and the unaccustomed authority of women created severe tensions. As if this were not enough, Shakers also faced persecution from Americans who castigated them as marriage-busters. As late as 1810, for example, an Ohio Shaker meetinghouse was mobbed by five hundred angry men.

It took six bitter years to establish equilibrium in the commune. By then, the Shaker core had become Americanized. New rituals and traditions replaced the lost ones, and internal harmony developed. And, thanks to Shaker industry and ingenuity, poverty gave way to prosperity and financial security.

By day, though not by solitary night, Shakers lived much as their neighbors did, except for their excessive prayerfulness. Women labored in kitchens and dairies, at looms and spinning wheels. Men toiled outside on farms or in forges or tanneries. They worked steadily, avoiding boredom by trading jobs. More significantly, they were encouraged to express their imaginations in practical ways, which explains the impressive roster of Shaker inventions: the clothespin, the buzz saw, the cut nail, the flat broom, the revolving oven, and an apple paring/coring/quartering machine.

In later years, however, the very core of Shakerism grew shaky. The ambivalence and outright rebellion of younger Shakers cannot be explained solely by Mother Ann's death in 1784; most likely even she would not have been able to stave off the decline. The reason was that the Shakers, like all celibate communities, had to rely for maintenance and growth on proselytization. Yet far from waging a perpetual propaganda war to attract newcomers, they failed to interest even their growing children in staying. The most serious point of dissension was the most fundamental: celibacy, which dictated the Shakers' architecture, regulations, and way of life.

When dissension occurred, panicked Shakers used various tactics to stave off communal collapse. Some tried more intense worship. Others shucked off their dingy clothes and danced naked, supposedly to conquer their pride. A few refused to sleep after dances, preferring to subdue their flesh like medieval nuns, lying down "on chains, ropes, sticks, in every humiliating and mortifying posture they could devise!"

Nineteenth-century Shakers continued to modify rituals. Their dramatic Midnight Cry, which lasted for two weeks, was a frenzied midnight march with candles and singing. Mountain Meetings resembled Haitian vodoun ceremonies, with spirits ranging from Mother Ann to Napoleon possessing mediums who later recounted their revelations. Significantly, these communications often denounced celibacy, the dogma at the core of Shaker theology.

The elders were aware that rebellion, almost always about celibacy, was intensifying. Instead of trying to communicate its benefits, they simply watched—forbidding and helpless—as it became the focus of discontent. The seriously disaffected began to leave even as newcomers joined. After a time, turnover rates rose so high that proselytization failed to hold the numbers steady.

Celibacy, which had inspired Shakerism, seemed to be destroying it. Yet it was not the principle itself but how it was presented and perceived. As the Shakers prospered in a prosperous land, they may have lost sight of how far they had come materially. Better nutrition and health diminished the perils of childbearing, previously one of celibacy's greatest advantages. Gender equality was tainted by the drab Shakeress cloak. And though charismatic Shakeresses preached and practiced celibacy as Mother Ann had, ultimately the movement ceased to offer enough rewards to keep its members or attract large numbers of new ones. Finally, it dwindled down to a handful of believers.

The Shakers' worst failure was with their children, most of whom rejected the austere religion and lifestyle. At New Lebanon between 1821 and 1864, of 144 boys admitted, some foundlings but most with their parents, 8 died, 10 were "carried away," 2 were sent away, 22 became Shakers, and 102 left "for the world." They did so because the Shakers suppressed the parent-child bond, which their theology denied even existed yet which we know all too well is crucial if the child is to develop properly. Instead, the Shakers rejected their youngsters, then expected them to embrace a way of life that seemed irrelevant or hostile to youthful needs, questions, and possibilities. Hormonal adolescents sullenly resistant to the strict regimen, and raised with work habits that surely filled them with confidence they would succeed in the scorned outside world, had little to which they could relate. No wonder the typical rite of passage into maturity was to take the road out of the commune toward the beckoning world they refused to despise.

FATHER DIVINE

"Peace!" was the watchword of the world into which baby George Baker was born in 1879, in Rockville, Maryland. The founder of the USA's most successful twentieth-century Christian celibate communities was the son of former slaves whose struggling family needed even the tiny wages he earned as a part-time child laborer. George also attended school long enough to become an avid reader and a lifelong devotee of his teachers' dogma of punctuality, cleanliness, temperance, and hard work.

Rockville's Jerusalem Methodist Church was George's other transformative experience. Its black lay preachers inspired him and its tightly knit community embraced him, protecting him against those who sneered at his slight stature: a mere five foot two when fully grown.

When he was a teenager, George's mother died, at 480 pounds "the largest woman in the county, if not the state," the local newspaper noted. Soon after Nancy Baker's death, George left home for Baltimore. In a permanent break with his past, he renounced all family ties and set out alone in pursuit of his personal truths.

Baltimore taught the newcomer about urban-style brute labor, poverty, unionism, and racism as destructive as the lynch mobs of rural Maryland. But God had not abandoned the wicked city. George took refuge in its storefront churches, where he molded his oratorical powers and deepened his religious commitment. Gradually he developed a theology that combined African-American spirituality with current beliefs about the power of positive thinking, achieving oneness with God, embracing celibacy, and obliterating not merely racism but race itself, a construct he came to believe did not exist.

George Baker's intense religiosity led to a mystical experience in which he spoke in tongues and reached a new level of being. Afterward, he began to call himself the Messenger. "By 1907," writes his biographer Jill Watts, "the Messenger believed he was the son of God and that his destiny was to spread God's word to the ignorant and unredeemed."

Once again, the God of celibacy had chosen as His representative one of the reviled, this time a man from a people recently delivered from slavery, still ground down by hatred and fear, habit and history, the might of unmajestic law and the forces of repressive order.

The Messenger's antiracist mission sent him south, to destroy Jim Crowism—"if it costs me my life," he declared. It well could have—lynching, often accompanied by castration, was a common enough fate for unlucky or unwise black men. Ignoring these dangers, the Messenger traveled to Georgia. There, the electrifying itinerant preacher exhorted his audiences to follow a loving God who had created a world where gender and race were meaningless labels.

How were his listeners to experience this world, to defy the illusory existence of gender and race? Through the power of thought, the Messenger taught, for thought, clarified through celibacy, could overcome the terrible obstacles that race and gender created. This was a unique and stern message gently told: transform society by conquering your own most basic urges.

In challenging the notion of race, the Messenger struck at the very foundations of American social structure. At the same time, his espousal of celibacy tempered the heresy of his message by nay-saying the legend, both galling and terrifying to whites, of unbridled black sexuality. Here was a black preacher, handsome and adored by his congregations, so scrupulous in his personal chastity that no undercover investigator or dissident follower would ever find a particle of evidence to suggest even a single lapse. A sexually active leader who denied that race existed would automatically have been suspected, even accused, of encouraging black men to coerce white women into sex. The primacy of celibacy in the Messenger's teaching strongly suggested he had no such agenda.

The Messenger's devotees found his strictures against sexual activity unusual and exacting. However, to overburdened black women, celibacy had the same enormous appeal Mother Ann Lee had encountered generations earlier. Before long, many wives attempted to break off sexual relations. Several even left their homes and moved in with the celibate Messenger. Suddenly, through celibacy, the Messenger had liberated the women in his improvised commune. These were not strutting seventeen-year-olds souped up with sexual tensions but women exhausted from lifetimes of drudgery, prolapsed uteruses from too frequent childbearing, and subservience to their "so-called males"—for the Messenger, remember, taught that gender, like race, did not exist.

Frustrated husbands and African-American religious leaders banded together against the diminutive but handsome preacher. He had cast spells, they charged, and caused their wives and mothers to lose their minds. "If something wasn't done, the whole community would be crazed." The police were brought in and the Messenger's black male accusers backed them up. Their combined strength overpowered the phalanx of enraged women protecting the Messenger and he was thrown into jail.

The Messenger flourished. Visitors swarmed to his cell and converted en masse, even white men who "seemed to be as wild over him as the negroes," a jail guard noted. In segregated, small-town Georgia, this was a near miracle and strong testimony to the Messenger's sincerity and charisma.

Afterward, the Messenger led his mainly female followers throughout the South on a punishing, five-year trek of proselytizing. Finally, in 1917, with the handful of faithful who continued to travel with him, he settled down in Brooklyn. He also married the most devoted woman in his entourage, tall, stately Penniniah, who lived with him in obviously contented celibacy until her death.

Why would this virgin bachelor who preached the sanctity of celibacy get married? Of course, skeptics questioned whether the marriage was, indeed, nonsexual, but all evidence indicates it was. It seems likely that, from the Messenger's perspective, Mother Penniniah fended off seductive women attracted to the larger-than-life (figuratively if not literally) leader. She also lent credibility to her husband's mission and, with the power of her own religious fervor, attracted many new disciples to the former bachelor's movement.

About this time, the Messenger adopted a new name, the Reverend Major Jealous Divine, implying religious and military authority, the jealousy of the biblical God, and his own divinity. His flock shortened this to Father Divine and chanted, "God is here on earth today. Father Divine is his name." Penniniah, of course, became Mother Divine.

Soon after, Father Divine scraped together $700 plus a mortgage and purchased a Sayville, Long Island, property to house his commune. To maintain it, he established the Busy Bee employment agency, which furnished his neighbors with trustworthy hired help made up of his own people.

In this commune, everyone worked, with evenings and Sundays devoted to religious services. Even Father Divine tended chickens and gardened on top of his onerous pastoral duties. The difference between the new and old way of life, however, was that through his savvy management, Father Divine provided the Busy Bees with lodgings in a fine home, generous quantities of food, security from all want. On their own, as they well knew, they could never have achieved this.

Like the old Shaker communes, Father Divine's household was rigidly structured and monitored to ensure strict celibacy, devout religious observance, hard work, and shared prosperity. Smoking, swearing, drugs, and alcohol were banned. The house was "heaven" and Father Divine was "God." His followers were "angels" who addressed each other as "brother" and "sister." Each angel had a single room—surely a luxury for most—with men and women separated except when religion or business required their collaboration.

As in Shaker communities, with their vitriolic, self-righteous lyrics, language in heaven was also regulated. But Father Divine forbade his angels to use negative words and banned (rather than trumpeted) *hell, Devil,* and even *hello,* which he believed was a corruption of *hell.* He originated today's wide-spread greeting "Peace!" and the mantra "It is wonderful," which dispelled negative ideas and conjured up positive thoughts that would lead, one day, to a peaceful world.

Like the Shakers, Father Divine welcomed parents and their children, though he believed the latter were products of the sin of sex that drained the body of "spiritual energy." Also like the Shakers, he required his disciples to renounce earthly kinship, including marriage, and substitute fraternal kinships with his other angels.

Like Mother Ann, Father Divine devised mechanisms to enforce celibacy by providing acceptable outlets for sublimating sexuality. Not surprisingly, given Nancy Baker's fatal obesity, her son was so obsessed with food that he used it as a tool of ministry. The tasty fare at his bulging tables consoled, nursed, and converted, and his "Holy Communion banquets," modeled on the Last Supper, were legendary. Decades earlier, he had inaugurated them in the South as potlucks. Later, they nourished overworked, underpaid African-Americans who packed into his dining room in such numbers that he had to host multiple sittings rather than turn anyone away. On weekends, Father Divine often spent twelve hours daily hosting them. The banquets also plumped up his angels and ensured that at least one of their earthly appetites was sated.

For Father Divine, eating was a consuming passion. Twice weekly he weighed the angels and chided any who lost weight. This, it would appear, was difficult to do. Consider a typical, Depression-era Holy Communion banquet menu: macaroni, rice, potatoes, peas, tomatoes, turnips, baked beans, turkey and pork chops, corn bread, biscuits, Graham bread, cake, pie, peaches, tea, milk, and Postum.

After these feasts, the stuffed diners burst into song and prayer, witnessing and confessing, shouting and dancing and speaking in tongues. Like Mother Ann, Father Divine favored these exhausting and emotional outpourings, which obviously served to dissipate any erotic feelings that gluttony had not obliterated.

Father Divine's commune differed from Mother Ann's in one important respect. Whereas hers was an essentially rural movement, his was urban, with white, mainstream neighbors in close proximity. After an initial period of tolerance, these neighbors decided they hated living close to a large, pulsating community of black people. They went on the attack, beginning with false rumors. The only actual scandal involved "John the Revelator," a white, Californian millionaire disciple, who lured a seventeen-year-old he christened "Virgin Mary" into the movement, seduced her, then confessed his evildoing. Father Divine immediately expelled him and separated him from the young woman. Yet despite Father Divine's overwhelming probity, the heavenly movement was tarred by gossipmongers skeptical about the dapper little preacher's personal chastity.

His neighbors' hostility, coinciding with an intensive crusade in New York City, finally drove Father Divine to relocate to welcoming Harlem. There an explosion of disciples recast his sect into a movement, as new angels replicated his commune in other locations and baptized his crusade the Peace Mission.

Ironically, the Peace Mission's expansion into businesses, and from East to West Coast, precipitated its decline. Its mainstay continued to be poor blacks, though a small number of wealthy whites also joined. One problem was that the public vastly overestimated the movement's membership, making Father Divine more influential than the true number of his followers warranted. In consequence, the Mission was increasingly drawn into political debates and destructive ideological battles with other black movements that deplored Father Divine's steadfast refusal to champion blacks over whites. Yet how could he, when a fundamental part of his creed was that race did not exist?

By the end of the Depression, the Peace Mission was restructured as a church. Its membership shrank and new orders were born. A flamboyant California branch sprouted the Rosebuds, young virgin females who swore eternal celibacy, wore uniforms emblazoned with *V*s for *virginity,* and celebrated Father Divine in giddy song. The male Crusaders, though not necessarily virginal, pledged themselves to celibacy and to Father Divine's theology.

But the Rosebuds' subservience—they strove to be "submissive, meek, and sweet; they have hearts where Christ alone is heard to speak"—and the Crusaders' militancy clashed with Father Divine's genderless teaching. They were celibate but far from egalitarian. By 1943, when Penniniah died, Father Divine and his churches were in free fall.

In 1946, he made the situation worse by marrying Edna Rose Ritchings, aka Sweet Angel, a pretty, white, twenty-one-year-old Canadian. Father Divine justified this risky adventure by claiming that the new Mother Divine was Penniniah and the Virgin Mary reincarnated, and he likened their union to "the Marriage of CHRIST to HIS Church."

Ah, Father Divine! At sixty-seven, he was suddenly seized by irresistible longings and reincarnated in the skin of the young George Baker so long ago shucked off. Yet from all accounts, this second marriage was as successful as the first, with the new Mother Divine thriving on the same celibate regimen as her predecessor. And celibate she was, for Father Divine preempted suspicion about any possible sexual activity by assigning a black angel to monitor her and presumably be a living witness to his heavenly wife's intact virginity.

From a larger perspective, its leader's questionable remarriage and, in 1965, his death certainly did not help the Peace Mission. However, the root causes of its decline lay elsewhere. By then, in a new era of sexual permissive-ness, widely available birth control, and the civil rights movement, celibacy was a harder sell except to those who could be convinced it was a moral imperative. The Peace Mission's communal life seemed rigorous and restrictive, even bizarre. Its insistence on severing the parent-child bond had serious psychological and judicial implications. And though he was very old, Father Divine made the tactical error, nineteen years after he married again, of anointing his untested young wife, rather than a well-groomed protégé, to head his shriveled church.

Today the Peace Mission sighs on in anachronistic relics, including Mother Divine's mansion. Another is Philadelphia's Divine Tracy Hotel, which segregates guests in gendered floors and prohibits tobacco, alcohol, and swearing. Women, in obligatory dresses and hosiery, and men, in pants and shirts, mingle together only in the lobby. In the Divine Tracy Hotel, only the most determined guests can avoid a celibate sojourn. It is an odd but fitting monument to a movement that, at one time, ushered thousands of weary and oppressed converts into similar heavens on earth.

America's Shakers and Father Divine's angels had much in common, and he proudly acknowledged his debt to Mother Ann Lee's theology. Most important of their shared tenets was that sex was at the root of human evil and therefore celibacy was essential in a righteous life. Their notion of celibacy stretched further than mere sexual negativism. It allowed them to redefine gender differences, so they effectively offered feminist lifestyles to their followers.

Unlike cloisters, however, their communes included men and women, and Father Divine's heavens were located in the world into which most angels trooped out to work. Just as important, in America's racially troubled society, celibacy defused the minefield of interracial sex. It permitted black Shakers to head communes and black angels to live alongside white ones, all under the guidance of a black leader who dismissed race as a meaningless designation and celebrated chaste marriage, first with a black woman, then with a white one.

Both Mother Lee and Father Divine proselytized among people oppressed by an unfair world and offered them safe haven in a new, righteous one. They taught that celibacy was a great moral good that required the sacrifice of all blood ties, including with children, who became the responsibility of the commune rather than individual parents. The rewards for joining either sect were immediate and substantial. Women won unheard-of equality, while hard work, discipline, and obedience provided collective material comfort, security, and the camaraderie of the spiritual fraternity that replaced blood relationships.

Mother Ann and Father Divine adopted remarkably similar strategies to enforce celibacy. They segregated men and women, permitting them to mix only in controlled situations. They addressed the need to sublimate sexual passions through rituals of frenzied dancing and singing, speaking in tongues, public confession, and near-hysterical worship. They even regulated language to promote their sectarian metaphors. Above all, Mother Lee and Father Divine exemplified the celibate life they demanded of others and never succumbed to temptation.

Ironically, the twice married but never bedded Father Divine faulted Mother Ann for having once had a sexual life. That she had terminated it, after divine revelation taught her that sex was the root of all evil, was not sufficient. From the vantage point of his own sinlessness, the virgin Father Divine judged the long-celibate Mother Ann and found her wanting. He believed her sexual experience in marriage, though short-lived and unwilling, had deprived her of immortality.

Shakerism and the Peace Mission were not failed experiments, though neither outlasted its founder for more than a few decades. What has endured are their legacies of a courageous celibacy that dared to challenge society's underpinnings of women's inequality and racial subjugation. The illiterate immigrant woman and the disempowered black man defied their social realities and bestowed on their followers the equality and personal dignity the law denied. Celibacy, combined with highly structured discipline and hard work, was briefly the answer for thousands of alienated, mostly lower-class Americans.

CHAPTER 4

Other Major Religions and Rites

Christianity, a mere two thousand years old, is one of the world's youngest religions. Hinduism, Buddhism, and Jainism are millennia older and, by the time of Christ's birth, already counted millions of Asian devotees. Each of these different faiths extols celibacy as one of the highest expressions of earthly existence, a crucial element in the lifelong endeavor to extinguish human passions and the longing for possessions. Each views sex as an element in relationships, and for certain stages of life, Hinduism prescribes and Buddhism tolerates marriage. All three religions teach, however, that erotic longing implies possessiveness of another person, in itself a condition to be avoided. Above all, celibacy is an essential condition to end the suffering of continuous rebirth and to achieve moksa or nirvana, the spiritual liberation that is the believer's ultimate goal. In each of the three belief systems, celibacy is a crucial means to an all-important end.

In Hinduism, with its semen-centered understanding of human physiology and spiritual development, celibacy has a crucial physical as well as spiritual dimension. Hindus regard semen as a powerful and enriching substance that should be conserved. This precept provides men with enormous impetus to abstain from wasteful sex. Instead of squandering semen by indulging in uncontrolled concupiscence, they can store it as creative energy that will add to their intellectual vigor, physical stamina, and moral worth. Semen is such a powerful elixir, it even keeps men more youthful.

Mainstream Hinduism, Buddhism, and Jainism all share the negative and suspicious assessment of women that later characterized much of Christian thought. Women are depicted as seductive temptresses, voraciously erotic and morally weak. Their lustful nature makes celibacy an even greater challenge for men, who also have to overcome their own wayward impulses.

Hinduism, Buddhism, and Jainism all require their maidens to remain virginal, but as in Christianity, celibacy can sometimes empower women and not just guarantee their marriageability. This is particularly true of nuns. In this context, their voluntary commitment to celibacy allows them, too, to aspire to moksa or nirvana. At the same time, it frees them from the burdens of marriage and motherhood and may provide opportunities for learning, scholarship, and public service otherwise prohibited to women. In the case of the Brahma Kumaris, a renegade Hindu sect, celibacy completely inverts the status of women. Its doctrine analyzes and explains the low status of women in terms of the great evil of sexual intercourse, and it preaches celibacy as the only way to rectify this great evil. In this sect, celibacy is paramount and women are hoisted to heights unheard of in the Hindu religion.

Hinduism, Buddhism, and Jainism are ancient religious philosophies that provide metaphysical explanations of the world that in most ways differ entirely from those of Christianity and the traditions in which it is rooted. Over the centuries, Hinduism and Buddhism have embraced billions of believers, Jainism millions. Their doctrines are sophisticated and sectarian, and infinitely complex. As they move through time and place, they continue to modify and vary. The following overview, therefore, is limited to the simplest sketch of each religion, glimpsed through the lens of celibacy. Nonetheless, it reveals just how integrally celibacy is located at the core of each of these creeds, and hence in the moral heart of so many human lives.

HINDUISM

SHIVA, EROTIC AND CELIBATE GOD

In the Hindu pantheon, the god Shiva is powerful, popular (especially in southern India), and highly revered. He is known as "the great ascetic" and worshiped by abstinent ascetics and religious mendicants as a model of celibacy and ascetic power. At the same time, Shiva is intensely erotic. In Hindu thought, this is not seen as a contradiction. Indeed, Shiva's nature as simultaneously celibate and erotic is "a unified concept central to Indian thought from prehistoric times."

From the Hindu perspective, Shiva's celibacy and eroticism are entirely compatible. They are not seen as conventional opposites—up and down, hot and cold—which by definition cannot coexist. Rather, Shiva's sexuality and chastity are understood as two forms of heat: kama, the heat of passion or desire, and *tapas,* the heat of creativity. Both kama and *tapas* are valued, but in terms of asceticism, *tapas* is far more important as it generates wondrous powers and attracts great respect.

Shiva's story, like Shiva himself, is a towering, suprahuman drama, a raging contest between this paradigm of chastity and Kama, the great god of desire and physical love and the only being who had any hope of subverting the mighty deity famous for his commitment to brahmacharya or sexual abstinence. Kama is cunning. He chooses as bait the splendid and irresistible Parvati. Parvati's famously glorious derriere drives Shiva wild. Despite his anguish, he resists her velvety charms, but his suffering is transformed into rage against Kama's audacious scheming to corrupt him. In revenge, Shiva incinerates his enemy with his "third eye," a searingly hot protuberance on the middle of his forehead. Ironically, this third eye, which becomes an instrument of destruction against Kama, the personification of lust, has been generated by the *tapas* of Shiva's determined celibacy.

The story does not end with Kama's death. It so troubles Shiva that he restores his nemesis to life. Kama reappears, but in invisible form, ubiquitous in the world. He is still dedicated to perverting his chaste adversary, and Hindu literature is replete with accounts of how Shiva deals with each new trap. Finally, Shiva marries the enchanting Parvati, won over by the strength of her *tapas* as much as her charm. This is where the uniquely Hindu comprehension of celibacy arises, in the realm of deities, though not mortals. Despite the apparent ambiguity—Shiva's occasional indulgence in erotic relations with Parvati—he is celibacy incarnate, powerful enough to sublimate the mighty force of his virility into an equally powerful *tapas*.

Traditional images of Shiva manifest his enigmatic nature. Often, this paragon of celibacy is represented by a raised phallus in full erection. It does not symbolize eroticism or sexuality, an aroused penis, but depicts, instead, a penis thickened with semen conserved through Shiva's celibacy and raised upward so it will not spill its seed. Another popular rendition of Shiva's celibacy adorns his head, usually a bumpy crescent or horns, or hair styled to convey a similar shape. Here, Shiva has forced his semen up through his spinal column and into the various protuberances. In these effigies, his vaunted celibacy crowns him with a hot, semen-rich coronet.

CELIBACY IN STAGES

Hinduism is a vastly complex religious system as rich in diversity of precepts as its Indian homeland. In fact, its differing beliefs and practices reflect India's cultural and regional distinctions and function more as instruments of unification than, for example, Christianity and its divisive sectarianism. The Hindu pantheon accommodates hundreds of deities of varying significance, and Hindu practice is similarly varied. Unlike Christianity, which values, strives for, and wherever possible, imposes unity of doctrine and practice, Hinduism is remarkably flexible and free of the Christian concept of dissension as heresy. By the same token, that very ideological pliancy means that explaining Hinduism, even from the limited perspective of celibacy, is a supremely challenging task.

In general, Hinduism aspires to purge human existence of its afflictions, the root of which is the perpetual cycle of birth, death, and rebirth. At the core of these afflictions is the physical body, an entity at the mercy of nature and simultaneously an illusion that conceals both human immortality and latent divinity. How then to achieve the goal of eliminating mortal misery by ending the cycle of rebirth and revealing the godliness present in every individual?

Hinduism's answer is to follow the asramas, the four stages of life that characterize ideal existence and in three of which celibacy is paramount. This is because individuals will experience cyclical rebirths until they achieve moksa, the spiritual liberation that is the ultimate goal of Hindu life. Rebirths are determined, in part, by karma, the goodness or badness of actions in previous lives, a kind of spiritual justice system that leads to continuous rebirth. To Hindus, these rebirths are not miracles of eternal life, as they might be to Christians, but rather the terrible price exacted for wrongful deeds committed earlier.

The way to end this relentless cycle of rebirths is to obliterate earthly longings and desires, including kama or sexual desire, and cultivate higher knowledge. Modest phrases encompassing lifetimes of travail, but the route to liberation, though rigorous, is at least clearly defined as a series of four life stages: brahmacharya or student, grihastha or householder, vanaprastha or forest dweller, and sannyasi or total renouncer or religious mendicant. Each asrama evokes "toil and suffering," steps in the gradual process of purification from "earthly taint." At the last step, the pilgrim is deserving of his spiritual home.

These asramas are, of course, more ideal than real; few Hindus become forest dwellers or religious mendicants. Members of more privileged castes, however, become brahmacharins, and even those deprived of this stage become grihasthas. Hindu women are largely excluded from this spiritual journey. Those who observe the asramas are almost exclusively male.

Ideally, a boy enters brahmacharya between the ages of eight and twelve years and remains for anywhere from nine to thirty-six years, though leaving after twelve is common. A dedicated few choose lifetimes as brahmacharins, students of the sacred texts. Traditionally, the brahmacharin lived with his guru in a forest, but urbanization has produced the phenomenon of urban gurus whose students commute from their parents' homes. The object of brahmacharya, however, has not changed: the guru trains the boy, in mind and body, for a virtuous adulthood of good habits and excellent character, formed through devotion to self-discipline, sacred knowledge, and complete chastity.

This commitment to sexual abstinence is so total that the very word *brahmacharya* has become synonymous with celibacy. It means a lifestyle of intense self-control, in which the rational mind reduces all the carnal appetites to nothingness. Only thus purified can a man attain the state of self-lessness and sufficient stores of semen necessary for the realization of truth.

In the past, if a young man lapsed and indulged in sex, he was subjected to severe penances. Manu, the Hindu lawgiver, decreed a humiliating year of wearing a donkey's skin, begging food from seven houses, admitting at each how he had sinned, eating only a single meal each day but bathing three times.

The chaste brahmacharin absorbs a wide range of knowledge during his apprenticeship: the sacred Vedic texts and rituals, his social and religious duties and responsibilities as a member of his caste, and proper codes of behavior. Together, this education sets him on the path that will reveal the Supreme Being, the ultimate goal of Hinduism. His celibacy is an essential instrument of learning and, in conjunction with his other austerities, helps him achieve control over all his senses.

Subduing sexual passion focuses the brahmacharin's attention on his studies and duties, and on drawing closer to the Supreme Being. But abstaining is not enough. The sexual urge must not merely be dominated but sublimated, transformed into energy and redirected into godliness. Celibacy is as much mental as physical. It is also an essential means to Hinduism's most important end: moksa, the ultimate liberation.

Celibate energy has a tangible physical dimension: semen. In no other religion is the power of semen as pronounced as in Hinduism and related religious traditions. Semen is a vital fluid, the essence of life. In some of the writings in the Upanishads, a set of sacred Hindu texts, for instance, the loss of seed is lamented as a kind of death. Semen is the creative force, and it is calculated that to produce one mere drop, sixty drops of blood are required. By retaining their semen, ascetic men generate *tapas,* the inner heat or energy that Shiva used to destroy Kama and the energy that imparts aspects of godliness to celibate mortals. Given its power, a brahmacharin who discharges semen risks at best serious waste, at worst dangerous loss. Instead, the precious fluid should be retained as an internal resource. He who treasures his semen and channels its power upward may attain personal and spiritual power and also sustain high levels of physical and mental agility, all invaluable to a student's success.

The grihastha or householder stage of life is the only one in which celibacy is inappropriate. Indeed, husband and wife should not merely indulge in sexual intercourse, they may even enjoy it. Despite this joyous view of sexuality in its season, some married couples practice brahmacharya. Mahatma Gandhi, who continually tested his resolve by sleeping with lovely and usually naked young women, is the most famous example. Gandhi, like many Hindus, equated eroticism with animal passion and believed that "a man who is unchaste loses stamina, becomes emasculated and cowardly . . . [in]capable of any great effort." In this stage of life, the householder, duly and ritually married, pursues the things of this world, including material and professional success. He tends faithfully to his family and acquits himself of his debts to society.

The householder is especially diligent about spiritual obligations to the gods and the ancestors. He performs the customary rituals to the gods, and he fathers sons who will later make funeral offerings to the ancestors. In fact, procreation is central to marriage, and Hindu gods, usually portrayed alongside their unvirginal consorts, are married. Hindu temple-goers do not see marriage as a concession to human weakness but rather as a stage in the lifelong journey of spiritual growth.

The householder stage of a man's life should end, Manu writes, when his flesh wrinkles and sags, his dark hair lightens to gray, and he is surrounded by grandchildren. His new asrama is that of the vanaprastha or forest dweller, and his wife, sworn to celibacy, may accompany him. Few Hindus, today as in the past, proceed to this stage. Those who do are mocked as fanatics but also respected for their asceticism and conformity to Hindu idealism.

A forest dweller is committed to asceticism. His foodstuffs are limited to vegetables, flowers, roots, and fruits. In the heat of summer, he may increase his physical discomfort by lighting five fires. In winter, he may wear damp clothes. He constantly recites the sacred texts of the Vedas and, Manu says, "should be controlled, friendly, and mentally composed; he should always be a giver and a nontaker, compassionate to all living beings." The forest dweller must also renounce sexuality and practice perfect celibacy. In old age as in his youth, he must relinquish all sensual desires, conserve what remains of his semen, and devote himself to a quest for self-understanding and fusion with the Supreme Being.

The fourth asrama, sannyasi, is even rarer than the third. Its goal, according to the Bhagavad Gita, is to become "one who neither hates nor loves anything," a prerequisite for escaping rebirth and achieving instead moksa, spiritual deliverance. This profound indifference, designed to obliterate the taint of karma, extends to the sannyasi's own body and social status, his past and his future. He must practice even greater austerities, notably giving up the use of fire. He also ceases to sacrifice to the gods because he no longer has earthly goals. He becomes a wanderer whom strangers feed or not, and he has no belongings, no expectations, no obligations, and no pride. He spends his time meditating on God and, say the sacred texts, "lives identified with the eternal Self and beholds nothing else." Ultimately, that oneness will allow him, at last, to escape the cycle of rebirth.

Classical Hinduism, like Christianity practiced mostly in the breach, nonetheless forms the worldview of countless millions of men and women about the meaning and nature of divine and human existence. Celibacy's crucial role in that metaphysical scheme of things is central to Hinduism, for two reasons: first to conserve the precious life force in semen, then transform it into creative energy, and second, as the only way to renounce and transcend earthly desires, to achieve moksa or liberation, the longed-for closeness or oneness with the Supreme Being.

MODERN CELIBACY IN SANNYASI ORDERS

Just as the apostolic life is at the heart of Christianity, asceticism is at the heart of Hinduism and also of Indian culture. However, Hindu asceticism differs fundamentally from Christian, in intent if not practice, because it is not grounded in mind-body dualism. Hindu ascetics do not aim to deny their bodies but to subject themselves to disciplines that enhance mental qualities and spirituality. To generate *tapas,* the internal heat or energy that will further their aim of liberating the soul, they often turn to yogic practice to "still the body, still the breath, and finally, to still the mind."

Today, some sannyasis, devotees of this extreme asceticism, live together in ashrams or communities. Others live alone. Women, too, may become renunciates, known as sadhvis or sannyasinis. Whether sectarian or solitary, these ascetics usually adopt a distinctive garb, ocher-colored gowns reminiscent of the costume of criminals, or the stark nakedness of the no-longer proud. Their hair—long and matted or shorn with a razor—reflects their indifference to both status and aesthetics.

When sannyasis join orders, they choose one led by a guru they consider powerful and perfect and to whom they owe unquestioning obedience. Each order has a specific doctrine with specific goals and ways to achieve them. Disciples are obliged to observe their order's regulations and basic principles, and to practice "moral purity, sincere thirst for ultimate reality, and trust in the guru." Celibacy, of course, is a fundamental dimension of moral purity.

The *ramanandi* order dates from the early fourteenth century. Its members are devotees of Lord Rama and his wife, Sita, major Hindu deities. *Ramanandi* monks accept members from all castes and once permitted women to join them, though they no longer do so. These monks, thousands strong, are often zealous though uneducated. During initiation rites, they sear the name Rama into their flesh and add the suffix *das*—slave—to their surnames. Many *ramanandi*s operate shelters for aged cows.

This fanatical devotion to their religious principles stems largely from Lord Rama himself. From the perspective of celibacy, Rama is notably detached in his marital relations, though he loves his wife. Both Rama and Lakshman, his bachelor brother, appear in sacred texts "as ascetics, living in the jungle of desire, where the demons reign." The *ramanandi* discipline of body and mind reflects this detachment from earthly senses and desires.

Each *ramanandi* must choose a guru to initiate him into the celibate Clan of God. He may select one of three suborders: *tyagis*, *nagas*, or *rasiks*. *Tyagis* travel about the countryside in monastic groups and are aggressively celibate, even to the point of castrating themselves. They concentrate on the positive spiritual energy created by conserving their semen. This *tapas*, accumulated through a regimen of strict ascetic discipline, gives the *tyagis* a special, supernatural power called *shakti*. Their celibacy also enables them to unite the masculine and feminine aspects found in all humans.

The suborder of *nagas* has radically different objectives. *Nagas* are fighting ascetics engaged in wrestling or military practices. They regard celibacy as a prerequisite for physical training, and so they store rather than discharge their semen, which they consider a crucial aspect of their spiritual power. The militaristic style of the *nagas* extends to their discipline and their organization into regiments and armies. During great festivals, the *nagas* defend their brothers in other, more vulnerable orders.

The third suborder, *rasiks*, are celibate aesthetes who, unlike the other two, live in stable temple communities and express their devotion to Lord Rama through ritual theater. They, too, consciously retain their semen, not to generate *tapas* but rather to sublimate it into a god-directed, selfless love, the chaste joy of longing for the untouched beloved, a pure passion much like the agape ideal of many early Christian nuns. *Rasiks* believe their hoarded semen will convert their masculinity into feminine qualities. This feminization is so important that many *rasiks* imitate Rama's wife, Sita, by putting on women's clothing.

The unifying and common denominator among these three diametrically different *ramanandi* suborders is their focus on celibacy and the conservation of precious semen, the source of their spiritual power and their mystical ability to partake of Rama's transcendental nature. In *ramanandi* doctrine, as in Hinduism generally, semen is a life-giving force that, properly conserved, transforms sexual into spiritual energy and endows its semen-rich devotees with special powers. Celibacy, therefore, is a critical instrument for achieving spiritual goals. On another plane, it also serves as a social boundary between monks and laymen and is essential to the *ramanandis*' institutional survival.

The supreme importance of semen in this religious scheme of things effectively excludes women from gaining acceptance as fully initiated *ramanandis*. The order has nuns, but they are seen as disciples rather than holy women. In fact, they so closely resemble the legions of lay widows who congregate at holy places to await death that little or nothing distinguishes one group from the other. Furthermore, *ramanandi* nunneries are known as *maiwaras*, where mothers live. This is consistent with Hinduism's view of women as unsuited to a religious vocation, both because of their ungovernable passions and because their main purpose in life is to procreate, a noncelibate function. Holy Hindu men renounce women. Women, the renounced, cannot join their renouncers.

THE DAUGHTERS OF BRAHMA

One unique sect embraces devout Hindu women, and it has celibacy, not semen, at its spiritual core. The Brahma Kumaris—Daughters of Brahma—are a modern sect and today number about a hundred thousand members, the majority of them men. In fact, their founder was a male—Dada Lekhraj, a wealthy jeweler from Sind, then part of north India, now part of Pakistan.

Until just before 1937, when he founded the Brahma Kumaris, Lekhraj seemed a devout and decent family man, exceptional only in the extent to which his profession permitted him access to unrelated women. This included even the residents of the women's quarters in the palaces of several rajas and maharajas. Probably Lekhraj's years of relatively intimate contact with so many women inspired the views he would later promulgate as doctrine, views about women's nature and status that ran counter to traditional Hinduism and scandalized his social circles.

Lekhraj's elite and affluent merchant men ordered their women's world in typical upper-caste and upper-class fashion, based on centuries of tradition. Men were revered as homegrown gods and sages and maintained their superior position by ensuring their wives and daughters had almost no education and were seldom permitted to sample life outside the family home. This was true even when business took the menfolk away from home for months, sometimes years. During these long separations, the women were supposed to remain at home, cherishing their men's memories.

But in many a household, a persistent rumor began to poison the domestic harmony. Unlike their chaste and secluded wives, this story went, the absent husbands were sexually profligate and some took mistresses. Before long, wives rebelled. Many no longer honored as deities and gurus the men who debased their marriages. The women also resented being seen as mere dolls designed for male sexual entertainment.

Some of these women were Lekhraj's clients, and sometimes they confided in him about their dissatisfaction and unhappiness. But until he was nearly sixty, Lekhraj seemed unaffected by what he heard. Then came the visions that transformed his life and radicalized many bitter Sindi women. First the gods Vishnu and Shiva appeared to him, then an apocalypse, the world destroyed by civil war and natural catastrophes. The souls of the dead flew upward by the millions, "as moths flutter in the direction of a light."

Lekhraj was profoundly shaken. He liquidated his successful jewelry business. The visions intensified. His wife and daughter-in-law found him in a trance, his eyes glowing red, a human candleholder for a fire within. Much later, Lekhraj interpreted this as instructions from a supreme being to "make such a world as this," the one that had just been revealed to him.

Lekhraj was a changed man. "I am a soul, you are a soul," he would intone. He also preached, and a stream of people began to gather around him, most of them wealthy women from his community. In 1937, he named several of them to a managing committee, the nucleus of the Brahma Kumaris. Soon after, he transferred his personal fortune to the committee.

The Sindi community reacted unfavorably. One man later recalled that after it became generally known young wives were attending Lekhraj's ashram and a vow of celibacy was involved, "there was a lot of resistance from husbands . . . a real 'hue and cry' both in the city and in the province as a whole." The merchants in particular were hostile. Many of them were wealthy and accustomed to good living, which included sex. By demanding a vow of chastity that extended even to married women, the largest constituency among them, the Brahma Kumaris had declared war on traditional Hinduism.

Lekhraj's teachings, from which the theology derived, not only put celibacy at dead center of the movement but simultaneously condemned sexual intercourse as the depravity that had transformed paradise into hell. (A hint of lapsarian Christianity, perhaps, but an isolated one. Nothing else in the Brahma Kumari belief system suggests similar beliefs.) The Brahma Kumaris believe all people are souls coupled with physical bodies, and they exist within the chronological context of historical cycles of moral and physical decline, each totaling five thousand years, divided into four equal ages.

At the beginning, the ages were pure and perfect. Men and women were equal, and neither adversity nor affliction existed. The principal cause of this flawlessness was the absence of sexual intercourse, which a yogic power to reproduce nonsexually rendered unnecessary. But erotic couplings entered the scene. Gradually, these godly folk deteriorated, morally and physically, until corruption and torment prevailed. Heaven became hell, and the fleshly desires of the body came to dominate the world.

Hand in hand with the degeneration of human standards came the bondage of women, enslaved by men's increasing lust. Wives and mothers were especially vulnerable and suffered all the indignity and misery imposed by their inferior status. The goal of the Brahma Kumaris is to end this cycle and purify themselves on earth so they may be reborn at or soon after the pristine beginning of each successive cycle. They wish to be liberated from sinful births rather than, as in mainstream Hinduism, rebirth itself. The only way they can achieve this is by renouncing the evil that is sexual intercourse and adopting complete celibacy.

To the frustrated women chafing under the domination of their free-living men, celibacy promised enormous rewards. To begin with, it fulfilled the theological condition for assuring perfect future births. It also relieved women from either the chains of marriage or the ignominy of spinsterhood. Cleansed of sexuality, they would find their true spiritual identities and shuck off their ties with the ungodly, material world.

Brahma Kumarism responded to the discontent among Sindi women. Some men were also persuaded of its essential truths and joined the movement. But this was radical new metaphysics that reevaluated women and presented them positively, postulating a higher status. It ran counter to Hindu thought, which, like classical Christianity, portrayed women as inferior and the root of evil. In religious terms, it suggested society could be different. In social terms, it promised women unheard-of opportunities—in the movement, for instance, they could be teachers and leaders. It also implied an affirmation of their gender and a scathing reassessment of their current status. Inspired with these new ideas, the women explained to their incredulous husbands that, henceforth, they should live together chastely, loving each other with a pure and asexual spiritual devotion.

Male, and husbandly, reaction to these scandalous teachings was violent. Brahma Kumari wives were beaten, evicted from their homes, locked away in solitary confinement, and sued through the courts for restoration of conjugal rights. Family pressures were applied—members of families with Brahma Kumari members were threatened with excommunication from their caste. Lekhraj himself was accused of everything from sorcery to lechery.

The Brahma Kumari movement proved impossible to eradicate. Lekhraj moved his followers from their city of persecution to Karachi, where they settled in a highly structured ashram that became their whole world. You have undergone a "death-in-life" birth, Lekhraj informed them. Because you have been reborn as children into a "divine family," I shall rename you. This was not all: Lekhraj revealed as well that he was Brahma, Hinduism's Supreme Being.

Life in the community was a tightly regimented, inner-directed round of yoga, devotional rituals, Lekhraj's daily sermons, divine revelations, and perfect celibacy. Discipline was quasi-military, but the members considered each other siblings under the tutelage of their spiritual guru. The Brahma Kumaris were indeed the daughters of Lekhraj-cum-Brahma.

After the 1947 partition of India and Pakistan, the Brahma Kumaris moved again, to Mt. Abu in India. Lekhraj began to understand that a celibate order could not sustain itself in disdainful isolation from the world. Proselytization was essential to survival. By the time he died in 1969, his Brahma Kumari sect had international roots and was flourishing. Though the majority of today's membership is male, women hold the key positions. Many are married but live chastely with their spouses. Celibacy continues to dominate their spiritual agenda; it is, they believe and preach, the virtue at the origin of all other virtues.

The Brahma Kumaris' understanding of celibacy has evolved to mean a kind of presexual quality. Converts are spiritually reborn as children and reclaim the innocent purity of childhood. Sex poisons and weakens the body and leaves it vulnerable to disease. Sex has overpopulated and made a slum of the planet. Brahma Kumaris liken the sexual act to foraging about in a sewer.

Sexual love has no vindicating features, either. True love is loving someone's essence—his soul. Sexuality expends precious energy (not semen) and women are its principal victims. They are rendered powerless by men's lust and demands for its fulfillment. Their rebirth as sexually pure children and their consequent renunciation of sex liberate women from this bondage and free them to achieve the enormous power of absolute chastity.

BUDDHISM

BUDDHA AND HIS PRECEPTS

Buddhism originated in the sixth century B.C. as an Indian metaphysical system steeped in the Hinduism its founder, Siddhartha Gautama, pondered, challenged, and rejected. Siddhartha was a wealthy Indian prince born into the Kshatriya caste, whose warrior and politician members are second only to Brahmans. The prince grew to detest the materialism of his privileged world, so contrary to Hindu ideals of asceticism and renunciation of human desires. By the time he was thirty, Siddhartha rejected outright his way of life and its luxurious trappings. He left his sorrowing family and plunged into a very different existence as a wandering ascetic in search of spiritual enlightenment. For six years he tramped through India, hoping that through his austere lifestyle, he would discover the truths he was seeking.

Those truths continued to elude him. At last, the prince rejected the life of extreme asceticism and turned to intense meditation. For forty-eight days he meditated, but without effect. But on the forty-ninth day, as he sat under a pipal tree, he was suddenly overwhelmed by the enlightenment he had yearned for. Finally, Prince Siddhartha—now Buddha, the Enlightened One—understood the nature and causes of human suffering and what people had to do to eliminate it.

Buddha began to preach, sharing his revelations. They were complex and interrelated, a metaphysical necklace constructed with three jewels. Buddha himself was the first. His teachings constituted the second. The third jewel was the Order of Disciples, ordained men and women sworn to live in communal obedience to Buddhist doctrine. Before the third jewel could be strung onto the necklace, however, Buddha had to enunciate and elaborate on the beliefs to which disciples would commit their lives.

Buddha's first sermon, Turning of the Wheel of Law, began this process, articulating the creed—his Four Noble Truths—at the heart of his teaching. In capsule form, these truths are that suffering is ubiquitous and caused by human desires that, if renounced, lead to the knowledge of reality's true nature and the path of salvation.

Salvation, or nirvana, was absolute freedom from the wheel of rebirth, a concept similar to that in the Hinduism in which Buddha had been raised. But Buddhism differs fundamentally from Hinduism in that it rejects the belief that deities govern the cosmos and the mortals who inhabit it. Instead, humans determine their own destiny through the manner in which they live their lives.

This precept was particularly radical in caste-ridden India, and it led Buddha to reject the caste system. This former prince of the second-highest caste not only welcomed members of the lowest into his fellowship, but he did so in the people's language of Maghadi, not the learned vehicle of Sanskrit. Masses of the lowest castes, hearing that they, too, could aspire to nirvana and escape the strictures and degradations of membership in a low caste, renounced Hinduism and converted to Buddhism.

The route to nirvana, Buddha taught, is via the Eightfold Path, simple propositions known as Buddhism's Middle Way. The eight principles are typically pragmatic. Believers should follow a life of moderation and balance, which meant they should hold correct opinions and aspirations, practice right speech, conduct, livelihood, effort, mindfulness, and meditation. To accomplish all this, they had above all to be faithful to vows of brahmacharya, abstinence from the passion that consumes both body and soul; ahimsa, nonviolence; and *aparigraha,* poverty. The ultimate goal was nirvana, absolute freedom from the wheel of rebirth, with all the suffering it engenders.

Part of the Middle Way's simplicity lay in its austerity. Right conduct, for instance, meant forswearing earthly appetites, and so Buddhism, like Hinduism, made lasciviousness an obvious target and brahmacharya the only remedy. Celibacy, in other words, was mandatory for anyone who aspired to salvation.

In his sermonizing about celibacy, Buddha sounded much like the Hindu he had once been. A Buddhist should avoid unchastity like "a pit of burning cinders," but the nature of lust in general, and of women in particular, made this immensely difficult. Women, Buddha declared, were lustier and weaker-willed than men, endlessly conniving to seduce wavering males. Despite this, men should suppress their lust, women their wiles, and both should observe strict celibacy.

Buddha acknowledged the likelihood that marital celibacy might prove unworkable. In that case, he exhorted spouses to be faithful to each other and, at the very least, strive for periods of sexual abstinence. Buddhism recognizes that most people cannot maintain marital celibacy; it tolerates sexually active marriage, sometimes even concubinage. However, at some point eroticism must come to an end, for all Buddhists who hope to achieve nirvana must adopt a life of renunciation, with celibacy at its core.

Buddhism's jaundiced view of womankind—as an obstacle to would-be celibate males—is reflected in its teachings. One scripture describes how Mara, sovereign over the realm of desire, struggled—fiendishly but unsuccessfully—to prevent Buddha from achieving enlightenment. Her daughters, Lust, Aversion, and Craving, sharpen the Buddhist portrait of womanly evil, personifying the lustful female devoted to destroying spirituality through her uncontrollable seductiveness. The all-important Buddhist concept of celibacy, therefore, can be neither defined nor understood without special reference to women's nature.

It happened that Buddha's extraordinary rejection of caste mitigated the effect of his negative views about women, which explains why so many from among the low castes converted to his liberating new religion. They may have been inveterate seductresses, but at least they were on a spiritual par with women born into even the highest castes. Furthermore, by pledging themselves to celibacy as well as to nonviolence and poverty, these women could become Buddhist nuns. While ensuring their spiritual salvation, they could evade the burdens and obligations of marriage and motherhood that would otherwise be their fate. Some even dared dream of lives rich with learning and preaching. For them, Buddhist brahmacharya was an albatross escaped, an opportunity for a life most other women could scarcely even imagine.

MEN AND WOMEN OF THE MONASTERIES

Buddhism has traditionally been a monastic religion, and its sanghas—religious communities—are its third (and last) jewel. This is a logical consequence of the second jewel, teachings that counsel an abstemious way of life incompatible with mainstream, married society. The possibility of attaining nirvana was the most compelling reason for joining a monastic community, but it is also difficult to overestimate the lure that escaping the burdens of lay life held for members of lowly castes.

This was even truer of women than of men. Life as a Buddhist nun was a refuge from the otherwise inescapable grind of wifehood, motherhood, and often, widowhood. Even as Buddhism spread beyond India and into China, Nepal, Tibet, and beyond, women both of high rank and low understood what a nun's life could offer. Monasticism held out opportunities, namely education, otherwise unobtainable by women and most men.

Monastic life was rigidly structured and governed by the Vinaya, texts that define ethical standards, the rules of daily conduct, exceptional situations, and the penalties for violations. Novices made ten vows, which included the five taken by lay Buddhists—not to kill any living thing (which led inexorably to vegetarianism), not to take anything not given, not to lie, not to engage in sexual misconduct, and not to consume intoxicating substances. The additional five focused on more minute details of life—not to sing, dance, or attend entertainments, not to use cosmetics or other adornments, not to use luxurious seats and beds, not to touch gold and silver, not to consume unfitting foodstuffs. Once ordained, monks had to pledge another two hundred precepts, while nuns faced a staggering three hundred.

Most of these additional one hundred precepts addressed unchaste nunly behavior. They enumerated the worst transgressions: having sexual relations, conniving to meet, flirt, or have bodily contact with a man for erotic or amorous reasons, even helping or failing to report another nun who had so transgressed. For these and a host of other sins, the penalty was expulsion from the order. Compared to Christianity, Buddhism punished its sexual sinners harshly, for ejection from the religious community, especially for women, was tantamount to social death.

In China, where Buddhism struggled against Confucianism and finally made great inroads, monasteries were havens from civil unrest and war, poverty, homelessness, and orphanhood. In spite of the stricter rules for nuns, women's convents could nevertheless also provide refuge from unwanted marriages, security when there was a dearth of male protectors, and the sole means of satisfying intellectual ambitions. In a society where most women were illiterate, Chinese nuns could read and write and often pursued scholarly vocations unthinkable in the outside world.

Like Christian nuns, Chinese Buddhist nuns were often drawn from the upper classes, and their biographies, not those of their less-privileged sisters, dominate the literature. As a result, it is far more difficult to portray the life of average nuns than of their (formerly) high-ranking peers, though we know that meditation, studying and chanting scriptures and holy readings, and asceticism were fundamental to all Buddhist nuns and monks. Some records of important nuns, almost all from privileged backgrounds, prove how liberating convent life was. As teachers and preachers, for instance, they grew famous for their work, something they could never have achieved as wives and mothers.

Two fourth-century Chinese women are living proof of what Buddhist nuns could accomplish. An Ling-Shou managed to convince her father that the convent life would bring greater honor to her family than her marriage. As a nun, she astonished her contemporaries with her wisdom and learned interpretations of sacred texts. She also built Founding of Wisdom Convent and several other sanctuaries and inspired hundreds of women to emulate her and pledge themselves to the religious life.

While celibacy was one tool for greater things in An Ling-Shou's case, in Chih-Hsien's story it plays a central role. Chih-Hsien, the virtuous and exquisitely beautiful daughter of a magistrate, joined a Buddhist order. In a society that demanded premarital virginity of its daughters, and as a nun dedicated to a religion that defined celibacy as a precondition for salvation, she is famous for defending her chastity against a vicious and lascivious public official. This man, who hated Buddhist religious, assaulted her sexually. When Chih-Hsien resisted forcefully, her enraged assailant stabbed her more than twenty times. She lost consciousness. At that, the lusty official departed. Chih-Hsien eventually recovered, her indomitable spirit vindicated, her virtue intact.

Sixteen centuries later, the metaphysical importance of celibacy has lost none of its force. Buddhist nuns still observe rigorous strictures against eroticism. To help negate its dangers and consequences, they are defeminized with an androgynous look: heads shorn of enticing hair and figures kept boyishly slight from fasting. Any breasts that survive the austere diet are concealed by a length of strategically draped cloth. The nuns live regimented lives of meditation, prayer, and ritual, with periodic fasting during which they must remain silent. Celibacy remains an absolute, with dismissal from the order the consequence of transgression.

Buddhist monks, too, pledge and practice celibacy, though unlike Buddhist nuns, many find this a greater struggle. Testimonials to this are found in extensive early-twentieth-century records of a monastic order, Thailand's *thudong* or forest monks. These men owned almost nothing, slept in forests or cemeteries, and ate only once daily. Sometimes, during the rainy season, they retreated to monasteries. Others dwelt there permanently but spent considerable time outside, helping overburdened villagers, often relatives, work the land. The contact these forest monks had with laywomen did not conform to strict Buddhism, which commands men and women to segregate themselves and warns men about the temptations women will place in their way. Instead, these Thai monks maintained easy relations with women, even frolicking with them at traditional boat races held during rice festivals. Inspectors sent from Bangkok continually reported that scandalous conditions prevailed among the monks.

Much evidence supports the contention that Thai monks found eroticism a far greater challenge than hunger, illness, social alienation, and loneliness. Women were the enemy—or at least their irresistibility was. Waen and Fan, two wandering monks, fought hard against unbidden lust stirred by encounters with ordinary women for whom they developed obsessions. Such encounters, according to one troubled soul, were "worse than a tiger, a bear, or an evil spirit." When Waen was seized by sexual passion, he meditated hard, then turned to fasting and imagining his beloved's body as it decomposed. Fan battled alone, unsuccessful in his efforts to disengage his thoughts from a certain woman, until his spiritual adviser locked him up in a temple room. The lovelorn monk meditated for a week. Then, realizing the woman must have been his mate in a previous life, he was able to forget her.

Sometimes, aroused monks failed to conquer their desires and either disrobed and married, were expelled, or else sneaked sinful and surreptitious sexual moments. Surprisingly, older monks fell victim to their erotic feelings even more than the younger men they counseled. One teacher taught that the danger age was between forty-five and sixty years, when the aging body rebelled against the inevitable decline that would end even the possibility of sexual experience. Then, he warned, chaste monks railed against their bodies. Sometimes they succumbed to carnality and disrobed, both literally and figuratively, always to the disgust of lay commentators and fellow monks, who found the spectacle degrading, a travesty of Buddhist belief and monastic purity.

Errant religious are, however, exceptions to the rule of absolute celibacy. In the main, Buddhist nuns and monks have been scrupulously chaste and battle temptation with the usually successful strategies of meditation and physical privation. Women suffered less because they had so much more to lose if they succumbed and so much more to gain through committed celibacy. It helped, too, that their convents were so strictly regulated and that they were seldom alone in circumstances that might have compromised their resolve.

Monks, on the other hand, were more often exposed to women than nuns were to men. The itinerant ascetics who begged for their sustenance routinely met laywomen and often fantasized about their charms, sometimes obsessively. The extent of their efforts to eradicate lust actually underscored the centrality of celibacy in Buddhist thought. The monks understood this only too well. They persevered in their ongoing struggle to stifle their sensuality, helped by watchful and experienced colleagues.

A demographic postscript to this brief glimpse of Buddhism underscores its importance as one of the world's major belief systems. As Buddhism matured and converted millions in its native India and influenced Hinduism as well, worried and jealous Hindu leaders campaigned to eradicate it from Indian soil. In the thirteenth century, nearly two millennia after its birth,

Buddhism was virtually exiled from its homeland. By then, however, it was spreading into Nepal, Tibet, China, Japan, and most of Southeast Asia. It continued to make enormous inroads and today dominates Eastern religious belief. In 1954, Buddhists were invited to return to India, where they now constitute a tiny but growing minority.

JAINISM

To Westerners, the most well-known Jain perhaps is Merry Levov, the fatally rebellious teenager who destroyed her parents' idyllic life in Philip Roth's Pulitzer Prize–winning novel, *American Pastoral.* Filthy (because washing with water destroys microorganisms), veiled by the reeking heel of a discarded panty hose (to avoid inhaling tiny insects or exhaling a gush of hot breath onto them), and piteously emaciated by her vegetables-only diet, Merry is a frail, putrid, feces-fouled, loose-toothed parody of Jainism, American radical-fanatic style.

Over 3 million real-life Jains, most of them in India, profess the same beliefs, including celibacy, unmentioned by rape victim Merry. In North America, however, they are better known for their vegetarianism and the extreme lengths to which they take ahimsa, nonviolence toward all life-forms including insects and even invisible organisms. Toronto's Bata Shoe Museum, for example, displays a pair of Jainist high-platformed shoes with the center of the soles hollowed out. Only the outer rims touch the ground, so the wearer crushes as few invisible organisms as possible.

The history of Jainism is shrouded in obscurity. It is, indisputably, a very old Indian religion. Its adherents date its origins thousands of years before Buddhism's, though Mahavira, its most hallowed teacher, lived around the same time as Buddha. Jainism shares many fundamental principles with Buddhism and Hinduism. Jains also strive to break the cycle of rebirth that moksa or nirvana alone can effect. They emphasize celibacy as an instrument to achieve this, relinquishing worldly pleasures and desires, including the desire for possessions and, through lust, for other people.

Nonviolence is paramount and is the source for most other Jainist beliefs. For the same reasons as Merry Levov, many Jains wear mouth masks called *muhpatti.* They avoid eating after dark, when their cooking fires would be a fatal attraction to insects. Mendicant monks even stop their wandering during the four months of the monsoon season, not to protect themselves against pounding rainstorms but rather to spare the lives of the seething life-forms that emerge and thrive during that season. For the same reason, they do not bathe with organism-filled water and are often described—by admiring observers who do not include Philip Roth—as filthy. With their fanatical reverence for all life, the Jains also practice total vegetarianism.

Jains believe time is like a wheel, with six spokes that are like six ages. With each slight revolution of the wheel, twenty-four teachers emerge to teach righteous living that will lead to moksa. The greatest and last of these teachers is Mahavira, a sixth-century, upper-caste member who married and fathered a daughter. At the age of thirty, this privileged young Jain went through the rite of renunciation, stripping off his elegant garments and slowly tearing out his hair in five painful handfuls. Then he began to wander the countryside as a (probably naked) mendicant, suffering abuse, confronting danger, and meditating. After twelve years, as he meditated in the field of a farmer named Samaga, he received *kevala,* the supreme knowledge or enlightenment that Jains consider omniscience.

Mahavira's status was affirmed in Jainist literature, which describes his unwashed flesh as milky white (the same color as his blood) and odorless, while his breath (unlike Merry Levov's overpowering stench) had the fragrance of a lotus flower. Now he had to disseminate his newfound wisdom, the great truths revealed to him. Four of his five Great Vows were classical Jainism: nonviolence to all life-forms, truthfulness, nonpossessiveness, and renunciation of all desires of the senses. The fifth was total celibacy, which Mahavira considered so important, and so central to the tenets of his religion, that he separated it from the category of general renunciation and articulated it as a specific vow.

Celibacy was centrally linked to nonviolence by Jainism's concern for sparing microbes. Female and male sexual organs are aswim with them, and so intercourse becomes a murderous activity. Celibacy was also linked to the vow to extinguish all sensual desires. For that reason, too, intercourse had to be avoided as a great evil.

For thirty more years, Mahavira proselytized, traveling and preaching continuously, staying in one place only during the monsoon season. In his seventy-second year, after delivering over one hundred lectures despite the debilitating effects of a total fast, he achieved his goal of moksa. Through carefully planned and executed death by starvation, the venerable ascetic achieved his final liberation.

After Mahavira's death, Jains split into two sects. One important difference between them, even today, is their dress code. The Digambara monks say they are emulating Mahavira's unclad state and go about stark naked, while the Shvetambara monks are garbed in white. The Shvetambaras do not see clothing as an obstacle to salvation. The Digambaras, however, condemn it as property to be rid of and something that might endanger the insects it would attract. They also scorn it as an instrument of society with its rules about humility and shame. Clothing, Digambaras believe, implies a regard for the things of this world, and they are so literal in how they interpret nonowner-ship that they also refuse to carry alms bowls and use their cupped hands as receptacles for their begged food.

The status of women is the other major doctrinal difference. Digambara doctrine denies women can achieve nirvana, though they are accepted as nuns to whom, significantly, nudity is forbidden. Despite their nunly vows and dedication to spirituality, their seductive womanly forms cannot be displayed. Shvetambaras have a more positive view of women. They evoke Mahavira, whose legacy included a legion of converts, both ascetic and lay, with females predominating by a ratio of over two to one. They also recall that Malli, a famous sage, was a woman.

Shvetambara nuns take the same five Great Vows as monks. They also swear obedience to their superior and to abstain from eating after dark. Strictures against contact between monks and nuns are severe. They must not cohabit nor be alone together. Digambara nuns are not permitted to roam the coun-tryside begging, but male and female Shvetambara religious wander, except during rainy seasons.

The object of the religious life is nirvana, which can only be achieved in slow stages. The ascetic relinquishes all possessions and relationships and becomes indifferent to the longings of his senses, for sexual satisfaction, phys-ical comfort, even tasty food. Meditation is paramount, and avoiding injuring life-forms. The only possessions Digambara monks always carry are a *rajoha-rana*—a small peacock-feather whisk for tenderly sweeping away insects with-out harming them—and a water gourd. Shvetambara monks own three lengths of cloth, an alms bowl, a blanket, a walking stick, a *muhpatti* mouth mask, a few volumes of holy scripture, and a *rajoharana* made of woolen tufts.

The appeal of Jainist monasticism is deeply spiritual, for unlike monasticism in Christianity and Buddhism, as an alternative to mainstream life it is limited. Some women join to avoid marriage, others the shame and misery of widow-hood. Some men find the rituals, such as the hair-pulling ceremonies, irre-sistible. However, unlike Buddhists, Jains seldom accept lower-caste members as initiates, so escaping the harshness of life in low-ranking castes is not a moti-vation.

In the Jain religion, the precepts of nonviolence, nonpossessiveness, and celibacy are so intertwined that each partially defines and explains the other. The chaste monk symbolizes the Jainist creed. Naked or lightly covered in the simplest cloth, roaming through village and forest, he is Jainism incarnate as he begs his meager rations from housewives and other strangers. When insects buzz around his vegetarian repast or alight on his lean body or bald head, he brushes them away gently with his *rajoharana*. He is careful not to squash even the tiniest bug, and before drinking, he peers into his water

gourd to make sure he sees no living creature in it. When he is tempted by unbidden lust, he remembers the sexual organs are hotbeds of microbic life that, in copulation, he would be responsible for pulverizing.

In any case, the mendicant monk knows the unchaste cannot achieve nirvana. He has renounced not only the material things of the world but possessiveness itself, including desire for another mortal's body. He has sworn off lust as a human passion to be avoided, even in its mildest form of unrequited titillation. And he has studied and pledged himself to the precepts of Jainism's greatest teacher, Mahavira, who so valued celibacy that he highlighted it as a separate vow, instead of incorporating it into the vow of nonpossessiveness. To the Great Ascetic and his followers ever since, celibacy is a form of mental discipline and an instrument of nonviolence, and an absolute prerequisite for achieving the nirvana of spiritual liberation.

Given the paramountcy of celibacy in Jainism, Westerners might wonder how they expect to shore up their numbers, already relatively small. The internal logic of the religion answers this nicely. Their scriptures teach that Jain membership will shrink until the fifth spoke of the wheel of time. The last Jains will be a monk and a nun, Duhprasabha and Satyashri, and a layman and his wife, the merchant Nagila and Phalgushri, as well as the last Jain king, Vimalavahana. This select band will die and be reborn in different heavens, and the sixth spoke of time's wheel will revolve. An apocalyptic inferno will consume the debased remnants of humanity, cave-dwelling dwarfs, and the world as we know it will cease to exist.

RITUAL CELIBACY

In the world's atavistic religions, where omnipresent gods reside in the trees, rocks, rivers, and earth, and in animals, shamans or priests are charged with the delicate task of communicating across earthly boundaries into the realm of the supernatural. Most come to the vocation at the invitation of divinities who appear to them in dreams. These men and women require a special sensitivity, and their training requires intense concentration, profound spirituality, and psychic and carnal purity achievable only through ritual purification. Usually this involves a retreat from daily life, dietary restrictions or fasting, and prayer and other devotions. Almost always, a period of enforced celibacy is essential. Removed from intimate human relations, the shaman or priest experiences heightened spirituality and can focus fully on the spirits and the work at hand.

CELIBACY CHARMS SHAMANS

In the stark, late-nineteenth-century northern world of the Caribou Inuit, heaven had no snow, ice, or storms, and hell was a sunless darkness with raging snowstorms and massive ice blocks that kept it cold. Every object was governed by an invisible force, and spirits could be contacted by wise men or shamans. This communication could take place only when a hooded, well-mittened shaman sat and, being careful not to spit on the ground or to take off his mittens, surrendered to a trance. Often he would have visions or successfully summon his spirit helpers. Such a shaman had undergone initiation rites so rigorous he risked dying at any moment from cold, hunger, drowning, or bullets. The powerful Igjugarjuk, described as an "outstandingly clever" shaman, described the suffering he personally chose for his novitiate.

Igjugarjuk endured "the two things that are most dangerous to us humans . . . hunger and . . . cold." His monthlong fast, doubly dangerous in the arctic chill, was broken only twice, by single mouthfuls of warm water. For the next year, he ate only certain foods. When he was exhibited to the spirits, he sat for a month, without daring to lie down, in an unprotected snow hut on an exposed ledge, with no caribou cover and only a scrap of hide to sit on. As his novitiate took place in the dead of winter, "I, who never got anything to warm me, and must not move, was very cold, and it was so tiring having to sit without daring to lie down that sometimes it was as if I died a little." This torment continued for a month, after which Igjugarjuk no longer had the strength to stand. "I was not very much alive anymore," he recalled, and "now so completely emaciated that the veins on my hands and body and feet had quite disappeared."

For an entire year, Igjugarjuk was forbidden to sleep with his wife. Even his food, which she cooked in a separate little pot, was segregated. No one else was permitted to share his meat. After Igjugarjuk had recovered from his ordeal and maintained strict chastity, his reward was that his village approved him as the new shaman.

Such extended celibacy in Caribou Inuit culture was exceedingly rare for any but shamans, though among ordinary folks it was fairly common in the short term—for example during mourning, the whaling season, and the Bladder Festival, when the spirits were known to be deeply offended by any violation of the prohibition against sex. The Bladder Festival lasted one month, during which the men moved into the dance house and women visited them only to bring food. Even then, they had to bathe before their daily visit and swaddle themselves in waterproof raincoats. These precautions were crucial, for without the assistance of the spirit world, starvation was inevitable. When the spirits demanded that the mortals abstain from sex, defiance would have been suicidal—there was simply too much at stake.

Igjugarjuk's rites of passage were, in their intensity, harshness, and celibate isolation, typical of shamans everywhere. In many societies, shamans are the only religious practitioners, and they hone their ability to communicate with the spirits through subjecting themselves, body and psyche, to grueling and terrifying experiences. The other denominator that cuts across cultures north to south, east to west, is celibacy, which is always required at least for short periods and often extensively, even for years. Far away from the frozen north, shaminism in the Amazon exacts similarly distinctive requirements, with strict observance of celibacy always a crucial factor in strengthening candidates for their roles as mediums between mortals and spirits.

Like Igjugarjuk's barren wastelands, the world of the Amazonian shaman is a treacherous quagmire of mystic forces, spirit helpers, cunning enemies, and vengeful clients. The Jivaro Indians of Ecuador know that witchcraft causes most sicknesses and nonviolent deaths and that daily, waking life is mere illusion, "a lie." Reality is supernatural, and the key to perceiving it is hallucinogenic drugs.

Only shamans, however, can traverse the barriers between the human and the supernatural worlds and interfere with the spirits sent to work there by rival shamans. Shaminism has two dimensions: bewitching or cursing, and curing, the opposite sides of the same machination. Both kinds of shaman rely on *natema,* a tisane of locally grown hallucinogenic substances, for the power to penetrate and interpret the supernatural world. *Natema* potions induce the trances that become bridges between the spirit and the real world and are so widely available that anyone can experience their wonders. As a result, about one in four Jivaro men are shamans.

Shamans must prepare themselves for their job and continually test and retest themselves to ensure their power is not waning. It often is, and so they are in a constant state of professional flux. Today's powerful shaman may be tomorrow's feeble failure.

These shamans work through *tsentsak*—spirit helpers or magic darts— who cause illness and death. To summon them, the shaman drugs himself with *natema.* Once they appear, or rather, once he is sufficiently intoxicated to see them, he directs them to enemies' bodies, which they infect with illness or kill.

Shamans learn and teach by apprenticeship. They accept novices, who pay them to reveal their skills and transmit their knowledge. To initiate a novice, the shaman will vomit up a bright substance with spirit helpers embedded inside. He hacks off a piece and the novice ingests it, his stomach aching as he does so. He gulps more *natema* and for ten days lies on his bed dosing himself with the drug.

To fortify himself for upcoming battles with the otherworld, the novice must rest for three months and abstain from sex. If he is too weak to observe this rule, he will be a feeble, unsuccessful shaman. After one month, he will spit up a spirit helper. Now he faces a curious decision. He will long to send this *tsentsak* to bewitch someone, and if he surrenders to this desire, he will become a bewitching shaman. If he stifles this impulse and instead swallows the *tsentsak,* he will become a curing shaman.

Celibacy plays a crucial role in the shaman's future. A bewitcher must maintain it for five months to acquire the power to kill; a healer must abstain for the same length of time to undo the effects of the opposing bewitcher. Shamans of both persuasions require a full year's celibacy to gain truly great power. This prolonged chastity is, however, considered an ordeal that deters many men from pursuing a career as a shaman.

The period of celibacy is not wasted. The novice makes use of the energy he is conserving by collecting the materials he will need in his work: insects, plants, worms, an entire arsenal he can then transform into *tsentsak* to use in his campaigns to hurt or heal.

When the period of abstinence is over and he has amassed all the flora and fauna he intends to use, the new shaman sets about invading his neighbor's body, or alternately, setting spirit helpers to suck out evil *tsentsak* another shaman has lodged inside the ailing person. About five years after his novitiate, when he swallowed his first *tsentsak,* the shaman subjects himself to a sort of performance review. He attempts to bewitch a tree, then decides whether he has lost his potency. If he has, he must repeat the cycle of accumulating enough goods to pay another, more successful shaman to supply him with a new *tsentsak.* More rest, lots more *natema,* energizing celibacy . . . Finally, he is again ready to make a foray into the world of the magical spirits.

Elsewhere in the Amazon, in the valleys of the Río Donachui of northern Colombia's Sierra Nevada de Santa Marta, where the rays of the sun activate the world beneath, the Kogi and Ika people turn to sun priests or *mama*s to guide them through their complicated and confusing world. *Mama*s do not choose their vocation, which is revealed at birth by divination. Infants born to be *mama*s become the wards of a *mama,* who removes them from their parents and takes them high into the mountains for years of preparation.

The *mama* and his wife raise the child in darkness, forbidden to look upon the sun or even the moon when it is full. The child sleeps by day and rises at night to eat and learn all the *mama* has to teach him: songs, dances, legends, divine secrets, the language known only to priests. This lasts nine years and is followed by deeper education in the mysteries of the earth and the sky.

During this period, the novice *mama* eats only simple, traditional food and must never taste salt. At puberty, he is first given meat. After eighteen years of instruction, the young man is taken outside at dawn and for the first time permitted to see the world illuminated. He is ready to receive its knowledge, the next stage in his priesthood.

Until then, the young man who has never seen sunlight has also been prevented from seeing a woman of reproductive age. During adolescence, when he is absorbing the accumulated wisdom of his priestly mentor, the *mama* ensures he is never exposed to temptation. Strictest celibacy is necessary if he is to concentrate all his energy and force on assimilating the vast amount of material the *mama* has spent so many years imparting.

VIRGIN PRIESTESSES OF THE SUN

The *Acllas* of the Incan Empire

The Jesuit fathers who had joined the Spanish military conquerors were shocked and distressed. Incan maidens, they complained, were quite unlike their counterparts in Europe. There, virginity was highly prized in brides, but in the far-flung Incan empire of the Andes, young women were as free to indulge in sexual dalliances as young men. The priests, metaphorically wringing their hands, deplored this behavior. "Women are considered of less value while they are virgins," lamented Jesuit father Costa, "and thus, whenever possible, they give themselves to the first man they find."

Given the Incas' pragmatic approach to sexuality, so different from the Europeans', the divinely inspired institution of the *acllas*—chosen women—is all the more intriguing. At first, these cloistered virgins seem like the Incan version of the vestals. The reality was different. The *acllas'* religious role did parallel that of the vestals, but unlike them, the *acllas* also had significant political impact.

By 1532, when Pizarro and his conquistadors arrived and crushed the Incas into defeat, the Incan empire extended from what is today Quito, Ecuador, down to central Chile. As imperialists ruling a patchwork territory of defeated enemies, the Incas faced constant opposition, ranging from sullen subterfuge to outright rebellion. Their genius was to devise a multifaceted administrative apparatus that melded the diverse conquered cultures into a cohesive political structure and made them governable.

The Inca himself, absolute ruler and descendant of the Sun God, was at the apex of the Incan pyramid. Underneath were his officials, privileged and educated nobles whose positions were hereditary and whose children were sent off to Cuzco, the administrative capital, for formal training. These curacas were highly paid and, unlike the millions of toiling peasants, did not pay taxes.

The cleverness of this system was how it co-opted the intellectual elite and former rulers of conquered peoples. Most curacas belonged to vanquished peoples, so the Incas bestowed on them the enviable status of Inca-by-privilege, which was not noticeably different from Inca-by-birth. The more talented and loyal they were, the more gifts and promotions they could expect.

Through this rigidly hierarchical structure, the Incan bureaucracy imposed its imperial standards and demands—heavy taxes, for example—on millions of Indian peasants. It certainly did not eliminate dissension, but it greatly facilitated the work—and the rewards—of empire.

The parallels between the imperial function of the curacas and the *acllas* are striking, except the *acllas* derived their power from the very different sphere of religion. Religion suffused Incan life. Ritual was paramount, for ceremonies and sacrifices ensured the fecundity of crops and animals and the health of the humans who tended them. The Incan pantheon was crowded, but Inti the Sun God, founder of the Incan dynasty, was among the most important deities.

As the Sun God's earthly descendant, the Inca had unique needs. Unlike other men, for example, he required virgin wives. With typical Incan brilliance, he sent his agent to locate the most beautiful virgins in every province of his dominion. Because Andean women had no predilection for chastity, the girls chosen were sexually immature ten-year-olds.

These *acllas* were selected strictly for beauty, rank, and of course, virginity. Once chosen, neither they nor their parents could object. Henceforth the new *aclla* was alienated from her community and belonged only to the Sun or Inca.

The *acllas* went into training, sequestered in convents called *acllawasis*, under the guidance of *mamaconas*, older *acllas* promoted to this rank. One crucial lesson was that for the rest of their lives, they must remain virginal. Four or five years later, the Inca intervened, reserving some novices for wives. Those he married, though exempted from virginity, were honored and held in awe and respect, "and Indian men and women greatly venerated them."

Most *acllas*, however, were ritually wed to the Sun, and as his wives, shared his divinity and were referred to as "sainted people." Like the Inca's wives, the *acllas* were revered throughout the empire. A popular myth even held that they were so spiritual, they subsisted only on the odor of certain fruit.

Daily life in the *acllawasi* was structured and busy, as befitted the industrious Incas. The *acllas* learned both religious duties and womanly chores, though the latter were always performed in a religious context. The *acllas* spun and wove fine, brightly colored cloth to adorn the idols, to burn in sacrifice, and for the Inca's garments. They brewed chicha liquor and cooked, and at sunrise they said, "Sun, eat this food that your wives have cooked for you." After sacrifices, this food nourished the Sun's priests, attendants, *acllawasi* guards, and the *acllas* themselves. Like the vestal virgins, they also tended the temple fire, feeding it special carved and painted wood.

Older *acllas*—the *mamaconas*—had even greater responsibilities. During a month devoted to special ceremonies, for example, they distributed vast quantities of balls of bread baked with the blood of animals sacrificed in religious ceremonies. They gave tiny bits to all the foreigners in Cuzco and sent larger portions to all the foreign temples throughout the kingdom and to various curacas, as a token of political bonds and their loyalty to the Sun and to the Inca. By this simple ritual with its powerful symbolism, the venerated *mamaconas* demonstrated what a valuable role they played in the Incan political strategy of strengthening the bonds between Cuzco and the provinces.

Their virginity underlay the *acllas'* existence. The *acllawasis* were heavily guarded and the *acllas* could leave them only to perform liturgical duties such as processions. But sexual longings sometimes overpowered them, and the male gatekeepers, the custodians of the *acllas'* virtue, were sometimes the thieves who stole it. Once, four *acllas* had sexual relations with certain men who were posted to guard the *acllawasi* gates. When it was discovered they had broken their sacred vows, the offending *acllas* and their lovers were arrested and the high priests sentenced them all to death. The *acllas* had been warned. They were the brides of the Sun, and their divine husband demanded perpetual celibacy.

Still, it is said that, more than once, an Inca crept into an *acllawasi* and had his way with a virginal *aclla*. After one such tryst, one of the elderly guards respectfully clasped the Inca's robe as he sat in the Square of the Sun. "Inca," he murmured, "last night you went into the House of the Sun and you were with one of his women."

"I sinned," replied the Inca in a muted voice.

The guard went away, satisfied he would not be executed for negligence for not defending the virtue of the *acllas*.

Most *acllas*, however, fell victim to neither the Inca nor their own passions. These women shared "the life of great queens and ladies, and a life of tremendous pleasure and amusement, and they were very highly regarded, esteemed, and loved by the Inca and by the Great Lords." And as unwitting agents of imperial reconciliation and consolidation, the *acllas* were so effective that twice, when Cuzco was sacked, the conquerors spared only two places: the Temple of the Sun and the *acllawasi*, the home of the revered Incan virgins.

In legend at least, the *acllas* live on today. Peruvian descendants of the Incas tell this story. A young *aclla* and a peasant boy became lovers. The Inca learned the maiden had violated her vow of perpetual chastity. He condemned the young couple to a living burial, faceup in the ground.

That night, the elements were so agitated that rivers dried up, stars shifted positions, and all the soil was contaminated, except the earth where the lovers were interred. The priests were alarmed. They decided the bodies should be dug up and burned. But instead of corpses, they found only two tubers lying side by side.

These were the first potatoes. One of the world's best-loved staple foods was the product of divine retribution against a sinning *aclla* and the lover with whom she had violated her sacred vow of perpetual virginity.

*Naditu*s of Babylonia

Babylonia also had cloisters of wealthy women—the *naditu*s—dedicated to Samas, the Sun God. Though many cities had these convents, only the *naditu*s of Sippar were celibate. The *naditu* institution existed in the Old Babylonian era and peaked under Hammurapi and his son Samsuiluna (1792–1712 B.C.). In fact, Hammurapi had a personal stake in it, because his sister Iltani was a *naditu.*

*Naditu*s dedicated to Samas, as opposed to other gods, enjoyed the highest status of any nuns and, like the vestal virgins, had unusual economic clout for women. Becoming a *naditu* was a family decision, never a question of religious vocation. First daughters were designated at birth as future *naditu*s and were "raised to the god" until they entered the cloister.

*Naditu*s were initiated when they were about fifteen years old, always in the first three days of the Babylonian month of Tebet, our December-January. On the first and third days, offerings were made to Samas and his wife, Aja. Day two was a festival in memory of deceased *naditu*s and ended with a banquet. On this day as well, a thread symbolic of her future union with the god Samas was placed on the *naditu*'s hand, and the cloister made her a bridal gift of food, drink, and silver. Additional ceremonies were performed for high-ranking *naditu*s, such as the Princess Iltani, to obtain divine consent before the initiates could be consecrated.

The initiation, like that of the vestal virgins, included important financial transactions between the *naditu*'s family and the cloister. The family provided an impressive dowry consisting of a portion of the father's estate, jewelry, furniture, dishes, looms, cows, and sheep. One *naditu* also received nine slave girls, twenty-four gowns, forty-two headdresses, and even the shroud for her far-off funeral.

Initiated *naditu*s gained the legal authority to administer their own property or they could appoint their brothers to do so. A *naditu* whose dowry did not include property had the right to share her father's estate equally with her brothers.

Oddly, many of the initiates could not enter the cloister until years later, when space became available. It was, in fact, unlike any other cloister. Instead of communal buildings, such as the Atrium Vestae, the *naditus* lived in individual houses within a walled compound. The houses were expensive, and though some *naditus* bought more than one, others had to be content with renting rooms.

The cloister housed one hundred to two hundred *naditus*, and though they were not forbidden to leave, this rarely happened. Several male administrators also lived there, and male relatives visited. Nonetheless, the *naditus* were expected to maintain lifelong celibacy, though the penalty for lapses was less severe than it was for unchaste high priestesses or wives, who were executed. In fact, during Hammurapi's reign, two *naditus* gave birth and were neither disgraced nor expelled from the cloister. *Naditus* who lived outside its walls, however, or who entered a tavern, were sentenced to death by burning.

The daily life of a *naditu* was a mixture of religious and secular activities. She made twice-daily offerings, and on the twentieth of each month, a day sacred to Samas, she had to provide a heartier oblation of meat and beer. She also participated in some of the seven annual festivals and in various religious banquets.

A typical *naditu* also devoted much energy to managing her estate, trading in silver and barley, and renting out fields, orchards, houses, barns, shops, slaves, and oxen. One *naditu,* for instance, supervised 117 employees. Many *naditus* were involved in cooperative ventures, and they often acquired lands adjacent to each other's and co-owned fields.

Though the *naditus* were an economic force, their power and privileged status embittered some male business associates. After business had been transacted, it was not uncommon for these men to turn on the *naditus* and pummel them.

Because the celibate *naditus* remained childless, they were permitted to adopt younger *naditus* or slave girls to care for them in their old age. This was an important consideration, for *naditus* were typically long-lived. The Princess Iltani, for instance, served for over sixty years before "her gods invited her to a feast," the happy euphemism for a *naditu's* death.

The cloistered *naditus* survived for over three centuries. Their dedication to Samas and Aja provided religious security for their families because of their intimate connection to these important deities. The secular benefits were equally significant. Their celibacy was a guarantee against the overpopulation that divided inherited Babylonian estates into puny strips. In return, the *naditus* were rewarded with status and privilege, and financial independence unique among Babylonian women.

SEX-POSITIVE RELIGIONS:
JUDAISM AND ISLAM

JUDAISM

Judaism and Islam are the world's only major religions that neither revere celibacy nor demand it of their faithful. They are rigid about virginity in unmarried women, but afterward, exalt marriage and its erotic dimension. Judaism, the older of the two religions, teaches that because God is just, He would not subject them to pain or suffering without a divine purpose. Such a God, therefore, wants His people to experience all the wondrous aspects of the life He created, including sexuality. However, this does not imply free love. Within Judaism, marriage alone is the proper context for sex.

Once married, Jewish spouses may glory in their sexual relations within certain limits. Masturbation and intercourse during menstruation are prohibited, and the only acceptable orifice for ejaculation is the vagina. Judaism values semen as the means of procreation and consequently deplores its loss as the male's failure to replenish the earth. Sexual intercourse is for pleasure as well as procreation, a belief stemming in part from ancient Jewish medical wisdom that regarded female and male sexual gratification as essential for conceiving a child. As well, sexual relations may continue well into old age, like the relationship between the aged Abraham and Sarah, his elderly wife.

The only form of celibacy permissible is vigilantly monitored female premarital virginity. Indeed, it is essential. Everyone else should be married, reveling in what one authoritative rabbi calls "legitimate physical satisfaction." Marriage has the added advantage of promoting the spiritual salvation of both husband and wife by keeping them from carnal sin. Marriage also advances God's grand design of perpetuating humankind, and it sustains the family as a social unit.

For Jews, fertile marriage had additional blessings. As a people battling exile, defeat, and other calamities, it was, by fusing family and spirituality, a key instrument of unity. This was so well understood that Jewish law specifically outlaws celibacy. Celibacy does more than violate Genesis 1:28's commandment to "be fruitful and multiply and replenish the earth." It is actually a crime akin to murder, by reducing the number of God's souls born onto this earth. After all, the tradition was that each Jewish man should produce at least one son and one daughter. In the Middle Ages, zealous rabbinical courts exercised their powers to force bachelors into fruitful marriage by fining, expelling, or even whipping them.

Jewish interpretations of what happened to Adam and Eve in the Garden of Eden demonstrate how differently Judaism and Christianity viewed sexuality and, by extension, celibacy. Rabbinical literature sees Adam and Eve as a married couple who consummated their union in the Garden. The snake, at first an innocent bystander, sees them doing this and is passionately smitten by Eve. This version of events in the Garden is too early to have been designed to counter a Christian one. It simply represents Judaism's pro-marriage precepts and explains the tone of these ancient blessings: "May you make joyful these beloved companions just as you made your creatures in the Garden of Eden. . . . Blessed are you, O Lord, who makes bridegroom and bride rejoice."

Another blessing exalts the glorious sound of the laughter and jubilation of brides and bridegrooms as they dance and sing with delight: "Blessed are you, O Lord, who makes the bridegroom rejoice with the bride."

Yet despite their religion's wholehearted endorsement of marriage, some Jews were attracted to celibacy. Much Talmudic literature deals with Noah's and Moses' supposed celibacy, and spokesmen for medieval Hasidism, an orthodox Jewish sect, attempted to reconcile the command to procreate in marriage with their misogynist, often demonic views of women. As Jews, they could not proscribe sexual intercourse, but they could and did demand it be performed without lust or physical pleasure. Similarly, they instructed men to care for their wives only as instruments for procreation. An analogy was the rhetorical question about the merchant who needed his horse to ride to market: "Should he therefore love the horse?" Some Hasidim carried this misogyny so far that it led them to celibacy, but this has never been anything but a Judaic anomaly.

A more delicate and ambivalent situation arose when some Talmudic rabbis swore to be celibate so they could devote themselves more completely to the study of the Talmud, the body of civil and ceremonial traditional Jewish law. The most famous example is the second century's Simon b. 'Azzai, who blasted celibacy in his teaching, yet practiced it throughout his life. When colleagues reproached him for this inconsistency, 'Azzai responded, "What shall I do? My heart desireth the Torah; let the world be maintained by others."

In harsh economic times, devoted students of the Torah, the five books of Mosaic law, were permitted to abstain from sex and from their duty to procreate while they pursued their education. A lifelong scholar could even remain unmarried so he could dedicate his life to his studies. But in direct contrast with Christianity, Judaism tolerates no monasticism, and the notion of celibacy remains a foreign and unwelcome one. As one ancient rabbi expressed it, "We are holy and more virtuous for we bear children and multiply seed in the world."

ISLAM

From the perspective of celibacy, Islam shares much with Judaism. Islam's prophet Muhammad had several wives and joyously indulged in sexual intercourse with them. "O you young men!" he exclaimed. "I recommend sexual intercourse to you." This was no single errant comment. Muhammad also said, "No house has been built in Islam more beloved in the sight of Allah than through marriage" and "Whosoever likes to follow my tradition . . . should know that marriage is from my tradition." Indisputably, loving women through erotic contact is fundamental to Islam.

This exuberant delight in marital love stems from the Koran and its story of creation. Allah created man from dust, earth, drops of semen, and congealed blood, which He, too, possessed. The knowledge that semen was also a divine attribute led to the view that marriage is the highest good. In fact, Muhammad expressly opposed celibacy and urged all men capable of marriage to marry.

Islam does not, however, countenance unrestrained licentiousness. Certain guidelines are provided, such as the stricture, shared with Judaism, to abstain from sex during a woman's menstrual cycle and to observe purification rituals before resuming it. For "truly Allah loveth those who turn unto him and loveth those who have a care for cleanness."

Islam's ideal is the responsible fulfillment of sexual urges. Attraction between the sexes is seen as divinely given and natural, "an absolutely universal divine wish," and "love is a mimicry of the creative act of God." The mystery of sexuality is equally blessed, the culmination of God's work. Even orgasms are wonderful phenomena, and Islam has succeeded in integrating "the orgasm into the transcending self."

Like the Jewish sages, the Prophet also condemned celibacy and monasticism. When the wife of Uthman bin Maz'ûn, his close friend, complained her husband had become an ascetic who fasted and abstained from sex, Muhammad was furious. He did not even wait to put on his slippers but snatched them up in his hands and raced unshod over to Uthman's house. "O Uthman!" he cried. "Allah did not send me for monasticism. . . . I fast, pray, and also have intimate relations with my wife."

Women as well as men are encouraged to marry. A Muslim holy man rebuked a woman who had become an ascetic so she could win favor in God's eyes. Asceticism was not the route to pleasing God, he assured her. The Prophet, in fact, regarded single people as the lowest ranked of all, whereas "one who marries has already guarded half of his religion, therefore he should fear Allah for the other half." In other words, because husbands and wives can legitimately indulge their erotic longings, no obstacles remain to obstruct their pursuit of spirituality.

One Muslim sect that defies these orthodox teachings is the Sufis, who preach and practice celibacy. The Sufis are mystics who liken women to Satan and evil and therefore shun them. However, they are minor, albeit well-known, exceptions to the rule.

In both Judaism and Islam, celibacy is a little-known and alien concept, and their theologians regard it with deepest suspicion. Virginity in unmarried women is fiercely upheld, but marriage is extolled as a virtue, with joyous, fulfilling procreation its prime function. The God of the Jews and the Muslim Allah both laid this down as a fundamental truth.

CHAPTER 5

Celibacy to Conserve Semen

So strict is the Catholic prohibition against onanism—casting sperm upon the ground, as the biblical Onan did—that on the one hand, nocturnal emissions have always been a major concern, while on the other, masturbation, coitus interruptus, and most birth-control devices other than abstinence are unmitigated sins. The Church even refuses the marriage sacrament to men who cannot ejaculate. Eunuchs, therefore, may not marry. For the same reason, nonconsummation because of impotence constitutes grounds to annul a marriage.

The nature of semen has long been of obsessive interest to philosophers, medical men, social reformers, religious thinkers, and athletic trainers throughout the world. It is a key concept in two of the world's largest religions, Christianity and Hinduism. As we have seen, Hinduism emphasizes the crucial importance of conserving semen, linking this to spiritual and moral development and with physical health.

The properties and essence of semen have also underscored medical thought, from Hippocrates in the fourth century B.C. on through William Acton in the nineteenth. For more than two millennia, athletes, too, have fretted as they struggled to honor their coaches' strictures against preperformance sexual activity, for few able-bodied young men have dared risk defeat by rashly expending their vital energy.

This chapter considers the importance of conserving semen—a uniquely male form of celibacy—from several perspectives: medicine from ancient to recent times; the nineteenth-century Moral Purity movements in the USA and Canada; Indian wrestlers caught up in anticolonialist, nationalist fervor; and the famous brahmacharya experiments of the great Mahatma Gandhi, who tested the state of his sexual indifference through intimate and intensely emotional relationships with a series of devoted young women.

TOTUS HOMO SEMEN EST

Conserving the Vital Life Force

Historically, male sexuality has been perceived as both a moral issue and a physical phenomenon. The moral plane involves passion and lust, seduction and conquest, lack of restraint and weakness. The physical manifestation has two principal players—penis and semen—which act out their ejaculatory themes of fertilization, satiation of pleasure, and onanism.

What is semen? In ancient times, the Chinese, Indians, and Greeks defined it as an essential substance or humor. Greek doctors refined this and taught that semen, intestinal juices, and lymph were in a category of fluids different from blood, mucus, yellow and black bile, and that good health depended on a proper equilibrium among them.

Hippocrates, the great medical authority, supported sexual restraint but not abstinence and taught that chaste women suffered dreadfully because their womb, dry from lack of semen, traveled restlessly throughout their body. When a woman with hysterical symptoms visited a Hippocratic doctor, he would immediately examine her genitals, assuming the cause to be an errant womb protesting lack of sexual activity. The prescription, of course, was intercourse and pregnancy.

Hippocrates described another female medical condition—menstrual-blood blockage, which caused madness and suicidal thoughts because it pressed against the heart, the center of consciousness. Again, intercourse was the prescribed remedy, and married women confirmed the benefits of intercourse because it eased the pain of their menstrual cramps. For women, therefore, virginity and celibacy were bad and intercourse was good.

Hippocrates had a different message for men, whom he advised to retain their semen, which energized their bodies. Sexual activity, though salutary for women, was detrimental to men because it drained away their semen. He cited as warning a sexually overactive young man who had actually died, raving mad, after a simple stomach ailment escalated to fatal illness, so drastically had he weakened his body by recklessly depleting his stores of semen.

The practical significance of this was not entirely clear, because what was beneficial for women might be detrimental for men. In fact, Hippocratic medical wisdom merely reflected Greek contempt for women as alien creatures who needed domestication—marriage and motherhood—by their male superiors. In practice, this dichotomy presented no real problems. Male health was the top priority, so men initiated sex or chose celibacy on the basis of their personal needs and beliefs. If they concluded that sex—the ejaculation of sperm—was beneficial to their health, they engaged in it. If they were more interested in the benefits of retaining semen, which conserved strength, they opted for celibacy.

So rooted in "science" was this sperm-related celibacy that contradictory points of view could lead the (usually short-term) celibate to trade abstinence for indulgence. Celibacy was, after all, simply another tool, like diet, exercise, massage, and bathing, to improve health in a fanatically health-conscious people.

By the early second century, creeping asceticism was reflected in medical writings. Galen, the great second-century Greek doctor who supplanted Hippocrates as the medical genius, reached conclusions that clashed with previous medical wisdom. Galen's personal preference was virginity for both men and women, but as a doctor, he worried about the disorders celibacy could cause. Specifically, a glut of surplus sperm, like putrefying garbage, could cause health problems such as slothfulness and listlessness. His prescription? Sexual activity. This advice applied equally to women, as Galen believed they, too, produced sperm. However, he warned that sex was tiring because sperm consisted of pneuma or vital spirit, and orgasms warmed the blood, a debilitating process. Young men who overindulged in sex, for example, dried out their bodies and required humidification. In Galen's reasoning, sex as a chore was the alternative to health-conscious chastity. Balance and extreme moderation were the operative principles.

Nocturnal emissions, the inadvertent wet dreams that plagued men from St. Augustine to Martin Luther, were also an integral part of this fluid discussion, as the liquid leaked was identified as semen. Reactions ranged from outright condemnation to acceptance. Soranus, physician to the emperor Hadrian, for instance, simply noted that "in general, nocturnal emission at the outset is not a disease . . . and results from a longing for sexual enjoyment . . . or, on the other hand, from continence or a long interruption of sexual activity."

Monastic wisdom (based on long experience) held that two or three nocturnal emissions per month were morally acceptable, mainly because they seemed to be unavoidable. This religious perspective, of course, did not factor in sperm's value as an essential bodily fluid.

The most bizarre interpretation of sperm's role in the sexual act came from St. Augustine. Through Adam's semen, he wrote, the entire human race had inherited a nature irrevocably marred by sin. The mechanism for this tragic collective flaw? "The nature of the semen from which we were to be propagated." Adam's semen was "shackled by the bond of death," and so every human born through semen is contaminated by sin. Only Christ, conceived without semen, is devoid of sin. In Augustine's mind, semen was inherently evil, a virulent poison that has infected the world since the time of the Fall.

At their core, these discussions and arguments about sexuality and celibacy were based on notions of sperm as a vital substance. Moral and social issues—the dynamics of relationships, for example—did not arise, and celibacy and its opposite were seen purely as prescriptions for health, little different from a course of exercise or a modified diet. This focus on semen is common to most societies and has had an enormous influence on male decisions about celibacy. (This was in blinding contrast to contemporary Christian debates about celibacy, which scorned this carnal perspective for a totally spiritual one.)

Over a millennium later, medical science had not advanced much past the Greek doctors. Its underlying premise was that a "vital force" or "life force"—a notion Galen would have felt comfortable with—controlled the human organism and could unite or enervate its parts. Some thinkers interpreted this vital force as magnetism, electricity, galvanism, animal heat, nervous energy, or nerve force; others preferred simply the vital force. What all systems had in common was the belief that vital energy transmitted life itself and that sexual energy was the great conductor.

One of the most important exponents of these two main schools of thought—vital force and electricity—was the Swiss doctor Samuel A. Tissot. Tissot's 1758 classic treatise on onanism, which inspired medical thought until the late nineteenth century, was a volte-face from the eighteenth-century medical notion that orgasm was healthy, and celibacy was therefore unsound and extreme. Tissot argued that semen was unadulterated, concentrated vital energy that the blood secreted to generate new life, a concept encapsulated in the phrase *totus homo semen est*. Semen, Tissot explained, is "the Essential Oil of the animal liquors . . . the rectified spirit, the dissipation whereof leaves the other humors weak, and in some degree vapid. . . . [The] loss of an ounce of this humor would weaken more than [the loss of] forty ounces of blood."

At the core of this theory was the crucial belief, common to Hippocrates, Galen, and Greek philosophers, notably Pythagoras, that each body has only so much vital fluid or energy and each ejaculation taps some of the precious stock. Other related theories taught that sperm preserved in the chaste body was reabsorbed, enriching the blood and revitalizing the brain. Obviously, sexual restraint was the only logical solution, for if a sexual wastrel expended all his life force through excessive sexual intercourse—always defined in astonishingly frugal terms; for example, more than once a month—he would then have exhausted his life's supply, and progressive and fatal debilitation would inevitably follow. (Even the radical, mid-nineteenth-century American free-love movement recommended once every two years as a safe formula.) This is why not only sex but also wet dreams and masturbation were condemned. They dissipated precious ounces of semen, draining away the finite stock each man was equipped with. Celibacy, therefore, was presented not merely as a moral choice but a physiological necessity.

Across the Channel, the late-nineteenth-century English debate on sex—in which sex was understood as the ejaculation of sperm rather than one dimension in an amorous relationship—was also framed in quasi-medical terms liberally mixed with moral dicta, and also with metaphors from contemporary economic models—the "thrift in semen" concept. Chastity was in vogue as part of the respectable gentleman's gear, with John Locke and William Pitt held up as models for lifetime celibates.

Some sternly austere medical writers taught that even nocturnal emissions were polluting. "Men of scrupulous conscience . . . look on them as tokens of a prevalent impurity of mind which they must cure," declared Sir James Paget. The well-known Dr. T. L. Nicols helped contribute to the wet dreamers' guilt by defining their dreams as manifestations of disease, 90 percent of the time as a result of masturbation. "Hundreds of young men are driven to suicide by this disease," he reported, no doubt with grim satisfaction. "A man who has a vivid sense of right and duty of refraining from sensuality, and preserving his own purity of mind and body, and chastity of all women, will do so even in his dreams."

This sort of chastity was close to impossible to enforce, of course, even for men who subscribed to its moral premises. Linking morality to a purely mechanical process cheapened it and, worse, made it ridiculous, as when, for instance, determined or neurotic young men attempted to thwart their undisciplined sleeping moments by tying string around their penises to prevent involuntary erections.

Respectable gentlemen were encouraged to adopt a regime that was not quite ascetic. Dr. William Acton, a British proselytizer for the ideal of respectable chastity, recommended daily baths, a hard bed, a bland diet without alcohol, intellectual stimulation, religious study, and rigorous physical exercise. The latter was incorporated enthusiastically into school curricula and idealized as Muscular Christianity.

In late-Victorian England, proponents of respectable gentlemanly chastity elaborated a nonmedical rationale, based on a current economic model. It proceeded from a general idealization of self-control in all spheres and argued that, like fiscal continence, sexual continence was good and could be achieved through self-control and sublimation, preferably by industrious use of time. The result of this sort of celibacy would be the accumulation of capital. Incontinence, on the other hand, was bad and provoked too early marriages and poverty.

Based on these premises, it followed that celibacy—until appropriately late marriage, after enough wealth had been amassed to buy a decent house—

should be an integral part of England's new industrial society. After all, weren't sexual continence and industry linked as values in a single system? The same vaunted thrift that had built England's industrial empire could, applied to an individual's limited supply of semen, stabilize society and produce fewer but superior citizens.

A homier, rural-nineteenth-century version of the gospel of thrift in semen transmogrified it into seed, the agrarian metaphor common in biblical times. Semen as seed, however, had quite different connotations from semen as a limited biological force. Seeds rot if unplanted, and poor farmers extended this analogy to sperm, useless if unused. Moreover, if the seed did not root and grow, it was equally useless. Similarly, rural men typically married women already pregnant with their sperm. Thrift in semen for the middle classes made no sense to laborers and farmers, who put their trust in swollen-bellied fertility from seed.

In North America as in Europe and India, with its own rigorous and sophisticated brahmacharya system of conserving semen, various social movements developed in response to the urgent proselytizing of eloquent crusaders. The Male Purity Movement, as it was known everywhere, rolled over the decades until, like a hoard of precious semen, it, too, was finally spent.

DAVY CROCKETT AND THE MALE PURITY MOVEMENT

Ah, Victorian-age America, what deliciously convoluted sexual repressiveness you inspire! And for once, young bachelors are its targets rather than the usual victims, the swish-skirted women who, if not Very Good, are Very Bad. But down to business. Let us meet an errant bachelor, before he finds salvation and we can no longer recognize him.

Let us call our young man Davy—he'd like that—for Davy Crockett is his idol. Our Davy knows his namesake well, through *Crockett's Almanacs*. In fact, he pants with envy as he reads these ranting, illustrated yarns about the cunning, hustling, womanizing, boozing daredevil who fled his mean pa's switch and has lived thrillingly ever since.

But our Davy does not live thrillingly. He hails from his father's shrinking farm in rural New England and he drifted into this port city to hire out his unskilled services. The year is somewhere in the first half of the century, before the devastating Civil War, and Davy has been finding brute labor in a factory. He shares miserable lodgings with several of his chums and, at night, hating to go home, wanders through the scramble of gaslit streets.

Sometimes, rarely, Davy sups in a restaurant. He finds the food prickly spiced and queer and washes it down with unaccustomed strong coffee. Then, pulling out a plug of tobacco, he muses as he chaws, spitting his phlegm far onto the filthy sidewalk like the contempt he feels for his life back home and his prospects here in the city. If he has enough money left, he might wink back at some Very Bad misses and who knows? He might even succumb without a struggle to the blandishments of their whorish seductiveness.

Fortunately for Davy, redemption is at hand. Put aside your *Almanacs*, young man, and pick up instead some edifying broadsides. How about Sylvester Graham's *Lectures to Young Men on Chastity?* Or S. B. Woodward's *Hints for the Young?* Or perhaps William Alcott's *Young Men's Guide?*

This trio of Graham, Woodward, and Alcott were among the founders of America's Male Purity Movement, dating from the 1830s when Davy and hordes just like him began to pour into New England's cities. The chaos, formlessness, and surging changes in this new America horrified these men. Paternal control over sons was eroding and with it, the attendant lessons in discipline, manhood, and morality. Apprenticeships, the traditional job-training system, were disappearing. Davy and his pals, unskilled, unattached, owning nothing and with nothing to lose, seemed like a threatening and dissolute urban mob. The Male Purity friends suspected that they—the students, salesmen, clerks, and tradesmen—also masturbated.

The Male Purity Movement did not, because it could not, force all American males into premarital celibacy. It did, however, influence many—how many we shall never know—and was the only concerted chastity campaign ever to focus exclusively on bachelors. However, a parallel development directed to women preached purity in the context of piety, submissiveness, and domesticity, with motherhood the only possible object of sexual intercourse—postmarital, of course. Pure women deserved the pure males the reformers were attempting to create.

The Male Purity Movement's propagandists preached temperance, vegetarianism, moral reform, and chastity before marriage. Alcohol and rich, spiced foods overstimulated and led to eroticism, and eroticism, often self-administered, corrupted, caused mental illness, disease, and the decay of the entire society.

Male orgasms were especially terrifying, "convulsive paroxysms attending venereal indulgence . . . [causing] the most powerful agitation to the whole system that it is ever subject to. The brain, the heart, lungs, liver, skin and the other organs feel it sweeping over them with the tremendous violence of a tornado," wrote Graham. From his appalled perspective, the earth not only moved, it heaved with the force of cyclonic devastation.

Despite this, Graham viewed sexuality as not entirely bad. It was merely a rational and, he believed, humane way to channel limited resources. Rather than squandering the vital force of semen on a few moments of sensual pleasure, much better to channel it into what Canadian historian Michael Bliss calls "creative sexual repression." Semen should be expended solely for propagating children and otherwise stored up as energy to be directed to the higher things in life.

However, because their ovulation cycle left women at the mercy of their impulses, they were helpless to resist men's cajoling. Useless, then, to enlist women in the struggle. Instead, go right to the source—Davy and his kind—with the clarion call of male celibacy. Fear of disease and insanity was part of the message and so was the recommended bland diet—"the diet that cured sex"—unseasoned vegetables and wholesome, taste-free bread and biscuits, Graham crackers, made of Graham's new flour, and Dr. John Harvey Kellogg's breakfast cereal—cornflakes, then advertised as a healthsome aid to subduing eroticism, now (more accurately) touted as a healthsome aid to sound nutritional balance and good, plain, time-honored taste.

Masturbation was roundly condemned; it was said to be dangerous to its perpetrator and caused "insufferable mental and physical problems" such as infant paralysis and rheumatism. It led to a terrible disease, spermatorrhea, which slowly, dreadfully, and inexorably killed the masturbator. Masturbation was also credited with causing homosexuality—indeed, was often a euphemism for it. Graham and others, for example, believed young men who showed each other this particular skill often ended up as each other's sexual partner and refused to marry women.

Davy was, the literature assured him, "thoughtless, rash and unwilling to be advised." If only he would listen! If only he could grasp the danger and accept that he must modify his coffee-guzzling, spice-jolted, homoerotic life. From the dangerous age of adolescence, he should spend fifteen years in celibate Christian courtship, preparatory to marriage. When he finally wed his frigid, Very Good wife, he could indulge himself sexually with her about twelve times per annum. More frequent ejaculations put him at risk of early death because each ounce of lost semen equaled four ounces (thirty-six fewer than Tissot's estimated forty) of precious blood. Nor was this once-monthly ration a privation, so boring did marital sex become after husband and wife "become accustomed to each other's body, and their parts no longer excite an impure imagination."

The American Male Purity Movement rolled through the decades, converting some bachelors, many more parents, a host of other reformers, and briefly, physicians. By the late 1860s, when our Davy had mercifully survived the Civil War and was now a married man carefully monitoring his sperm, the crusade had peaked, though young men were still encouraged to retain their semen. Outside his austere home, Davy II would hear little about its teachings. But Davy III, and even IV and V, might well be converted anew if they became Boy Scouts and were persuaded by Scouting's celibacy-promoting, masturbation-bashing tracts and other literature.

Pure Books on Avoided Subjects, as some booksellers discreetly advertised them, approached this most delicate of subjects from male and female perspectives: *What a Young Boy Ought to Know*, *What a Young Man Ought to Know*, *What a Young Husband Ought to Know*, and *What a Man of 45 Ought to Know* were the male offerings, written by Lutheran minister Sylvanus Stall. Masturbation was denounced as a terrifying curse that caused weakness and ill health, "and in extreme cases imbecility and insanity . . . as the inevitable result." Masturbators, lacking strong bodies, faced consumption and certain death.

To impress upon young readers the deadly consequences of autoeroticism, Stall reported how some parents dealt with the problem: tying their children's hands behind their backs or to bedposts, or even immobilizing them in straitjackets. Boys had to understand what genitals were for: "only for throwing off the waste water of the system. . . . Handling them at all will hurt them and make them sick."

Stall also warned against nocturnal emissions. "Few men can suffer emission more frequently than once in two weeks without serious physical loss," and so suitable physical and mental exercises and thoughts should be invoked to end the problem forever. Cold morning showers, coarse toweling, restricted meat and spices, and frequent defecation were highly recommended.

Even marriage could not be regarded as a license for sexual expression. After all, wedding or not, the groom had only so much semen, and when that was gone, he faced physical erosion. Once a week was the maximum permissible, once a month was better, and best of all was celibacy except for sexual coupling for the sake of conceiving children. Though men would have difficulty with this, God in his wisdom had made women passive and sexually indifferent, ruling out mutually irresistible passion.

Women were instructed similarly. *What a Young Wife Ought to Know* admonished that too much sexual activity makes a marriage "little better than licensed prostitution," and explained, "There is a vast amount of vital force used in the production and expenditure of the seminal fluid. Wasted as the incontinence of so many lives allows it to be, and prostituted to the simple gratification of fleshly desire, it weakens and depraves. Conserved . . . it lifts him to a higher plane of being."

At age forty-five or thereabouts, sex was to be completely terminated. Enough semen had been lost, and any further droplets could "ill be spared." Fortunately, sexual desire would wane and die, so celibacy would be fairly easy. The new celibates would feel "the grateful sense of relief [that] the stress of the sexual impulse is gradually passing away."

The Male Purity Movement, and the related Moral Purity Movement, which also included women, cut an ideological swath in the fabric of American society that resonates to this day. Its fervor and authoritarian tone were captivating. The prestige of many of its crusaders and its temporary endorsement by much of the medical profession lent it great credibility. Its Christian base and its rigorous formula for a pure life appealed to those distressed by the turbulence of changing America. A century and a half later, echoes of its urgent message resound in the agenda of the Moral Majority, the Promise Keepers, and True Love Waits.

JOHN HARVEY KELLOGG'S DIET TO CURE SEX

Snap, crackle, and pop they didn't, for Dr. John Harvey Kellogg (1852–1943) designed his cornflakes to soothe and numb all taste buds, from tongue to toe. The successful physician, a Seventh-Day Adventist greatly influenced by Sylvester Graham, had such a strong aversion to sex that he spent the nine decades of his life without ever indulging in it. "The reproductive act," Kellogg declared, "is the most exhausting of all vital acts. Its effect upon the undeveloped person is to retard growth, weaken the constitution and dwarf the intellect."

Kellogg never risked this. Even during his honeymoon, he and his new wife spent a chaste but bonding six weeks revising his books, *Plain Facts about Sexual Life* and *The Proper Diet of Man*. Afterward, Kellogg never faltered. If he felt any temptation, he must have staved it off with one of the many sex-killing tools he urged on others: a spiceless, wholesome diet, routine exercise, hard work, daily bathing, and religion. To this he added a personal, unpublicized fillip—a cold-water enema, administered each morning after breakfast by one of the orderlies at his prestigious Battle Creek Sanitarium. Perhaps, speculates his biographer John Money, this was symptomatic of klismaphilia, "an anomaly of sexual and erotic functioning traceable to childhood, in which an enema substitutes for regular sexual intercourse. For the klismaphile, putting the penis in the vagina is experienced as hard work, dangerous, and possibly as repulsive."

Money may be wrong about klismaphilia, but Kellogg's relentlessly sound diet should have ruled out sluggish bowels as an explanation for why he needed these continual intestinal irrigations. Perhaps he was simply frightened of constipation, which, he taught, caused "local excitement" as unexpelled feces pressed on the genitals.

What is certain is that Kellogg was a brilliant medical thinker and practitioner whose published views on sexuality strongly influenced a generation of his peers. He came late onto the Moral Purity scene, but his contributions to it refined and elaborated on earlier theories, notably Sylvester Graham's.

Kellogg's views on the causes of unchastity were particularly far-ranging.

Heredity was one. Others were exciting stimulants and condiments that "irritate the nerves and derange the circulation," working directly on the sexual organs by increasing the local supply of blood to the genitals. These foodstuffs worked bad miracles. They caused even pious visiting clergymen to metamorphose into lechers who victimized their female hosts after the latter inadvertently served up the instruments of their own seduction in the form of "the richest cake, the choicest jellies, the most pungent sauces and the finest of fine-flour breadstuffs." Who could resist such temptation? "Ministers are not immaculate," Kellogg warned his readers.

Other obstacles to continued chastity were more obvious than tasty tea cakes. Tobacco and liquor, for instance, transformed male youth into a "veritable volcano of lust," while pornographic books promoted obscenity. Idleness led to depravity, especially in the form of loafing in barrooms or lounging on sofas reading romance novels.

Women's clothes were particularly dangerous. Excessive love of fashion doomed young women to sacrifice their virtue to men who could keep them suitably attired. Corsets forced the flow of blood downward "into the delicate organs of generation" and excited the genitals. Heavy clothing below the waist generated "unnatural local heat." To Kellogg, a tightly corseted, thick-skirted woman was an ideal candidate for nymphomania.

Other problematic activities were waltzes, which stimulated the passions and provoked unchaste desires; superheated rooms; overly long confinement of students in a sitting position; most forms of public amusement; "lascivious day-dreams and amorous reveries"; and young boys' overtly filthy stories. Kellogg also slammed women's veiled remarks as hiding "in loose insinuations more smut than words could well express."

In his own long life and marriage, Kellogg practiced what he preached. After one pretty young woman jilted him, he unexpectedly proposed to and married Ella Eaton, a kind and intellectual nurse-in-training at his sanitarium. The honeymoon produced only clean copies of his manuscripts, and soon afterward, the chaste, childless Kelloggs announced they planned to open their home to needy children, including several Mexicans, blacks, and Puerto Ricans. Forty-two children later, the Kellogg family was also a societal experiment: Could Kellogg love, and moral instruction salvage, even disadvantaged, abused youngsters from slums? Sadly, the answer seemed to be no. Most of the successful junior Kelloggs came from good family backgrounds, while most tragically hopeless cases slouched forward into equally dissolute adulthood.

Ella and John, their virginal foster and adoptive parents, lived together in their mansion, publicly respectful of each other, privately affectionate, perpetually celibate. Much besides forty-two little people bound them together:

their committed Christianity; their obsession with proper vegetarian eating and food preparation; their profound interest in child-rearing. After two decades of marriage, however, Ella fell ill and effectively withdrew into her own rooms, dying over twenty years later without ever having emerged again into the Kellogg world. Nothing suggests her virginity tormented her any more than his did John. What is certain, however, is that the Kelloggs constructed a unique marital relationship based on mutual respect, shared ideals and goals, and an unshakable will to avoid sex, and they died as celibate as they had been born.

THE POWER OF SEMEN IN SPORTS

Movie idol Robert De Niro in the movie *Raging Bull* is body-locked in a no-holds-barred sexual skirmish. He and his sparring partner, his seductive young wife, are loving every minute. But he has a date in the boxing ring, and he has warned her they must abstain from sex for weeks beforehand. This time, though, as they writhe together on their marriage bed, it looks as if he will weaken. Then, at the last minute, he pushes away and escapes into the bathroom. There he takes up a pitcher of ice water and, wincing slightly, pours the contents down over his bulging penis. In the next scene, we see him in the boxing ring, cheered on by shrieking spectators, savagely pummeling his opponent.

Raging Bull is the movie rendition of the very real life of boxer Jake LaMotta, and this incident pitting him against sexual arousal and temptation is a drama that has been played out between male athletes and their lovers since antiquity. Eubatus of Cyrene, who at the Ninety-third Olympiad won the stade, the ancient equivalent of today's hundred-meter sprint, and became the fastest man alive, could have sympathized with *Raging Bull*. Eubatus' prerace sexual nemesis was the stunning hetaera or courtesan Lais, who was so enthralled by the Olympic star, she set out to seduce him. Eubatus was as leery of antagonizing her as of sacrificing victory by sleeping with her. He wriggled out of the impasse by agreeing that, after the race, he would take her home with him, a promise he acquitted—deceitfully—by carting off her portrait instead. But had the chaste (though married) young runner unleashed his power-laden sperm into a lover rather than his performance, he would never have succeeded in capturing the ultimate prize.

Athletes are—and always have been—notorious for the lengths to which they will go to enhance their performance. Rigorous training, special dietary regimes, regulated sleeping patterns, performance-enhancing substances such as steroids—all have been integral parts of athletic training programs. Celibacy is another common feature of a sportsman's discipline, necessary to avoid the debilitating consequences and wasteful emotions of sex. Usually, its advocates promoted it as a way to store up precious semen, the vital bodily fluid that determinedly chaste men could transform into a God-given, performance-enhancing substance. This was true for the ancient Greeks, the Victorians, and the Cherokees, among others, and it remains true for Indian wrestlers and the football players, soccer stars, boxers, and other male athletes who prefer to stockpile their precious semen rather than yield it up in a single self-indulgent spasm.

THE GREEKS TRAIN SOUND MINDS IN CHASTE BODIES

Eubatus was a superb athlete who "knew" what all his competitors "knew"—that semen was a vital fluid and releasing it weakened the body. He may not have studied the great philosophers and medical writers who dispensed this wisdom, but he and his cohorts had absorbed their teachings. So had their coaches, who appreciated the specific advice the philosophers gave to sportsmen. These trainers applied their knowledge to fashioning programs that would maximize performance. In the fiercely competitive world of athletics, where winners were their city-state's superstars and victory or defeat carried ominous international significance and symbolism, the stakes were enormously high.

Greek athletes were living testaments to sound minds in sound bodies, revered (when they won) by their countrymen and admired (even in defeat) by philosophers, who lauded their immense discipline and self-control as qualities to be emulated. Their celibacy, in particular, was esteemed. Plato, for instance, raved about Olympic victor Ikkos of Tarentum, who "because of his desire to win, his ability, and courage in his heart along with self-control . . . never touched a woman, or a boy either, in the entire course of his training." The same was also true, Plato added, of several other notable sportsmen, despite the fact they were citizens of less refined states than Athens and "possessed much stronger sexual drives."

In ancient times, Olympians were so intent on maintaining celibacy that some practiced *ligatura praeputii,* tying back the foreskin. Such men looked peculiar, as Dionysus remarked to them in Aeschylus' *Theori Isthmiastae:* "Cum decurtatas, tanquan murium caudas, mentulas vobis video"—I see your pricks cut short just like the tails of mice. "You've practiced hard . . . you haven't been slack but have trained properly." Presumably Dionysus spoke with authority, for except in the earliest years when they wore shorts, Greek athletes took pride in competing naked.

Their vaunted celibacy was not the only strategy Greeks employed to excel in sports. For centuries, the month before competing, they observed an austere and unvaried vegetarian diet of cheese and figs. They also exercised, rested, and maintained a schedule comparable to those of ambitious athletes everywhere. But their semen-rich celibacy was especially important, and as they worked out and competed, they could feel it powering their muscular strength, making them, as one first-century expert commented, "bold, daring, and strong as wild beasts." They were equally aware that sexually active athletes, even those with superior physiques and skills, were so weakened by losing their semen that they became "inferior to their inferiors." After all, it was "semen, when possessed of vitality," that made men manly, "hot, well-braced in limbs, hairy, well voiced, spirited, [and] strong to think and to act."

The power of semen in athletics, as in life, had various theoretical sources. From the sixth century B.C. until well into the early centuries of Christianity, Greek philosophers and medical thinkers constructed theories about semen and the weakening effects of losing it. The Pythagoreans and Kroton medical-school thinkers located semen in the brain and spinal cord, which meant that discharging it would specifically undermine those two vital areas of the body. Democritus' pangenesis theory took a ubiquitous perspective and saw sperm in all body parts, so that excreting it would dilute a man's overall strength. The third major concept was hematological and propounded by writers from Aristotle to Galen. Sperm was created from the best elements of the blood, and blood might even be the conveyer of each mortal's spirit. The obvious effect of losing such an indispensable fluid was to severely undermine the whole man. No matter which of these precepts a coach or his athletes subscribed to, the end result was the same: celibacy was essential.

A doctrinal subtext was the Greek belief that sex with a woman was both debilitating and contaminating. This alone was reason enough for an ambitious young man to abstain. Sex with boys lacked this flaw, but as it caused seminal loss, it, too, was dangerous. Even nocturnal emissions drained their involuntary victims. In his work *On Athletics,* philosopher Philostratos counseled wet dreamers to exercise cautiously and rebuild their strength, "since they now have a deficit in their system."

Heroic Greek athletes were often known for their feats of celibacy as well as their triumphant races and matches. Ikkos of Tarentum, who won the Olympic pentathlon in 472 and afterward established himself as a coach, was commended by Plato for his sexual abstinence. Cleitomachus of Thebes, who won three Olympic crowns for wrestling and the *pankration,* a unique ancient sport combining aspects of wrestling and boxing, and who in 216 B.C. surpassed even these achievements by winning three events on the same day, was famous for his chastity. Cleitomachus could not tolerate even a ribald story and would spring up and out of the room if someone began to tell one. In fact, he was even repelled by the sight of dogs coupling in the street.

The great interpreter of dreams, Artemidorus of Daldis, concluded his book on them with the cautionary tale of an athlete who dreamed he had castrated himself and subsequently achieved glorious victory. The athlete construed this to mean he should remain celibate and so abstained completely. As a result, he won many more prizes, but when he grew cocky and indulged in sex, his winning streak ended and he "retired ingloriously" from the competitive stage.

The triumphant Greek athlete, splendid in his chaste nakedness, was also the unwitting fountainhead of a legacy that endures to this day, the belief that conserving semen will enhance strength and improve performance. Ironically, the athlete had only to control his urges for women and boys until the race was done, when he was given free rein to indulge his lust. The average Greek citizen neither aspired to celibacy nor admired it, except as an instrument to hone the state's finest sportsmen. Champions such as Cleitomachus, who abhorred sex at any time, were exceptions to their culture's rule. So were certain philosophers and their acolytes, who idealized abstinence. Women, excluded from this sperm-derived perspective except as agents of lasciviousness, could only look on as the lovely Lais did. But over two millennia later, when the Olympic torch signals the opening of yet another Olympiad, lusty but abstinent young competitors are modern disciples of the ancient Greek legacy.

THE VICTORIANS EXERCISE MUSCULAR CHRISTIANITY

The young American Davy we met earlier knew—or at least he should have—about the great dangers of self-indulgence, the worst of which were masturbation and its awful cousin, illicit sexual intercourse. Davy also treasured—or at least he should have—his semen, that precious store of God-given fluid he had to dispense frugally enough to last his entire virile lifetime.

This was all the negative side of the semen ledger: how to avoid debilitating/exhausting/weakening his manly self. Even the prescribed regimen—wholesome and spiceless food, purity of body and soul—was designed to dodge trouble. But how was Davy to energize himself? Well, he could throw himself into a sport, which by midcentury, was being touted as an ideal way to stimulate the physical man. One delightful consequence of sport was that it would not merely invigorate or reroute a man's sexual longings but recharge his strength at the same time.

This ideology of the "spermatic economy"—budget your sperm and spend it wisely—endured for over half a century. A man's body, unlike his finite volume of sperm, could thereby become a renewable resource. He would be a walking, flexing, pulsating specimen of Muscular Christianity.

From 1850 to 1890, schools in both North America and England made playing games an important part of their curriculum, and the obsessive role of sports in these cultures dates from that period. It became a major instrument in male bonding and in teaching men to be men. It also inculcated in them the notion that they were biologically superior to women and to other, effete breeds of man. (Unlike the Greeks, however, the Victorians were too modest to prove this by competing in the nude.) Sperm played an equally vital role in this sports-mindedness, partly through seminal sublimation, partly through an unexplained physical process.

Sports, this semen-efficient activity, became associated as well with moral asceticism—temperance, in the nineteenth-century sense of avoiding all evils such as liquor and women. "What are you running here, a Sunday school or a baseball team?" demanded Chicago Cubs star player King Kelly of puritanical manager A. G. Spalding. Spalding's answer might have been that the two were inseparably connected, moral purity and sportsmanship being two sides of the same coin. In fact, he hired Pinkerton detectives to tail his players and report on their extracurricular movements. At playgrounds, schools, and professional ball fields everywhere, the sportsman's code applied: no tobacco, booze, gambling, womanizing, or ungentlemanly behavior. Underlying these strictures was the most outlawed of all sins—onanism, casting irreplaceable sperm into a moral void.

In 1889, the Brooklyn Bridegrooms baseball team put their collective celibacy into the headlines when they adopted it as a talisman and won that year's pennant. This was, admittedly, a desperate measure for a desperate team. But despite the above-average number of newlywed team members who gave the Bridegrooms their nickname, the players cooperated and avoided their wives until after the play-offs. Pitcher Bob Carruthers went so far as to decline visiting his newborn baby, presumably a consequence of his preseason unchastity.

The ideology of Muscular Christianity faded slowly. Today, it still permeates some sports, notably boxing and soccer, and some football teams, all manned by players seeking every possible physical and psychic advantage. Everywhere in the world, men have pondered their physical makeup. Often, the result of such meditations has been the conclusion that sperm is an immeasurably important substance and that it plays a role in men's activities from the cognitive to the carnal, of which sports is arguably the most widespread and beloved.

THE CHEROKEES PLAY BALL

The Cherokee game of ball play—*anetsâ* in the Cherokee language—was so popular that in the state of Georgia, local tradition holds that the Cherokee won large land tracts from the Creeks in a ball-play wager. Many place names testify as well to the game's prominence in the southern states: Ball Flat, Ball Ground, and Ball Play, for example.

Anetsâ was a fierce game similar to lacrosse, played with a deerskin ball that the naked players caught and threw with two sticks. The sticks were under three feet long, with a wooden stem and a string or thong bowl, not unlike tennis rackets. The object of *anetsâ* was to score goals, and one American anthropologist who observed it played likened it to a mélange of baseball, football, and the historical game known as shinny. The rules of *anetsâ* permitted almost anything short of slaughtering members of the opposing team, and strategy often included maiming the leading rival players. This might mean, for instance, purposely smashing an opponent onto the ground to break his bones. The game continued despite injuries, until twelve goals had been scored. During this time, usually from sunrise to sunset, the athletes ate nothing and drank only a sour concoction made from green grapes and wild crab apples. Afterward, the losers surrendered their often substantial goods as they settled their pregame wagers, and the winners performed rituals to alleviate their rivals' vengeance.

Much rested on the outcome of the ball play, whose opponents were usually rival bands or settlements. Anything of value to the group might be gambled on their team's victory—guns, blankets, horses, even land. Because of this, preparations began weeks before games and involved shamans, tribal elders, and ceremonial dancers, as well as an intense training regimen. Players were the tribe's most athletic young men, because *anetsâ* required speed, nimbleness, and muscularity, a formidable combination. And—shades of ancient Greece—fame as a ballplayer was almost as enviable as prowess as a warrior.

The athletes went into training usually four weeks before the season opened in September, after the corn harvest. Training consisted of secret ceremonies and ritual incantations, bathing and fasting. The men could not eat rabbit, a timid beast, or frog, whose bones are fragile, or any other creature of unmasculine, feeble, or fainthearted nature. They had to forgo hot and salted food. *Anetsâ* was so manly a sport that if a woman merely touched one of the ball sticks or one of the players, her contaminating powers guaranteed her team would lose. For the same reason, players had to maintain complete sexual abstinence. In earlier, precolonial times, the penalty for violating this taboo against women was sometimes death.

The antiwoman aspect of *anetsâ* extended to pregnancy. The player husband of an expectant mother was banned from the field, for like his wife, who carried the child they had both created, he was too heavy and sluggish to perform properly during the grueling game.

The players observed other important pregame rituals. They underwent a torturous scratching ordeal in which a shaman's assistant gouged them nearly three hundred times with a seven-toothed comb fashioned from the splintered leg bones of a turkey. The blood was then rinsed off and the player was supposedly energized for the brutal bout of *anetsâ*.

Descriptions of *anetsâ* paint a picture eerily similar to that of the ancient Greek Olympics, with rigorously trained men staking their nation's prestige on the outcome of the sport. The proud nudity, the brutally tough nature of the events, the overriding importance of the game to the entire tribe, and the mandatory celibacy invoke the Greek games as much as the Cherokee.

This is not to say, however, that the two were identical. The Cherokee had no sperm-based ideology, but probably saw it as a potent fluid like blood and womanly excretions, capable of rendering great harm to its originator if a conniving enemy used it in magic spells. But the absolute celibacy required before these crucial *anetsâ* matched the Greek's, as did their mutual certainty that contact with a woman ensured defeat. The Cherokee power of semen is, in other words, of a special, unrelated order, but the single-minded chastity it demanded earns it a place in this record of celibacy in sports.

TODAY'S CHASTE ATHLETES

Muhammad Ali struggled to remain celibate for six weeks prior to each fight—when you don't get sex for a while, you get mean and angry and it makes you a great warrior, he explained. The Greatest is not alone among modern athletes in espousing chastity for the sake of his sport, though his reasons hark back more to the ancient Greeks than to the modern Muscular Christianity of A. C. Green's Athletes for Abstinence and the Life Athletes. These movements include scores of professional and Olympic sportspeople who pledge premarital virginity and moral purity, and stars such as Andy Pettitte of the New York Yankees pledge the Life Athlete Commitment, which reads:

1. I will do what is right, even when it is difficult.
2. I will give myself only to that special person that I marry as my partner for life.
3. I will respect the lives of others, especially the unborn and the aged.
4. I will not quit or make excuses when I fail. I will try again.

"We exist," the Life Athletes proclaim, "to survive in a world where the misuse of sex has hurt many of us. We don't want disease, divorce and death to keep us from what we want in life." This return to abstinence is a moral stance in the age of AIDS and differs fundamentally from the traditional view of sexual activity as an impediment to athletic performance. Like their Muscular Christian forerunners, the Life Athletes and Athletes for Abstinence strive for celibacy until they are legally married.

Traditionally, coaches and their athletes have believed that sexual activity undermines sports performance. "It is well known," two experts wrote in 1995, "that athletes in the United States are told to abstain from sexual intercourse prior to athletic competition." Several studies, including the first one, conducted in 1968 by William Masters and Virginia Johnson, have investigated the relationship of sex and performance and have concluded that there probably is none. However, the notion of moral purity or at least superiority may in fact boost an athlete's self-esteem and hence motivate him to excel. By the same token, knowledge of an opponent's ascetic regimen may spook a less-disciplined rival into underperforming as a form of conceding moral defeat.

The abstinent-champion theory is both die-hard and long-lived. Coaches still advocate it because they believe sex devours energy and debilitates, reducing concentration, muscle strength, aggressiveness, and the will to win. They also rate premarital sex and masturbation as fractionally more enervating than marital sex. The more strenuous and competitive the sport, the more its coaches tend to hold this view. Boxing, weight-lifting, football, and soccer coaches are much more likely to enforce celibacy than those overseeing yachters and golfers. This attitude carries over onto the playing field. College footballers are more likely than baseballers to credit celibacy for better play, and to believe that it increases physical strength by preserving energy.

In soccer, the world's most popular sport, celibacy is often an important training tool. To this day, soccer fans in Peru blame their country's 1982 World Cup loss, 5–1 to Poland, on those Peruvian players who broke the ban on sex the night before the game. Prior to the 1998 World Cup, coaches from around the world admitted they enforced the ban on their players. Brazilian wives and girlfriends were ordered to stay away and not to distract their men's attention during the tournament. For much the same reason, Chilean and Scottish players agreed to a "no-sex" time-out. Only England's coach, Glenn Hoddle, stood alone and, in the name of creating a happy atmosphere, encouraged pregame sex by flying in wives and girlfriends. This was in striking contrast to 1966, when England enacted the celibacy rule—and won its first and only World Cup title.

This determinedly celibate thrust in soccer, which draws on an increasingly discredited belief in the power of semen, is more than an anachronistic marvel. Soccer is one of the world's greatest common denominators, and its appeal converts new devotees, both spectators and players. In Europe and South America in particular, soccer players are akin to deities, often surpassing movie stars and other celebrities. Their professional careers are documented and their personal lives scrutinized for the edification of their voracious, adoring fans. On top of this, players collectively, as representatives of their nation, bear enormous responsibility. By winning the World Cup, they bestow glory on their compatriots as well as themselves. Conversely, by losing, especially early on in the tournament, they heap shame and humiliation on their co-nationals' heads; losers returning home may be hooted at or even pelted with debris. Given the importance of their sport, it is no wonder soccer players and coaches grasp at any method that promises to help them. Celibacy, a time-honored athletic tradition, is an obvious possibility.

Coaches also justify celibacy as the solution to the problems of sexually active players. Lovemaking, they remind naysayers, involves relationships and their commitments and complications. Sex takes time and energy and is often associated with alcohol and late nights, or in Casey Stengel's words, "It isn't sex that wrecks these guys, it's staying up all night looking for it." These aspects of active sexuality in themselves can be major hindrances to an athlete's conditioning and workouts and ultimately, his actual performance.

Implicit in all these debates—for celibacy is not swallowed whole by all the hardy men on every team—is that intercourse is especially taxing for males because they lose semen. But this does not mean that women athletes, who are in no such danger, are given different guidelines. At least one study has found coaches consider women vulnerable to sexual encounters because they experience them as emotionally draining. Men, on the other hand, suffer physical consequences. The very existence of their semen, therefore, holds men hostage to its extraordinary power.

The astonishing spread of soccer keeps celibacy in the media limelight. Other sports figures employ it as well, usually weeks before a competition. Boxers traditionally do so. Some footballers abstain at least the night before a game and feel strengthened and energized. For these sportsmen, celibacy is both discipline and ritual. Psychologically, it empowers them, and they experience this physically. It also lends a certain élan to their lives, an idealism and superiority of purpose appropriate for folk heroes. The historical theories of the power of conserved semen are now mere echoes, but in their temporary and self-conscious celibacy, these men have embraced the legacy of the legendary athletes of yesteryear.

So, in a very different way, have the men and women of the purely moralistic school of celibacy, the Life Athletes and Athletes for Abstinence. They, too, revere sports as a higher calling and speak with deepest respect of "an athlete's heart," a pure entity that evokes self-sacrifice for higher goals in all senses of the word. Their inclusion of women eliminates at a stroke the invocation of the magic of sperm, as well as the misogyny that underlies much of the raison d'être of sporting celibacy—manfully dodging the erotic snares of the weak and wayward gender. These inheritors of Muscular Christianity hold each other's hand with fraternal chastity and mutually pledge to lifetimes of virtue and sexual purity.

INDIAN WRESTLERS

A continent away, the power of semen retains its hold. In India today, wrestlers are so dedicated to conserving and enriching semen that they are fervently celibate. "Celibacy is the paramount means by which a wrestler establishes his character. He is a disciple of celibacy," wrote a leading exponent of modern brahmacharya, a key element of Hindu religious thought.

Indian wrestling—*Bharatiya kushti*—is tremendously popular and quite unlike its rigged, showboating, and institutionalized American counterpart. *Bharatiya kushti* is a sport-oriented way of life in which celibacy and self-control are absolutes. Wrestlers—*pahalwans*—are a kind of brahmacharin, ascetic, righteous, and extraordinarily healthy men devoted to seeking a level of selflessness that will permit them knowledge of pure truth. However, even more than other brahmacharins, *pahalwans* are deeply concerned about losing semen, which Hindus believe contains the essence of life. Even the loss of a slight dribble during involuntary nocturnal emissions alarms *pahalwans*. Semen is fundamental to their athletic vocation and they shudder at losing one drop, which they equate to sixty drops of blood. It is not just one more fluid rather a distillate of blood, marrow, bone, and other bodily substances and so incorporates within itself the very nature of human existence.

"A person should guard his semen just as a jeweller guards his most valuable diamonds," explains one Indian authority. Another elaborates with similar imagery: "We emphasize brahmacharya—never to lose one's semen. It is the essence of power; the essence of strength; the essence of endurance; the essence of beauty. . . . Brahmacharya gives something special to the lips, a special light to the body, a shine to the eyes, and something special to the cheeks."

The *pahalwans* have an elaborate system to manage this semen retention, which is important because, being so big and strong, they are thought to have a correspondingly larger store of it. When they wrestle, they wear a *langot*, a tight G-string that trusses the genitalia up between the legs. They think, speak, and as much as possible, hear no evil and keep their distance from women. They force their minds away from lascivious thoughts and confine their fellowship to like-minded men. They practice austerities, the most obvious one being celibacy. They chant and pray, for faith in the supreme deity underlies every spiritual success.

The *pahalwans* have busily structured lives. Never sit around and daydream, they admonish newcomers, for daydreaming can easily lead to circumstances that deplete semen. Masturbation, a massive waste of semen, is strictly forbidden. So are unbidden wet dreams, which can be eliminated by a series of measures as diverse as washing one's feet in warm water before bed, reflecting on the Supreme Being, and urinating when the urge comes.

Diet, too, is crucial because a *pahalwan* must do more than conserve his semen; he must recharge and enrich it. Milk is at the heart of his nutritional regimen, and the stereotype of a wrestler is a burly man who can guzzle bucketfuls of milk. Men drink milk to intensify their virility—Hindu myths describe milk, especially cow's milk, as an ideal liquid—and, as they gulp, assume they are adding to their body's reservoir of semen.

Ghee, clarified butter, also produces semen, and strong semen at that, the stuff of physical, moral, and spiritual strength. Indeed, it is a more important source of semen than milk. "Just like ghi fuels the dias [lamps] of religious worship, so does semen fuel the fire of one's own body," explained one wrestling guru.

Pahalwans also devour vast quantities of almonds smashed into a thick paste and mixed with milk and honey. After practice, this is a fine pick-me-up. Some also pulverize and eat hashish, which calms or erodes passion. Otherwise, they eat only lightly spiced food, avoid pickles and chutneys that stimulate sensuality, and abstain entirely from tobacco.

Pahalwans are teetotalers because liquor is antithetical to semen. "Wrestlers are uniformly vehement in their advocacy of temperance," writes scholar Joseph S. Alter. "They literally cringe at the thought of so much energized semen—and all that it represents by way of the nation's potential energy for growth and development—going to waste."

The importance of sperm-retaining celibacy to a *pahalwan* is obvious. For this reason, some writers recommend wrestling as a way to maintain celibacy, and as the majority of wrestlers are young men in their late teens and early twenties, guilt at erotic thoughts and deeds drives many to take up the sport. As well, they are motivated by the widespread conviction that brahmacharya is so powerful it can transform even the frailest and sickliest boy into a champion.

The actual wrestling takes place in an *akhara,* a simple gymnasium with an earthen pit for wrestling, a floor for exercise, a well, and a temple or shrine to Lord Hanuman, a celibate god. The *akharas* are free to all men but outcasts and Muslims and, of course, women, who are forbidden to enter the premises. The manager/owner is a guru who instructs his disciples in wrestling and devises a total life program for each one, including exercises, food, and rest. He also counsels them spiritually.

Pahalwans regard themselves as "extraordinary men who do extraordinary things to and with their bodies." Before independence, wrestling was an important channel for nationalist ideology. Now it is a physical activity with rules similar to Olympic wrestling's, as well as a spiritual quest by men pledged to physical strength and competence, celibacy, duty, obedience, honesty, and humility. The role of religion is so pervasive that *akhara*s have shrines or temples on-site, and *pahalwan*s are compared to the Hindu god Lord Hanuman, as he struggles with his demonic enemies.

*Pahalwan*s do not live at the *akhara* but at home and also either attend school or work. Ideally, a *pahalwan* rises at 3 A.M.—in reality, most are up by 4:30 or 5 A.M. A glass of water and lime juice is followed by forest or jungle ablutions and careful defecation, which guarantees total control over semen. At 9 A.M. the *pahalwan* arrives at the spacious and breezy *akhara,* works out, wrestles, and performs a litany of routines before he finally leaves for the crowded bustle of his other life. Ideally, *pahalwan*s would rest, eat, and sleep the rest of the day, but in practice, this is impossible.

The *pahalwan*'s lifestyle is both austere and complex, integrated as it usually is into mainstream Indian life. At its core is the special, powerful wrestler's celibacy, which seeks not merely to retain semen but to create it through carefully structured diets. The self-discipline of a regimented daily life; the guidance of a wrestling guru and the companionship of *pahalwan*s or other brahmacharyas; a strict adherence to the regulations forbidding sensual thoughts, autoeroticism, wet dreams; and daily exercise and wrestling matches—all are carefully designed to achieve the strictest celibacy and, with it, the augmentation and enrichment of semen, the living quick of human existence.

BRAHMACHARYA AND THE POWER OF SEMEN

Celibate Selflessness

By itself, the Hindi word *brahmacharin* probably conjures up little more than ascetic Hindu men in loincloths avoiding women's eyes and abstaining from sex. But pair it with Mahatma Gandhi and suddenly a kaleidoscope of images flashes onto our mental screens. Ironically, the most startling is of a tiny, gnarled, jug-eared old man lying naked next to a haremlike procession of lovely, trusting, birthday-suited, and very young women: elder statesman Gandhi, testing his vow of brahmacharya.

Whether we see this as salacious old goatery or delightful innocence, it is an unforgettable introduction to India's complex ideal of brahmacharya. Brahmacharya means much more than mere abstinence. Traditionally urged on married couples as, in Gandhi's words, the "only noble and straight method of birth control," it embodies a lifestyle of intense self-control in which the rational mind reduces all the carnal appetites to nothingness. Only thus purified can a man—for brahmacharins are, by definition, men—attain the state of selflessness necessary for the realization of truth.

Brahmacharya is based on traditional thought, including medical writings, and depicts successful brahmacharins as virtuous men with supremely healthy bodies purified, paradoxically, by conquest of their carnal desires through an austere lifestyle, exercise, and celibacy. The overall fitness this produces owes much to the brahmacharin's semen, the essence of life, which is no longer wasted but retained as an internal resource. Gandhi lamented that, as a sexually active husband and then a brahmacharin plagued by nocturnal emissions, he had spilled so much semen that he regarded himself as "an incomplete brahmachari. . . . This shortcoming of mine is known to the world."

"The whole purpose of brahmacharya," concludes American anthropologist Joseph S. Alter, "is to build up a resilient store of semen so that the body—in a holistic, psychosomatic sense—radiates an aura of vitality and strength." Unchaste men, to the contrary, were morally weak, incapable of leading. In Gandhi's view: "Chastity is one of the greatest disciplines without which the mind cannot attain requisite firmness. A man who is unchaste loses stamina, becomes emasculated and cowardly. He whose mind is given to animal passions is not capable of any great effort."

But awareness of semen is only part of the brahmacharin's path to realization of truth. The steps along the way are simple to enunciate, murderously difficult to master. Gandhi's instructions for achieving it are fourfold. First, understand that brahmacharya is necessary. Second, gradually control all the senses, especially through fasting and a careful diet that must never include animal flesh. Third, consort only with clean companions, both human and literary. Lastly, pray.

The focus of brahmacharya being spiritual enlightenment, bodily celibacy alone does not suffice. A true brahmacharin will not even entertain erotic thoughts. That is not to say such fantasies will not insinuate themselves. The trick is to refuse to focus on them. "Victory will be ours in the end," Gandhi wrote, "if we non-co-operate with the mind in its evil wanderings." Hence his controversial brahmacharya experiments.

GANDHI'S WOMEN

"Celibacy . . . is like walking on the sword's edge, and I can see every moment the necessity of continued vigilance," the struggling Gandhi confessed. The world's most famous and flamboyant proponent of celibacy was not blessed with a propensity for it. As a youth and even an old man, he was tormented by his raging sexuality.

Gandhi was the spoiled, favorite, and youngest son of a provincial prime minister. At thirteen, he was married to Kasturbai Makanji, also thirteen, whom he at first regarded merely as "a strange girl to play with." Two years later, coached by his sister-in-law, he initiated sexual relations and, despite Kasturbai's obvious "disinclination," gave full vent to his adolescent lustfulness. Later, with repentant hindsight, Gandhi confessed that the urgency of his sexual desire had blinded him.

Three years after Gandhi's marriage, his father fell deathly ill. The young Mahatma was at the sickbed, massaging the ailing man's legs, when his uncle suggested he take a break. Gandhi eagerly complied and raced to force himself on his pregnant wife. In the midst of their lovemaking, a servant knocked at the door to announce his father had just died.

This incident permanently scarred Gandhi, who always blamed his lust for depriving him of rendering some final service to his dying parent. His guilt deepened when, months later, Kasturbai delivered a stillborn baby. Gandhi was devastated. "What other outcome could there have been?" he lamented, convinced the infant's death was linked to his own sinful carnality.

Two years later, Gandhi set off alone for a three-year stint in England, fortified by a pledge to his beloved mother that he would shun wine, women, and meat. At least once he was severely tempted, by a fun-loving landlady, but managed to flee intact. Meanwhile, he sought spiritual wisdom from many sources, including Christian clergymen, and reflected deeply on this verse from the Bhagavad Gita:

> If one
> Ponders on objects of the senses there springs
> Attraction; from attraction grows desire
> Desire flames to fierce passion, passion breeds
> Recklessness; then the memory—all betrayed—
> Lets noble purpose go, and saps the mind,
> Till purpose, mind, and man are all undone.

Back in India, Gandhi's chastity continued because his irrational jealousy of his wife so agitated him that he sent her back to her parents for a year. Furthermore, he spent much time with a spiritual guru whose views on celibacy profoundly influenced his impressionable disciple. However, Gandhi resumed marital relations until he set sail again, this time for South Africa. He begged Kasturbai not to follow him immediately, arguing that in India, she could live splendidly on the South African wages he would send her. The real reason, however, was his longing to live chastely, without the wife who, quite unintentionally, inflamed his sexual passions.

However, Kasturbai was not interested in separation and joined her husband in South Africa, where he had founded an ashram or commune based on brahmacharya, ahimsa (nonviolence), and *satya* (truth). Gandhi's first shaky vow of abstinence, in 1901, was succeeded in 1906 by a final vow of lifelong celibacy: brahmacharya. A life of guilt-ridden reflection on the effect of his lustfulness on his father's and his stillborn son's deaths, powerful cultural traditions celebrating celibacy, familiarity with Christian asceticism and other influences, including Leo Tolstoy's metamorphosis in *The Kreutzer Sonata*—all culminated in this decision.

Gandhi was fully aware of all Tolstoy's hedonistic vices, his partying and mistresses, his dependence on alcohol and tobacco. When the great writer renounced them all to follow an ascetic, prayerful life, Gandhi was one of his most sympathetic supporters. And when Tolstoy failed to sustain this lifestyle, Gandhi refused to condemn him. Instead, he reminded Tolstoy's critics that only the man himself could know how terribly he had fought in his struggle for spiritual purity or how many times he had triumphed against temptation.

(Ironically, *The Kreutzer Sonata* was Tolstoy's marriage manifesto in principle only. Sadly, he could not sustain the celibacy he preached. His wife becoming pregnant again was "the real postscript to *The Kreutzer Sonata*," she wrote sardonically. But Gandhi understood Tolstoy, who would be eighty-two years old before he felt free of lust.)

Brahmacharya, regrettably absent in the Tolstoy marriage, greatly improved the Gandhis'. Kasturbai was compliant and the Mahatma stopped blaming her for sabotaging his resolve to be celibate. "I could not steal into my wife's heart," the formerly autocratic husband wrote, "until I decided to treat her differently than I used to do, and so I restored to her all her rights by dispossessing myself of any so-called rights as her husband."

Gandhi's brahmacharya was Hindu-derived, modified by Christianity and his own precepts. He longed to be "God's eunuch," a Christian metaphor. He also linked celibacy with fasting or special food, his lifelong obsession. "I have found from experience that the observance of celibacy becomes comparatively easy, if one acquires mastery over the palate."

At one time or another, onions, salt and other condiments, sugar, dates, currants, and milk were all banished from the ashram kitchen. Inhabitants of the ashram spent what seemed to some of them a disproportionate amount of time discussing food, namely what at any given time they could or could not eat. "Sometimes I think it would be better if we just ate anything and did not think about it at all," one of them remarked. Fasting was also frequently observed, an important prop in the battle to quell sexuality.

Gandhi found that battle even more taxing and discouraging than the fight for Indian independence, his final mission after he returned to India. Yet he routinely violated the customary brahmacharya precaution of avoiding temptation by avoiding women. Instead, he actually invited it by his ongoing intimacy with women he welcomed into his ashram and by the quagmire of emotions he stirred in their hearts.

For instance, Gandhi liked to stroll with his favorite young women, his arm draped around their shoulders. The jealousy among his devotees was ferocious, and they tallied scores and quarreled among themselves. An outstanding new disciple, Prema Kantak, hurt by the other girls' taunts—"Bapuji does not put his hands on your shoulders!"—was devastated to discover the ashram rule: Bapu could only embrace girls under sixteen years. She was seven years over the age limit. She confided her pain to Gandhi, who advised her to ask permission from the ashram superintendent. Prema recoiled. "Why should I hanker after your hand so much that I have to go and get permission?" she snapped.

But one night she heard Gandhi fall down near the toilets, weak from diarrhea due to a food experiment. Prema supported him back to bed, his limp body sagging against hers. Afterward, the ashram rule was forgotten and Bapu often took his evening walk with Prema, who once kissed his hand and cried, "The hand that has shaken the British throne is resting on my shoulders!"

Like her rivals—and they were legion—Prema suffered the anguish of competing for the beloved Bapu's favor. In *Intimate Relations*, psychoanalyst Sudhir Kakar analyzes the nature of Gandhi's tactics. He strove to intensify the intimacy between himself and these special women but immediately withdrew if one of them responded by requesting a closeness he felt crossed an invisible line he had drawn between them. He then tried to control the rebuffed woman's pain or withdrawal from him so the relationship would continue. The consequence of this constant emotional turmoil, in the women and sometimes even in Gandhi himself, was that the emotional ambience in the ashram often reached fever pitch and produced frequent explosions.

Yet Gandhi tolerated, indeed fostered, this emotional climate, all the while stressing how integrally linked brahmacharya and ashram life were and how crucial for the development of women.

> A woman, as soon as she enters the Ashram, breathes the air of freedom and casts out all fear from her mind. And I believe that the Ashram observance of brahmacharya has made a big contribution to this state of things. Adult girls live in the Ashram as virgins. We are aware that this experiment is fraught with risk but we feel that no awakening among women is possible without incurring it.

Some of these adult women experienced their lives differently. Prema left to found another ashram only after years of emotional turmoil, victim of Gandhi's relentless manipulations—gentle, mocking rejection alternating with cajoling invitation. She accused him of emotional seduction, luring people into his trap. Gandhi denied her charge, but added that even if he were to do such a thing, she should remain self-confident.

Another casualty was Madeline Slade, an aristocratic Briton who descended on the ashram, and Gandhi, with unstoppable enthusiasm. Before long Gandhi began to respond, and for most of their twenty-four years together, he and Mira, as she was called, were, except for their chastity, much like ill-fated lovers. When the tensions became unbearable, Gandhi would send her away. Mira, unable to endure these heartbreaking episodes that Gandhi preferred to think of as spiritual struggles, would suffer nervous breakdowns. Then she would reappear at the ashram, only to be banished once more.

Gandhi softened her exile with tender words in letters indistinguishable from lovers' missives everywhere. "The parting today was sad, because I saw that I pained you. I want you to be perfect woman . . . to shed all angularities," he wrote after one such tumultuous parting. After another: "I could not restrain myself from sending you a love message on reaching here. I felt very sad after letting you go." Another day, on a postcard: "This is merely to tell you I can't dismiss you from my mind. Every surgeon has soothing ointment after a severe operation. This is my ointment . . ." In a letter, he lamented, "I have never been so anxious as this time to hear from you, for I sent you away too quickly. . . . You haunted me in my sleep last night and were reported by friends to whom you had been sent, to be delirious, but without any danger."

So went Gandhi's exquisitely refined handling of the women in his ashram harem. His was brahmacharya-style womanizing. Prema and Mira led the pack of his favorites, both intelligent and resourceful women he would/could not bring himself to relinquish or rather liberate from the steely bonds of his love. This, despite the cost to their—and certainly his own—serenity. And to his wife's, for feisty, loyal, and loving Kasturbai had to witness it all, and despite her own intimacy with Gandhi, she remained rightfully jealous of all her husband's women.

Gandhi's understanding and practice of brahmacharya was clearly unorthodox. Though committed to controlling his bodily senses, he felt no need to restrain his passionate emotions. He permitted himself intense relationships with many women and never attempted to sublimate his feelings, which he openly reflected upon and articulated. Instead, he cultivated and kindled love in the yearning breasts of a succession of appealing acolytes, then dampened it down whenever it threatened to rage out of control.

Gandhi's famous experiments with young, naked women were actually not as dangerous as his relations of the heart, which kept the ashram's emotional climate at boiling pitch and promoted bickering resentment and divisive rivalry. Gandhi did not see it that way. Instead, he boasted to Prema about how he had resisted the temptation to make love with thousands of women who had lusted after him. God had saved the women and Gandhi, too.

Gandhi considered his sexually unconsummated trysts as feats of moral strength that compared favorably with those of men who had the same inclinations but merely avoided women. Other brahmacharins controlled only their bodies and not their passions and were filled with lust even though they shed no semen. He, on the other hand, practiced purity of thought as well as sexual abstinence.

Gandhi's famous experiments, involving strictly sexual temptations, were not inconsistent with one ancient Indian tantric custom that trains the celibate to perform the sexual act without desire or ejaculation of precious semen. However, his experiments were much closer in design to the strategies employed by illustrious Hindu holy men of old, in particular Ramananda, who successfully tested himself with two lovely temple prostitutes. Alone with them in an isolated garden, Ramananda would strip them, oil and bathe their bodies, then dress them again, all the while remaining unaroused. And long ago, the philosopher Viswanatha had managed, by concentrating on his guru's instructions, to lie chastely with his wife.

Seen in this light, Gandhi's experiments seem like twentieth-century repetitions. They began after he complained of nightly "shivering fits" and requested that various young women—teenaged virgins or newlyweds—sleep next to him to warm him. Sushila Nayar, who later became his physician, masseuse, and secretary, was unaffected by her nights next to the man they affectionately called Bapu. But Abha Gandhi, Bapu's great-nephew's sixteen-year-old wife, had a different experience. She had to remove her clothes so Gandhi could judge whether he, like Ramananda, was sufficiently chaste to be unaffected by her nakedness. Abha's husband was so distressed he offered himself in his wife's place; he, himself, would keep the old man warm at night. But no, Gandhi wanted Abha for his brahmacharya experiment.

Another teenager, distant cousin Manu Gandhi, bathed and shaved Gandhi, slept with him, monitored his physical condition during his fasts, and gave him enemas. Manu reveled in the status these intimacies earned her and the edge she acquired over other women jockeying for position in Gandhi's affections. Gandhi, meanwhile, congratulated himself on his unresponsiveness to the warmth of her body next to his and the sensation of her hands as she ministered to him. Manu headed the list of nubile young guinea pigs in the brahmacharya experiments.

As modern India's greatest sage and leader, the man who inspired millions in the fight for Indian independence, Gandhi's brahmacharya was not the personal eccentricity or curiosity it might have been in another man. He and his countrymen saw it as an essential and appropriate instrument to ready himself for a crusade. Obliterating the carnal desire for sex, stimulating food, wealth, and possessions was an essential step in this process, and Gandhi took it. In consequence, he achieved brahmacharya, which freed him to operate in the highest political sphere and, in particular, to develop the concept of militant nonviolence that inspired India's fight for independence, won him the title of Mahatma—Great One—and singled him out as a role model for independence and social-justice movements worldwide.

Gandhi's celibacy was diametrically opposite to that practiced by the ancient Christians he also admired. Unlike them, he refused to renounce intense, intimate relationships with attractive women, many of them openly in love with him. Gandhi's was a unique, personal version of Indian brahmacharya, in which the power of the mind dominates the body. Sexual abstinence is only one dimension. Because self-control is paramount, testing to see whether that control is truly in place makes logical sense. Gandhi certainly justified his demand for alluring young bedmates on these grounds, though from any perspective, he was guilty of exploiting them. His emotional abuse of Kasturbai, Prema, Mira, and a throng of other wronged women was, however, most egregious of all.

Despite his unacknowledged mistreatment of the women he loved and was loved by, Gandhi's celibacy had implications for the amelioration of the condition of women in general. Living in intimacy with as many of them as he did, including his wife, Kasturbai, he grew to empathize with them on many issues. He remarked, for example, that mentally, he had become a woman. He argued strongly against marriage between old men and young women, so common in India, and suggested debauchery as an apt word to describe it.

Gandhi also credited his wife's early "resistance" to his domineering ways with instilling in him a great respect for women. "If they will only learn to say no to their husbands when they approach them carnally," he said. "I want women to learn the primary right of 'resistance.'" He was not advocating celibate marriage but rather a desexualized relationship in which women's primary function was motherhood. Indeed, in idealizing motherhood, perhaps because he had so adored his own young mother, Gandhi implicitly denied women's sexuality, despite daily evidence of it at the ashram.

The concept of brahmacharya itself, of course, does not and cannot relate to women, who have no semen to conserve. Gandhi believed, however, that sexual chastity was an option for them, though most were destined to be wives and mothers. Gandhi's unusual version of brahmacharya, however, is instructive not so much as a model for abstinence but as an example of a tool for political action. A pale analogy would be the public hunger fasts endured to protest certain conditions. An individual transforms his lifestyle—permanently, in Gandhi's case, or temporarily, in the case of hunger strikers—for the sake of a principle. The difference is that brahmacharya is achievable only after great struggle, and even a lifetime of effort is no guarantee of success.

The philosophy, tradition, legends, and value system underlying brahmacharya elevate it to the highest level of human endeavor. The strength it injected into Gandhi's psyche and the enormous prestige it brought him among his countrymen are its most wondrous dimensions. His coupling of an elaborate philosophy of militant nonviolence with brahmacharya also affirmed the power of a celibate lifestyle in the creative process—in this case, the birth of a political movement.

SEMEN AS PATRIOTIC ELIXIR

In modern India, brahmacharya has a new agenda. It is rooted in the same traditions and philosophy but it is no longer essentially the pedagogical principle it once was. It was never conceived as a general moral rule. "What was good for one was by no means food for all, particularly when it came to abstinence," Joseph S. Alter argues persuasively in "Celibacy, Sexuality, and the Transformation of Gender into Nationalism in North India."

In North India, brahmacharya has become a postcolonial, anti-Western concept, specifically designed to counteract Indian modernization, including the slackening of religious observance and the current rampant sexual activity attributed to Western influences. One of its proponents writes despairingly of the situation he hopes the new brahmacharya will rectify:

> Because the youth of today are destroying their semen they are courting the worst disaster and are daily being condemned to hell. . . . Mother nature stands, stick in hand, watching their abominable behavior, and for every drop of semen spilled she lashes out and strikes their vital organs. . . . Now tell me, what future do such people have?

Brahmacharya literature is directed at teenaged boys and college students, and school bookstores carry it alongside textbooks. It does not gather dust. The young men read it and relate the truth of its message to celibate men they admire—the popular wrestlers whose training regime centers on their practice of brahmacharya, an important element of Hinduism's long and respected ascetic tradition.

This literature, unlike what existed in Gandhi's day, includes brahmacharya manuals with explanations about celibacy's benefits and explicit instructions about how to control desire and maintain good health. The wrestlers provide excellent examples of how conserving semen strengthens both character and body, enabling the brahmacharin to perform otherwise impossible feats.

The new brahmacharya has a scientific tinge and concentrates on the physiology of male sexuality. The books "analyze the mechanics, hydraulics, and chemistry of sex with particular emphasis on the various properties of semen, since semen is regarded as the most essential fluid of life," Alter writes. A modern writer enthuses, "To tell the truth, semen is elixir."

The second most important factor is a proper diet, avoiding foods that enervate, agitate, excite, or inhibit semen production. Generally, spicy, fried, and oily items should be avoided.

Brahmacharya literature also includes alarming passages describing the fifteen to thirty symptoms the semen-deficient may suffer: drooping posture, averted eyes, constant perspiration, irritability, sunken eyes, restlessness, gum disease, halitosis, tooth decay, addiction to alcohol, tobacco, and drugs, a habit of chewing on pencils, chalk, dirt, and paper, memory loss, depression, dull wits, mental anguish, and dementia.

If readers believe even half of this list—if they have personally sniffed in disgust at the bad breath or sweat of a sexually active companion—they may be frightened or inspired enough to adopt the brahmacharya lifestyle urged on them by the authors.

These authors, Alter believes, are inspired by their sense of powerlessness in dealing with profound socio-moral changes. This march backward into Indian tradition is both deliberate and desperate. Brahmacharya, the time-honored, holistic path to purity on earth, is a proud and powerful weapon to employ against Western sexual exploitation and degradation.

British imperialism, with its lingering remnants, has its own typical culture. In it, powerful white men have defeated and triumphed over Indian men, whom they then characterize as effete and impotent, unable to protect themselves or their women from a superior force. This imperialism has, as well, a distinctly sexual thrust. Virility is transmogrified from a metaphor for political and cultural power into an actual physical attribute of the conquerors: British men are more virile than the vanquished Indians. The measure of power, Alter argues, was both literally and figuratively a man's capacity to spend semen. For the imperialist, spilling semen has a diametrically opposite meaning to the Indian's: the one empowers, the other enervates.

Carrying the real-life metaphor further, the British contempt for Indian men extended to Indian women, whom they eroticized and had their sexual way with, through rape, seduction, prostitution, concubinage, even intermarriage. Sperm was spilled wantonly, and the conqueror measured his worth by a body count of women defiled.

In North India especially, intellectuals have overcome their bitterness and despair in favor of counterattack. In every possible way, brahmacharya is the perfect weapon, an all-dimensional, honorable, and practical life choice that the wrestlers have even made fashionable. It is another, uniquely Indian way of measuring virtue. It is a regimen of self-control, balance, and understanding truth, and of the body's integration with nature, with vital semen stored up as an empowering resource and not squandered after the fashion of colonial sexuality. One advocate urges:

> Open your eyes and set your resolve in order to regain the glory of the past through the regimen of celibacy. One who is able to control a single drop is able to control the seven seas. There is nothing in the world—no object or condition—which a celibate man cannot overcome.

CHAPTER 6

Female Celibacy Transcends Gender

CROSS-DRESSING FOR MILITARY SUCCESS

JOAN OF ARC

Fierce flames incinerated the maverick warrior Joan of Arc, one of the world's most celebrated virgin martyrs. She was condemned to burn at the stake, however, not for her chastity, which had been judicially verified and confirmed, but for wearing male clothing, usually sumptuous knightly garb and suitable weapons. One of the charges against her reads:

> Her hair cropped short and round like a young fop's, she wore shirt, breeches, doublet, with hose joined together and fastened to the said doublet by twenty points, long leggings laced on the outside, a short mantle reaching to the knees, or thereabouts, a close-cut cap, tight-fitting boots and buskins, long spurs, sword, dagger, breastplate, lance, and other arms in the style of a man-at-arms.

Sporting a boyish bob and knightly attire, accessorized with crossbow and sword, the uniform of fighting men—capitally offensive? Yes, *if* you are a teenage peasant girl living in early-fifteenth-century France, *if* you take your orders directly from divine voices, and *if* those voices urge you to defy the authorities' explicit interdiction against transvestism, which they based on Deuteronomy 22:5: "A woman shall not wear a man's apparel, nor shall a man put on a woman's garment: for whosoever does such things is abhorrent to the Lord your God." Such a woman was equally an abomination unto medieval cultural and religious standards, which interpreted Joan's fashion sense as morally dissolute, culturally inappropriate, socially insolent, and politically seditious.

In the fall of 1428, when she was sixteen, a trio of heavenly voices—St. Margaret of Antioch, St. Catherine of Alexandria, and St. Michael the Archangel—spoke to Joan of Arc through the wind and the bells of her village's little church. Go, Joan, they murmured, seek out Charles, the Dauphin, who will give you an army to drive the English invaders out of France. Off

Joan went, a tall and shapely teenager in a red dress, utterly confident that all would come to pass as the voices dictated.

Joan had not miscalculated. First, she persuaded the local commandant to escort her across enemy-occupied territory to the Dauphin. She also sheared off her black hair and donned a black doublet, short black tunic, and black cap. Once at court, she easily triumphed, though Charles first tested the veracity of her story through weeks of close observation, an intensive two-week ecclesiastical examination, and an intimate physical probing by the queen and two matrons.

The status of Joan's hymen—intact—was a crucial factor in the king's investigation, and she helped by explaining that her virginity was not happenstance but deliberate. Her divine mentors had first spoken to her at the age of thirteen. On the spot, she had pledged her chastity to St. Catherine and St. Margaret, "for as long as it may please God." (She had even successfully defended herself in consistory court against her local bishop, who accused her of denying she had married a village lad.)

These multiple testimonials to the young woman's absolute purity convinced the Dauphin of her divine mission. Accordingly, he entrusted some of his best troops to her so she could accomplish her first goal: to raise the siege of Orléans and lead him to Reims to be crowned and consecrated king. She fought her way to victory and led the Dauphin and twelve thousand troops through English-occupied territory to Reims Cathedral, where he was crowned Charles VII.

The Dauphin had taken a staggering risk. No woman had ever commanded troops during the Hundred Years' War. Joan was an untrained nobody, whose main selling points were her resolute confidence, convincing story, and confirmed virginity. Yet her soldiers responded enthusiastically. With one single exception, noted an eyewitness, "they all had great confidence in God and in the good justice of their king and their lord." A contemporary war chronicler added, "All regarded her with much affection, men and women, as well as small children. And there was a very extraordinary rush to touch her, or even to touch the horse on which she sat."

This loyalty continued throughout Joan's short career, though she deprived her men of their usual booty by outlawing looting and pillaging. Instead of these material rewards, she awed them with her military virtuosity and offered salvation as their *muliere santa,* holy woman.

On the battlefield, Joan was spectacular. Miraculously, she commanded armies and motivated her soldiers, drew up battle plans and waged war as if she had had a lifetime of military training and experience. As the Duke d'Alençon recalled, "Everyone marveled . . . that she acted so wisely and clearly in waging war, as if she was a captain who had the experience of twenty or thirty years; and especially in the setting up of artillery, for in that she held herself magnificently."

Joan's religious values reinforced her genius and personal courage. She refused to shed blood and carried her standard rather than her sword into battle. She refrained from fighting on Ascension Day, prayed "assiduously," heard daily mass, and often celebrated the Eucharist. She banned blasphemy, gambling, and camp-following prostitutes.

Joan's intense spiritual presence also numbed men to her beauty and sexual allure. Indeed, she felt so secure that she took no precautions to protect herself. She slept next to Jean de Mertz, who swore on oath he "never had any desire or carnal feelings for her." The Duke d'Alençon was more precise: "Sometimes, when we were in the field, I slept with Joan and the soldiers 'on the straw,' and sometimes I saw Joan get ready for the night, and sometimes I looked at her breasts, which were beautiful. Nevertheless I never had any carnal desire for her."

The depositions go on and on. The soldiers uniformly "believed it was impossible to desire her," so much so that in her presence, they ceased to desire any woman at all. So strongly did they feel this that many worried about their failure to respond.

Lovely, cross-dressed Joan remained safe from her own men's lust but not from the fortunes of war. On May 23, 1430, while defending the town of Compiègne, north of Paris, the Burgundians captured her and sold her to their English allies for the substantial sum of twelve thousand crowns.

The English threw her into prison and forced her to wear women's clothes. They also maligned her as a camp-following whore, after which Joan begged to be officially examined. The duchess of Bedford had her subjected to another gynecological examination, which confirmed her virginity. In fact, Joan so impressed the duchess that the latter forbade all males, including guards and soldiers, to touch their prisoner. She also sent a tailor, Jeannotin Simon, to make Joan a dress. During a fitting, Simon "softly put his hand on her breast," but Joan smacked his face. Without her soldier's apparel, she had become vulnerable to male sexual attraction.

Joan was transferred to Rouen, and in February, March, and April of 1431, a contingent of over one hundred members of an ecclesiastical court of the Inquisition, including the bishop of Beauvais and the papal deputy inquisitor, tried her for heresy and sorcery. Her inquisition was grueling, but as the weeks passed, her inquisitors increasingly focused on her idolatrous worship of false gods—the three saints of her vision—and for transforming her own person into a masculine idol—"a false lie"—by wearing her doublet and breeches.

What ultimately damned Joan was that, unlike such venerables as the transvestite saints who totally obliterated their identity as women to live as monks, she in no way hid her gender. Sometimes she even revealed it, as, for example, when she bared her wounded leg so her squire could medicate it with olive oil and bacon fat, or when she undressed at night. No one ever mistook Joan for a man.

Until the day she was sentenced to death, Joan seemed unable to grasp the seriousness of her "sin" of cross-dressing. "Dress is a small thing, among the littlest," was one of her recorded comments. She also connected it with the military profession and swore she "would never for anything swear not to arm herself and wear men's clothes." Leading the troops became Joan's justification for her masculine attire, but as her inquisitors so forcefully pointed out, that did not explain why she persisted in cross-dressing in every possible circumstance: in prison, church, court.

Finally, faced with their inexorable logic and also their refusal to allow her Holy Communion until she wore a dress, she invoked the highest authority for her attire: "It pleases God that I wear it. I do it on the command of our Lord and in His service. . . . When I have done what I was sent to do by God, I will take women's clothes."

Why, in the face of such grave and obvious danger, was Joan so obstinate on this point? In prison, shackled and guarded solely by men, she was in continual danger of rape. Yet she never suggested she wore men's clothing to protect herself. Instead, she defended her choice as obedience to divine instructions and as her means of self-definition. In her medieval context, her pledge of chastity coupled with her transvestism defined rather than concealed her sexual identity.

Joan's choice of epithet, Jeanne la Pucelle rather than la Vierge, is telling. The latter had saintly and religious connotations, but la Pucelle referred to the secular maidenhood that preceded marriage and, often, widowhood. Joan did not see her gender as a spiritual obstacle that cross-dressing surmounted. Unlike the transvestite saints, whose chastity and sartorial disguise allowed them to bury themselves in monasteries, Joan used both her virginity and her manly garb to gain greater access to the world.

As her trial progressed, Joan linked her chastity and cross-dressing together as elements of God's will, though she let it slip that she preferred men's clothes to women's. She made it clear as well that she rejected feminine occupations and argued that "there are enough other women to do them." Thanks to her mother, she could sew as well as any woman, but preferred instead to honor her divine instructions to save France. Her commitment to virginity was an essential precondition to this form of life—a sexually active or receptive woman would not have survived a single day as commander of her male troops.

On May 23, the inquisitorial court summarized Joan's "faults, crimes, and errors" and exhorted her to "correct and reform herself." On May 24, she made a panic-stricken recantation by signing a document confessing to "adoring and calling up evil spirits," "breaking the divine law, Holy Scriptures, and the canon laws . . . [and violating] against the decency of nature" by wearing men's clothing. As proof, she shucked off this clothing, put on a dress, and submitted to having her hair "shaved off and removed" to obliterate her boyish haircut.

The court, reassured, commuted her sentence of death to life imprisonment. Presumably Joan brooded and prayed in her cell, begging God and her spiritual mentors for guidance. St. Margaret and St. Catherine complied, reproaching her for her lifesaving recantation. On May 28, her jailers discovered their famous prisoner once again clad in manly costume. A retrial on May 29 established her guilt. On May 30, she was released to the secular authorities, who gave her a cap embroidered with her sins: heresy, relapsing, apostasy, and idolatry. Then, in the churchyard of St. Ouen, they burned the virgin warrior at the stake.

Joan's virginity, tested over and over, including twice during her inquisitorial trial, was not enough to save her from the mortal sin of cross-dressing. Until her capture, however, that much certified virginity, combined with her casually affected garb, catapulted this military superstar into the highest ranks and won her power, obedience, honor, and trust. Then, as enemy troops faltered and fell to her superior force and strategy, her legendary virginity was so omnipotent, it killed sexual arousal in any man who saw her. Cloaked in protective chastity and a warrior chief's mantle, Joan defied the natural order of marriage and housewifery, trading sewing needles and cooking pots for sword and dagger, breastplate and lance.

A CROW NATION GENDER-BENDER

In the early nineteenth century, Crow nation warriors captured a ten-year-old girl of the Gros Ventre of the Prairie tribe and, as was their custom, gave her to a Crow family as an adopted daughter. The tomboyish Woman Chief— her name in later years—found womanly ways and such pursuits as tanning, sewing, quilling, and beading distasteful, but she loved horseback riding, archery, and hunting. Her indulgent adoptive father was so proud of her skill that he designated her guard of the family's horses, usually a son's responsibility. This was not considered bizarre, for Plains Indians permitted females who swore they had never menstruated to cross the gender boundary and act like boys, though we do not know if Woman Chief, too, claimed amenorrhea.

As she matured, Woman Chief grew taller and stronger than most women.

She was taught to shoot a gun and became an expert markswoman. Soon she could equal or surpass the braves and became a single-minded hunter. From the birds of her childhood she graduated to deer and bighorn, which she butchered and brought back to the camp on her back. She also joined the buffalo hunt and routinely hauled home the meat and hides of four or five of the enormous animals.

Though Woman Chief was attractive enough, the young men had no romantic interest in her, and she apparently reciprocated their indifference. When her adoptive father died, therefore, it seemed natural for her to assume his role as head of both lodge and family, a hunter whose quarry fed her stepbrothers and stepsisters and their mother.

Woman Chief's most striking achievement, however, was becoming a valiant warrior. After a murderous Blackfoot raid on Crow people who were camped near a trading fort, she volunteered to parley with the enemy, whose language she understood. As she rode up to the rendezvous, Blackfoot envoys began shooting, certain this woman would be easy to capture. "Stop!" Woman Chief shouted several times. When they continued firing, she took aim with her rifle and shot one to death, then killed two more with her bow and arrow. Two escaped and pounded back to their encampment for reinforcements. A party of enraged Blackfoot pursued Woman Chief right to the gates of the fort where, to the collective cheers of white and red observers, she raced to safety.

This risky escapade earned Woman Chief the title of "brave"—a warrior— though her society normally permitted women onto battlefields only as cooks and caretakers. One year later, Woman Chief enlisted a troop of braves and led them into her first military skirmish against the Blackfoot, during which her band stole seventy horses and scalped two Blackfoot. Woman Chief personally slew and scalped one and disarmed the other. Her reputation grew, and she followed up with so many other victories, always emerging unscathed, that the Crow honored her as they honored no other woman. They sang songs about her courage and admitted her to the tribe's decision-making council. During a tribal council, she stood with the chiefs and was ranked third out of 160 family heads.

By this time, Woman Chief was wealthy, for she had hundreds of captured Blackfoot horses and could barter them for whatever she wanted. She was also extremely generous and shared her wartime booty with her friends. She decided to make even more money by becoming a trader, dealing in traditionally decorated quill hides. However, as she refused to lower herself to the womanly arts needed to transform raw hides into salable items, she dipped into her large reserves and paid the bride-price for a wife to do it instead. This proved such a lucrative collaboration that in a few years she bought three more wives.

For the next twenty years, Woman Chief lived as a celibate warrior with four wives who cared for her and did all her handicraft work. No hint exists that she had sexual relations with any of them, and she continued to enjoy the high regard of the Crow nation. Everyone understood perfectly why she had entered into this arrangement, peculiar because other cross-gendered women married only males. Her people noted that no man had wished to marry her, probably because no one wanted a wife who bested him in male pursuits and refused to turn her hand to anything "womanly."

In 1851, a contemporary observer described Woman Chief as "neither savage nor warlike. . . . She is about forty-five years old; appears modest in manner and good-natured rather than quick to quarrel."

Soon after this encounter, Woman Chief was killed. A tentative peace existed between the Crow and the Blackfoot and associated tribes, including the Gros Ventre, the people to whom she had been born. As Woman Chief still spoke their mother tongue, she determined to venture into their territory to discuss various important issues of mutual concern. Despite the urgent warnings of experienced fur traders, she set out on her mission. As she parleyed and smoked with a group of Gros Ventre, she decided it was safe to reveal her identity, but she had badly miscalculated their response. They probably knew from reputation how many of their tribesmen she had slain, and outraged at her presence, they murdered her and her four Crow companions.

Like Joan of Arc, Woman Chief defied the natural order of her society by becoming a warrior. However, her motivation was entirely different. Woman Chief had no divine inspiration, no mission. She simply had a strong preference for manly occupations and a correspondingly deep loathing for womanly ones. Also unlike Joan, Woman Chief did not cross-dress. Throughout her military career, she wore the dress of a Crow woman, except that her accoutrements were bows and arrows and guns.

Woman Chief's celibacy was almost certainly a combination of choice and circumstance. She never expressed the least desire to marry a fellow brave nor made the slightest attempt to promote her eligibility by displaying any womanly wiles or skills, but seemed content with how the Crow men respected and honored her and accepted her leadership. Woman Chief was already a family head, capably supporting and running her own household. Any Crow woman who wished to marry, especially an exceptional one such as Woman Chief, would have behaved to suit. She never did.

Woman Chief was simply a career hunter-warrior who maintained the highest standards for professional and social success. She might have accepted celibacy for want of marriage proposals, but it is more likely she chose it because she found such intense personal satisfaction, social honor, and financial gain in her unwomanly life as a Crow leader and family head.

AMAZONS OF OLD DAHOMEY

Legends of Amazon women warriors have enriched the storytelling of countless adventurers. These fantastic and largely fantasized females were splendid and towering, courageous and ferocious, and they fought like crazed tigers, governed their own villages, captured male prisoners for stud, and generally operated with grandiose recklessness. Often, they had only one breast, having sliced off the other so they could rest their bows comfortably against their now-smooth chests. However, credible eyewitnesses to their existence have always been impossible to find. The exceptions are the many reliable European soldiers and slave traders who met and sometimes battled the Amazons of Dahomey in West Africa.

Captain William Snelgrave first reported the Amazons in 1727, when he ventured into the Dahomean forest to establish contact with the king of Dahomey. Snelgrave shipped slaves to the West Indies and the king was in the slave-napping business. When they met, His Majesty sat surrounded by his elite Amazon guard, all naked to the waist, adorned with gold arm rings and sporting muskets.

The Amazons were such trustworthy warriors that the king and his successors expanded their military role. By the mid–nineteenth century, a British anti-slavery crusader, Frederick Forbes, forayed into the depths of Dahomey and also encountered the Amazons. "The Amazons are not supposed to marry," he wrote, "and, by their own statement, they have changed their sex. 'We are men,' say they, 'not women.'" The women dressed alike, ate the same food, and carried firearms of which they took great care. They lived inside the barracks under the care of eunuchs. Forbes counted about twenty-four hundred Amazons, who were an elite part of the regular army as well as the king's bodyguards.

Other English visitors described the Amazons' costumes and military role. They wore blue-and-white-striped, cotton, sleeveless dresses, with knee-length skirts and then short trousers underneath. Each of the king's three brigades had its own elaborate hairstyle, including heads shorn of all but one or two lone tufts.

The Gbeto, or elephant huntresses, were thought to be the bravest and proudly bore the scars of their battles with dangerous and wounded elephants. The Nyekplehhentoh, or razor women, specialized in hatred for the enemy's chief; they carried a hinged sword about one and a half feet long. Even young girls could be Amazons—members of the Gohento, or archers. Though they, too, had weapons—a bow with poisoned arrows and a small knife lashed to their wrist—they were rarely sent into battle but worked as scouts and porters.

The Amazons apparently reached their peak of power in 1850 under King Gezo, who elevated them to a status at least equal to that of his male soldiers and perhaps superior to it. His selection process was simple: every three years he ordered all his subjects to introduce their teenage daughters to him. From their number he chose the likeliest as officers and others as soldiers.

Observers noted that celibacy was a strict requirement for Amazons, and apparently the penalty for violating it was death for both the soldier and her lover. The consequence, Dahomeans liked to quip, was that more soldiers died after scaling the walls into the Amazons' quarters than they did in battle. Explorer Richard Burton believed the Amazons' celibacy inspired their fierceness. "They are savage as wounded gorillas, more cruel by far than their brethren in arms," he declared. The more likely reason the king prohibited them from engaging in sexual relations, however, was because he understood that only abstinent women could guarantee him undiluted loyalty and devotion. He only exempted a few select Amazons from the chastity he imposed on their sisters. These were his personal concubines, known as the Leopard wives.

In 1892, despite the best efforts of its Amazon warriors, the Dahomean kingdom fell to the French, and the famed women warriors passed into history. Impressive but less spectacular than their mythical sisters, they are the sole Amazons whose existence is historically verifiable. Their celibacy, which ensured the king of their allegiance and perhaps drove them to perform admirably warlike feats, earned them great respect and is probably their most celebrated characteristic.

DEFYING THE NATURAL ORDER

Elizabeth I, the Virgin Queen

Elizabeth Tudor's virginity was such a striking feature of her reign that when she was nearly fifty and enamored of Walter Raleigh, she agreed to his suggestion that a new American colony be named in her honor—Virginia. Until her death, contemporaries speculated and gossiped, blithely slandering their queen, but all evidence, including the correspondence of dozens of informed foreign diplomats, confirms that Elizabeth truly was, as she claimed, the Virgin Queen.

Why did this lovely, brilliant, accomplished, and ambitious young woman, whose passionate and jealous heart was legendary, never succumb to her sweethearts? Her reasons were both psychological and political. Throughout her childhood, Elizabeth was exposed to marriage Henry VIII–style. This began when she was two and a half years old and Henry, her father, ceased to love her mother, Anne Boleyn. Instead, he fixed his fickle heart on Jane Seymour, Anne's radiant, slender, meek, and sly young lady-in-waiting. The raucous, impetuous, vain, and silly Anne was devastated when she stumbled across Jane perched on her husband's knee. Soon after, she delivered a premature, stillborn son. Instead of offering sympathy on their shared loss, Henry stormed into Anne's sickroom, ranting that she had deprived him of an heir. Divorce, Henry VIII–style, was close.

Anne's enemies trumped up adultery charges against her, and Henry, longing for an excuse to be rid of her, pretended to be enraged. Anne went from brief imprisonment in the Tower of London to mock trial to execution by beheading, denying her infidelity with her last breath. Elizabeth, far away at the nursery palace at Hunsdon, never saw her mother again. Before her death, Anne made arrangements for Elizabeth's religious instruction but left no other instructions or final message. She died blaming her little daughter for ruining her by not being a boy.

The baby princess was in grave danger from her father, just as her half sister Mary had been when Anne Boleyn replaced *her* mother, Spain's Catherine of Aragon. Elizabeth's caretakers, understanding her precarious situation, were petrified. Justly so, because Henry soon had Parliament declare Elizabeth a bastard, just as he had done to Mary, with whom he sent her to live.

When Elizabeth was four, the new queen, Jane, delivered Edward, Henry's longed-for son and heir. As Elizabeth and Mary were driven to their half brother's christening, they passed the gruesome spectacle of rotting limbs and severed heads, blackened from boiling pitch, nailed to walls, bridges, posts, and monuments everywhere, unforgettable reminders of the savagery of Henry's reprisals. His victims in this case had been the Pilgrimage of Grace rebels. The ex-princesses, now formalized bastards, must have trembled and even wept— their father, who had killed Elizabeth's mother, was capable of terrible things.

Elizabeth's next experience of marriage came when Henry decided to remarry after Jane Seymour's premature, natural death. However, when he first saw his intended, the supposedly beautiful Anne of Cleves, he was furious. She was "not . . . *fair*," he bellowed, "but . . . of a *brown complexion*. . . . I love her not." He could not wriggle out of marrying her, but he refused to sleep with her and divorced her almost immediately.

Soon Henry married again. This time his bride was young Catherine Howard, an orphan whose past included a beastly guardian and seduction by an older man, Francis Dereham. Unfortunately, she went on to cheat on the king with Thomas Culpepper, a courtier. After blackmailers and plotters revealed this to Henry, Queen Catherine Howard, too, was beheaded. An apocryphal rumor spread that she had died whispering, "I die queen of England, but I would rather die the wife of Culpepper," fueling the storm of popular hatred against her.

Henry's last wife, Catherine Parr, specialized in elderly husbands, Henry being her third. She was kind to the neglected Elizabeth, installed her at the court, and mentored her. Before Henry could weary of his new wife, he died. Elizabeth was thirteen, a reinstated princess who had to kneel before her nine-year-old brother, the obnoxious Edward.

Teenage Elizabeth had more firsthand experience of yet another marriage. When she was fourteen, the widowed Catherine Parr married Admiral Thomas Seymour. When Catherine was very pregnant, the admiral stole Elizabeth's bedroom key so he could prance uninvited into her room, grab her from her bed, embrace and kiss her, and slap her buttocks, all the while cracking ribald jokes. At first, he inveigled Catherine into joining him in his sport of tickling Elizabeth in bed. Once, Catherine immobilized her stepdaughter while Seymour cut her dress into a hundred scraps.

Elizabeth tried hard to resist, sticking her nose into a book as Seymour talked or, if she knew he was coming, hiding behind the curtains. His attentions escalated—he crept into her room bare-legged, still in his nightshirt. The court began to gossip. Then Catherine caught him alone with Elizabeth in his arms. Immediately, she sent her stepdaughter away. Elizabeth, precocious and sophisticated, understood the implications of her exile. When Catherine died a year later, Elizabeth refused to write the admiral a letter of condolence. "I will not do it, for he needs it not," she said bitterly.

Despite Catherine's death, the scandal continued to dog Elizabeth. The affair had been more than a near-seduction. Though her moral standards and her love for Catherine drove her to resist him, she had been attracted to the handsome and jovial Seymour. Her banishment from court was shattering, humiliating, and dangerous. She heard the swirl of gossip—that Seymour had hoped Catherine would die in childbirth so he could wed the little princess and that she, Elizabeth, had had an illegitimate baby with him and was again pregnant. Elizabeth was still an adolescent but she was learning a harsh lesson—because she was a princess, her flirtation was no longer an affair of the heart but an affair of the state.

It was true that Seymour, now a suspiciously merry widower, sought to marry her. Meanwhile, he was accused of high treason and Elizabeth had to answer questions about her own participation in his schemes. She had the sense to write the protector exonerating herself, calling the rumors "shameful Slanders" and offering to appear at court where her flat stomach would confirm her innocence. She also noted she would not marry without the Privy Council's consent, a sentiment she would never modify. Ultimately, Seymour was beheaded and Elizabeth was absolved, but the rumors never stopped, and for two years, her brother, King Edward, refused to receive her at court.

Reprieved, Elizabeth learned invaluable lessons from the incident. She had been betrayed by the loose, thoughtless tongues of her serving women. Nothing she did was private from these women, who spent most of each day with her and were always a source of potential spying. (As queen, she had eighteen of them.) From then on, she governed her private behavior accordingly.

Elizabeth also took away the lesson that her body belonged not to her but to England, and that her marriage would be a political event, decided and approved by government councilors. When it happened, she had to be virginal and unstained, absolutely above suspicion. And in her circles, as she had had impressed upon her during Henry's multiple marriages, even a hint of infidelity in a queen could easily be fatal. Virginity quickly suggested itself to her as a solution to a quagmire of potential problems.

Elizabeth's formidable intelligence and extensive education also reinforced her sense of personal independence and ambition. Despite her traumatic childhood, she had had a series of excellent Cambridge tutors. She was fluent in five or six languages. She was a student of classical literature and had an expert knowledge of painting and poetry. (In later years, she patronized and protected Shakespeare.) She did exquisite calligraphy, danced brilliantly, and was an excellent musician. She knew her history, politics, and diplomacy, both formal and behind the scenes. She understood finance and accounting. She was a master of riposte and wrote elegant, sophisticated English.

In character, Elizabeth was steely, the iron will that her childhood nurses had remarked upon forged by the passage of time. She cursed and spat and punched when she was annoyed. She howled with laughter when she was amused. She loved to hunt and play practical jokes. She ate moderately and preened immoderately, plastering her face with cosmetics, adorning herself with fantastic gowns, elaborate wigs, and precious jewels.

Elizabeth became a veteran nonmarrier. After Henry's aborted schemes to betroth her in childhood, Queen Mary—widely despised as Bloody Mary because of the blood shed in her persecution of non-Catholics—had tried her awkward hand at finding her half sister a Catholic prince. Young Elizabeth, by now an experienced survivor, chose the safest route and swore "she would not marry, even were they to give her the king's son." Nonetheless, Mary and her Spanish consort continued to negotiate a husband for the princess, who persisted in refusing to approve one.

Then in 1558, after Mary's death from deepest melancholy after a series of false pregnancies and very real disease, Elizabeth became queen. She was Christendom's greatest catch, and her marriageability was a political and diplomatic issue of the highest importance. The Council and the House of Commons discussed it ad nauseam, and it was easily the most bruited topic of conversation among knowledgeable people throughout Europe. Elizabeth's advisers perfunctorily evaluated candidates for personal qualities, eliminating truly hideous, deformed, or stupid men, but they gave far more weight to national and family connections, finances, religious affiliations, and professional experience. Elizabeth reveled in the intrigue of it all and encouraged her councilors to propose as many names as possible, raising hopes everywhere, creating panic, force-feeding gossip. Finally, the Commons addressed their queen, requesting her to marry. Unspoken but understood was their panic that, unmarried, she had no heir and was vulnerable to assassination or overthrow by sideline contenders, beginning with her royal relative Mary, Queen of Scots, whom she ordered executed in 1587.

Elizabeth's reply was lengthy, gracious, and unequivocal. She would abandon spinsterhood whenever God so inclined her, and until then, she would rule with England's best interests always in mind. Unlike other royals—her deceased half sister Mary, with her Catholic husband, sprang to mind—*she* would never sacrifice national or religious interests to wed an individual. "In the end," she concluded with great prescience, "this shall be for me sufficient, that a marble stone shall declare that a Queen, having reigned such a time, lived and died a virgin."

This was all true as far as it went, but Elizabeth's motives were far more complicated. She was well aware of the implications of an unwisely chosen husband such as Mary's. She was equally aware of how powerfully she could manipulate politics and diplomacy by endlessly negotiating a future marriage that would ultimately fail to materialize, leaving her free to raise—and then dash—the hopes of another candidate or suitor. Moreover, what had marriage to offer her personally? She was already a queen, immensely wealthy and secure. She was able to command the admiration, feigned or not, of any man in her realm. Marriage could only compromise her independence, diminish her power, and tax her limited patience. It might also threaten the stability of the nation, as Mary Tudor's marriage to Philip had.

No man could win her hand, but Elizabeth's heart was a different matter. She fell tempestuously in love, usually with dashing younger men. Her longest love affair, never consummated, was with Robert Dudley, later Earl of Leicester, a married man whose wife's peculiar death—she broke her neck in an accident while her husband was away with Elizabeth—prompted all sorts of evil rumors about how conveniently she had died.

Elizabeth's love for her "Sweet Robin" lasted for thirty years, and when he died in 1588, she went into seclusion in her room and refused to see anyone. Finally her most senior officials risked ordering her door smashed in so they could go inside and speak to her. Elizabeth's deep attachment to her Robin, however, had not prevented her from considering marrying him off, for diplomatic reasons, to Mary, Queen of Scots. Nor did she wish to marry him herself. "I will have here but one mistress and no master," she once shouted at him during a quarrel.

For his part, Leicester never expected her to marry him because from the time she was eight years old, she had sworn to remain unmarried. "I hate the idea of marriage for reasons that I would not divulge to a twin soul," she once confided to Lord Sussex. The reasons remain mysterious, but it is not difficult to imagine what some of them were.

Throughout her lifetime, however, Elizabeth flaunted her tantalizing spinsterhood and toyed with foreign diplomats about various marriage proposals. Each time this happened, her virtue was carefully investigated, with serving maid, ladies-in-waiting, and courtiers all eager to disclose their confidences. The verdict was always the same: "she has truly and verily been praised and extolled for her virginal and royal honor, and . . . nothing can be said against her; and all the aspersions against her are but the spawn of envy and malice and hatred."

Elizabeth passed every inspection but still refused to finalize any marriage arrangements. Parliament and her councilors, anxious about who would succeed her, argued that her marriage was England's business rather than her own and pressured her to decide.

Elizabeth responded by defending her virginity and unmarried state: she was a loyal Englishwoman and would marry "as soon as I can conveniently . . . and though I be a woman, yet I have as good a courage, answerable to my place, as ever my father had. I am your anointed Queen."

The Virgin Queen developed a discernible pattern. She encouraged suitors, wasted their time in protracted talks, then discarded them. This worked to her political advantage because her potential suitors, seeing her as a valuable marriage partner, were unlikely to cause problems for her. The only exception was François, Duke of Alençon, at twenty-three half her age when they met. For eleven years Elizabeth vacillated between love and indifference. Finally she consulted her councilors, and their lukewarm assent frightened her off as much as popular outrage at the notion of such an unlikely match.

Toward the end of her life, the virgin who had loved and been loved so often, who had flirted, teased, courted, quarreled, and even executed beaux, bade farewell to her greatest love of all, the parliament of the English people. No prince loves his subjects more than I do, she declared, and no queen could ever be happier to risk her life for them, as I have mine. Though she was a woman, God had bestowed upon her a manly heart that had never been afraid of any enemies, domestic or foreign.

On March 23, 1603, the dying Elizabeth called in Archbishop Whitgift, her "little black husband," whom she favored because, like herself, he had remained celibate. Whitgift knelt at her bedside, held her hand, and for hours kept a prayer vigil until she fell asleep. She died without waking, and the balladeers lamented:

> She rul'd this Nation by her self
> And was beholden to no man,
> O she bore the sway end of all affairs
> And yet she was but a woman.

This ditty nicely sums up Elizabeth's life. She was first and foremost England's queen, and unlike her father, who could marry and divorce at will, she knew a male consort could undermine her, divide her power, humiliate and harm her. Just as nuns were Brides of Christ, Elizabeth was the Bride of England, albeit a bride with a roving eye for a handsome face, a muscular physique, and a persuasively flattering tongue. She was far too brilliant and ambitious to subordinate herself to a man and used her famous virginity like a moat that protected her from anyone seeking to get too close to the reins of power. In persistently defying the explicit wishes of her councilors and parliament to marry and provide England with a successor, she consolidated her own power and did what no other woman ever had: gave her name to an entire era.

FLORENCE NIGHTINGALE

"My life is more suffering than almost any other kind, is it not, God?" wrote Florence Nightingale, in despair at the futility of existence under her parents' roof. With her mother, Fanny, and her sister, Parthe, the privileged thirty-one-year-old's life was confined to an endless round of social visits, teas, and parties. Florence loathed it all, even the "charity" balls and concerts where "people bamboozle their consciences and shut their eyes."

Over a decade earlier, on February 7, 1837, God had spoken and called her to his service. But unlike the message Joan of Arc had received, Florence's had been vague about what this service entailed.

In any case, her parents rejected their daughter's desire for a career or profession. In Victorian England, women like Florence were supposed to marry. She was an excellent catch—attractive, wealthy, clever, fluent in several languages, widely read, dynamic, witty. She had "adored" her longtime suitor, Monckton Milnes, but after nine years of courtship, she had rejected him. Afterward, she suffered terribly when he would scarcely speak to her, but she never regretted her decision. Monckton would have satisfied her intellectual and passionate nature, Florence explained, but "I have a moral, an active, nature which requires satisfaction and that would not find it in his life. . . . I could be satisfied to spend a life with him in combining our different powers in some great object. I could not satisfy this nature by spending life with him in making society and arranging domestic things."

God, she believed, had marked her out to be one of the single women, whom He "organized . . . accordingly for their vocation." The Nightingales were furious. Florence had turned down the perfect husband. Family quarrels escalated into bitter battles.

On her thirtieth birthday, Florence confronted her life: "Today I am thirty—the age Christ began his mission. Now no more childish things. No more love. No more marriage. Now Lord let me think only of Thy Will, Oh Lord Thy Will, Thy Will." Slowly, this will was revealed to her: she should devote her life to nursing, the profession of slatterns, drunks, prostitutes, and criminals.

Hospitals in Florence's day were cesspools of filth, degradation, abuse, and death. Only the most destitute and desperate would go to an institution where the floors were slimy with vomit, feces, and blood, where patients were jammed together in filthy, linenless beds, and surgeons routinely seduced the degenerate nurses.

Predictably, Florence's parents angrily refused even to consider her request to enter this world. Again, Florence was thrown into despair. "In my thirty-first year I see nothing desirable but death," she wrote. "Why, oh my God, can I not be satisfied with the life that satisfies so many people? . . . My God, what am I to do?"

Finally she rebelled. She bullied her parents into allowing her to go to Germany for a training session at a medical establishment, Kaiserwerth Institute on the Rhine. The family fought her every inch of the way. Her sister, Parthe, flung bracelets into her face with such force that Florence passed out. Despite it all, she went to Kaiserwerth.

At the Institute, training began at 5 A.M. and ended with a nightly Bible reading. Food was poor, accommodations Spartan, and nursing instruction "nil." None of this mattered, for in the lacunae, Florence identified her calling. "This is the life," she wrote to her mother. "Now I know what it is to live and love life. . . . I wish for no other earth, no other world but this."

Back home, her family's opposition was unabated. Nonetheless, Florence triumphed, and in 1853, she was named superintendent of the Institution for the Care of Sick Gentlewomen. Though she despised the charitable matrons in charge, dismissing them as "Fashionable Asses," she overrode her family's hostility and accepted the position. After she was installed, the Fashionable Asses were horrified at her energy and zeal. She reorganized their operation from the revolutionary perspective that the patient was paramount and forced the Institution's directors to agree to accept all sick women, not just Anglicans.

A contemporary character sketch by the celebrated writer Elizabeth Gaskell painted Florence as a driven, compassionate, but cold near-saint. Her soft voice and gentle mannerisms belied her unyielding character and her irresistible force of personality. She had causes rather than friends, and she hovered, Gaskell concluded, somewhere between God and the rest of mankind.

One of Florence's attributes was strict celibacy, easy to abide by after her momentous decision not to marry. For her, it was a cheap price to pay for her freedom from marriage. She harmoniously incorporated this chastity and the chance to pursue the profession to which God had called her into her increasingly austere lifestyle. Even her intense relationships with the men who revered her seemed to lack a sensual dimension. Instead, she always ensured their admiration was sublimated into unremitting toil for her current cause. This nonthreatening fervor enabled Florence to deal openly with the most important officials of the day—doctors, politicians, and military officers—without the least whiff of scandal. This extended even to her brother-in-law, who married Parthe only after Florence had turned him down.

The next stage of Florence's mission saw her orchestrate a move from Harley Street to Scutari in Turkey, as superintendent of nurses in the hospital there. With a ragtag band of nurses and nuns, she arrived in 1854 to an edifice groaning with wounded soldiers dying of malnutrition, gangrene, and infection, and medical wards teeming with rats, decomposing garbage, even a festering corpse, but innocent of furniture, operating tables, cooking utensils, or supplies. In the basement, two hundred starving women were crammed together, quarreling, sickening, and dying. Outside, stopped-up latrines overflowed and poisoned the air.

Despite these horrendous conditions, Florence's worst enemy was officialdom, for the doctors refused to even acknowledge her existence. Barred from the wards, she waited it out until an influx of casualties following the Battle of Balaclava shook hostile doctors into enlisting her. War wounds, cholera, frostbite, and dysentery ravaged the troops. Nearly three out of every four soldiers were ill or injured. Florence threw herself into the struggle to save them, scrubbing, feeding, soothing, hearing them, raising funds, visiting them at night with one of her famous Turkish lanterns—the Lady with the Lamp. Finally, mortality at the Scutari Hospital dropped from 42 percent to 2.2 percent.

Florence was a hero to her patients and to the general public. She knew, however, that if it weren't for the public support making it too awkward for the War Office to get rid of her, many a military doctor or official would sacrifice her like Joan of Arc. She had accomplished miracles, but only by defying authority, recruiting support from influential individuals, including Queen Victoria, and imposing her systems and values with an iron will.

Florence had also driven her own slight body too far, with sleepless nights, insufficient food, and no relief from relentless nursing, management, and intrigue. Twice she fell gravely ill, perhaps as a result of post–traumatic stress disorder, and never really recovered. Back in England, she adopted nunlike clothing—simple black dresses and prim caps. She was emaciated from illness and her abstemious diet. Her quiet melancholy stemmed from grief at leaving so many soldiers in their Crimean graves, as well as lingering memories of the war. But the wounds and blood and dysentery, the cold and heat and hunger, did not haunt her as much as "intoxication, drunken brutality, demoralization and disorder on the part of the inferior; jealousies, meanness, indifferent, selfish brutality on the part of the superior."

Semi-invalided, Florence spent the next half century reclining on a sofa or bed with her Persian cats, often tormented by the unwanted company of her blatantly insensitive mother and sister. "The whole occupation of Parthe and Mama was to lie on two sofas and tell one another not to get tired by putting flowers into water," she said disgustedly. The Nightingale women were a study in contrasts, with Mama and Parthe lolling through life while Florence, who never ceased carping about their idleness, demanded slavish loyalty from her friends and admirers and worked them as mercilessly as she did herself.

For the rest of her life, Florence conducted her crusades from bed. She prepared reports, exposés, and projects: the construction of hospitals, Indian public health, workhouse reform, the world's first training system for the nursing profession, which she had single-handedly transformed from a disgraceful, low-life occupation into a respectable, even noble calling. She also wrote a book, *Notes on Nursing: What it is, and What it is not,* still one of the best texts available.

At the end of her long life, Florence had not a single regret about her decision to nurse rather than marry. She was also very firm about advising other women "to keep clear of . . . the jargon, namely, about the 'rights of women,' which urges women to do all that men do, merely because men do it . . . and the jargon which urges women to do nothing that men do, merely because they are women. . . . Surely woman should bring the best she has, *whatever* that is, to the work of God's world, without attending to either of these cries."

To the end, her ever-active, analytical mind was impatient with ideology and rote thought. Personal rebellion had been the price of her success, but when she died, aged ninety, she had enormous accomplishments to her credit.

Apart from these successes, Florence was admired by and corresponded with the highest in the realm, including Queen Victoria. She measured her friendships and her life in goals achieved—nothing else mattered. Life was not a journey but a destination. This was true from her earliest years, when she had refused to be submerged within a stifling Victorian marriage and, in defiance of her genteel world's natural order, embraced celibacy and freedom.

CHASTITY WITH AN AGENDA

British Spinsters Strike against Sex

There's little new under the sun. Who hasn't sniggered about the legendary "headache" that grips angry/resentful/exhausted/repulsed women when their husbands demand sex? One woman or even millions clutching their head at bedtime do not constitute a celibate society. But when they are acting deliberately, and each "headache" is a political tool rather than a personal ploy, the case is very different.

In *Lysistrata,* as we have seen, a legion of battle-weary soldiers' wives unite to force their husbands to cease hostilities. Their weapon, withholding sex until the bellicose men lay down their swords, is celibacy at its strategic purest, employed in the great cause of peace.

In the late nineteenth century, thousands of British women staged their own real-life version of *Lysistrata.* Their agenda was quite different from the Greek model—they were all unmarried, and they celebrated their spinsterhood as a deliberate strike against women's inferior position.

In feminist writer Lucy Re-Bartlett's ringing words, "In the hearts of many women today is rising a cry somewhat like this . . . *I will know no man, and bear no child* until this apathy is broken through—these wrongs be rights. . . . It is the 'silent strike' and it is going on all over the world."

What had the "silent strike" to do with communal celibacy? And what, apart from political sensitization and moral courage, lay behind the women's truculence?

The answers were several and echoed well beyond Britain, into North America. The first answer was simply demographic: nearly one in three women was single and one in four would remain so. Thanks to men's higher death and emigration rates, there were significantly fewer males. From 1821, when the British census reported 1,036 women for every 1,000 men, the discrepancy in this gender ratio rose until after World War I, it stood at 1,096 to 1,000.

Interpreting these figures is not as transparently obvious as it might first appear. Such severely skewed ratios had an undeniable impact on individual women's chances for monogamous marriage. But much, much more was at play.

The 1880s saw a relaxation of the rules and some of the laws that had condemned women to social and economic dependence. This was particularly true for women in the more advantaged classes. Higher education, for example, was more accessible and so were some of the professions. White-collar employment mushroomed, opening so many new positions that women were actually hired. Because of the 1870 Married Women's Property Act, women could keep their wages and no longer had to surrender them to their husbands, so the idea of salaried employment was far more alluring than it had been.

These changes were not gifts from a munificent government. They were the outcome of decades of agitation, mostly by middle- and upper-class women, against their oppression. Many of them had also spoken out on behalf of the millions of their working-class sisters, whose oppression was manifested differently but stemmed nonetheless from the same patriarchal domination.

Had the laws changed in tandem with social customs and granted professional women the same legal independence as their brothers, spinsterhood might not have seemed so enticing. What was still so galling, however, was that in marrying, a woman merely exchanged her father's authority for her husband's. True, the 1882 (revised and upgraded) Married Women's Property Act permitted women to own property in their own right, but in other crucial areas, they remained legally subservient. All too often, the transfer of subservience from father to spouse proved a sorry bargain.

As a female writing team had observed a decade earlier, "A woman should be reminded . . . that in marrying she gives up many advantages. Her independence is, of course, renounced by the very act that makes her another's. Her habits, pursuits, society, sometimes even friendships, must give way to his."

Hadn't Florence Nightingale earlier warned that women who marry "must sacrifice all their life . . . behind *his* destiny woman must annihilate herself"? She, like so many other women of her class, remained single—and celibate— to guarantee the personal independence she needed to fulfill her ambitions.

The statistical odds against finding a suitable husband ensured that many a woman languished in despised spinsterhood, pining for the children she would never have, writhing under the contempt of relations obliged to harbor her upon the death of her parents, facing an interminable life of bleak boredom. (Had some talented members of this class undertaken to research the fate of young Hindu widows, a heartrending and significant genre of literature might have developed.)

But the dearth of British men certainly cannot explain why one-quarter of British women never married—after all, at the worst of times, the imbalance never even quite reached eleven to ten. And determinedly marriage-minded women could and did emigrate to Australia, where the gender imbalance was reversed, though the quality of available men was somewhat questionable.

What, then, explains this sweeping wave of middle-class womanly singleness? In *Marriage as a Trade,* playwright Cicely Hamilton argued the phenomenon was a political tactic to create a significant class of spinsters prepared to challenge male domination, including what she styled sexual abuse. Except for those who turned to other women for sexual satisfaction, as a small percentage did, these spinsters adopted celibacy as a necessary tool in their campaign.

Another spinster-by-choice noted that "wherever women are admitted to sex intercourse to such a degree that the celibate class is practically nonexistent, there the position of women socially, economically, and intellectually is of a low order."

Thus a considerable slice of late-nineteenth-century celibacy was the deliberate choice of frustrated, rebellious, and politically astute middle-class women. Sexual intercourse with a man, they believed, was a surrender of judicial and (despite the 1882 legislation) property rights, and an abdication of personal independence. They seized on celibacy as a strategy to improve the female condition and, with quiet determination, earned their own living and simply refused to marry.

Spinsters United

"Wanted," the notice might have read, "Spiritual community for determinedly single, rebellious, and politically astute professional women." The time and place: late-nineteenth-century England. The players: the "silent strikers" described above, educated young women who opted for celibacy in protest against the double standard that clawed at them in every aspect of life—the law, the workplace, politics, overall society.

In the 1880s, a generation of these women matured to adulthood and set out on their personal journeys. One lively and ambitious group included writer/activist Beatrice Potter and novelists Margaret Harkness, Amy Levy, and Olive Schreiner. They chose to move out from under their fathers' (overly patriarchal) roofs, but not into communal, single-sex residences such as those set up by an earlier wave of female teachers, nurses, and social workers. These young women were more adventurous and went off instead to live in their own lodgings.

Compared to their comfortable childhood homes and neighborhoods, these residences were extremely modest and deliberately chosen to be agreeably distant from those of their families. Central London was especially appealing, far away from prying, critical relatives. It permitted an ease and anonymity of movement. Best of all, so many like-minded women lived there that they formed, within the heart of the bustling metropolis, a community of kindred spirits whose mutual support was a continual reminder of what they wanted to achieve.

None of this, however, made their lives easy. Independent or not, decent women did not wander about alone or eat alone. Parts of London, as Virginia

Woolf wrote in *The Pargiters,* were "as impassable, save with their mother, as any swamp alive with crocodiles." And "to be seen alone in Piccadilly . . . was equivalent to walking up [residential] Abercorn Terrace in a dressing gown carrying a sponge." Despite these constraints, the determined young women set themselves up downtown and prepared to lead self-directed, satisfying, worthy, and celibate lives.

These women differed from millions of other chaste working women supporting and discovering themselves in their own digs because their celibacy was a purely political stance. It had nothing to do with perceptions of morality, fear of pregnancy, or keeping pure until Mr. Right materialized with a proposal of marriage. Sometimes even the women were astonished that they had rejected bourgeois marriage and motherhood and had hammered out a notch for themselves in the real world of gritty, grimy London. As social worker Beatrice rhapsodized in her journal:

> "Who would have thought it," [Maggie and I] . . . said constantly to one another, "when we two as schoolgirls stood on the moorland near Bournemouth . . . discussed our religious difficulties and gave vent to all our world-sorrow, and ended by prophesying we should in ten years be talking of cooks and baby linen . . . who would have thought of our real future?"

Strengthened and deeply influenced by each other's ideas and experiences, including Beatrice's many stories about her needy clients, the women produced an impressive body of work. All wrote about London's poor, and all rejected the patronizing attitude of charitable middle-class women. Instead, they portrayed their subjects with empathetic clarity.

In her novel *Out of Work,* Maggie Harkness scarcely disguised her own tenement and melodramatically depicted the life of casual laborers down at the docks. In *Reuben Sachs,* tormented and depressive Amy Levy pilloried the values of bourgeois Jewish life. She also wrote brave poetry about platonic lovers:

> Ere all the world had grown so drear,
> When I was young and you were here . . .
> And all our observations ran
> On Art and Letters, Life and Man.
> Proudly, we sat, we two, on high,
> Throned in our Objectivity;
> Scarce friends, not lovers (each avers),
> But sexless, safe Philosophers.

Most tellingly, Maggie's and Amy's novels ring truest when their heroines are like themselves. Maggie's alter-ego narrator Mary Cameron lives in Ladies'

Chambers, "a funny place, full of medical students—she-boys she called them—lady-journalists, artists, and widows." Mary furnishes her room "with Japanese ware, art muslin, and the various knick-knacks that lady-students and their consoeurie gather." Since leaving her parents' rural rectory, Mary has supported herself as a proofreader and typing and shorthand teacher. Mary is, in other words, Maggie and all her community of friends rolled into one.

Mary and the other heroines vindicated the real women's carefully constructed, resolutely celibate lifestyle. As writers, they not only sampled and supped on the raw lives of the industrial poor but wrote about them so proficiently, they earned their keep doing so.

Their proud celibacy sustained without obsessing them. They were too busy experiencing and working and enjoying life. This included romance—Beatrice, for example, dallied with (chastely, of course), then declined to marry, Radical politician Joseph Chamberlain. No, their collective commitment to celibacy simply shored up their confidence and guarded them against succumbing to male dominance. Beatrice, who was intensely attracted to the much older, powerful, and prosperous Chamberlain, is an excellent case in point. Despite her feelings, she was frightened off because she recognized he was a dominant personality: "If the fates should unite us (against *my will*) all joy and lightheartedness will go from me. I shall be absorbed into the life of a man whose aims are not my aims; who will refuse me all freedom of thought in my intercourse with him; to whose career I shall have to subordinate all my life, mental and physical."

Yet despite its success, this spiritual community of celibate women was as vulnerable as other communes. The problem was not celibacy, its original glue, but ongoing life itself: money problems and professional achievement, emigration, and in the case of Amy Levy, profound, incurable melancholy. After nearly a decade, the women parted ways, shutting the doors forever on their once tremendously productive celibate community.

The community did not fail so much as wither away, a shriveled vine impervious to pollinating bees or restoring rainfall. In earlier times, it had borne profusely. Its luscious grapes had fermented into heady wines. They banished shyness and inspired ideas that, in their turn, gave birth to the prose and poetry that had been the community's raison d'être, tangible evidence that independent women could, in celibate community, create and succeed. Its heroines, however, faithful reflections of their now-dispersed authors, lived on in their fictional celibate communities, touching other women, moving some to stake their futures on themselves.

Sexology versus "the Stinging Weapon of Death"

The "silent strike," with its contingent of proud spinsters, generated an inevitable backlash. This came in the guise of sexology, the latest entry into the field of "scientific" inquiry, and the Motherhood movement. Sexology's founding fathers, England's Havelock Ellis, Germany's Iwan Bloch and August Forel, stressed the innate biological differences between men and women. In Ellis's words, "women's special sphere is the bearing and the rearing of children, with the care of human life in the home. Man's primary sphere remains the exploration of life outside the home, in industry and inventions and the cultivation of the arts."

With this observation of the status quo cloaked in scientific garb, Ellis proceeded to extrapolate conclusions. One was that ideal sexual relations would be between male dominance and female submissiveness. Another was that the ideal female, a paragon of Motherhood, was very definitely not a spinster, a word that in Ellis's writings elaborated on the nasty connotations our century has inherited from his.

Like so many Motherhood aficionados, Ellis claimed and was credited with a feminist agenda: surely praising the wonderful work of mothers must be women-positive. In Ellis's case, this seemed irrefutable, for he also preached the novel idea that women should, indeed must, enjoy sex. No more lying rigid, clenching fists and teeth, enduring bimonthly genital invasion by obliterating it with thoughts of England and the empire. (Ironically, Ellis himself had earlier lost an adored lover because he failed to reach a full erection during a romantic interlude. His sexual predilection was to observe women urinating, which stemmed from his unforgettable boyhood experience of watching his mama pee in the garden.)

Ellis's espousal of the great Motherhood or, in Germany, Mutterschutz, movement partially explains his enormous influence. From the 1880s onward, fewer children were born but infant mortality soared. Physical exams revealed the poor condition of many schoolchildren, and military recruits were rejected at a high rate for a plethora of disabilities. Something was wrong—at least, the authorities now knew something was wrong—and the solution seemed to be a nation of Super Moms who would reverse the physical decline. In Ellis's words, these women would undertake the "regeneration of the race" and the "evolution of a supermankind."

Women, too, bought into the Motherhood ideal. Some felt it validated the roles they had chosen or that had been chosen for them. Others were persuaded that sexology was scientific truth and so believed the conclusions its thinkers so convincingly reported.

These conclusions clashed with feminist beliefs, particularly the silent strike, the voluntary spinsters' movement in which women took control of their lives by refusing to surrender their rights to husbands. Censuring spinsters became the keynote of antifeminist attacks. One Motherhood proponent, herself a woman, decried spinsters with an analogy to a beehive, in which infertile workers were like "surplus women" who refused or had no opportunity to marry. Since the worker bee's poisoned sting required the egg-laying tube, spinsters who relinquished "the power of life" would, by definition, gain possession of "the stinging weapon of death."

Another male antifeminist spoke in alarmist terms of eventual civil war between wives and spinsters, "the waste products of our female population." In *Modern Woman and How to Manage Her,* another male writer called spinsters "man-condemning, man-hating . . . women who are 'independent of men,' a motley host, pathetic in their defiance of the first principle of Nature, but of no serious account in the biological or social sense." He even proposed polygamy as a solution to "spinsterhood, and the right to live one's own life—the supreme consummation of a large number of revolutionary British women."

In later years, charges of lesbianism and frigidity, both caused or worsened by spinsterhood, bolstered the attacks on single, independent women. Given that British women outnumbered men by 2 million, this was heavy artillery indeed. These women were acknowledged—negatively—as the prime movers behind reforms for all species, human and animal. The "fanaticism and crankiness" of these dangerous virgins, charged virulent antifeminist Charlotte Haldane, impelled them to espouse "freak science, freak religions, and freak philanthropy," and to embrace wholeheartedly such contemptible crusades as antivivisection, the bane of England's scientific advancement, dogs' homes and cats' homes, missionary endeavors, and "'Kill-joy' propaganda."

Furthermore, "enough is known [about the psychological effects of permanent virginity]," Haldane opined, "to make us aware that in entrusting responsibility towards individuals and the State to elderly virgins we may be acting unwisely."

Lesbians, styled "intermediate women," were even more problematic. They should be allowed only inferior jobs because as educators or nurses or doctors, "intermediate women may do an enormous amount of harm."

In the manipulative hands of the sexologists and their unlikely Motherhood allies, the celibacy that women seeking independence had once embraced with such delight and firm purpose was now portrayed as sullied and suspicious, a witch's mantle for freaky madwomen or a masquerade for reviled lesbians. Society still demanded virgin brides, but their virginity was their supreme offering to a husband who would maneuver them through the rest of their life. Aging girls—women—who failed to contract a marriage were pitied, but self-styled spinsters with agendas, no matter how noble and important, were condemned in vitriolic terms, their brand of feminism repudiated as antisocial and unworthy of any regard but the most evil eye. Their celibacy had become as loathsome as its object: women's independence and personal fulfillment.

CHAPTER 7

Celibacy as Womanly Duty

CELIBACY AS A GUARANTEE FOR MARRIAGE
Chaste Brides Guarantee Paternity

When and where was the concept of celibacy first articulated? Did it originate as a shamanistic instrument later adopted by ambitious hunters and warriors? Or was it first imposed on nubile women to guarantee their purity for the men they would later breed with? The story of celibacy, in the guise of virginity and chastity, is shrouded in the mists of eons past. Though the hunger to know is too urgent to dismiss, we can only suckle it on pap distilled from prehistoric gleanings, glimpses, and guesses and hope that some true nourishment seeps in.

Myriad pieces of data confirm the near-universal subordination of women from the earliest times. Despite consoling myths about great matriarchies, it is a rare society where women are equal to their men. One study of over eight hundred societies reveals how overwhelmingly males dominate leadership positions, including in their kinship groups. Enormous China, with the world's largest population, typifies humankind's perspective. China has traditionally undervalued women, and even today in its rural areas, women have a 40 percent higher suicide rate than men because they, too, undervalue their lives. The mechanics of this process of universal inferiorization can only be guessed at. What is certain is that, unlike hunter/gatherers and horticulturists, most stable agricultural societies base social continuity and internal stability largely on female celibacy—virginity in girls, chastity-cum-fidelity in wives—the best guarantee for a successful genetic transfer.

This rule's rare exceptions underlie its universality. The male virgins of Papua New Guinea's tiny Enga culture are prime examples of the infrequency of the phenomenon of compulsory male virginity. Conversely, a few cultures value fertility so greatly that their men refuse to waste themselves on women who have not proved themselves by bearing a child. As we shall see, these, too, are anomalies.

Less rare is the societal standard that accepts or even expects premarital sex with the intended spouse, with pregnancy followed swiftly by marriage. A European example is eighteenth-century Georgian England, where in rural parishes—the overwhelming majority—illegitimate births not followed by marriage were a mere 1.5 percent of births in the early seventeenth century, 3 percent in 1750, and still only 6 percent in 1810. However, births within seven months of marriage—though conception was prior to it—were 10.2 percent of first births from 1650 to 1699, 25.5 percent a century later, and by the nineteenth century, over 30 percent. Clearly, in most cases, premarital sex was acceptable with the intended mate and pregnancy precipitated the actual marriage ceremony.

However, many societies that tolerate a lack of chastity among lower-ranking women demand premarital virginity of women of higher status. This class element is complex. It operates partly to reinforce more stringent moral standards on members of its female elite, thereby emphasizing their superior moral worth. Paradoxically, the opposite is often true for its males, who are permitted or even encouraged to indulge in sexual experimentation.

A second major reason for valuing chastity is moral or religious. As humankind evolved, so did belief systems, and we have already seen how spiritual values deal with sexuality and govern its expression. Celibacy, one such manifestation, has its advocates and practitioners such as widows and shamans or priests. Except in isolated communities, it is only selectively practiced; after all, wholesale enforcement would be collective genetic suicide. Virginity in brides, however, is the religious ideal of the great majority of societies.

The third and perhaps the driving force behind this policy is economic. In many societies, a wealthy man's daughter used to be his chattel and, as such, a vehicle for distributing his land and other holdings through a dowry or for acquiring property through a bride price. Chastity, as evidence of the pure and pristine nature of the goods, was at the forefront of qualities necessary in the bride-as-merchandise.

Here is a brief breakdown of the most important considerations underlying this fixation on virginity. First, the bride's chaste maidenhood carries several important guarantees for her husband: (1) that the children she conceives—at least the first one—will be his; (2) that she has not dishonored him by allowing another man to take her maidenhead and have intimate knowledge of her body; (3) that by refraining from sexual activity, she has demonstrated the likelihood of marital fidelity; (4) that by obeying the dictates of her relatives, her culture, and/or her religion, she has proved she is dutiful and likely to submit as well to her husband's authority; and (5) that by coming to her husband unburdened by a child, her dowry and future labor will be devoted exclusively to the new family he and she have just founded.

The bride's family and in-laws also benefit, because (6) her virginity enables her family to negotiate favorable marriage terms; (7) she has shamed neither her own nor her husband's family by acquiring a bad reputation; and (8) she has not violated her religion's strictures against premarital sex, bringing down on her family's head the wrath of offended deities.

For a combination of these reasons, defloration has developed an almost mystical significance. Its imperatives override the urgent stirrings of awakening young bodies and impose chastity. This despite the fact that chastity runs counter to the human female's evolution as a creature unique in her capacity for seasonless, round-the-clock copulation.

This is why, of course, most societies that insist on maidenly virginity tacitly acknowledge that it is unnatural. They do this variously. They devise stringent methods to enforce it—foot-binding and female genital mutilation are examples. They inculcate the principle of virginity into their youth or preach it as a religious tenet. They punish the unchaste, often severely. They marry girls off when they are still too young to be lustful. Lastly, they reward virgins and/or their families. Young women who sacrifice immediate, intimate pleasure may gain considerable economic payback: husbands who will support them, who may even pay—to their families—a hefty bride price for the virtuous young bride.

This trade-off has its ironic dimensions. The indefatigable sexuality that virgins must suppress was part of an evolutionary strategy to attract the strongest, most productive males. Now women must achieve the same goal by repressing that very sexuality, tantalizing prospective mates to purchase it for the price of a marriage vow. (As late as 1981, when the British royal family calculatingly selected an appropriate consort for the heir to the throne, they let the world know that the teenage Diana Spencer's vaunted virginity was one of her most important qualifications.)

This social construct places an enormous responsibility on a woman's shoulders. If, in a single weak or willful moment, she surrenders to her physical nature, she can destroy her future or shame her family.

VIRGINS AND DISGRACED MAIDENS

Now a quantum leap, from reasoned deductions about the general principles governing the behavior of long-vanished societies to three real societies: traditional and modern China, ancient Greece, and several nations in today's Muslim Middle East, all demanding brides preserve their virginity for their husbands to deflower.

For long periods of history, the Chinese increased the chances of maintaining large-scale chastity by crippling little girls' feet so that, as nubile women, they could barely hobble from room to room, much less down past the garden gate to indulge in sexual adventures. Nonetheless, some unmarried women—maimed and unmaimed—were unchaste. Of these, many concealed the fact or got caught by their families or were publicly exposed—for example when the bridegroom fled from the wedding chamber, bleating about having married a "wing-broken bird." How did these lapses occur? In the usual way, and sometimes, even women with bound feet defied probability and were wanton, willful, or seduced.

These unmaidenly maidens felt no spiritual guilt, for their deed had no religious connotations—as females, after all, they were considered lesser beings than males. But they had violated China's pervasive principle of yin and yang, the essential harmony that governs society. Those who were caught dreaded the consequences, for the price of unchastity was dishonor for the entire family. They had defiled the traditional culture of *mianzi*, honoring one's family's prestige.

For women, a sexual peccadillo was costly in other ways. It was difficult or impossible to find a husband for a sullied woman except by subterfuge—passing her off as a virgin. And if a man agreed to accept a nonvirgin, he would not send his bride's family the expensive gifts they could otherwise have expected five or six times a year.

In China today, the old values have not disappeared, though Communism and modernity have modified cultural expectations. In 1985, in an informal survey conducted in Tongxi village, both men and women told researcher Xiao Zhou that female virginity was crucial to a love relationship. In Tongxi, the average groom's family paid four thousand yuan for a wedding, while collectively earning only nineteen hundred yuan per year. *Mianzi* still carries a high price. A soiled bride, on the other hand, does not merit an elaborate wedding, nor will her family's gifts be as fine or as frequent. She herself will receive inferior items: cotton, for instance, instead of precious polyester.

In a curious twist of values, materialism sometimes prevails over *mianzi*. Then a young man's family resorts to "mother's-lock" sex, a common form of entrapment. This happens when they calculate the cost of honor versus dishonor and opt for the latter. A mother will lock her son in a bedroom with his girlfriend, assuming, and desiring, the worst. Once this happens, the ensuing wedding will be an economical affair. Just as important, the mother-in-law will forevermore taunt her daughter-in-law about her indiscretion, thereby controlling the younger woman.

As in China, celibacy in ancient Greece was also a uniquely female virtue. As we have seen, the Greeks did not value celibacy, but their daughters had to remain virginal. Because they regarded girls as lustful, early marriages seemed sensible—less time for brides to succumb to temptation. In this line of thinking, fourteen-year-old girls were considered marriageable, though the men they married were much older.

Sometimes, however, marriage did not come soon enough. If she was caught, the young woman was in terrible trouble. Fathers were obliged to obliterate all reminders of such shameful daughters from the household. Selling them into slavery was a common solution. One Athenian official took more drastic action: he fed his "ruined" daughter to a starved horse. Why not? By her unchastity, the girl had rendered herself a nonentity whose worthless body might as well sate another sort of bestial hunger.

It was, of course, natural for a young woman whose secret lover had actually impregnated her to fight with the wiliness of desperation against her dreadful fate. The most common ploy was to swear the sperm inside was holy and that one of the gods had done this thing to her. Any girl *(parthenos)* who managed to pull this off—and a few did—was not merely saved but was afterward treated as someone protected by divine immunity. After all, punishing a *parthenos,* whom a god rather than a mortal man had deflowered, would inevitably provoke divine retribution.

Palestinian Muslims are reminiscent of the ancient Greeks in their fanatical concern about premarital virginity. If they even suspect a girl has been unchaste, then brothers and fathers storm into action, murdering their own sisters and daughters in "honor killings." Often, these are disguised as accidents by burning the body. In 1991, in the Israeli-Arab town of Ramle, Israeli police detained a sixteen-year-old Arab runaway girl they had caught driving in a stolen car with a married man. The girl begged them not to inform her parents, who would kill her. The police disregarded her pleas and called her parents. "We've got your daughter here. She's very scared—you have to promise you won't hurt her," they said. The parents assured the police they would do no such thing and came to take custody of their daughter. Soon afterward, she was murdered.

So many victims of honor killings are discovered that Suheir Azzouni Mahsi, director of the Women's Affairs Technical Committee in Ramallah, West Bank, estimates one woman a week is murdered in Gaza and the West Bank. "They feel that women should take care to be a virgin when married, and not sleep around," she said.

Palestinians are not alone in their fury at unchaste young women. In 1977, a Saudi princess, Mishaal, faced with an unwelcome arranged marriage, decided to flee her family and country to marry Khalid Muhallal, a man she loved. Before escaping from the country, she and Khalid had to spend a few nights together at a hotel. When they checked out, Mishaal disguised herself as a man and attempted to board a plane at the Jedda airport. She was discovered and turned over to her family.

No trial took place. However, Mishaal's defiance and her bad judgment (perhaps it was her only option) in meeting Khalid in a hotel were unforgivable—she had compromised her virginity, whether or not she had actually lost it. Guilty or not, Mishaal was guilty. The family disagreed about her punishment, but those who begged for her life were overruled. She was shot to death in a parking lot and Khalid was beheaded. As with countless unfortunate women before her, Mishaal's chastity was deemed more valuable than her very life.

TESTING FOR MAIDENHEADS

Throughout the ages and the world, virginity is essential in as-yet-unmarried women. Culture, religion, and societal values demand it; the law enforces it. But how, precisely, does one go about proving virginity? For want of a better method, many cultures have relied on examining the hymen. This is unfortunate, because it is a little-understood membrane, and inspecting a quaking woman's genitalia to ascertain the state of her hymen is, at best, a hit-and-miss affair.

"The Very Fine Membrane Called Honor," a chapter in N. El Saadawi's *The Hidden Face of Eve,* provides the following breakdown about various types of hymens: 11.2 percent of girls have elastic hymens; 16.16 percent delicate hymens that are easily damaged; 31.32 percent thick, elastic hymens; and 41.32 percent hymens that resemble what people suppose is normal.

Nonetheless, this elusive and irritatingly variable membrane has been and still is the object of intense scrutiny, though it is likely that only highly trained physicians can correctly interpret what they see or feel. For every test there is an anti-test, and as many people specialize in concealing or repairing torn hymens as in recognizing them. In the contests between the two groups of "experts," the great moral issue of virginity is reduced to true absurdity.

A common and obvious test for virginity is to stick in a prying finger and investigate. In her haunting novel about a young Haitian girl, *Breath, Eyes, Memory,* Edwidge Danticat describes these "tests." "When I was a girl," Sophie's mother told her, "my mother used to test us to see if we were virgins. She would put her finger in our very private parts and see if it would go inside. . . . A mother is supposed to do that to her daughter until the daughter is married. It is her responsibility to keep her pure."

The Apocryphal Gospels describe how a skeptical Salomé, who had witnessed Jesus' birth, tested Mary just as Sophie's mother tested her. She stuck her fingers into Mary's vagina, but before she could touch the hymen, she felt a searing burn and had to terminate her examination. The divine significance of the incident was not lost on Salomé. Postpartum Mary had passed her test.

Zulus and other South African peoples are currently reviving a similar testing ritual that had all but died out decades ago. With AIDS and other sexually transmitted diseases terrifyingly rampant, the value of virginity has suddenly increased. Virginity testers are often traditional healers who, for a small fee, examine each young client, then issue certificates of virginity to all the girls they believe have not had sex. In the past, virginity testing determined the bride price—a virgin was worth an additional cow, for example. Today, virginity has profound health implications, though some South Africans worry that instead of setting new standards of sexual morality, the certified virgins may be at risk of rape thanks to a widespread myth that sex with a virgin will cure AIDS.

On wedding nights throughout the world, proof of virginity is almost universally required. The commonest form is the bloodied sheet, proudly waved to inquisitive onlookers. Luckily, the sheet test is also the simplest to cheat on. Poor Sudanese girls, including virgins simply taking extra precautions, turn to bribable *dayas,* the local midwives who also perform FGM (female genital mutilation). For a fee, a *daya* will cook her divinations and set the marriage date to coincide with menstruation. If this is not feasible, she will, at the last moment, insert a tiny bag of chicken blood into her client to substitute for any failure of the hymen to bleed. Variations on this method, such as using congealed balls of sheep's blood, are common everywhere.

Greece, where the hymen was believed to be a membrane located in all organs except the vagina, developed different tests for virginity. Herodotus describes a festival at which two groups of supposed virgins armed themselves with sticks and stones and fought fiercely. "Those who died of their wounds were called false virgins," he noted.

In Algeria, the older women say they can spot unchastity in how a deflowered woman walks or hear it when she urinates. Certain Algerian midwives boast they can tell from the color of the genitals. Medical doctors, too, are consulted, so worried parents can produce a *qamija,* a medical certificate. The doctor's examination, however, is easy to circumvent. A real virgin is presented to him or her and the certificate obtained in the false virgin's name.

Physicians sometimes collude in hiding the evidence. In Sudan, for example, wealthy nonvirgins have gynecologists surgically reconstruct the missing membrane. In ancient Greece, where the hymen was not linked with the genitals, perfumed pessaries were used to rejuvenate vaginas.

Repaired, disguised, and substituted hymens, rejuvenated vaginas, false virginity—the forces of deception are powerful. They have to be. The stakes are immense, the consequences of failure unthinkable. Preventive measures, therefore, have been correspondingly harsh: seclusion, genital mutilation, foot-binding, child marriage, terrorization.

The paradox is that all this heavy-handedness and torture are orchestrated to ensure nubile, hormonally driven young women resist every carnal instinct and remain celibate until a suitable man becomes available. If this does not happen—for instance, because a society has a skewed gender ratio or a young woman must wait until a homely older sister finds a mate—the forced virginity is lifelong.

The virgins, alas, are often coerced rather than converted. They understand the gravity of violating the celibacy commandment, if only by witnessing what happens to other women whose unchastity is revealed, but the message is a mechanical one: getting caught brings terrible retribution. The issue is couched in rhetoric about family honor and shame, *mianzi* in almost every language known to man. It is seldom if ever approached from the perspective of the young woman who must bear the burden of abiding by it.

Again, that familiar irony: the least-valued member of society is the one whose virtue is crucial to the honor and prosperity of her entire family. Even to herself, she is inferior, weaker in all ways than males, less deserving of food, education, leisure, personal choice. Temptations abound. Her heart is treacherous and her loins throb. Importuning, testosterone-ridden males make many promises. But if she is caught surrendering her virginity, she becomes society's pariah, scorned, cast out, sold away, stoned by her brother's hand, fed to hungry horses.

This scenario is timeless and international. It both reflects and results from the moral and cultural conundrum on which most societies are constructed. Western nations have only recently slackened their rules and evaluation of unmarried women who are no longer virginal. Elsewhere, the old ways often still reign supreme. And somewhere, even as these lines are written, a hymen has burst and with it, an ex-virgin's world.

Exceptional Aztec and Enga Virgin Bachelors

Though premarital female virginity is one of humankind's great common denominators, most societies impose standards of conduct on young males as well. These range from strict celibacy to licentious experimentation, often with prostitutes or women of low social rank who may be seduced without consequence to the seducer. Curiously, most cultures either frown on masturbation or flat out condemn it, as a dangerous squandering of precious semen or at the very least, a serious breach of decent behavior.

Tellingly, most societies that urge virginity on their young males do little or nothing to punish those who disobey. At various times in the nineteenth and early twentieth centuries, for instance, British and North American mores included caveats against male premarital sexuality. But these changed moral precepts never permeated mainstream culture, and in any case, a penalty for randy male sexuality was nonexistent. The only attempts made to enforce male chastity—of which the Male Purity Movement was the most widespread, cohesive, and forceful—were based on moral suasion and/or fear, usually of disease, sterility, permanent damage to the tender organ, or the loss of vital powers through the lost semen.

Two societies, one cosmopolitan and sophisticated, one isolated and backward, are the exceptions that prove the rule: the ancient Nahuas or Aztecs of Mexico and the Enga people of Papua, New Guinea. Like most others, the culture of the Aztecs was based on male domination, but in terms of its bachelors, it operated rather differently. The Aztecs revered celibacy for both men and women, though like some Greeks, they also believed it had harmful side effects. The virgin daughter of a leading Aztec once came upon a naked man and was consumed by desire for him; afterward, she sickened and swelled up. This was a cautionary tale, but it was one to which the Aztecs had no easy solutions.

Aztec society reflected this dichotomy. Celibacy was requisite for youth from high-ranking families; indeed, it distinguished them from plebeians, whose sexual indulgences were regarded as a mark of inferiority. Among the privileged, celibacy was rigidly enforced for both males and females. Harsh physical punishment awaited transgressors, but the belief that the bodies of the unchaste would remain immature and their brains degenerate was just as compelling a reason to remain chaste. There was also the fear of exposure during penitential exercises. To honor the gods, young men pierced their penises, and anyone who fainted was automatically considered wanton.

Celibacy was also mandatory for students at the *calmecac* or temple. All of these privileged youth from high-ranking families had to swear an oath of chastity, and violators—boy or girl—were executed: either strangled, roasted alive, or pierced by arrows.

Female virginity was so exalted that an unbroken hymen was spoken of metaphorically as a precious jewel. A young woman was motivated to preserve hers by pride, reinforced by her terror of retribution. The disgusted gods would rot her flesh and her husband could reject her if he suspected her hymen was not intact.

Rejection would happen during the marriage festivities, on the sixth day. An unhappy husband would announce his wife's misconduct by serving wedding guests their food in pierced dishes. She would not be stoned to death, as both men and women were for adultery, but she could expect either divorce or an eternally suspicious husband.

In reality, this seldom happened, for Aztec maidens were thoroughly indoctrinated from childhood. A lyrical folk tale repeated a loving father's counsel to his little daughter. "My precious necklace, my precious quetzal plume, my human creation, my offspring," he croons. "You are my blood, my color, in you is my image." Then he warns her: "Do not give up your body in vain, my little daughter, my child, my little dove, my little girl. . . . If . . . you cease being a virgin . . . you will be lost . . . you will never be under the protection of someone who truly loves you." The ecstasy of lovemaking will become your bitterest memory and will haunt you forever, he concludes, because even your husband will always suspect your chastity.

The Aztec preoccupation with premarital celibacy stemmed from their religious convictions and worldview and forged a golden mean between excess and abstinence. By eliminating sexual rivalries, it greatly reduced tensions between the military and the collective laborers. Another important feature of virginity was that it emphasized the difference between youth and adulthood. The Aztecs feared that emotional attachment resulting from an early sexual experience might foster individuality or rebellious independence. This would seriously affect a young person's relations with his family and his future life as a citizen in this highly regulated and hierarchical society.

For quite different reasons, the tiny Enga societies of the New Guinea Highlands also stress bachelor virginity. After a half century of foreign contact, often with Australian and American anthropologists, the Enga number about 180,000 and live on the western side of the Hagen mountain range. The Enga are subsistence farmers who specialize in cultivating sweet potatoes and raising pigs as symbols of wealth and prestige. They share a religious belief system that leads the unmarried men to accept celibacy. Indeed, this precept is so thoroughly instilled that few of them have the slightest desire to disobey it.

The Engas' supreme creator is Aitawe, who inhabits the upper world along with the sky beings, the *yalyakali.* The underworld is populated by ghosts, or *timango,* mighty spirits who interfere constantly in human affairs and sometimes kill humans by biting them, though each *timango* is restricted to a single death-by-biting. *Timango* are mainly malign, and the Enga devote much time to placating them. In particular, they must observe tradition, for the *timango* strike the entire clan to punish a single clan member's transgression.

The Enga must also maneuver between the negative and positive forces of their world. Some negative forces are women, mothers, grandmothers, vaginas, and ghosts. Their positive opposites are men, fathers, grandfathers, penises, and sky deities. Marriage, then, is a union of polarities, often contracted between members of warring clans: "We marry the people we fight!" one Enga clan trumpets.

This is not as anomalous a system of marital selection as it might first appear, because the Enga notion of war is more stylized than real—one anthropologist describes them as "balletic episodes." To foreign eyes, Enga battles resemble fencing matches or duels between fight leaders or bands of warriors armed with bows and arrows. Bloodshed is limited and death infrequent. After a day of fighting, the combatants engage in ritual rhetoric. Later, Enga Big Men on both sides present each other with impressive gifts of pork to mark the return of peace.

Men marry for the first time at twenty to thirty years old, women between fifteen and eighteen years. Both should be chaste, the bride so her clanspeople may arrange a suitable marriage, the groom because only upon marriage can he acquire magical protection against the dangerous consequences of sexual intercourse with women or contact with his wife when she menstruates. The bachelor "knows," for example, that touching a menstruating woman will "in the absence of magic sicken a man and cause persistent vomiting, turn his blood black, corrupt his vital juices so that his skin darkens and wrinkles as his flesh wastes, permanently dull his wits, and eventually lead to a slow decline and death."

This "knowledge" is just the beginning. At about fifteen years, Enga boys join bachelor associations and remain members for about a decade, when they marry. Ritual baths protect them from female influence, and ceremonies preserve the flora that is their subclan's heritage. Ritual retreats enhance the bachelors' physical appearance, including growing their hair, a symbol of masculinity and physical stamina, which must never be cut or even coiffed against the proud possessors' wishes.

Sexual activity by any of these bachelors would endanger them all and kill their precious plant life. The bachelors beat any offender and fine him the price of a pig in compensation for the harm he has done them. They avoid looking at each other's genitals and prudishly refrain from mentioning sex or bodily functions in their conversations. At four-day retreats, essentially bachelors' purification rituals, the agenda is instruction in Enga lore and magic and preparation of appropriate costumes and wigs.

The bachelors also attend dull and decorous courtship ceremonies where they meet chaperoned girls. During these encounters, the men finger their penises with their left hand, guarding them against the fertilizing powers of the right, contaminated by women's touch. In most Enga societies, everyone but disabled adults will marry, so these preparatory activities for future husbands are compulsory, and participants take them seriously.

For the first several weeks after marriage, both bride and groom wear their wedding clothes and decorations and remain chaste. The woman devotes herself to good thoughts about her husband to protect him from the polluting effects of her gender and the sexual intercourse they will soon indulge in. To reinforce this, his clansmen visit her nightly, singing about his virtues and purposefully keeping her awake. Her husband, meanwhile, who is absent during these nocturnal songfests as well as during most of the days, spends his time learning magic to shield him from the perils of imminent coitus and menstruation.

When the new and still-virginal husband is adept enough at magic to copulate, he leads his wife to their fields, and there they finally come together. For four or five days they perform this ritual. Then the husband and his clansmen go hunting for the possums due to his father-in-law as "payment for the wife's vulva."

Enga premarital chastity is integrally linked to ghosts, the wrathful *timango* who serve all human activity and even penetrate thoughts. Without magical interventions that may be acquired only after marriage to ward off the evil consequences of sexual intercourse and contact with women, Enga males feel vulnerable and responsible for potential—indeed, probable—harm that will befall their clanspeople. Premarital chastity may also serve another, unacknowledged purpose: to limit population growth, desirable in this cramped society with such limited resources, where wars perpetually flare between clans trying to subsist on barely adequate land. This extends to the sexual mores of married couples, who make love infrequently and, apart from their initial coupling, never near their gardens, whose fertility they fear contaminating.

THAT PESKY DOUBLE STANDARD

The double standard is a worldwide phenomenon that has many layers of meaning. The first is that one and one is not always two, because a whore is a criminal but her john is a client, and also because a woman must be virginal at marriage and chaste afterward but her husband is not bound by the same constraints. The double standard implies, in other words, that chastity is primarily a woman's domain.

Most of the world's societies—with the exception of the aforementioned ancient Aztecs and the Engas of Papua, New Guinea—observe this double standard. Even in the modern era of the liberal Western world, sexually indulgent or aggressive women are judged much more harshly than men whose conduct is identical. In previous eras, the discrimination was thunderously obvious, preached from pulpits and parliaments and specifically mandated in the law.

The double standard was nefarious not only because it embodied egregious gender inequality but because it condoned prostitution as a sexual outlet for unchaste men. Though it condemned prostitutes as social scum and consigned them to lives of degradation, danger, and disease, it sanctioned their profession. The reason was obvious: without prostitution, lascivious men might seduce rather than marry the virgins of their own social class. It is particularly chilling that the Catholic Church, from St. Augustine on, supported the double standard and, albeit reluctantly, swallowed the equation that no prostitution equals no chastity.

This moral conflict is evident in Catholic Church or canon law, a mélange of moral theology and Roman legalistic thinking that first took coherent form in the mid–twelfth century when the monk Gratian issued his *Decretum*. Soberly considered, the Church's basic premises were ambiguous and morally wobbly. Its laws forced women to abide by a higher standard of sexual conduct than men. They also denounced prostitution but at the same time partially exonerated it as the safety valve that kept virgins pure.

The Church's teachings on this issue colored and reinforced the morality of centuries of Christian civilization. It is unsurprising, then, that the double standard matured as a code of sexual conduct that demanded female chastity and at the same time approved, or at least tolerated, male carnality expressed in the use of prostitutes, though this meant sacrificing certain women to sexually unrestrained men.

In most places, the double standard had its own double standard: it operated differently among different classes. Though a privileged young woman was utterly ruined by the discovery that she had been unchaste, the great mass of workers, industrial and agricultural, had less rigid constraints. In England in 1843, a rural vicar complained to a royal commission that women were so deficient in virtue that they seemed scarcely able to comprehend what chastity meant or to regard it as a virtue. In fact, in the countryside and among much of the urban proletariat, premarital sex between serious beaux was common and acceptable, and pregnancy commonly preceded rather than followed marriage. The vicar misunderstood this and mistook sincere commitment for sexual wantonness.

However, the custom did not exempt working-class women from the deleterious effects of the double standard. Not all males honored their obligations to marry their child's mother. And when men who came from a higher social echelon seduced a working-class girl, they almost never honored that class's code. Domestics and shop girls in particular were the prey of privileged men, but pregnancy destituted these women rather than pushing them into marriage with the baby's father.

Among the middle and upper classes, chastity's double standard wreaked havoc on social decency. This had reached a frenzied peak centuries earlier, during the Restoration inaugurated by Charles II's triumphal return to London in May 1660. Liberated from fourteen years of Cromwellian parliamentarian government and puritanical morality, which even frowned on premarital male sexual activity, young women were coached to trap husbands without surrendering beforehand even a taste of the delights to come. Men were frustrated at this implacable wall of chastity and took it as a challenge. They began, in large numbers, a kind of unholy crusade to seduce young virgins. "Resist, resist!" the virgins' elders urged them. "Just say a resounding 'No' to your pleading, inveigling, deceiving young suitors." After all, as the old adage went, "Who would keep a cow of their own that can have a quart of milk for a penny?" But at the same time, ladies, forgive them for trying to ruin you. This double standard of sexual conduct is necessary, because unlike you, men by nature have urgent, irrepressible needs.

Indeed, prostitution in lecherous, virgin-deflowering, dual-standard England had always flourished, though individual prostitutes or "stews" were seldom prosperous. From the reign of Henry II to Henry VIII, brothels were officially licensed. When the bishop of Winchester took over as supervisor, the stews were renamed "Winchester geese." The eighteenth century was much the same. Prostitutes continued to ply their trade, servicing clients who had either to pay for sex or do without until they married their chaste brides.

This legion of prostitutes, common all over Europe but notoriously plentiful in England, played a crucial role in upholding their societies' notions about chastity. Ironically, the stew was to the virgin as the savior is to the saved. St. Augustine ("Remove prostitutes from human affairs, and you would pollute the world with lust") had, centuries earlier, articulated this famously.

The classic historian of European morals, W. E. H. Lecky, elaborated on Augustine's premise, sensitively casting "the most mournful, and in some respects the most awful," figure of the prostitute as a tragic actor in the human morality play.

> Herself the supreme type of vice, she is ultimately the most efficient guardian of virtue. But for her, the unchallenged purity of countless happy homes would be polluted. . . . She remains, while creeds and civilizations rise and fall, the eternal priestess of humanity, blasted for the sins of the people.

Lecky was right. Prostitutes, reviled though they were, effectively accommodated enough male lechery to ensure "good girls" remained just that. This made prostitution an essential service, without which society's moral standards would collapse under the burden of pent-up lust.

HARLOTS FOR HIRE

The double standard in England was proof incarnate of St. Augustine's observation about the dynamic and essential link between prostitution and enforced chastity. But the credit for the most striking elaboration of the equation—no whores, no chastity—goes to the eighteenth-century medical doctor and writer Bernard Mandeville. In *A Modest Defence of Publick Stews: or an Essay upon Whoring,* Mandeville proposed to protect a great many virgins by legalizing a limited number of prostitutes. He justified his rationale for this moral triage—three virgins to the right so there'll be only one harlot to the left—and then recommended a state-administered system of public whores, civil servants who fornicated for pay.

Whoring, Mandeville began, had become so widespread that Societies for the Reformation of Morals, moral vigilantes who hunted down and prosecuted sinners, had sprung up everywhere.

> The gravest consequences . . . are the *French Pox* [venereal disease], which, in two Centuries, has made such incredible Havock all over *Europe.* . . . The Innocent must suffer by it as well as the Guilty: Men give it to their Wives, Women to the Husbands, or perhaps their Children . . . so that no Age, Sex, or Condition can be intirely [*sic*] safe from the Infection.

Other terrible consequences of "this uncontrolled debauchery" are that "Bastard Infants" are murdered, lascivious young men refrain from marrying because they prefer to indulge in sexual relations with prostitutes, and marriages are destroyed by errant husbands. Seduced young maidens are ruined when "a Slip of this nature is discover'd" because afterward, they have no chance of marrying and are often forced into prostitution.

At bottom, Mandeville felt, human nature is the real culprit, for both men and women are hopelessly lustful. "Alas! this violent Love for Women is born and bred with us; nay, it is absolutely necessary to our being born at all." So, too, women, who were physically constructed for erotic passion: "All our late Discoveries, in Anatomy, can find out no other Use for the *Clitoris,* but to whet the Female Desire by its frequent Erections; which are, doubtless, as provoking as those of the *Penis,* of which it is a perfect Copy, tho' in Miniature."

No wonder that, when they are gripped by "the Violence of Female Desire," women risk anything to satiate it—even "Shame and Poverty are look'd upon as Trifles."

To counterbalance their innate sensuality, social pressures are employed.

> All young Women have strong Notions of Honour carefully inculcated into them from their Infancy. Young Girls are taught to hate a *Whore,* before they know what the Word means; and when they grow up, they find their worldly Interest entirely depending upon the Reputation of their Chastity. This Sense of Honour and Interest, is what we may call artificial Chastity; and it is upon this Compound of natural and artificial Chastity, that every Woman's real actual Chastity depends.

Mandeville's shrewd analyses of seduction and courting rituals, painfully reminiscent though cleverer by far than the offerings in many modern women's magazines, explained how women calculate their lovers will continue to love them as long as they have struggled to maintain their chastity and surrendered it only after being "storm'd" or seduced. Wrong, wrong, wrong, of course—but by then, chastity is a thing of the past.

Before zeroing in on his solution to the problems caused by women's inability to withstand importuning men, Mandeville also dealt with male virginity, which he castigated as strongly as he recommended it in most females. Virgin bridegrooms, he declared, are "mightily shocked at the Disappointment" of the marriage bed. An unchaste man, on the other hand, has totally different reactions: "When he enters into Matrimony, he is prepar'd against any Disappointments . . . and is ready to make Allowance for those Faults and Imperfections which are inseparable from Human Kind. This is so true, that Women have establish'd a Maxim, that Rakes make the best Husbands."

After his elaborate and accurate description of the mechanics of the double standard, Mandeville got to the heart of the matter: "The only way to preserve Female Chastity, is to prevent the Men from laying Siege to it: But this Project of the *Publick Stews* is the only Way to prevent Men laying Siege to it: Therefore this Project is the only Way to preserve Female Chastity."

Legislating against sexual impropriety, he argued, won't work well, but "a Licence for *Publick Stews,* which is a Kind of legal Evacuative," will provide lusty men with a clean, safe outlet. They will "prefer the ready and willing Embrace of a Courtezan, before the doubtful and distant Prospect of enjoying a modest Damsel, whose Coyness will cost so much Pains, as well as Time, to overcome; and when overcome, may probably occasion a future Uneasiness, and give them more Trouble after Enjoyment than they had before."

One of these "Troubles" is venereal disease. In Mandeville's clinical experience, young girls who cave in then proceed to sleep around with such abandon that they contract diseases, and should be avoided for that reason alone. A "Publick Stew," however, would undergo routine medical inspections, and if she reported any suspicious symptoms herself, would be treated free of charge. (However, two such strikes and she was an out-of-work, ex–Public Stew.)

As a bleak and unblinking look at the double standard this medical doctor knew so well—venereal disease, abortion, infanticide, young women ruined—*A Modest Defence of Publick Stews* is a brilliant document. Even more shattering is Mandeville's sincerity in proposing a system of carefully regulated prostitution as a solution. The double standard would remain in full force, laundered and made tolerable by decriminalizing prostitution.

As Mandeville would undoubtedly agree, the effects of the double standard he tackled so long ago still resonate today. He might even nod approvingly at feminist writer Naomi Wolf's statement that "all women suffer a hangover from our long understanding of the relationship between wives, nuns, and virgins, on the one hand, and prostitutes and courtesans, on the other. . . . Virtually every woman who was not an aristocrat had to uphold an ideology of respectability and chastity that distinguished her from a prostitute."

OUTRAGED WOMEN DEMAND CHASTE MEN

Mandeville's recommendations notwithstanding, prostitution evolved and flourished as a nongovernmental operation. Legions of Victorian men accepted and honored the code of premarital celibacy, but many spoiled and randy young blades saw no need to repress their erotic longings. When women of their own class refused to succumb, they found a vulnerable and cooperative woman elsewhere. She was, perhaps, a domestic servant that a higher-ranked young man could force himself on, or the shop girl he paid or flattered for a few minutes of extracurricular pleasure. At one time or another in his life, she was likely the "public stew," the prostitute whom that compromised servant or shop girl might eventually be forced to become.

To desperate, reckless, or ruined women, the calling of the streets was irresistible. It supplemented the pittance they earned elsewhere at their day jobs. Henry Mayhew, an investigative journalist and author whose exposé of London's seething, suffering laboring class in the mid–nineteenth century continues to shock, discovered, for instance, that a seamstress who stitched together moleskin trousers could earn five shillings and sixpence a week, scarcely enough to survive, if she worked sixteen hours daily. When work was slack, she could either starve or "go a bad way" and sell her body.

Because so many women were struggling to survive by needlework, lacemaking, and other trades, with occasional forays into prostitution, the competition was ferocious. As a result, incomes remained low, arrests and imprisonment common, and their unhealthy bodies were susceptible to venereal disease. Some managed to support themselves by prostitution alone, and a few lucky and clever ones did better—they parlayed their amorous skills into marriage. "Why shouldn't we?" inquired one confident streetwalker. "We are pretty, we dress well, we can talk and insinuate ourselves into the hearts of men by appealing to their passions and their senses."

But in the last half of the nineteenth century, venereal disease invaded the latter-day flock of Winchester geese, and prostitution and the double standard became the concern of reformers of every ilk. In earlier centuries, and despite Mandeville's alarm, only inconsequential numbers of deaths were attributed to the so-called French pox, as syphilis was called in England. In

London, according to the Bills of Mortality, it struck down eleven victims in 1813, eighty-six in 1817, and only nineteen and fourteen in 1818 and 1819. Prostitutes and their clients, and those secondarily infected, endured nasty and debilitating symptoms, but doctors could provide effective treatment and restore most patients to health. For centuries, venereal disease was seen as a disturbing problem rather than a critical one.

In 1864, a drastic change occurred, after horrified medical officers reported that gonorrhea and syphilis affected up to 30 percent of the troops in British garrison towns, including many ports. The military capacity of the nation was called into question. In panicky attempts to stamp out or at least control these diseases among soldiers and sailors, Parliament passed a series of Contagious Diseases Acts between 1864 and 1869. These Acts authorized police in towns with substantial military installations to seize any suspected prostitutes and force them to submit to a vaginal examination every two weeks. Infected women (but not men) could be confined to a hospital for up to nine months.

The object was to diminish venereal infection by controlling prostitutes, but the real effect was to persecute thousands of women, sexually active or not. Any woman out alone in public without a reasonable excuse was a target. Homeless girls were routinely hauled off and painfully examined, and one widow afterward committed suicide. Women plucky enough to resist were charged in police court, where it was their word against that of a plainclothes government spy. Furthermore, prostitutes but not their clients were charged in criminal court. "What think you of sending a wench to Bridewell [prison], and doing nothing to the fellow that debauch'd her, tho' sometimes the first is single, and the other married?" demanded one opponent of the double standard.

Until the passage of the Contagious Diseases Acts, prostitution and its underlying moral duplicity had had mainly muted challengers. The Acts, embodying the worst features of the double standard, provoked sustained and widespread protest. One group of critics proposed a novel solution that Dr. Mandeville had left unexplored in his essay on Rampant Whoring: that men stop doing it. Chastity in men? How preposterous, given their naturally lecherous natures and irrepressible sexual impulses! (This would have surprised the ancient Aztecs, Chinese, Greeks, and a few million other people who "knew" that women were the culprits when it came to sexual desire.) And yet, if men could only get a grip on themselves (but absolutely not with the masturbatory handshake that so distressed the Male Purity contingent) and just tell themselves, "No!"

This at least was the thinking of the Church of England Purity Society, as well as thousands of feminist activists in late-Victorian England. The Purity Society was formed at the instigation of Jane Ellice Hopkins, a lifelong celibate dedicated to ending the degradation of women through prostitution by the novel expedient of reforming men's bad behavior. Hopkins also worked with young women at risk for prostitution, providing counseling, clothes, lodging, and a job registry with real jobs rather than the fake come-on ads that duped gullible, desperate, and unemployed girls into servitude as harlots.

Men's chastity leagues, Hopkins declared, should be developed to deal with the "real cause" of Rampant Whoring and moral decay—that pesky double standard. "What I crave," she wrote, is to instill in wayward men "a good, strong passionate sense of the pitifulness of degrading women, inflicting a curse which they do not share with so much as their little finger." These men indulge, then return to their "jolly" lives and friends, their "pleasant" homes and their careers, their "power of marrying" intact. Behind them, in the debris of their sexual fling, are their female victims, destined to lives as social outcasts, barred forever from the safety and comforts of marriage and motherhood. The women might be infected with a "hideous" disease and could expect only "a degraded life and [then to] die a Godless, Christless, hopeless death."

After Hopkins exposed the Anglican Church's complacency and tacit complicity in upholding the double standard, the Church was shamed into creating its Purity Society. Its pledge cards, signed by hundreds of men and strikingly reminiscent of today's Promise Keepers, listed five obligations: to respect all women and defend them from wrong; to reject indecent language and jokes; to maintain sexual purity equally for men and women; to proselytize these principles; and to maintain personal purity.

Contrary to Dr. Mandeville, with his hypothetical, well-regulated sexual civil service, Hopkins hated prostitution and blamed men for driving women, consumed by "disease, degradation, curses, drink, despair," into it. "Ay, I know that it is often the woman who tempts; these poor creatures must tempt or starve. But that does not touch the broad issue, that it is men who endow the degradation of women; it is men who, making the demand, create the supply."

And thunderingly, "Is it fair for you men, who can compel a fair wage for your work, to sit in judgement on her, and say it is her fault?"

Hopkins's dream for starving out (rather than institutionalizing) prostitution consisted of three kinds of coexisting municipal societies: male purity leagues to inspire men to learn self-control; vigilante committees to see that they did and to prosecute those who failed; and women's associations to work directly with at-risk girls. Hopkins's was as radical a proposal as Mandeville's. Each individual man provoked into feeling his guilt could be induced to take responsibility for his actions and stop sinning.

Another group to which Hopkins belonged, the Moral Reform Union, founded in 1881, rejected the double standard and accepted as a principle that men and women should abide by the same morality. They were convinced that both could be chaste and denounced as a blasphemous fiction the age-old, Mandeville-endorsed premise that prostitution was essential for a few to ensure moral purity in the majority. What the Union members wanted was quite simply virtue and rectitude in men. The Contagious Diseases Acts were, the Union said, inequitable laws based on the double standard and its outrageous hypothesis that a group of bought women was necessary to the smooth functioning of a society. *Et tu,* Dr. Mandeville!

Decades of sustained outrage against this monstrous assumption and against the Acts themselves produced their suspension in 1883 and their repeal three years later. Feminist purists rejoiced, but their rapture was modified by the reality that prostitution continued to thrive as a nightmarish degradation of womanhood. The seduced maid was still kicked out onto the street if she became pregnant. The streetwalker caught soliciting was still locked up in jail. The battle against the Contagious Diseases Acts had been won, but not the greater war against prostitution and the double standard.

The moral purists attacked the issue from several angles. One was to stamp out the notion that men's sexual desire was too urgent to curb. For centuries, ever since sex-crazed women had been erased from the moral lexicon and replaced by sex-crazed men, this unstoppable male urge had justified prostitution and other sexual abuses. If it could be exposed for what it was—an unscientific fabrication—then self-control would take on new possibilities as men (and women) learned to regard male sexuality as a normal physical trait, akin to any other hunger. A man who overpowered a vulnerable woman by subterfuge or muscles would be judged as reprobate as one who stuffed food into his mouth before the grace or snatched cutlets from other people's plates. As one suffragette put it, "The man or woman who is incapable of sexual self-control should be walking about on four legs, and not on two, because lack of self-control is incompatible with human nature."

The other myth to be combated was that celibacy weakened the male physiology, for ironically, while millions of men worried about the loss of even one drop of semen, others anxiously observed their chaste genitalia for signs of atrophy. The medical establishment was also coming around, and some physicians admitted publicly that modern scientific thought ran counter to a persistent superstition that chastity was physically harmful to men. (Even today the old heresy limps on, as some men and some women weigh celibacy against the mantra "If you don't use it, you lose it.")

Over a century and a half after Mandeville's *Modest Defence of Publick Stews,* the moral purity movement took on the same issues but proposed diametrically different solutions. For its members, chastity in vulnerable young women was a right that self-indulgent men imperiled. Chastity in men, on the other hand, was a proud, moral measure of self-control and constituted the best possible protection against sexual abuse of women.

After the repeal of the Contagious Diseases Acts, the moral purists and other reformers focused on the age of prostitutes. In England, the age of consent was twelve. Grown men eagerly sought out prepubescent girls, knowing they had nothing to fear from the law. Some were pedophiles, but often their concern was to protect themselves against venereal disease, which virgins did not carry. In consequence, a supply of very young girls, often spurious virgins, came onto the prostitution market.

The opposition to changing this was powerful and persistent. Many legislators were themselves unrepentant brothel habitués and resisted all efforts to modify the legislation. In 1875, they relented slightly and raised the age of consent to thirteen. Moral reformers saw this as a cynical reaffirmation of the double standard. Underclass women over the age of thirteen remained virtually unprotected, and men of all classes considered them fair game.

For an entire decade, nothing changed while the spotlight was on the Contagious Diseases Acts. Then in 1875, the Herculean efforts of reformers and a crusading journalist named William Thomas Stead convinced the reluctant lawmakers to raise the age of consent to a more acceptable sixteen.

Stead was the son of a Congregational minister and the doting father of six children. At the age of sixty-two, he went down on the *Titanic,* quietly reading in the first-class smoking room, a Nobel Peace Prize nominee on a doomed journey to a peace conference. In his prime, Stead used his editorship of *The Pall Mall Gazette* to research and expose flaws and inequities in his society. His grandstanding journalistic campaign on behalf of ruined young girls was startlingly unorthodox. First, he found a London police officer willing to be quoted about how abysmally the law protected girls. When Stead inquired, "Is it or is it not a fact that, at this moment, if I were to go to the proper [whore]-houses, well introduced, the keeper would, in return for money down, supply me in due time with a maid—a genuine article, I mean, not a mere prostitute tricked out as a virgin, but a girl who had never been seduced?"

The police source replied without a moment's hesitation, "Certainly."

Having established the situation surrounding his issue, Stead proved his point in a manner that went far beyond investigative-reporting techniques. Through a brothel-keeper, he actually negotiated with a certain Mrs. Armstrong, an alcoholic mother, to purchase her virginal daughter Eliza (a pseudonym for Lily), "a bright, fresh-looking little girl, who was thirteen years old last Christmas." Stead and Armstrong struck a deal, and Eliza was his for the price of five pounds. However, before he paid the entire sum, Stead had the girl's virginity professionally certified by Madame Mourez, an abortionist/midwife, "whose skill in pronouncing upon the physical evidences of virginity is generally recognized in the profession." After a brief examination, Madame Mourez issued a written certificate of virginity. She was even moved to exclaim to Stead, whom she assumed was about to deflower young Eliza, "She is so small, her pain will be extreme. I hope you will not be too cruel with her."

With his certified virgin in tow, Stead stepped firmly off the path of acceptable journalistic practice and into a netherworld of quasi-criminality, morally justified, tactically sound, but legally indefensible. Stead instructed his brothel-keeping agent to take Eliza to a whorehouse on Regent Street. There, "despite her extreme youth, she was admitted without question," Stead reported. She was also undressed and put to bed, quieted with chloroform purchased from Madame Mourez, the abortionist, who had enthusiastically recommended it for deflowering virgins. Stead then entered Eliza's room, closing and locking the door. Silence. Then, with a scream "like the bleat of a frightened lamb," the drowsy child cried, "in accents of terror, 'There's a man in the room! Take me home—oh, take me home!'"

Eliza need not have worried. She was in no danger of being raped. She was merely the sacrificial lamb in Stead's blazing crusade to reform the age-of-consent laws. Once his cautionary drama had been played out and documented, Stead arranged for Eliza's passage out of merciless England to France. Then he sat down at his desk and penned his account of Eliza's adventure.

"The Maiden Tribute of Babylon" caused a sensation. "An Earthquake has shaken the foundations of England," proclaimed the bishop of Truro. Ironically, Stead soon replaced Eliza as principal victim of the exposé. He was charged, convicted, and condemned to three months in prison for exporting a minor without parental consent. Stead responded bitterly. "What else could one expect?" he declared, given that the very legislators he had hoped to prod into reform were themselves patrons of Mrs. Jeffries's brothel in Chelsea or Berthe's on Milton Street. Despite this, Stead's revelations created an outpouring of public outrage, including a four-hundred-thousand-name petition that, unrolled, was two and a half miles long. The legislators, secret clients of brothels or not, caved in and raised the age of consent to sixteen. Though women over sixteen remained unprotected against sexually predatory males, this legislation was nonetheless a heavy blow to England's historically entrenched double standard.

Today, hard-won laws in North America and much of Europe have established a measure of equality that has deeply eroded the most blatant manifestations of the double standard. Feminists of both genders keep vigilant watch to ensure the old ways of thinking, acting, and legislating do not creep back into use, at least in the law. However, even now, remnants linger on. Randy young men still sow their wild oats, but the girls they sow them with are sluts. The double standard is eroding, but chastity still bears a woman's face.

White Women, Black Men

The American South shared this double standard, but its unique society—white and black; free, freed, and slave—so complicated the issue that it was played out quite differently, though the racial caste system shared some elements of the class divisions elsewhere. And because slavery was a legal institution, only after the Civil War abolished it was the race-muddled double standard even dented.

Delicate as lilies, spotless as doves, polished as alabaster, fragile as porcelain—such creatures as these certainly belonged high up on a secure, untouchable pedestal. In the South, that was where, metaphorically, the antebellum white women were stashed away. Their flesh-and-bloodedness was ignored, their sexuality and passions denied. "In Georgia," one observer commented wryly, "a woman was not supposed to know she was a virgin until she ceased to be one."

White female chastity was so prized that impugning it carried a monetary penalty; one smeared South Carolinian woman was awarded $1,000 from a defendant of modest means. Southern gentlemen seducers, despite the oxymoronic term, were deemed guilty primarily of betraying their society's moral code, while their victims were blamed for the actual seduction. Certainly a seduced woman would pay the price of a ruined life with no remission for subsequent blameless conduct.

So far, business as usual—the double standard nicely trimmed and flying at full staff. But in the American South, slavery and racism contributed their special leaven, imposing double standard upon double standard. The tension here was not merely between white men and white women, but between white men and black women and white women and black men. (Black men and black women pursued their own paths, following remembered West African standards and pitting themselves as best they could against white men's sexual predations.)

White men, whose own women were supposedly brushing heaven atop the proverbial pedestal of chastity, had no compelling reason for sexual purity. Unlike the Cheyenne, for example, who bound their women into chastity belts, then remained celibate as well, the Southerner turned his lust on captive black women without means to resist him. One British visitor put it nicely:

"The men of the South especially are more indelicate in their thoughts and tastes than any European people; and exhibit a disgusting mixture of prudery and licentiousness combined . . . one of the effects of the system of slavery, and the early familiarity with vicious intercourse to which it invariably leads."

In fact, the mixed-race population of the American South was almost exclusively the product of white-men/black-women relationships, though a few lower-class white women opposed society's norms and slept with or married black men.

Miscegenation, the inelegant and condemnatory term for interbreeding, accounted for 4 to 8 percent of all slave births during the 1850s. One Louisiana planter commented that no pretty black woman in his state could escape being a white man's concubine. (This phenomenon was less widespread in the other slave states.) It was essential, however, for the liaison to be secret or at least discreet. Kentucky politician Richard Johnson, who during the 1820s and 1830s unwisely lived with, loved, and educated the daughters he had with his mulatto housekeeper, Julia Chinn, could make no headway in Southern Democratic politics because of his "scorn of secrecy."

Usually, the offspring of black women and white men were simply treated as slaves, for the child of a slave inherited his mother's legal status. Some were freed and cared for, but far more simply served in lighter-skinned bondage. Plantation mistress Mary Boykin Chestnut lamented in her journal:

> God forgive us, but ours is a monstrous system, a wrong and an iniquity! Like the patriarchs of old, our men live all in one house with their wives and their concubines; and the mulattoes one sees in every family partly resemble the white children. Any lady is ready to tell you who is the father of all the mulatto children in everybody's household but her own. Those, she seems to think, drop from the clouds.

This legacy of slavery died a slow death. Twentieth-century, Mississippi-born writer Willie Morris recalled that he was twelve years old before he realized sexual intercourse was not the exclusive province of animal-passioned black women with white men, but that white women, too, were sexual beings.

The Southern double standard, coupling as it did white female chastity and white male lasciviousness, primarily with black women, meant white and black women had radically different personal experiences. White women had to preserve their chastity at any cost, all the while aware their men were indulging at will with black women, often without bothering even to conceal their infidelities. The myth of the white belle's innocence must have been galling indeed to the woman whose husband was obsessed by a slave woman he was bedding in his family's home. Black women, for their part, had to deal with both their own men and white aggression. Many successfully fought off unwanted attention, and some black men died defending their women. The high rate of miscegenation, however, is proof that slavery empowered white men at the expense of everyone else.

Contemplating this, as millions did prior to the Civil War, led to a scarifying question: What if black men were to turn their sights to—God and the law forbid!—white women? What if, as the pro-slavery folks often demanded of the abolitionists, a black man wished to *marry* a white man's daughter?

The abolitionists confronted this horrid notion head on. A few, such as William Lloyd Garrison, were blunt: "Slaveholders generally should be the last persons to affect fastidiousness on that point; for they seem to be enamoured with amalgamation." Others argued white men had so wronged black women that they had put their own wives and daughters at risk from enraged black men. Abolition of slavery would hasten the end of this intolerable situation and liberate vulnerable white women as well as slaves. In fact, this was one of the abolitionists' strongest counterarguments to slavery defenders' fears about rampaging black male sexuality.

The abolitionists' other strategy was to shore up their own morality through strict adherence to the tenets of Moral Purity, from suppressing lust to dampening their physical appetites with bland concoctions of Graham flour. (Many were fanatical believers in the flour's properties of moral purification, though one felt it improved only his bowel movements.) The abolitionists yearned to eradicate not merely the double standard of slavery, in which different-hued men and women were unequal, but also the double standard of gender. Southern white women, however, did not lend their support to this campaign. They wanted an end to the sexual double standard and the grievous humiliation and jealousy it caused them. Most had not, however, the slightest interest in stamping out slavery, the institution that exempted them from the unremitting round of household chores their sexual rivals performed for them.

Of course, not all white Southerners were unbridled lechers. In *Roll, Jordan, Roll,* Eugene Genovese quotes David Gavin, a forty-four-year-old bachelor worried that his continued celibacy is causing various health problems. This virgin was certainly an exception but not a freakish one. Enough men practiced prolonged celibacy for the *New Orleans Medical and Surgical Journal*'s editors to publish an article warning of its consequences: "irritable state of the testes, headaches, malaise, etc. and from nocturnal emissions." Like the North, the South was changing. "By the early nineteenth century," Genovese concludes, "many slaveholders had become prudes, with enough exceptions to torment the quarters."

The South's double-double standard, integrating sexism and racism in a complicated brew and forcing virginity only on unmarried white women and celibacy on white widows, survived and flourished after emancipation. Antebellum uneasiness about black males, however, intensified to collective paranoia. Centuries of sexual wrongdoing convinced white men that black men, too, were lustful and hankered after all white women. As a result, any black man even suspected of sexual misconduct with a white woman was a candidate for vigilante justice. (This was the hostile and suspicious ambience Father Divine survived during his years of proselytizing throughout the South.)

Prior to 1880, lynch mobs were often equal-opportunity killers, stringing up black and white alike. Afterward, about 80 percent of victims were black males. The lynchings, which tended to occur during the hot summer months, were frequently accompanied by torture. Castration was common. The October 1934 lynching of Claude Neal in Marianna, Florida, was typical: "After taking the nigger to the woods . . . they cut off his penis. He was made to eat it. Then they cut off his testicles and made him eat them and say he liked it." After prolonged and unspeakably grotesque torture, Neal died.

Any miscegenation that occurred, the lynching mentality vowed, would be the offspring of black women and white men, not white women and black men. Sexual innuendo was by no means the only cause of the 2,805 confirmed lynchings in the Southern states between 1882 and 1930. But the genital mutilation that so often preceded execution speaks volumes about white preoccupation with black male sexuality and underscores how guilty terror was transmogrified into obscene hatred. Not only did the abolition of slavery fail to crush the South's double standard, it may even have intensified and hardened it, in all its complex intricacies.

AIDS TO CHASTITY

Chastity Belts

We have all heard, and probably joked, about chastity belts. We know, vaguely, that they were used in the olden days. If pressed, we might even cobble together a description. Weren't they gruesome contraptions, bolted around hapless women's loins like enormous, saw-toothed, metal Kotex pads? Didn't jealous husbands use them before setting out on long voyages? Weren't some of these husbands holy Crusaders, leaving civilized Europe to Christianize the heathen? Or was it the opposite, that Crusaders returning from foreign conquests carried with them as booty these exotic monstrosities?

In fact, chastity belts were exceedingly rare. They were not unicorns—they did really exist—but they are far more common in literature and in the popular imagination than as actual hardware, and in Europe, only the cruelest, most obsessive men forced their women into one. Those unlucky women, however, numbered at least in the hundreds. The discomfort, inconvenience, humiliation, and often agonizing chafing they suffered was the terrible price exacted from them to guarantee exclusive access to their body.

In Europe, chastity belts as genital chain mail were designed to enforce fidelity in women. As far as we know, they were unlike the Cheyenne Indians' rope-and-rawhide device, China's bound feet, and Africa's female genital mutilation, which were used primarily to protect maidenly virginity.

Most authenticated chastity belts are from the late sixteenth and early seventeenth centuries. Several court cases resulted from the injuries they caused their wearers. One involved a jealous Danish husband who bolted his wife into a chastity belt. For months she endured the pain it caused her, until her friends intervened and insisted she have it removed. Her predicament became public and an outcry ensued. Her husband was summoned to court, which banished him for his cruel treatment of his wife. But as late as 1892, a Frenchman named Hufferte seduced a young girl, then became so ragingly jealous that he put her into a chastity belt. What happened afterward is uncertain, but newspapers of the period reportedly sometimes carried advertisements for these items.

Information about chastity belts comes from several sources: actual specimens found in museums throughout Europe, including many in out-of-the-way villages; historical documents; records of judicial proceedings; and in literature and art. The British Museum, for instance, has a copy of a Heinrich Aldegreyer engraving portraying a love-struck young couple, naked except for her chastity belt. In one hand she grips a key, evidently to the one garment she wears, and stares uncertainly into his pleading eyes. Dare she or daren't she? That is the unanswered question.

The final consideration is how, precisely, did chastity belts work? If they were like coats of armor for the genitals, how did their unfortunate wearer urinate, menstruate, and move her bowels? How, after performing these functions, could she clean herself?

First of all, surviving belts are all slightly different, but their essential design is the same. They have hip bands formed of anywhere from four to ten iron-jointed strips. The portion that passes between the legs is also jointed so it bends back up again, behind the woman's posterior. Some attention was given to decoration and the wearer's comfort. Designs are etched into the surface, and the insides are padded with velvet or silk. There is a slit in the front for urine and blood, and a hole, often heart-shaped, in the rear for feces. These openings are surrounded by saw-edged teeth that would quickly lacerate or mince any penis inserted into them.

An obvious problem was that the metal dug or bit into the flesh and, at the very least, chafed it. Unless the woman could urinate and defecate with unusual precision, the interior of the belt must soon have been fetid, soiled, and caked with errant excrement. Sleeping must have been nightmarishly difficult, as the belt pressed down onto the flesh. Washing the enclosed areas was impossible, for the sharp metal teeth at each womanly aperture would be as lethal to fingers holding a cloth as to a penis.

The chastity belt tortured real women, but as a metaphor in literature and popular culture, it has titillated millions. As a genital shield, it kept individual women chaste. As a symbol, it has been a powerful reminder to millions of how important chastity is and to what stupendous lengths men have gone to ensure their women observe it. The belts, of course, have nothing to do with the positive aspects of chastity and everything to do with the double standard and the outmoded concepts of male dominance over women's bodies that are associated with it.

Clearly the idea of guaranteeing women's virtue by locking up their genitals has a universal appeal to men petrified of the possibility of unchaste brides. In North America, the Cheyenne people also invented the chastity belt. The Cheyenne view of premarital chastity was so grim that a young woman had no hope of a respectable marriage if a boy had so much as touched her genitals or breasts—Cheyenne virginity was a deadly serious business. As soon as a girl first menstruated, she had to wear a rope-and-rawhide chastity belt that circled her waist, was knotted in front, then drawn down and backward between her thighs in two pieces. Each piece was curled around and around each thigh to just above the knee. This contraption guarded the genitals but did not interfere with the woman's gait, so she could walk normally even when it was on. She always attached it at night and, when she was away from home, during the day as well. Even after marriage, her husband might oblige her to resume wearing it during his long absences during hunting season or war parties.

The Cheyenne regarded the belt as perfect protection, and each man knew that if he attempted to undo it, his victim's male relatives would probably kill him and her female relatives would destroy his family's property. At the turn of the twentieth century, for instance, when a lustful man called Lone Elk untied a girl's belt, her family's furious women stormed his lodge, killed his horses, and smashed everything they could find. Next they proceeded to his parents' lodge, where his father, in accordance with Cheyenne custom, stepped aside as they trashed his possessions.

The Cheyenne chastity belt was a less drastic contrivance than the European model. On the other hand, it was universal and by custom assured a girl's inviolability, hence chastity. Males respected it and the penalties for tampering with it were draconian enough to enforce that respect. As a result, Cheyenne women were famed for their chastity, and those few who willingly surrendered it were disgraced for life.

This sexual austerity extended into marriage. Cheyenne husbands punished unfaithful wives by "putting them on the prairie," a form of institutionalized gang rape, sometimes followed by cutting off their noses. In one tribal version, "they post some thirty young men on the road by which they know their wives must pass . . . the husband issues from the ambuscade and says to his wife: 'As I know that you are fond of men, I offer you a feast of them—take your fill.' Her cries are futile; several of them hold her, and they enjoy her one after the other." (Virgins unwilling to marry were subjected to the same sexual violence in an attempt to force marriage on them.)

Cheyenne society was unusual in that male chastity was also highly regarded. (This is dealt with in chapter 8, "Abstaining in a Good Cause.") Obviously a society with virtually no available women must develop an ethos of chastity for all its members, in contrast to the double standard, which can operate only with prostitution as an integral element. Seen in this light, the Cheyenne chastity belt was as much symbol as it was physical obstacle to sexual activity. What made it so successful was the community's commitment to chastity as the only acceptable way of life.

Female Genital Mutilation

Chastity belts are deplorable, but they can be unlocked or hacked off, and the women imprisoned inside them healed and perhaps restored. The ultimate chastity device, however, is irreversible, and tragically, it forces millions of women into a premarital celibacy they might just as easily have adopted through religious or intellectual conviction. This device is actually a surgical procedure: the amputation of part or all of the body parts that sexual intercourse normally involves. It is usually called female genital mutilation, or FGM.

FGM has three versions. In ascending order of brutality they are excision or clitoridectomy; intermediate; and infibulation or pharaonic circumcision. The following definitions are taken from Alice Walker's documentary *Warrior Marks: Female Genital Mutilation and the Sexual Blinding of Women:*

Excision or Clitoridectomy: Removal of the clitoris and all or part of the labia minora.

Intermediate: Removal of the clitoris, all or part of the labia minora, and sometimes part of the labia majora.

Infibulation or Pharaonic: Removal of the clitoris, the labia minora, and much of the labia majora. The remaining sides of the vulva are stitched together to close up the vagina, except for a small opening, which is preserved with slivers of wood or matchsticks.

FGM plunges both its practitioners and its victims into a time warp. In most parts of the world where it thrives, nothing much has changed in centuries. Old women with grimy hands slice off unanesthetized small girls' genitalia with sharpened (or worse, blunt) stones or knives, scrape off resistant flesh, sometimes with their fingernails, then sew up this handiwork wound with thorns, all the while ignoring the shrieks and protests of their delirious and often dying "patients." *The Economist* estimates that, currently, six thousand girls are mutilated every day.

P.K., a Malian woman, recalls the experience from her own childhood. Her mother, anticipating her child's agony, was terribly upset. The excisor was an old woman from the blacksmith caste. P.K. was anxious, having "seen recently excised girls walking. I can tell you it was not a pretty sight. From the back you would have thought they were little bent old ladies, who were trying to walk with a ruler balanced between their ankles."

But the women lied to P.K., denying her circumcision would be painful. Then they grabbed her and pulled her legs apart. They poured sand over her genitals, perhaps to stanch the blood. She felt a hand clutching her genitals, and a fierce pain. The excision of the labia minor and the clitoris was already under way. As P.K. lay helpless, the agony seemed interminable, and though girls her age were not supposed to cry, she wept and shrieked as the searing pains racked her young body. She felt the wetness of blood gushing out of her gaping wounds. The women stanched the bleeding with a concoction of butter and medicinal herbs, but the pain was excruciating, and it continued. After she was mutilated, P.K. had more terrible moments whenever she had to move her bowels.

The death rate from FGM is unrecorded, but it is believed to be high, and the genitally mutilated are much more likely than intact women to die in childbirth. In survivors, the long-term medical consequences are enormous. Urination through a tiny, unsewed-up hole is often difficult, menstruation always so. Dr. Saida, a Sudanese female gynecologist, explains, "Blood cannot be passed normally. It is retained for a long time and results in a great deal of pain. . . . The blood is black by the time it is passed, and there is much clotting."

Other problems may never be treated. Dr. Saida says internal examinations are impossible to perform. This includes vaginal smears or even inserting a catheter. Even if a physician were able to see up into the mutilated woman, her insides are so abnormal that it is easy to make a wrong diagnosis.

FGM also assists in the relentless spread of AIDS. As the incisor cuts child after child without sterilizing her bloodied knife or blade, she may also transmit HIV from one infected child to all the rest. As the number of HIV-positive children born of HIV-positive parents increases, AIDS as well as chastity is a consequence of FGM.

These primitive operations have one principal purpose: to render their subjects incapable of illicit sexual activity or indeed, as pharaonically infibulated brides experience on their dreaded wedding nights, of any sort of sexual activity performed without cruel and unusual force. "There is nothing left to feel," says Fahtma, the educated wife of a U.S.-educated Sudanese government official. "When your husband comes to you, it is the same as if he came with a stick to a piece of leather."

Ahmed, a young veterinarian, describes a typical wedding night with a wife like Fahtma. First, penetration on the first night "is virtually impossible. You are dealing with heavy scar tissue that is overgrown, and you are using flesh to penetrate it, and not iron." Traditionally, men open up their terrified wives with knives or swords. Otherwise, they will emerge from the bridal chamber with penis throbbing and abraded, as if they had violated a saw-toothed chastity belt instead of their wife's mutilated vagina. These honeymoon ventures often land both husband and wife in the hospital. In Ahmed's Sudanese culture, nuptial sex is so perilous it frequently requires medical intervention.

It is, of course, unlikely such unbreachable women will stray before marriage or even succumb to rapists, who are as inadequately equipped as husbands. FGM assures celibate brides but at unimaginable cost. "Pharaonic circumcision," as Fahtma says, "is essentially something that is meant to control something that people feel they will not be able to stop otherwise, and that is women's free expression of sex."

Fahtma is an educated woman. Most genitally mutilated women are not, and usually, they do not have the slightest idea of what FGM is supposed to accomplish. Two weeks after their circumcisions, two young Gambian girls spoke with American writer and anti-FGM crusader Alice Walker. We were not told why we were circumcised, they said to her, except that it is a tradition. Even if we asked our parents, they would not tell us, nor do we wish to know. But we will do this to our own little daughters, as our mothers' mothers did, and our mothers to us. Though people elsewhere in the world may not observe this tradition, we will continue to practice it.

All that suffering, and the mutilated girls do not even know why! At least when she was strapped into a chastity belt, a European or Cheyenne woman knew what it was for and what it was designed to prevent. But FGM, the most barbaric chastity tool of all, has taken on a life of its own. In too many societies, it represents tradition and family life and continuity—indeed, everything that matters.

FGM is an ancient practice probably dating from ancient Egypt. The pharaonic variation seems to have spread through Africa via the north-south and east-west caravan routes that linked so much of the continent. Today, it is prevalent in Somalia (whose women are known as "the sewn-up women"), in

Sudan (which has a saying that girls "are like a watermelon because there is no way in"), and is widely practiced in forty other countries, including Ethiopia, Egypt, Kenya, most of West Africa, and in the Arabian Peninsula. African animists and Christians practice it, and it is identified with Islam, though the Koran does not mention it and Muhammad was notably ambivalent. "If you circumcise," the Prophet wrote, "take only a small part and refrain from cutting most of the clitoris off. . . . The woman will have a bright and happy face, and is more welcome to her husband, if her pleasure is complete."

In Islam, however, female chastity represents the family's honor, and women even suspected of having contaminated themselves are severely punished. In fact, it is not at all uncommon for male relatives to administer the death penalty personally and justify it as honor killing. In this culture, FGM is a surefire adjunct to veiling, segregating, and secluding to guarantee that virgins remain virginal and married women faithful.

FGM, like chastity belts, purdah, veiling, and crippled little "golden lotus" feet, is man's response to the exigencies of Virginity, Chastity, Celibacy—the nonsexual trinity at the core of many cultures. It assumes women will not abide by the rules except if imprisoned, preferably within their own mutilated flesh. Why, then, bother educating them about why they must endure this mutilation of their sensitive genitalia? Just invoke the mantra of Tradition, keep the Grandmothers at hand, and hold down and slash away at the maidens, all the while chiding them for sobbing out their anguish. Womanly celibacy is the reward for their lifetimes as victims.

BOUND FEET

Foot-binding, often wrongly described as a cultural fetish or aesthetic standard, was actually a chastity belt applied to the feet. Like female genital mutilation, it was mutilating, excruciating, irreversible, and inflicted by self-righteous women in the name of community and tradition. When the little girl grew into a woman, the four-inch knobs of crushed bones and tendons that were no longer real feet guaranteed her husband that she had never strayed from her father's home and that she would never, could never stray from his.

Foot-binding probably began at the end of the T'ang dynasty (618–907) when palace dancers' feet were compressed rather than bound. By the twelfth century, during the Sung dynasty, upper-class court patrons began to display feet they had made smaller and smaller, and this painful fashion became a standard feature of imperial society. Slowly, the custom spread, outward and downward, until even the poorest peasant girls had at least slight bindings to shorten their feet.

Since antiquity, Chinese men had admired small feet and women whose gait was delicate and measured. Larger feet were disdained as ugly and lower-class. Tiny feet were erotic and beautiful, the epitome of gentility and elegance. Men even fantasized about seeing a naked foot, a golden lotus. A Taiwanese doctor added a medical explanation for the extraordinary appeal of bound-footed women. The deformity affected a woman's walking posture, tensing her lower body and tightening the skin and flesh on her legs and her vagina. Walking also affected her buttocks. They became larger, and men found them more sexually appealing. Tiny, maimed feet, well-bathed and perfumed, were sucked and nibbled, fondled and stroked, in sexual foreplay. Usually, they remained chastely encased in embroidered silk, even in bed, but some men were so aroused by the rank odor and deformity that they insisted on caressing the naked flesh. A few even used the crevice created by the broken heel and toe as a sexual orifice. Devotees swore these golden lotuses, named after an ancient Indian fable, were the most gorgeous appendages in the world. How ironic that these symbols of womanly chastity were simultaneously objects of sexual fetishism!

At first, when they were solely a palace affectation, bound feet were a cosmetic curiosity. As the ritual spread, however, a philosophical interpretation gained currency: "Why must the feet be bound? To prevent barbarous running around!"

The Sung dynasty (960–1279), locus of foot-binding, was also home to a conservative moral renaissance that clashed with previously tolerant attitudes toward chastity, divorce, and remarriage, among other issues. Scholars and philosophers recommended tighter control over women, who should be less educated and more obedient. Sung philosopher Ghu Hsi exhorted widows to remain chaste, arguing they would do better to starve than to remarry. Unsurprisingly, he was an enthusiast of foot-binding and introduced it into southern Fukien province as a way of spreading Chinese culture, in particular the notion of separation between men and women.

Ghu Hsi had an ideological ally in Chu Hsi, a governor of a prefecture in Fukien. Chu Hsi detected lasciviousness in the local women and decreed all women's feet should be severely bound so that they could scarcely move about. In consequence, Fukien women's feet became so crippled they could only totter about supported by canes, and large gatherings such as funerals were nicknamed "a forest of canes."

Crippled-feet women were, perforce, homebodies. As they wobbled along, clutching at walls or companions to steady themselves, their husbands could gaze admiringly at the contorted little stumps stuffed into pretty three- or four-inch embroidered shoes and know for a certainty that their wives could never gallivant as they did, or indeed go anywhere on their own.

The craze became deeply embedded in Chinese culture. By the time of the Yu'an dynasty (1271–1368), it was a recognized way of guaranteeing female chastity—young girls remained virgins, matrons remained faithful. A manual designed for women informed them that they had to bind their feet not to beautify them but to ensure they could not wantonly stray from their quarters. What probably originated as a fashion fad came to define female erotic appeal and trapped women inside their houses, helplessly chaste. One woman explained to her curious daughter that upper-class women had to bind their feet because the ancient sages recommended foot-binding as a way of preventing them from leaving the women's quarters, except in a covered sedan, supervised by the menfolk. Their lifestyle became as constricted as their feet, which they no longer needed to use.

Bound feet also became a status symbol, with the upper classes striving for a goal of three inches of crushed-toed golden lotuses. Such women were so obviously immobilized that they were completely dependent on their husbands, who basked in the glory of being wealthy enough to support such delightfully inactive wives. Conversely, lower-class girls, whose labor was essential in the home, had to be content with four-inch versions. "If you care for a son, you don't go easy on his studies; if you care for a daughter, you don't go easy on her foot-binding" was the motto of conservative families.

As it spread throughout China, from the north to the center and then south, foot-binding took on even more symbolic meaning, emphasizing yet another physiological difference between men and their tiny, fragile women. During the period of the Mongol conquest, it also distinguished the tiny-footed Chinese women from the larger-, natural-footed Mongolian women.

By the Manchu dynasty (1644–1912), foot-binding had become a fine art practiced by most mothers on their shrieking, tormented daughters. Long experience taught that five or six years of age was the optimal time to begin binding. The girlish feet were still small and malleable, and the idea of prettiness might help the child endure her agony.

The first day of the years-long process was carefully chosen. The parents burned incense and prayed. In Ta-t'ung, Shansi province, renowned for tiny-footedness, a lamb's belly was slit and the little girl's feet forced inside for two hours, while the lamb whimpered and died and the girl sobbed from fear and pain. Then her blood-softened feet were removed from the carcass and swiftly bound with white silk. The girl lay down for a week, then her feet were rebound, minus the first layer of skin, which, deprived of proper circulation, had peeled off. Mrs. Hsui-Chen, a southern woman born at the turn of the twentieth century, recalled that her mother started the binding when she was just seven years old. "I was used to freedom and wept, but mother did not pity me in the slightest. . . . 'No matter how it hurts, I forbid you to loosen the binding.' I was formerly very active, but became as dull as a wooden chicken and tearfully endured my suffering."

The suffering, to force feet into the grotesque shape, toes bowed underneath, unbendable big toe stuck straight up, was terrible. Ten feet of two-inch bandage was the instrument of torture. From the inside of the instep it was drawn over the small toes, straining them in toward the sole. From there it went around the heel and was pulled tightly to bring heel and toe closer. Round and round the bandage went, tighter and tighter, all ten feet of it. Often the flesh putrefied, so that strips of sole, even a toe or two, rotted away. At first the pain was nearly intolerable, especially when mothers compelled their daughters to walk on the mangled feet.

One woman recalled how her feet never stopped aching and the pain kept her sleepless. As the feet lost all circulation and sensation, it eased. Every third or fourth day, her mother bathed the bloodied stumps with alum and wiped away the oozing pus. If the girl wept, her mother beat her.

The stench of rotting flesh plagued all foot-bound girls. Wealthier mothers reduced the sweating and cut the odor with alum; poorer women used a borax solution. Often the process sickened the children, who suffered fever and stomachache in addition to the unrelenting pain of their ruined feet.

After a few years, the golden lotus was perfected and proudly displayed in miniature shoes that the young, chair-bound victims often spent their days sewing and embroidering. If they wanted, they could share their victory over nature and anguish by competing in the annual Assemblage of Foot Viewing. Rival tiny-footed women vied for attention with bells or silken butterflies with flapping wings on their wee shoes. Later, others even dyed their feet red. As they hobbled about on their heels—their toes could not take the pressure of their body weight—eager men gawked and gaped at the spectacle. Of course, they were not allowed to touch these delightful lumps. Their blinding beauty, after all, was also their possessor's guarantee of chastity.

Like female genital mutilation, foot-binding deformed, enfeebled, and disabled women. Slowly, through the wonders of mass psychology and culture, bound feet were transformed into an ideal of beauty and erotic appeal that doomed millions of women to unimaginable pain, permanent loss of independence, and unnatural confinement. As chastity in women dominated the social agenda, feet were bound ever more severely, sacrificing circulation, flesh, toes, and health to the fetish of auto-shackling virgins and the dutiful matrons they subsequently became.

Foot-binding did not so much end as limp to a slow death. In 1906, the Manchu government ordered all women to unbind their feet or risk having both legs chopped off. Many women were so horrified at this violation of tradition that they disobeyed or rebound the feet later, when it became safer to do so. The rest began the long process of taking off their bindings, but most could achieve, through ointments, lotions, and massage, only the pitiable semblance of a normal foot. The reintroduction of women's natural feet into Chinese life did not mean, however, that female chastity had been eliminated along with foot-binding. It remained a cultural imperative, but one that would subsequently require enforcement through indoctrination and other social pressures.

CHAPTER 8

Abstaining in a Good Cause

Abstinence—voluntary restraint—is celibacy's simplest manifestation, and it is practiced worldwide for a multitude of reasons. The most common is as a surefire and free method of contraception and as a way to generate or restore fertility after childbirth. Another form of abstinence is the renunciation of sex by older women to free themselves from the burdensome life of child-rearing, to protest the presence of a new and younger wife, or as a personal declaration of their desire to change their status and lifestyle. Abstinence may also have political roots, as was the case in the Voluntary Motherhood Movement, whose adherents wished to control their husband's access to their body by agreeing to sexual intercourse only for procreation.

No Loving, No Baby

No loving, no baby. It seems axiomatic that abstinence is the most obvious and easily administered birth control of all. In India, brahmacharya is promoted as the most natural and finest technique. The Catholic Church incorporates partial celibacy into the rhythm method, and the more frequently used sympto-thermal method, and censures other forms of contraception as onanistic and therefore sinful, because sperm redirected into condoms or diaphragms or killed by foam or chemical douches is no better than Onan's sinful casting of his seed upon the ground.

Interestingly, the world's most intensive birth-control campaign ever, China's 1979 One-Child-Only Policy, did not endorse abstinence. Before the campaign, 5 to 10 percent of couples used contraceptives. By 1982, this figure had risen to 70 percent. Half chose IUDs, a quarter tubal ligations, one-tenth vasectomies. About 8 percent relied on steroid pills, 2 percent on condoms, and the remaining 4 percent on either diaphragms or coitus interruptus. Only an infinitesimal, unmeasured percent abstained.

The Chinese political mind-set explains this anomalous situation. China leapt into the program, considering it crucial for future prosperity. One-Child-Only was conceived—not just metaphorically—as a surgical operation, and so it was implemented medically through the vast public-health network, one of the few innovations that survived Chairman Mao's death and the overthrow of the Gang of Four.

Ninety percent of Chinese communes had their own medical station, and contraceptive services were an integral part of them. Barefoot doctors were trained to insert IUDs and perform tubal ligations, vasectomies, and vacuum-aspiration abortions. Apparently, the leaders put all their faith in these methods, which the system was well equipped to deliver.

How to persuade people to resort to them? By really attractive incentives, that's how, such as fourteen days fully paid leave for an early abortion, thirty days for one in midterm, twenty-one to twenty-eight days for tubal ligation, or two to three days for an IUD. For a fertile young woman, why simply abstain if, for the price of a simple medical procedure, you could get a fully paid holiday?

Presumably the gigantic surveys that elicited this information missed the voluntary celibates, but that is not the point. Here was an opportunity for China to extend its proscription against premarital sex for both men and women—"Sex is a mental disease," factory walls proclaimed—to the marital arena. Obviously even China's harsh government could not enforce wholesale celibacy, which it apparently rejected out of hand as a contraceptive method. Certainly, compared to medical procedures, celibacy was less dependable and harder to reward because it was voluntary and out of the loop of the impressive primary health services.

Ironically, the success of the uncelibate, surgical One-Child-Only program has led to an upsurge today in enforced celibacy—of male bachelors. The birth rate plunged, but not indiscriminately—millions of son-obsessed couples aborted fetuses after ultrasound identified them as female, or they exposed or otherwise destroyed infant daughters if ultrasound had not been available to forewarn them. If they could have only one child, they would not settle for a girl.

Today, those favored boy children are growing into frustrated adolescence and manhood because their greater number has skewed the gender ratio. Though millions of men will find women to marry, many will not. Some are already chafing under their enforced celibacy, and articles regularly appear describing their schemes for importing foreign women and other strategies to nullify the man-heavy world their parents inadvertently created.

Postpartum Abstinence

In sex-obsessed modern Western culture, celibacy outside cloisters and religious orders is much less common than in restrained China. Western women who have just delivered babies seek advice about when they can resume sexual relations—usually, as soon as it no longer hurts too much. Not so in much of the rest of the world. One massive survey sampled 863 societies and determined that in 302, sexual abstinence is practiced, usually in association with childbearing. Those societies, in other words, consider it quite normal that, in the prime of their lives, men and women purposely forsake conjugal relations, often for years. To them, postpartum celibacy in particular, and often other types as well, are essential, rational, and well-respected rites of passage.

Throughout the world, postpartum sexual abstinence is a widespread phenomenon. In cultures where it is integral, it does more than prevent births. As an after-birth ritual, it greatly enhances each infant's health and chances of survival. It controls child spacing and, by allowing time for the mother's body to recover from her pregnancy, increases the fertility of the abstaining parents for their next bout of procreative sexual relations.

The mechanics of this are complex, and mother's milk figures largely. Many cultures continue the taboo against sex for as long as a mother suckles her infant. Some even credit breast milk with having birth-control properties. For these reasons, lactation prevents more births than any other form of contraception.

Of course, it is not the actual milk that works this magic, but rather in large part lactation, which extends postpartum amenorrhea. When mothers suckle every few hours, ovulation is depressed, so even if sexual relations occur, the chances of conceiving are much lower.

In hundreds of traditional, non-Western societies, however, those sexual relations are unlikely, for celibacy typically accompanies breast-feeding and is not terminated until after the child is weaned. How do fertile, celibate parents tolerate this prolonged abstinence? How do nursing mothers respond? What about their husbands? A brief tour of several societies reveals a wide range of responses.

At least one people, the Kafa of southern Ethiopia, believe periods of celibacy greatly improve a man's chances of fathering a son. They think that the quantity of sperm in an ejaculation determines gender: copious amounts form boys, smaller amounts girls. Because they blame frequent intercourse for depleting the sperm supply, they conclude that moderation in sexual matters is advisable because, after all, "men want sons" and so do women. Consequently, they both accept celibacy as a welcome boy-making tool.

Other peoples are rigorous postpartum celibates for quite different reasons. The Grand Valley Dani of Irian Jaya, Indonesia, for example, are the world's most abstemious people. Anthropologist Karl Heider, who lived among them for two and a half years, reported that after the birth of a child, the parents abstain from sex for between four to six years. No one deviates from this practice or looks for sexual release elsewhere. Men with other wives abstain from them as well, unlike polygamous husbands in societies where long-term postpartum abstinence is the custom. The Dani do not appear unhappy or stressed about these lengthy periods of celibacy; nor do they seek out activities to sublimate repressed sexual energy.

Most intriguingly, Dani society does not preach abstinence or have sanctions in place to punish transgression. Apparently the culture simply does not focus on sexuality, either to encourage or discourage it. Marriages, for example, occur only during important pig feasts, which are held every four to six years. Even then, the newlyweds must wait an additional two years before they have sexual intercourse, after they have participated in a special ritual. In Dani society, postpartum celibacy is in harmonious synchronization with their generally low-key sexuality.

The Cheyenne people of the North American plains used to abstain for even longer periods than the Dani, about ten years after the birth of each child. The couple swore a sacred oath of chastity, which was seen as both sacrifice and commitment. They clearly understood between-child celibacy as their people's form of birth control and explained that they did it "to give the first child a chance." As a Cheyenne named Dog put it, "If I were to have had too many children, I'd be whipping first one, then the other." Because the Cheyenne hated any punishment, they considered it wiser "to let the first child grow up before there were others."

The fierce warrior Sambia of the New Guinea Eastern Highlands have a unique take on their after-birth taboo against sex. The men are deeply suspicious of women because they consider their menstrual and vaginal fluids contaminating. To avoid being poisoned, they divide the hamlet into male and female sectors. Even pathways are designated by gender, as are parts of each house.

The Sambia see semen as quite different from female liquids. Far from being polluting, it is a uniquely vital force, essential to manhood. Unfortunately, from their misogynist perspective, semen is equally crucial for women, who need to draw it up inside themselves for strength, breast milk, and to create babies. This means that, for men, sexual intercourse is as much a debilitating drain as a pleasure.

After a baby is born in the menstrual hut, the Sambian father avoids both mother and child for months. He might dry up the breast milk with a glance.

He might also be so aroused by the sight of his wife suckling their child that he might weaken and violate the taboo against postpartum sex. To guard against this, he stays safely away and initiates sexual relations only after the child can walk, at two or three years, much later than the North American standard.

Fathers often become moody and irascible during this extended period of abstinence. Mothers, on the other hand, revel in deeply intimate relations with their children, particularly their sons. After anywhere from seven to ten years, these relations are abruptly terminated when the boy is forcibly snatched away from his shrieking mother. For Sambian women, these profound emotional and physical attachments with their children more than compensate for the loss of sexual relations with their husbands, who are hostile and violent at the best of times.

Though these cultures are radically different, their long observance of postpartum celibacy probably originates from the same forces of nature: the precariousness of infants' lives, which is countered by allowing the mother to concentrate all her efforts and breast milk on one child at a time, and an environment that cannot sustain much population increase. So like it or not—and the violent, suspicious Sambia clearly do not—they have developed strict regimens of postpartum celibacy.

In Africa, particularly West Africa, postpartum celibacy generally lasts longer than anywhere else except in tiny societies in New Guinea and in the Cheyenne people of North America. Because millions of people observe them, African practices likely permit more significant insights into human celibacy generally. Happily, they are relatively well-documented.

The intensely child-centered nature of African families is a crucial factor in how society after society has fashioned its particular variety of postpartum abstinence. Children are in many ways their families' chief assets, and parents strive to produce as many as possible. Even when they are quite small, children make useful economic contributions to their household. More importantly, in cultures without government and retirement pensions, children are their parents' main security against unforeseen financial or medical crises and to ensure a comfortable old age. When they marry, they extend and reinforce connections between their birth and in-law families. Children are crucial in maintaining the intergenerational links that underpin African social systems.

These considerations explain the general desire for many children, but there are also compelling reasons for wanting to ensure that a sufficiently long period elapses between births. Infant and child mortality is closely related to inadequate nutrition and maternal debility, which are in turn related to too little time between births. Child spacing, therefore, has developed as the great if unarticulated goal of these societies. Postpartum abstinence, in conjunction with lengthy terms of breast-feeding, is one of the prime instruments to achieve birth spacing that will keep massive child mortality in check, improve survivors' health, and—as a byproduct—increase parents' fertility.

Of all the tribes, the Yoruba of Nigeria have been the most rigorously scrutinized. Generally, they observe about three years of postpartum celibacy until the child has been totally weaned. Older women and farmers' wives advocate even lengthier spans. The Yoruba know this prolonged ban on sex protects their children's health. They breast-feed until the child is an active toddler, and they understand that the nutritional properties of mother's milk guard against such diseases as kwashiorkor, which turns its little victims' hair reddish and bulges out the bellies on their skinny, protein-deprived bodies.

The Yoruba also believe breast-feeding, like pregnancy, depletes a woman's strength. This is another important reason for abstaining during lactation, for the double burden of supplying milk and growing a baby would be too onerous. To avoid it, the Yoruba usually remain celibate until about six months after the child has been weaned.

Yoruba postpartum abstinence, in other words, is a custom that has, over generations, protected babies and their mothers from nutritional deficiencies. It has also resulted in children being spaced several years apart and, therefore, in fewer being born to each woman. The benefits of this are that the babies' chances of survival are much higher than of those born one after another by exhausted, debilitated women.

Polygamous Yoruba men, however, may seek release with another wife. Women have no such option, yet only 15 percent profess to be bothered by this lengthy deprivation. This becomes understandable when we consider the nature of Yoruba marriages. They do not share the kind of intimacy for which Westerners strive. Yoruba women seldom eat with their husbands, and in fact nearly half never do. They rarely share a bed, and a vast majority do not even sleep in the same room. The loss of sexual relations with a spouse clearly cannot have the same emotional impact as it does between more codependent men and women, for example the better-educated Yoruba elite, whose relationships more resemble Western ones. Though these advantaged women abstain for a shorter period after childbirth, they claim to suffer more from forgoing their conjugal sexual relations.

The other factor—deprivation of sexual satisfaction—should be seen in light of the Yoruba habit of genitally mutilating their young women. Because these clitoridectomies deaden sexual response, the women bear the loss of sexual relations much better than the men.

The changing times, with their heavily westernized and westernizing advertising campaigns for both "drugstore" contraception and powdered baby formula, have begun to erode the need for postpartum abstinence. High-ranking Yoruba who can afford artificial birth control and/or baby formula, or who can compensate for a swift succession of pregnancies with rich, nutritious food, see no reason to abstain from sex for the long periods traditionally observed.

Interestingly, this and other African societies have accomplished child spacing and procreative fertility without resorting to strategies at one time common in Europe: delayed marriage, abortion, and infanticide. From the perspective of the Africans' child-oriented lives, the violence of abortion and infanticide would be unthinkably wicked deeds of cruelty. Through celibacy, they exercise control from the outset, and with its companion breast-feeding, they nurture and protect their planned children.

Granny Time Ends Sex

In tropical Africa, what anthropologists call terminal abstinence is a widespread phenomenon. What it refers to is the deliberate—and often deliberated—decision to terminate conjugal sexual relations. For example, Yoruba women—but not men—know that permanent celibacy awaits them down the road. Sometimes husbands impose celibacy on their wives because they wish to take or concentrate on a younger wife, but twice as often the women themselves decide to adopt it. Most commonly, this happens when a woman becomes a grandmother.

Throughout Africa, and in Yoruba society in particular, child-rearing is predicated upon extensive grandmotherly participation. The transition from mother to grandmother is complex. Each has different rights and obligations, and sometimes the simplest or only way to navigate between their conflicting demands is to renounce childbearing altogether. Renouncing sexual relations is no hardship for these grandmothers. Usually, a woman's greatest emotional satisfaction comes from her children and family, not from an intense love affair with her husband.

A woman may also declare terminal celibacy as a protest against a new wife or because she has proven her fertility and can now rest. It is not a rejection of her husband so much as a redeployment of energies. For women whose marriages represent dynastic bonds and courtyards full of children rather than romantic attachments to their husbands, and for the millions of women who are genitally mutilated, terminal celibacy can be a release rather than a loss. Indeed, it is often no loss at all.

In North America, many aging (genitally unmutilated) women also retire from sexual service without the slightest regret. Some consider sex as purely for reproduction, while others say that, at their age, it is no longer necessary, proper, or dignified. Many older men and women claim they must abstain from sexual activities because of illness, though the medical reality is that their arthritis, heart disease, or hypertension does not require it. In fact, their newly adopted celibacy may disguise or excuse an antipathy to sex.

VOLUNTARY MOTHERHOOD

In the late 1870s, when pregnancy was an interesting condition, underwear one of many of life's unmentionables, and death a delicate passing away, feminists cleverly softened their demands for an instrument to control when and how often they gave birth by referring to it as Voluntary Motherhood. After all, birth control had ugly connotations, namely, freedom from the consequences of, well, a coming together, as it were, a very intimate sort of carnal knowledge.

From one perspective, feminists shared the common fear that contraceptives would lead directly and inevitably to wanton sexuality. The various "washes, teas, tonics, and various sorts of appliances . . . [were a] standing reproach upon, and a permanent indictment against, American women," declared one feminist, articulating the disgust shared by many antifeminist men. So pronounced was their alarm that legislation actually prohibited the distribution of information about birth control.

From a different optic, birth control was criticized for being unromantic and removing the spontaneity from lovemaking. Women's greatest fear, however, was that widespread contraception would work against them. They would no longer be able to keep their husbands at arm's length by invoking the argument that sex might lead to conception. These devices also smacked of "looseness" and sexual abandon and seemed unsuited to respectable people living respectable lives. Contraceptives might also send husbands galloping off to bed with "fallen women" they no longer needed to worry about impregnating. Jealousy was only a partial factor. Horror of the venereal diseases that unfaithful husbands quite frequently passed on to their wives was a more urgent issue. For all these reasons, many women, including Voluntary Motherhood feminists, accepted birth control in only one form: sexual continence, the world's oldest and most widely practiced method of contraception.

Voluntary Motherhood supporters were concerned above all with a woman's right to control her body and, by extension, her fertility. They saw celibacy as the only moral way to achieve this and condemned artificial devices as instruments of immorality that permitted consequence-free sexual indulgence. In an era where women had few legal and social rights, demanding control of their sexual relations with their husbands was considered extremely radical. Their endorsement of celibacy softened its impact, but only slightly.

Under the aegis of Voluntary Motherhood, married celibacy could take two forms: the couple's mutual or the woman's unilateral decision. Usually, the wife's unilateral declaration of celibacy was at the core of Voluntary Motherhood. On the difficult battleground of her home, each determinedly celibate woman defied not only her husband and her society's norms but even the law, which required her to submit both body and will to her husband. In these circumstances, she needed immense courage to dictate her sexual availability and to withhold it except when she was prepared to conceive a child. "Our religion, laws, customs, are all founded on the belief that woman was made for man," remarked feminist Elizabeth Cady Stanton. "Womanhood is the primal fact, wifehood and motherhood its incidents. . . . Must the heyday of her existence be wholly devoted to the one animal function of bearing children? Shall there be no limit to this but woman's capacity to endure the fearful strain on her life?"

Like a great many other nineteenth-century women, Stanton had no romantic notions about sexual intercourse. It led to endless pregnancies, and when desperate mothers sought advice on how to avoid conception, they were given false information. Medical "expert" Dr. Ezra Heywood, for example, told them that conception could be avoided if they abstained from sex until ten to twelve days after menstruation. This woefully wrong interpretation of the fertility cycle misled women, who ended up pregnant yet again. No wonder, then, that sex soon lost its magic. Too often, it exhausted, impoverished, disabled, and killed. A woman grieving for a miscarried child was a typical victim: "I am nearly wrecked and ruined by . . . nightly intercourse, which is often repeated in the morning. This and nothing else was the cause of my miscarriage . . . he went to work like a man a-mowing, and instead of a pleasure as it might have been, it was most intense torture."

To end these all-too-frequent personal tragedies, the Voluntary Motherhood movement preached that women had the right to practice celibacy. Any other form of contraception was not only morally questionable, but would deprive her of the ability to control when she had intercourse.

The Voluntary Motherhood movement was both inherently radical and relatively conservative in its stance. In an era when the notion that a man could rape his wife was seen as ludicrous because marriage gave him unlimited access to her body, wives who resisted on ideological grounds were social rebels. Their commitment to Voluntary Motherhood, and to celibacy except for procreation, was their means of empowering themselves vis-à-vis their husbands, and in a larger sense, within the families they wished to space out and control, and even within the society whose laws they so quietly and privately defied. In this context, they justified their celibacy as an instrument or a weapon they needed to fight for the very noblest of causes.

CHAPTER 9

Coerced Celibacy

INVOLUNTARY CELIBACY

Often, celibacy is an unbidden state, imposed by circumstances—a lack of available partners, for instance, as in modern China with its skewed sex ratio, or in apartheid-bound South Africa, where rigid work and travel permits could confine one marriage partner to the white city, the other to a black township. The American Civil War, which killed off a generation of young men, also doomed their sisters to spinsterhood as maiden aunts, burdensome family charges, and underpaid schoolmarms.

In societies with strict social and moral standards, financial constraints may also necessitate celibacy. In Victorian England, middle-class spinsters were expected to abstain from sex until marriage, and most brides sashayed chastely up the aisle. But they often took an inordinately long time to do so because before the final vows were exchanged, the bridegroom was supposed to accumulate enough money to buy a proper house in an approved neighborhood: "Virtue is good, but a house in Belgravia is better," as the aphorism went. As the young men waited out their long courtships and engagements, they practiced frugality but not always celibacy; thanks to the license the double standard permitted English males, the percentage of prostitutes in England was higher than in anywhere else in Europe.

In the twentieth century, the Great Depression squeezed more than pockets and stomachs as it pushed millions into unemployment and underemployment. This relentless poverty forced the postponement of thousands of marriages, and it convinced the unmarrieds to remain celibate or face the unmentionable—another mouth to feed when their own were flapping with unsated hunger. Country folks who lacked access to reliable birth control or who had religious or moral concerns about it simply waited it out.

Social values may produce the same effect. In Asian societies that bar young women from marrying before their older sisters are suitably disposed of, unwelcome premarital celibacy may be extended indefinitely by the impossibility of marrying off a homely, disabled, or disagreeable sibling. In India, Hindu widows could not remarry even if they were widowed as children and were forced into lifelong celibacy. Even today, this has changed only slightly. In some societies, lack of dowries has also doomed women to celibacy, and as we have seen, medieval convents expanded their numbers and their coffers by accepting dowries far too modest for a mortal husband.

Other times, celibacy is directly coerced. A man or woman is tossed into prison, where sex is forbidden. Until this century, European domestic servitude entailed celibacy, often for life. In England, some male servants could marry, but women could not because employers refused to inconvenience themselves by dealing with the pregnancies and babies their domestics' marriages would produce. The countess of Carlisle aggressively monitored her female servants, instructing her head housemaid to tattle on any underlings not "regularly washing their monthly-napkins," which "proved they were not having a baby." Many women lived out their lives in chaste service, fending off the sexual advances of their domineering employers.

Bachelorhood or celibacy was also mandated for certain trades and professions. Apprentices could not marry even when they became journeymen, but had to wait for years until they were masters. Often their delayed marriages followed either resentful chastity or cheap whoring. In the Middle Ages, male serfs were often lifetime bachelors.

Educators on all levels often faced a traditional ban on marriage—celibacy or your job was a common choice. Quite unlike brahmacharya, the orthodox learning tool for Indian students and scholars, celibacy was often inflicted on reluctant Western academics. Until 1882, when the requirement was relaxed, Oxford and Cambridge dons accepted their positions on condition of celibate bachelorhood. Some observed it cynically, in the breach, keeping mistresses or frequenting whores, but many dons were conscientious men who lived in scholarly celibacy in the comfortable, well-catered, and companionable digs of their ivory towers. Until the twentieth century, throughout Europe and North America, female teachers faced the same stricture from rigid, misogynist educational bureaucracies that cringed at the thought of sexually active or bulgingly pregnant women forming tender young minds.

Instances of coerced or de facto celibacy are legion, and those mentioned above represent a tiny sampling. Nonetheless, any kind of celibacy unwillingly embraced is substantively different from committed celibacy. The hormonal young woman pledged to chastity because it will guarantee her a suitable marriage or the athlete striving for greatness in the next competition is motivated in ways the coerced or happenstance celibate is not. A look at five cases of such unwilling celibacy confirms this.

Doing Celibate Time

In the litany of deprivations in a male prison, the absence of available women probably heads the list. Indeed, an inmate sees almost no women save a few guards and classification officers and perhaps a chaplain, nurse, or librarian and the occasional visitor. Mainstream correctional thinking endorses this—womanlessness or celibacy, it is argued, is part of the punishment. A few institutions, concerned about widespread homosexual activity in the primarily heterosexual population, have instituted conjugal visiting programs. Many others permit contact visits so that, under the vigilant eye of the visiting-room guards, a prisoner may embrace family and friends, even hold hands or cuddle children.

The biggest issue in single-sex prisons—at least, what should be the biggest issue—is rape among inmates. Ever since *Fortune and Men's Eyes,* the 1971 movie based on John Herbert's play, which treated the subject with sensitivity and compassion while portraying several rapes in all their terrible brutality, the public has known what happens "inside." A vulnerable, terrified, inexperienced young inmate—if he is attractive and has alluring buttocks, so much the better—is targeted from the moment he meets his colleagues. Whether he likes it or not, he has become a "punk" and will probably not sleep that night without being raped by either a special "daddy" or a gang of inmates who will hold him down, pull off his trousers, and spread his legs, then violate him one after the other in an assembly line of abuse.

Quite apart from the physical pain and injury, the psychic trauma, unending shame, and terror of realizing this is just the beginning, the punk and his assailants have just played out the penal system's most common nightly drama. Quite likely his assailants, too, are heterosexual and somewhere, deeply buried, wish they were not doing this, know they should not be doing this, not the rape, not the penetration of another male's anus.

The destruction of esteem is as intense as in any violated woman. The helplessness, the horrifying knowledge that authority stands idly by and does not intervene, the glimpse of the hell of his future life in prison, are just part of it. With ever-rising rates of HIV-positive inmates, as well as those living with AIDS, the chances of contracting the deadly virus are enormous.

The inmate predators and their victims by no means represent the majority of the population. Many men look away or frown at rape, understanding it as the violence it is. They may themselves, however, engage in sexual intercourse with a special partner and rationalize this unaccustomed homosexuality as "jailhouse love." This can vary from the tough-master/submissive-"mistress" relationship to mutual affection expressed not only in constant companionship, protection, and other assistance but physically, with hugging and kissing as preliminaries to mutual masturbation or penetration.

Other inmates—roughly half or more, depending on the institution—engage in no sexual activity other than autoeroticism. These men accept and endure their celibacy as part of the overall prison experience. Some have wives or girlfriends on the outside, others are merely able to maintain the values that most of them shared before incarceration—on the street, men do not attack and gang-rape other men.

These celibates are the prison system's excuse for permitting what is, in fact, an intolerable status quo; not every inmate goes in for homosexuality, correctional apologists say. In fact, much of "jailhouse love" and prison rape is only peripherally homosexual. Rather, both are responses to coerced celibacy in a system inmates hate and defy, a system solidly maintained by the outside world against which they have also rebelled. That these sexual episodes take place between men is pure necessity and has nothing to do with the essence of the acts.

Men who assault and injure and humiliate are, among other things, protesting their incarceration with its attendant womanlessness. They are proving to themselves, their peers, and their guards that they are still powerful, that, although they, too, are humiliated daily, they can instill terror and dominate others. They create solidarity with other men with the same needs. They protect their reputations—in prison, a reputation that includes toughness is crucial for survival—and ensure that they themselves will never be victimized.

What they say they are doing is quite different, and many are probably unaware of their true motivation. The excuse or explanation they articulate—to themselves as much as to each other—is that they need some outlet to release their sexual energy. In fact, the violence and bullying are far more integral to the act than ejaculation and even serve as foreplay.

Much the same is true of men who strong-arm a weaker inmate into serving as their punk. They are not as violent, but develop unequal relationships based on their dominance—which requires constant reasserting—over the submissive and defenseless but resentful and sometimes rebellious young inmate.

The cost, of course, is enormous, especially to the punk, whose loss of self-esteem is incalculable, but also to the daddy. If he is heterosexual—and the great majority are—he has to deal with his own internal conflicts, his basic contempt for what he is doing versus his urgent need to prove he has resisted the total disempowerment of prison. He is, he tells himself, not queer, even if he does sleep with other men who can, he now admits, sexually arouse him. He is, he says, just fooling around with jailhouse love, just sticking it to "the system," whose henchmen, the detested guards or screws, ridicule what they call his homosexuality but—oh, so complicit in this travesty of life—do absolutely nothing.

The rare man acknowledges as well his need for affection. "Can you imagine not being able to touch another human being for twenty-three fucking years?" demands inmate Carl Bowles in the maximum-security Leavenworth Penitentiary in Kansas.

Because he has resorted to jailhouse love, Bowles scorns the celibates who manage without sexual partners. "Why? Because they are scared of becoming homosexuals," he sneers. And "'Oh my God, am I turning gay because I want someone to hold, to touch, to love me?'" they wonder. Prison authorities may call him a predator, Bowles says, but like most jailhouse daddies, Bowles portrays himself as a misunderstood, caring guy, improvising as best he can in an inhuman system.

Prisoners respond differently to their coerced celibacy. Typically, some accept it for want of an alternative. Others rebel, sublimating their rage against the authorities and presumably life itself—for rage is what drives so many of them inside in the first place—into physical assault on other, weaker men. There are certain parallels to unwilling nuns in medieval convents, namely overt resistance to celibacy and the collective creation of a tolerable way of life, despite their grievous circumstances. The more brutal the coercion, the more determined and audacious the opposition. Celibacy is seen as part and parcel of an alien lifestyle and brings no rewards at all. Without any stake in respecting it, the captive is usually an unwilling collaborator in his celibate condition.

VESTAL VIRGINS OF ST. PETERSBURG

Schoolteaching in Tsarist Russia was little different from anywhere else. The profession was undervalued, underpaid, and overworked, and subject to unutterably petty rules and regulations spewed forth by a strangulating educational bureaucracy. Russia's legal code granted government officials the right to deny any soldier or civil servant permission to marry, but by the late nineteenth century, only schoolteachers who married lost their rent-free lodgings, seniority, even their jobs.

In fact, women teachers were the real target and were routinely fired for marrying, while men seldom were. In 1897, the St. Petersburg Duma (the name for elective municipal councils) formalized this discrimination, passing a law that banned the hiring of married women teachers and terminated those who married after their appointment.

The reasons? With fewer employment opportunities than men, single, well-educated young women were grateful for teaching positions. Since they needed less money to live (so the authorities reasoned), they demanded lower salaries. Teaching youngsters was natural for them and prepared them for marriage, at which time they would be dismissed. Off they went to their husbands, at a net saving to St. Petersburg because they were given no pension benefits and were replaced by another contingent of eager, hardworking, docile young spinsters. Why were women singled out for singleness? Married men, after all, were permitted to teach. The reasoning was that a man merely provided his family's living, but a mother had much heavier responsibilities. She might, for example, have to nurse a baby during school hours or stay at home to nurse a sick child or husband. She might even transfer to her family some of the interminable hours previously dedicated to her teaching.

Elementary-school teaching in St. Petersburg paid better than elsewhere in Russia, and the city's rich cultural life, with concerts, ballets, and lectures, was an additional lure for eager young minds. School conditions, on the other hand, were less delightful. Classes were held in the teachers' rented apartments, dark and cramped, unequipped and noisy, and scattered throughout the city, preventing camaraderie with other teachers. Their often cold, hungry, desperately poor, and sometimes abused pupils were divided into three grades, for which one teacher alone was responsible. To ease the children's suffering, teachers were supposed to dip into their own meager purses and provide after-hours food, clothing, and lodging. When teachers dared complain, it was of overwork and nervous exhaustion.

This, however, was not the end of their employer's demands. Teachers had to provide certificates of political reliability, and in some areas (but not St. Petersburg), the women had to submit medical proof of virginity. In Moscow, female but not male teachers had to abide by a strict 11 P.M. curfew and were monitored to ensure they did so. Clearly, women teachers were expected to be more than just unmarried. Virtue and virginity were of the highest importance.

Frightened teachers dared protest only collectively, through the women's movement and teachers' mutual-aid societies. A 1903 survey revealed their conflicting views on the issue of celibacy as a prerequisite to teaching, which many abhorred but practiced for want of alternatives. As one liberal legislator expressed it, "This situation weighs heavily upon city teachers and is tantamount to serfdom. Women teachers are primarily poor girls, needing a scrap of bread; the city administration gives them the chance to work and not die of hunger, but under conditions which cripple their natures, condemning them to eternal celibacy."

Thirty-five teachers reported financial insecurity as their motivation for remaining single and celibate; twenty-nine were afraid of losing their jobs; seven were too exhausted by their teaching responsibilities to lead a personal life; and seven worked too long hours to meet potential husbands.

A minority of women teachers readily accepted the celibacy imposed on them. Two did not want to marry anyway, one to avoid wedding an unsuitable man, as she noticed so often happened. A few believed teaching was emotional reward enough: "THEY DO NOT NEED A FAMILY. They have found their family among those whom the Lord called His pupils." Others argued that teaching provided them with independence and a satisfying profession without the constraints of marriage or parental authority, and they defended both their celibacy and their right to reject marriage.

The vast majority, however, would have loved to marry and raise families and believed married women were better teachers than spinsters. One anonymous writer agreed: "The Duma's vestal virgins! How sad and pitiful that sounds. . . . What intelligent woman would give up her right to be a mother? What educated young woman, having known the soul of a small child, would give up the right to bring up her own children and give the motherland useful citizens?!"

Some blamed a host of physical and emotional problems on their legislated celibacy: "Celibacy has a harmful effect on everything—on health and on character: it causes selfishness, irritability, nervousness, and a formal relationship to the children," one woman declared. To avoid all this, a tiny number of defiant women teachers simply had secret love affairs or married and hid the fact. If discovered, they were summarily fired.

The simmering discontent boiled over late in 1905, when the Duma voted, by a majority of one, to maintain the marriage ban. The authorities had won, just barely, their "battle against the laws of nature." Eight years later, the "laws of nature" were reestablished, when in a nearly unanimous vote, the marriage ban was repealed. Celibacy was no longer a requirement for St. Petersburg's women teachers.

This episode, replayed in variations throughout the Western world, including Canada, was a telling indictment of coercive celibacy. Most teachers observed it, reluctantly and even bitterly, simply to keep their jobs. The professional and economic risks were too great, and the news of cheaters caught and fired maintained the ambience of fear. Far from finding it rewarding, these unwilling teachers attributed a multitude of ailments to their unnatural celibacy. The few who embraced it voluntarily, on the other hand, respected it as a means to an independent and respected profession and adopted it as a desirable and fruitful way of life.

CELIBACY IN MAO'S CULTURAL REVOLUTION

In Communist China in 1974, seventeen-year-old schoolgirl Anchee Min was carted away to Red Fire Farm in a convoy of eleven trucks. She was excited because it was an honor to be chosen for such a prestigious assignment. But during her time at the collective farm, Anchee Min's emotional, moral, and ideological worlds were turned topsy-turvy when her friend Shao Ching's young lover was executed after the couple had been caught making love. Shao Ching, also seventeen, was breathtakingly lovely, slender as a willow, and rebellious. She copied out forbidden literature and shared it with her special friend Anchee Min. Instead of tying her braids with brown rubber bands like the other girls, Shao Ching bound hers with colored string. She scrounged tiny remnants of cloth and designed elegant underwear that she embroidered with flowers, leaves, and lovebirds. In the stark dormitory, her drying laundry hung like artwork.

Shao Ching also altered the standard-issue clothes so that her shirts tapered in, nipping her tiny waist, and her trousers emphasized her long legs. She enjoyed her full breasts and sometimes, in warm weather, shucked off her bra. One admiring soldier reportedly wept when he heard she had fallen ill.

During Chairman Mao's Cultural Revolution, a good female comrade was supposed to reserve all her energy and thoughts for the revolution. Until she was in her late twenties, she was not so much as to contemplate men or marriage. "Learn to have a stainless mind!" people recited. The girls at Red Fire Farm tried to model themselves on the heroines in revolutionary operas, paragons of virtue who never had men, either husbands or lovers. No wonder, then, that Shao Ching expressed no interest in men, even to Anchee Min, her closest friend. She was already suspect enough for her fine underwear, which had been criticized at a Party meeting.

One night, Anchee Min and her companions in a military training program were called out to a "midnight emergency search." With loaded pistols they were led through the reeds and toward a wheat field, silent and watchful. The order came to drop to their bellies, and they began to crawl through the night. Mosquitoes buzzed and stung, but that was the only sound. Suddenly, Anchee Min heard the murmur of two voices, a man's and a woman's. "I heard a soft, muted cry. And then my shock: I recognized the voice as Shao Ching's."

Anchee Min's first thought was to warn her friend—the consequences of being caught with a man were unthinkable. Shao Ching had never even hinted that she was romantically involved, but why would she? At Red Fire Farm, such an admission would be shameful.

The brigade acted in unison, flashing thirty flashlights at once, exposing Shao Ching's buttocks and a skinny, spectacled, bookish young man. They took Shao Ching away, leaving a group of soldiers to beat her lover. "Make him understand that today, lustful men can no longer force themselves on women," Anchee Min heard Yan, their leader, instruct. Shao Ching's studious young lover displayed no sign that he felt guilty. As the soldiers began to beat and whip him, he made a visible effort not to cry out.

Four days later, a public trial was held in the mess hall. Shao Ching had undergone "intensive mind rebrushing" and testified in a quavering voice, reading from a paper she held in hands that shook so much, she twice dropped her statement. "He raped me," she said. Her words convicted her lover and he was executed.

The fastidious Shao Ching stopped bathing and cut up her pretty underwear. After months, other girls complained that she stank. She was sent to a hospital in Shanghai and treated for a nervous breakdown. She returned to the farm, fat as a bursting sausage from medication, hair matted, eyes vacant. Later she was found dead, drowned among a tangle of weeds. At a special memorial service, Shao Ching was honored as an "outstanding comrade" and was admitted posthumously into the Youth League of the Communist Party. Her grandmother was given money in condolence.

Celibacy at Red Fire Farm was so strictly enforced that violators were executed. Shao Ching had been saved only because Yan had insisted she recant and blame her lover. Shao Ching had done so, but the mental stress destroyed her mind and she never recovered—no doubt haunted by memories of how her teenage love affair had condemned a young man to torture and death.

CELIBACY IN A CROWDED MARRIAGE

In 1972, tiny, seventeen-year-old Rahme, a devout Palestinian girl, was married to fifteen-year-old Mahmoud and went to live in his refugee camp in the West Bank. The babies began to arrive. Rahme was pregnant with the fourth when Mahmoud fell head over heels in love with Fatin, a ravishingly lovely teenager. "I adore Fatin," he informed Rahme, "and she has accepted my proposal of marriage. You may have a divorce."

Rahme would not have minded leaving her hot-tempered and abusive husband, but Islamic law would have required her to leave the children as well, to be raised by their father's new wife. "I don't want to divorce you," Rahme said. "I want to keep my family."

Mahmoud warned her that if she stayed, he would blame her for any friction with Fatin, and he had no intention of ever again sleeping with Rahme. If she remained in her crowded marriage, the apt name Princess Diana used to describe her own unhappy ménage à trois, Rahme would be doomed to celibacy at the age of twenty-three. But she accepted because she could not bear to leave her four children.

Rahme made good her promise and cooperated with Fatin in every possible way. Eleven children later—Fatin's—Rahme swept and scoured and cooked and prayed, all without complaint. She and her eldest son, who liked Fatin but also hated her "for being the cause of my mother's suffering, not for who she is herself," endured the situation because they planned to escape sometime in the future, when he could support Rahme and his little sisters.

Rahme is one of millions of women whom crowded marriages, or harems, have made celibate. Their levels of endurance vary from woman to woman. Rahme's motivation is simple and unshakably strong—four children. For their sakes, she shares an impossibly overpopulated household with the wife who is her husband's lover and the eleven children who have resulted from the lovemaking Rahme probably overhears as she lies alone, a reborn virgin under her husband's rowdy roof.

CELIBATE VICTIMS OF SKEWED GENDER RATIOS

Celibacy can creep up in myriad unexpected ways. Skewed gender ratios, a global fact of life, often produce unwilling celibates. The ratios are distorted by any number of phenomena. Wars are a major contributor, killing off enormous numbers of men in a narrow age range. Female infanticide, the consequence of the world's preference for male children, warps populations so that women become much rarer—modern China, with 118.5 males for every hundred females, is now experiencing this disconcerting reality. Celibacy is one important response to these skewed ratios, especially in light of predictions by Chinese officials, who estimate that "the number of hopeless bachelors could mushroom to 80 million." (Polyandry would also be a solution.)

Old age also creates celibates, usually women. Many are married to men who have become impotent, a common problem in older males. Unless these women turn to extramarital affairs, they are forced into celibacy. So are the millions of wives who outlive their husbands, another common phenomenon. Their situation garners little understanding or support. Society assumes these old women and the few men also in their category have become asexual and ridicule them as obscene if they show interest in pursuing a sexual relationship. North American nursing homes, for example, usually enforce celibacy. At the end of their lives, even sexually interested women and some men are obliged to retire into a chaste existence they neither seek nor enjoy.

Their unwanted lifestyle is reinforced by adult children who are often deeply distressed or disgusted at any hint of sexual activity or even desire in their mothers. They find such eroticism inappropriate and threatening, even selfish—they believe good mothers live for others, whereas sexuality satisfies deeply personal needs. In old age, women are expected to revert to the undefiled state of early childhood when they were sexless, virginal, and pure. As a result, many respond by stifling their sensuality. They are made to feel guilty and inadequate and accept the celibate role they are expected to play.

In any case, the dearth of suitable partners effectively imposes celibacy on even the most amorous older women. On the positive side, they are forced into it relatively late in life, unlike other coerced celibates.

WIDOWED CELIBACY
CHASTE HINDU WIDOWHOOD

Today, widowhood connotes sadness, seniority, whitened hair, and the fragility of aging bones. Young widows exist, but because they may remarry, they are not strikingly sadder than divorcées of the same age. To a great extent, our image corresponds to the reality. This was not always so. Until medical advances became widely available, at different times in different places, widows and widowers could be any age. Death respected neither youth nor maturity, carrying off its victims in childbirth, plagues, epidemics, drought, famine, and a host of other natural catastrophes. Widows, in those times, could be teenaged, middle-aged, or very old.

From our perspective of celibacy, what really mattered was the future as either perpetual widows or remarried wives. (Widowers, of course, are much rarer and are much more likely to be encouraged to remarry.) All societies have policies about widow remarriage, with many permitting it, some to the extent of making specific provision for them to marry brothers-in-law, who will be fully invested in parenting any children and in caring for the now-single woman. Other societies are—or were—neutral or hostile to widow remarriage. Early Christianity falls into the latter category. Marrying another man, even after the first one was dead, sounded far too much like sexual license. It was, therefore, severely frowned on. The assumption was that widows would/should remain perpetually chaste. Once a woman had been married, society recognized her husband's right to exclusive sexual ownership, which continued in force even after his death. The general view was that a widow's remarriage violated that ownership by transferring it to a new man, which was widely regarded as a betrayal of her first husband.

Hinduism's take on widowhood incorporates elements of this fundamental revulsion for female sexuality with reincarnation, producing a conclusion that is a merciless condemnation of widows. Basically, Hinduism understands the husband's death—especially from an accident, disease, or chronic condition, as opposed to old age—as caused by his wife's sinful behavior in a previous life. How to challenge such an interpretation, which is at the core of the religion's worldview? And so instead of sympathy for her bereavement, concern for her economic plight, anxiety about her fatherless children, Hinduism turns accusingly on the widow and consigns her to, at best, a living hell and, at worst, to an agonizing death.

Until recently in the Hindu world, widows of any age were reviled and cursed. "Some say that child marriages cause early widowhood," wrote a Brahmin. "I say that widowhood is not caused by child marriages, but by those child widows having acted against their husbands in previous births. Adultery, teasing, etc., might have been the cause. . . . Child widowhood is horrible, no doubt, but it is the effect of the wrath of God upon man."

In other words, widows were criminals, virtual murderers. What sort of life does such an evil creature deserve? The most brutish possible, and the most chaste. Manu, the Hindu lawgiver, decreed a widow should starve herself by eating only herbs, roots, and fruit, and so a widow traditionally ate once a day, only the plainest foods, and was always hungry. To ensure her chastity and her family's honor, she had to remain in her family's home, was made ugly, and was condemned to emotional and physical torment. Her hair was shaved and she no longer wore the red dot of marriage—the *tilaka*—on her forehead. She was stripped of all her jewelry, her earrings, nose-ring, bangles, chains, and bracelets. She wore only a white sari without a blouse underneath and went barefoot. Except to do chores everybody else rejected, she could no longer leave her home, but worked there as a drudge, reviled and cursed. At night she slept on the floor, sometimes on a hard mat. In ancient times, she had to cake her head with mud and sleep on a bed of stones. She could join in no family outings, ceremonies, or celebrations.

Despite every privation, a widow's chastity was always suspect. In a folk song, a widow moaned to her mother-in-law, "I shall be alone in my bed, O mother-in-law, and not just for a few days; Immature before marriage, I was totally inexperienced; Now, how will I spend my nights and days alone?"

Of course, a widow was easy prey, and the predator was often a male relative. Because the double standard in India thrives as solidly as elsewhere, if a pregnancy occurred, the widow was shunned and could expect no pity from any quarter. Her seducer, however, being a man, escaped all consequences of the affair. Even if he wanted to, he could not marry her. A widow was forever her husband's and remarriage was absolutely forbidden.

Millions of widows suffered grievously. Many were children who had never even lived with their husbands. Often they were toddlers. Not surprisingly, throughout Indian history the number of child widows has been enormous. The last census of the nineteenth century recorded that Calcutta alone had ten thousand widows under four years of age, and over fifty thousand between five and nine. Between 1921 and 1931, in all of India, the number of child wives rose from 8,565,357 to 12,271,595, creating the potential for millions of future child widows.

The Hindu religion taught that before marriage and childbearing, boys and girls should spend years as chaste brahmacharins. Gandhi, too, hated child marriage. "Where," he demanded in 1926, "are the brave women who will work among the girl-wives and girl-widows, and who will take no rest and leave none for men until girl-marriage becomes an impossibility?" He lamented as well "the inhuman treatment often accorded to our widows."

Inhuman, indeed, and based solidly on traditional teachings about women. These do not make lovely reading. How, for instance, to digest this ancient wisdom: "A man with a hundred tongues would die before finishing the task of lecturing upon the vices and defects of women, even if he were to do nothing else throughout a long life of a hundred years."

And, continues this litany of condemnation, "women combine the wickedness of a razor's edge, poison, snake and fire," and their natural faults are "falsehood, thoughtless action, trickery, folly, great greed, impurity and cruelty." They are "lascivious, fickle-minded and falsehood incarnate" and "have the hearts of Hyaenas." Manu the lawgiver expressed it pithily: "Stealing grain or cattle, having intercourse with a woman who drinks liquor, or slaying a woman, are all *minor* offences."

Manu's views are tremendously important because they influenced two thousand years of legislation and custom. Women had no rights and lived only to serve their husbands, who could abuse, discard, or sell them with impunity. Above all, women had to be chaste. The greatest calamity that could befall a woman was to compromise her chastity. Widowhood was, therefore, doubly incriminating, as incontrovertible evidence of previous sin and as a vulnerable state in which weak, lascivious, fickle women were more than ever tempted to stray. The merciless treatment of widows was therefore perfectly logical. It punished them for killing their husbands and, like the best military offense, struck out and incapacitated them before they could so much as fantasize about resistance.

SUTTEE AS THE ULTIMATE CHASTITY BELT

The wretchedness of a widow's life was, however, perhaps not the worst consequence of her husband's death. After all, she was still alive, in a manner of speaking. Many Hindus, mostly men, considered this intolerably lenient. They believed that if a woman's husband was happy, so should she be. If he was sad, so should she be. And if he was dead, so should she be. So even creeping miserably around a relative's or spiteful in-law's home was too soft an existence. Any good widow (a Hindu oxymoron) would know better than to impose her tainted self on this world. That was what suttee—immolation on the husband's funeral pyre—was for.

The "paramountcy of a woman's chastity" was the most compelling reason for suttee, although financial and property considerations also cost many an inconvenient widow her life. One anti-suttee crusader explained that relatives and in-laws feared that "if there was no cremation, widows may go astray; if they burn, this fear is removed. Their family and relations are freed from apprehension." From this perspective, suttee becomes "the ultimate chastity belt."

The widow who willingly clutches her husband's sandals and climbs up unaided to lie beside his corpse as the fagots are fired is truly reverenced. Once they are safely crisped, such widows are lauded and mythologized, much like Muslim suicide bombers who eagerly launch themselves as human explosives to ascend directly to paradise. The great difference is, huge numbers of suttees have not gone willingly to their incineration.

Those who did were driven either by religious conviction or, more probably, by despair at their lot. Though suttee was legally banned in 1829, it has flourished until well into the twentieth century—a mere decade ago—when teenaged Roop Kanwar shared her husband's cremation in September 1987.

For centuries, witnesses have reported force in supposedly voluntary suttees. In the seventeenth century at Lahore, Frenchman François Bernier watched as a few Brahmins and an old woman immobilized a shivering and sobbing twelve-year-old widow with ropes, then forced her onto the pyre. He saw another suttee prevented from escaping the billowing flames by men carrying long poles. In the eighteenth century, a Western observer saw a widow tied down beside her dead husband on heaped logs that were then set ablaze. But in the dark and rainy night, the widow managed to free herself from the scorching flames and hid nearby. Soon, however, her relatives noticed only one body on the pyre. They raised the alarm and quickly found the wretched woman cowering under some brushwood. Her son hauled her back and ordered her to either hurl herself back onto the funeral pyre or at least to drown or hang herself. If she refused, he warned, she would cause him to lose his caste.

Such stories abound. Widows were drugged, beaten, bound, terrorized, and tied down beside their dead husbands. Often, they were bound with slow-burning shoots of green bamboo that would hold them until they died. In 1835, despite livid protests by the British agent, the five queens of a deceased ruler were hauled, screaming and protesting, to their death on his pyre. In the 1950s, a suttee who escaped from the flames lay charred and dying for two days under a tree, and nobody offered her the slightest assistance.

Roop Kanwar was eighteen when her husband of eight months died of gastroenteritis in Deorala, a village in Rajasthan. Hours later, still on September 4, 1987, stern men armed with waving swords escorted her to her husband's hastily contrived funeral pyre. Some eyewitnesses thought she walked unsteadily and foamed at the mouth, while to others she was cheerful and composed. (Statements were impossible to corroborate, with participants understandably reluctant to admit they had attended the illegal event.) "Mummy! Papa!" Roop cried, thrashing her hands as the flames, ignited by her conveniently unindictable, underage brother-in-law, licked at her body. Neither Mummy nor Papa were there, of course; they were informed of their daughter's "courageous decision" only after the fact.

Roop Kanwar was the (hopefully) last victim of centuries of tradition, her death facilitated by authorities who civic-mindedly seized upon this fortuitous opportunity to bring some pilgrimage business into their little village. As Roop's in-laws swaggered about, proclaiming their honor, Deorala suddenly became a shiny new dot on the religious map.

The heat of passion is ice-cold compared to the inferno of a suttee's sad ending. Millions of suttees have undoubtedly quavered to their terrible deaths, secure in their righteousness and proud of, or at least grateful for, the honor the flames will soon reflect on their entire family. Millions more have been forced onto the flames by relatives and in-laws. These latter are determined to eliminate the unwanted presences of the widows, and above all, to guarantee they will never disgrace themselves or their loved (even if unloving) ones by an unchaste thought, much less a deed. Suttee is, after all, a preemptive strike against potential unchastity.

CASTRATED CELIBACY

Celibacy necessitated by castration—the excision of the sexual parts—sends shudders through our modern sensibilities. Yet for more than four thousand years, millions of males have endured this mutilation. The Persians were perhaps its first authors. As an eighteenth-century scholar noted, "The Latin word *spade*, which comprehends several sorts of eunuchs, was taken from a village of Persia called Spada, where . . . the first execution of this nature was made. . . . The first eunuch mentioned in the holy scriptures was Patiphor . . . who bought Joseph from the Midianites . . . and it is observed . . . that Nebuchadnezzar caused all the Jews, and all other prisoners of war, to be gelt or cut."

Throughout the centuries, a large percentage of eunuchs have been youngsters from families whose poverty precipitated the decision to castrate the child. In these cases, parents expected to advance their son's career in areas closed to all but eunuchs: certain types of domestic service in aristocratic homes or royal courts, or as castrati opera singers. Other boys were neutered after their enslavement by enemies victorious in wars: Nebuchadnezzar's policy of castrating male prisoners of war "that he might have none to attend him in his private service but eunuchs" is a case in point.

Sometimes older males voluntarily sought out the surgery, almost always as a means of earning a living as an entertainer or court functionary. Occasionally, men gelded themselves in full adulthood for religious reasons—the Church Father Origen; the obscure Valesii, a heretical Christian sect of the third century about whom little is known; and the nineteenth-century Russian Skopts are examples of these self-determined celibates. Much closer to home and closer in time is California's Heaven's Gate celibate computer cult, the members of which committed mass suicide in 1997 and whose leader, Marshall Applewhite, had turned to castration as a desperate measure to obliterate his uncertain sexuality.

Hundreds of thousands of people have also been subjected to castration as punishment for imagined or real crimes ranging from masturbation to rape. The mentally or physically disabled have been neutered to prevent them from reproducing. African-American men have been brutally desexed by lynch mobs terrified of their sexuality.

We shudder at castration for a host of reasons. It assaults the private core of human existence. It has almost always been a butchery, performed inexpertly by unqualified quacks and costing the lives of a majority of its victims. Its consequences are lifelong, visible, and far-reaching, affecting appearance, stance, and above all, psychological development and adjustment. We know now how important, perhaps crucial, the penis is to psychosexual development. Lessons harshly learned from routine circumcisions gone wrong have taught us that sexuality is not an amorphous variable physicians can successfully alter simply by radical surgery. When we read about eunuchs, whether in medieval China or the Ottoman empire, or as victims of Nazi eugenics, our growing knowledge of the effects of castration colors our perceptions.

The issues surrounding castration are complex and as fascinating as they are disturbing. Eunuchs who have left written records reported that they reflected deeply and incessantly on their mutilation. Though a dearth of such documents prevents a thorough study of eunuchs' reactions, all anecdotal evidence suggests that most of them brooded bitterly about the physical effects of castration and about the contempt and ostracism that mainstream society directed at them, including the mightiest military commanders of the Byzantine empire.

However, eunuchs often simultaneously understood and valued another dimension of their condition, seeing it as a means—their only means—of gaining access to certain positions. They or their parents neutralized poverty by trading their sexuality for opportunity, often but not always realized.

Afterward, eunuchs had lifetimes of confronting the other, less desirable consequences of the procedure. In particular, they had to deal with incessant humiliation and enforced celibacy, though much evidence exists that they experienced sexual longings their ravaged bodies could not satisfy. And these were the luckier men who could at least rationalize about their situation. Others, victims of brute force alone, had not even that consolation.

EUNUCHS IN GREEK MYTHOLOGY

After the earth goddess Gaia was created out of primeval chaos, creation proceeded briskly as, in a pre–Virgin Mary virgin birth, she brought forth the sea, the mountains, and the sky, whose name was Uranus. Gaia and Uranus became lovers, and mother and son begat a slew of children, notably the Titans and Titanesses. Among them were Cronos and Rhea, Zeus' parents, a lexicon of other major deities, and the Cyclopes and Hundred-Armed giants. These latter were, from Uranus' perspective, problem children, and he hated them so intensely he refused to let them into the light. The only way he could accomplish this, however, was to shove them back inside poor Gaia's womb, despite the agonizing pain this caused her.

Gaia was furious at Uranus' insensitivity and his domineering ways. She confided these sentiments to Cronos and the Titans, and together they conspired to retaliate against Uranus. Gaia provided Cronos with weaponry—a flint sickle she herself built—and instructions. The next time Uranus mounted her, the Titans were to grab and immobilize him while Cronos sliced off his genitals.

This came to pass according to plan. After he castrated Uranus, Cronos hurled the missing members, along with the sickle, down into the sea. As the salty foam churned around them, miraculously and ironically they were transformed into Aphrodite, goddess of love. The drops of blood became the Three Furies, who avenge parricide and perjury. From the first years of the Greek world's creation, one of its key deities was a eunuch who metamorphosed into the goddess still revered today for her devotion to love.

While the desexed Uranus remained up in the sky, Cybele, a Phrygian goddess, moved into Grecian mythology and gave eunuchism a much more active role in popular religion. In all its versions, Cybele's story is a delirium of castration. She originated as a strange, dual-gendered creature who so alarmed the gods that they castrated her. She then grew into the goddess Cybele, the Great Mother, while her severed male genitalia became an almond tree.

A nut from the almond tree fell down and impregnated a river goddess, who bore a son, Attis. Like a typical Greek who wished to get rid of an unwanted baby, the goddess abandoned him on a mountainside, where a billy goat suckled him. Attis grew into beautiful manhood and Cybele fell passionately in love with him. (Of course, she did not know that he was, via the remove of the almond tree, either her son or her postcastration clone.)

Attis, for his part, did not reciprocate Cybele's frenzied love and proposed instead to a king's daughter. Cybele was enraged with jealousy and, in her wrath, maddened Attis and his future father-in-law so that they castrated themselves. When Attis died of his wound, Cybele was devastated. She turned him into a pine tree and decreed that, as a memorial to him, only eunuchs could serve as priests in her temple. And indeed, this, too, came to pass.

The cult of Cybele was introduced into Rome in 204 B.C. The priests, or *galli*, castrated themselves with old-fashioned tools such as sharp stones or potsherds, and they wore women's clothes, grew their hair long, and styled it in womanly fashion. Romans, forbidden by law to join the priesthood or to castrate themselves, mocked the *galli* as half-men. The Roman poet Martial penned the following scornful lines, falsely accusing the *galli* of the sexual impropriety of cunnilingus.

> They cut your cock off, but not so to bed,
> Cunt-lover: what needs doctoring now's your head.
> For while your missing member can't but fail,
> Your tongue still breaks Cybele's rule: it's male.

Emperor Julian, however, considered emasculation "that holy and inexpressible harvest," while others believed *galli* were Wise Ones, Pure Ones, and Holy Ones. Their castration was an act of purification, endowing them with the innocence of virgins and children because only the chaste could perform certain rites. Cybele's priests were not the classical world's only eunuchs; eunuch priests also served Hecate at Lagina in Caria, and the Megabyzi, Artemis' chief priests at Ephesus, were eunuchs. Relatively rare and self-castrated, they were utterly pure and possessed far more spiritual power than voluntary celibates, who could err at any moment. By taking matters into their own hands, as it were, eunuchs rejected worldliness and attained instant superiority.

CHINESE EUNUCHISM AS A CAREER OPPORTUNITY

In December 1996, China's last eunuch passed away, ending a centuries-old tradition of castration as preparation for important civil-service positions. The divine origin of this custom was astrological and led the Chinese to believe that certain stars proved that eunuchism was the route to brilliant career opportunities.

From the Yin dynasty (221–206 B.C.) and probably as early as the Chou dynasty (1027–256 B.C.), eunuchs served in the palace, an isolated city the emperor was forbidden to leave. At first, eunuch sentinels called *an jen* guarded the imperial palace; others, known as *ssu jen,* monitored the emperor's harem and punished errant court ladies. The eunuchs had been forcibly castrated and came from either conquered peoples or the ranks of prisoners condemned to lose their sexual organs for the crime of seducing unmarried women. (The women, still fully sexed, were locked up for the remainder of their days.)

The great advantage of eunuchs was their inability to procreate, which meant they would never be driven by ambitions for their children. Isolated from their human families, who could never enter the palace, they could turn to the emperor as the family they would never have. For these reasons, they seemed more trustworthy in affairs of state. They might embezzle money, but at least they would not plot to advance a son's interests. They might manage some mangled lovemaking when they guarded concubines, but there would be no pregnancies as a result. As not-quite-men, eunuchs seemed appropriate buffers between citizens and the emperor, a divinity who could not have contact with ordinary humans lest they notice that he, too, was an ordinary man.

After a while, ambitious Chinese took note of the splendid career possibilities for eunuchs and began to castrate either themselves or their children, much like students taking exams in the hopes of future employment. By the tenth century, a special form of castration was officially recognized. Approved applicants went to a *ch'ang tzu*—a little hut—outside the palace where a freelance, government-certified castrator and his apprentices operated.

The patient's abdomen and upper thighs were tightly bound and his genitalia bathed three times in hot pepper-water, an unfortunately mild anesthetic. The future eunuch was placed in a semirecline on a heated couch, and assistants gripped his waist and legs. The castrator stood before his client, clenching a small, curved blade. "Will you regret it or not?" he intoned. At the least sign of hesitation, the operation was off. Otherwise, he leaned over, made an expert excision, and voilà! A new eunuch.

With scrotum and penis gone, the castrator plugged up the urethra. Then his helpers covered the wound with soaking paper and bandaged it. Now the eunuch had to stand and, clutching the assistants, walk around and around the hut for two or three hours before he was permitted to lie down and rest. For three days he drank no liquid, so terrible thirst compounded his suffering. After three days, the castrator unplugged him. If urine poured out, the operation had been successful. If not, he was doomed to agonizing death.

Now came the crucial disposal of the *pao,* or treasure, as the butchered genitalia were referred to. Only the most careless castrator forgot to preserve the genitalia, for without this powerful item, a eunuch could expect no professional promotions. He also needed them when he died, so he could enter the next stage of life complete if not intact.

Often, the trauma and torment of his castration drove the thought of his *pao* out of the new eunuch's mind and he forgot to ask for it. Technically, it then reverted to the castrator, who routinely sold it to its original owner for a sum of up to eight times the cost of the actual procedure. In later years, if the *pao* was lost or stolen, the eunuch would purchase or rent someone else's to continue in his job.

One hundred days after surgery, the wound was usually healed—that is, if the patient survived. The castrator was now entitled to his fee, which he would not otherwise receive. This sum was so enormous that poor eunuchs, which almost all were, could pay only by installments drawn on the anticipated imperial salary. The typical eunuch was a child or man from a poor family, his manhood the price of otherwise unattainable prosperity and power. (Unlike a cultured, high-ranking man, he could not attempt to pass the state exam that admitted men to high office.) After his recovery, the eunuch was sent to the palace. If he was commissioned for a post, his castration date became the birthday of his new life.

Sadly, there were no guarantees, and rejected eunuchs faced miserable lives as beggars or petty criminals, despised by society as deficient half-men. At the end of the Ming dynasty, in 1644, twenty thousand castrated applicants vied for three thousand positions. The situation was so critical that the government set aside a park to house those creatures whose manly sacrifice had been in vain.

Eunuchs neither looked nor dressed like other men. They wore black trousers topped by a long, gray garment, a dark blue coat, and a cap. Those castrated in childhood were called *t'ung cheng,* those in adulthood *cheng.* They all had high voices. Most were beardless and pudgier than sexed men. Younger eunuchs tended to wet their beds, and the Chinese had the expression "as stinky as a eunuch."

In character, they were perceived to be highly emotional and kindhearted and were said to enjoy lapdogs. They developed a sort of professional camaraderie and sometimes united to intrigue in political affairs. They were said to be so sensitive about their missing genitalia that acquaintances dared not even mention a broken teapot or a tailless dog in their presence.

Successful eunuchs, about three thousand at any one time, were employed in a wide range of offices, from engineering, interior decorating, agriculture, cleaning, cooking, music, warehousing, even making toilet paper or caring for imperial cats. Most of these were lowly jobs, yet even the humblest or a formerly depraved eunuch could aspire to one of the few lofty posts, which usually involved direct contact with the emperor.

One such powerful eunuch, the Ching Shih Fang, monitored the emperor's sexual relations with his empress and also his concubines and recorded the date of intercourse so that if conception took place, the emperor's paternity would be assured. At dinnertime, the Ching Shih Fang would select about twenty concubines' nameplates and offer them to the emperor like an after-dinner delicacy. After the emperor had made his selection, the chosen woman was stripped and carried to the imperial bedchamber on another eunuch's back. Later, the Ching Shih Fang would call out, "Time is up!" and unless the emperor wished that night's favorite to bear his child, she was dismissed.

Curiously, eunuchs also supervised the emperor's sexual education, using erotic images as teaching aids. They also taught him speech, table manners, correct behavior and etiquette, and developed unheard-of intimacy with their great ruler. Ming dynasty emperor Wu was so comfortable with one eunuch, Wang Wei, whom he called Pan Pan, friend, that he ignored his counselors if Wang Wei offered different advice. Emperor Ling of the later Han dynasty liked to lie with his head in a eunuch's lap and called his two special eunuchs "my mother" and "my father." This relaxed intimacy is not surprising, given the emperor's alienation from real life and the constant care, instruction, and solace his favorite eunuchs would have provided him since his confined and lonely childhood.

Besides the emperor, other members of the imperial family sometimes took a fancy to individual eunuchs. The nineteenth-century Empress Dowager Hsi favored eunuch Li Lien Ying, a onetime petty criminal and shoemaker who had had himself castrated, learned hairdressing, and with his skilled comb, insinuated himself into the Empress Hsi's heart. For forty years, always with her blessing, Li Lien Ying wielded tremendous power and acquired a fortune through systemwide bribery.

Predictably, court jealousy and gossip magnified and perpetuated the stories of such imperial-eunuch relationships, to the point where they reached the ears of even the general population. These ordinary folks, who would never set foot inside the imperial city, despised all eunuchs for their apparent invincibility, their corruption, their physical appearance, and the nature of their deformity. They acknowledged and resented the eunuchs' power in equal measure and both feared and scorned them as powerful freaks.

But what about sexuality? How did these thousands of men cope with their surgically imposed celibacy? Some were permanently embittered about their mutilation, and a few tried desperately to reverse it. Lao Ts'ai, a hated tax-collector, allegedly murdered virgin boys then devoured their brains, hoping to regrow his genitals. Another eunuch did the same with the brains of seven executed criminals. Others married and attempted sexual relations, sometimes with artificial devices. Some kept concubines. The vast majority, however, were celibates who never lost their sexual desire, merely the means of expressing it.

For its initiates, after all, eunuchism was not primarily about sexuality. These young men resorted to castration only as a desperate means to catapult themselves or their families out of unremitting poverty and up into wealth, influence, security, and prestige. About three-quarters were children of impoverished parents, the rest young men ambitious or lazy enough to submit their bodies to the castrating knife. They understood what the operation entailed, but when they weighed a sexed life of indigence and hardship against a desexed career that could lead as far as access to the imperial family, choosing sexlessness did not seem intolerable. The stories about court eunuchs certainly horrified many, but a few interpreted them as beacons of hope in an otherwise hopeless world. And when prospective eunuchs nodded briskly at the fateful question "Will you regret it or not?" prosperity and power, not celibacy, were uppermost in their minds.

BYZANTINE EUNUCH PARADISE

Like prostitution, robbery, murder, and other crimes, castration was illegal in both Christian theology and Roman law. In the sixth century, the Byzantine emperor Justinian, who ruled from 527 to 565, decreed harsh punishment for the crime—perpetrators could themselves be castrated and, if the surgery did not kill them, be sent to work in the mines, as well as have their property confiscated. But such dire risks only helped drive up the value of eunuchs so that, also like prostitution, robbery, and murder, castration flourished, to the point where one writer describes the Byzantine empire as a "eunuch's paradise."

Although the Council of Nicea banned self-castration and barred eunuchs from the priesthood in 325, and Roman legislation from the first to the fifth centuries forbade the castration of slaves, even the noblest families often opted to castrate their sons. The reason? Social and professional advancement, especially in the military. By the tenth century, eunuchs dominated the imperial court, took precedence over everyone else during ceremonies, and in the church, army, and civil service rose to the highest offices.

Their success was due to one simple factor—their sterility. No matter what, no eunuch would intrigue on behalf of a son. In consequence, eunuchs were considered so reliable they formed the core of the bureaucracy and provided an important balance to the hereditary nobility.

The eunuch Narses was the Emperor Justinian's immensely powerful and successful grand chamberlain and later, in ripest old age, the general known as the Hammer of the Goths after he demonstrated great military prowess, even genius, in routing them. Narses' birth date is uncertain, but he died sometime between 566 and 574, at anywhere from eighty-six to ninety-six years of age, famous, fabulously wealthy, and widely esteemed, "among the few [eunuchs] who have rescued that unhappy name from the contempt and hatred of mankind."

At first, only foreigners or slaves were castrated, but as the institution of eunuchism developed, even emperors castrated their sons to eliminate rivals or to place them in such high positions as the Orthodox Church's bishop, patriarchy of Constantinople, which required celibacy, preferably of the eunuch variety. Military eunuchs had brilliant careers as admirals and generals. The grand chamberlain, a supremely powerful imperial official, was usually a eunuch. In the palace, eunuchs were wardrobe-keepers, controllers of the imperial purse, estate managers, majordomos, and highest of all, superintendents of the sacred bedchamber and, inevitably, repositories of the empire's most intimate secrets.

Eunuchs were often the booty of piracy, kidnapping, and tribal wars. Because so few castrates lived—Emperor Justinian believed that only slightly more than 3 percent survived the operation—they were extremely valuable, fetching three times the price of a genitally intact boy. Unlike the Chinese and Ottoman equivalents, many Byzantine eunuchs had the less radical testicles-only operation.

A doctor sometimes forced to perform these mutilations described the two procedures. The compression method consisted of soaking young boys in hot water and then squeezing their testicles until they were crushed into nothingness. In the more drastic excision method, both testicles were surgically removed, which produced eunuchs who, unlike their testicularly compressed brothers, allegedly experienced no erotic sensations at all.

Excision was preferable to compression because it eliminated even more sexual desire. However, when the operation was performed on a postadolescent youth, there was no guarantee it would remove his ability to achieve erection. It happened, therefore, that on rare occasions, a eunuch had sexual relations with a palace woman. Whenever such a liaison was discovered, the eunuch offender was executed. The mere possibility of such a scandal was so great that eunuchs who displayed homosexual tendencies were tolerated and sometimes even welcomed. Ironically, homosexuality was punished by castration, leading the public to equate eunuchs with homosexuals. Homosexuality was also the preferred charge against those suspected of plotting against the emperor.

As was the case with their desexed compatriots elsewhere, the sexual incapacity of the Byzantine eunuchs earned them their masters' trust, and they were often assigned to positions that involved considerable intimacy with women. Their presence bolstered the separation between the sexes—eunuchs were, after all, the "third sex."

Sometimes, though, members of this third sex acted suspiciously as if they belonged to the first. The more gently castrated Byzantine eunuchs managed to escape enforced celibacy far more often than their more damaged, penis-lacking peers. This, despite the threat of death if their lovers were palace women. When the lure of lust was too strong, eunuchs indulged as best they could, the spirit urging them on even when the flesh was seriously flawed. Others, less lascivious or more sexually incapacitated, focused instead on the career opportunities available to a talented and industrious eunuch. If intense ambition drove them more than sensuality, they were admirably positioned to reach the highest ranks of either civil administration or military command, and to influence imperial policy, amass personal fortunes, earn enduring reputations, and satisfy almost every human craving except sexual desire.

BLACK AFRICAN EUNUCHS OF THE OTTOMAN EMPIRE

Islam honored eunuchs and considered them "neutral emissaries in a moral universe highly charged with sexual tension." Eunuchs guarded the Ottoman imperial harems and were bulwarks against *fitnah*—chaos. Each eunuch's castration personified his office and was one of three modes: the radical *mamsuh*, excision of both penis and testicles; *khasi*, only testicles removed; and *majbub*, penis severed but testicles intact. Virtually all Ottoman court eunuchs were *mamsuh*s.

Eunuchs first surfaced in the Muslim world in the twelfth century, as priests in a cult known as Eunuchs of the Prophet. Forty eunuchs with lifetime appointments kept perpetual vigil at the Prophet's tomb in Medina. The tombs of Shiite imam Ali at Najaf, Sultan Hasan at Dome of the Rock, Jerusalem, and of Saladin also had eunuch guards.

Later, eunuchs were brought into households as servants and into the Ottoman sultan's palace, despite Islamic law's proscription of castration. At first, the Ottoman eunuchs were white, bought from European dealers. Vienne, in France, was the center for the actual surgery. Later, most eunuchs were either Ethiopians or black Africans, enslaved and mutilated outside the boundaries of the empire to avoid legal problems. By the reign of Suleiman (1520–66), black eunuchs were more powerful than white. The African eunuchs' behavior could be peculiar, petulant, and socially inept, and they were known as eccentrics.

Young boys were the usual victims. They were also the most valued eunuchs because they had not already had, and could never have, any offspring to dilute their loyalty to their owners. In the early nineteenth century, these children were taken to Egyptian villages for castration, often performed by Coptic priests.

Frequently, the surgeries were fatal, thanks to incompetent castrators and unhygienic conditions. Pus often clogged the urethra, killing the wounded boy. Scores of contemporary accounts testify that throughout their lives, surviving eunuchs suffered hormonal and psychological disorders, and many were intensely bitter about their deformity, about which, unlike their Chinese counterparts, they had had no consultation and over which they had no control.

The eunuchs who emerged alive from the ordeal, however, were precious commodities, expensive, rare, and difficult to obtain. What better gift to impress and ingratiate oneself with the sultan, the man with everything else? So the palace seldom needed to purchase eunuchs as the vast majority were given as gifts.

Once "manufactured," the young eunuchs were sent to a highly regimented school where strict, elderly, castrated instructors taught them Turkish high-court culture, the etiquette of the palace, and how to perform their duties there. Playtime was allowed, and the youngest eunuchs mingled with harem slave girls, who were also learning their future trade. When the eunuchs graduated, they entered into service with the rank of *en asagi*—the lowest. Older eunuchs were sometimes brought to the palace after long service in high-ranking private households in Istanbul or the provinces.

The Ottoman eunuchs' duties varied, but usually centered on the imperial household, although the Mamluk dynasty employed large numbers of eunuchs as military guards. Sultan Abdulhamit II's daughter provided this job description: "to lock and unlock the doors of the Imperial Harem every evening and morning, to take shifts guarding the doors, to watch those entering and leaving, and not to allow in anybody from the outside."

In this era, 1876–1908, two head eunuchs were officially recognized for their high governmental standing. However, their real importance stemmed from their manipulation of courtiers and their intimate knowledge of palace intrigue and gossip. Who was better positioned to garner information about the personal habits and innermost secrets of the sultan's family and inner circle?

In general, the more powerful the court women, the more influential the eunuchs. The second half of the sixteenth century until well into the eighteenth, for example, has been called the Sultanate of the African Eunuchs, a period during which the harem played an increasingly meaningful role in politics. The sultan himself ruled from the harem where his mother, the *walide* sultan, all-powerful because of her lifelong influence on her son, headed the cast of women. The others, especially the competing mothers of the sultan's children, devoted their confined, restricted lives to seething intrigue. Their agendas frequently involved the question of which of their sons would succeed their royal father onto the throne.

The nature and urgency of their goals, and their varying impact on the sultan, gave these women, imprisoned in warrens of tiny, dark rooms guarded night and day by black eunuchs, enormous power. It also pushed them to enlist the eunuchs, who spied on them and controlled their movements, in their struggles and alliances. In particular, they sought to persuade the *kizlar aghasi,* the chief black eunuch, to lobby on their behalf with the sultan, to whom he had unlimited access. One classic example was the 1618 alliance between the *kizlar aghasi* and a harem mother to elevate her fourteen-year-old son, who became Osman II, to the throne.

Besides the enormous power that eunuchs derived from their close relationship with harem women—modern historians have variously described it as a sinister alliance and a cancer at the heart of the empire—their chief, the *kizlar aghasi,* had other major resources. He managed the estates and properties owned by the denizens of the seraglio, a very profitable occupation. From 1595, he was also superintendent of the royal mosques, which gave him the right to dispense immense patronage and to pocket a fortune from the well-regulated tariff of bribes associated with that patronage.

Compared to China's imperial palace, the sultanate required relatively few eunuchs—in 1903, for example, 194 African eunuchs guarded the harem. They enjoyed unusual job security and over half were never transferred, a token of their owners' attachment to them. They also amassed fortunes, strong motivation to continue their spirited service as almost coconspirators with their master or, more particularly, mistress.

The eunuchs' sexuality was, of course, supposedly nonexistent, hence their appointment to the harem. Mainstream society both dreaded and shunned them, so they had no outlet for relationships outside the world of their sultan owner's court. Furthermore, the authorities believed—wrongly—that black men were unattractive to women and so thrust them among women. Naturally, emotional attachments developed, though unless an operation had been incomplete, no sexual activity was possible.

Unlike their Chinese counterparts, the Ottoman eunuchs were reluctant celibates, their psyches as mutilated by involuntary castration as their bodies. The *kizlar aghasi*s, for instance, were reputedly cruel, their ruthlessness supposedly the consequence of their castration. Yet they greatly enjoyed the perquisites that constituted the flip side of being a eunuch, their prestigious, lucrative, and secure positions and the high esteem in which their owners held them.

THE *HIJRAS* OF INDIA

In ancient times, a lovely young maiden, Bahuchara, was traveling through the forest in Gujarat. Suddenly, thieves attacked her group. Devastated by the fear that they would rape her, Bahuchara drew out her dagger and sliced off her breast, offering it to the bandits in place of her virginity. This self-sacrifice, and her ensuing death, led to Bahuchara's deification as the goddess Mother Earth.

Bahuchara intervenes actively in mortals' lives. One important folklore story is about a king who prayed for her to bring him a son. Bahuchara complied, but Prince Jetho was impotent. One night as Jetho lay dreaming, Bahuchara appeared to him and ordered him to chop off his genitals, dress like a woman, and become her servant. Jetho did so, and from then on, Bahuchara has singled out impotent men and given them the same command. If they refuse, she punishes them by arranging that during their next seven incarnations, they will be impotent. This is how the cult of Bahuchara Mata, whose devotees are required to mutilate themselves sexually and remain celibate, developed.

In the nineteenth century, some people reported that impotence was an essential prerequisite to acceptance as a *hijra*, the Urdu word for these genitally mutilated males. Some communities observed novices for as long as a year before castrating and admitting them. Others imposed temptations—for example, four nights with a prostitute—as tests of genuine impotence. Celibacy was equally essential. Today, many *hijra*s—perhaps a majority—engage in homosexual prostitution, while a large minority remain true to the traditional principle of sexual abstinence. These *hijra*s are strictly monitored so they have no contact with men or *hijra* prostitutes, and they earn their living entertaining by singing and dancing at weddings and at births.

Emasculation, and the ritual powers Bahuchara then bestows on them, is how they obtain a special place in Indian society. They call the castration process *nirvan,* a total calmness devoid of desire, the beginning of a higher consciousness. Hindu scriptures and the *hijra*s define it as rebirth, and quite literally it is, for afterward, men have become "not men." (They also prefer to be referred to as "she" rather than "he.")

A *hijra* midwife performs the operation. "She" has never undergone any training but trusts entirely in divine power and takes no responsibility for either success or failure. The first step is to invoke the goddess by making offerings to ascertain if the time is propitious. Then comes the decisive moment. The midwife splits open a coconut; if Bahuchara Mata wishes the operation to proceed, the two halves will separate cleanly.

Next, the future *hijra* is sequestered for up to a month in a house he may not leave, even for his ablutions. He must abstain from sex, from looking into a mirror, and from spicy food. One morning before dawn, the client is stripped—"they must be as naked as the day they were born"—and bathed. He sits on a low stool, held from the back by assistants. The midwife ties his penis and scrotum with a string and pulls tightly. He, meanwhile, stares at Bahuchara Mata's image and repeats her name as a mantra, inducing a trance. The midwife slips out the knife she has concealed in her sari and severs his genitalia, inserting a small stick into the urethra. *Hijra*s claim they feel no pain other than "a small pinch" or a sensation "like an ant bite."

The blood gushes unchecked to the floor, ridding "her" of male ingredients. This first hour is crucial, for the *hijra* will either live or die. The midwife slips the excised genitalia into a pot, creeps out, and buries them under a living tree. Then, for the next forty days, she tends the wound. It remains unstitched but is repeatedly soothed with hot sesame-seed oil. The *hijra* follows a rigid diet and never leaves the room, even to go to the bathroom. Other *hijra*s tend to her every need.

On the fortieth day, the reincorporation ritual is performed. The *hijra*'s facial hair is tweezed out, turmeric is powdered onto her face and body, then washed away, and she dons bridal garb, makeup, and jewelry. Late at night, she is taken to a lake, ocean, or temple tank where milk is thrice poured over her head and into the water. She is now reborn, freed of her cursed impotence. Henceforth, she can call on her goddess, who may use her as an instrument to do her will.

The *hijra* joins a religious community of her "sisters" and "aunts," an institutionalized third gender with a special place in Hindu society and ritual. A guru leads them, and they live together in groups of five to fifteen, oblivious to the distinctions of caste or religion so divisive in mainstream Indian society. The *hijra*s worship Bahuchara Mata and earn their keep through performances on ritual occasions, particularly marriages and feasts celebrating a boy's birth. Sometimes they are invited, but often they simply arrive, decked out in full regalia, including ankle bells and spangled scarves. They drum, dance wildly, singing and shouting, even mocking their hosts. They flirt grotesquely with men, crack ribald jokes, and make obscene gestures.

When a boy's birth is being celebrated, the *hijra*s arrive and inspect the infant's genitals. If they conclude he is impotent, they inform his parents that he must be emasculated and become a *hijra*. "These children belong to us because they are like us, neither man nor woman," as one *hijra* said. Otherwise, the child will continue impotent for seven more rebirths. At weddings, *hijra*s insult the groom and his family in a burlesque of the reality, by pretending that their status is lower than the bride's and her family's.

The *hijras'* real importance at ritual celebrations stems from their powers of ensuring fertility. Their feminized persons possess the power of *shakti,* the creative dynamism of the Mother Goddess, which she transmits to them through their impotence. The *hijras'* emasculation, which kills sexual desire, combined with their renunciation of sex, is central to their new powers. The *hijras* are well aware of this and allude to themselves as sannyasis, wandering beggars dedicated to the attainment of spiritual purity.

Today, however, many Hindus of the upper classes fear that the *hijras'* sterility will contaminate rather than help their newlywed daughters, and so, making gentle excuses, they prevent them from dancing together. In fact, dread and derision are common reactions to *hijras,* who crash ceremonies uninvited though not unexpected, then demand recompense. This is, after all, their traditional way of earning a living. "God has made us this way," a *hijra* explained, "neither man nor woman, and all we are left with is to go wherever a child is born or a wedding is performed and sing a couple of songs so that we can sell our art or talent and make a little money and fill our stomachs."

When hosts chase them away penniless, *hijras* employ their other major power, laying curses that will come true. One *hijra,* literally kicked away from a child's birth party, saw her curse come true the next day when the boy sickened and died. "Our respect was at stake," the *hijra* explained afterward.

Such *hijras* bitterly resent the *hijra* contingent that consists not of ascetic celibates but rather of homosexual prostitutes. True *hijras,* of course, are only too well aware that their status, such as it is, depends on their celibacy as well as their relationship with the goddess. They refer to the prostitutes as false geldings and charge—justifiably—that they ruin all *hijras'* reputations.

In modern India, for instance, accusations fly that *hijras* augment their ranks by kidnapping and forcibly castrating victims. Despite the shocking thrill these cases generate, researchers have determined that most *hijras* are voluntarily castrated. Many have transsexual tendencies from childhood and for this reason are often ostracized by society, even by their families. Some simply conclude that this is a better job than whatever else lies in store for them.

Despite accusations and public ambivalence, the *hijras* remain a centuries-old, institutionalized third gender. Their impotence, emasculation, and commitment to sexual abstinence combine to create a vehicle for Bahuchara Mata's powers, an anomaly whereby she and her sexually mutilated acolytes confer fertility and other blessings on mortal humans. The goddess also provides *hijras* with the means to earn a living by either blessing or cursing their reluctant hosts. Though rogue *hijras* who practice male prostitution are increasingly prevalent, true *hijras* cherish their celibacy as the characteristic that, above all others, brings them a modicum of social acceptance and respect.

THE CASTRATI OF THE OPERA

In 1737, Philip V of Spain suffered from such relentless and chronic depression that his wife, Elisabeth Farnese, feared he would die. To stave off death, she engaged the superb opera singer Carlo Broschi, known only as Farinelli, to enchant her melancholy husband. Each night, the Italian would sing four songs and Philip would listen, entranced. Perhaps because of this, Philip survived another nine years.

What manner of music was it that could save a life? Imagine a voice as sweet as a flute and with tones as subtle as the human larynx can produce, a voice that soars upward through the air "like a lark . . . intoxicated with its own flight." Imagine a voice that transforms emotion into sound as glorious as a soul rising upward with it, clinging to its wings. Imagine, finally, "a calm, sweet, solemn, and sonorous musical language" that leaves its audience thunderstruck, transported into ecstasy by the power and grace of the most splendid music under the heavens.

This was the soprano or contralto voice that combined the power of male lungs and physical bulk with a woman's high, sweet range. This was the voice of a castrato, a gelded boy grown into manhood after years of intensive opera training in the finest conservatories.

This jeweled musical miracle did not, however, come cheap, even for the castrati who enjoyed splendid careers in the opera. The cost included a slew of boys killed by botched surgeries explained away as accidents and even more live boys ruined for normal life but equally unsuited for opera. These pitiful rejects, whose talents failed to meet the rigorous standards of operatic maestros and demanding audiences, were cast aside to live as they could, sexually mutilated and untrained for any trade.

The few truly successful castrati, however, were catapulted from ordinariness to glorious achievement, endless adulation, and careers replete with personal and professional satisfaction, material wealth, and secure retirements. Farinelli, perhaps the greatest of all, epitomizes the triumphant consequences that genital surgery could coax out of natural musical brilliance. "One God, one Farinelli!" groaned a fashionable admirer, unwittingly coining her hero's most memorable epitaph.

The origins of the castrati are hazy, but the cause is not—the prohibition against women singing in church and appearing onstage. Until the fifteenth century, high-voiced boys had substituted. The Spaniards devised a way of singing that forced light male voices into trilling warbles that strained vocal cords but produced femalelike sounds. These "falsettists" performed the new a cappella compositions that became wildly popular in the mid–fifteenth century and created greater expectations in musical range and timbre.

By 1600, castrati began to appear, and in considerable numbers. (Some speculate that earlier falsettists had actually been disguised castrati. This is plausible but unprovable.) In 1599, the first castrati were admitted into the Vatican Church choir, despite the official Church ban on castration. In the seventeenth century came the invention of Italian opera, a popular, quasi-international style of entertainment that required contingents of singers with women's voices. Since women were still banned from the stage, castrati were the perfect solution. Indeed, until the late eighteenth century, Italian opera and castrati were indistinguishable concepts, and 70 percent of male opera singers were castrati.

In the eighteenth century, castrato Filippo Balatri composed a witty and poetic account of his life as a revered soprano. Balatri's was an ironic commentary tinged by bitterness about his fate and was the first public revelation about the life castrati were compelled to lead.

By the nineteenth century, Balatri's keen sense of the indignity of his castration was seeping into the collective conscience of opera lovers. Choirmasters and guilty parents began to lie about how the perpetual male sopranos in their charge had been created: "A pig attacked and injured his privates, necessitating the operation" was a typical explanation. Eventually, after two hundred entrancing years, it ended. Opera no longer demanded gelding, though the Vatican chapel and other Roman choirs continued to employ castrati especially maimed for the purpose. The last known castrato was Alessandro Moreschi, who made recordings as late as 1903 and performed in the Sistine Chapel until 1913.

Most castrati (but not Farinelli) were poor boys whose parents aspired to greater things. The first stage was a visit to a conservatory for a voice evaluation. A positive response gave the nod to castration, and the parents rushed to make private arrangements. Doctors specializing in the illegal operation were centered in Bologna. The child was drugged with opium or another narcotic and seated in a tub of very hot water until he was nearly unconscious. Then the surgeon pared off the ducts leading to the testicles, which later shriveled and dried up.

Surviving patients were admitted to music conservatories, where they studied for up to ten years. Because they were considered delicate, they were given better food and warmer rooms than sexually unmutilated music students, and their health was carefully monitored. However, many hated the school and ran away. Others, though sopranos, proved to have indifferent voices. The real problem was probably the intensity and quantity of the work:

six hours daily of lessons, plus additional hours of harpsichord practice and music composition.

Somewhere between the ages of fifteen and twenty, after he had passed a series of tests, the successful castrato made his operatic debut—as a woman. His immaturity, slightly effeminate physique, and wondrous voice earned him instant adoration. Fans mobbed him, and both ladies and gentlemen fell in love with him. Casanova, for example, described his first impression of a certain castrato: "In a well-made corset, he had the waist of a nymph, and, what was almost incredible, his breast was in no way inferior, either in form or in beauty, to any woman's; and it was above all by this means that the monster made such ravages."

Indeed, contrast how a slender, beardless, sweet-voiced young man with rouged lips, flowing locks, and woman's dress would compare with the uncastrated male actors who had previously played damsels: "One sees a stout shepherdess in virgin white with a soft blue beard and a prominent collarbone . . . clenching a nosegay in a fist that would almost have knocked down Goliath, and a train of milkmaids attending her enormous footsteps."

In addition, castrati were superbly trained and musically knowledgeable. Nonetheless, some did not make the grade and were relegated to touring provincial opera houses.

Despite star status, castrati faced considerable resentment, even hatred. Jealous colleagues and the general public disdained their neutered state, accused them of luring other men into homosexuality, and detested their arrogance and conceit. Yet many castrati were famous paramours with legions of female followers eager to make love with a man who could not impregnate her and curious to see what their famous, much discussed genitalia looked like. All this attention, of course, did not improve the castrati's image with fully sexed men. From the castrati's own perspective, these sexual conquests were bittersweet, for they were forbidden by law to marry, and at least one died brokenhearted because of this ban.

What about celibate castrati? They were rare indeed, though the brilliant Farinelli was likely chaste, perhaps because of shame. Castrato Filippo Balatri, too, opted for celibacy. He feared a woman would soon find him sexually inadequate and tire of him, and he explained in his own ironic words why he never married: "By the grace of God, by my industry, and thanks to surgeon Accoramboni of Lucca, [I] never took a wife, who after loving me for a little would have started screaming at me."

Balatri also specified in his will that his corpse was not to be bathed in the customary way, "not only for the indecency I see in it but because I do not want them to amuse themselves by examining me, to see how sopranos are made."

The operatic castrati were a unique kind of eunuch. Unlike the Chinese, Ottoman, and some Byzantine eunuchs and the true *hijras*, they were seldom celibate, and chastity was never mentioned as one of their qualities. What mattered was the timbre, range, and power of their voices, not their lives outside the opera house. Though they were often scorned for their incompleteness and, like all eunuchs, legally proscribed from marrying because of their inability to procreate, most were as sexually active as other men. Nonetheless, they belong in this account of castrated celibacy because of their great fame. In fact, the castrati are proof par excellence that unless castration is so severe that it kills sexual drive, its victims seldom voluntarily opt to abstain from whatever sort of sexual relations their mutilated condition permits. Even then, there must be a combination of important rewards to maintain celibacy and strong disincentives for violating it. Most castrati, partial castrates with little motivation to remain chaste and no punishment if they were not, indulged their sexuality in about the same measure as other male entertainers with retinues of adoring and available women (and a few men).

CASTRATION TO PUNISH OFFENDERS

There is a certain simplicity to the idea of hacking off offending appendages—the hands of thieves, for example. By the same token, why not the genitalia of sex offenders? Or of the genetically offensive, who might otherwise produce similarly disabled offspring? Or of masturbators or homosexuals, who challenge the standards of decency and risk their health? Throughout the ages, the logic of such proposals satisfied many of the authorities responsible for enforcing the law. And so off with their—well, whatever would eradicate the problem.

Mutilating genitals is a time-honored practice. As medieval punishment for rape or adultery it satisfied the *jus talionis,* an eye for an eye. In Europe, from 1906, it was a common sentence for sex offenders. In the nineteenth century, Charles Darwin's cousin Francis Galton coined the term *eugenics* to describe the systematic upgrading of the human gene pool by selecting "better" people to reproduce. Sterilization was the obvious way to prevent "inferior" people from doing so. In 1931 the British parliament roundly defeated eugenics legislation, but elsewhere in Europe it was enthusiastically embraced. Hundreds of thousands of unfortunates were sterilized, both to "improve the nation" and, more usually, to save it money.

Physical castration—removing the testes—is the same process that was used on castrati to arrest development of their laryngeal structures. In adults, it inhibits sexual desire and decreases sexual activity, which has made it an attractive option for treating sex offenders. It has also been used for eugenics.

In the USA, castration for eugenic reasons continued from 1899 until the 1930s, and in several Southern states was the punishment of choice for black males convicted or even suspected of raping white females.

In Europe, Germany enthusiastically embraced eugenics, and its 1933 Eugenic Sterilization Act made sterilization obligatory for everyone suffering from hereditary disabilities. The Kaiser Wilhelm Institute assisted, by instructing physicians in the niceties of "race science" and training them to carry out their related duties. Nazi "justice," too, often involved genital mutilation. During the Third Reich, four hundred thousand people judged unfit to reproduce were sterilized, many by castration. One of the first groups earmarked were the "Rhineland Bastards," mixed-race children of German mothers and African-American post–World War I occupation troops. Others were those afflicted with blindness, deafness, physical disabilities, feeblemindedness, schizophrenia, and manic-depression. With suitable semantics, vagrants and alcoholics, too, could be classified as feebleminded and thus desexed.

Sexual deviancy was particularly targeted, and homosexuals were hounded down. The Reich Ministry of Justice decreed that every homosexual act between adults was almost certainly the consequence of an instinct derived from poor heredity. One prison doctor performed so many castrations that he streamlined his technique and speed to the point that he could whip off each patient in eight minutes flat, using only local anesthesia.

By 1929, twenty-four American states, notably California and Virginia, had enacted sterilization laws to prevent future genetic defects. By 1958, 60,926 people had been neutered, with police hunting down escapees and forcing them back to undergo the procedure.

In Canada, only the provinces of British Columbia and Alberta passed eugenics laws. British Columbia sterilized at most a few hundred. Between 1928 and 1971, Alberta's Board of Eugenics ordered 2,822 citizens neutered. About 700 survivors are currently suing for compensation.

Castration for sexual offenses often produced eunuchs, and the older the castrate, the more likely the surgery would render him impotent. Studies of these castrates have concluded that immediately after surgery, at least 60 percent lost their sexual drive and potency, and with time, so did another 20 percent. Other side effects—hot flashes, decrease in beards and body hair, and the development of fatty tissue, softer, slacker, and flabbier skin, the so-called puckered and lightly wrinkled castrate face—were common. Castration also caused the recidivism rate of sexual offenders to plunge from 84 percent prior to their surgery to about 2.2 percent afterward.

Today, asexualization of sexual offenders is now achieved through chemical rather than physical castration. The former is seen as less drastic and is also reversible. Hormones or other medications are injected, reducing the sex drive and thereby improving the subject's ability to respond to various sorts of psychotherapy and behavior modification. Chemical castration is used in the USA, Canada, and Europe, though it produces more recidivists—about 6 percent in one study—than surgical castration.

Currently, overpopulated China's new Eugenics and Health Protection Law attempts to prevent "inferior births" through a mixture of mandatory castration, sterilization, abortion, and celibacy. It is aimed at people with hereditary, venereal, or contagious diseases—for instance, hepatitis B—or severe psychoses.

In Thailand, an amateur form of unofficial but radical castration is on the rise. Over one hundred vengeful women have drugged unfaithful husbands, then hacked off their penises. Authorities consider the problem so serious they have formed a Penis Patrol. This patrol is summoned whenever another victim awakes to discover his genital region bloody and minus its most crucial member. Like a search party, they look in nearby fields for the butchered penis, racing against time to rush it to the hospital for reattachment. Often they locate it, but one enraged wife fooled them by attaching her husband's penis to a helium balloon to ensure he'd never get it back.

One consequence of this wave of penis amputations is that Thai surgeons are now world authorities on penis reattachment. One surgeon alone has reconnected thirty-one penises to their original owners. Another is that Buddhist monasteries are gently swelling, as some of the new castrates reconcile themselves to their desexed state and seek spiritual solace in religion as monks.

The amputators, women unwilling to tolerate their spouses' philandering and mistresses, are escalating their illicit but effective campaign. They face ten years' imprisonment if found guilty of the crime, but the cutting edge of this story is that they are prepared to serve their time as long as they make their point by nipping their husbands' infidelities in the bud.

CHAPTER 10

Celibacy to Repress Unconventional or Sorrowful Sexuality

Celibacy is the most obvious way to avoid revealing or experiencing unconventional sexuality, in particular homosexuality and pedophilia. At various times throughout history, these forms of sexuality have been outlawed. People discovered indulging in them have risked a plethora of penalties, often severe, including imprisonment, humiliation, professional disgrace, social ostracism, and religious censure. In these circumstances, adopting celibacy has been an excellent way to hide, deny, or even "cure" both homosexuality and pedophilia.

Celibacy also serves as the most convenient way to dodge various sexual fears, including revulsion for the genitalia, the act of sexual intercourse, or both. To some people, it is the easiest way to deal with a broken heart, self-protection against a repetition of the sorrow following a failed relationship.

All these scenarios for celibacy are simple to imagine, and most thoughtful adults can identify celibates of their own acquaintance who probably fit these categories. Of course, this often remains speculation. Individuals who choose celibacy to conceal, deny, or repress sexual expressions they consider unacceptable, harmful, or nasty are unlikely to be forthcoming about these issues. This is even truer of historical figures. The nature of the beast often makes it difficult to be certain about their celibacy and even more so about their reasons for it. Nonetheless, the following celebrities are generally acknowledged as true celibates, each for his own reasons.

LEONARDO DA VINCI AVOIDS PRISON

Leonardo da Vinci (1452–1519) was an artistic genius of the Renaissance, a painter, sculptor, musician, scientist, and inventor whose work still seems breathtakingly inspired. Da Vinci was also a complicated individual, and much of the intimate detail of his personal life remains tantalizingly hidden. However, considerable evidence points to his homosexuality. This includes scholarly analyses of his crude, often inaccurate depictions of female genitalia, his paintings and sculptures, and a host of little clues susceptible to this interpretation. Sigmund Freud is probably correct in saying that it is "doubtful whether he ever embraced a woman in passion."

Homosexuality in Renaissance Florence, da Vinci's home base, was so unremarkable that the German nickname for gay men was *Florenzer*. Legal penalties against it were seldom enforced, and a man who was reasonably discreet could anticipate few problems. However, in his early twenties, da Vinci had been enmeshed in an ugly situation that colored all his later perceptions of how he ought to live.

In 1476, he and three other young men were charged with having sodomized seventeen-year-old Jacopo Saltarelli, an apprentice goldsmith and part-time prostitute. In theory at least, da Vinci and his co-accused risked the death penalty. They were arrested and, for a few terrifying hours, imprisoned. They were interrogated and humiliated. Afterward, between hearings, they had to endure a two-month wait. Finally they were acquitted, but the scandal, innuendos, gossip, slander, and speculation tormented da Vinci for years afterward. Among his earliest inventions were an apparatus to yank bars off windows and another to open a prison from the interior. Clearly, the Saltarelli fiasco had seared da Vinci to the core.

What lesson did he learn from it? Most likely that he should do nothing, ever, to provoke a similar nightmare. From then on, at the slightest hint of impropriety, he would protest he was being victimized, attacked, maligned, insulted, and would vigorously insist on his childlike innocence of all wrongdoing. After the Saltarelli affair, da Vinci intended to be the world's most cautious man.

Does this mean that Leonardo da Vinci was celibate? The answer is that it is quite likely he actually earned his reputation for perpetual chastity. His declarations support this view. He condemned sexual intercourse as "so disgusting that human beings would soon die out if it were not a traditional custom and if there were no pretty faces and sensuous dispositions." He also feared syphilis, known (in Italy but not France) as "the French disease," and the mental degeneration he associated with active sexuality.

Da Vinci's long beard is sometimes cited as his attempt to obscure his beautiful face, a way to stave off tempting others. "Avoid lustfulness," he urged. "He who does not restrain his lustful appetites places himself on the same level as the beasts." Freud's conclusion was that da Vinci "appears to us as a man whose sexual drives and activity were extraordinarily low, as if some higher aspiration lifted him above ordinary animal necessity."

Again, the Saltarelli affair insinuates itself into this interpretation. Da Vinci had probably engaged Jacopo Saltarelli as a nude model. Afterward, though he was surrounded by male models and in his latter years lived with Francesco Melzi, his student, who also became his heir, he seems to have ensured that he never gave cause for another accusation. The most plausible and consistent explanation for da Vinci's chastity is that he found the sexual act grotesque and was almost paranoically afraid of a repetition of the Saltarelli scandal. To minimize or deny his homosexual orientation, he probably opted for the safe device of chastity.

LEWIS CARROLL ALLAYS SUSPICION

Today, Lewis Carroll would be shunned or indicted as a raging pedophile. A century ago, however, the Anglican deacon and mathematics and logic don at Oxford University's Christ Church College managed to indulge his sexual passion for little girls—the littler, the better—with only mildly unpleasant repercussions. A shy, pleasant, and youthful-looking man who lost his habitual stutter only in the presence of children, Carroll adored the company of nymphets. "I am fond of children (except boys)," he wrote to a friend. "To me they [boys] are not an attractive race of beings."

But girls were. Carroll would invite them to accompany him on excursions to the beach, to his summer place, to tea, to dinner. He had definite views about his guests. They should be upper class, pretty and lithely built, intelligent and dynamic. Their mother's permission for the outings was essential, but the girls should come alone, without even another child. As he wrote to one mother of his acquaintance,

> Would you kindly tell me if I may reckon your girls as invitable . . . to tea, or dinner singly. I know of cases where they are invitable in sets only . . . and such friendships I don't think worth going on with. I don't think anyone knows what girl-nature is, who has only seen them in the presence of their mothers or sisters.

Carroll also believed it was proper to kiss those under age fourteen without first asking their mother, but on the rare occasions when he entertained older girls, he scrupulously requested prior parental consent. "Are they kissable?" he asked one mother of two daughters, one of whom he judged to be over fourteen.

One of Carroll's favorite activities was regaling his little visitors with fantastic tales. In 1862, as he chatted with ten-year-old Alice Liddell, he conceived the idea behind *Alice's Adventures in Wonderland*. Three years later it was published, and Carroll was famous. Despite this charming opus, something went very wrong between Carroll and the real Alice, whose mother furiously destroyed all the letters he wrote her daughter. Largely because of his new glory as the creator of *Alice's Adventures in Wonderland,* however, Carroll had no difficulty in finding other mothers thrilled to lend him their girls.

Apart from the delight of their companionship, Carroll enjoyed photographing these children. Sometimes he would dress them up in costumes, but he greatly preferred nude poses. Even here, he always obtained the mother's consent before stripping and photographing the little girl. Incredibly, mothers would agree. However, his unusual hobby provoked considerable comment and gossip, much of it scandalized. In 1880, suddenly, and sagely, Carroll abandoned photography.

The stream of girl friends, however, continued to flow. When the girls reached sixteen and ripened into maturity, Carroll dumped them. One of the few who remained in his life after her sixteenth birthday commented, "Many girls when grown-up do not like to be treated as if they were still ten years old. Personally I found that habit of his very refreshing."

Another lifelong friend, actress Ellen Terry, whom Carroll had first contacted when she was an eight-year-old actress and he already twenty-four, laughingly dismissed a rumor that she and Carroll had had a romantic interlude. "He was as fond of me as he could be of anyone over the age of ten," she wrote.

Biographers agree on two facts: Carroll died a virgin, and in his lifetime of chaste liaisons, he had over one hundred girl friends. One reason for his celibacy is obvious. Since his propensity was exclusively for the very young, the mere suggestion that he had made a sexual approach would have destroyed him. His "friends" were upper-class girls, "lent" him by their parents, and had a single one of them reported any wrongdoing or the suspicion of it, Carroll would have faced ruin. As it was, he prudently scotched quite nasty gossip when it became obvious that his foray into nude photography would not go unchallenged. Throughout his lifetime, Carroll walked a careful line between his belief that "if you limit your actions to things that *nobody* can possibly find fault with, you will not do much," and the realities of the society of which he was a respected member.

John Ruskin Shuns Repellent Sex

John Ruskin, the celebrated Victorian writer, artist, and critic, wooed teenage Euphemia Gray for two years before their marriage. Their courtship was largely literary, an intense correspondence that led them both to longingly anticipate their wedding night. Both were virgins, Effie only nineteen, John a decade older. In their bridal bed, John delicately tugged his beautiful new wife's dress from her shoulders and discovered, apparently to his amazement, certainly to his horror, that poor Effie had pubic hair.

John was revolted. He had never before seen a naked woman and had supposed they were somehow more different from men than Effie proved to be. He actually concluded she had a deformity because she was "not formed to excite passion." (An alternate theory is that her womanly breasts were the problem because he had expected a smooth, hairless, and tiny-breasted figure much like the ten-year-old child he fell in love with a decade later.) Given John's tempestuous state of mind, he was remarkably calm. He merely embraced his wife, turned over, and slept. Effie, who had been prepared to follow her older husband's more knowledgeable, perhaps experienced lead, was dumbfounded.

In the chaste postnuptial period that followed—six years, to be exact—John artfully rationalized his refusal to consummate their marriage. He hated children, he said, and could not tolerate the inconvenience of lugging a pregnant or nursing Effie with him on his European travels. Effie countered with the observation that people married in order to have and rear children, and that abstaining verged on the sacrilegious. Nonsense, John replied, surely she was aware that the holiest people were chaste?

The shock of Effie's body was John's first inkling that he was totally unsuited to a carnal relationship. His odd upbringing, almost devoid of playmates and toys, had certainly not prepared him for the realities of marital life. Above all, he was so inseparably bonded with his parents that he lacked any notion of independence from them. Throughout his lifetime, they remained his sole financial support and provided him with emotional comfort, personal counsel, and moral authority. The Ruskins had been deeply disappointed when John married Effie rather than a more spectacular socialite and had refused to attend the ceremony. Afterward, with some justification, Effie attributed the failure of her marriage to her in-laws' nonstop interference in it.

The Ruskins developed a modus vivendi that satisfied both, though Effie never ceased to yearn for children. (Her mother had been pregnant with her thirteenth when Effie married.) They lived separate lives, and Effie soon developed a reputation as such a charming, witty, and intelligent guest that she was greatly sought after. Moreover, the care she took to maintain her chastity and keep her reputation unsullied ensured that she could never be justly accused of sexual impropriety.

In fact, Effie not only was a married virgin, she adored her husband. "I never could love anybody else in the world but John. . . . I am one of the odd of the earth and have no talent whatever for intrigue as everything with me must be open as the day." John, however, was different and slyly tried to insinuate Effie into compromising situations with men. His most reprehensible attempt was with brilliant young painter John Everett Millais, whom he invited to spend weeks in a tiny rustic cottage with the chaste Ruskins. The sexual tension between Millais and Effie was palpable, and Millais himself became convinced that John had engineered the situation to rid himself of Effie. Indignant and determined, he made sure not to fall into John's trap.

By this point in the marriage, John openly admitted it had been a mistake. For her part, Effie was devastated when he told her, on her twenty-fifth birthday, that he would never consummate their marriage, that it would be "*sinful* to enter into such a connexion, as if I was not very *wicked* I was at least insane and the responsibility that I might have children was too great, as I was quite unfit to bring them up."

They had reached the point of mutual hatred. In 1854, Effie finally confided her wretched situation to her friend Lady Eastlake, wife of Sir Charles Eastlake, president of the Royal Academy. "Tell your parents," Lady Eastlake advised, "because the law has provisions to help in such a situation." The Grays and their daughter began a clandestine campaign to extricate Effie from her marriage. They engaged lawyers and had Effie examined by two doctors. Both declared her a virgin and one was "thunderstruck." Soon, Effie escaped and went home to live with her parents.

The legal machinery was activated. John was served divorce papers and defended himself by explaining that Effie was insane. Lady Eastlake was outraged. She began a campaign to counter John's accusation, visiting hordes of friends to whom she carefully detailed Effie's plight. Soon London society turned on John, for sexless marriage was as unthinkable and as wrong as sex before marriage.

An ecclesiastical court heard witnesses, and court-appointed doctors, including Queen Victoria's accoucheur, the unfortunately named Dr. Locock, examined Effie and confirmed her virginity. So, in an affidavit, did John. Afterward, the marriage was annulled on the grounds that "John Ruskin was incapable of consummating the same by reason of incurable impotency." (This was not strictly true, for as he indirectly confessed in a letter to a confidante, he masturbated throughout his life.)

A year later, Effie and Millais married. Poor Effie was in for a second unusual wedding night, for Millais wept and confessed that he, like John, knew nothing about women or sex. What if he, too, was unable to perform? Effie soothed and encouraged him, and two months later, she was pregnant with the first of their eight children. Her ex-husband, relieved to be rid of his wife, went back to live with his ecstatic parents. He remained chaste but (shades of his contemporary Lewis Carroll) fell in love with little girls "just in the very rose of dawn," but grew increasingly indifferent as they matured into grittier puberty.

However, nymphet Rose La Touche was different. John longed to marry her, despite the several decades' difference in their ages. But Rose's mother was concerned. She very sensibly contacted Effie, who vindicated her own honor by revealing the intimate details—or rather the lack of them—of her marriage with John. That was the end of John's proposed marriage to the budding Rose. He died a virgin, masturbation his only sexual outlet, driven into lifelong celibacy by his revulsion for the adult woman's body.

Sir Isaac Newton Mends a Broken Heart

Sir Isaac Newton was either a virgin or a nearly lifelong celibate. His only great love affair was unconsummated and began quite late in life, when he was already well into his forties. His companion was Fatio de Duillier, an attractive, twenty-three-year-old Swiss mathematician. Fatio lived in London, shared Newton's passion for their common discipline, and reciprocated his affection.

For six years the pair were inseparable. Then Fatio was struck by a serious illness. At the same time, he was shaken by unsettling news about his family and financial crises in Switzerland. For a time, it seemed he would have to return home. Newton was frantic at the thought and implored Fatio to move to Cambridge, where Newton had teaching appointments and would support him. For reasons that remain unknown, Fatio declined, and in 1693, he and Newton broke off their relationship.

As a direct result, Newton plunged into delirious, delusional depression. He became paranoically suspicious and turned on his friends, accusing them of abandoning and betraying him. "Sir," he wrote to John Locke, "being of opinion that you endeavored to embroil me with women and by other means, I was so much affected by it . . . 'twere better if you were dead." To Samuel Pepys he directed a missive terminating their friendship. After his friends reacted with kindness and understanding, Newton apologized, blaming sleeplessness for his unprovoked attacks.

Newton endured eighteen months of severe depression. He recovered emotionally, but never regained his scientific creativity. Instead, he was appointed to the Royal Mint, first as warden, then master, with a large salary. Though the position was generally regarded as a sinecure, he chose to take it seriously. He saw himself as watchdog of the nation's currency and sought out and prosecuted counterfeiters with the same intensity of passion he had formerly invested in Fatio. A number of these criminals died on the gallows as a direct result of Newton's efforts, perhaps victims of the same smoldering rage he had earlier leveled at his friends.

For the rest of his life, Newton seemed immune to love. He and Fatio corresponded desultorily but never again rekindled the intensity of their former relationship. Newton was absentminded and ascetic. His austerities came about more from inattentiveness than principle, and he went hungry and sleepless simply because he forgot to eat, forgot to sleep.

His celibacy was probably a combination of the same sort of asceticism and a literally burned-out capacity for love. He had met and fallen for Fatio relatively late in life, and for six years sustained an almost feverish passion for the young mathematician. When Fatio's circumstances changed and their platonic affair ended, Newton was so brokenhearted that his life ground to a halt for well over a year. His recovery was only partial, for he was never again able to systematically apply his great scientific mind to the studies that had made him so famous. Instead, he went off on tangents, hectoring colleagues, tyrannizing the Royal Society, feuding with other scientists. Though he lived to the old age of eighty-four, he never again ventured into an affair of the heart. His obsessive love for Fatio had shattered his life and probably so seared his heart as to permanently disable it.

BOSTON MARRIAGES CELEBRATE ROMANTIC FRIENDSHIP

Once upon a time, before the late nineteenth century introduced the shocking notion of lesbianism into their ken, little American girls matured into womanhood unafraid to indulge and express their intense affection for their women friends. The wellborn remembered fondly the childhood sleepovers when they shared a bed, chatted and giggled all night long, and if they were so inclined, kissed and fondled each other as well. Had anyone queried the special affection they were expressing, they—and their society—would have justified it as the delightful phenomenon of romantic friendship.

And why not? In the genteel nineteenth-century world, women were asexual creatures who ungirdled and surrendered their unwilling loins to their husbands solely to fulfill their wifely duties and to procreate. From many accounts, they performed this unpleasant task with even less enthusiasm than they churned butter or embroidered butterflies onto the edges of tea towels. Could these creatures incapable of lusting after their own husbands possibly possess erotic feelings about members of their own sex? The general consensus was certainly not, and based as it was on contemporary medical science, who but the most suspicious could doubt it?

In fact, "the friendships of young girls prefigure the closer relations which will one day come in and dissolve their earlier intimacies," writer Oliver Wendell Holmes observed in his novel, *A Mortal Antipathy.* What were they, after all, but girlhood rehearsals for marriage, the great drama of a woman's life, wrote Henry Wadsworth Longfellow in *Kavanagh.* In *The Bostonians,* Henry James portrayed "a very *American* tale . . . [about] one of those friendships between women that are so common in New England" and thereby inadvertently christened the most enduring of these relationships as Boston marriages.

Boston marriage was the recognized term for committed and usually chaste romantic relationships between women. Most were unmarried, professional working women, but the occasional wife also pledged herself to another female as well as to her husband. Romantic friendships, complete with longing gazes, passionate letters, and emotional outbursts, were the first stage of Boston marriages. They flourished in women's colleges and in circles that permitted ambitious women to dream of forgoing marriage and motherhood in favor of a career—a radical stance for the period. They provided companionship, mutual support, nonrivalrous encouragement, emotional passion, and essential security. Almost certainly most were also chaste, for despite their vows of eternal love and devotion, these women would have rejected overt sexuality as an "immodest act." This was as true of those who recognized that they were lesbian as it was of those who were heterosexual.

The feature of romantic friendships that transformed them into Boston marriages was cohabitation, though some Boston marriages were conducted from separate dwellings. It was, of course, not unheard of for single women to live together, particularly after the American Civil War. This national butchery had widowed hundreds of thousands of young women and destined legions of others to mostly unwelcome, often needy spinsterhood. Financial constraints forced some of them to form joint households, just as in the eighteenth century "spinster clustering" had permitted manless and penurious European women to survive together with a modicum of comfort and stability. American widows and spinsters, thrown unexpectedly and unpreparedly onto their own resources, found salvation in the same arrangements. Enough of them did so that the notion of unrelated, unattached women living together became acceptable.

Cohabitational Boston marriages were cloaked in the same social respectability, though they were motivated not by economic desperation but by deep emotional commitment. Social acceptance of romantic friendships, coupled with an absence of speculation about possible sexual dimensions, extended to the notion of shared residences. Indeed, the Boston married shared their society's innocence or ignorance about female eroticism and most probably refrained from expressing it. Chaste or unchaste, what differentiated Boston marriages from other relationships was that they were founded on love, equality, mutual support, common professional passions and ambition, and personal fulfillment achieved in the absence of a controlling male. "Out of the darkness of the nineteenth century," writes Lillian Faderman, "they miraculously created a new and sadly short-lived definition of a woman who could do anything, be anything, go anywhere she please."

In the 1890s, English writers Katharine Bradley and Edith Cooper, who coauthored twenty-five plays and eight books of poetry published under the name Michael Field, proclaimed, "My love and I took hands and swore / Against the world to be / Poets and lovers evermore." North American soul mates linked their lives in the same fashion, but as physicians, clerics, social workers—dedicated to satisfying, worthy, and remunerative professional careers. A few even adopted children.

Boston marriages permitted these pioneering women to achieve what, in orthodox marriages, they could not—working lives free of the constraints of managing a house and rearing children. Nineteenth-century sculptor Harriet Hosmer articulated this forcefully. It was a "moral wrong" for a woman artist to marry, she said, because either her profession or family would suffer, and she would become a poor mother and an equally poor artist. Hosmer herself aspired to be a good artist. As a result, she wrote, "I urge eternal feud with the consolidating knot."

Others redefined the battleground and tied their consolidating knots with other women.

The most often cited exemplars of Boston marrieds were nineteenth-century writer Sarah Orne Jewett and poet/hostess/pioneer social worker and community organizer Annie Fields, who were for over twenty-five years the mainstay of one another's existence. They met as geese rather than goslings, at an *Atlantic Monthly* breakfast reception in honor of Oliver Wendell Holmes. Annie, forty-five, sat at the head table with James, the husband she adored. During the celebration she was introduced to the thirty-year-old Sarah, placed at a middle table that reflected her less illustrious status in the world of American literature. A little later their paths crossed again, and slowly they drew closer as friendship ripened into deep affection. Early on, Sarah interpreted a gift from Annie "as a sign of something that is between us, and since we have hold of each others [*sic*] hands we will not let them go."

These sentiments were heartfelt, mutual, and unexceptional—Sarah felt and expressed herself similarly to her beloved sister Mary, for instance. The foundation of her lifelong Boston marriage with Annie was built on many blocks: their commitment to literature and learning, their social consciences, their unique combination of conservative values, privileged backgrounds, and eighteenth-century manners, and their joyous sense of humor. Even their prior partnerships with a man—Annie with James, Sarah with her father—

were common denominators. They shared such a unique spiritual and intellectual affinity that, before his death, James Fields named Sarah "the friend he would choose for her [Annie] above all others."

Two years into her relationship with Sarah, Annie lost her husband. She plunged into mourning, and her friends, including Sarah, worried about her relentless and profound depression. Sarah was especially sympathetic—her father's death had wounded her almost as terribly. Fortunately, the women found solace in separate séances, during which James Fields and Theodore Jewett revealed to the spiritualist medium their approval of their womenfolk's relationship and urged them to travel together to restore their health and happiness.

The famous Boston marriage began. The women's living arrangements were little affected. Sarah divided her time between her family's rural home in South Berwick, Maine, Annie's bustling house-cum–literary salon at 148 Charles Street in Boston, and Annie's summer home in Manchester-by-the-Sea, Massachusetts. South Berwick was more leisurely and provided more writing time. Boston was exhilarating, with never-ending intellectual stimulation and the joy of writing in the library, with Annie, her dear "Fuff," "Fuffy," "Fuffatee," "Mouse," or "Mousatee," working silently nearby at her own desk. As Sarah reminded their friend Willa Cather, "To work in silence and with all one's heart, that is the writer's lot; he is the only artist who must be a solitary, and yet needs the widest outlook upon the world."

The women also traveled extensively abroad, in the USA, and in Canada, for leisure and to assuage Sarah's chronic and debilitating rheumatism. Their friends, family, literary acquaintants, and society in general accepted their friendship—Boston marriage—as the nurturing and committed way of life it was. They were inveterate hostesses, often entertaining a dozen visitors a day, a few men and many women from their extensive circle of accomplished and talented associates. No hint of scandal or even suspicion darkened their shining household, which remained until Sarah's death in 1909 a model of respectable and estimable living.

Modern literature about the women's shared lives explores the issue of their sexuality and reveals only the depth and satisfaction of their mutual love, never any hint that it had an erotic dimension. Certainly in the minds of the thousands who knew them, their chastity was unquestioned. Annie had been a devoted wife to her husband and Sarah a determinedly ambitious writer for whom the exigencies of marriage would have diluted the energy and focus she required in her work. In Annie, Sarah found her soul mate and life companion; in Sarah, the bereaved Annie found the same. Their Boston marriage was a rock-solid partnership based on reciprocal values, interests, and goals, bonded by unjealous affection and respect, and for over a quarter of a century it provided a safe haven for two of the most gifted women of their era.

A more modern, noncohabitational Boston marriage grounded Rachel Carson, whose *Silent Spring* was the catalyst for the foundation of the environmental movement. On the surface, compared to Sarah Jewett's extraordinary Annie Fields, Dorothy Freeman, Rachel Carson's great love, was an unremarkable woman. For Rachel, however, she was the "white hyacinth" who would sustain her until death, whose love reflected and magnified her own. "All I am certain of is this," Carson confided to Dorothy, "it is quite necessary for me to know that there is someone who is deeply devoted to me as a person, and who also has the capacity and the depth of understanding to share, vicariously, the sometimes crushing burden of creative effort, recognizing the heartache, the great weariness of mind and body, the occasional black despair it may involve—someone who cherishes me and what I am trying to create, as well."

They met when Rachel was forty-six and Dorothy nine years older, two conservative, permed-haired, tailored naturalists linked by passionate affection and common interests and problems, including caring for their aging mothers. Rachel was an already famous spinster, Dorothy a contented wife and mother whose husband, Stanley, welcomed this celebrated new friend into his life with genuine pleasure.

Rachel and Dorothy spent little time together—a lifetime total, estimates Rachel's biographer Linda Lear, that could be counted in months, not years. They nourished their romantic friendship mainly through phone calls and letters, a profusion of confidences and reminiscences, hopes and dreams. "I do know that we are, to an incredible degree, kindred spirits," Rachel wrote. Both she and Dorothy wanted Stanley to understand their devotion. "I *want* him to know what you mean to me," Rachel declared.

But the core of their relationship was private, and so they devised a system whereby they composed passages they called "apples" for each other's eyes only. These "apples" they would cherish and hide, while placating Dorothy's husband (and Rachel's inquisitive and demanding mother) by reading them the text that remained. These bowdlerized epistles, however, were their only indulgence in deception. They did nothing else to incur Stanley's displeasure or disappointment, though their obsessive affection for each other naturally impinged on the Freeman marriage. "The suddenness and intensity of this feeling between us has obviously brought great changes into both of our lives," Rachel observed to Dorothy. "As far as I'm concerned, it is so exactly what I needed that it is all, not only beautiful and wonderful, but truly constructive; but for you I have sometimes feared I have too greatly disturbed the normal flow of your life, causing too much preoccupation with 'Us' and too much emotional upset."

The intensity of their affection drove the women to their writing tables, and an enormous correspondence flowed between them. Rachel particularly railed against their separation and longed for the summer, when they would be together. "I know I need you terribly," she wrote. "(And I believe you need me, too. Shameless!)" If only, she lamented, we could see each other even monthly, "I really don't think I'd ever sink into the state of despair that so often comes over me."

But the Carson-Freeman Boston marriage was not an equal one. Rachel was its star, and Dorothy both accepted and accommodated to that. In the words of Linda Lear, "Rachel's letter left Dorothy no doubt about the responsibilities involved in loving Rachel Carson or with what other invisible forces she would have to share her." Dorothy responded gallantly to the challenge. Rachel's neediness sparked her nurturing instincts, and the intensity of their love kindled Dorothy's frustrated creative longings. Imagine, too, her rapture and pride when Rachel wrote her that the title of *The Sea Around Us* "has a new and personal significance—the sea around Us."

Years passed. In 1960, Rachel's health deteriorated—a serious ulcer, viral pneumonia, and a sinus infection. Then cancer—a radical mastectomy, though her physician lied and denied she had a malignancy. As the cancer eroded her body, Rachel wrote a series of letters that would comfort Dorothy after her death. "I think that you must have no regrets in my behalf," she assured her beloved friend. "I have had a rich life, full of rewards and satisfactions that come to few, and if it must end now, I can feel that I have achieved most of what I wished to do. . . . My regrets, darling, are for your sadness. . . . What I want to write of is the joy and fun and gladness we have shared—for these are the things I want you to remember—I want to live on in your memories of happiness."

In 1964, months before her fifty-seventh birthday, Carson's weakened body gave out and she died of a heart attack. Reading lines from T. S. Eliot, Dorothy scattered her beloved Rachel's ashes, the final rite of their Boston marriage.

Boston marriages have probably always existed in fact though not name, as women loving women have paired off in devoted couples and pledged, if only between one another, to be "lovers evermore." Some expressed their love erotically. Others did not, either because they feared terrible social consequences or because they had no need. Sarah Orne Jewett and Annie Fields, Rachel Carson and Dorothy Freeman, are chaste representatives of these relationships. They met and were smitten, then committed themselves to each other until death tore them asunder. Most Boston marriages were distinguished by the equality between the partners and their unusual ambition and focus, their determination to forge ahead in the world and renounce marriage and motherhood, women's destiny. Whether or not they embraced celibacy, these women were sexual deviants—the unchaste because of the lesbianism their society denied or condemned, the celibate because they disdained the prescribed path and carved out a different sort of womanhood. The latter were, perhaps, the greater rebels, for theirs was not a choice dictated by the exigencies of their bodies but the reasoned workings of their informed minds, abetted by the stirrings of their passionate hearts.

CHAPTER 11

Impotent Celibacy

UNWELCOME CELIBACY

Illness, disease, and accidents erode more than good physical health. They may also ravage a previously healthy sexuality, so that eroticism gives way to impotence that may not be reversible. Obviously, ailments affecting the sexual organs greatly increase the chances of impotence. Prostate cancer in men and vaginismus in women are examples, but generalized conditions are just as lethal to sexuality. Almost half of impotent North American men over fifty are victims of atherosclerosis, the hardening of artery walls because of fatty-material buildup, which blocks the flow of blood to the arteries supplying the penis. Diabetes, hypothyroidism, low testosterone or high estrogen, depression, and anorexia are among scores of ailments that can be sexually inhibiting. Obesity is an immensely complicated disorder that can engender so much personal shame in an individual that he or she effectively represses all sexuality. Conversely, people may intentionally resort to overeating to achieve a sort of protective obesity that shields them from unwanted sexual encounters. The range of conditions leading to impotence is vast and creates celibates in all walks of life.

LIMP AS YESTERDAY'S LETTUCE

Ancient Roman males suffered impotence caused from the overingestion of lead from their magnificent aqueduct system. Many found the condition so distressing and comical that it became a recurring theme in their literature. In *Satyricon,* the poet Titus Petronius Arbiter describes how he feigned illness to disguise his impotence, then decided to attack his flaccid penis, the cause of all his troubles.

With dreadful Steel the Part I would have lopt,
Thrice from my trembling Hand the Razor dropt.
Now, what I might before, I could not do,
For, cold as Ice, the fearful Thing withdrew,
And shrunk behind a wrinkled Canopy,
Hiding his Head from my Revenge and me.
Thus by its fear I'm baulked of my Design,
When I in Words more killing vent my Spleen.

Having spared his "sullen Impotent" penis from castration, Petronius demanded of it, "Have I deserv'd from you, when rais'd within Sight of the Greatest Joy, to be doom'd to the highest Misfortune? To have a Scandal fix'd on the very Prime and Vigor of my Years, and to be reduc'd to the Weakness of an old Man?" His guilty penis, however, did not rise to the occasion, but

He still continu'd looking on the Ground;
Nor more, at this had rais'd his guilty Head,
Than wither'd Poppies on their tender Stalks.

The great Ovid, too, had his problems. In a poem on impotence, ironically in his series titled "Amores," he describes his humiliation:

What's the matter? Isn't she, in fact,
the elegant object of my every prayer?
And yet when I held her I was limp as yesterday's lettuce
a useless burden on an idle bed.
Although I wanted to do it, and she was more than willing,
I couldn't get my pleasure-part to work.
She tried everything and then some . . .
It was as if my body had been stung numb by hemlock
and would no longer carry out my plans.
A sorry sight! I lay there like a rotten log, a dead weight.
I even thought that I might be a ghost.
. . .
As far as she knew, I was neither young
nor a man. She left me, pure as any Vestal virgin,
polite as any sister to her brother.
. . .
I would not be at all surprised to learn that witchcraft lay behind my present
torpor—yes, that must be it.
. . .

Well, you may say, maybe she wasn't so great.
Maybe she wasn't the best kisser in the world,
or didn't try very hard. Didn't try! She could have moved solid oak, hard
    adamant, dull stone
with those kisses. Any man alive would have responded,
but I was neither living nor a man.

The self-mockery of these Latin poems belies the real impact impotence often has, on both men and women. Roman males, unable to hide their inability to achieve erection, bemoaned their fate, sought medical advice, and if that didn't work, resorted in desperation to quackery. Some retreated into shamed celibacy. In the poetry, however, what we see is a combination of clever, self-deprecating satire and the frustration and impatience of men not yet in total despair.

Testing for Impotence in Prerevolutionary France

Had John Ruskin lived in prerevolutionary France rather than Victorian England, his medically certified virgin wife Effie's divorce petition might have forced him into proving his virility the hard way. That is to say, he would have had to demonstrate before court-appointed witnesses that he could indeed achieve erection.

Almost from the beginning, the Catholic Church condemned marital sex for any reason but procreation. It forbade eunuchs to marry because they could not breed. It also granted annulments to husbands or wives who could prove sexual nonconsummation of their marriage, with the best proof being medically authenticated virginity or impotence. (An impotent female, defined as "so narrow that she cannot be rendered large enough to have carnal relations with a man," was a virtually uninvoked category in canon law.) In Catholic France, up to the mid–sixteenth century, "fraternal cohabitation" was cause for divorce only as a last resort. Then, suddenly, Churchmen turned the screws on marriage and the heyday of the impotence trials was born.

These trials, which sound like a Jonathan Swift farce, were designed by ecclesiastics obsessed by the notion that an impotent man who married committed "an attack upon the authority of the Church." The marriage itself they condemned as "a mortal sin," a "sacrilege," and "an insult to the sacrament and a profanation of its sanctity." As if he did not have enough trouble, the impotent man was widely reputed to be extraordinarily lustful, given to secret vices outlawed in Christianity. These men supposedly enjoyed bizarre sexual positions that defiled the marriage bed. Furthermore, they were so lascivious that nothing could defuse their burning passion, which sexual intercourse merely inflamed.

In 1713, the unfortunate Marquis de Gesvres was subjected to an impotence trial, which discovered no such passions and was public, acrimonious, and ended only when his wife, the complainant, died. The marquis allegedly cuddled throughout the night, whispering tender pledges of love, but even when the marquise summoned up the courage to touch him, he "did hide himself in his nightshirt" and held her hands for fear she would molest him. After this encounter, he exiled his wife to the country for ten months, where she contracted "nettle rash, smallpox, measles, and fever together with an infinity of alarming symptoms such as the vapors and fainting fits." When she finally returned to Paris, she was "half-dying." The trial, sensational in its testimony, also engendered "poetry," or narrative limerick, titillatingly descriptive. A sample:

> Of a certain young Marquis it's said
> He did nothing but sleep when in bed

These trials demanded inspection of the genitals to prove that the man could achieve erection. Sometimes judges insisted on more elaborate evidence that the couple could consummate their marriage and called for "trial by congress," which forced a husband and wife to attempt to copulate in front of staring, note-taking witnesses.

The Marquis de Gesvres's trial judges confined themselves to the issues of erection and ejaculation. As was routine after an inconclusive physical examination, the marquis had to demonstrate his ability, but could choose the locale and time of the experiment. Like most men, he preferred his own house. Obediently, he lay abed there for two nights, but could report no erection. He was given more chances. Once, his examiners noted harshly that they had observed an erection, but because of its "tension, hardness, and duration" they discounted it as evidence of the ability to procreate.

The experts scorned a later attempt at an erection on the same grounds: inadequate hardness, tension, and duration. "Critical and superstitious experts, just looking at you makes me wilt," the despairing marquis complained. Had his virginal wife not soon after expired, the marquis was certainly headed for a verdict of "Impotent!"

Similarly humiliating invasions performed on women also did not necessarily lead to a conclusive verdict. Too many plausible excuses could explain away any number of suspicious findings. For example, a virgin's cervix might have been dilated if, for example, she had inserted her finger into it to soothe an internal itch. Her pubic hair might be matted because of her style of horseback riding. And a broken hymen might easily be caused not by a husband falsely accused of impotence but by the examiners themselves, who poked too hard "out of spite or ignorance."

The competence of the midwife examiners to whom women complainants were entrusted was problematic. Ideally, they ought to have been old enough to have experience, but young enough to have a steady hand and good eyesight. Unfortunately, they often lacked these qualities.

Women's examinations, usually for the virginity that they charged their husbands were incapable of eradicating, were horrendous. They were first bathed, to dissolve any materials used to simulate virginity. A male jurist described how the woman had to lie spread-eagled before the examining midwives, matrons, and physician. They spent considerable time prodding at her genitals, their expressions so solemn that the judge was visibly amused. The doctor was the worst offender, his invasive weapon either a specially designed, mirrored instrument or a dildolike wax tool. His extensive probing alone would deflower a virgin, the jurist protested, even if she had been intact before the examination began.

The French Revolution put an end to these risible trials. Marriage became a civil contract, divorce laws were instituted, and when impotence inspired separation proceedings, civil rather than religious authorities dealt with the petition, sparing both defendant and complainant the ordeal of a Church trial.

The impotence trials were horrendous procedures that masked the human tragedy of unconsummated marriages, broken promises, dashed hopes, and individual despair. The fraudulent cases—women who resorted to artifice to simulate virginity, men who pretended they could neither harden nor ejaculate—were just part of the larger picture of misery in marriage. The genuine cases, which were legion, transformed human frailty into canonical absurdity with a nearly scatological veneer. In these cases, at least one partner was a bitter celibate longing for release from frustration and childlessness. The Catholic Church, through theology and legislation, transformed impotent celibacy into the cruelest of human conditions.

CELIBACY IN RESPONSE TO VAGINISMUS

Celibacy from impotence as a consequence of various genital cancers, particularly if the disease or treatment is mutilating, is presumed and understood. The same is true of paraplegia or quadriplegia. Diabetes is another condition that may provoke impotence in men. So are some psychiatric disorders that include symptoms of shame and despair. Another common one is anorexia, which in severe form effectively neuters the victim, who becomes too weak to contemplate, desire, or partake in sexuality.

Other conditions that may induce celibacy are less well known. One of these is vaginismus, in which muscle spasms around the vagina are so severe that a penis either cannot penetrate it or causes extreme pain when it does. It is difficult to know how many women are affected by it. In the 1970s and 1980s, Masters and Johnson found it in about 5 percent of research volunteers at their institute. They suspected it was generally underestimated in medical diagnoses of the general population because many women sufferers opt for celibacy to avoid the pain and embarrassment of dealing with it. Because these women do not seek help for sexual dysfunction, they are medical research's unknowns.

Vaginismus can be so severe that sexual intercourse is impossible. Masters and Johnson have been consulted by desperate couples unable to consummate their marriages after ten years. Often they are driven to seek help because a longing for children overpowers their embarrassment or their refusal to acknowledge they have a problem.

Sometimes vaginismus develops after years of normal sexual functioning. Traumatic events such as rape may provoke it. So may serious pain during intercourse, for example if an episiotomy has not properly healed. Other painful conditions may also provoke vaginismus as a defensive response.

Sex-negative psychological conditioning can also produce vaginismus, as a reaction to feelings of extreme guilt. Many women reported to Masters and Johnson that their mothers were intensely puritanical about sex and refused to allow their daughters to do anything they labeled sluttish, including wearing makeup before age eighteen, dressing in typically teenage style, or having boyfriends. One woman's mother had zealously clipped newspaper articles describing rapes and, throughout her daughter's four years at university, sent them to her weekly.

In the sexual sphere, though some women avoid sex altogether, others "service" their husbands through fellatio or masturbation. They are distraught that they cannot offer genital sex and worry that their spouses will find a more sexually responsive partner. Some do, engaging in extramarital affairs for sexual release and also to verify that they themselves are still sexually capable.

Couples forced into celibacy that is the direct consequence of a medical condition, as opposed to a religious, ascetic, or idealistic principle, see their abstinence as an unfortunate, even tragic condition that requires professional intervention. It subtly alters the form of a relationship and is extremely stressful. In rare instances, this unwelcome celibacy is seen for what it is: a bearable way of life precipitated by a regrettable medical condition.

You *Can* Be Too Thin: Anorexic Celibacy

She is stick-thin, and if we could see under the baggy sweatshirt and pants, we would gasp at her withered thighs and bony buttocks. If we could touch her, we would feel her cold flesh with its furring of soft, fine hair. Sniff, and turn sharply from her sour breath. Observe and marvel at how this emaciated woman jogs with the dedication of a marathoner, then caps this feat with one hundred perfect sit-ups. Later, she sips spring water so sparingly that hours later, the small bottle is still nearly full. Sometime that day she might eat—*nibble* is more exact. An apple perhaps, or a piece of dry bagel. This, in its way, is another miraculous performance, for who could have imagined that one small apple could last three hours, then be stashed away in the fridge only half-gnawed, neatly wrapped in Saran Wrap, for tomorrow's sustenance?

What else do we see as we watch this gaunt young woman stalk through her day, minute by orchestrated minute? She sleeps rather a lot, for merely existing overtaxes her meager resources, and she does not merely exist. She is a perfectionist whose life is geared to the mechanics of self-imposed starvation. She exercises relentlessly, working off bulges and softness only she perceives. She may continue with her studies, perhaps falling behind as her priorities subtly change and she devotes every iota of her energy to her brutal regimen.

Oddly, she will hide her hard-won leanness under bulky clothing instead of flaunting it before her plumper peers. In other ways, too, she is secretive. If she sometimes succumbs to an overwhelming urge to eat, she gobbles forbidden food, which is mostly everything but lettuce, raw vegetables, and unbuttered bread, wolfing it down into her deprived system. But it will not stay there for long. Almost immediately she will panic at the crime she has committed and remedy it. She will stuff herself with the laxatives she is never without or lock herself in the bathroom with the shower running full blast so nobody can hear her as she inserts a practiced finger down her throat and efficiently vomits up every morsel she has just consumed.

She no longer menstruates, and her body resembles that of a famished child. She is uninterested in sex, for her little remaining strength is exhausted by her daily routine. She has nothing left to give and has withdrawn her carnality into herself, devouring it as she no longer devours nourishing food. But you simply must eat, her horrified mother/doctor/sister implores her. She smiles beatifically, for she knows better. She has no intention of eating. She is, for the first time in her life, in utter control of every moment of each day, of every inch of her shrunken but obedient body. If she cannot be stopped, and if no medical intervention is made, she will often continue to refuse food and die.

Sadly, this young woman is legion. She is the classic case of anorexia nervosa. She generally comes from a comfortable family whose high standards, like society's expectations, she believes she fails to meet. "The main theme [of the disease]," explains Hilde Bruch, a pioneer in this field, "is a struggle for control, for a sense of identity, competence, and effectiveness."

The eminent psychiatrist Pierre Janet analyzed the stages and progress of the disease and concluded that anorexia nervosa is "due to a deep psychological disturbance, of which the refusal of food is but the outer expression." One of its many consequences, apart from permanent infertility or even death, is asexual celibacy. As her breasts and buttocks shrivel and her energy flags, the starving woman is more concerned with her regimen of strenuous exercise than the disappearance of her menstrual periods. This amenorrhea is accompanied or followed by asexuality, a diminution or annihilation of sexual interest or desire. The full-fledged anorexic, secreting her ravaged body from prying eyes, is indifferent to her losses, having gained in their place near total control over her bodily functions. Hers is the celibacy of starvation, and she experiences it with indifference, so obsessed is she with bodily self-control.

The first documented case of anorexia nervosa was the thirteenth century's Princess Margaret of Hungary, declared a saint in the twentieth century. So many medieval female saints fasted to the point of starvation, however, and from such vastly different motives from today's anorexics, that "holy anorexia" is considered a unique category.

Today, one theory is that, in general, the disorder "is a manifestation of anxiety over, and avoidance of, maturing sexuality." It is equally true that the biochemical consequences of anorexia eventually dictate asexuality. These chicken-and-egg, egg-and-chicken scenarios apply in different measure to different people and underscore the strong link between sexuality and eating disorders. Even today, anorexic women are much less likely than their nonanorexic sisters to be involved in an erotic/romantic relationship or to be married. As the disease progresses to "the acute stage, victims become asexual beings. . . . The same biochemical imbalance that halts menstruation also impacts sex drive." Whether at the outset or at the end of the journey, impaired sexuality is the handmaiden of anorexia nervosa.

As anorexia proceeds inexorably through Western populations, consuming its victims, studies about it also proliferate—diagnosis, treatment, causes. Feminist psychoanalysts often interpret it as a protest against patriarchal and misogynist society in the form of a refusal to participate in "adult" or penetrative genital sexuality.

One version of this thesis maintains that anorexics equate food with all carnality, which they strive to control by denying it. Susie Orbach, trailblazing author of the 1976 *Fat Is a Feminist Issue,* links anorexia, which obliterates

both feminine curves and menstruation, with a subversion of the traditionally rounded female shape. The anorexic "is oddly desexualized and degen-
dered" and symbolic of the confusing messages modern society sends its
women: nurture and feed others, but restrain your own intake, lest you swell
up and exceed the new standard of femininity as slenderly chic.

Other writers believe that for overstressed, overstretched women, food is
both a symbol and actual substitute for erotic pleasure. This metaphor is
extended with grotesque logic to jaw-wiring, a version of a chastity belt,
which prevents the consummation of eating/sex by damming shut the craving cavity. In this bleak parallel, food/sex equals anorexia/celibacy, and the
jaw-wiring is the chastity belt that guarantees its wearer will remain pure.

Although anorexia is primarily a female condition, males are not immune.
German writer Franz Kafka is a famous example. Even as a youngster, Kafka
had eating problems. He fasted rigorously, abstaining from meat and, later,
alcohol, to ensure physical purity and strengthen his affinity with nature. At
the same time, he fantasized about gluttonous binges, larded his writing
with over five hundred food-related passages, and savored the sight of other
people eating. He also flung himself into physical activities, notably swim-
ming, gymnastics, and running. The result of this lifestyle was, of course,
extreme thinness, which Kafka agonized over. "I am the thinnest human
being I know," he confided.

Like most anorexics, Kafka suffered impaired sexuality. From childhood,
his psychosexual development was "disturbed" and the sexual act appalled
him. Several psychiatrists have attempted retroactive psychoanalysis. Among
other factors, one psychiatrist mentions "the problematic development of his
[Kafka's] sexual identity," another his "simulated asceticism in the form of an
aversion to filth." The evidence of Kafka's anorexia is overpowering, the suggestion that it had a quasi-sexual locus strong though unprovable.

Ultimately, whether anorexics are female or male, the latter stage of their
disease strips them of the physical powers of sex. Their impotence probably
reinforces their initial desire to stave off sexual maturity—most anorexics
begin their sad journey in adolescence or soon afterward. It also fulfills their
ambivalence, fear, or outright loathing of sex.

CHAPTER 12

Celibacy in Literature

Celibacy in literature is a topic so vast that one thousand people could have shaped this section in one thousand different ways, without duplicating each other's selections. Only one—*The Kreutzer Sonata,* Leo Tolstoy's long short-story rant about celibacy—would inevitably have anchored all thousand lists. The following literary samples reflect works diverse in time, genre, style, and readership. Chaucer could have substituted for Milton; Dorothy Sayers's *Gaudy Night* might nicely have replaced Virginia Woolf's *Room of One's Own*; only Tolstoy's terrible *Sonata* was destined to make its sonorous appearance.

This section opens with a brief consideration of courtly love, the centuries-long literary phenomenon that matured and developed and meandered along several paths, including real life's. No one author dominates. Courtly love was a formulaic theme, and the troubadours and poets who celebrated its rituals did so within the framework of its elaborate rules and story-line possibilities.

COURTLY, ENNOBLING, AND UNREQUITED LOVE

Courtly love, the literary invention of medieval troubadours, is no one thing and, unlike the proverbial and unchanging wheel, was constantly reinvented. Often, its poetic creators presented it as ardent but sexually unrequited love between an adoring man and his lady. In these manifestations, courtly love acknowledges human sexual longing but incorporates it into a great passion guided not by carnality but rather by the highest moral and aesthetic values.

Courtly love is an exalted state between a man and a superior woman he both respects and adores with quasi-religious fervor. Her love tests his resolve, firmness, and loyalty, for it is difficult to obtain. It is also immensely ennobling, so that his very suffering strengthens every aspect of his being: his military prowess, social standards, even his moral and religious perspectives. Sometimes, the mere thought of his beloved triggers these holistic improvements.

The twelfth century's Andreas Capellanus actually enumerated the rules of courtly love, which he defined as the inherently painful ceaseless meditation on the beauty of one's beloved, whom one glimpses from time to time but cannot possess. The ideal, seldom fulfilled, is total union with the beloved, to whom one is almost never married.

Some of Capellanus's more universal rules are that love is always in a flux, either growing or diminishing. Making it public usually kills it. Its very nature as next to impossible to consummate is also its most powerful stimulus, and during its fleeting lifetime, jealousy will sharpen the intensity of the courtly lovers' feelings. Courtly love is obsessive and best endured by constant contemplation of the beloved.

By the fourteenth century, an anonymous poet was refining the notion of love. In his "Ten Commandments of Love," he advocated faith or honesty, attentiveness, discretion, patience, secretness, prudence, perseverance, pity, measure or moderation, and mercy. The lover in Chaucer's "Complaint to His Lady" is so excessively long-suffering that he swears to obey his lady in whatever she desires, would rather die than offend her, and begs only for a drop of her grace. Here is his version of courtly love:

> But I, my lyf and deeth, to yew obeye,
> And with right buxom herte, hooly I preye,
> As [is] your moste plesure, so doth by me;
> . . .
> And therfor, swete, rewe on my peynes smerte,
> And of your grace, graunteth me some drope;
> For elles may me laste no blis no hope,
> No dwelle within my trouble careful herte.

Courtly love was agonizing and admirable, the source of chivalrous virtue. For these same reasons, it was often chaste, both because the logistics of consummation defeated the would-be lovers and also because, in some manifestations, courtly love was inherently pure. As one troubadour sang, "Out of love comes chastity."

An enormous but logical stretch puts courtly love together with the secret feudal societies that adopted then institutionalized a collective devotion to an unattainable woman who inspired their members to deeds of greatest daring and valor. The woman? The Virgin Mary, whose immaculate conception the early medieval Church had just begun to celebrate. The most famous of these secret societies was the Knights Templar, excommunicated knights who swore oaths of poverty, obedience, and chastity and dedicated themselves to the (newly immaculately conceived) Virgin Mary. Unlike their secular counterparts, however, whose courtly love involved personal grooming as a token of respect to their lady loves, virginal or otherwise, the sexually abstinent Knights Templar, according to St. Bernard of Clairvaux, "never combed, rarely washed, [and wore] their beards bushy, sweaty and dusty, stained by their harness and the heat."

Centuries of literature and lives imitating art transformed courtly into romantic love, intense and unattainable, a phenomenon too high-mindedly impractical to survive marriage and the trials of time, routine, and old age. The precious instant of recognizing the beloved, the stylized pursuit, the exchange of extravagant words penned on scented paper, the self-indulgently obsessive meditating on each other—these became the characteristics of this new kind of love. Sexual attraction fueled it, just as it had the courtliest of loves, but in this case as well, sex never dominated the lovers' agenda.

As literature, romantic love flirted and seduced as it inflamed and seared, titillating its aficionados with its stately rituals of gallant chase, heartsick suffering, rapturous encounters, gushing epistles, all in the name of profoundest if evanescent love. Sometimes this love was chaste by intention. Even when it was not, sex was usually overpowered by complications of plot and character that, depending on your point of view, either reprieved the lovers from the banality of sex or condemned them to its nonconsummation. Centuries of courtly and romantic love challenged thousands of lovers. Ultimately, most emerged from its clutches with their virtue intact.

MILTON AND THE CHASTE LADY

John Milton's Lady, one of the lovely maidenly "stars breathing soft flames," is captured by a despicable gang of men with evil intentions. The leader, Comus, exhorts her to swallow a magic potion:

> List, Lady; be not coy, and be not cosen'd
> With that same vaunted name, Virginity. . . .
> What need a vermeil-tinctur'd lip for that,
> Love-daring eyes, or tresses like the morn?
> Fortunately, the Lady knows better:
>
> Thou hast nor ear, nor soul to apprehend
> The sublime notion, and high mystery,
> That must be utter'd to unfold the sage
> And serious doctrine of Virginity. . . .

After much debate, the Lady's two brothers dash onto the scene, swords at the ready, and save their sister from the repulsive fate Milton described as coupling "in the rites of nature by the mere compulsion of lust, without love or peace, worse than wild beasts."

Underlying *Comus* was Milton's revulsion for the bestiality of sex and his yearning for celibacy. His chaste love affair with a young Italian man was his most cherished relationship, and when Charles Diodati died in 1638, Milton's literary epitaph was a passionate ode to their restraint: "Because the flush of innocence and stainless youth were death to thee, because thou did'st not know the joys of marriage, lo, for thee virginal honors are reserved."

But Milton violated his own precepts. A mission to collect a bad debt was somehow transformed into a proposal of marriage, and instead of the money, he arrived home with Mary, his sixteen-year-old wife. The marriage was unhappy for both husband and wife. Mary found the dour John a bore, and he found her flighty and incompatible. "It is not strange though many who have spent their life chastely, are in some things not so quicksighted, while they haste too eagerly to light the nuptial torch," he wrote in self-exculpation.

Mary was the real loser, for though her mother and sister moved in with her and Milton, she died delivering their fourth child. Milton, meanwhile, was going blind, but his daughters scorned him as brutally as Mary's mother. He endured a wretched domestic life. His girls stole housekeeping money and sold his books until he finally sent them off to learn the lace-making trade. He remarried, but his second wife died within a year. Throughout this torturous period, Milton was trying to write *Paradise Lost.*

In 1663, understanding friends introduced Milton to his third wife, Elizabeth Woodhull. She was a much younger woman who cared for him until his death in 1674 and provided the tranquillity and stability he needed to complete *Paradise Lost,* published in 1667. His personal life, specifically his three marriages, was a constant reproach to his values, and this is reflected repeatedly in his poetry.

In the magnificent epic poem *Paradise Lost,* Milton again celebrated chastity, coupling it with an exploration of the terrible temptations to transgress. "Judge not what is best / By pleasure, though to nature seeming meet," he warns:

> For that fair female troop those saw'st, that seem'd
> Of Goddesses, so blithe, so smooth, so gay,
> Yet empty of all good wherein consists
> Woman's domestick honor and chief praise;
> Bred only and completed to the taste,
> Of lustful appetence, to sing, to dance,
> To dress, and troll the tongue, and roll the eye;

To these that sober race of men, whose lives
Religious titled them the sons of God,
Shall yield up all their virtue, all their fame.

In another harsh description of temptation triumphant, "Adam and Eve after they Fell," Milton laments that

So rose the Danite strong,
Herculean Samson, from the harlot-lap
Of Philistean Dalilah, and wak'd
Shorn of his strength, they destitute and bare
Of all their virtue. . . .

Much later, a repentant Eve tells Adam,

. . . and miserable it is
To be to others cause of misery,
Our own begott'n, and of our loins to bring
Into this cursed world a woeful race,
That afte wretched life must be at last
Food for so foul a monster. . . .

In the poetry of the great John Milton, chastity is the ultimate virtue, sex a mortal sin, and woman the seductive snake who entices wavering men to lie with her. Doctrinally speaking, Milton's lyrics hark back to the early Christian Fathers. In that respect, *Comus, Paradise Lost,* and his other masterpieces are like St. Augustine togged out in gilt-embroidered poetics.

Pamela, Shamela

Samuel Richardson's *Pamela or Virtue Rewarded,* published in 1740, was a literary milestone of massive proportions. When the kindly and sympathetic Richardson penned it, he was merely an accomplished, professional how-to letter-writer who expanded his craft into narrative form, told a true story that had deeply affected him, and unwittingly produced the English language's first novel.

For fifteen years after "a gentleman" had recounted it to him, Richardson had pondered the story of a young servant girl and her unpleasant and all-too-representative experience in service. As a mere slip of a twelve-year-old, this child had been forced to go into service because of her family's financial problems. She became the personal maid of a woman who died three years later, whereupon her dead mistress's son attempted, "by all manner of temptations and devices, to seduce her." So far, so ordinary—this was, after all, the lot of hundreds of thousands of young domestics throughout England.

But here the story deviated from the usual path of pregnancy, discovery, disgrace, expulsion from service, childbirth in a hovel or even a ditch, ruin, misery, perhaps death. For in the story Richardson heard, the bonnie lass "had recourse to . . . many innocent stratagems to escape the snares laid for her virtue," which included nearly drowning herself. However, she persevered, and finally, "by her noble resistance, watchfulness, and excellent qualities, subdued" her tormentor so that he actually did the decent but astonishing thing and married her.

Even more astonishingly, the bride managed to vault the social abyss between herself and her husband and "behaved herself with so much dignity, sweetness, and humility, that she made herself beloved by everybody." Both rich and poor adored her and her grateful husband blessed her. Apparently this was what had really happened, and Richardson set himself the task of committing the story to paper. He painstakingly presented it from the heroine's perspective, with all the nuances and judgment a beleaguered fifteen-year-old might have had. *Pamela* is the 533-page result.

Pamela was staggeringly successful, to its publisher's delight, selling out five editions in its first year. (Nearly 260 years later, it is still required reading for thousands of postsecondary literature courses.) Its message—that maidenly virtue and virginity were marketable commodities that could greatly advance both their owner and her family—resonated with the rising middle class. The great poet Alexander Pope raved that *Pamela* would do more for virtue than volumes of sermons. But vociferous critics also emerged, foremost among them Henry Fielding, who detested Pamela's cloying and calculating coyness. Months after *Pamela*'s triumphant appearance, Fielding counterattacked with *Shamela,* subtitled "An Apology for the Life of Mrs. Shamela Andrews. In which, the many notorious Falsehoods and Misrepresentations of a Book called Pamela, Are exposed and refuted; and all the matchless Arts of that young Politician, set in a true and just Light . . . Necessary to be had in all Families. . . ."

Ten months later, Fielding's lengthier novel *Joseph Andrews* appeared, still parodying *Pamela.* Here the hero is the virtuous Joseph Andrews, in dire danger from his aggressive, lascivious, and upper-class female employer. When he resists her advances, she is aghast.

> "Have you the assurance to pretend, that when a lady demeans herself to throw aside the rules of decency, in order to honor you with the highest favor in her

power, your virtue should resist her inclination? That when she had conquered her own virtue, she should find an obstruction in yours?"

"Madam," said Joseph, "I can't see why her having no virtue should be a reason against my having any: or why, because I am a man, or because I am poor, my virtue should be subservient to her pleasures."

"I am out of patience," cries the lady: "did ever a mortal hear of a man's virtue! Did ever the greatest, or the gravest, men pretend to any of this kind! Will magistrates who punish lewdness, or parsons who preach against it, make any scruple of committing it?"

Fielding was getting in his own strikes against what he regarded as the preposterous and morally revolting *Pamela,* in which virginity is called virtue, ticketed with a price tag, and hawked to the highest bidder. In his own moral scheme, chastity—true chastity—is essential, for men as for women. He slips in lessons about the consequences of debauchery—a ruined young woman condemned to Newgate Prison for prostitution, while her seducer suffers only pangs of remorse. Joseph Andrews's chastity is more than his physical virginity. It is his commendable ability to master his sensuality. Chastity is not some smug item for barter. It is a religiously derived way of life and deserving of more profundity than *Pamela* was able to give it.

TOLSTOY'S *KREUTZER SONATA*

After the Bible, *The Kreutzer Sonata* is possibly the world's best-known literary endorsement of chastity. Written in 1890, eleven years after Leo Tolstoy's religious conversion, its central theme is the chastity that Tolstoy fervently believed was essential to mankind's moral health. It was in many ways a fictionalized and wildly fantasized account of his own marital struggles and resonated so deeply that Mahatma Gandhi acknowledged the profound influence *The Kreutzer Sonata* had on his own thinking and way of life.

Tolstoy had, after his religious metamorphosis as a reborn Christian in 1879, attempted to reconcile his new beliefs with his daily life. Far from the monkish asceticism he dreamed of, his fame and fortune supported an indulgent family lifestyle he came to abhor. Tolstoy gave up drinking and smoking and embraced vegetarianism. He often wore simple peasant clothes, cleaned his own room, worked in the fields, and made his own boots. He tried hard but unsuccessfully to convince his wife to give away their possessions and join him in an ascetic, contemplative religious life.

Perhaps even more importantly, from Tolstoy's perspective, was his attempt to transform his marital relations from sexually active to purely platonic. His ideal in marriage was chastity, and for the briefest of periods, he succeeded. *The Kreutzer Sonata* is a tormented diatribe against marriage, lust, romantic love, and sexuality. The narrator is Pozdnischeff, an elderly man who pours out his vitriolic story to a lawyer, a fellow train-traveler. *The Kreutzer Sonata* is the name of a Beethoven sonata, and we learn that Pozdnischeff's wife has been playing it with a musician friend. Pozdnischeff, consumed by jealousy, suspects her of infidelity. His poor wife has no chance. He procures a dagger, bursts in on her and her friend, and though the lawyer (and readers) understand she is completely innocent of any wrongdoing, her crazed husband stabs her to death. Pozdnischeff's views on marriage reflect his chillingly murderous past:

> Marriages . . . have existed and still exist for some people who see in marriage something sacred, a sacrament which is entered into before God. For such people it exists. Among us, people get married, seeing nothing in marriage but copulation, and the result is either deception or violence.

The narrator has, furthermore, concluded that sex is unnatural, shameful, and painful. The Shakers, he says, are right.

> Passion . . . is an evil, a terrible evil, to be combated, not fostered, as it is in our society. The words of the Gospel that "whosoever looketh on a woman to lust after her, hath committed adultery with her already in his heart," apply not only to other men's wives, but also and mainly to one's own. In our world as at present constituted, the prevalent views are exactly contrary to this, and consequently to what they ought to be.

Relating this to Darwinism and evolution, he adds:

> The highest race of animals is the human race. . . . To hold its own in the struggle with other races it must . . . unite like a swarm of bees, and not go on endlessly multiplying and increasing; and like the bees it should bring up the sexless, that is to say, it ought to aim at restraint, and not by any means contribute to inflame the passions.

He realizes, however, that most people will strenuously object to his theory, for *"try to persuade people to refrain from procreation in the name of morality—ye gods, what an outcry!"*

The old man denounces sexual, carnal love as "the most powerful and vicious and obstinate" of all human passions. Were it annihilated, however, "the aim of mankind [for] happiness, goodness, love," would be fulfilled. The human ideal, he continues, is for "goodness attained by self-restraint and chastity."

Sexual intercourse, he elaborates, breaks the moral law. Honeymoons, therefore, "are nothing but a sanction for lewdness." The vilest aspect of love, he says bitterly, is that

> whereas in theory love is described as an ideal state, a sublime sentiment, in practice it is a thing which cannot be mentioned or called to mind without a feeling of disgust. . . . It was not without cause that nature made it so. But if it be revolting, let it be proclaimed so without any disguise. Instead of that, however, people go about preaching and teaching that it is something splendid and sublime.

The old murderer's rant even detours toward pregnant or nursing women, for whom he articulates deep sympathies. Because lustful men force them into sexual activity, he says angrily, the hospitals are full of hysterical women driven there by psychic anguish after they have broken the laws of nature.

The Kreutzer Sonata maintains its enraged tone until the end, a diatribe against sexuality and carnality, against marriage and the hatred that too often develops between husband and wife, and against the theories and arguments that encourage procreation. It is also, like a message reflected in a mirror, a monologue in defense of sexual chastity based on the murderer's, and Tolstoy's, conviction that moral law and moral health demand humans renounce sexuality. Ironically, soon after *The Kreutzer Sonata* was published, Tolstoy was unable to abide by his own impassioned pleas. He violated his vow of chastity by forcing himself on his wife, simultaneously impregnating and embittering her.

JUDITH SHAKESPEARE

In *A Room of One's Own,* Virginia Woolf's ringing essay about women's need for personal autonomy including independent means, she fantasizes that William Shakespeare had a sister Judith, every bit as gifted and imaginative as he was. But as she was a girl, the Shakespeares did not send her to school as they had her brother, for in those days, girls stayed home, apprentices training for their futures as housewives and mothers. Judith was restless as she mended William's torn trousers, absentminded as she bent over to stir the oily stew pot. Sometimes, rebelliously, she would snatch up a book and read a few pages, until Mistress or Mr. Shakespeare caught her slacking and sharply rebuked her for mooning about. In wilder moments, perhaps Judith even scribbled down her thoughts and dreams, then burned her work to hide all traces of her insubordination.

Before Judith was out of her teens, the Shakespeares arranged her betrothal to the son of a neighboring wool stapler. "Marriage is hateful!" she cried out in desperation when her parents informed her of their decision. Alarmed and angry, Mr. Shakespeare beat her severely, then relented and, instead, implored her not to shame him with her sullen behavior. He even resorted to bribery, promising her a necklace or a fine petticoat in return for her sunny cooperation.

Judith was brokenhearted, torn between loyalty to her parents and to the fierce longings of her unquiet heart. Her heart prevailed, and with a bundle of her meager possessions, she ran away and set out for the theaters of London. However, the managers were blind to her genius for fiction, her lust "to feed abundantly upon the lives of men and women and the study of their ways." She might be as talented as young William, but Judith Shakespeare was a female, and that was all anyone needed to know.

At last Nick Greene, an actor-manager, took her in. He also deflowered her and made her pregnant. Driven by "the heat and violence of the poet's heart when caught and tangled in a woman's body," Judith killed herself.

Judith's dilemma was every Elizabethan woman's. The brilliant, artistic soul trapped inside her body would, Woolf said, "certainly have gone crazed, shot herself, or ended her days in some lonely cottage outside the village, half witch, half wizard, feared and mocked at." In Judith's case, attempting to breach the dramatic world of actor-managers was fatal, for it meant compromising her chastity. And "chastity had then, it has even now, a religious importance in a woman's life, and has so wrapped itself round with nerves and instincts that to cut it free and bring it to the light of day demands courage of the rarest. . . . It was the relic of the sense of chastity that dictated anonymity to women even so late as the nineteenth century."

Chastity in this Woolfian sense extends far past inviolate genitalia and encompasses both intellect and spirit. Their purity, like the body's, is defined by rigid conventions, penetrable only by appropriate agents designated by social and cultural mores. A wild spirit, free-ranging and unfettered, was unchaste. A surging ambition, longing to communicate to the world, was unchaste. Judith Shakespeare combined these with a grateful heart and surrendered her chastity, forking it over in return for the chance—unrealized!; stolen from her by Nick Greene's lustful bullying—to touch the world in iambic pentameter.

GARP'S MOTHER

In John Irving's *The World According to Garp*, the mid–twentieth century's Jenny Fields was a privileged young woman whose wealthy parents expected her to snare a suitable husband at her exclusive college. But Jenny rebelled, dropped out, and entered the socially unsuitable profession of nursing. She also remained single and celibate. However, nobody seriously believed she had no lovers and assumed that "Jenny's sexual activity was considerable and irresponsible." This, of course, was why her mother presented her with a douche bag every time she visited home.

The truth was, Jenny relished being "a lone wolf" uninterested in either men or sex—"she wanted as little to do with a peter as possible, and nothing whatsoever to do with a man." In her autobiography, Jenny described herself this way: "I wanted a job and I wanted to live alone. That made me a sexual suspect. Then I wanted a baby, but I didn't want to have to share my body or my life to have one. That made me a sexual suspect, too."

Her scornful colleagues nicknamed her Old Virgin Jenny and asked mockingly, "Why not ask God for [a baby]?"

But Jenny persisted, a virgin determinedly scouting for a man to father her child. Technical Sergeant Garp's shrapnel-smashed brain made him the perfect candidate. He could utter only one word—"Garp"—and his sole remaining pleasures were radio and masturbation. Even better, he was terminally injured, so would not be around to interfere in Jenny's life.

Jenny's decision was made. She had sex with Garp, just once, and conceived her son. When Garp died, Jenny "*felt* something," but mainly that "the best of him was inside me." In keeping with her antisex feelings, Jenny found compatible employment with the Ellen Jamesians. These were a society of women who cut out their tongues to protest the rape of Ellen James, an eleven-year-old whose rapists had thought they could prevent her from denouncing them by cutting out her tongue. Fortunately, she wrote out a detailed description that identified them. The rapists were caught, convicted, and murdered in prison.

Jenny told the world about her aggressive feminism and her quest for celibacy in her book *A Sexual Suspect.* Finally she was assassinated, shot through the heart as she began a speech in a parking lot. She was buried in New York's first feminist funeral, for women only. Afterward, her son, T. S. Garp, who could no longer hide behind her crisp, white nursing uniform with its little red heart stitched over the breast, took over the management of his own troubled life, and also of the novel.

Vampire Celibacy, Medium Rare

Are vampires eternally celibate lovers or is vampirism antithetical to celibacy? A bloodless look at some of the literature leaves the question largely unanswered, but serves up delectable literary tidbits suitable for nibbling. Bram Stoker's *Dracula,* properly interpreted, was likely Victorian pornography, but pornography with a difference. Where other authors titillated with seductions, orgies, and sadomasochistic drills, Stoker mesmerized with scenes of fantasized eroticism in which, for example, "lamias" or female vampires set upon hero Harker, trapped in the castle, and barely miss "seducing" him, while *nosferatu* the "vampyre" is a constant menace, "drawing the life's blood" of his victims.

What does this really mean? Is the *nosferatu* akin to a ubiquitous, unkillable needle-happy doctor? Or are his biting kisses, at least metaphorically, seductive? Perhaps just bewitching? Tantalizing? Is this orgasmic sex without intercourse, without even the possibility of intercourse?

The classic early vampire tales never clarify whether their characters actually have sex with vampires, though certainly they pique the reader's interest—and libido?—with their innuendos. In the end, the vampire is the ultimate seducer, and descriptions of his bloody conquests are metaphors for the reader's dark and hidden sexual fantasies. After all, who wouldn't be charmed by an immortal, omnipotent being invisible in mirrors, perhaps presenting as a savage dog or wolf, whose Achilles' heel is his aversion to religious paraphernalia, garlic, sunlight, and running water? Who cannot imagine the shivery thrill of blowing away this ancient predator with a hefty puff of garlicky breath or the production of a gleaming crucifix?

Modern vampires are very, very sexy, with all manner of erotic imagery— heterosexual, bisexual, and homosexual—quite prominent. Vampire sex or celibacy—this is, of course, the stickiest question—is the ultimate kind, dangerous and deadly, with a quasi-surgical finality. Vampire sex or celibacy, depending on your take, is the cutting edge of erotic fantasy and has led to admirably serious debate on the issue of whether vampires actually exist. (They don't, even in Transylvania.)

CHAPTER 13

The New Celibacy

SHRINKING CLOISTERS

The frenzied, joyous, righteous irreverence of the early 1960s stemmed from a plethora of circumstances: widespread challenges to American racial inequities; rumblings of protest against the war in Vietnam; an indulged generation maturing in suburban security; growing articulation of widespread female discontent; and the development of the birth-control pill, which revolutionized young people's perceptions of sexuality and tantalized adults with spectacular new possibilities.

In combination, these were staggeringly potent influences. In particular, they transformed modern notions of sexuality. One of the innumerable examples is the young people who detected in their own mothers what Betty Friedan dubbed "the feminine mystique" and subsequently rebelled against the gilded cage of dependent, stay-at-home marriage. Later, as flower children exploring new dimensions of erotic expression, they created shock waves throughout their societies.

The Catholic Church was far from immune to the tumultuous events of the secular world. An extraordinarily high number of priests and nuns entered holy orders during the 1950s and early 1960s—and the convictions of many of them showed that the more antiquated notions of the Church, like the times, were a-changin'. One of these antiquated notions was clerical celibacy. For centuries, it had been embraced, accepted, or swallowed by millions of religious whose complaints about practicing it tended to focus on their own inadequacies rather than the basic unsoundness of obligatory celibacy. Then, as the 1960s swept conventions aside and challenged tradition, a groundswell of clerics squinted hard at celibacy and frowned at what they saw.

Celibacy as a permanent way of life had always been difficult to observe. We have seen how unwilling female religious, shunted into cloisters, bitterly resisted this rejection of their sensuality and the possibility of establishing intimate relationships in which they could express it. On the other hand, women who voluntarily entered holy orders as a vocation had much less of a struggle, for the rewards of celibacy far outweighed its disadvantages. Male religious, however, often fought lifetime battles with their sexuality; their lives became ordeals against the enemies of wet dreams, masturbation, and obsessive fantasizing. Many violated their vows, with women or each other. For them, celibacy was the most exacting religious pledge and the most often breached.

Celibacy was much more than a burdensome vow, arguably the most burdensome. It was also the state that distinguished Catholic clergy from most others. Anglicanism and Buddhism, among other religions, are also served by some celibate religious, but in no other religion does celibacy dominate the moral agenda as it does in Catholicism. Centuries of thunderous theologians championed it as a supreme virtue, pleasing to God and paralleling Christ's own chastity. Even in the 1960s, Catholic Church spokesmen lauded it. Celibacy was "far more precious to God" than matrimony, wrote one. "The objective excellence of virginity over marriage cannot be called into question," declared another.

But some conscientious Church people reflected differently. The director of a treatment center for psychologically disturbed religious revealed that "many of the neuroses we treat are aggravated by styles of spirituality and community life that encourage religious . . . to try to be happy without giving and receiving genuine affection and warm love."

The Jesuit Rule 32, *Noli me tangere,* for example, forbade Jesuits from touching each other, even in jest. They also banned PFs—Particular Friendships—between individuals.

In 1967, a majority of nuns responding to a sisters' survey believed that "the traditional way of presenting chastity in religious life has allowed for the development of isolation and false mysticism among sisters." Two thousand years of theology was sinking beneath the force of accumulated discontent, disbelief, and disobedience. Suddenly, long-term celibate religious had to justify their psychological depth, maturity, and integrity. This was the hopeful context in which Churchmen began their massive preparations for what came to be known as Vatican II.

VATICAN DECREES CELIBACY A BRILLIANT JEWEL

The 21st Ecumenical Council of the Roman Catholic Church, or Vatican II, began in 1962 as liberal Pope John XXIII's initiative to deliberate on the issue of Christian unity. The swinging pendulum of perspective deeply influenced

Catholic clerical attitudes. A golden glow of optimism warmed religious yearning for fundamental change.

And why not? Unwillingly celibate—or guiltily uncelibate—religious were convinced optional celibacy would solve the age-old dilemma, making honest men and women of those called to the service of God but without the concomitant sacrifice of their sexuality. Some confident priests even took the extraordinary step of marrying, certain that Vatican II would vindicate and legitimize their status.

The sudden death of Pope John XXIII in June 1963 killed this ambience of hope. Less than three weeks afterward, white smoke wafted from the iron stovepipe on the Sistine Chapel, announcing the election of Paul VI, the pope who would quash all hope that Vatican II would alter Church dogma on celibacy. On October 11, before the issue had been discussed, the new pope advised the Council that public deliberations on celibacy were totally inappropriate and that he was determined to preserve the rule of celibacy. The ensuing vote to continue the age-old rule of celibacy passed smashingly, with 2,243 bishops overwhelming 11 lonely dissenters. Enforced celibacy as a concomitant of religious vocation remained untouchable. Shaken and often bitter, religious everywhere heard and understood.

If the message of Vatican II was not clear enough, Paul VI reiterated it in 1967 with his *Sacerdotalis Caelibatus*, his encyclical letter on priestly celibacy. "Priestly celibacy has been guarded by the Church for centuries as a brilliant jewel," he trumpeted, "and retains its value undiminished even in our time when mentality and structures have undergone such profound change. A desire [has been] expressed, to ask the Church to reexamine this characteristic institution of hers. It is said that in the world of our time its observance has come to be of doubtful value and almost impossible."

Paul VI then listed some of the anticelibate arguments current among Catholic religious: (1) Jesus did not exact celibacy of his disciples; it was a freely chosen act of obedience to either a special religious or spiritual gift. (2) The Church Fathers wrote long ago—different times, different mores. (3) The rule of celibacy bars devout Catholics blessed with a religious calling from joining holy orders if they cannot accept lifetime celibacy. (4) The Church values clerical celibacy more highly than the need for priests in desperately undermanned parishes worldwide. (5) A married priesthood would eliminate most of the harmful deceptions and hypocrisy currently eroding its membership. (6) Perpetual celibacy has detrimental physical and psychological effects, including alienation and bitterness. (7) A religious's acceptance of celibacy is passive rather than voluntary.

Convincing? Shatteringly so? Even Paul VI conceded that "the sum of these objections would appear to drown out the solemn and age-old voice of the pastors of the Church and of the masters of the spiritual life, and to nullify the living testimony of the countless ranks of saints and faithful ministers of God, for whom celibacy has been the object of the total and generous gift of themselves to the mystery of Christ, as well as its outward sign."

But this was merely cerebral, while Paul VI was spiritual. Without ado, therefore, he dismissed all these compelling arguments and reaffirmed what his heart and soul assured him was gospel truth: "the present law of celibacy should today continue to be firmly linked to the ecclesiastical ministry . . . [and] should support the minister in his exclusive, definitive, and total choice of the unique and supreme love of Christ."

Paul VI proceeded to hammer out his personal convictions about celibacy: (1) Christ was a lifetime celibate and recommended celibacy as a special gift. (2) Celibacy denotes and also generates great charity, love, and spiritual devotion. (3) Priests "made captive by Christ" come to share his essence, of which celibacy is an essential feature. (4) Priests who face "a daily dying," or renunciation of legitimate families, will draw closer to God. (5) Celibacy liberates religious from familial demands that would take time away from ministry. (6) Celibacy is not unnatural, for God-given logic and free will can overcome sexuality. (7) Solitary religious are not lonely but rather filled with God's presence. Occasional loneliness replicates the life of Christ, who "in the most tragic hours of his life was alone." (8) The "lamentable defections" of priests are not a reflection on the rigors of celibacy but on the inadequacies of the initial screening process. (9) Rather than warping personalities, celibacy contributes to maturity and psychic integration. Paul VI's conclusion? "The law of priestly celibacy existing in the Latin Church is to be kept in its entirety."

Incredibly, many Catholics still hoped. In 1970, the Jesuit magazine *America* predicted that by middecade, married priests would be a reality. Optimistic Dutch and Brazilian priests married. Optional celibacy, they believed, was almost certainly in the offing. How wrong intransigent Churchdom proved them! Not only did marriage remain strictly forbidden, but the Church subjected those requesting release from their vows to treatment many described as demeaning, even traumatizing.

A decade later, a new pope, John Paul II, dashed any speculation that he was a breath of fresh theological air. Not at all. On such matters as celibacy and birth control he stood solidly behind his predecessors' pronouncements and pontificated, "Virginity as a deliberately chosen vocation, based on a vow of chastity, and in combination with vows of poverty and obedience, creates particularly favorable conditions for the attainment of perfection in the New Testament sense."

American cardinal John J. O'Connor expressed an earthier viewpoint. Categorizing anticelibate arguments into three main points—celibacy as the cause of priestly sexual sinning, as a barrier to the religious vocation, and as a violation of human rights—he replied, "To all three categories I say, 'Bah humbug!' Every virgin can give spiritual birth to countless souls, if the virgin offers himself or herself to Christ with the passion and commitment with which a man and a woman can offer themselves to each other. This is to become a virgin for the kingdom of heaven, as was the case with Mary. The virgin can become a wonderful channel of grace to the world, as was Mary."

Such certainty, such serenity in response to such churchly turmoil, personal despair, and spiritual anguish! Meanwhile, entire Catholic congregations go unministered for want of priests. The problem is critical in Brazil, Indonesia, and parts of Africa, and these are only a few examples. Indonesia is a primarily Muslim country where women are relatively emancipated and celibacy (as opposed to premarital virginity) is not highly regarded. How, then, to attract priests and even converts to Catholicism? In 1982, in a meeting with John Paul II, Indonesian bishop Justin Darwajuomo staked his bishopric on the pope's willingness to permit him to ordain married men into his nation's priesthood. The result? Permission denied, resignation accepted.

In Africa, too, in countries where polygamy is common, clerical celibacy is an enormous obstacle to the recruitment of indigenous priests. It directly contradicts the traditional view that "marriage is the focus of existence . . . a duty, a requirement from the corporate society, and a rhythm of life in which everyone must participate. . . . He who does not . . . is a curse to the community, he is a rebel and a law-breaker, he is not only abnormal, but 'underhuman.' "

In Africa, clerical celibacy is practiced mainly in the breach, so the issue becomes not celibacy but limiting priests to merely one wife. "In African culture," a missionary says, "if you are somebody, you have two wives. Sometimes four or five. Now a priest is a man of honor: if he has two or more wives, no problem whatsoever." Except that he cannot marry legally, and so his common-law wives cluster nearby him in separate huts. No wonder African bishops demand the right to ordain married priests.

Latin America is another teeming morass of underserviced Catholics and surreptitiously uncelibate priests. Despite a policy of proselytizing among natives to recruit priests, the Church's position on celibacy blatantly ignores cultural realities, specifically traditional perceptions of celibacy. Peru is an excellent case in point. Life in the Andes centers around the notion of the *pareja,* the couple, and a man's authority is based on his having a family. Celibacy is neither understood nor respected. Responsible men are supposed to have families and support them. The idea of a celibate Peruvian leader is an oxymoron. Is it any wonder that an estimated 80 percent of Peruvian priests cohabit with women?

A majority of Brazilian priests are also noncelibate, perhaps 60 to 70 percent. As many as a third of Western missionaries, either succumbing or adapting, do the same. The "naturalness" of their lifestyles prompts parishioners to respect them and alleviates the suspicion often held toward men who are apparently immune to innate sensuality.

In the Philippines, a small majority of priests live with women. Rural manses are always peopled by the priest's extended family, and a priest's wife is introduced as an aunt or sister, his children as his nieces and nephews. So widespread is this practice that most parishioners are reluctant to donate to Sunday's collection plate, knowing it is destined for the support of the priest's family.

What about European and Catholic Poland, John Paul II's own homeland? Or Polish priests elsewhere, for one in three European priests are Polish? No statistics exist, but what is certain is that celibacy is frequently an easily shrugged-off obligation, though they seldom actually marry. A young Polish priest places this attitude in context: "Compulsory celibacy is just a human law. Everyone knows it's going to change eventually. So why should our lives be spoiled by something that's going to change in twenty years' time?"

Compelling logic, as forthright as the widespread Polish clerical lack of celibacy John Paul II knows about but addresses with the silence of either confusion or complicity.

Everywhere in the Catholic world the same story is told. Most German priests responding to a 1985 survey in Cologne agreed that some priests are false celibates who secretly violate their vows of chastity. Many North American priests also observe their vows of celibacy in the breach. A few marry secretly and resort to the medieval priestly tradition of passing off their wives as housekeepers. Most who are uncelibate simply have lovers or indulge in affairs. And, says married ex-priest David Rice in *Shattered Vows,* "there is the priest who uses his Roman collar as a tomcat uses his miaow, to charm all the women he can, and to lure them to bed—and then uses his collar a second time round, to break the relationship or evade his responsibilities."

An extensive study by Richard Sipe titled *A Secret World: Sexuality and the Search for Celibacy* calculates that about 40 percent of U.S. priests are routinely uncelibate, a figure that excludes those whose lapses are infrequent.

David Rice concludes that ultimately, unless compulsory clerical celibacy is ended, millions of Catholics will be deprived of priests and therefore of mass. "Thus it is a choice between celibacy and the Mass," he warns. But an equally alarming scenario is just as likely—the sacraments dispensed by clergy who routinely desecrate their holy vows, thereby inspiring in their congregants the notion that sifting through Church dogma and rejecting what seems inconvenient or incompatible with their deepest beliefs is perfectly acceptable.

For three decades now, through its strident reaffirmation of clerical celibacy, Vatican II and subsequent papal authority have effectively muzzled concerned Catholics who argue for optional celibacy. This includes laypeople, who in North America, for example, increasingly embrace the idea of married priests. A *Newsweek* poll in the USA, for instance, shows that lay support for married priests grew from 53 percent in 1974 to 71 percent in 1993. A *Maclean's* magazine poll in Canada found that 84 percent of Canadian Catholics would allow priests to marry.

This represents, of course, only one dimension of priestly sexuality. Many priests, whether celibate or not, are homosexual in orientation; Sipe interprets data gathered between 1960 and 1980 to mean that about 20 percent of priests acknowledged either celibate or sexually active homosexuality, and later surveys indicate that their number has rapidly increased, perhaps even doubled to between 38 percent and 42 percent. The figures also suggest that only about half of all priests are celibate.

Gay priests share some issues with their heterosexual brothers, but whereas the Church openly addresses the issue of priests who wish to marry, it is reticent, almost secretive, about the very existence of gay priests. Fundamentalist Christians, whether Catholic or not, cite scriptural prohibitions against men lying with men as evidence that homoeroticism is evil. This conservative stance calls into question the right of gay priests to be ordained in the first place. It also flatly denies their right to have sexual intercourse, both on the grounds that it would be perverse and that it would violate their vow of celibacy. The priestly rebellion against that vow has hidden dimensions that have figured only peripherally, if at all, in the ongoing worldwide debate about Catholic clerical celibacy.

Indisputably, vast numbers of priests are either openly or clandestinely uncelibate, and in many countries large contingents are even married, either legally or de facto. How does the Vatican respond? Like a tongue-tied mute, incapable of so much as a squeak of disapproval. Yet it cannot be impervious to conditions within its own temporal body, not with the Vatican's intelligence system operating even more efficiently than the CIA's. Astonishingly, and pityingly, we are forced to conclude the Vatican chooses to trumpet the inviolability of clerical celibacy against a backdrop of a priesthood writhing, figuratively and literally, against that very ideal.

But what about religious who prefer to operate within the Church's defined spiritual parameters? Who prefer public battle to clandestine defiance? Who agonize about their role in an institution whose principles they reject? The resounding answer may be heard in the thunderous sound of a stampede of priests and nuns into secular life. Like the steady tramp of feet around Jericho, their exodus continues to shake the foundations of the unheeding Vatican.

MISOGYNOUS EXCEPTIONS
TO THE PAPAL RULE OF CELIBACY

Enforced clerical celibacy is a principle Church theologians cherish largely on the specious grounds of tradition, despite an avalanche of evidence that it has usually been widely ignored or violated, sometimes more, sometimes less than it is today. They also mouth rigid interpretations of the same scripture that all other Christian denominations find compatible with their own married clergy. They brush away all else—loneliness, depression, alienation, for example—as featherweight concerns. Yet in the mid-1990s, a new situation crushed all their previous objections to dust. Married Roman Catholic priests? Certainly—at least when those priests were converted, ex-Anglican clergymen who had staked their professional lives on a principle of misogyny so breathtaking, it resonated like a familiar echo in the hallowed precincts of the Vatican.

This principle was, of course, that women must never be ordained, and the new—and married—priests were former Anglican priests who bucked their Church when, finally, toward the end of the twentieth century, it lurched into the minefield of female ordination.

For decades, Rome had already made exceptions to the rule of celibacy in isolated cases, usually of priests converting from other churches, such as the Greek Orthodox, which permits married priests. However, North America and Australia were specifically exempted from this indulgence, though married priests were sometimes "lent" to them by European dioceses. Unlike these men, however, attracted to the Roman rites by any number of factors, the outraged ex-Anglicans were egregious misogynists, united in their rage over female ordination.

Many of the ex–Anglican priests who quit their church because of its decision to permit women into the priestly ranks turned to Rome as a solution and requested permission to become Roman Catholic priests, despite their married status. With an alacrity astounding in such a sluggish institution, the pope approved these requests. The United Kingdom's five Roman Catholic archbishops explained this ruling in a letter to their Church's other, forcibly celibate priests. "At the present time the Catholic Church is welcoming into full communion a number of married clergymen of the Church of England, often together with their wives and in some cases their children," their letter began. "Many of these clergy wish to be ordained priests in the Catholic Church. . . . We are convinced that their ministry will enrich the church. . . . The Holy Father has asked us to be generous. We are confident that you also will welcome and appreciate these new priests when, in due course, they . . . take their place in the presbyterate of many of our dioceses."

The archbishops, anticipating outcries of resentment from some priests and joy from others, attempted to forestall both. Ordaining these ex–Anglican husbands as Catholic priests in no way implied a change in the ages-old rule of celibacy: "The special permissions needed in these cases are by way of exception from the general practice of . . . accepting only single men for priesthood." The new priests would be required to "accept the general norm of celibacy and will not be free to marry again"—in fact, the bishops would investigate the stability of their new members' marriages and evaluate the strength of their wives' support for this new priestly venture. As well, the Church limited the admissions procedure to four years, so that the dissidents had to act relatively quickly. It also prohibited the suddenly Catholic clergymen from assuming all the duties of regular parish priests.

What about former Catholic religious who, forced to choose between ministry and marriage, had opted for the latter? Would they be eligible to resume their places in the Church? Not at all. Unlike the Anglicans who had taken the holy vow of matrimony, the Catholic ex-religious had sworn their vows fully aware that celibacy was an integral component of their vocation. In other words, it was unthinkable that they could be exonerated after having defiantly broken those vows.

The most truly stunning aspect of these Statutes for the Admission of Married Former Anglican Clergymen into the Catholic Church is their unbridled misogynism. How else to explain the otherwise inexplicable reversal of the celibacy-principle-cum-policy sanctioned by centuries, popes, and canon law? How else to understand how the same Church that shrugged off the protests, pleas, and anguish of its own Catholic clergy was suddenly so responsive to the spirituality of clergymen whose sole reason for resigning from their God-given vocation was their church's decision to permit the ordination of women? Why else would the pope and his advisers, who normally proceed at a maddeningly sluggish pace, hurtle forth to snatch up this gang of ultraconservative Anglican dissidents?

Certainly, after years of indifference to them, the Church did not have a *crise de conscience* about its unmanned pastorates, nor a *moment de panique* about the relentless flight of conflicted religious from their cloisters back into the uncelibate world. No, what motivated the Church was the strength of the Anglican rebels' conviction about the fundamental unsuitability of women as priests, a conviction today's Church Fathers share and are committed to sustaining.

Indeed, so strongly did this antiwomen ideology resonate with the Catholic hierarchy that it drowned out questions about just how sincerely these Anglican newcomers could ever accept such tenets as papal infallibility and the Immaculate Conception. The Church's enthusiastic embrace of the resolutely misogynist ex-priests was, in a general atmosphere of ecumenicism and good-will, an uncontrolled outburst of antiecumenicism. It was, in fact, nothing less than the public salvaging of men who had defied and challenged the Church of England, the self-serving gesture of fellow loyalists who recognized, and immediately recruited, these fundamentally kindred spirits: Celibacy might be a brilliant jewel, but it pales beside the harsh light that directs women away from the path men tread and blinds them whenever they band together to challenge the dogma that deems them unfit for priestly ordination. This is because, as we have seen, official Church celibacy stems largely from fear of women's sexual allure—an oft-cited image describes them as temples built over sewers—which only complete abstinence can successfully counterbalance.

Now-married priest and Johns Hopkins Medical School lecturer Richard Sipe writes in *A Secret World: Sexuality and the Search for Celibacy:* "It is hard to overestimate the importance of antifeminism in the formation of celibate conscientiousness and priestly development for over two centuries when the discipline of celibacy was being solidified (1486 and following)."

CATHOLIC PRIESTS VOTE WITH THEIR FEET

Today, as in the past, hundreds of thousands of Catholic priests question and rail against the discipline of celibacy. Those tormented by doubt have options. They may take leaves of absence of up to a year, to meditate, pray, and resolve their personal crises. They may seek counseling within the Catholic framework. They may also abandon their vocations and return to the world, a course of action once unthinkable and even now, difficult to negotiate successfully.

No Catholic religious doubts that celibacy freely chosen, or granted by God's grace, has the power of infusing the priest with a profound love and serenity that strengthen his ministry and enrich his relations with parish-ioners. Coerced celibacy, on the other hand, weakens and saddens, embitters and alienates. Some priests simply endure, with loneliness their overriding companion. Many cheat and take lovers they either disguise as housekeepers or friends or flaunt as mistresses. Others find the struggle intolerable and finally leave; of those who do so, 94 percent identify their discomfort with celibacy as their prime motive. Since Vatican II, over one hundred thousand have joined the exodus, more than one every two hours, nearly one-quarter of the world's working priests. In the United States, 42 percent of priests leave within twenty-five years of their ordination, which translates into the bleak statistic that half of American priests under the age of sixty have already gone. In Canada in the past two decades alone, the number of priests and nuns has dwindled by a quarter, though 45.7 percent of Canadians are Catholic and the vast majority—84 percent versus 71 percent in the USA—are amenable to ministry by married priests.

At the same time that droves of priests have been defecting, far fewer novices have felt called to join holy orders. Swiftly and steadily, the world's complement of Catholic clergy is dangerously eroding, so that nearly half of all parishes have no priest at all. At the root of this phenomenon is compulsory celibacy, the issue that has racked the Church since its earliest days.

"It was mainly about celibacy," said Dominic, an American ex-priest, about his decision to leave. "I was spending too much of my time, my energy, my inner strength, on coping with it. Celibacy was preventing me from being the priest I wanted to be . . . the Christian I wanted to be. Celibacy had become an end rather than a means. That's the case with any number of priests."

Another priest, returning to his empty house after the emotional outpouring of Sunday mass, felt he "was like a diver who had gone down deep and did not have a decompression chamber when he came up."

William Cleary, a Jesuit for twenty years, left the priesthood when he became convinced that celibacy is not a virtue and, in its denial of God-given sexuality, may even be "a vague kind of sin." After all, Cleary argues in "A Letter to My Son: The Sin of Celibacy," sexuality is God's vehicle for perpetuating life on earth and "reveals the Divine Being, and . . . reveals who we humans are, the incredible depths of this world's goodness . . . [and] helps toward prayer, contemplation, and all the religious and human values."

No wonder that Dean R. Hoge notes, in *The Future of Catholic Leadership,* that "the celibacy requirement is the single most important deterrent to new vocations to the priesthood, and if it were removed, the flow of men into seminaries would increase greatly, maybe fourfold."

It should also be emphasized that traditionally the Church has treated apostates with brutal indifference; leaving is often a miserable experience, emotionally, psychologically, professionally, and financially. In the USA, they were "solitary, shuffling pariahs, from whom Christian society asked only that they should disappear off the face of the earth." Italians refer to them as the Church's "White Homicides" because despite years of service, they are pushed out into the world jobless, scorned, with only about $300 to their name, bereft of friends, ostracized by former colleagues. Even in countries where the Church does not actively persecute those who renounce their vows, the transition from religious to secular life is almost always trying and often frightening. Ex-priests who continue to work for the Church—as pastoral assistants, for example—report that they are underpaid, stigmatized, and humiliated, and that celibate coworkers are unfriendly, hostile, and envious of them.

Too often, ex-priests are dismissed as if they are in the same category as disbarred lawyers or other disgraced professionals. But the majority remain devout Catholics who long to continue practicing their profession of serving God. Thousands of them attempt to do so through Rent-A-Priest, a nonprofit agency begun in 1992 in Framingham, Massachusetts, which now has branches in Canada and South Africa. In the U.S., Rent-A-Priest claims a database of over two thousand estranged priests available to conduct baptisms, funerals, and other sacraments. The majority of these men are now married and call themselves "married Catholic priests." But the Church does not acknowledge them as such—the Canadian diocese of Toronto, for instance, refers to them as "laicized priests," an ambiguous and unsatisfactory classification. Worldwide, the Church deplores Rent-A-Priest's swelling ranks as a manifestation of the raging conflict over celibacy. More seriously, it refuses to sanction the sacraments they perform.

No wonder, then, that so many priests prefer to remain in holy orders and defile the vow of chastity they find so onerous. But how many is "so many"? Sipe's study estimated that nearly 40 percent of American priests are chronically uncelibate, 20 percent in stable relationships with one or more adult women, nearly as many with adult men. A minority, the pedophiles, foist themselves on minors both male and female.

Subtract this cheating 40 percent from the priesthood and 60 percent remain. Are its members at least celibate? Not necessarily. Many of them indulge in occasional erotic adventures, but slack Church tallying of sexual lapses permits about four such episodes annually before it labels their perpetrator sexually active. In other words, about half the Catholic clergy sworn to celibacy is uncelibate.

THE THIRD WAY OF SOPHISTRY AND CHEATING

A number of religious abide by The Third Way, a clerical lifestyle that sprang up after the 1960s sexual revolution, during which priests would frequent bars where they picked up women for necking and petting sessions but steered clear of sexual intercourse. In the 1970s, this behavior matured into The Third Way, a more thoughtful venture shared by nuns and priests as partners who shared affection and personal confidences in dating/necking/petting relationships that seldom led to overt sex. Decades later, nuns and priests continue to practice The Third Way, though less publicly.

Others, dissatisfied with these attempts to indulge sensuality and deepen personal development without actually having sex, maintain that, after all, celibacy prohibits marriage, not sex, an argument that permits them guilt-free sexual expression. These priests, and the nuns who often share their beds, claim to believe that by not creating families, with all the concomitant responsibilities and duties, they retain at least a technical celibacy that permits them to "devote themselves full-time to the service of the larger human family after the pattern of Christ."

Alas, the Church hierarchy lends a certain credence to this sophistry. Too often, when a troubled priest seeks advice about his involvement with a laywoman, his bishop will have him transferred away from her, hoping this will end the relationship. In this equation, the woman is a mere obstacle to be escaped—her life and love, future, and (frequently) fetus *her* problem, *her* responsibility.

Claire-Voie (Open Road) provides ample evidence of this unfortunate tendency. Claire-Voie is a France-based support group for priests' lovers, the mistresses hidden in the shadows, the mothers who cannot name the man who fathered, and also bastardized, their children. The stories are legion. When Father Ghislain's superiors discovered his intimate relationship with Monique, a parishioner, they relocated him and ordered him to keep Monique a secret. Pregnant Maya Lahoud's lover was transferred across the ocean to Quebec. Before he left, he asked her to sign a legal document in which he acknowledged paternity of her child whom he pledged to support, but only if Maya agreed never to reveal his identity. Other priests with mistresses report their superiors maintain discreet silences about their affairs, tacitly sanctioning profound hypocrisy and, from their own professional perspective, sin.

Yet no official Church pronouncement will ever define celibacy as bachelorhood. Churchmen know very well what celibacy is. So should those defiant clergy who propose The Third Way. In the cruel glare of publicity focused on religious sexual sinning, their reasoning seems specious at best, cynical at worst. How, given the cross fire of pronouncements supporting and denouncing clerical celibacy, and Pope John Paul II's declaration that priests who desecrate their vows of celibacy bring tragedy upon themselves, can any religious genuinely suppose they can hide behind a shallow definition? How, drenched in the tears of hundreds of thousands of defecting priests, can they dismiss the anguish of these men who understand celibacy as a much greater commitment than merely retaining legal bachelorhood? How, deafened by the cries of women abandoned or ignored by the priests who impregnated them, can other priests pretend that celibacy only means being unmarried? How, in the shadow of groups like Corpus (Corps of Reserve Priests United for Service), can they persist in denying that priestly celibacy is a complex and profound condition not susceptible to alteration by blithe redefinition? Surely it would be far more fruitful for them to harken to the men of Corpus and like-minded organizations, whose painful decisions to leave the priesthood expose the real issues involved and whose lobbying seeks to clarify and, of course, to change the canon law that even the pope has admitted is not Church doctrine but discipline.

Divorce à la Catholic Church

Corpus began in 1974 in response to an American bishop's dismissal of married ex-priests as of no further use to the Catholic Church. This, at a time when ten thousand ex-priests had married and polls showed that 79 percent of Catholics would welcome married priests, galvanized Corpus's founders to create an advocacy group that is now greatly expanded and highly professional.

Corpus's original cause was simply to work toward an acceptance of a married priesthood—in other words, to end compulsory clerical celibacy. Today, its mission has expanded to locating and communicating with ex-priests, providing media information about related data such as the number of priests who continue to leave, and endorsing other concerned Catholic groups that aim to smash the rule of mandatory celibacy.

One such international group, or rather movement, is the Austrian-originated We Are Church, which mounts intensive public campaigns for optional priestly celibacy and other Church reforms. By 1996, We Are Church claimed it had collected 2.3 million signatures on a petition demanding change. Canada's Catholics of Vision, supported by Corpus, has begun a similar campaign, bitterly opposed by several bishops, five of whom banned participants from campaigning on Church grounds.

The flood tide of sexual scandals perpetrated by clergymen has also provided spokespeople from Corpus and other organizations with arguments for optional celibacy. These, reinforced by publicized studies about the psychological effects of coerced celibacy, lead them to conclude that sexual repression, the inevitable consequence of mandatory celibacy, creates legions of mentally or psychically unbalanced clergymen. Some of these act out in destructive and violent ways, grievously harming people they were supposedly dedicated to counseling, helping, and spiritually guiding. As one ex-priest reflects, "A relationship with God can be deepened by denial, by sacrifice . . . but it can also be soured and dirtied."

Sexual abuse by priests is so widespread and, today, so much more frequently reported that support groups for victims are springing up everywhere. Chicago-based Linkup is such an organization. According to Father Tom Economus, Linkup's president, 90 percent of charges against Catholic priests involve abuse of boys, which is consistent with Richard Sipe's estimate that 6 percent of the American priesthood are practicing pedophiles. Protestant clergymen, on the other hand, are mostly accused of heterosexual "counseling situations gone wrong."

The recent avalanche of scandalous revelations has forced Catholics, including pro–optional-celibacy groups, to confront the issue. The fact remains, however, that the percentage of clergy who commit criminal acts is tiny compared to those who violate their vows of celibacy with consenting adults, whether other religious or laypeople. And not all priests who marry were uncelibate when they resigned from holy orders. Ultimately, though, compulsory celibacy is the common denominator of their fight against Church discipline. Sexually active married priests can be just as effective as the voluntarily celibate, they argue. Both can function in states of grace, and God alone grants each soul his special gift.

THE BLEEDING

As priests wrench off their collars in record numbers, so do monks and other religious, in particular nuns. Since the sexual revolution, over three hundred thousand nuns have quit their orders, about one in five worldwide, a breathtaking statistic people in Catholic circles call "the bleeding." Interviews and surveys coincide in reporting that the vow of chastity is one of the main causes, just as it is among young Catholic women who decide not to join the convents they would have filled decades earlier. This, despite the fact that nuns rank their vows of chastity as "the most meaningful and the least difficult of the three vows."

Nunly life today is vastly different from in the Middle Ages, when wretched nuns were crammed into convents by harsh families or harsher circumstances. Then, they could never break out of the confines of their cloistered prisons. By the twentieth century, convents were populated primarily by women who had chosen the religious life as a vocation, though a small but constant contingent was composed of the one daughter that parents had promised to God. Mercifully, convents seldom accepted overtly mutinous or obviously unsuitable novices, so as a general rule, nunneries were overwhelmingly populated by dedicated nuns.

Until Vatican II, convent life was rigidly structured, censored, and chaperoned. Its inmates, visibly distinguished from the outside world by their ungainly and anachronistic medieval vestments, lived sternly segregated from all outside influences, from the media to their own families. Many congregations banned newspapers and magazines, and a select radio or television program was a rare, supervised treat. Contacts with the world were always monitored, so that even relations had to tolerate another nun's presence as they chatted with their daughter/sister/niece/aunt/cousin. The same protocol applied to dental, medical, and shopping expeditions, and to visits "home," which were limited to intervals of five or six years. The returning nun was accompanied to her parents' house by a sister from the local convent, and both returned to that convent to sleep at night. These regulations ensured celibacy and protected nuns from the contamination of any but churchly influences.

The rewards of this tightly controlled, celibate life were not just spiritual. Nuns were respected and honored in their communities. They were educated (though usually with no consideration for individual vocational proclivities) for whatever professions their order directed: teaching and nursing were the most common. Most orders were financially successful and many were actually wealthy. In sickness and old age, her order's resources assured a nun total security.

Vatican II turned this world upside down, and hundreds of thousands of nuns bailed out. First of all, it eliminated their specialness by declaring that *"all* members of the Church had received an equal call 'to the fullness of the Christian life and the perfection of charity,' simply by virtue of their baptism." Despite their vocation, it appeared that nuns were like any other devout Catholics, cherished but not unique. Moreover, Vatican II reaffirmed their exclusion from the priesthood, which remained a males-only preserve. How, then, were nuns, celibate, sacrificing, and dedicated to God's work, different from other pious but noncelibate Catholic women? Apparently they were not. "In one stroke," writes Patricia Wittberg in *The Rise and Fall of Catholic Religious Orders,* the Council "nullified the basic ideological foundation for eighteen centuries of Roman Catholic religious life."

Following Vatican II, radical changes swiftly transformed convents. The dress code changed and nuns began to look like other conservatively garbed women. They were sent to colleges and universities to study and mingled with whomever they wished. Often they lived in small groups or even alone, without a mother superior. Later, holding one of the interesting and responsible jobs by then available to educated women, nuns earned salaries they had to surrender almost in their entirety to their orders, which dictated the minutest details of their living allowances.

The world, too, was changing. Increasingly, the feminine mystique had new outlets for its energy: educational opportunities, career paths, jobs in industry, social freedom. The birth-control pill's liberating effect on women cannot be overestimated, even for some Catholics who defied their Church's teaching in the cause of controlling their own bodies. With priestly ministry still closed to Catholic women, convents no longer represented upward mobility—which, they saw, was widely available in the outside world. And as traditionally Catholic educational and medical institutions secularized, those drawn to lives of service could fulfill their goals outside holy orders. The respect they could formerly take for granted eroded, as critics attacked them for their collective wealth, accused them of smugness, and questioned their commitment to social problems.

Against this backdrop of two changing worlds, post–Vatican II Catholicism and reformist mainstream society, nuns and potential novices had to evaluate their lives. As they did so, "the bleeding" began. So did the drastic reduction in the number of new recruits. The consequence of both these processes has been the radical change in nunly demography, as aging sisters have come to represent the largest segment of their orders. Of Canada's thirty-six thousand Catholic nuns, 57 percent are over sixty-five, and of these seniors, more than half are older than seventy-five. A mere 1.4 percent are under thirty-five. These days, five to six times more nuns die than enter as novices.

One of many implications of the bleeding that affects younger nuns is financial: with resources drained by the needs of a top-heavy senior membership, working nuns' salaries are an important consideration in collective survival. Furthermore, the security that nunhood once represented is increasingly problematic: Decades from now, how will their impoverished orders maintain these women in their old age?

Many nuns who left in the initial stages of the bleeding cited problems with their vows of celibacy and obedience as the main reason for their decision. (Today, those in the outward trickle are more likely to point to finances. They resent relinquishing their salaries to superiors who then infantilize them by doling out personal allowances.) As always, sexual chastity itself was seldom the motive behind a woman's decision to commit to the spiritual life. Rather, it was an integral, inescapable part of the religious vocation, often the easiest with which to deal. Its costs—childlessness and singleness—seemed worth its rewards: a privileged position in the Catholic Church; honor to the earthly families left behind; educational, vocational, and professional opportunities; relief from financial worries.

After Vatican II, these rewards for taking the veil largely evaporated. Laywomen, too, could be educated and respectably employed, even in Church service, and could hold prestigious positions within the parish. Why, then, through a vow of celibacy, sacrifice the joy of marriage and motherhood, to say nothing of the erotic pleasures of sex? In the two decades after Vatican II, many nuns concluded there was no longer any valid reason to do so.

"Celibacy was an issue for me," reported an apostate nun explaining her decision to leave. "I missed male companionship." A second fell in love with a Jesuit for whom she conceived "an intellectual attraction, an emotional attraction, a comradeship of souls and physical attraction." When a teaching nun "started to have dreams and fantasies about my eighth-grade boys . . . I knew it was time to go." "I began to want children of my own," recalled another. Typical reasons that, after the 1960s, outweighed celibacy's payoffs for the devout nun and contributed more than a few drops to the bleeding.

Since Vatican II and the sexual revolution, over three hundred thousand nuns and two hundred thousand priests worldwide have formally renounced their sacred vows, including celibacy, and defected. Half a million men and women, former religious, are now integrated, with varying degrees of success, into the world. For a great many, celibacy had become the great stumbling block to their personal and spiritual missions.

New Age Monasticism

At the opposite pole, one sliver of society, tiny but disproportionately news-worthy, has incorporated a New Celibacy into a New Age monasticism. This monasticism owes much to a fascination with the asceticism and mysticism of both early Christianity and Buddhism, Hinduism, and Eastern Orthodoxy. But it is also impregnated with postrevolutionary notions of women's equal-ity and of the quest for intense, intimate, and nurturing relationships fostered by strict celibacy.

Benedictine monastics in the charismatic Our Lady of Guadalupe in Pecos, New Mexico, for example, pair up for prayer, and most pairs consist of a man and a woman. "We are celibate, but we love one another," one member explains. In contrast to monks throughout history, whose primary relation-ship was with God and God alone, these Benedictines foster their human connections, which they prize as an essential element of spirituality.

Hermits of the Spiritual Life Institute, a Christian organization, live in their Nova Nada communities in Arizona and Nova Scotia. They are also celi-bate and each year renew a vow of chastity. They "live together alone," staving off loneliness without compromising solitude and facilitating the mundane problems solitaries encounter in the wilderness.

California's Hindu ashram, Siddha Yoga Dham, in Oakland requires celibacy of its unmarried residents. "When you love God," a woman devotee says, "some things are given up, not because they're necessarily bad but because they're incompatible with the all-consuming love that you've found." One committed observer predicts: "The 'new monasticism' will provide a cat-alyst for change, will be a conscience for the nation, will change the values of many with regard to work and money, relationships, and the environment." In particular, its celibacy is conceived and practiced as a voluntary vehicle to deepen and harmonize the bonds of love rather than a privation or a sacrifice.

CELIBACY AS AN UNDIVIDED HEART

Kathleen Norris, the Protestant author of *The Cloister Walk,* was so drawn to monastic life that she became a Benedictine oblate attached to St. John's Abbey in Minnesota. This involved pledging to abide by the Rule of St. Benedict insofar as her personal situation permitted. Because Norris is married, she observes her vows by frequent visits to the monastery, by assiduous and contemplative reading of the Scriptures, and by learning from the wisdom of St. John's religious residents.

The Benedictine nuns' reflections on celibacy are so grounded in love that Norris titles one chapter in *The Cloister Walk* "Learning to Love: Benedictine Women on Celibacy and Relationship." Older sisters recall the days when they were taught to avoid sexual thoughts and, of course, sex itself. Surprisingly, several sisters confided that falling in love is an essential element of celibacy. One nun told Norris that she first realized what celibacy really meant when she fell in love with a priest. A prioress elaborated publicly on this theme:

> The worst sin against celibacy is to pretend to not have any affections at all. To fall in love is celibacy at work. Celibacy is not a vow to repress our feelings. It is a vow to put all our feelings, acceptable or not, close to our hearts and bring them into consciousness through prayer.

Another nun explained to Norris that when a nun falls in love—a common occurrence—she can use the occasion to shed her romantic images and develop her understanding of what being a nun is really about.

The Benedictines also realize that nuns and monks define celibacy differently. The men think of it as abstaining from sex, the women more as living together in a community and as a way to manage affective relationships. Celibate monks believe their celibacy conserves sexual energy, which they divert into church service or expend in consuming food and alcohol, playing sports, and working. Nuns, on the other hand, deal with their celibacy more directly, thinking, talking, and praying about it. Above all, they must accept it as a personal commitment. "It is a daily choice to live as a celibate," one nun concluded.

Norris extrapolates from nunly meditations on celibacy, particularly its roots in religion and love, to her own state of matrimony and its vow of fidelity. Like Benedictine celibacy, marriage begins as a sacred lifetime commitment that requires self-transcendence. Both celibacy and matrimony "are a discipline. Both can be a form of asceticism," Norris quotes one nun approvingly. She worries, however, that today's culture promotes an incompatible view of true love, equating it with possessing and being possessed, whereas the nature of the celibacy she celebrates is precisely the opposite because it "seeks to love non-exclusively, non-possessively." Indeed, mature Benedictine celibates often speak about their freedom "to love many people without being unfaithful to any of them." Simply put, their deepest wish is that celibacy will give them "an undivided heart."

THE POWER VIRGINS

Decades after it electrified, horrified, revitalized, and transformed Western society, North America's sexual revolution is now firmly entrenched as a mainstream way of life. By now, its effects are showing—for one thing, it has probably cropped years off the age of the average virgin. Today, the median age of losing virginity is 17.4 for girls, 16.6 for boys, about three years earlier than in the late, staid 1950s. Broken down, these figures are actually more startling: 19 percent of adolescents between the ages of thirteen and fifteen are nonvirgins. By age sixteen and seventeen, this rises to 55 percent, and fully 72 percent of all high-school seniors have had intercourse, at least half with more than one partner.

These figures do not paint a picture of uninhibited, liberating, and reward-ing sexuality. To the contrary, they are adrip with poisonous consequences: a rash of pregnancies—by the time American women reach twenty, 43 percent will have become pregnant once (one every twenty-six seconds)—among mainly unmarried, ill-prepared mothers. Another way to understand this is to compare it with the situation in 1960: then, 33 percent of teenage mothers were unmarried at the birth of their first child; by 1989, this percentage had shot up to 81 percent.

Rates of sexually transmitted disease (STD) have also skyrocketed, so that today, by the age of twenty-one years, about one in four is infected with such STDs as chlamydia, syphilis, or gonorrhea. More frighteningly, AIDS is mak-ing new inroads among young people. Despite impassioned warnings from such famous figures as basketball player Magic Johnson, who admitted that his reckless promiscuity had caused his tragic diagnosis, many young people still engage in unprotected sex.

Equally sobering is that teenagers do not practice what they preach: despite their own early indulgence in sex, few consider it "reasonable to first have sexual intercourse" before age sixteen or seventeen. Why, then, do they so blatantly jump the gun? Curiosity is the leading reason, and "being in love" a distant second—63 percent of girls and 50 percent of boys surrendered their virginity to consummate their love. Alarmingly, even more girls (but only 35 percent of boys) succumbed to pressure from their sweethearts, while 58 percent of both were driven by the desire to impress their friends and become more popular. This, despite the ever-hardy double standard by which they judge themselves: two-thirds agree that sexual experience enhances a boy's reputation while it damages a girl's.

Once upon a time, before the sexual revolution, chastity was easier for girls to maintain. For one thing, they menstruated later, at fourteen rather than twelve, as they do now, and married earlier, at twenty-one rather than today's twenty-five. Then, a young woman could reasonably calculate that she had only seven years of chastity to conquer before she married, at which point she could surrender her virginity with the full approval of parents, religious authorities, and mainstream society. Today, both she *and* her brother are under severe pressure from hormones, a sex-driven society that scorns virgins as geeks, friends and classmates who taunt virgins and boast of their own sexual prowess, and the personal pain of dealing with boyfriends who coax or coerce them to have sex when they would prefer not to.

Yet despite today's rampant sexual experimentation even among the very young, about 20 percent of all teenagers remain chaste until adulthood. Why do these young men and women defy the norm? How do they handle the forces that defeat most of their peers? In what fundamental ways are they different from them? And, having achieved chaste maturity, do they regret deferring their sexual initiation?

These issues must be examined against the backdrop of today's complicated social and moral climate, in particular the media and music worlds dedicated to millions of young people and the power of the purses they control. In those worlds, hedonistic values, sex-driven advertising, and musical presentations blare out the message that sex is good, natural, cool, and ubiquitous. Sex as they portray it is a physical maneuver preceded by seductive, flirtatious behavior and cloaked in suggestive clothing, come-hither stances, and an aroma of animal musk.

In this sex-sated world, feminists interpret the sexual act from the perspective of power politics, revealing how it, too, is integrally linked to the inequities between men and women. Unfortunately, their analyses have inspired some other women to conclude that righting the wrongs of the damnable double standard means adopting male sexual standards. Translated into action, this has led to belt-notching, score-keeping, power-play sex, initiated and controlled by women. They see nothing ironic about defining independence and equality as gaining mastery of infinite varieties of what Erica Jong famously dubbed "the zipless fuck." In their combative version of the sexual revolution, real women carry condoms in their jeans, grade (out of ten, for instance) the hard curves of men's buttocks, and initiate sex with partners who arouse their transient lust.

But in these very same worlds, vying with that overwhelming vision of life, is another powerful force, the aggressively proselytizing Moral Majority of the Christian right wing. It, too, has its youth wing and sponsors a countercultural movement that preaches sexual abstinence until marriage and heterosexuality as the only legitimate form of orientation, and it provides converts with accessories as trendy and upbeat as those of the rival ethic of sex-is-almighty. The best-known organization within this framework, one whose reach extends worldwide, is the aptly named True Love Waits.

True Love Waits

The crucial core of the True Love Waits philosophy is contained in this pledge that hundreds of thousands of young women and men have signed:

> Believing that true love waits, I make a commitment to God, myself, my family, my friends, my future mate and my future children to be sexually abstinent from this day, until the day I enter a Biblical marriage relationship.

True Love Waits is clear and uncompromising in asserting its values and assumptions about humankind. True love exists as a God-given emotional dynamic. It is an identifiable phenomenon that blesses only heterosexual couples—love intragender is neither true nor sacred. When true love strikes, the man and woman so blessed should respond by making their union permanent, legal, and honorable in a ceremony that is biblically inspired. Afterward, in the final sublime sequence, comes sexual consummation.

True Love Waits (to be wed in holy matrimony before going all the way) was founded in April 1993 in the U.S. Bible Belt city of Nashville, Tennessee, after youth minister Richard Ross was galvanized by two fourteen-year-olds who confided to him, "We're the only virgins left in our school." They may have been, and their plight was replicated in promiscuous educational institutions all over the Western world. True Love Waits, with its deceptively simple message cunningly touted, soon attracted hundreds of thousands of pledged Waiters. A movement had been born.

Celibacy is at the heart of True Love Waits, a positive, confident, reassuring celibacy. It validates and shores up those young people who remain chaste, but also embraces legions of remorseful nonvirgins it designates "secondary virgins." "Students who have failed sexually can be invited to seek God's forgiveness and make a True Love Waits pledge 'from this day forward.'" Ergo, instant redemption, and though even True Love Waits cannot repair broken hymens, it does comfort the contrite and pardon the penitent.

Amid the barrage of messages blasted forth by our ubiquitous media, the pronouncements of True Love Waits sound calm and clear in the cacophony.

God does not condone premarital sex. Virginity is a "gift you can only give once." "Put the focus where God does: on the heart." "Be willing to wait creatively." It is not wise for Christians to date non-Christians. God wants you to be in charge of your life. He will bring you the right partner at the right time. Homosexual attractions are not immoral, but sexualizing them crosses the biblical barrier and is sinful. Walk closer to God.

True Love Waits is aided by aggressive and savvy marketing. It offers typical teen paraphernalia: T-shirts, sweatshirts, jackets, scarves, baseball caps, wall banners and posters, pendants, pins, rings, necklaces, as well as Bibles, manuals, and general literature. Its slogans—"Stop your urgin', be a virgin," "Pet your dog, not your girlfriend," and for reborn virgins, the wistful "I miss my virginity"—rival in targeted triteness those of any other megasuccessful ad campaign.

True Love Waits promotes Christian music (the Newsboys, DeGarmo & Key, Steven Curtis Chapman, Geoff Moore and the Distance, DC Talk, Audio Adrenaline) and dances—no Waiter need forgo typical teen recreations. In fact, this music and these dances—free of drugs and sex—encourage energetic young people to socialize with each other and sublimate their sexual energies in recognizably typical ways, with no sense of deprivation. However, because of the movement's focus on sexual abstinence and the moral courage it inspires in believers, they have little difficulty in abiding by their vows.

True Love Waits also demands active proselytizing from its converts and orchestrates these drives with sophisticated and practical, detailed instructions. The object is usually to garner media attention as well as new and secondary virgins. In February 1996, for instance, True Love Waiters swarmed into Atlanta's Georgia Dome to attend a chastity rally. But the truly spectacular moment was when three hundred and fifty thousand signed pledge cards were hoisted on cables upward to the ceiling. Even more striking was *Life* magazine's September 1994 color spread of 211,163 of these cards staked into the ground near the Washington Monument.

The 1997 Valentine's Day Vision—displaying True Love Waits commitment cards on secondary-school campuses throughout the USA—demonstrates the organization's determination and ambition. Material from the True Love Waits/Goes Campus literature maps out the plan step-by-step: advance planning, conducting motivating True Love Waits retreats, Bible studies and ring ceremonies, communication with other Christian groups and clubs to muster helpful support, dealing with school administrations and the media, and after the great event, dismantling the display.

Should recalcitrant educational officials stymie the students' efforts during the long, complicated process preceding the Valentine's Day Vision, "the students should graciously say they will need to discuss the issue further and will return at a later time." Avoid emotionalism, the literature advises the students, it will probably work against you. Resort instead to either creative alternatives—perhaps a display across the street from the forbidden campus—or to the law, especially the Equal Access Act, included with the Valentine's Day Vision kit as an emergency contingency.

True Love Waits has spread from its American Bible Belt base through the USA, even to urbane Stanford University in California, the state where, TLW laments, a teenager gives birth every eight minutes. The Stanford group, originally named Students for a Traditional Sexual Ethic, was formed in 1994. True Love Waits has also taken hold in Canada, especially in the prairie Bible Belt. "This is no fad," asserts the coordinator of the Canadian Alliance for Chastity in Cornwall, Ontario. "Teachers tell me they talk about this [chastity] for days in the hallways and school yard."

This is also true in hallways and school yards worldwide, including South Africa, where in 1994, the first year of the True Love Waits initial campaign, sixty thousand students signed pledges. "I am a teenager who is really confused about life," confided one Waiter from KwaZulu/Natal. Another rejoiced that "I have always wanted to remain sexually pure but thought I was in the minority. I'm happy to discover that I was wrong! Signing an official pledge will help me stick to my decision."

Though True Love Waits evolved and matured in the heartland of Christian Protestant fundamentalism, its engineers have been canny or ecumenical enough to reach out to the twenty-three thousand parishes and millions of American Roman Catholics. The Church has clasped tight their outstretched hands and officially adopted True Love Waits. After all, what is chastity but "a new way of sharing an old message for us," remarked the executive director of the National Federation of Catholic Youth Ministry.

That message about chastity is attracting millions of youthful adherents, who at least temporarily abstain from the sexual activity so common among the great majority of their peers. Certainly part of the attraction is in the medium—hip, modern, sanguine, unabashedly commercial, morally authoritative. The new cliché is that thanks to True Love Waits, virgin geek has metamorphosed into virgin chic.

But the felicitous presentation of the chastity ideal cannot explain the breadth and depth of its appeal. Nor are converts only those parented by members of the Moral Majority, who presumably find the tenets of True Love Waits as reassuringly familiar as its trendy trappings. The children of less dogmatic Christians or of those of non-Christian religious persuasion or of agnostics or atheists, who lack this perspective, are nonetheless drawn to Power Virginity and the notion of chastity it preaches.

Chastity sanctioned by the moral context of religion is also authoritative. "God wants me to be pure," Waiters explain. "God says premarital sex is wrong." More imaginatively: "My Body is a Temple for GOD and I Will Not Defile It!" The promised rewards are also alluring—at God's behest, the right partner will materialize and true love and holy matrimony will follow. As husband and wife, the new couple will revel in eroticism intensified by the long dry season that preceded it. Meanwhile, Waiters indulge in romance instead of lust.

Hundreds of thousands of pledge cards later, Power Virginity has proven itself both powerful and empowering. It is assertive rather than defensive. Its assumption that virginity is noble and not embarrassingly old-fashioned or cumbersome, something to hide until one can get rid of it, gives its virgins a welcome sense of self-control and self-definition. Until True Love Waits appeared on the scene, virginity was too often a burden. Now virgins can say, "It is my life and it shouldn't matter to anyone if I have sex or not." Furthermore, "If you're secure in your decision, what other people say is not going to affect you." Power Virginity has become acceptably cool.

As an organization, True Love Waits is a brand-new phenomenon, its impact impossible to assess. At least a decade should elapse before we attempt to evaluate its influence and staying power. It may well prove ephemeral, a flash in the media pan. Significantly, a barrage of publicity surrounding True Love Waits petered out after 1994 and now surfaces only sporadically. At the same time, teenage pregnancies are again rising, most to unmarried mothers. No doubt thousands of young people still wait virginally for true love, but it is far from apparent that the True Love Waits movement has redefined the morality of the current generation.

YOUNG PEOPLE'S MOVEMENT

True Love Waits is the most celebrated and identifiable organization in the modern chastity movement, but many others urge the same message. Together, they have contributed to the persistent presence of chastity, albeit in tiny dollops, in today's youth culture. And virginity, rare though it remains, is no longer a shameful burden. The chastity movement has at the very least redeemed it as a socially acceptable human quality.

Several cultural icons have actually glamorized celibacy or at least coaxed it out of the closet. Well before True Love Waits surfaced, Juliana Hatfield, a rock singer popular with teenagers and young adults, informed *Interview* magazine that she was a virgin. MTV veejay Kennedy, "the ultra geek who made geek chic," made the same defiant announcement. In 1994, singer Morrissey claimed to be an asexual secondary virgin who last had sex years ago. "Sex is *never* actually in my life," he said. "Therefore I have no sexuality." And in 1999, the flamboyant, age-defying, and voluptuous movie star Cher revealed the startling news that ever since her last intimate relationship ended years earlier, she had been celibate. Decades earlier, she had named her only daughter Chastity. Nonetheless, she was finding her own experience of chastity a "strange" one due entirely to a dearth of suitable lovers. The men she met were either unappealing or unwilling to be marginalized as "Mr. Cher." The implication was that until she was offered steady affection and commitment, Cher would remain abstinent.

Chastity also has its small- and large-screen champions. Nubile young actress Cassidy Rae, star of the now defunct *Models, Inc.,* assured fans that despite her on-screen defloration, she was still, at age eighteen, a virgin. "I want to stay as pure as I can for my [future] husband," she said. Actress Tori Spelling's *Beverly Hills 90210* character, Donna Martin, was for several breathless television seasons one of the few virgins left on Rodeo Drive until she, too, joined the mainstream when she did the deed in 1997. In the movie *Clueless,* actress Alicia Silverstone as Cher was not only the coolest gal on campus, she was also a virgin saving herself for teen heartthrob Luke Perry.

Probably the most impressive celibate model for males is A. C. Green, a powerful (six-foot-nine-inch, 225-pound) forward with the National Basketball Association's Phoenix Suns. At thirty-three, Green may be America's most enduring famous virgin, and as founder of Athletes for Abstinence, perhaps its most vocal. "I am still a virgin," Green said in 1997. "I abstain as an adult for the same reasons I did as a teen—the principle doesn't change, or the feeling of self-respect I get. . . . From a sheer numbers standpoint, [abstaining] can be a lonely cause—but that doesn't mean it's not right."

The most toweringly important model for most males and many females is Los Angeles Lakers superstar Magic Johnson. Johnson's too-late damnation of the rampant promiscuity that led to his HIV infection has seriously sullied the hitherto dazzling image of the world of carefree sexual gratification. Johnson also spelled out the sad lesson his seropositivity has taught him: "The only safe sex is no sex."

This tiny cast of brave virgins (born and reborn) and one doomed libertine, however, plays against the relentless eroticism of popular music, television, and cinema; they are oases of purity in society's steamy sexual landscape. For this reason, they loom large in the lonely sights of chastity advocates, particularly professional ones.

The sexual revolution's legacy of skyrocketing teenage pregnancies, staggeringly high rates of abortion and illegitimate births, and raging STDs, including AIDS, has also shocked and alarmed people more concerned about the disturbing social consequences than the religious implications. Unlike the Moral Majority, which spawned True Love Waits, these men and women often tolerate or support premarital sex, but between consenting adults, not youth. For them, abstinence is a time-related issue, essential for young people, irrelevant or optional in maturity.

This very different focus has produced a drive for youth chastity with a wide range of strategies: educational, punitive, exhortatory. Though these are eerily comparable to the tactics employed in the perpetually losing war on drugs, and about as effective, the battle continues because the stakes are so high.

Some major contenders in the chaste-youth campaign are "tough love" enforcement of statutory rape and abortion laws, and enactment of laws against financially delinquent fathers, including teenagers. The fundamentalist-Christian True Love Waits movement represents the most significant exhortatory moral approach. So does the cheerier Born-Again Virgins of America—BAVAM!—which targets the already fallen. Last and perhaps most enduring are the sex-education programs that optimistically rely on the power of well-presented and accurate information to persuade young people that self-respecting, self-selected, disease-free sexual virtue is its own reward.

Legislative pressure—Thou Shalt Not Fornicate with Underage Children, Thou Shalt Not Easily Abort Unwanted Mistakes, Thou Shalt Not Evade Parental Financial Obligations—attaches consequences to actions, and the assumption is that most people will avoid incurring these consequences. Chastity as a model is inferred rather than cited as the obvious way to conform to the law. Safe sex, which solves every problem except illicit intercourse, is a close second. However, a major flaw of such attempts to bludgeon people into behaving is that monitoring all or even most violations is too monumental an operation to succeed. Most people soon understand that only the unlucky are caught and punished, and motivation to abide by these laws is at best halfhearted.

Morality messages about chastity undoubtedly have more impact than legal threats, and True Love Waits is the foremost example. BAVAM!, a society of "recovering sluts," appeals to a different constituency, but it, too, is grounded in a moral imperative: "to help regain the moral fiber America was once built upon and recognized as, and do it with a sense of humor."

BAVAM! was founded by twenty-five-year-old West Coast American landscape gardener Laura Kate Van Hollebeke, who, though unafflicted with "full-blown slutitis (the inflammation of a female's cerebrum causing irrational indecisiveness when met face-to-face with any eager male)," was very shaky with importuning men. To address this weakness, which created "a bothersome void where my healthy self-respect ought to have been," she took a vow of abstinence. From then on, she was committed to refraining from sexual activity "until the 'I do's' have been said before a priest." Via a much visited Web site, a newsletter, and T-shirts ("Sexless in Seattle," "I Love You Man . . . But I Won't Sleep With You"), she shared her experiences with other "recovering sluts." She notes, "I had the chance to challenge people to reassert power over their body, to gain self-respect; to really exhibit respect for others, for love, for commitments. . . . Now . . . the nonprofit organization BAVAM! is spreading like wildfire. It is a squealing, hearty infant."

BAVAM! has nothing of the structure, organization, and commercialism of True Love Waits. It is, its newsletter says, "simply an attitude and a behavior of one who wants to start over and does just that—starts over. In psychological and religious circles, it's known as secondary virginity." Membership is loose, but not intangible. There is a pledge, and a "Certified Born-Again Virgin" membership card and "Certificate of Virginity," both excellent props to ward off sexual advances. BAVAM! also offers T-shirts and sweatshirts, its quarterly newsletter, and advertises support groups and socials for members across the USA and Canada.

In contrast to True Love Waits, BAVAM! is a spontaneous organization of like-minded young adults who have fixed on celibacy in reaction to unpleasant, unsettling, and unhealthy sexual experiences.

The most intense, serious, and heavily funded campaigns for youth chastity are educational, and despite common goals, the rival systems are often predicated on bitterly opposed assumptions about human nature and behavior. A motion presented by a cochairperson of the HIV/AIDS Advisory Council of the Board of Education in New York underscores the magnitude of disagreement: "Children should not be having sex," he moved, confident he was articulating a proposition with which his fellow councilors would acquiesce. To his astonishment, the motion was soundly defeated.

Quite possibly the only motion that might have passed, the only common denominator of conviction, is that information is essential in guiding or shaping the target audience's future conduct. How much information, however, is a veritable minefield of contention. So is the ultimate goal of the informational campaign: Should it promote chastity until the young person is married, or until self-sufficient and truly in love in a committed relationship?

Obviously, religious and moral judgments govern opinions about these and other key issues: Should we offer information about birth control, or might that encourage sexual activity and increase the risk of pregnancy because teens are notoriously inefficient users of condoms? Should we terrify by painting scenarios about STDs and AIDS? Should we stress the emotional, social, and financial costs of unwanted parenthood? Should we rant about the horrors of abortion, legal and illegal? Should we preach "saved sex" through fear of a God devoted to chastity? Or should we present alternatives such as abstinence and safe sex? Should we concentrate on girls, the usual victims of sexual coercion, or should we pretend the sexual double standard doesn't exist and focus our attention equally on boys?

One simplistic approach was Maryland's billboard Campaign for Our Children, which featured slogans such as "Abstinence makes the heart grow fonder" and "You can go further when you don't go all the way." The goal of this sustained media blitz was "to extend the period of abstinence" to older teenagers.

Various sex-education programs are more sophisticated, though not necessarily more effective. Many rely simply on grindingly accurate information about the physiology but not the tumultuous emotions surrounding sex. The hope is that the enlightened student, understanding the mechanics of his body, will then make appropriate decisions about his personal path.

Other programs, designed by school boards for use as complete sex-education programs, err by their obsession with chastity and their blatant exclusion of other material. The widely disseminated American Sex Respect, a sex-education curriculum complete with textbooks and teaching aids, stands accused of urging sexual abstinence alone and failing to discuss birth-control methods and their relative merits. It also misleads students with such nonsense as "petting [before] marriage can sometimes harm our sex life within marriage." A similar curriculum, Teen-Aid, which has also been adopted by Canadian schools, also deceives with such fallacies as "the only way to avoid pregnancy is to abstain from genital contact" and "the correct use of condoms does not prevent HIV infection but only delays it."

Girls, Inc. and Postponing Sexual Involvement (PSI) are American community-based programs that invite girls to meet in small groups. Their approaches to the issue of teen sexual experimentation are very different from Sex Respect and Teen-Aid. Through its Preventing Adolescent Pregnancy (PAP) program, Girls, Inc. targets vulnerable teenagers and invites frank discussion of their problems, temptations, and the pressures their peers exert on them to experience life's sexual dimension. Like the Maryland ad campaign, PAP hopes merely to postpone sexual activity, not to quash all but intercourse between husband and wife.

PSI was developed by Atlanta-based Dr. Marion Howard after her survey of her teenage clients given birth-control literature revealed that "84 percent wanted to know how to say no to someone pressuring them for sex—and to say no without hurting their feelings." PSI uses celibate teens first to communicate its message that abstinence can be cool and then, through role-playing, to suggest realistic ways to deal with social situations that too often lead to coerced sexual relations.

Programs and propaganda notwithstanding, chastity remains a beleaguered phenomenon among North American youth. Troubled authorities scrutinize this uninhibited, indiscriminate writhing and wax eloquent in their laments. Afterward, they lunge to the rescue with questionnaires and studies that document the profligacy, then propose policies and programs cloned on policies and programs that have already failed as battleground weapons in the war against drugs and other societal evils.

This is not to denigrate the positive aspects of these weapons, nor to deny their resonance among the chaste few, the roughly one-fifth who exit their teenage years still virginal. For these young people, the chastity campaign carries proud messages that reinforce their commitment to Sex Saved for True and Married Love. They know what our sex-charged society seldom admits, that they have the right to say no to sex, and to do so with dignity and with confidence in their choice of virginity or chastity. Truly, they are Power Virgins, self-directed and determined.

This is particularly true of girls, whose post–sexual-revolution mass forays into erotic adventure were not necessarily liberating. Their ever-plummeting age of first sexual experience and their skyrocketing rate of pregnancies, abortions, and illegitimate births are evidence of the contrary, sad, and frightening consequences of ignorance, pressure by peers and society, and a craving for approval and love, however transitory and conditional.

The sexual revolution did and does challenge the double standard, and it has radically changed women's lot. But until the double standard is obliterated, the relations between males and females remain unequal. Translated into specific realities, this means that until randy males are not admired as studs while their randy sisters are vilified as sluts, until society and its laws genuinely accept that babies are created by fathers as well as mothers, sex between girls and boys is an unequal activity, with unequal consequences and penalties.

Girls who opt for Power Virginity shuck off much of the burden of this sexual standard. Like their celibate male peers, they also relieve themselves of the anxiety or even terror of STDs, in particular AIDS, and of pregnancy. They are in tune with the clarion cry that celibacy is noble and uplifting. Their skills in maintaining it enhance their sense of self-worth, facilitate the development of a positive identity, and are typically based on reason and gentle firmness designed not to hurt, offend, or repulse would-be lovers.

In other ways, these young women are like abstinent young men. Both see their celibacy as temporary and do not anticipate a lifetime without sex. They share the conviction that their virginity is a gift worthy only of bestowing on a beloved partner in a committed relationship, which many, including all those who are practicing Christians, equate with marriage. Abstinent teenagers also see abstinence as a way to enrich their future sexual lives, and they have taken to heart the chastity campaign's lesson that they should be proud rather than ashamed they have decided differently from the majority of their peers—not being geeks in a sexual world but chic dissenters every bit as cool as their mainstream comrades.

We do not know yet what happens to these youth in maturity, whether they stay celibate until they marry or enter stable relationships or instead abandon their idealism about celibacy if this does not happen. What is certain is that a romantic view of love figures largely in their worldview. This notion of a true love, whose identity will be revealed in due time, makes their chastity a sacrifice they joyously accept for the sake of the magnificence of their erotic future with the truly loved. At the core of this doctrine is an intensely inspiring romantic idealism.

But not all Power Virgins see love and sex in such idyllic terms. A notable example is Tara McCarthy, author of *Been There, Haven't Done That: A Virgin's Memoir.* "I'm twenty-five years old and I'm a virgin," McCarthy confides. "At least by popular standards. I've never had sexual intercourse." She has, however, enjoyed oral sex and mutual masturbation. Clearly, McCarthy's definition of sexual activity, and therefore virginity, is more idiosyncratic than universal.

McCarthy's determined refusal to "go all the way" through penetrative vaginal sex stems from her (True Love Waits reminiscent) decision to wait for Mr. Right, "who loves me and whom I love back—unconditionally. I also know that when I do have sex and do so for all the right reasons, it will be the biggest gift I've ever given anyone in my life."

Meanwhile, McCarthy chafes under the burden of her sexuality and sometimes wonders "whether it's really been worth the wait when the wait has proved to be so long."

McCarthy's memoir of unfound love, told mostly through accounts of her love affairs and (nonpenetrative) sexual encounters, is intriguing largely because she presents herself as a postrevolutionary anomaly. Her world is clearly far removed from the religious roots of her quiet True Love Waits peers, who have enormous numbers and an elaborate infrastructure in place to sustain them as they, too, wait for Ms. and Mr. Right. McCarthy, a columnist for *Hot Press,* Ireland's *Rolling Stone* magazine, repeatedly boasts of her allure and stresses that "I am not a right-wing religious fanatic nor am I a prude. I'm not a wallflower nor have I ever had any trouble finding guys who would sleep with me." She is, nonetheless, on a solitary mission. In her frenetic world, virgins *are* by definition right-wing religious fanatics, prudes, wallflowers, or geeks.

As her own unique kind of virgin, McCarthy admits that many of her friends scoff that she is "not *really* a virgin." After all, "the words *chaste* and *pure* often enter into the definition of *virgin* and I'd never claim to be either." However, she dismisses naysayers as victims of "this whole all-or-nothing mentality—the virgin or whore complex—[which] has really warped things."

Her own understanding of virginity is quite different: "Since it's the only act that physically joins two people together, in which the parts truly fit, I've imbued it with symbolic meaning and reserved a special place for it in my life."

As a statement of youthful sexual rebellion, McCarthy's *Been There, Haven't Done That* signals the advent of a new virginity-positive literature that thumbs its nose at society's credo that sex is an obligatory, normal, and readily available commodity.

REBORN CHASTITY

Among members of the unvirginal, older generations, a new celibacy is also casting down roots. Decades after the sexual revolution first stormed the puritanical primness of the postwar world, people began to take stock of its impact, and to tally their losses. Women who did not feel orgasms resented having to fake them, a direct result of the revolutionary fiat that the long-neglected female must now be brought to suitable sexual pitch. Some men, previously unaccountable for their amorous performances, agonized about their inadequacies, often brought to their attention by newly critical, score-keeping, note-comparing female partners.

As these nervous lovers have remarked, sex itself seems to have become a revolutionary casualty. Certainly it has been depersonalized and relegated to the category of other athletic activities. Popular magazines routinely feature how-to articles about it: how to achieve orgasm, how to excite him/her, how to avoid the sexual blahs, how to tease, tantalize, titillate, and tempt. Increasingly, sex is portrayed as a complicated, mechanical skill unrelated to tenderness, intimacy, and affection.

Sex—the New Sex, that is—is also demanding of its participants. Like other serious competitors, they must be in superb physical condition, with nary a flaw visible to their partner. Women's bodies especially must be thin and lean, fragrant and odorless, shaven of armpit and shin, glistening, moisturized, coiffed, and toned. Men are judged by slacker standards, but flabby bellies, jiggly breasts, and unimpressive penises are serious flaws, sometimes even shameful or risible. No wonder that the cosmetic, diet, fitness, and fashion industries reap windfall harvests, while plastic surgeons vie to lift or augment breasts, excise blubber, reshape limbs and torsos, and implant devices into small, unloved penises. No wonder, too, that anorexia stalks young women like a fiendish vampire bent on bleeding them of self-esteem, health, and ultimately, the ability and desire for sexual relations.

For men and women enmeshed in these debilitating and destructive realms, where is the revolutionary liberation? The exuberant freedom? The joyous self-expression? The heartening equality? Insofar as they see sex as an arduous, risky, and competitive drill rather than a loving intimacy between caring, responsive, and uncritical partners, they are increasingly unmotivated to venture into the erotic encounters they would much prefer to avoid. For them, celibacy takes on the image of a haven, an escape from a chore that affords them little pleasure, considerable vexation, and endless anxiety.

So, too, for those (usually women) who reflect deeply about the sex that permeates their world and then decide to forgo it. Coitus, they conclude, ought to transcend physical boundaries to touch the heart and soul. It should be a true coupling, a manifestation of affection, tenderness, and respect. If it cannot offer these essential dimensions, best forswear it as an unsatisfactory, sometimes demeaning pastime or sport.

These abstainers make a considered and purposeful choice that at least for the short term—the New Celibacy is still too new, too recent, to permit long-term analysis—vindicates their chaste lifestyle as an enrichment rather than a privation. Few of these New Celibates are virgins. They know what they are renouncing and why. They seek, and most find, empowerment and control over their lives, and more emotional passion in relationships. Some also achieve the heightened spirituality they formerly craved to erase the emptiness of their sexually active lives.

Enough New Celibates exist to speak of a trend if not a movement, and their spokesmen and advocates have begun to produce literature for and about them. Three of the best known are Gabrielle Brown's *The New Celibacy: A Journey to Love, Intimacy, and Good Health,* the first of this genre; Celia Haddon's *The Sensuous Lie*; and Sally Cline's *Women, Passion and Celibacy.*

The New Celibacy was first published in libertine, pre-AIDS 1980 and was addressed to those who rejected the boisterous new age and sought instead the path to deeper spirituality and better ways to express their sexuality. Celibacy was the most intense and attractive of these ways. It was, at the time, also startlingly radical, an outlandish notion that many people ridiculed. To counter this, Brown assumed a somewhat didactic tone and focused on presenting celibacy as a viable option even for healthy and committed people.

The New Celibacy created a sensation. It identified the problem so many individuals were experiencing and lent legitimacy to the discredited idea of celibacy. By the time it was reprinted in 1989, however, celibates were no longer regarded as peculiar. Thanks in part to AIDS and much more to a stultifying surfeit of mindless sex, celibacy had emerged from clandestinity and had crossed back into the mainstream.

Statistics confirm this. In 1986, Ann Landers, North America's doyenne of mores and morals, published the results of an immense survey of ninety thousand women. The world, but not Gabrielle Brown, was stunned to learn that 72 percent of Landers's respondents preferred "being held close and treated tenderly" to engaging in sexual intercourse. Nor were they mostly post-menopausal crones: 40 percent were under forty years old.

Two years later, *Maclean's* magazine reported that its annual Canadian "sex survey" revealed a 20 percent decrease in the category of the "somewhat [sexually] active," a 50 percent increase in those reporting less frequent sex, and a 25 percent rise in the number who had forsworn intercourse altogether.

Penthouse magazine had earlier polled its readers for its Celibacy Survey, which revealed that celibacy was "taking on a new respectability"—and seldom because of the lurking menace of AIDS. Less than half the men and fewer than 40 percent of the women had chosen celibacy because they feared disease. Instead, their concerns were emotional and spiritual. Further, over half of these celibates viewed their experiences as healthy, and 74 percent of the women and 68 percent of the men believed they had broadened their views about the opposite sex.

These widespread and highly credible surveys bolstered Brown's view that her contemporaries could choose and practice celibacy without fear of ridicule, and that celibacy had a great deal to offer them. First of all, coitus is about much more than mere physical expression. As soon as people realize that they are expecting sex to bring them something quite apart from the physical act, they may well begin to concentrate their attention elsewhere.

Precisely for this reason, Brown criticizes the common post–sexual-revolution notion that sex is normal, "*the* methodology for 'Total Expression of True Love.'" In this context, she denounces sex therapists and psychologists who accept this "normalization" of sex and therefore its concomitance, that a failure to engage in sex is unhealthy, something that therapy should strive to remedy.

Celibacy, too, is a form of sexuality, Brown reminds readers, but it has its "good" and "bad" forms. Good celibacy is a choice that feels "right" and "natural" and involves "a certain mental and emotional outlook through which the experience of celibacy can be fully enjoyed." The bulk of the book is devoted to Brown's message that celibacy can be a healthy, positive, life-affirming path to reducing stress, creating a union between mind and body, and reinvigorating relationships. "Physical closeness without physical sex is something that women tend to enjoy and quite a few prefer to the experience of orgasm because it incorporates so many of the subtleties of love and romance."

This cuddly, celibate, uninhibited intimacy can strengthen marriages as well as other relationships. Women are its principal beneficiaries because it allows them to identify and reject old patterns of behavior that have created and limited their scope. After they have achieved this nonpossessive intimacy, they will experience personal independence and freedom. Brown does not, however, venture beyond enthusiastic descriptions of this phenomenon to grapple for its cause—namely its power to dilute the hierarchical power relations between males and females. Instead, she prefers to enumerate its benefits for both genders.

The New Celibacy promises men many of the same rewards as women, including better relationships with women or new respect for them. It "can help a man explore new modes of personal communication and intimate relating to others" and "envision his life more clearly, take control of his activities, learn to choose what he wants and who he wants it with." He may also "come to grips with his masculinity by allowing him to separate his virility from his sexuality."

Brown also offers bare-bones pro-celibacy arguments reminiscent of those detailed earlier in the "Celibacy to Conserve Semen" chapter. She describes not having sex, for instance, as conserving "sexual energy" and says "celibacy has been a recognized cure for impotence for centuries." However, she hastens to add that celibate men are the antithesis of impotent and celibacy itself "can be considered 'the source of the very highest potency.'"

The New Celibacy's final chapter ends with "Some Guidelines on How to Be Celibate." "Think of it as a vacation," Brown urges. "During a vacation, you can expect to be more rested, more relaxed, less pressured, more open to new experiences. You can expect the same from celibacy."

Her other guidelines are equally simple: enjoy yourself, don't think about sex, don't think about celibacy as deprivation. "Just as when you're on a diet, you should feel so secure inside that you can sit and have tea with your friends in a pastry shop without feeling an unbearable desire to eat pastry."

In fact, Brown exhorts celibates to express themselves in new and satisfying ways: plunge into your work, she tells them, dine with a friend, eat to your heart's content, go home alone, fall in love, savor romantic encounters. In these and a host of other delightful ways, celibates can enjoy the richer and more balanced life that their chosen lifestyle can provide.

In *The Sensuous Lie*, Celia Haddon examines celibacy gently, in the context of the sexual hedonism that still reigns as a social standard. Through a series of anecdotes and intimate personal revelations, she explores the dilemma of today's voluntary and involuntary celibates. She probes the loneliness of the latter and their sense of alienation in a culture that has little understanding of their situation. She applauds the serenity of the former and likens it to the profound satisfaction of earlier centuries' religious.

Haddon also examines various forms of modern celibacy and its effect on the emotions. She arrives at no firm conclusion, but suggests that for most people, it is probably not unbearable. She also notes that former celibates, such as religious who leave their orders to marry, adapt readily to sexual activity.

In a series of comfortably connected anecdotes, Haddon builds up a case against today's obsession with sex and what she perceives as a bias against morality and spirituality as pressing personal issues. In the end, she looks to love as the important value, whether in celibate or uncelibate relationships. We should, she argues, "try to formulate a love and affection scale . . . touching, hand-holding, pats on the shoulder, hugging, playful sparring, words of endearment, smiles, crinkled eyes, kisses on the cheek—that might be ways of measuring affection."

What particularly frightens Haddon are the excesses of the sexual revolution, which she fears "will lead us away from intimacy, affection, and kindness toward a sexuality of cruelty, competitiveness, power, and domination. Something is rotten in the way we love now." Mostly, she longs for an end to a surfeit of sexual rules and measuring people "by the activities of the genitals rather than the feelings of the heart." Haddon neither endorses nor condemns celibacy or even pretends to understand why it liberates some people and oppresses others. What is significant in her musings is her frankness and perplexity, a guide who can point out only the problems and not the solutions. As a critical observer of social life during the sexual revolution, Haddon's sensitive consideration of a celibacy she has rarely experienced highlights the complexities of living as a celibate and validates it as a lifestyle that can incorporate as much love as any other.

In 1993, Sally Cline swept into the arena with *Women, Passion and Celibacy.* The title is apt and summarizes the book's basic theme, a plea for independent-minded women to passionately embrace celibacy for positive reasons. "Despite the functioning of the genital myth," Cline writes, "it is possible for women to have a passion for celibacy, a fact either overlooked or contradicted in our sexually satiated society, whose current orthodoxy is that life without sex and life without men is no life at all."

Unlike Brown, Cline identifies sexual activity as a site of power where men oppress their female partners. She points angrily to the dichotomy between women's supposed freedom and the reality, from cosmetic surgery intended to enhance their appeal to relentless media bombardment of messages, including pornography, that give the lie to the declaration of freedom. Mainstream magazines advise on how to appear younger and prettier and how to please/appease your man. Cosmetic products and services, including surgery, are multibillion-dollar businesses that would founder into bankruptcy should true gender equality ever materialize. All these values, propaganda, and related tools are cemented together by sex, which is everything and everywhere. In sad consequence, Cline argues, "women in particular should consume and accept sexual congress, along with beauty products, diet regimes, low wages and violent inflictions, as part of a contemporary cultural system which aims to checkmate power in aspiring women's lives." In this angry dialectic, celibacy "raises eyebrows because it is an act of rebellion against the sacred cow of sexual consumerism."

In her fierce fight to legitimize celibacy for women, Cline overstates and simplifies. The presence of True Love Waits alone, not to mention adult celibate movements, underscores how seriously she overstates her premise that a modern woman's celibacy is seen as immensely radical and subversive, an economic and ideological threat. (Other writers describe it in more detail and with less cant. Tuula Gordon, for instance, writes that a woman's celibacy is seen as "kinky but safe" and the celibate woman, "judged against a popular construction of the happy, companionate marriage," is pitied as "incomplete," "deviant," "a sort of shriveled-up old spinster." Kathleen Norris says society views celibacy as a "highly suspect" condition that "leaves celibates vulnerable to being automatically labeled as infantile or repressed.") Nonetheless, Cline's concern for women's inequality and the passion of her commitment to assuaging their pain and dissatisfaction are both convincing and relevant.

In keeping with her theme, Cline describes celibacy as a multifaceted condition that begins in the mind and both transcends, embraces, and expresses sexuality. It is derived from the notion of nonpossessiveness and personal freedom and may be a sexuality in which the woman is not possessed by her male partner. Lastly, celibacy is often a means to achieve spiritual, intellectual, political, and other freedoms.

In fact, Cline's interviewees identified many other reasons for their choice of celibacy. They saw celibacy as a way to gain more time for their work and other significant activities; for spiritual growth, autonomy, independence, and self-determination; or as a strategy for avoiding intense relationships. Others suffered sexual-performance anxiety; found sex boring; had suffered previously from sexual abuse or violence; feared AIDS and STDs; were ill, elderly, disabled, or genitally altered, such as by hysterectomies. Many were celibate to recover from troubled relationships; to reduce or eliminate problems such as jealousy, possessiveness, dependence, obsessiveness, or overattachment; or because they wished to form closer, more affectionate relationships.

Cline believes, however, that Passionate Celibates always opt for celibacy for reasons "*in some way related to a central notion of autonomy.*" She sums it all up in a description that serves to define Passionate Celibacy. Women who choose celibacy to express their sexuality and define it as passionate are renouncing old definitions based on male domination. Passionate Celibacy, therefore, is "a source of power and encouragement for celibate women previously labeled sick, prudish, or frigid. . . . As an alternative sexual strategy that takes power away from men, it allows women their own choices about what to do with their bodies."

Disregard the hyperbole and Cline's Passionate Celibates become thoughtful women who choose celibacy as a helpful means of achieving their various personal goals. This includes freedom from relationships that can oppress them because, for instance, they are mired in gender inequality.

Legions of other women have pondered their sexual expression, contemplated or adopted celibacy, and then shared their experiences in magazines and journals. Most chafe against involuntary singledom, but a great many who adopt it voluntarily describe it as deeply satisfying. American novelist Elaine Booth Selig, for example, declined to settle "for the fifty-fifty arrangement that is the ideal for so many couples" because, alone, she already had the whole hundred. "I have learned that the words *alone* and *lonely* are not synonymous," she concluded.

For quite different reasons, American editor Ziva Kwitney decided to become celibate. This happened after she horrified herself, and a decent man, by asking him to leave after they had made love. "I felt grotesque—*like the man I had already feared being intimate with,* the one who wants you out of his sight when the sex is over." Kwitney's eighteen months of celibacy were restorative. "I began to have a sense of myself as a universe, complete, without need of another."

Many reborn virgins miss the physical pleasures of sex but do without them because they treasure celibacy's rewards much more highly. One of these is the time and emotional energy freed up for friendships. "Friendships, with males, with females, and with couples, are . . . real sources of joy and support," French-Canadian journalist Francine Gagnon emphasizes.

A new and very young arrival on the literary abstinence scene is Wendy Shalit with *A Return to Modesty.* A sexually "inexperienced" and self-styled "extreme right winger," Shalit abhors her sad postfeminist world whose young women are self-mutilating, stick-thin anorectics stalked by sexual predators prowling unsafe streets, young women who are very very unhappy—"with their bodies, their sexual encounters, with the way men treat them on the street—unhappy with their lives." Their woes stem directly from our society's lost respect for female modesty, she continues, which can be remedied only by a return to *modesty.* Modesty, in this context, is at the heart of Jewish "modesty laws," and (Shalit wrongly believes) of Victorian society, fundamentalist Islam, and other delightful icons of feminine reticence.

Shalit hopes her proposed new modesty will so resemble the old that she provides an appendix entitled "Some Modest Advice." These coy tidbits, culled from the literature of romanticized yesteryears, include such goodies as "On How to Distinguish Between Blushes (blushing, as a manifestation of embarrassment, is good)," "On Parasol Elevation," and "On How to Walk Modestly in the Street." Her brand of modesty would flourish best, Shalit writes, in a society cleansed of pornographic television, "intrusive" sex education, the ubiquitous condoms that lead to self-deception, coed bathrooms, short, tight, décolleté dresses, and—of course—sex before marriage.

Premarital sex, indeed, even premarital touching (Shalit is at the opposite end of the virginity pole from Tara McCarthy), smash youthful innocence and often provoke the distressing situations, particularly the specter of divorce, that Shalit believes modesty can alleviate. Refusing sex before marriage gives heightened importance to sex *after* marriage, and saving this most private part of oneself is tantamount to "insisting on your right to keep something sacred . . . welcoming the prospect of someone else making an enduring private claim to you, and you to him." And most important of all, reserving sex for marriage implies that marriage will be "the most interesting" part of life, a precept that may make marriage endure.

In many ways, what Shalit proposes is a secularized version of True Love Waits. Though her inspiration comes from Jewish modesty laws, and she speaks approvingly of *hijab* as an accoutrement of modesty (rather than repression), her arguments have little religious base. In that sense, they reach out to women of all religions, because they are particular to none.

The very mixed response to *A Return to Modesty* suggests Shalit has touched a nerve—indeed, several nerves. Insofar as it is possible to consider her proposition without sliding into rightfully bitter ideological battles, and leaving aside the fact that her historical arguments and analogies are flawed, it is clear that she has evoked a positive response from a limited constituency of young, mostly white, upper-middle-class women who misunderstand, fear, or are oblivious to feminism. They share her disquiet about the likelihood of divorce and are eager to discuss ways to avoid it. The world Shalit paints—even if it did *not* exist in history—is an attractive world of gentle flirtation between respectful youth who later contract permanent, loving, and enriching marriages inhabited by happy wives. If (modestly) tantalizing men in a bid to hold out for marriage, redefining marriage as a wondrous communion, and reviving it through intermittent celibacy could actually bring that world into being, then it would certainly be difficult to argue against Shalit and her return to the modesty that never really was.

Women's modern literature about celibacy usually acknowledges that sexual yearnings are an issue, albeit a secondary one. So, therefore, is masturbation, one obvious solution. Many feminists consider it perfectly acceptable, indeed desirable. One writer elaborates on this theme: "While our culture ties our eroticism to heterosexual intercourse and reproduction, we can recall our sexuality without turning the world upside down. We can, through celibacy and masturbation, define our sexuality and satisfy ourselves sexually."

Sally Cline agrees and assures her Passionate Celibates that masturbation may well be an integral part of "purposeful, self-chosen chastity . . . combined with an independent, autonomous outlook." Maverick Tara McCarthy goes much further, satisfying her sexual urges through mutual masturbation and oral sex. Gabrielle Brown, however, frowns on autoeroticism. "Masturbation . . . is primarily a sexual activity . . . if you want to indulge in celibacy, you don't masturbate," she says. Clearly, the different ideologies behind celibacy dictate the approach to masturbation. Modern feminists see it as a beneficial adjunct to celibacy. Thinkers primarily concerned with celibacy as sexuality argue that masturbation defeats or nullifies the decision to be chaste. Christian religious concerned with observing the purity of their vows of sexual chastity denounce it on similar grounds.

Lesbian Celibacy versus Lesbian "Bed Death"

With regard to celibacy, lesbians and heterosexuals share most issues, but lesbians confront additional concerns. One obvious one is that despite the Western world's improved climate for tolerance, it is nonetheless far from axiomatic that homosexuals should reveal or at least not hide their sexual orientation. Once virtually unthinkable, self-disclosure is still problematic. This being the case, cautious or conservative lesbians may opt for celibacy as the safest way to protect themselves from social censure and disgrace.

Lesbian celibacy is by no means confined to hidden sexuality. For a plethora of complicated reasons, including societal disapproval, family disappointment, parental abuse, and rape, lesbians typically have sex much more infrequently than heterosexual women or male homosexuals. Ironically, as lesbian psychotherapist Marny Hall notes, "lesbians, diagnosed as mentally ill twenty years ago because they had sex with other women, are now deemed unhealthy because they don't." This condition, known as lesbian bed death, haunts countless women who, because of it, question their normalcy.

A major albatross for lesbians is today's widespread reverence for sex, proud product of the sexual revolution. The assumption that most "normal" people are sexually active and that celibates are therefore peculiar scars lesbian as well as heterosexual women, sometimes pushing them into unwanted sexual encounters. Nor are they helped by therapists trained, as most have been, in what Hall labels the "More-Is-Better school of sexual therapy." Though rape or abuse survivors often loathe sex with anyone, even a loving and beloved female partner, much relevant literature and many therapists focus on restoring these women to functioning sexual beings. They say (or they mean), in Carolyn Gage's bitter words, "We just want to help you get to the place where you will *want* to fuck," instead of the words that would begin to heal a woman's chronic pain: "You don't have to fuck. You *never* have to fuck."

The reality is, "nonsexual pair-bonding [today's Boston marriage?] is perfectly normal for many long-term lesbian couples."

Gage grounds her plea for the right to be celibate—"without stigma or penalty"—in the argument that lesbianism, "as a cultural sanctuary where violated women could define and customize our intimacy needs, is disappearing." In place of that traditional and consoling refuge, lesbians are now judged by postrevolutionary values that equate sexuality with normalcy, celibacy with dysfunction. For them, the psychological balm of abstinence is, if not strictly verboten, tantamount to being branded as an emotional deviant, an errant soul in a world where adult sexuality is a mark of mental health and a measure of social adjustment. These celibates suffer a double sadness: their victimization in childhood and their mischaracterization in adulthood.

Further complicating the matter is that lesbians are not always clear about how to define sex. Must it involve genital contact? Is a couple who merely neck and pet, cuddle and spoon, sexual or celibate? "The relentless quantification of what 'counts' in sex surveys and other research, no matter how well-intentioned, does not begin to illuminate the nature of many lesbian relationships."

In other words, definitional boundaries place enormous and unnecessary burdens on those lesbians who flounder in the uncertainty of understanding the nature not of their sexual orientation but of their sexual expressions.

CELIBACY IN THE AGE OF AIDS

The end of the millennium delivered the starkest challenge ever known to the Western world's notions of sexuality. At first, AIDS meandered into our ken as a curiously recalcitrant "environmental disease." Bit by bit, as scattered media reports described its seemingly bizarre symptoms—a generalized failure of the host body's immune system—Westerners were introduced to the twentieth century's plague.

AIDS revealed its nature with excruciating slowness. Much time elapsed before its initial victims were even diagnosed and even more before they began to die. As the band played on, the true scale of the horror began to emerge. At the very least, this was the deadliest sexually transmitted disease yet known to mankind.

At first, AIDS targeted homosexuals, then gradually stretched out its tentacles to intravenous drug users and the recipients of contaminated blood. Medically administered blood transfusions and unsterilized needles joined tainted human bodies as instruments of death. Debate raged about AIDS' origins, its treatment, its likely progress through unsuspecting, unprepared populations. AIDS struck out like a biblical plague and no one could be sure of being passed over.

The mounting hysteria spawned scapegoats: homosexuals, heroin users, hemophiliacs. The time lapse between infection and symptoms gaped longer and longer, from months to years, even decades. An industry of protective devices sprang up. Policemen joined dentists and doctors as mass consumers of rubber gloves, while blood, semen, spittle, and urine became terrifying effluvia. Workplace regulations were revamped after workers mutinied against assignments that risked contact with the incurable virus. And in sex-steamed bathhouses and bedrooms everywhere, men and women reacted, reevaluated, and revolted.

The interlude between the frisky young sexual revolution and the age of AIDS was a scant two decades. AIDS catapulted celibacy into the spotlight, to be debated in urgent public and private forums as an issue devoid of the moral and religious dimensions it had always previously engendered. Never before in human history had the decision to embrace celibacy—or reject it— seemed so vitally important.

The story of the actual epidemic is short, recent, and grievous. Once, syphilis and gonorrhea had been the world's most devastating sexually trans-mitted diseases, joined recently by stubborn, recurrent herpes. Unlike all its predecessors, though, AIDS was almost invariably fatal, and its advance through HIV-infected bodies was a tortuous, often hideous carnage. Since its initial hosts were primarily homosexual, people living with and dying from AIDS have been doubly afflicted—with the disease and with widespread sus-picion, fear, and even condemnation. AIDS literature has developed its own judgmental vocabulary, which makes implicitly moral distinctions between casualties. Children, hemophiliacs, and surgical patients infected through blood transfusions and heterosexual women contaminated by secretly bisex-ual men are *innocent victims.* By implication, gay men, drug users, and prosti-tutes are *guilty victims* who deserve the brutal punishment of this deadly syndrome.

In reality, even "innocent" victims have been shunned—children banished from their schools by administrators relentlessly pressured by terrified parents of other students; patients neglected by nervous nurses and medical workers; employees dismissed when their employers discovered their HIV-positive sta-tus. These twentieth-century lepers do not have to ring warning bells as they creep into unfriendly towns, but by and large, the HIV-negative population responds to them with the same frissons of revulsion and loathing that pro-pelled the stones of our leper-taunting forebears.

Four factors stamped AIDS as the terrifying malady of deviance: its incur-ability, its transmutability into new strains, its communicability through bodily fluids, and its primary identification with homosexuality. In common parlance, nice people do not contract such a filthy disease. Nice people are either monogamous or chaste heterosexuals, or those very few innocents who have, through no fault of their own, imbibed tainted blood.

The moral stance underlying AIDS discourse is hardly different from the thunderous tone of earlier centuries' rants against syphilis and gonorrhea. In them all, only one perspective is possible—the conservative. It is not a far leap to apocalyptic conclusions about AIDS and homosexuality as plagues threatening the very life of all humankind and as divine retribution for reprehensible wrongdoing.

"AIDS as deviance" is a ubiquitous metaphor, insidious in its repercussions, and its subtext, "AIDS as punishment," coincided with revulsion over the excesses of the sexual revolution, which included the promiscuous, bathhouse milieu of one all-too-visible and vulnerable segment of the gay male population. Even today's youth guru Katie Roiphe ponders about AIDS as a punishment for the modern view of sexuality as meaningless and inconsequential, shared with everyone and thereby stripped of specialness. Surely the signs were evident along the sexual revolution's carelessly erotic way? After all, "implicit in the idea of paradise is, of course, the premonition of a fall."

So ubiquitous was the perception of AIDS as divine retribution that an American Roman Catholic bishop felt compelled to write, "There are some misguided individuals who have declared AIDS to be a punishment from God. Deep in the Judeo-Christian tradition, however, is the knowledge that our loving God does not punish through disease."

But his was a lonely voice, and the discourse on AIDS as punishment swelled in volume and passion as even its mainly gay victims lamented the evil ways that had condemned them to early death.

This moralistic cast superimposed onto a medical condition leads to anti-AIDS educational campaigns designed, like certain anticrime programs, to scare the offender straight. In this case, it means to petrify people into monogamous heterosexuality or, failing that, outright chastity. This end-of-the-world urgency provides much of the atmosphere that permeates debates about celibacy in the age of AIDS. The disease itself, by its relentless killing, provides the rest.

SEX AND AIDS

AIDS first surfaced into public notice in 1981 as a mysterious killer that seemed to target gay men. By 1983, sexual behavior and HIV had entered the picture. Slowly, profiles of this "gay disease" grew more inclusive, as hemophiliacs, drug addicts (who shared needles), and heterosexuals also sickened and died. Doctors and researchers accumulated data. Mainstream and alternative media featured heartrending and frightening stories of infection, of truncated lives, of clocks that could never be turned back.

In July 1985, the drama escalated, as celebrities admitted they, too, were vulnerable. The first major one was probably Rock Hudson, who revealed both his homosexuality and his impending death from AIDS and died three months later. The great movie idol's announcement shook President Ronald Reagan, until then silent on the issue, to pronounce. His recommendation of sexual abstinence followed by monogamous marriage sounded typically simplistic and conservative, and egregiously unmindful of the reality of so many people's lives, most notably those at highest risk.

AIDS awareness exploded in 1991 when National Basketball Association champion "Magic" Earvin Johnson, an international hero to millions, gamely admitted that he, too, was HIV-positive. The shock of his announcement was palpable. Unlike Hudson, Johnson was an ardent heterosexual, but one who confessed that he had slept with legions of women, not always one at a time. A collective shiver of terror seized the heterosexual world. If Magic Johnson could get AIDS, then anyone could. And in his book *What You Can Do to Avoid AIDS,* Johnson sounded disturbingly like Reagan. "Take responsibility," he urged. "It's your life. Remember: the safest sex is no sex."

Millions heard this message and some were converted, but the idea that celibacy was the only proof against AIDS was both alarming and sobering. Celibacy seemed so crushingly absolute, and advocates such as Johnson offered no alternative.

Five years after Johnson's stunning revelation, American boxer Tommy Morrison walked into a press conference and tearfully disclosed that just forty-five minutes earlier, he had learned his second blood test for HIV was positive. Like Magic Johnson, he, too, had contracted HIV through promiscuous, heterosexual sex. "I honestly believed that I had a better chance of winning the lottery than contracting this disease," Morrison said. "I have never been so wrong in my life. The only sure prevention of this disease is abstinence." Then he added a plea to "a whole generation of kids out there like me that have totally disregarded the moral values that were taught to us by our parents. . . . If I help one person be more responsible about sex, then I'll score my biggest knockout."

Sports studs had been stricken and—tearfully, repentantly, generously— offered celibacy as the magical elixir that could have saved them, if only they had known. But celibacy is a long-term commitment. Could they, or their converts, sustain it for years, perhaps a lifetime, without a single, potentially fatal lapse?

The smash hit *Jeffrey*, a New York play subsequently made into a movie, focused on precisely this question. Jeffrey is the proverbial struggling young actor/waiter, a gay man who watches in horror as AIDS decimates his coterie. Finally, he weighs all his options and renounces sex. But Jeffrey is personable and attractive, and not long after, he meets Steve, aka Mr. Right, who kisses him, then reveals he is HIV-positive. Jeffrey is repelled by the danger, which reinforces his vow of celibacy, though he cannot stop himself from fantasizing about Steve. Jeffrey's friends, including the AIDS-struck Darius and his uninfected older lover, urge him to forget celibacy and celebrate life while he can and at least engage in safe sex. Jeffrey turns for counsel to a priest, who tries to seduce him and mockingly dismisses his query about the supposed celibacy of priests. Jeffrey flees the church and, though he longs to be with Steve, will not deviate from his decision.

The resolution to Jeffrey's story, however, comes after he experiences sudden psychic illumination. He contacts Steve, arranges a romantic, candlelit dinner, and pulls the other man toward him in a lingeringly tender kiss. Even in the context of life and death, *Jeffrey* reminds legions of viewers, celibacy is no easy proposition.

In a series of novels culminating in *The Death of Friends*, Hispanic-American detective writer Michael Nava follows his California-based criminal defense lawyer Henry Rios through a series of murders, as well as his private life with young Josh Mandel, who finally "crosses over" from being HIV-positive into AIDS. As Josh's blood count deteriorates, he taunts the uninfected Henry and cheats on him with other doomed lovers. Finally he leaves Henry for one of them. Later, Henry takes Josh back and nurses him through his final days. At the end of *The Death of Friends*, Josh dies. The message in these finely crafted detective stories is certainly not abstinence, but they do catapult AIDS into the literary limelight and detail the anguish of those trapped in its clutches.

Jeffrey and the bittersweet adventures of Henry Rios portray the realities of AIDS with infinitely more subtlety and sophistication than earnest messengers Magic Johnson, Tommy Morrison, and self-righteous moralists like Ronald Reagan. This is because they were premised on the fact that within the gay community, the associated issues were far more complicated than just saying no except within permanent and monogamous relationships. In the Nava novels, a woman is infected by her upstanding husband, a respected judge whose secret gay life she knew nothing about, and one of Josh Mandel's bitter last reflections is "I'm dying, and . . . the bottom line is another gay man did this to me." In real life, this fiction stresses, celibacy is no easy matter or even an option, particularly a grudging celibacy coerced by the raw fear of AIDS. *Jeffrey* and the Michael Nava novels have attracted a wide heterosexual audience, which has been informed as it has been entertained. But underneath all the artistry is the grim reminder that AIDS is a merciless killer spread primarily by sexual contact.

CELIBACY AND AIDS

Celibacy in the age of AIDS can be either the simplest, most obvious of responses or else a coerced resolution to a terrifying dilemma. The key to AIDS lies in its urgency, in how its implicit biological imperative is unlike that of any moral or religious doctrine. AIDS arrived as the sexual revolution was at its apex, and its devastation coincided with or perhaps precipitated that revolution's waning and the reemergence of conservative views on sexuality (and much else, including economic and social policy). With breathtaking swiftness, AIDS joined teenage pregnancy as a primary justification and facilitator for the renewed call to celibacy.

This celibacy is largely shrouded in fear and lacks the promise of energy and empowerment that has attracted so many other celibates across time and space. It resolves no moral crises and fulfills no religious strictures. It is not a social obligation, nor is it monitored by anyone but the individual practitioner. It is not reinforced by a solemn or sacred vow nor cheered on by an approving society. Especially in the gay community, celibacy may be experienced as a serious privation, with high psychic costs. "I'd rather be dead than celibate," one man told Masters and Johnson. Celibacy does, however, ward off death, no negligible consideration in a world where Masters and Johnson argue that "the sexual revolution is not yet dead—it's just that some of the troops are dying."

Celibacy, even the fear- and logic-coerced celibacy of the age of AIDS, is nonetheless a complex and sophisticated notion presented simplistically by many of its current proponents. Former U.S. vice president Dan Quayle mistakenly labeled it "the true cure" for AIDS. Reagan remarked, "When it comes to preventing AIDS, don't medicine and morality teach the same lessons?" To these spokesmen of the religious right, celibacy is so absolute a principle that even suggesting condom use—the other successful weapon against the HIV virus—seems outrageous libertinism.

"You're not going to be saved by condoms," argued one Canadian educator. "Condoms will help a bit, but you'd be far better off if you just didn't get to that situation at all." Others complain that advocating the use of condoms misleads people into believing they are infallible shields against HIV. A spokeswoman for the religious right's Concerned Women of America, which claims six hundred thousand paying members, explained to Katie Roiphe that "condoms *break*. It's like trying to stop water with a chain-link fence."

Much of the debate over eradicating AIDS through celibacy has homophobic nuances, as does much of the discussion about AIDS in general. As a result, gay communities have explored the issue separately, as it relates to their needs and perceptions of what is involved. After all, sexual expression has been fundamental to defining sexual orientation, and gay liberation, as part of the sexual revolution, developed a new, uniquely gay-male conceptualization of sexuality. It broadened the range of acceptable behavior, including multiple partners and anonymous sex, so that a sudden exhortation to celibacy was all the more startling. It even begged the root meaning of celibacy just as it did in the heterosexual world, where purists debate the acceptability of masturbation and other forms of eroticism. (Celebrated politicians, headed by U.S. president Bill Clinton, are clearer about what constitutes sexual intercourse—they insist it means penile penetration alone.)

Homosexuals, too, ponder these questions. If a man abstains from penetrative anal sex but engages in fisting (in which a fist substitutes for a penis), or oral sex including rimming (performed on the anus), or mutual masturbation, is he celibate? (The politicians would have to shout, "Yes!") In fact, celibacy to avoid AIDS, as opposed to its religious and spiritual forms such as brahmacharya, simply requires avoiding contact with bodily fluids. This points clearly to mutual masturbation as acceptable. In *Changing HIV Risk Behavior: Practical Strategies,* Jeffrey A. Kelly advises:

> We should not forget that curtailing sex for brief or long periods is an acceptable goal for some individuals (especially those whose partners, such as non-monogamous gay men or IDUs [intravenous drug users], have a relatively high probability of being infected), and that abstinence from sex under some circumstances and with some potential partners is an essential survival skill in an era of AIDS.

By the end of the 1980s, AIDS ceased to be associated primarily with homosexuality. In the wake of news reports from Africa documenting it as a devastating killer of heterosexuals, mainstream complacency about the gay disease quickly evaporated. That in Africa it struck women as heavily as men drew anxious attention to statistics indicating that in the Western world as well, heterosexual infection was on the rise. The magnitude of the AIDS epidemic in Africa also triggered concerns that it might be a biological juggernaut with inexhaustible reserves.

The volume of infection is terrible, and the majority of victims are heterosexuals, usually infected through heterosexual intercourse. Women are struck as often as men and frequently infect their babies either at birth or through breast-feeding. Ritual scarring and female genital mutilation, both invasive procedures performed with unsterilized implements, provide other routes for HIV infection.

Africa's different rhythms and customs demand different AIDS-prevention strategies. The marriage relationship seldom implies fidelity for husbands. In many countries, men may have several wives, and extramarital affairs are common. So is prostitution, and as most African prostitutes are HIV-positive, the virus is swiftly transmitted to clients, who infect their wives, who pass the infection on to their newborns. Throughout Africa, close to 2 million orphaned children are AIDS' most recent casualties.

Why does AIDS strike with such fury in Africa? One reason may be, research indicates, that people infected with other diseases are particularly vulnerable to HIV infection. In Africa, with its poorer population and inadequate health services, people suffering from venereal diseases, from genital herpes to gonorrhea and chancroid, are much more frequently infected than their healthier peers. So are those with tuberculosis, which is currently making a global comeback. In some African cities, as many as 80 percent of TB patients are HIV-positive, while TB itself is rising steeply, making its victims much more receptive to contracting the virus if they are exposed to it.

The first challenge for African anti-AIDS campaigners is to educate people about AIDS and to use that information to change their sexual habits. In Soweto Township in South Africa, AIDS educator Refilos Serote, whom men sometimes flirt with during her lectures, adds her own fillip to this message. "We need to teach our young girls to say 'No' at a tender age. We had been taught man is a god. You cannot refuse him."

And what about celibacy, so high on the Western world's list of anti-AIDS tactics? In Africa, abstaining from sex is neither admirable nor even acceptable, and voluntary celibates are considered aberrant, cowardly, and unmanly. This is because in most of that continent's nations, celibacy is an alien concept without the religious and moral overtones it has elsewhere. There, celibacy challenges manliness and the rights of men to sexually possess many women, and it offers little to women except to drive their men elsewhere for sexual gratification. When celibacy is expected, for example among lactating women, it is often risky, because husbands deprived of sex turn elsewhere, either to other wives or to Africa's ubiquitous and HIV-riddled prostitutes. After a new mother's infant is weaned, her possibly infected husband terminates her period of celibacy by sleeping with her and may infect her as well. The economic marginalization of women is another factor that militates against the possibility of their embracing anti-AIDS celibacy. Most women have no alternative to marriage as a way of supporting themselves and thus cannot avoid the risks of sleeping with unfaithful husbands or marrying much older men whose wide sexual experience is more likely to have exposed them to HIV.

Ironically, the tragedy of AIDS itself is frightening some Africans into celibacy, among other preventive measures. In Uganda, a government campaign targets young people and urges them to remain virginal until marriage. They are "bombarded with terrifying anti-AIDS propaganda everywhere—in theaters and community social halls, in churches and youth political meetings." A radio announces grimly, "Premarital sex [is] the sure way to an early grave." Another intones, "Love carefully. The person you so cherish might be the special one to lead you to your grave!" The dramatic impact has tangible results and the Ugandan rate of infection has begun to decline.

In societies decimated by the disease, the strategy of premarital virginity carries weight. However, the notion of adult celibacy is generally unpopular, even risible. Worse, many Africans are as deeply suspicious of celibacy as they are of condoms, which they see as the brainchild of whites plotting to rid the world of the black race. Only the reality of the AIDS apocalypse can shock its victims into action, including celibacy. Until then, its champions are brave but lonely voices pleading a cause that little short of a miracle will convince most Africans to adopt.

Back in the Western world, which has taken frightened notice, AIDS has begun to mimic the African experience and is spreading more and more into the heterosexual population. In Canada, the proportion of women to men infected has fallen from one in fifteen in 1993 to one in seven in 1997, or 14 percent of AIDS cases. American AIDS statistics mirror this tendency, as well as an enormous discrepancy among racial groups, with blacks and Hispanics infected at stunningly higher rates than whites and other Americans.

Suddenly, AIDS has become everyone's nightmare, and everyone has to grope his or her way through it. One young woman, Sonja Kindley, describes how some of her Generation X friends have reacted by adopting as personal mores what she calls "emotional promiscuity." In the age when "AIDS and STDs spoil all the fun," these "sex-without-sex experiences," she writes, stem from a "'90s spin on '70s promiscuity: sleaze *sans* STDs . . . verbal love affairs and electronic seductions, pursuing intimacy without getting naked."

The physical rewards of this low-risk lifestyle are obvious, but "intellectual seductress" Kindley also notes its high price: "the tease can become torture." This is celibacy at its most unsustainable: self-inflicted by sexually stimulated virgins, born and reborn, whose terror of AIDS and fear of less lethal STDs and of commitment inspire them to lose themselves in unrequited sexual titillation. If celibacy figures at all, it is merely a tactic to be weighed against other tactics such as condoms and spermicides. In this context, research into other agents to fight AIDS—chemicals, the foolproof latex, behavior-modification techniques—weighs heavily in the equation.

And in the time of AIDS, these other agents matter. After all, which is likeliest to crumble, a condom or a vow of celibacy? (*Jeffrey* is a perfect case in point.) This, then, is the battlefield where the anti-AIDS strategists mount their campaign. The crucial point of contention is whether advocating celibacy actually endangers its converts by offering them false protection. This is because only one violation, especially a spontaneous sexual act performed without benefit of condom or spermicide, can be fatal, and over the long term, such lapses are quite likely to occur. Condoms, on the other hand, can be stashed in pockets and handbags and are a barrier to the virus.

Anti-AIDS celibacy, stripped of its religious core, has become a tool comparable to any other and, like any other market commodity, must continually be reevaluated. Does it work? Is it risky? Is some other anti-AIDS device better? It is difficult to be certain, but celibacy seems to be making important inroads in the gay population. Some investigations have revealed that homosexuals are more likely than before the epidemic to be either celibate or monogamous, and many others have fewer partners and engage less frequently in anal sex, the riskiest practice of all. Generally, gay men appear to be making more changes in their sexual behavior than heterosexuals.

Celibacy in the age of AIDS and as a weapon in the battle against the disease is markedly different from celibacy inspired by religious or moral considerations or by cultural expectations. In the AIDS context, celibacy is a calculated strategy driven by fear and statistics, in which spontaneous erotic longings may vie successfully with the intellect's concern for physical self-preservation.

This is because neither homosexuals nor heterosexuals feel a long-term commitment to their tactical celibacy. Instead, they continually weigh its benefits against current research, new developments and data in the AIDS field, and evaluations about the relative effectiveness of condoms and various other methods to block HIV infection. Nonetheless, celibacy is also seen as a lifesaving device and plays an essential role in coping with the ever-present threat posed by AIDS and the constant mutations of HIV.

In Africa, celibacy as an anti-AIDS weapon is largely a failure. It remains to be seen if this will also be the case in hugely populous India and China, where the World Health Organization predicts an AIDS epidemic is on the verge of exploding. There, too, AIDS is striking primarily heterosexuals, and celibacy as well as condoms will be urgently touted. Probably, the identification of sexual abstinence with brahmacharya and virtuous self-discipline will lend it the legitimacy it lacks in Africa. In Asia, its advocates will not be seen as agents of genocide but as messengers of hope who offer an escape from impending catastrophe.

EPILOGUE

"So, are you for it or against it?" people continually ask me upon hearing that I have written *A History of Celibacy*. I find this question disconcerting. My purpose was to trace celibacy's history, not to evaluate its advantages and disadvantages so I could pronounce that celibacy is good or celibacy is bad. As well, celibacy is such a complicated phenomenon that I become almost tongue-tied trying to articulate abbreviated but meaningful responses to this irksome question.

Much of the problem is that celibacy is inextricably linked to how societies define sexuality and how this definition finds concrete expression in their family structures, social standards, and laws. Outside these specific contexts, celibacy is nothing more than not having sex, which tells us precisely nothing about how billions of humans have experienced it, chosen it, worked within it, rejected it, been coerced into it, and converted to or away from it.

All this means that the answer to the simplistic question, "Are you for it or against it?" must not—in fact, cannot—be equally simplistic. Of course I have developed strong opinions about celibacy, and I am vitally interested in its place in today's world, my own world. So my response has to be that I'm neither for celibacy nor against it, but that depending on the circumstances, it can be a sensible sacrifice or a vicious privation, a lifesaving device or a spiritual revelation.

The truth of this answer is particularly important, indeed urgent, in the Western world, which has lost its balance about the nature and value of eroticism. We are bombarded by sexual images, most notably in advertising, that are often so irrelevant that they are bizarre. Calculatedly lustful images hawk clothes, cosmetics, automobiles, and even household cleaning products, while fashion is dictated by emaciated and pouty women slinking seductively down runways, often in outfits that expose just how pathetically bony their young torsos are. Even intimate relationships are evaluated on their sexual content: Is the sex satisfying? Liberating? Frequent? Inventive? Fun?

In such a sex-dominated world, celibacy is pushed into the background. Apart from the small contingent of Power Virgins, True Love Waiters, Athletes for Abstinence, and other convinced celibates, most people view celibacy as sad and lonely at best, unnatural at worst, the preserve of priests and nuns, spinsters and prisoners, and other pitiable victims.

Yet until recently, for at least three thousand years in most parts of the world, celibacy has been far from uncommon and rarely considered unnatural. Billions of people have either chosen or been forced into celibacy for periods ranging from the few weeks of the whale hunter to the lifetime of the saintly nun or the bitter eunuch.

We have seen why this is so. Celibacy in the form of premarital female virginity guarantees the paternity of at least the first child and implies future fidelity. It bridges the chasm between the secular and sacred worlds, ushering shamans into communion with the gods and providing the path for devout men and women to attain spiritual perfection. Celibacy is the traditional path toward enhancing physical strength and endurance, mental concentration and intellectual prowess.

In the past, celibacy was particularly relevant to women. In a world that overwhelmingly portrayed them pejoratively, as creatures flawed by weak physiques, wills, morals, and intelligence, their societies' customs, laws, and institutions governed their sexuality and, more often than not, denied them the privilege of deciding when, and with whom, they could express it. On the other hand, many women have voluntarily embraced celibacy to gain a measure of control over their own bodies and destinies. Sometimes, their dedicated celibacy gained them access to education and trades usually restricted to men. More often, they avoided marriages their parents might arrange with unsuitable partners, and the excruciating and often dangerous childbirth that would follow. Among legions of others, who can forget eponymous Uncumber, the hairy patron saint of women who wish to unencumber themselves from their husbands?

But throughout the ages, celibacy has been a double-edged sword. As a chosen lifestyle, it may empower and liberate, but when coerced, it can repress and crush. Depending upon the nature of the experiment, celibacy sustains or torments, emboldens or embitters, protects or humiliates, comforts or punishes.

Usually, celibacy combines elements of each of these polarities, with one outbalancing the other. This is notably true in the case of voluntary celibates. The young female virgin may ache with unrequited erotic longings, but she provides for her future well-being by assuring herself of a suitable marriage. The long-term brahmacharin or priest may struggle with sexual impulses, but the reward is the achievement of ultimate knowledge, or union with God. An

Indian *sadhin* trades the delight of holding a child in her arms for the right to plow a field, smoke a cigarette, and express herself freely, like a man. The ambitious nun renounces her right to a human family, but glories in the opportunity to study and preach, to control her convent's finances, and to acquire a reputation for wisdom and knowledge. African-American Shakers or followers of Father Divine had to surrender their right to sexual expression, but they lived in communities that defied the racist standards of the outside world and permitted them to preach and lead their fellows, white as well as black.

On the other side of the ledger, those coerced into celibacy are much more likely to find its bitter liabilities outweigh its rewards. The young female virgin forced by poverty or another handicap into permanent spinsterhood may have endured a galling existence as an unwanted burden to her family, though she did not risk dying in childbirth. The Hindu child widow probably internalized her celibacy as one more in a long list of privations and understood it as her punishment for having caused her husband's death by her conduct in a past life. A convicted thief suffers sexual abstinence and the cessation of marital relations as a cruel part of his sentence and finds nothing redeeming in it. Similarly, the unwanted daughter shunted off into a nunnery pined forever for the children she would never have and cursed the celibacy to which her religious life condemned her.

For forcibly castrated eunuchs, the balance was the most precarious of all. Many eunuchs wielded power unimaginable to other men from their low-ranked caste or class, but they lost forever their chances of founding their own family. A few castrati achieved fame and fortune, thanks to their incomparably powerful, soaring, and hauntingly lovely voices, but like other eunuchs, they were mocked and ridiculed for their feminized bodies and effete mannerisms.

Today, the sexual revolution, the birth-control pill, and AIDS have drastically altered these equations. Virginity has lost much of its value as a prerequisite for marriage, and sexual experience, particularly if it has enhanced the young person's erotic skills, now often counts as an advantage rather than a drawback. The pill and other easily accessible birth-control devices have also contributed to changing the sexual stakes by reducing the likelihood of pregnancy to almost zero. AIDS, however, which can transform sex into a potentially lethal indulgence, to some extent offsets the benefits of protective devices such as condoms and spermicide.

These new factors have mitigated the old considerations, principally religious and moral issues, and social expectations, which now influence far fewer individuals' judgment and decisions about sex. As a consequence, sexual abandon far outweighs celibacy on the scale of acceptability. Active sexuality, though sometimes fatal, is the majority's lifestyle of choice, and celibacy is widely rejected as untenable, symptomatic of deep psychological problems or even a horrid punishment akin to death itself.

This revulsion stems in large part from the false assumption that celibacy is a form of sexual anorexia, a regimen designed for members of religious orders who only the most peculiar laypeople would voluntarily embrace. This is a blinkered view of celibacy, which can take immensely complex and different forms. As the millennia of its history have shown us, experiments in celibacy have ranged from the communal chastity of the Essenes and the Shakers, the individual commitment of the Christian Fathers and the Brides of Christ, and the utter repression of all sexuality by the brahmacharins. Celibacy can also be devoid of spiritual significance, like that of the Dahomeyan warriors, who used it to transcend the restrictions imposed on other women. It can be coerced, as it was on eunuchs or unmarried and unmarriageable virgins. Its longevity ranges from a monk's lifetime or the decades-long virginity of the vestal virgins to the six weeks favored by Muhammad Ali prior to his boxing bouts and the temporary chastity of shamans training for careers as conduits between mortals and their gods. And it can be sterile, like the everlasting virginity of the "official" Virgin Mary, or fruitful, like the briefer virginity of the actual Jewish maiden who gave birth to her holy infant in a stable, surrounded by gentle animals.

Contemporary celibates reflect both traditional modes of celibacy as well as the modern tendency to scorn it. Many Catholic priests and nuns, for example, retain traditional beliefs about celibacy's biblical origins in Christ's stricture to be "eunuchs for the kingdom of God." But large numbers of their fellows practice a querulous celibacy rooted in a fundamental denial of its legitimacy. They feel compulsory celibacy is archaic, emotionally stunting, and spiritually unrewarding.

A completely unrelated category of celibates—those abstaining in the shadow of AIDS—are equally reluctant. These men and women have calculated the odds that condoms might break or spermicides fail and have decided that celibacy is the lesser of life-preserving evils, but an evil nonetheless.

However, today's convinced secular celibates share none of these qualms. Power Virgins, for example, confidently proclaim the rightness of their belief—usually grounded in religion—that sex outside marriage is wrong. This shores them up through the years of waiting until Mr. or Ms. Right appears on their horizon. Unlike earlier centuries' not-yet-married celibates, who acted in conformity with social norms, the Power Virgins challenge society's view of adult celibacy as an oddity or even an unpleasant physical or emotional disorder.

This nonconformity is equally true of adult celibates. Some are "reborn" virgins who, for various reasons, have come to regret their previous erotic adventures. The majority are women who define sexuality in terms of relationships rather than pure physicality. They opt out so they can shed the element of possessiveness they consider contaminating, and they regain personal autonomy, renewed vigor, and a heightened sense of freshness and commitment in their friendships. Many cherish their celibacy because it enriches their lives and deepens their sensibilities. For them, it represents a space that is both safe and serene, a purposeful withdrawal from erotic intimacy with its concomitant obligations and responsibilities.

Other celibates rejoice at their sense of heightened spirituality. Quite apart from shamans and members of religious orders, these secular celibates have testified to their sense of profound connection with God and with the ambience of otherworldliness. Today, many still speak of inner exploration, of serenity, of connectedness.

My own newfound celibacy, which I am so often asked about, differs slightly from most of these experiences. This is undoubtedly because I have been deeply influenced by what I learned as I reflected on and wrote *A History of Celibacy*, which was the major impetus for my decision. First of all, I was not a dissatisfied person seeking spiritual growth or any other sort of inner illumination. I was, as I remain, a writer and a dean of students with a fulfilling and intense professional life. When I began the final stages of this project and understood that, at this juncture of my life, celibacy had a great deal to offer me, I happened to be celibate because I was not in a relationship. From the outside, my decision changed precisely nothing. Yet to me, the transition from circumstantial to convinced celibacy felt transformative. As for so many others, in history and in the present, the element of choice made all the difference in how I experienced celibacy. Instead of burdensome and frustrating, it now felt joyous and liberating.

This is because for me, as for most women, celibacy has major tangible benefits, namely respite from the time-consuming burdens of housewifery, to which even liberated professionals succumb. I am particularly grateful to be relieved of that aspect of previous relationships. No longer do I need to plan, shop for, cook, serve, and clean up after a week's meals, or iron the shirts I once foolishly boasted I could do better than the dry cleaner, or answer that infernal question "Honey, where are my socks?"

For this privilege of living according to my own rhythms and rationing my days to suit my own needs, I pay the price of sex. I could, of course, indulge in fly-by-night affairs, without having to iron a single shirt or locate even one elusive sock, but that solution is unappealing. I prefer the simpler path of renouncing sexual relations altogether. At the same time, I have several close male friends and feel even safer in our emotional intimacy now that I know nothing more complicated will ever evolve.

However, my personal experience is not a blanket recommendation for others. Without marriage and childbearing behind me, I know that I would not find celibacy so rewarding. For me, celibacy has not meant sacrificing the incomparable joys of rocking a tiny baby, and shaping and sharing the life of this beloved flesh of my flesh. There is no question in my mind that as a younger woman, I could never have chosen celibacy.

I differ from many other celibates in another way—I have not found celibacy spiritually enlightening. I seek spirituality in my religion, Christianity, but exploring its roots as I researched this book left me instead struggling to retain my religious faith. Celibacy's long history cuts to the core of Christian doctrine, and its pernicious portrayal of women and its fundamental misogyny caused me great personal pain. Ultimately, the examples of so many of the courageous and energetic women I wrote about, and the recent appointments of my Anglican Church's Bishops Victoria Matthews and Ann Tottenham, whom I know and admire, prevailed over my resentment and doubt, and I reclaimed Christianity, albeit my own unorthodox version. I now recite my Church's creeds with mental reservations, interpret the Scriptures my own way, and disdain my religion's teachings about the role of women. In my case, the history (as opposed to the practice) of celibacy shook and transformed but failed to destroy my faith.

A History of Celibacy is a descriptive and analytic narrative and neither advocates nor opposes celibacy. When brought from obscurity into light, celibacy is historically defined by the same core elements of human existence: sexuality, gender, rank and role in society, and collective and individual responses to these realities. Countless people have chosen celibacy and found it empowering, liberating, and energizing. Creative contemporaries may reclaim the phenomenon and redefine celibacy in unique ways. Then, according to their individual needs, drives, and desires, they can choose either to practice or to reject it. Either way, the element of choice is crucial.

ACKNOWLEDGMENTS

Researching and writing *A History of Celibacy* consumed nearly eight years of my life, but I was seldom alone. Many people have shared various stages of the project with me.

For their enthusiasm and intellectual support, I thank my research assistants Don Booth, Meredith Burns-Simpson, Christine Cuk, Zahra Hamirami, Marian Hellsby, Eva Kater, Antony Mayadunne, Paul Meyer, Gary Peters, Kim Réaume, Radhika Sambamurti, and Elaine de Vries.

I am indebted to my sister Louise Abbott for her editorial suggestions, and my mother, Marnie Abbott, for her indefatigable newspaper clipping.

My friends and writing buddies Pegi Dover, Chris Dunning, Gideon Forman, Laurie Freeman, and Anita Shir-Jacob were never-ending sources of encouragement.

Dolores Cheeks was always in the wings, nodding encouragement, never doubting that I could do it.

Paulette Bourgeois has been a Rock of Gibraltar, the kindest and wisest of friends, who provided solace and sound advice, critiqued my ideas, and always cheered me on.

Over the years, Rev. Joel and Yvonne Trimble, Rev. Daniel and Evelyn Poirier, Lorna Lebrun, and my cousins Ian Griggs and Denise Powell provided me with summer writing havens.

Rev. Lance Dixon steadied me with his calm counsel, spiritual guidance, and practical help during the difficult times.

I am infinitely grateful to my friends Michèle Leroux, John McIninch, Janis Rapoport and Doug Donegani, and Sarah Reid, and to my stepdaughter, Lisa Namphy, for their love and support.

I hope the past few years will inspire my son Ivan Gibbs to create a book of his own.

Iris Tupholme, publisher at HarperCollins, had another book in mind until she saw the shelves full of my research binders and heard and believed in my vision. Thanks, Iris, for being a miracle worker.

Great editors are a writer's best friend, and I've had two: Nicole Langlois, my editor at HarperCollins Canada, and Gillian Blake, my editor at Scribner. My deepest thanks to you both for your dedication to this enormous project.

Early on, my agent, Heide Lange, shared my dreams.

On the principle of saving the best for last, I acknowledge my research assistants and friends Kelly Thomas and Michal Kasprzak. Kelly's boundless excitement with each new discovery, her staggering powers of analysis, and the depth of her historical background were matched only by her research skills and sheer determination. When Michal joined us, she infected him with her commitment to this project. I will never forget the blur of the final days punctuated with brainstorming sessions, homemade bread, and always-brewing Chai tea, and our collective joy when the book was finally finished. Thanks, too, to Gabriela Pawlus for pitching in so wholeheartedly during the last, frenzied days. And thanks to University of Toronto's Trinity College Provost Tom Delworth for understanding the needs of a writing dean.

NOTES

Chapter 1: Divine Pagan Celibacy

23 Greek Myths: Sources for the section on Greek myths are Sue Blundell, *Women in Ancient Greece* (London: British Museum Press, 1995); Michael Grant and John Hazel, *Who's Who in Classical Mythology* (London: J. M. Dent, 1993); R. Graves, *The Greek Myths* (London: Cassell, 1958); A. W. Mair, trans., *Callimachus and Lycophron* (New York: G. P. Putnam, 1921); Mary L. Lefkowitz and Maureen B. Fant, *Women in Greece and Rome* (Toronto, Sarasota: Samuel-Stevens Publishers, 1977); Deborah Lyons, *Gender and Immortality: Heroines in Ancient Greek Myth and Culture* (Princeton: Princeton University Press, 1997); Sarah Pomeroy, *Goddesses, Whores, Wives, and Slaves* (New York: Schocken, 1975); and William Smith, ed., *Dictionary of Greek and Roman Biographies and Mythologies*, vol. 3 (New York: AMS Press, 1967). Each deity's Roman name follows in parentheses.

24 The three chief goddesses: Blundell, 33, notes that "Hera's yearly rebirth as a potential bride may well have been seen as an event which recreated and reaffirmed the marital relationship."

25 "Child sprung full-blown": *Eumenides*, 736–49, 664—65, cited by Blundell, 28.

25 When her brother: Graves, 96–97. Both Athena and Hephaestus were victims of a prank—he had been told that Zeus had sent her to the smithy expecting he would make violent love to her. Athena, on her part, misunderstood her brother's initial remarks about forging the weapons for the price of love.

25 "And give me arrows": Mair, 61.

26 Artemis was ruthless: Lyons, 91. Another, less common version is that Orion boasted of his skills to her. He may also have tried to rape Artemis herself.

26 Artemis' relations with women: At Halae in Attica, a festival of Artemis required a man's throat to be lightly slit with a sword so a few drops of blood fell. Blundell, 29.

27 "Zeus has made you": Ibid., citing the *Iliad.*

27 she was worshiped daily: And later, as Vesta, throughout the Roman empire.

27 "She was completely unwilling": Pomeroy, 6, citing Homer's "Hymn 5: To Aphrodite."

29 "Help me, Father": Smith, 166–68.

30 Hippolytus Opposes Love: Quotations from Euripides' tragedy *Hippolytus* are from the translation by Gilbert Murray, published in London by George Allen & Unwin Ltd., 1931. Other sources for this section are Plato (trans. R. Waterfield), *Symposium* (New York: Oxford University Press, 1994); and F. I. Zeitlen, *Playing the Other: Gender and Society in Classical Greek Literature* (Chicago: University of Chicago Press, 1996).

30 "No one should oppose": Plato, 29–30.

30 ". . . spurns my spell": Euripides, 4–5.

31 "O God, why hast": Ibid., 34–35.

31 "Dost see / This sunlight": Ibid., 52.

31 "One Spirit there is": Ibid., 67.

31 "Ah me! / Would": Ibid., 72.

32 "I know / How love": Ibid., 14.

32 For the rest: In addition to her charms, Aphrodite had a magic girdle. Anyone wearing it would automatically be the object of love. Even Zeus, the most powerful god of all, could not resist Aphrodite's power. Hera borrowed the magic girdle to capture his attention and distract him from the Trojan War.

32 Lysistrata's Ultimatum: Quotations from Aristophanes' comedy *Lysistrata* are from *Three Plays by Aristophanes* (trans. Jeffrey Henderson), published in New York by Routledge, 1996. Other sources for this section are Kenneth J. Dover, *Greek Popular Morality in the Time of Plato and Aristotle* (Oxford: Basil Blackwell, 1974); R. L. Fowler, "How the *Lysistrata* Works," *Classical Views* 15 (1996): 245–49; and Aline Rousselle (trans. Felicia Pheasant), *Porneia: On Desire and the Body in Antiquity* (Oxford: Basil Blackwell, 1988).

33 In the play at least: In fact, it lasted another seven years, until 404 B.C.

33 Aristophanes ignored these: Fowler, 245–49.

34 Women, Teiresias ruled, experience: Dover, 159.

34 "I haven't even seen": *Lysistrata*, lines 114–15. Rousselle, 65, notes that sometimes unsatisfied Greek matrons resorted to leather penises.

34 Thesmophoria: Sources for the section on the Thesmophoria festival are Sue Blundell, *Women in Ancient Greece* (London: British Museum Press, 1995); Babette Stanley Spaexl, *The Roman Goddess Ceres* (Austin: University of Texas Press, 1996); and H. S. Versnel, *Transitional Reversal in Myth and Ritual* (London: E. J. Brill, 1993).

34 Men were strictly excluded: In another nocturnal festival for Demeter, even male dogs were shooed away.

35 the chaste tree: This tree is a member of the verbena family and smelled quite like pepper.

36 Cult of Isis: Sources for the sections on the cult of Isis, oracle of Delphi, and special virgins are Apuleius (ed. J. G. Griffiths), *The Isis Book* (Leiden: Brill, 1976); Sue Blundell, *Women in Ancient Greece* (London: British Museum Press, 1995); Walter Burkert, *Ancient Mystery Cults* (Cambridge: Harvard University Press, 1987); Michael Grant and John Hazel, *Who's Who in Classical Mythology* (London: J.M. Dent, 1993); Robert Graves, *The Greek Myths*, vol. 1 (London: Cassell, 1958); Sharon Kelly Heyob, *The Cult of Isis Among Women in the Graeco-Roman World* (Leiden: Brill, 1975); Robin Fox Lane, *Pagans and Christians* (San Francisco: Harper & Row, 1988); Ovid, "Amores," in Diane J. Rayer and William W. Batshaw, eds., *Latin Lyric and Elegiac Poetry: An Anthology of New Translations* (New York: Garland Publishing, 1995); Robert Parker, *Miasma* (London: Oxford University Press, 1983); Propertius (ed. G. P. Goold), *Elegies* (Cambridge: Harvard University Press, 1990); William Smith, ed., *Dictionary of Greek and Roman Biographies and Mythology*, vol. 3 (New York: AMS Press, 1967); Tibullus (trans. J. P. Postgate), *Tibullus* (Cambridge: Harvard University Press, 1962); and Marina Warner, *Alone of All Her Sex: The Myth and the Cult of the Virgin Mary* (London: Weidenfeld and Nicolson, 1976).

36 Isis was a gentle: In Egyptian mythology, Isis was the wife and sister of Osiris and the mother of Horus.

37 "how extremely hard were": Apuleius, 93.

37 "Because lying apart was": Ovid, 493, 495.

37 Apollo, for example: Blundell, 160. Zeus' oracle at Dodona had a similar arrangement.

37 The most popular was: It became the most popular after the sixth century B.C.

37 On the seventh day: Except for three months in winter, when it remained closed.

38 Pagan religions rarely: Parker, 77–80, gives examples of short-term celibacy or virginity as requirements to plant and harvest the olive, for beekeeping, and perhaps for food preparation.

Notes

39 Vestal Virgins: Sources for the section on vestal virgins are J. P. V. D. Balsdon, *Roman Women: Their History and Habits* (London: The Bodley Head, 1977); Mary Beard, "The Sexual Status of Vestal Virgins," *JRS* 70 (1980): 12–27; Richard Cavendish, ed. in chief, *Man, Myth & Magic: The Illustrated Encyclopedia of Mythology, Religion and the Unknown*, vol. 2 (New York, London, Toronto: Marshall Cavendish Ltd., 1983); Jane F. Gardner, *The Legendary Past: Roman Myths* (Great Britain: British Museum Press, 1993); Judith P. Hallett, *Fathers and Daughters in Roman Society: Women and the Elite Family* (Princeton: Princeton University Press, 1984); Mary R. Lefkowitz and Maureen B. Fant, *Women in Greece and Rome* (Toronto, Sarasota: Samuel-Stevens Publishers, 1977); E. Royston Pike, *Love in Ancient Rome* (London: Frederick Muller, 1965); Herbert Jennings Rose, *Ancient Roman Religion* (London: Frederick Muller, 1965); and Paul Schilling, "Vesta," in the *Encyclopedia of Religion* (New York: Macmillan, 1987).

40 "Are you watchful": Schilling, 251. Other sources translate "watchful" as "wakeful." In her fascinating article, Mary Beard also offers strong evidence that the vestals may have represented royal wives, as their garb was similar to a Roman bride's, and after their shorn hair regrew, they dressed it in the style suitable for the day after marriage.

40 And when, under the: After this initial shearing, she could grow her hair long and dress it, though fancy styling was frowned on.

40 This haircut was not all: Descriptions of the vestals' clothes and induction rituals found in most sources originate from Plutarch's *Life of Numa* and other contemporary sources.

41 In adulthood, however: Balsdon, 238–39, suggests "there were undoubtedly periods of persistent religious and moral laxity when the whole College was corrupt, and from early days the novice was exhorted not to be a prig, but to follow the example of the rest; it was perfectly safe, she would be told." However, Balsdon does not document this assertion, though she points to national calamities that were blamed on vestals' lack of chastity.

42 They ran a terrible risk: Most sources cite Plutarch's description of an amorous vestal's fate. The rationale was that if a condemned vestal were innocent, Vesta would rescue her. As this never happened, each live burial was considered justified.

42 Of the ten documented: Balsdon, 240. However, at the end of the second century B.C., allegations against the College led to a full-scale inquiry and a vestal was convicted of being unchaste. The following year, two who had been acquitted were also condemned. In 83 and 90 A.D., Emperor Domitian declared the College to be a sinkhole of corruption. These possible exceptions aside, most vestals were celibate.

43 The Influence of Greek Philosophy: The main sources for this section are Vern L. Bullough, *Sexual Variance in History* (New York: John Wiley & Sons, 1976); Kenneth J. Dover, "Classical Greek Attitudes to Sexual Behavior," in Andreas Karsten Siems, ed., *Sexualität und Erotik in der Antike* (Darmstadt: Wissenschaftliche Buchgesellschaft, 1988); Kenneth J. Dover, *Greek Popular Morality in the Time of Plato and Aristotle* (Oxford: Basil Blackwell, 1974); Sarah B. Pomeroy, *Goddesses, Whores, Wives, and Slaves* (New York: Schocken, 1975); Pythagoras (trans. R. S. Guthrie), *The Pythagorean Sourcebook and Library* (Grand Rapids: Phanes Press, 1987); and Ute Ranke-Heinemann, *Eunuchs for the Kingdom of Heaven: Women, Sexuality, and the Catholic Church* (New York: Doubleday, 1990).

44 "When you want": Ranke-Heinemann, 329.

44 "How about your service": Plato, Book I, 11.

44 Stoicism had similar: All such views of sexuality ran counter to the relaxed Greek view of homosexual relations, which Stoics condemned as being, by their nature, for mere sensual pleasure rather than for procreation.

44 "[A] wise man ought": Bullough, 166. Seneca was Nero's tutor. Later, Nero had him killed.

45 The Essenes Prepare for Armageddon: The main sources for this section are David Flusser (trans. Carol Glucker), *The Spiritual History of the Dead Sea Sect* (Tel Aviv: MOD Books, 1989); and Duncan Howlett, *The Essenes and Christianity: An Interpretation of the Dead Sea Scrolls* (New York: Harper & Brothers, 1957).

45 "Israel that walks": Flusser, 11–13.
46 "when he knew what": Ibid., 31–32.
46 Perhaps this was true: Howlett, 90, writes that no conclusion is possible; possibly women were once part of the sect but, later, celibacy was imposed.
46 They saw instead: Flusser, 52–56. This requirement did not limit their membership, estimated to be about four thousand at their peak.

Chapter 2: Early Christianity

47 A Tale of Two Women: The main sources for this section are Peter Brown, *The Body and Society: Men, Women and Sexual Renunciation in Early Christianity* (New York: Columbia University Press, 1988); John Bugge, *Virginitas: An Essay in the History of a Medieval Idea* (Hague: Martinus Nijhoff, 1975); Manuela Dunn-Mascetti, *Saints: The Chosen Few* (London: Boxtree, 1994); Robin Lane Fox, *Pagans and Christians* (San Francisco: Harper & Row, 1988); *Holy Bible,* NSRV; and Joyce E. Salisbury, *Church Fathers, Independent Virgins* (New York: Verso, 1991).
47 "dismiss her quietly": Matthew 1:18–19.
47 "Joseph, son of David": Ibid., 1:20–21.
48 "took her as his wife": Ibid., 1:24–25.
48 "Look, the virgin shall": Ibid., 1:23.
48 "You know that after": Ibid., 26:2.
48 "Go therefore and make": Ibid., 28:19–20.
49 "For there are eunuchs": Ibid., 19:12.
49 "Who are my mother": Mark 3:33–35. Jesus probably knew that Mary and his brothers were worried he was working too hard and taking too little nourishment. They had probably come to whisk him home for supper.
49 "Gateway to the Devil": Salisbury, 113.
50 "you are dust": Genesis 2:15–25, 3:1–24.
50 Martyrdom Toughens the New Religion: The main source for this section on Christian persecutions is Robin Lane Fox, *Pagans and Christians* (San Francisco: Harper & Row, 1988), 419–612. Manuela Dunn-Mascetti, *Saints: The Chosen Few* (London: Boxtree, 1994), is also used.
51 "No rain, because": Fox, 425.
51 campaign against Christians: Ibid., 456. Fox describes an instance in which nineteen people under threat of persecution for their Christianity sought certificates attesting to their lifelong paganism. Of these nineteen, at least thirteen were women, and of the men, one was sixty-two years old, another disabled.
51 "When torn by all": Ibid., 440.
52 The Second Coming: The main sources for this section are Ambrose, "Concerning Virgins," *Nicene and Post-Nicene Fathers,* vol. 10 (New York: Christian Literature Co., 1896); Peter Brown, *The Body and Society: Men, Women and Sexual Renunciation in Early Christianity* (New York: Columbia University Press, 1988); Peter Brown, "Bodies and Minds: Sexuality and Renunciation in Early Christianity," in David M. Halperin, John J. Winkler, and Froma I. Zeitlin, eds., *Before Sexuality: The Construction of Erotic Experience in the Ancient Greek World* (Princeton: Princeton University Press, 1990); Peter Brown, "The Notion of Virginity in the Early Church," in B. McGinn, J. Meyendorff, and J. Leclercq, eds., *Christian Spirituality: Origins to the Twelfth Century* (New York: Crossroad, 1985); John Bugge, *Virginitas: An Essay in the History of a Medieval Idea* (Hague: Martinus Nijhoff, 1975); Vern L. Bullough, *Sexual Variance in Society and History* (New York: John Wiley & Sons, 1976); John Chrysostom, *On Virginity; Against Remarriage* (Lewiston, N.Y.: Edwin Mellen Press, 1983); St. Cyprian (trans. Roy J. Deferrari), *Treatises* (New York: Fathers of the Church, 1958); *Holy Bible,* NSRV; Jerome, *Post Nicene Fathers,* vol. 6 (Leiden: Fathers of the Church Press, 1991; also avail-

able on-line: http://ccel.wheaton.edu/fathers2.html); Joyce Salisbury, *Church Fathers, Independent Virgins* (New York: Verso, 1991); and Tertullian (trans. S. Thelwall), "One Exhortation to Chastity," *Ante-Nicene Fathers*, vol. 4 (Washington: Christian Classics Ethereal Library, 1951; also available on-line: http://ccel.wheaton.edu/fathers2.html).

52 "[In the desert] where": Jerome, "To Eustochium," 25.

53 "There is no greater": Jerome, "Against Jovinian," 386.

53 "It is laws which": Ibid., 14.

53 ". . . But because of": 1 Corinthians, 6:13, 7:2, and 7:6–7.

53 in fact, angels were: Gregory of Nyssa and later John Chrysostom wrote that Adam and Eve led an angelic life before the Fall. Bugge, 5–29.

53 "shall not perform": Jerome, "Against Jovinian," 374.

53 "While you remain": St. Cyprian, chap. 22, 50.

53 "For chastity has made": Ambrose, "Concerning Virgins," vol. 10, Book I.

53 "pressing their teeth": Jerome, "To Eustochium," 35.

53 "The smell of your": Ambrose, "Concerning Virgins," vol. 10, Book I.

54 "It is not the harlot": Jerome, "Against Jovinian," 367.

54 "[to be in the womb]": Jerome, "Against Helvidius," 344.

54 "Christianity did not make": Bullough, 160.

54 "the things of the": Chrysostom, 73.I.6.

54 "How can you possibly": Brown, "Bodies and Minds," 482.

55 The Christian sexual revolution: In the West, the superiority of celibacy remained unchallenged until the Reformation. The Eastern Church, on the other hand, never adopted the West's strict adherence to celibacy among its married clergy. Brown, "The Notion of Virginity," 427.

55 "For you have received": Ibid.

55 The Fathers understood: Gregory's brother was St. Basil the Great, who defended studying pagan literature, admired Platonic thought, and organized monasteries. Their sister was St. Macrina/St. Thecla.

56 Hail Mary? The Progressive Virginities of the Holy Mother: The main sources for this section are Vern Bullough, *Sexual Variance in Society and History* (New York: John Wiley & Sons, 1976); *The Catechism of the Catholic Church* (London: Geoffrey Chapman, 1994); John McHugh, *The Mother of Jesus in the New Testament* (New York: Doubleday, 1975); Ute Ranke-Heinemann, *Eunuchs for the Kingdom of Heaven: Women, Sexuality, and the Catholic Church* (New York: Doubleday, 1990); Jane Smith and Yvonne Haddad, "The Virgin Mary in Islamic Tradition and Commentary," *Muslim World* 79, no. 3–4 (July/October 1989): 161–87; and Marina Warner, *Alone of All Her Sex: The Myth and the Cult of the Virgin Mary* (London: Weidenfeld and Nicolson, 1976).

57 How, then, had the conception: Al-Tabari, the most famous of the classical commentators, presented three possibilities: God manifested as an angel blew into Mary's pocket until his breath reached her womb and she conceived; he did the same into her sleeve; or he breathed into her mouth.

58 "I have tempted the living": Ranke-Heinemann, 343–44, citing the Proto-Gospel of James. Ranke-Heinemann says this book had an "enormous" influence on the development of Mariology. Other sources, such as *The Ascension of Isaiah* in about the second century, also described a painless, hence virginal, birth.

58 "Jesus would not have": Ranke-Heinemann, 5, citing Pope Siricius in a letter to Bishop Anysius in 392.

59 Nonsense, said many: McHugh, 200–201. This is known as the Epiphanian view, advocated by St. Epiphanius of Salamis in Cyprus. Those who believed this included Clement of Alexandria, Ambrose, Gregory of Nyssa, and Origen.

59 "He who was worthy": Warner, 23; McHugh, 200–201, 223–25.

59 "it was fitting": Bugge, 150–54, 110.

59 "remained a virgin": St. Augustine, Sermon 186, *The Catechism of the Catholic Church*.

Notes

61   Encratites and Gnostics Boycott the Womb: The main sources for this section are *Acts of Judas Thomas* (trans. Klijn) (Leiden: E. J. Brill, 1962); "Acts of the Holy Apostle Thomas," *Ante-Nicene Fathers*, vol. 8 (Washington: Christian Classics Ethereal Library, 1951; also available on-line: http://ccel.wheaton.edu/fathers2.html); Peter Brown, "Bodies and Minds: Sexuality and Renunciation in Early Christianity," in David M. Halperin, John J. Winkler, and Froma I. Zeitlin, eds., *Before Sexuality: The Construction of Erotic Experience in the Ancient Greek World* (Princeton: Princeton University Press, 1990); Peter Brown, *The Body and Society: Men, Women and Sexual Renunciation in Early Christianity* (New York: Columbia University Press, 1988); John Bugge, *Virginitas: An Essay in the History of a Medieval Idea* (Hague: Martinus Nijhoff, 1975); Vern L. Bullough, *Sexual Variance in Society and History* (New York: John Wiley & Sons, 1976); Minucius Felix (trans. G. H. Rendall), *Octavius*, vol. 9 (London: William Heinemann, 1931); E. Henneche and W. Schneemelcher (trans. McL. R. Wilson), *New Testament Apocrypha* (London: Lutterworth Press, 1963); *Holy Bible*, NSRV; "The Interpretation of Knowledge" (trans. J. D. Turner), *Nag Hammadi Codices,* XI (Leiden: E. J. Brill, 1990); W. Schneemelcher, ed., *Acts of John;* "Sophia of Jesus Christ" (trans. M. Parrott), *Nag Hammadi Codices,* III (Leiden: E. J. Brill, 1990); Tatian (trans. J. E. Ryland), "Address of Tatian to the Greeks," vol. 3, chap. 15; also available on-line: http://ccel.wheaton.edu/fathers2.html; and Tertullian, "Concerning Virginity"; also available on-line: http://ccel.wheaton.edu/fathers2.html.

61   Two other major sects: This is true despite the Fathers' denunciation of Gnosticism. By the second century, it was discredited as a distortion of Christianity.

61   "polluted and foul way": "Acts of the Holy Apostle Thomas."

61   But, lured by the: Jewish thought took an opposite tack: Adam and Eve taught the animals how to have sex.

61   "And marriage followed": "Origins of the World," *Nag Hammadi Codices,* II, 5:109, in Brown, *The Body and Society,* 94.

61   "For that which befalleth": Ecclesiastes 3:19.

61   "for it is ordained": Henneche and Schneemelcher, citing *Acts of Andrew* 5, 2:410.

62   In Encratite tradition: This was written about 220 in Syria and embodies Encratite thought.

62   "marriage passeth away": *Acts of Thomas* 88, 101.

62   One of the leaders: Marcion was a church reformer excommunicated by the Church in Rome in 144. He set up a rival organization.

62   "repudiate the fruit": Bullough, 184.

62   Marcion based his: Marcion believed the message of Jesus had been written down some time after the events in question, and the Gospels represented false apostles brainwashed by Judaism. Only Paul and Luke had written truthfully, but errors had been inserted in their Gospels. Ibid., 185.

62   "Enter through the rib": "Interpretation of Knowledge," 53.

62   "the unclean rubbing": "Sophia of Jesus Christ," 220.

63   "the unseen springs": Schneemelcher, *Acts of John* 53–54, 2:241.

63   Give Me Chastity . . . but Not Yet: The main sources for this section are Augustine (trans. R. S. Pine-Coffin), *Confessions* (Baltimore: Penguin, 1961); Augustine (trans. Mary Sarah Muldowney; ed. Roy J. Defferrari), *Treatises on Various Subjects* (New York: Fathers of the Church Press, 1955); Augustine (trans. Matthew Schumacher), *Against Julian* (New York: Fathers of the Church Press, 1957); Augustine (trans. Charles T. Wilcox; ed. Roy J. Defferrari), *Treatises on Marriage and Other Subjects* (New York: Fathers of the Church Press, 1955); Peter Brown, *The Body and Society: Men, Women and Sexual Renunciation in Early Christianity* (New York: Columbia University Press, 1988); Vern L. Bullough, *Sexual Variance in Society and History* (New York: John Wiley & Sons, 1976); Minucius Felix (trans. G. H. Rendall), *Octavius* IX:4 (London: William Heinemann, 1931); *Holy Bible,* NSRV; Joyce E. Salisbury, *Church Fathers, Independent Virgins* (New

York: Verso, 1991); and Tertullian, "Concerning Virginity"; also available on-line: http://ccel.wheaton.edu/fathers2.html.

64 Since childhood, Augustine: Augustine, *Confessions*, 45.

65 "The law in our": Augustine, *Treatises*, vol. 14, 213.

65 "that bestial movement": Augustine, *Against Julian*, vol. 16, 130.

65 "Not in rioting": Romans 13:13–14.

65 "You converted me": Augustine, *Confessions*, 178.

65 "the manly mind": Ibid., 193.

66 Over his long life: Some of these are *The Catholic and Manichaean Ways of Life; Confessions; City of God; The Good of Marriage; On Marriage and Concupiscence; On Adulterous Marriage;* and *Against Julian*.

66 "a man eighty-four years": Augustine, *Against Julian*.

66 "Your flesh is like": Brown, 426.

66 "descend with a certain": Ibid.

67 "The evil of carnal": Augustine, *Against Julian*, vol. 16, 203.

67 "greater, indeed, is": Augustine, *Good of Marriage*, chap. 23, 45.

67 Church Mothers: The main sources for this section are Robin Lane Fox, *Pagans and Christians* (San Francisco: Harper & Row, 1988); Otto Kiefer, *Sexual Life in Ancient Rome* (London: Constable, 1994); Aline Rousselle (trans. Felicia Pheasant), *Porneia: On Desire and the Body in Antiquity* (Oxford: Basil Blackwell, 1988); Joyce E. Salisbury, *Church Fathers, Independent Virgins* (New York: Verso, 1991); and Joyce Salisbury, "Human Beasts and Bestial Humans in the Middle Ages," in Jennifer Ham and Matthew Senior, eds., *Animal Acts: Configuring the Human in Western History* (New York: Routledge, 1997).

67 Stories about outstanding virgins: These stories were preserved in the Escorial manuscript, which was a *Codex Regularum*, a collection of monastic writings that served as guides for monks and nuns to follow in their own lives.

69 "In truth, virgins have": The quotations in the account of Constantina are taken from Salisbury, *Church Fathers*, 63, citing "Vita Ste Constantine."

69 The real Constantina: The origin of this legend was probably the misidentification of Constantina with the emperor's devoutly Christian sister Constantia, for whom he probably built the Basilica of St. Agnes.

70 Our second Church Mother: The quotations in the account of Mary of Egypt are from Salisbury, *Church Fathers*, 70–72, citing "Vita Domne Marie Egiptie."

73 The last in our tales: The quotations in the account of Helia are taken from Salisbury, *Church Fathers*, 75–80, citing "Vita Sanctae Helia."

74 "When she accepts": Ibid., 77.

75 "threw himself at me": Fox, 424.

75 "By idealizing virginity": Ibid., 310.

76 Female Transvestite Monks: The main sources for this section are Vern L. Bullough, *Sexual Variance in Society and History* (New York: John Wiley & Sons, 1976); and Joyce E. Salisbury, *Church Fathers, Independent Virgins* (New York: Verso, 1991). Quotations are taken from Salisbury, 105–7, citing "Vita Sanctae Castissimae."

77 Her monkish accomplice: He did so, apparently, without first attempting to dissuade her from this illegal act. Christian women were supposed to cover, not cut, their hair. But in excesses of zeal, so many had that in 390 a law forbade the practice. "Women who shall have shorn their hair contrary to divine and human laws . . . should be debarred from the doors of the church," it declared. In Deuteronomy 22:5, men and women are also barred from cross-dressing.

78 Pelagia of Antioch: Citations in the account of Pelagia are taken from *Holy Women of the Syrian Orient* (trans. Sebastian P. Brock and Susan Ashbrook Harvey) (Berkeley: University of California Press, 1987).

78 "She will have looked": Ibid., 44.

79 "I am a prostitute": Ibid., 49–50.

79 "You will have": Ibid., 50–51.

80 The most famous of these: This story is taken from the following sources: Rosemary Pardoe and Darroll Pardoe, *The Female Pope: The Mystery of Pope Joan* (Wellingborough: Crucible, 1988); Clement Wood, *The Woman Who Was Pope: A Biography of Pope Joan, 853–855* (New York: William Faro, 1931); and Vern L. Bullough, *Sexual Variance in Society and History* (New York: John Wiley & Sons, 1976), 368–69.

82 Uncumber was the daughter: The story of Uncumber is taken from Bullough, 367–68.

83 The Desert Fathers' New Alphabet of the Heart: The main sources for this section are Christopher Brooke, *The Monastic World, 1000–1300* (London: Paul Elek Ltd., 1974); Peter Brown, *The Body and Society: Men, Women and Sexual Renunciation in Early Christianity* (New York: Columbia University Press, 1988); Manuela Dunn-Mascetti, *Saints: The Chosen Few* (London: Boxtree, 1994); Michel Foucault, *Western Sexuality: Practice and Precept in Past and Present Times* (New York: Basil Blackwell, 1975); Graham Gould, *The Desert Fathers* (Oxford: Clarendon Press, 1993); Elaine Pagels, *Adam, Eve, and the Serpent* (New York: Random House, 1988); Aline Rouselle (trans. Felicia Pheasant), *Porneia: On Desire and the Body in Antiquity* (Oxford: Basil Blackwell, 1988); Norman Russell, trans., *The Lives of the Desert Fathers: The Historia Monachorum in Aegypto* (London, Oxford: Mowbray, 1981); Tim Vivian, trans., *Histories of the Monks of Upper Egypt and the Life of Onnophrius by Paphnutius* (Kalamazoo: Cistercian Publications, 1993); and Benedicta Ward, trans., *The Sayings of the Desert Fathers: The Alphabetical Collection* (London: Mowbray, 1975).

83 "He who wishes": Rouselle, 143.

84 After eighteen years: His wife then transformed her house into a private convent.

85 "more dead than": Pagels, 89.

85 Thirty-two men: These calculations were made by Rouselle, 175–77.

85 "transcend the laws": Ibid., 171, quoting Abba Dioscorus. However, Dioscorus added that "imaginings are the result of deliberate choice and are a sign of an evil disposition."

86 One young girl: Ibid., 144. The monks took her to the river and "made love" with her.

87 "the same feelings": Ibid., 150.

87 "If you were a": Ibid., 141.

87 "When you see": Ibid., 148.

87 "Do not bring young": Ward quoting Isaac, Priest of the Cells.

88 "thinking about bricklaying": Foucault, 19–20.

88 "rightly hailed as the": Brown, 229.

88 St. Simeon's Chastity at Sixty Feet High: The source for the following section and for quotations is Susan Ashbrook Harvey (trans. Robert Doran), *The Lives of Simeon Stylites* (Kalamazoo: Cistercian Publications, 1992).

89 Simeon's object in: Other saints stood all day, and some alternated between standing and sitting. But they did not do this on a pillar. A Greek cult at the temple of Aphrodite in Hierapolis, 144 kilometers distant from Simeon's pillar, had immensely high phalli or pillars, which a man climbed twice a year and lived on for seven days. Up there he communed with the gods and asked for blessings for all Syria.

90 Marrying "the True Man": The main sources for this section are Ambrose, "Concerning Virgins," *Nicene Fathers,* vol. 10 (Leiden: Fathers of the Church Press, 1991; also available on-line: http://ccel.wheaton.edu/fathers2.html); Ambrose, "Concerning Virgins," book 2, chap. 3 (Leiden: Fathers of the Church Press, 1991; also available on-line: http://ccel.wheaton.edu/fathers2.html); Ambrose (trans. Daniel Callam), *On Virginity* (Saskatoon: Peregrina Publishing Co., 1987); Virginia Burrus, *Chastity as Autonomy: Women in the Stories of the Apocryphal Acts* (Lewiston, N.Y: Edwin Mellen Press, 1987); Averil Cameron and Amélie Kuhrt, eds., *Images of Women in Antiquity* (London: Routledge, 1983); Jerome, "To Demetrias," "To Eustochium," "To Laeta," *Nicene Fathers,* vol. 4 (Leiden: Fathers of the Church Press, 1991; also available on-line:

http://ccel.wheaton.edu/fathers2.html); John Moschos, *The Spiritual Meadow* (Kalama-zoo: Cistercian Publications, 1992); Elizabeth Alvida Petroff, *Medieval Women's Vision-ary Literature* (Oxford: Oxford University Press, 1986); and Joyce E. Salisbury, *Church Fathers, Independent Virgins* (New York: Verso, 1991).

93   Thecla, obsessed with Paul: Burrus, 125–26. Toward the end of his life, Paul was arrested in Jerusalem, transported to Rome, released from prison, then continued his missionary work. After his final imprisonment, again in Rome, he was beheaded out-side the city.

93   Thecla insisted on traveling: Petroff, 126. There is a discrepancy in the stories of Thecla's ordeal among the beasts. My version borrows from each.

93   "offered her vital parts": Ambrose, "Concerning Virgins," book 2, chap. 3.

94   "I wish to present": Salisbury, 32–33, citing Jerome, "To Demetrias."

94   "Do not seek the": Jerome, "To Eustochium," 32–33.

94   "Jesus is jealous": Ibid., 32.

94   "If all this is true": Jerome, "To Demetrias," 270.

94   "a deliberate squalor": Jerome, "To Eustochium," 28; "To Laeta," 194.

94   "Your mouth should": Ambrose, "Concerning Virgins," 382.

95   "virginity may be lost": Ambrose, *On Virginity*, 40.

96   Alexandra and Melania: The story of Melania is from Salisbury, 114–22.

97   an outstanding example: Ecdicia and Egeria, for example.

Chapter 3: Later Christianity

99   Medieval Eastern Monasteries: The main sources for this section on monasteries are Peter Abélard (trans. Henry Adams Bellows), *The Story of My Misfortunes* (Glencoe: Free Press, 1972); Anne L. Barstow, *Married Priests and the Reforming Papacy: The Eleventh-Century Debates* (New York, Toronto: Edwin Mellen Press, 1982); Peter Brown, *The Body and Society: Men, Women and Sexual Renunciation in Early Christianity* (New York: Columbia University Press, 1988); Vern L. Bullough, *Sexual Variance in Society and His-tory* (New York: John Wiley & Sons, 1976); Norman Cantor, "The Crisis of Western Monasticism, 1050–1130," *American Historical Review* 66, no. 1 (1960–61): 47–67; Manuela Dunn-Mascetti, *Saints: The Chosen Few* (London: Boxtree, 1994); Robin Lane Fox, *Pagans and Christians* (San Francisco: Harper & Row, 1988); Michael Goodich, *The Unmentionable Vice: Homosexuality in the Later Medieval Period* (Santa Barbara: ABC-Clio, 1979); Susan Ashbrook Harvey (trans. Robert Doran), *The Lives of Simeon Stylites* (Kalamazoo: Cistercian Publications, 1992); C. H. Lawrence, *Medieval Monasti-cism: Forms of Religious Life in Western Europe in the Middle Ages* (New York: Longmans, 1989); Aline Rousselle (trans. Felicia Pheasant), *Porneia: On Desire and the Body in Antiquity* (Oxford: Basil Blackwell, 1988); and Herbert Workman, *The Evolution of the Monastic Ideal: From the Earliest Times Down to the Coming of the Friars* (London: Epworth Press, 1927).

99   "For nothing displeases": Brown, 228.

99   It came to be: Ibid.

99   "great, walled-in monasteries": Ibid., 435. According to Susan Ashbrook Harvey, in her foreword to *The Lives of Simeon Stylites*, 27–28, "Every Syrian monastery contained—besides the church, the common cemetery, a small enough house for the abbot or for guests—one of several buildings for common use: refectory, chapter-room where the superior instructed his monks and . . . the bakery, the kitchen and . . . a forge, a shoe-maker, a room for weaving . . ." The monks lodged in cells "sometimes grouped around the monastery. . . . They were made of very poor materials, with the result that nothing remains."

100   "To save souls": Workman, 88.

100   "the Invisible God": Fox, 415.

101 "With wine and boys": Brown, 230.
102 "We must create": Lawrence, chap. 2.
102 "to form a school": Workman, 143.
103 "supported himself and": Abélard, 63.
103 "He was indeed": Goodich, 10. Emphasis added.
104 The truth was: This Church-monastery link had begun under Pope Gregory I, 590–604.
105 "What else do worldlings": Dunn-Mascetti, 31. Cantor, 69, suggests St. Bernard's crabbiness might have stemmed from his awareness that the political world was becoming more, not less, grasping, penetrating, and secular.
106 "conceded that anybody": Bullough, 433.
106 Celibacy One, Lust Zero: The source for this section on Scuthin is Richard Zacks, *History Laid Bare: Love, Sex and Perversity from the Etruscans to Warren G. Harding* (New York: HarperCollins, 1994), 41.
107 To Wed or Not to Wed: The main sources for this section are Clarissa W. Atkinson, *Mystic and Pilgrim: The Book and the World of Margery Kempe* (Ithaca: Cornell University Press, 1983); Anne L. Barstow, *Married Priests and the Reforming Papacy: The Eleventh-Century Debates* (New York, Toronto: Edwin Mellen Press, 1982); Peter Brown, *The Body and Society: Men, Women and Sexual Renunciation in Early Christianity* (New York: Columbia University Press, 1988); Vern L. Bullough, *Sexual Variance in Society and History* (New York: John Wiley & Sons, 1976); Margaret Gallyon, *Margery Kempe of Lynn and Medieval England* (Norwich: Canterbury Press, 1995); Michael Goodich, *The Unmentionable Vice: Homosexuality in the Later Medieval Period* (Santa Barbara: ABC-Clio, 1979); Margaret King, *Women of the Renaissance* (Chicago: University of Chicago Press, 1991); W. E. H. Lecky, *History of European Morals*, vol. 11 (New York: Longmans, Green and Co., 1911); Martin Luther (ed. Jaroslav Pelikan), *Luther's Works* (St. Louis: Concordia Publishing House, 1955–86); Eileen Power, *Medieval English Nunneries, c. 1275 to 1535* (New York: Biblo and Tannen, 1964); Aline Rousselle (trans. Felicia Pheasant), *Porneia: On Desire and the Body in Antiquity* (Oxford: Basil Blackwell, 1988); and Joseph R. Strayer, *Dictionary of the Middle Ages*, vol. 3 (New York: Charles Scribner's Sons, 1983).
108 "Nothing," Luther thundered: Luther, "Letter to Nicholas," *Luther's Works*, vol. 48, 321–22.
112 "as if they were": Brown, 443.
112 The *focaria* or: Power, 436. *Focaria*, and not the acronym of For Using Carnal Knowledge, may also be the origin of the word *fuck*.
114 "You lucky man": Luther, "Letter to Nicholas," *Luther's Works*, vol. 48, 321–22.
115 Begin the Beguine: The main sources for this section are Clarissa Atkinson, *Mystic and Pilgrim: The Book and the World of Margery Kempe* (Ithaca: Cornell University Press, 1983); Carolly Erickson, *The Medieval Vision: Essays in History and Perception* (New York: Oxford University Press, 1976); Jerome, "To Eustochium," *Post-Nicene Fathers*, vol. 6 (Leiden: Fathers of the Church Press, 1991; also available on-line: http://ccel.wheaton.edu/fathers2.html); Margaret King, *Women of the Renaissance* (Chicago: University of Chicago Press, 1991); Ernest McDonell, *The Beguines and Beghards in Medieval Culture, with Special Emphasis on the Belgian Scene* (New York: Octagon Books, 1969); Elizabeth A. Petroff, *Medieval Women's Visionary Literature* (Oxford: Oxford University Press, 1986); Eileen Power, *Medieval English Nunneries, c. 1275 to 1535* (New York: Biblo and Tannen, 1964); and Joyce E. Salisbury, *Church Fathers, Independent Virgins* (New York: Verso, 1991).
115 Marie, the best known: This is an approximate date. Sources give 1176, 1177, and early 1178 as Marie's probable birth date.
115 Marie was renowned: From Petroff, 7, citing Marie d'Oignies's *Life* by Jacques de Vitry. "From the horror she felt at her previous carnal pleasure, she began to afflict herself and she found no rest in spirit until, by means of extraordinary bodily chastisements, she had made up for all the pleasures she had experienced in the past."

116 Certainly their preservation: McDonell, 228, citing Joinville's *Histoire de S. Louis*. Also, page 137 notes that a thirteenth-century will indicates Beguinage was equated with chastity.

117 "pregnancy, the crying of infants": Jerome, 23.

117 Women who married: King, 135, reiterates how convents or Beguinages offered women the dual advantages of allowing them to pursue their personal goals in dignity and the celibate existence that freed them from the risks of childbearing and family life.

118 "sin came from a woman": Erickson, 189.

118 Women Out of This World: The sources for this section are Margaret King, *Women of the Renaissance* (Chicago: University of Chicago Press, 1991); and Ernest W. McDonell, *The Beguines and the Beghards in Medieval Culture, with Special Emphasis on the Belgian Scene* (New York: Octagon Books, 1969).

118 In Milan such women: The *beatas* took informal vows of chastity, claimed exemption from sexual passions, and were dedicated to charity and visionary piety.

119 A number found their: Franciscan third order or tertiaries "strive in the world and under the tempering of a religious order and in conformity with the spirit of that order to attain Christian perfection in a manner appropriate to secular life by practice of a rule approved for them by the Holy See." McDonell, 132–33.

119 Mary Ward, Who Was "But a Woman": Sources for Mary Ward are Olwen Hufton, *The Prospect Before Her: A History of Women in Western Europe, 1500–1800* (New York: Alfred A. Knopf, 1996); Margaret King, *Women of the Renaissance* (Chicago: University of Chicago Press, 1991); Marie Rowlands, "Recusant Women, 1560–1640," in Mary Prior (ed.), *Women in English Society, 1500–1800* (London, New York: Methuen, 1985); and Retha Warnicke, *Women of the English Renaissance and Reformation* (Westport: Greenwood Press, 1983).

120 "It seems that the": Rowlands, 169.

120 "Wherein are we so": Warnicke, 180.

120 Worse was in store: Hufton, 384, says Mary Ward was as much victim of rumors as of her actual activities.

121 Achieving sainthood was: King, 130.

121 Catherine of Siena: The main sources for this section are Electa Arenal and Stacey Schlau (trans. Amanda Powell), *Untold Sisters: Hispanic Nuns in Their Own Works* (Albuquerque: University of New Mexico Press, 1989); Clarissa Atkinson, *Mystic and Pilgrim: The Book and the World of Margery Kempe* (Ithaca: Cornell University Press, 1983); Rudolph M. Bell, *Holy Anorexia* (Chicago: University of Chicago Press, 1985); Marcello Craveri, *Sante e Streghe: Biografie e documenti dal XIV al XVII secolo* (Saints and witches: Biographies and documents from the XIV to XVII centuries) (sections trans. Michal Kasprzak) (Milano: Feltrinelli Economica, 1980); Elizabeth A. Petroff, *Medieval Women's Visionary Literature* (Oxford: Oxford University Press, 1986); and Eileen Power, *Medieval English Nunneries, c. 1275 to 1535* (New York: Biblo and Tannen, 1964).

122 "Now I betroth you": Craveri, 70.

123 "Vilest girl, you": Bell, 41.

123 "God watch over you": Ibid., 42.

123 "Daughter, I see": Ibid., 43.

125 Not only did: Today we might be tempted to identify it as anorexia. However, Catherine's variety, common among holy women, was rooted in an asceticism that included but in no way focused on controlling food intake. Unlike with today's anorexics, who are obsessed with body image and often couple food deprivation with excessive physical exercise, the holy variety was accompanied by mortification of the flesh and spiritual exercises designed to express personal humility while glorifying God. For these reasons, I am reluctant to label Catherine of Siena an anorexic.

127 Hildegard of Bingen Frowns on Fasting: The main sources for this section are Tamara Bernstein, "Holy Hildegard: a medieval nun with '90s sex appeal," *The Globe and Mail*,

May 6, 1995; and Matthew Fox, ed., *Hildegard of Bingen's Book of Divine Works with Letters and Songs* (Santa Fe: Bear & Co., 1987).

127 "poor little figure": Bernstein.

127 Her advice, imparted: The following section quotes from Hildegard's letter to Elisabeth, who died on July 18, 1165, and is taken from Fox, 341–42.

128 Mohawk Saint Kateri Tekakwitha: The following are sources for the section on Kateri Tekakwitha: Henri Bechard, "Kateri (Catherine) Tekakwitha," *Dictionary of Canadian Biography*, vol. 1 (Toronto: University of Toronto Press, 1966); K. I. Koppedrayer, "The Making of the First Iroquois Virgin: Early Jesuit Biographies of the Blessed Kateri Tekakwitha," *Ethnohistory* 40, no. 2 (spring 1993): 277–306; Alison Prentice, Paula Bourne, Gail C. Brandt, Beth Light, Wendy Mitchinson, and Naomi Black, *Canadian Women: A History* (Toronto: Harcourt Brace Jovanovich, 1988); Nancy Shoemaker, "Kateri Tekakwitha's Tortuous Path to Sainthood," in Nancy Shoemaker, ed., *Negotiators of Change: Historical Perspectives on Native American Women* (New York: Routledge, 1995); "Lily of the Mohawks," *Newsweek*, August 1, 1938; and "The Long Road to Sainthood," *Time*, July 7, 1980.

128 In 1656, Tekakwitha: Tekakwitha was born at Ossernenon (Auriesville, New York), but spent much of her brief life near Montreal. She is, therefore, considered Canadian.

128 Tekakwitha recovered: Shoemaker, 60, says Tekakwitha was self-conscious about her appearance and, unlike other Indian women, tried to hide her face under her blanket. When she died, some people said mockingly "that God had taken her because men did not want her." Jesuit father Chauchetière, however, saw her disfigurement as a blessing that enabled her "to renounce all attachment to the flesh and embrace the state for which she was destined"—cited by Koppedrayer, 282.

129 "burned with an": Koppedrayer, 283.

129 "she had none of the": Ibid., 284.

129 "One sees savages": Ibid., 284–85.

129 "Catherine, in whom": Ibid., 284.

130 "I have deliberated": Ibid., 287.

132 Worse, she might: Prentice et al., 36, note: "Some native women met the Jesuits on their own ground by adopting celibacy, thus protecting themselves from the trials of European-style marriage, as did . . . Kateri Tekakwitha."

132 "Married people separated": Koppedrayer, 288.

133 Convents of Joy: The main sources for this section are Electa Arenal and Stacey Schlau (trans. Amanda Powell), *Untold Sisters: Hispanic Nuns in Their Own Works* (Albuquerque: University of New Mexico Press, 1989); Clarissa W. Atkinson, *Mystic and Pilgrim: The Book and the World of Margery Kempe* (Ithaca: Cornell University Press, 1983); Catherine Brown, *Pastor and Laity in the Theology of Jean Gerson* (Cambridge: Cambridge University Press, 1987); Margaret King, *Women of the Renaissance* (Chicago: University of Chicago Press, 1991); Margaret King and Albert Rabil, *Her Immaculate Hand: Selected Works by and about the Women Humanists of Quattrocento Italy* (Binghampton: Center for Medieval and Early Renaissance Studies, 1983); Elizabeth Petroff, *Medieval Women's Visionary Literature* (Oxford: Oxford University Press, 1986); Eileen Power, *Medieval English Nunneries, c. 1275 to 1535* (New York: Biblo and Tannen, 1964); Arcangela Tarabotti (sections trans. by Michal Kasprzak), *La Semplicita Ingannata* (A simple deceit) (London: Institute of Romance Studies, 1994); Foster Watson, ed., *Vives and the Renascence Education of Women* (New York: Longmans, Green and Co., 1912).

133 The thirteenth-century *Hali Meidenhad*: As devotional literature of this era, it was typical in devaluing marriage between mortals in favor of a spiritual union with Christ. All quotations from *Hali Meidenhad* are taken from Atkinson, 185–86.

135 "You sing a new song": Brown, 226–27.

135 "The virginity of the body": Watson, 87.

136 "The majority of people": Tarabotti, 202.

136 "a career, a vocation": Power, 25.

136 "I thought that from": Petroff, 256.

137 "So many pains": Arenal and Schlau, 241.

138 Unwilling Nuns: The main sources for the following section are Electa Arenal and Stacey Schlau (trans. Amanda Powell), *Untold Sisters: Hispanic Nuns in Their Own Works* (Albuquerque: University of New Mexico Press, 1989); Margaret King, *Women of the Renaissance* (Chicago: University of Chicago Press, 1991); and Eileen Power, *Medieval English Nunneries, c. 1275 to 1535* (New York: Biblo and Tannen, 1964); Guido Ruggiero, *The Boundaries of Eros: Sex Crime and Sexuality in Renaissance Venice* (New York: Oxford University Press, 1985); and Arcangela Tarabotti (trans. Michal Kasprzak), *La Semplicita Ingannata* (A simple deceit) (London: Institute of Romance Studies, 1994).

138 "My mother wished": Ruggiero, 77.

139 "Now earth to earth": Power, 31. The large number of idiots accepted into convents was a frequent complaint.

139 "imprisoned in monasteries": Ruggiero, 182, n. 23.

140 "For the physical cell": Madre Marcella de San Félix, "Loa to the Solitude of the Cells," in Arenal and Schlau, 236.

140 "I, poor and alone": Weaver, 192.

140 "guileful, weaving the web": Tarabotti, 200.

141 "There is an inscription": Ibid., 205.

141 Penalties were degrading: Arenal and Schlau, 12–13. An ex-nun of my acquaintance was accused of haughtiness and forced to clean her convent's floors with a handkerchief.

141 Saint Douceline whipped: Power, 29.

143 "as hot . . . and": Ibid., 452.

143 "Turning like a": Ibid., 453.

143 The record of documented: Ibid., chap. 11, "The Old Daunce," is filled with reports of investigations, documented sexual misadventures, charges, punishments, penances, relapses, and comparisons of the sinfulness of various cloisters.

144 An Unwilling Nun's Love Cut Short: The source for the following section, and all quotations, is Giles Constable, *Monks, Hermits and Crusaders in Medieval Europe* (London: Variorum Reprints, 1988).

145 Secular Celibates and Agape Love: The main sources for this section are John Boswell, *Same-Sex Unions in Premodern Europe* (New York: Villard Books, 1994); Peter Brown, *The Body and Society: Men, Women and Sexual Renunciation in Early Christianity* (New York: Columbia University Press, 1988); Vern L. Bullough, *Sexual Variance in Society and History* (New York: John Wiley & Sons, 1976); Averil Cameron and Amélie Kuhrt, eds., *Images of Women in Antiquity* (London: Routledge, 1983); Louise Collis, *Memoirs of a Medieval Woman: The Life and Times of Margery Kempe* (New York: Harper & Row, 1983); Aline Rousselle (trans. F. Pheasant), *Porneia: On Desire and the Body in Antiquity* (Oxford: Basil Blackwell, 1988); and G. Rattray Taylor, *Sex in History* (New York: Vanguard Press, 1954).

147 Thanks to the intimately: Her *Life* is thought to be the first extant autobiography written in English, the only language she spoke.

148 The Shakers: The biographical section on Mother Ann Lee is taken from Nordi Reeder Campion, *Mother Ann Lee: Morning Star of the Shakers* (Hanover, London: University Press of New England, 1990); Lawrence Foster, *Religion and Sexuality: Three American Communal Experiences of the Nineteenth Century* (New York: Oxford University Press, 1981); M. Gidley and K. Bowles, eds., *Locating the Shakers: Cultural Origins and Legacies of an American Religious Movement* (Exeter: University of Exeter Press, 1990); Robert Lauer and Jeanette Lauer, *The Spirit and the Flesh: Sex in Utopian Communities* (Metuchen, London: The Scarecrow Press, 1983); Raymond Muncy, *Sex and Marriage in Utopian Communities in Nineteenth-Century America* (Bloomington: University of Indiana Press, 1989); Diane Sasson, *The Shaker Spirituality Narrative* (Knoxville: Uni-

versity of Tennessee Press, 1983); and *Testimonies of the Life, Character, Revelations and Doctrines of Mother Ann Lee* (New York: AMS Press, 1975).

149 "He that is unmarried": 1 Corinthians 7:32–33. This is from the *Holy Bible*, St. James Version, that Ann would have known.

149 Reluctantly, rather than: "Her husband's conversion to Shakerism and to celibacy is the first proof we have of the power of Ann Lee." Campion, 16.

150 Slowly, the number of Shakers: The movement was also called the United Society of Believers in Christ's Second Appearing.

151 Somehow, she managed: Gidley and Bowles, 103, n. 9, suggest Stanley left Ann for a prostitute.

151 "a solum female": Ibid., 128–29.

151 "swiftly passing and": Campion, 84.

151 "Oh ho! I will": Ibid., 85.

152 "You are a filthy": Foster, 31.

152 "clad in garments of": Ibid., 62.

152 "Of all the relations": Lauer and Lauer, 220–21, 163.

153 "no pity, in their": Foster, 31, citing Hervey Elkins, who left the community after fifteen years. Though the Shakers annulled existing family relationships, many newcomers to the movement were related to already converted Shakers.

153 As late as 1810: Mother Ann herself was relentlessly persecuted, even beaten and whipped.

154 "on chains, ropes": Foster, 42, citing ex-Shaker Thomas Brown.

154 Significantly, these communications: For example, a young Shakeress claimed Mother Ann had appeared to her and revealed the Shakers should move up into the higher, married state.

155 Father Divine: This section on Father Divine relies exclusively on Jill Watts, *God, Harlem U.S.A.: The Father Divine Story* (Berkeley: University of California Press, 1992). After reading this book, I scrapped all my other sources. They were either incomplete or erroneous and portrayed him as a porky buffoon quite unlike the elegant, eloquent, and charismatic religious leader he actually was.

155 Rockville, Maryland: Watts shows convincingly that, contrary to popular myth, Father Divine did not grow up in the Deep South.

155 Gradually he developed: In this he presaged modern scientific thought, which supports this view.

155 "By 1907": Watts, 27.

156 "seemed to be as wild": Ibid., 36.

157 Like the old Shaker communes: This information was reported by Susan Hadley, a young African-American woman sent by the county district attorney to spy on Father Divine in 1930. Instead of exposing him as a scoundrel, Hadley had only praise for the blameless lifestyle she shared in his "heaven."

Chapter 4: Other Major Religions and Rites

164 Hinduism: The main sources for this section on Hinduism are Michael Aloysius, *Radhakrishnan on Hindu Moral Life and Action* (Delhi: Concept Publishing Co., 1979); Joseph S. Alter, "Celibacy, Sexuality, and the Transformation of Gender into Nationalism in North India," *Journal of Asian Studies* 53, no. 1 (February 1994): 45–66; Lawrence A. Babb, "Indigenous Feminism in a Modern Hindu Sect," *Sign: Journal of Women in Culture and Society* 9, no. 3 (1984): 399–416; Lawrence A. Babb, *Redemptive Encounters: Three Modern Styles in Hindu Tradition* (Berkeley: University of California Press, 1986); Durga Das Basu, *The Essence of Hinduism* (New Delhi: Prentice-Hall of India, 1990); Peter Brown, *The Body and Society: Men, Women and Sexual Renunciation in Early Christianity* (New York: Columbia University Press, 1988); Baba Hari Dass,

Silence Speaks (Santa Cruz: Sr. Rama Foundation, 1977); M. Dhavamony, *Classical Hinduism* (Rome: Gregorian University Press, 1982); Gavin Flood, *An Introduction to Hinduism* (Cambridge: Cambridge University Press, 1996); Sudir Kakar, *Intimate Relations: Exploring Indian Sexuality* (New Delhi: Penguin Books, 1989); Klaus K. Klostermaier, *A Survey of Hinduism*, 2nd ed. (Albany: State University of New York Press, 1994); Yogi Raushan Nath, *Hinduism and Its Dynamics* (New Delhi: Rajiv Publications, 1977); Wendy Doniger O'Flaherty, *Eroticism in the Mythology of Siva* (London: Oxford University Press, 1973); Wendy Doniger O'Flaherty, *Women, Androgynes, and Other Mythical Beasts* (Chicago: Chicago University Press, 1980); Troy Wilson Organ, *The Hindu Quest for the Perfection of Man* (Athens: Ohio University, 1970); A. C. Swami Prabhupada, *The Science of Self-Realization* (New York: Bhaketivedonta Bode Trust, 1977); Hoston Smith, *The World's Religions: Our Great Wisdom Traditions* (New York: Harper Collins Publishers, 1986); Peter Van Der Veer, "The Power of Detachment: Disciplines of Body and Mind in the Ramandandi Order," *American Ethnologist* 16 (1989): 458–70; and Stanley Wolpert, *A New History of India*, 4th ed. (New York: Oxford University Press, 1993). All quotations in the section on Shiva are from O'Flaherty, *Eroticism in the Mythology of Siva.*

164   "a unified concept": O'Flaherty, *Eroticism in the Mythology of Siva*, 8.

165   This is where the: Certain radical ascetics attempt to subdue all human lust by having sexual intercourse devoid of sensation. This, however, is not mainstream Hinduism.

166   "toil and suffering": Aloysius, 111.

166   Hindu women are: The sacred texts refer primarily to men, and in secondary literature, only a few texts suggest women may follow parallel life stages. The fundamental role that semen plays in the Hindu belief system, of course, reinforces the view of women as different beings with different destinies.

167   Celibate energy has: In chapter 5, "Celibacy to Conserve Semen," the role of semen is elaborated. See particularly the sections entitled "Indian Wrestlers" and "Gandhi's Women."

167   By retaining their semen: Sometimes, *tapas* even lends a pleasant odor to some yogis or sannyasis.

167   "a man who is": Brown, 86, cites Gandhi's comment as evidence that conservation of semen was thought to conserve a man's strength.

168   "should be controlled": Flood, 63.

168   "lives identified with": Smith, 53–54.

169   "still the body": Flood, 93.

169   "moral purity, sincere thirst": Klostermaier, 348.

169   "as ascetics, living": Van Der Veer, 462.

171   The Daughters of Brahma: This section on the Brahma Kumaris is drawn from Lawrence A. Babb, "Indigenous Feminism in a Modern Hindu Sect," *Sign: Journal of Women in Culture and Society* 9, no. 3 (1984): 399–416; and Lawrence A. Babb, *Redemptive Encounters: Three Modern Styles in Hindu Tradition* (Berkeley: University of California Press, 1986).

172   "there was a lot": Babb, *Redemptive Encounters*, 101, citing the author's interview with an elderly man.

174   Buddhism: The main sources for the section on Buddhism are Roy Amore and Julia Ching, "The Buddhist Tradition," in Willard Oxtoby, ed., *World Religions: Eastern Traditions* (Don Mills: Oxford University Press, 1996); Tessa Bartholomeusz, "The Female Mendicant in Buddhist Sri Lanka," in Joze I. Cabezon, ed., *Buddhism, Sexuality and Gender* (New York: State University of New York Press, 1992); Roger J. Corless, *The Vision of Buddhism: The Space under the Tree* (New York: Paragon House, 1989); Rita Gross, *Buddhism After Patriarchy* (New York: State University of New York Press, 1993); Hanna Havnevik, *Tibetan Buddhist Nuns* (Oxford: Norwegian University Press, 1957); Peter Hawey, *An Introduction to Buddhism: Teachings, History, Practices* (Cambridge: Cam-

bridge University Press, 1985); Shih Pao-ch'ang (trans. Kathryn Ann Tsai), *Lives of the Nuns*, 2nd ed. (Honolulu: University of Hawaii Press, 1994); Diana Y. Paul, *Women in Buddhism* (Berkeley: University of California Press, 1985); Hammalawa Saddhatissa, *Buddhist Ethics: The Path to Nirvana* (London: Wisdom Publications, 1987); Dale E. Saunders, *Buddhism in Japan* (Philadelphia: University of Pennsylvania Press, 1964); Alan Sponberg, *Attitudes Towards Women and the Feminine in Early Buddhism* (New York: State University of New York Press, 1992); S. Tachibana, *The Ethics of Buddhism* (London: Curzon Press, 1975); Kamala Tiyanavich, *Forest Recollections: Wandering Monks in 20th Century Thailand* (Honolulu: University of Hawaii Press, 1997); Karma Lekshe Tsomo, *Sisters in Solitude* (New York: State University of New York Press, 1996); Stanley Wolpert, *A New History of India*, 4th ed. (New York: Oxford University Press, 1993); and Leonard Zwilling, "Homosexuality as Seen in Indian Buddhist Texts," in Joze I. Cabezon, ed., *Buddhism, Sexuality and Gender* (New York: State University of New York Press, 1992).

175 In his sermonizing: Saddhatissa, 88.

177 Even as Buddhism spread: Buddhism spread to Nepal, Tibet, China, Japan, and most of Southeast Asia.

177 Compared to Christianity: In Japan and Tibet, however, local Buddhist practice permitted, in some circumstances, nuns and monks to marry.

179 "worse than a tiger": Tiyanavich, 134–35.

180 In 1954, Buddhists: See Wolpert, 108–9.

180 Jainism: The main sources for this section on Jainism are Paul Dundas, *The Jains* (London: Routledge, 1992); Jagdishchandra Jain, *The Jain Way of Life* (Gurgaon: Academic Press, 1991); Padmanabh S. Jaini, *The Jaina Path of Purification* (Berkeley: University of California Press, 1979); Mohan Lal Mehta, *Jaina Culture* (Varanasi: P.V. Research Institute, 1969); and Ashim Kumar Roy, *A History of the Jains* (New Delhi: Gitanjali Publishing House, 1984).

183 An apocalyptic inferno: So celibacy presents the Jains no problems of the sort faced by the Shakers or Peace movement celibates, for whom proselytization was essential.

183 Ritual Celibacy: The main sources for this section are Elizabeth Abbott, *Haiti: The Duvaliers and Their Legacy* (New York: Simon & Schuster, 1990); Frank Boas, *The Central Eskimo* (Lincoln: University of Nebraska Press, 1888 [reprinted in 1964]); Karen McCarthy Brown, *Mama Lola: Voodoo Priestess in Brooklyn* (Berkeley: University of California Press, 1991); Wade Davis, *One River: Explorations and Discoveries in the Amazon Rain Forest* (New York: Simon and Schuster, 1996); Philippe Descola (trans. Janet Lloyd), *The Spear of Twilight: Life and Death in the Amazon Jungle* (New York: New Press/HarperCollins, 1996); Katherine Dunham, *Island Possessed* (Garden City: Doubleday, 1969); James Frazer, *The Golden Bough: A Study in Magic and Religion*, vol. 2 (London: Macmillan, 1911); Michael Harner, "The Sound of Rushing Water," *Natural History* 77, no. 6 (June/July 1968): 28–33; James Peoples and Garrick Bailey, *Humanity: An Introduction to Cultural Anthropology*, 2nd ed. (St. Paul: West Publishing Co., 1991); Knud Rasmussen, "Observations on the Intellectual Culture of the Caribou Eskimos," in *Report of the Fifth Thule Expedition 1921–24*, vol. 11 (New York: Arts Press, 1976); and Edward Moffat Weyer, *The Eskimos: Their Environment and Folkways* (Hamden: Archon Books, 1969).

184 "I was not very much alive": Rasmussen, 53.

185 The Jivaro Indians: Harner, 28–33.

186 Elsewhere in the Amazon: The source for this section on the Kogi and Ika peoples is Davis, 56–57.

187 The *Acllas* of the Incan Empire: The main sources for the following section are Constance Classen, "Aesthetics and Asceticism in Inca Religion," *Anthropologica* 32 (1992): 101–6; Bernabe Cobo (trans. and ed. Roland Hamilton), *Inca Religion and Customs*, Book 1 (Austin: University of Texas Press, 1990); Mark J. Dworkin, *Mayas, Aztecs, and Incas* (Toronto: McClelland & Stewart, 1990); and Irene Silverblatt, *Moon, Sun, and*

Witches: Gender Ideologies and Class in Inca and Colonial Peru (Princeton: Princeton University Press, 1987).

187 "Women are considered": Silverblatt, 102.

188 Once chosen, neither they: Silverblatt stresses the significance of the *acllas'* selection process.

188 "and Indian men": Silverblatt, 104.

188 "Sun, eat this food": Cobo, 174.

189 They were the brides: Classen, 105, n. 5, notes the Inca's male servants, the yanacona, also remained celibate during their youth and may have been the *acclas'* male counterparts.

189 Still, it is said: Cobo, 173.

189 "the life of great queens": Silverblatt, 103.

190 These were the first: This delightful myth is recounted in Davis, *One River,* 439.

190 *Naditus* of Babylonia: The source for this section on *naditu*s is Ulla Jeyes's "The Naditu Women of Sippar," in Averil Cameron and Amelia Kuhrt, eds., *Images of Women in Antiquity* (London: Routledge, 1983), 260–72.

192 Judaism: The sources for this section on Judaism are Gary Anderson, "Celibacy or Consummation in the Garden? Reflections on Early Jewish and Christian Interpretations of the Garden of Eden," *Harvard Theological Review* 82 no. 2 (1989): 121–48); David Biale, *Eros and the Jews: From Biblical Israel to Contemporary America* (New York: Basic Books, 1992); Vern L. Bullough, *Sexual Variance in Society and History* (New York: John Wiley & Sons, 1976); Louis M. Epstein, *Sex, Laws and Customs in Judaism* (New York: Ktav Publishing House, 1967); and Robert Gordis, *Love & Sex: A Modern Jewish Perspective* (Toronto: McGraw-Hill Ryerson Ltd., 1978).

192 They are rigid: See "Celibacy as a Guarantee for Marriage," in chapter 7.

192 Masturbation and intercourse: Ironically, this has led many Israeli men "whose lives are guided by the *halachah* [religious law], which tells them when they can and cannot have sex with the wives," to seek out prostitutes, mainly from the former Soviet Union. "So, on Thursday afternoons (boys' night out in Israel), busloads of ultra-Orthodox Jews travel . . . to Tel Aviv for a few moments of passion in a massage parlor, behind a sand dune, or in an alleyway." Samuel M. Katz, "Hookers in the Holy Land," *Moment,* April 1998.

192 Marriage has the added: Epstein, 14–15.

192 In the Middle Ages: This practice stopped after the fifteenth or sixteenth century.

193 "Blessed are you": Anderson, 132.

193 "Should he therefore": Ibid., 136.

193 "What shall I do": Epstein, 141–42.

193 "We are holy": Anderson, 122.

194 Islam: The sources for this section on Islam are Abdelwahab Bouhdiba, *Sexuality in Islam* (London: Routledge & Kegan Paul, 1985); Vern L. Bullough, *Sexual Variance in Society and History* (New York: John Wiley & Sons, 1976); and Sayyid M. Rizvi, *Marriage and Morals in Islam* (Richmond: Vancouver Islamic Educational Foundation, 1990).

194 "O you young": Rizvi, 24.

194 "truly Allah loveth": Bullough, 218.

194 "the orgasm into": Bouhdiba, 7, 8, 247.

194 "O Uthman": Rizvi, 25–26.

194 "one who marries has": Ibid., 29.

Chapter 5: Celibacy to Conserve Semen

198 *Totus Homo Semen Est:* The main sources for this section are Michael Bliss, "Pure Books on Avoided Subjects," *Historical Papers* (1970): 89–108; Sue Blundell, *Women in Ancient Greece* (London: British Museum Press, 1995); Max Braithwaite, *Never Sleep Three in a*

Bed (Toronto: McClelland & Stewart, 1969); Peter Cominos, "Late-Victorian Respectability," *International Review of Social History* 8, nos. 1, 2 (1963): 18–48, 216–50; Amma F. Angell Drake, *What a Young Wife Ought to Know* (Philadelphia: Vir Publishing Co., 1908); Robin Lane Fox, *Christians and Pagans* (Harmondsworth: Viking, 1986); Sylvester Graham, *Graham's Lectures on Chastity, specially intended for the serious consideration of young men and parents* (Glasgow: Royalty Buildings, [1848], 1900); John S. Haller and Robin M. Haller, *The Physician and Sexuality in Victorian America* (Urbana: University of Illinois Press, 1974); Brian Inglis, *A History of Medicine* (London: Weidenfeld and Nicolson, 1965); J. H. Kellogg, *Plain Facts for Young and Old* (first published as *Plain Facts about Sexual Life*) (Buffalo: Heritage Press, 1974); Rosalyn M. Meadow and Lillie Weiss, *Women's Conflicts about Eating and Sexuality* (New York: Haworth Press, 1992); John Money, *The Destroying Angel: Sex, Fitness and Food in the Legacy of Degeneracy Theory, Graham Crackers, Kellogg's Corn Flakes & American Health History* (Buffalo: Prometheus Books, 1985); Stephen Nissenbaum, *Sex, Diet, and Debility in Jacksonian America* (Westport: Greenwood Press, 1980); Elaine Pagels, *Adam, Eve, and the Serpent* (New York: Vintage Books, 1989); Jody Rubin Pinault, *Hippocratic Lives and Legends* (New York: E. J. Brill, 1992); Ute Ranke-Heinemann, *Eunuchs for the Kingdom of Heaven: Women, Sexuality and the Catholic Church* (New York: Doubleday, 1990); Aline Rousselle (trans. F. Pheasant), *Porneia: On Desire and the Body in Antiquity* (Oxford: Basil Blackwell, 1988); Richard W. Schwartz, *John Harvey Kellogg, M.D.* (Nashville: Southern Publishing Association, 1970); M. L. Shanley, *Feminism, Marriage and the Law in Victorian England, 1850–1895* (Princeton: Princeton University Press, 1989); Carroll Smith-Rosenberg, "Sex as Symbol in Victorian Purity: An Ethnohistorical Analysis of Jacksonian America," *American Journal of Sociology* 84, supp. (1978); Jayme Sokolow, *Eros and Modernization: Sylvester Graham, Health Reform, and the Origins of Victorian Sexuality in America* (London, Toronto: Associated University Press, 1983); Gerhard Venzmer, *Five Thousand Years of Medicine* (London: Macdonald & Company, 1972); Ronald G. Walters, *Primers for Prudery: Sexual Advice to Victorian Americans* (Englewood Cliffs: Prentice-Hall, 1973); and Barbara Welter, "The Cult of True Womanhood," *American Quarterly* 18, no. 2 (1966): 151–74.

198   Hippocrates, the great: Hippocrates lived from 460–377 B.C.

199   "in general, nocturnal": Rousselle, 66.

199   "The nature of the": Pagels, 109.

200   "the Essential Oil": Sokolow, 79.

201   "Hundreds of young men": Cominos, 32.

202   Similarly, rural men: Smith-Rosenberg, 237, discusses this same concept in the USA. There, fathers preserved their seed for the future well-being of their children, born and unborn.

202   Let us call: This composite Davy is drawn from data in Smith-Rosenberg, 212–47.

203   The chaos, formlessness: Smith-Rosenberg; Walters; Graham; Kellogg; and Haller and Haller.

203   "convulsive paroxysms attending": Sokolow, 92. For these reformers, male urban youth "represented the struggle between order and formlessness. . . . The sexual and social temptations that endangered his body threatened the order and structure of society."

204   Fear of disease: These bland foods replaced rich, spicy, tempting, stimulating tastes that the trio taught led to moral corruption and wanton behavior. Meadow and Weiss, 114, write: "No wonder our mothers gave us milk and Graham crackers before shipping us off to bed! How come we did not suspect all this time that these innocent crackers would quiet our stirrings? We also did not suspect that when Mom fed us Kellogg's Corn Flakes the next morning for breakfast, it was to reinforce the last night's quietings of our passions. Isn't it strange . . . that Mom insisted on a good breakfast when we reached adolescence and might harbor erotic thoughts? We marvel at the heights to which society has gone to curb women's appetites!"

204 "insufferable mental and": Sokolow, 79.

204 "thoughtless, rash and": Smith-Rosenberg, 231, citing Alcott's *Young Men's Guide.*

204 "become accustomed to": Nissenbaum, 119.

205 Pure Books on Avoided Subjects: The female equivalents, *What a Young Girl Ought to Know* and *What a Young Woman Ought to Know,* were by Dr. Mary Wood-Allen. *What a Young Wife Ought to Know* and *What a Woman of 45 Ought to Know* were the work of Dr. Emma F. Angell Drake.

205 To impress upon young: Other medical treatments for masturbation were suturing with silver wire and applying blisters and tonics.

205 "only for throwing": Drake, 88–89.

205 The Male Purity Movement: In England, the parallel social purity movement sought to stamp out many kinds of illegal sexual activity: premarital sex, prostitution, child prostitution, and white slavery. Shanley, 92.

206 "an anomaly of sexual": Money, 84.

207 Other problematic activities: Ibid.

207 In his own long life: The above exposition of Kellogg's views comes from Kellogg, 182–96, 174–77.

209 The Greeks Train Sound Minds in Chaste Bodies: The main sources for this section on Greek athletics are Sue Blundell, *Women in Ancient Greece* (London: British Museum Press, 1995); Walter Burkert, *Homo Necans: The Anthropology of Ancient Greek Sacrificial Ritual and Myth* (Berkeley: University of California Press, 1983); Clement of Alexandria (trans. J. Ferguson), *Stromateis* (Washington, D.C.: Catholic University of America Press, 1991); Robin Lane Fox, *Christians and Pagans* (Harmondsworth: Viking, 1986); H. A. Harris, *Greek Athletes and Athletics* (London: Hutchinson & Co., 1964); Hugh Lloyd-Jones, "Artemis and Iphigeneia," *Journal of Hellenic Studies* 103 (1983): 87–102; Jody Rubin Pinault, *Hippocratic Lives and Legends* (New York: E. J. Brill, 1992); Plato (trans. R. G. Bury), *Laws,* vol. 11 (New York: G. P. Putnam's Sons, 1926); Pliny (trans. W. Jones), *Natural History,* vol. 8 (Cambridge: Harvard University Press, 1963); Plutarch (trans. E. L. Minar), *Moralia,* vol. 9 (Cambridge: Harvard University Press, 1961); Ute Ranke-Heinemann, *Eunuchs for the Kingdom of Heaven: Women, Sexuality and the Catholic Church* (New York: Doubleday, 1990); H. W. Smyth, trans., and H. Lloyd-Jones, ed., *Aeschylus,* vol. 11 (Cambridge: Harvard University Press, 1987), app.; and Waldo E. Sweet, *Sport and Recreation in Ancient Greece* (New York: Oxford University Press, 1987).

209 "possessed much stronger": Sweet, 115.

209 "Cum decurtatas, tanquan": From *Aeschylus.* Latin translated by Paul Mayer.

210 "bold, daring, and": Pinault, 127.

210 "semen, when possessed": Ibid., 128, citing Arteaeus.

210 "since they now": Sweet, 227.

211 The Victorians Exercise Muscular Christianity: The main sources for this section are G. J. Barker-Benfield, *The Horrors of the Half-Known Life: Male Attitudes Toward Women and Sexuality in 19th-Century America* (New York: Harper & Row, 1976); Ray B. Browne, *Objects of Social Devotion: Fetishism in Popular Culture* (Bowling Green: Bowling Green University Popular Press, 1982); Pat Caplan, "Celibacy as a Solution? Mahatma Gandhi and Brahmacharya," in Pat Caplan, ed., *The Cultural Construction of Sexuality* (New York: Routledge, 1987); Michael A. Messner, *Power at Play: Sports and the Problem of Masculinity* (Boston: Beacon Press, 1992); M. A. Messner and D. F. Sabo, eds., *Sport, Men, and the Gender Order: Critical Feminist Perspectives* (Champaign: Human Kinetics Publishers, 1990); Donald J. Mrozek, *Sport and American Mentality, 1880–1910* (Knoxville: University of Tennessee Press, 1984); Stephen J. Overman, *The Influence of the Protestant Ethic on Sport and Recreation* (Aldershot: Avebury, 1997); and David Q. Voigt, "Sex in Baseball: Reflections of Changing Taboos," *Journal of Popular Science* 12, no. 3 (1978): 389–403.

Notes

212 "What are you running": Overman, 199.

212 The Cherokees Play Ball: The source for this section on Cherokee ball play is James Mooney, "The Cherokee Ball Play," *American Anthropologist* 111, no. 2 (April 1990): 105–32.

214 Today's Chaste Athletes: The main sources for this section on modern sports are Lisa Alther, *Kinflicks* (New York: Alfred A. Knopf, 1976); Mark H. Anshel, "Effects of Sexual Activity on Athletic Performance," *Physician and Sportsmedicine* 9, no. 8 (August 1981): 64–68; Tommy Boone and Stephanie Gilmore, "Effects of sexual intercourse on maximal aerobic power, oxygen pulse, and double product in male sedentary subjects," *Journal of Sports Medicine and Physical Fitness* 35, no. 3 (September 3, 1995): 214–17; *The Complete Runner* (Mountain View: World Publications, 1974); B. J. Cratty, *Psychology in Contemporary Sport: Guidelines for Coaches and Athletes* (Englewood Cliffs: Prentice-Hall, 1973); Gloria J. Fischer, "Abstention from Sex and Other Pre-Game Rituals Used by College Male Varsity Athletes," *Journal of Sport Behavior* 20, no. 2 (1997): 176–84; Lloyd Garrison, "Has the Bear Lost Its Claws?" *Time* 131, no. 6 (February 1988): 54; Michael Gordon, "College Coaches' Attitudes toward Pregame Sex," *Journal of Sex Research* 5 (1988): 256–62; Nathan Hare, "A Study of the Black Fighter," *Black Scholar* 3, no. 3 (1971): 2–9; Warren R. Johnson, "Muscular Performance Following Coitus," *Journal of Sex Research* 4, no. 3 (August 1968): 247–48; Jules Older, "New Zealand Coaches' Attitudes to Pre-Event Sex," *Journal of Popular Culture* 19 (1985): 93–96; "Sex and Sports: To partake or abstain before games, that is the question," *Sports Illustrated*, posted on CNN/SI June 2, 1998; Richard Starnes, "Sex Added Incentive for England to Shine," *Ottawa Citizen*, June 15, 1998; and James S. Thornton, "Sexual Activity and Athletic Performance: Is There a Relationship?" *Physician and Sportsmedicine* 18, no. 3 (March 1990): 148–54.

214 The Greatest is not: This will be discussed at greater length in chapter 13, "The New Celibacy."

215 "It is well known": Boone and Gilmore, 214.

216 "It isn't sex": *The Complete Runner*, 159.

217 Indian Wrestlers: The source for this section is Joseph S. Alter, *The Wrestler's Body: Identity and Ideology in North India* (Berkeley: University of California Press, 1992).

217 "Celibacy is the paramount": Ibid., 90, citing K. P. Singh.

217 Wrestlers—*pahalwans*: See below for the section on Gandhi and brahmacharya.

217 "We emphasize brahmacharya": Alter, 129. Personal interview with Narayan Singh.

218 "Just like ghi": Ibid., 151.

218 "Wrestlers are uniformly": Ibid., 134.

218 As well, they are: Ibid., 134–35.

218 "extraordinary men who": Ibid., 3.

219 Brahmacharya and the Power of Semen: The main sources for this section are Joseph S. Alter, "Celibacy, Sexuality, and the Transformation of Gender into Nationalism in North India," *Journal of Asian Studies* 53, no. 1 (February 1994): 45–66; *Bapu's Letters to Mira (1924–1948)* (Ahmedabad: Navajivan Press, 1949); Judith Brown, *Gandhi: Prisoner of Hope* (New Haven: Yale University Press, 1989); Mahatma Gandhi, *My Religion* (Ahmedabad: Navajivan Publishing House, 1955); Mahatma Gandhi (trans. Mahadev Desai), *An Autobiography or The Story of My Experiments With Truth* (Ahmedabad: Navajivan Publishing House, 1959); Pushpa Joshi, *Gandhi on Women (Collection of Mahatma Gandhi's Writings and Speeches on Women)* (Ahmedabad: Navajivan Publishing House, 1988); Sudkir Kakur, *Intimate Relations: Exploring Indian Sexuality* (Chicago: University of Chicago Press, 1990); Millie G. Polak, *Mr. Gandhi: The Man* (London: George Allen & Unwin Ltd., 1931); and Irving Wallace, Amy Wallace, Sylvia Wallace, and David Wallechinsky, *The Intimate Sex Lives of Famous People* (New York: Delacorte Press, 1981).

219 "only noble and": Gandhi, *An Autobiography*, 112.

220 "an incomplete brahmachari": Kakur, 105, citing Gandhi's letter to a confidante, Prema Kantak.

220 "is to build up": Alter, 51. According to Kakur, 119, "Indian metaphysical physiology maintains that food is converted into semen in a thirty-day period by successive transformations (and refinements) through blood, flesh, fat, bone, and marrow till semen is distilled—forty drops of blood producing one drop of semen. Each ejaculation involves a loss of half an ounce of semen, which is equivalent to the vitality produced by the consumption of sixty pounds of food. . . . Each act of copulation is equivalent to an energy expenditure of twenty-four hours of concentrated mental activity or seventy-two hours of hard physical labor."

220 "Chastity is one": Brown, 86, cites Gandhi's comment as evidence that conservation of semen was thought to conserve a man's strength.

220 "Celibacy . . . is like": Gandhi, *My Religion,* 152.

221 "a strange girl": Wallace et al., 340.

221 "What other outcome": Gandhi, *An Autobiography,* 20–22.

221 "If one": Ibid., 48.

222 "the real postscript": Wallace et al., 112.

222 "I could not steal": Ibid., 96.

222 "I have found": Ibid., 102.

222 "Sometimes I think": Polak, 83–84.

223 "The hand that has": Ibid., 111–12.

223 "A woman, as soon": Joshi, 274.

224 "The parting today": *Bapu's Letters to Mira,* March 22, 1927, 30.

224 "I could not": Ibid., September 26, 1927, 46.

224 "This is merely": Ibid., September 29, 1927, 47.

224 "I have never been": Ibid., October 2, 1927, 47.

225 Seen in this light: Anthropologist Alter, 61, believes the most striking feature of Gandhi's experiments is "their utterly banal character."

226 Indeed, in idealizing: Gandhi also believed menstrual blood was a stigmata of *vikara,* the sexual distortions of a woman's soul, and that truly celibate women ceased menstruating.

227 Semen as Patriotic Elixir: My main source for this section is Joseph S. Alter, "Celibacy, Sexuality, and the Transformation of Gender into Nationalism in North India," *Journal of Asian Studies* 53, no. 1 (February 1994): 45–66.

227 "Because the youth": Ibid., 49.

228 "analyze the mechanics": Ibid., 50–51.

228 "To tell the truth": Ibid., 52.

229 "Open your eyes": Ibid., 59, citing Shivananda, 1984.

Chapter 6: Female Celibacy Transcends Gender

231 Joan of Arc: The main sources for this section are Marie-Véronique Clin, "Joan of Arc and Her Doctors," in Bonnie Wheeler and Charles T. Wood, eds., *Fresh Verdicts on Joan of Arc* (New York, London: Garland Publishing, 1996); Susan Crane, "Clothing and Gender Definition: Joan of Arc," *Journal of Medieval and Early Modern Studies* 26, no. 2 (spring 1996): 297–315; Kelly DeVries, "A Woman as Leader of Men: Joan of Arc's Military Career," in Wheeler and Wood; Marjorie Garber, *Vested Interests: Cross-Dressing and Cultural Anxiety* (New York: HarperPerennial, 1992); *Holy Bible,* NRSV; Henry Ansgar Kelly, "Joan of Arc's Last Trial: The Attack of the Devil's Advocates," in Wheeler and Wood; Melanie Perry, ed., *Biographical Dictionary of Women* (Edinburgh: Chambers, 1996); Jane Marie Pinzino, "Speaking of Angels: A Fifteenth-Century Bishop in Defense of Joan of Arc's Mystical Voices," in Wheeler and Wood; and Susan Schibanoff, "True Lies: Transvestism and Idolatry in the Trial of Joan of Arc," in Wheeler and Wood.

231 "Her hair cropped": Schibanoff, 42.

231 "A woman shall": *Holy Bible,* NRSV.

232 "for as long": Crane, 305.

232 "All regarded her": DeVries, 7.
232 "Everyone marveled": Ibid., 9.
233 "softly put his": Schibanoff, 54.
234 "Dress is a small thing": Crane, 301.
234 "It pleases God": Ibid., 302–3.
234 "there are enough": Ibid., 310.
235 "shaved off and": Schibanoff, 37–38.
235 A Crow Nation Gender-Bender: The sources for this section are Edwin Thompson Denig (ed. John C. Ewers), *Five Indian Tribes of the Upper Missouri* (Norman: University of Oklahoma Press, 1961); Judith Lorber, *Paradoxes of Gender* (New Haven: Yale University Press, 1994); and James Peoples and Garrick Bailey, *Humanity: An Introduction to Cultural Anthropology* (St. Paul: West Publishing Co., 1991).
237 "neither savage nor": Denig, 195–200.
237 Woman Chief was: Woman Chief also inspired other native women interested in the warrior life. However, an Assiniboin woman who tried to emulate her was killed in her first war expedition. Running Eagle, a Piegan woman warrior, was killed after successfully leading several war parties. She, too, may have been inspired by the famous Woman Chief.
238 Amazons of Old Dahomey: The source for this section is Tim Newark, *Women Warriors: An Illustrated History of Female Warriors* (London: Blandford, 1989). During a recent summer I spent in Benin, the former Dahomey, two knowledgeable princes assured me that the Dahomean Amazons were historical realities. They also mentioned that these women had been celibate.
238 "The Amazons are": Newark, 42.
239 "They are savage": Ibid., 48.
239 Their celibacy, which: However, we do not know if they were lifelong celibates or if, like the vestal virgins, they could opt for marriage after a set period of service.
239 Elizabeth I, the Virgin Queen: The sources for the following section are Edith Sitwell, *Fanfare for Elizabeth* (London: Macmillan & Co., 1946); Lytton Strachey, *Elizabeth and Essex* (Oxford: Oxford University Press, 1981); and Neville Williams, *The Life and Times of Elizabeth I* (London: Weidenfeld and Nicolson, 1972).
240 Anne went from: Anne held the forlorn hope that she might be sent to a convent rather than executed.
240 Elizabeth's caretakers, understanding: They must have known—and may have discussed in front of Elizabeth—that as soon as Henry had heard the axman had severed Anne's head, he had leapt onto the royal barge and spent the day with Jane.
240 Henry's last wife: Her first left her a widow at age fifteen.
241 "I will not do": Sitwell, 183.
242 Elizabeth's advisers perfunctorily: One candidate, Charles IX of France, was only fifteen when she was over thirty.
243 "In the end": Williams, 102–3.
243 "I will have here": Ibid., 131.
244 "I hate the idea": Strachey, 17.
244 "she has truly": Ibid., 129.
244 "as soon as I": Ibid., 138–39.
244 "little black husband": Williams, 215.
245 "She rul'd this Nation": Ibid., 354.
245 Florence Nightingale: The main sources for the following section are Monica Baly, ed., *As Miss Nightingale Said . . .* , *Florence Nightingale Through Her Sayings—A Victorian Perspective* (London: Scutari Press, 1991); Vern L. Bullough et al., eds., *Florence Nightingale and Her Era: A Collection of New Scholarship* (New York: Garland Publishing, 1990); Elspeth Huxley, *Florence Nightingale* (London: Weidenfeld and Nicolson, 1975); Florence Nightingale, *Notes on Nursing,* new ed. (London: Harrison & Sons, 1914); and Martha

Vicinus and Bea Nergaard, eds., *Ever Yours, Florence Nightingale: Selected Letters* (Cambridge: Harvard University Press, 1990).

245 "people bamboozle their": Vicinus and Nergaard, 40.

246 "organized . . . accordingly": Ibid., 40–41.

246 "Today I am": Baly, 19.

246 "In my thirty-first": Ibid., 15.

246 "This is the life": Ibid., 19.

247 Twice she fell: In Bullough et al., 23–29. Marian J. Brook is very plausible in support of this theory.

248 "intoxication, drunken brutality": Ibid., 26.

248 "The whole occupation": Ibid., 32.

248 "to keep clear of": Huxley, 190.

249 British Spinsters Strike against Sex: Most material for this section is taken from Deborah Epstein Nord, "Neither Pairs nor Odd: Female Community in Late Nineteenth Century London," *Signs: Journal of Women in Culture and Society* 15, no. 4 (summer 1990): 733–54. Also used are Lucy Bland, *Banishing the Beast: Sexuality and the Feminists* (New York: New Press, 1995); Havelock Ellis, *Sonnets with Folk Songs from the Spanish* and *Man and Woman* (Waltham Saint Lawrence: Golden Cockerel Press, 1925); Phyllis Grosskurth, *Havelock Ellis: A Biography* (Toronto: McClelland & Stewart, 1980); Olwen Hufton, *The Prospect Before Her: A History of Women in Western Europe 1500–1800* (New York: Alfred A. Knopf, 1996); Sheila Jeffreys, *The Spinster and Her Enemies: Feminism and Sexuality, 1880–1930* (London: Pandora Press, 1985); Melvyn New, ed., *The Complete Novels and Selected Writings of Amy Levy, 1861–1889* (Gainseville: University Press of Florida, 1993); Beatrice Potter Webb (ed. Norman and Jeanne MacKenzie), *The Diary of Beatrice Webb,* vol. 1 (London: Virago, 1982); and Virginia Woolf (ed. Mitchell A. Leaska), *The Pargiters* (London: Hogarth Press, 1978).

249 "In the hearts of": Jeffreys, 90.

249 From 1821, when: Bland, 162, offers these statistics: in 1881, 1,055 women to every 1,000 men, rising by 1911 to 1,068.

250 "must sacrifice all": Ibid., 88.

250 Except for those: Hamilton was also a member of the Actresses Franchise League.

251 "wherever women are": Jeffreys, 93.

251 Beatrice Potter: Later Webb, when she married Fabian socialist Sydney Webb.

252 "as impassable, save": Woolf, 37.

252 "Who would have": Webb, 139.

252 "Ere all the world": New, 401.

253 "a funny place": Ibid., 746.

253 "If the fates": Webb, 111.

253 After nearly a decade: Amy Levy committed suicide. Olive Schreiner and Maggie Harkness went abroad. Beatrice Potter became more politicized and later married Fabian socialist Sydney Webb.

254 Sexology's founding fathers: The introduction to the Sex Reform Congress of 1929 so acknowledged the trio. Jeffreys, 128.

254 "women's special sphere": Ellis, *Man and Woman,* 447.

255 "spinsterhood, and the right": Jeffreys, 144–45.

255 The "fanaticism and crankiness": Ibid., 175. Haldane omitted their work in the movements against slavery, child labor, and war.

255 "intermediate women may": Ibid.

Chapter 7: Celibacy as Womanly Duty

257 Celibacy as a Guarantee for Marriage: The main sources for this section are my overall research for this book and also Helene Fisher, *Anatomy of Love: The Natural History of*

Monogamy, Adultery and Divorce (New York: Norton, 1992); A. D. Harvey, *Sex in Georgian England* (London: Duckworth, 1994); Beverley Jackson, *Splendid Slippers: A Thousand Years of an Erotic Tradition* (Berkeley: Ten Speed Press, 1997); Howard S. Levy, *Chinese Footbinding: The History of the Curious Erotic Custom* (New York: Walton Rawls, 1966); Lynn Margulis and Dorion Sagan, *Mystery Dance: On the Evolution of Human Sexuality* (New York: Summit Books, 1991); Xiao Zhou, "Virginity and Marital Sex in Contemporary China," *Feminist Studies* 15 (summer 1989): 279–88; and Richard Zacks, *History Laid Bare: Love, Sex and Perversity from the Etruscans to Warren G. Harding* (New York: HarperCollins, 1994).

257   One study of: Martin Whyte extrapolated from the Human Relations Area File of over eight hundred societies. From this data bank, Whyte studied ninety-three societies and concluded that in 88 percent, all local and intermediate political leaders are male and that in 84 percent, males are also the leaders in the kin group. Fischer, 286.

257   China has traditionally: According to *The Economist*, November 8, 1997, a researcher into the suicide phenomenon reports that girls "are not 'highly valued' and so learn to place little value on their own lives."

257   What is certain: Nonagricultural aboriginal societies in North America, Australia, and Africa operate in a manner that may once have been typical of most societies: with relative equality between men and women and without the obsession with female chastity. They usually value chastity for its spiritual power, and shamans and warriors practice it for prescribed periods. Examples are the Igbo people of Nigeria, the Montagnais-Naskapi Indians of eastern Canada, and the aborigines of the Australian outback. Fisher, 211–14. Also Zhou, 279: "As in most societies, virginity in China is only a concern for women."

257   Conversely, a few: Amerindian societies, for instance, and among the Incas, the lower-ranking classes.

258   Clearly, in most cases: Harvey, 3–5, citing statistics reconstructed by the Cambridge Group for the Study of Population and Social Structure.

258   A second major reason: See chapters 2 and 3.

258   Virginity in brides: Zhou, 287. Even today in China, "a woman's power resources come from her virginity" but also her "resistance to early marriage." Traditionally, her family arranged the marriage.

258   that the children: Despite this, far-ranging studies of men from the jungle-dwelling Yanomamo of Venezuela to American Midwesterners show that about 10 percent erroneously believe they are fathers of children sired by someone else. These cuckolded men demonstrate the importance of a bride's intact hymen. Margulis and Sagan, 120.

259   The indefatigable sexuality: As Margulis and Sagan, 96, tell it, "Women enchanted men with their rotundity and curves, becoming sexually attractive virtually all the time—and therefore eluding the attempts of selfish males to mate with women only when they were ovulating."

259   Virgins and Disgraced Maidens: The main sources for this section are Geraldine Brooks, *Nine Parts of Desire: The Hidden World of Islamic Women* (New York: Anchor Books, 1995); A. D. Harvey, *Sex in Georgian England* (London: Duckworth, 1994); Sarah Pomeroy, *Goddesses, Whores, Wives, and Slaves: Women in Classical Antiquity* (New York: Schocken, 1975); Roy Porter, *English Society in the Eighteenth Century* (London: Penguin, 1990); Guilia Sissa, *Greek Virginity* (Cambridge, London: Harvard University Press, 1990); and Xiao Zhou, "Virginity and Premarital Sex in Contemporary China," *Feminist Studies* 15 (summer 1989): 279–88. Several newspaper accounts of recent events in Muslim countries were also used.

260   "wing-broken bird": Zhou, 80, 84.

260   These unmaidenly maidens: Often, girls were not even named. They were regarded as temporary residents of their homes who would soon leave their parents' roof to live with their in-laws.

261 In this line: "A girl was ideally first married at fourteen to a man of about thirty." Pomeroy, 64. The age of menarche was usually later than fourteen, so girls weren't yet in physical, hormonal turmoil.

261 "honor killings": Palestinian authorities treat these killings as crimes of passion, which carry reduced sentences. "Upholding Men's Honor Takes a Deadly Toll," *Toronto Star,* September 8, 1996.

261 Soon afterward, she: Brooks, 53.

261 "They feel that": *Toronto Star,* September 8, 1996.

262 She was shot to death: This is my interpretation of one version of the Mishaal story told by Brooks, 50.

262 As with countless unfortunate women: In 1997, a Cairo bride's father beheaded her for the crime of having eloped. He then strutted about his low-income neighborhood boasting, "Now the family has regained its honor."

262 Testing for Maidenheads: The main sources for this section are Jan Bremmer, ed., *From Sappho to De Sade: Moments in the History of Sexuality* (London, New York: Routledge, 1989); Edwidge Danticat, *Breath, Eyes, Memory* (New York: Soho, 1994); N. El Saadawi,· *The Hidden Face of Eve: Women in the Arab World* (London: Zed Press, 1980); Lynn Margulis and Dorion Sagan, *Mystery Dance: On the Evolution of Human Sexuality* (New York: Summit Books, 1991); Lawrence Osborne, *The Poisoned Embrace: A Brief History of Sexual Pessimism* (London: Bloomsbury, 1993); Guilia Sissa, *Greek Virginity* (Cambridge, London: Harvard University Press, 1990); and Richard Zacks, *History Laid Bare: Love, Sex and Perversity from the Etruscans to Warren G. Harding* (New York: HarperCollins, 1994).

262 This is unfortunate: Margulis and Sagan, 118, quote Robert Smith, ed., "Human Sperm Competition," in *Sperm Competition and the Evolution of Animal Mating Systems,* 642: the hymen is "one of the great unsolved mysteries of human anatomy." Perhaps, they suggest, the hymen was originally a minor defect like webbed fingers or toes.

262 "When I was a girl": Danticat, 60–61.

262 She stuck her fingers: First Gospel of James 19–20, Pseudo-Matthew 13:3–5.

262 Postpartum Mary had: So, centuries later, did Joan of Arc. Her captor, the Duke of Bedford, ordered two women to examine her and allegedly spied on the proceedings. Joan's hymen was still in place, though horseback riding had scarred her bottom.

263 Variations on this method: French medical professor Nicolas Venette gave this advice in a 1687 sex manual. Bremmer, 91.

263 "Those who died": Sissa, 83.

263 In Algeria, the older women: This is a common test. "My mother always listened to the echo of my urine in the toilet, for if it was too loud, it meant that I had been deflowered," writes Danticat, 154.

263 In ancient Greece: In Isabel Allende's novel *Eva Luna,* Eva's godmother uses a knotted cord to measure the circumference of her head, which will reveal whether she is a virgin.

264 Exceptional Aztec: The main sources for this section are Miguel Léon-Portilla, *The Aztec Image of Self and Society: Introduction to Nahua Culture* (Salt Lake City: University of Utah Press, 1992); and Alfredo Lopez-Austin, *The Human Body and Ideology: Concepts of the Ancient Nahuas* (Salt Lake City: University of Utah Press, 1988).

264 Enga: The main sources for this section are Paul W. Brennan, *Let Sleeping Snakes Lie: Central Enga Traditional and Religious Belief and Ritual* (Adelaide: Australian Association for the Study of Religions, 1977); B. Carrad, D. Lea, and K. Talyaga, eds., *Enga: Foundations for Development* (Armidale, Australia: University of New England, 1982); Robert J. Gordon and Mervyn J. Meggitt, *Law and Order in the New Guinea Highlands* (Hanover, London: University of Vermont Press, 1985); Shirley Lindenbaum, "Sorcerers, Ghosts, and Polluting Women: An Analysis of Religious Belief and Population Control," *Ethnology* 11 (1972): 241–53; Carol P. MacCormack, ed., *Ethnography of Fertility and Birth* (London: Academic Press, 1982); J. Meggitt, *The Lineage System of the Mae-*

Enga of New Guinea (New York: Barnes & Noble, 1965); Mervyn Meggitt, *Blood Is Their Argument* (Palo Alto: Mayfield Publishing Co., 1977); and Eric Waddell, *The Mound Builders: Agricultural Practices, Environment, and Society in the Central Highlands of New Guinea* (Seattle, London: University of Washington Press, 1972).

266 "My precious necklace": Abridged from citations in Léon-Portilla, 190–94.

266 "We marry the people": Meggitt, *Lineage,* 101.

267 "balletic episodes": Meggitt, *Blood Is Their Argument,* 19.

267 "in the absence": Lindenbaum, 311.

267 At four-day retreats: Meggitt, *Lineage,* 234.

267 During these encounters: The men finger their penises during the entire unmarried period. Lindenbaum, 312.

268 "payment for the": Meggitt, *Lineage,* 127.

268 That Pesky Double Standard: The sources for the section on canonical law are James A. Brundage, "Prostitution in the Medieval Canon Law," *Signs: Journal of Women in Culture and Society* 1, no. 4 (1976): 825–45; and Keith Thomas, "The Double Standard," *Journal of the History of Ideas* 20 (April 1959): 195–216.

269 This moral conflict: This was about 1140.

269 Though a privileged young: In contrast to Georgian times, when among the very high-born, a certain latitude existed.

270 "Resist, resist!": Thomas, 195–96.

270 "Winchester geese": Ibid., 198.

270 "Remove prostitutes from": Ibid., 197.

270 "Herself the supreme": Ibid.

270 Harlots for Hire: The sources for this section are Bernard Mandeville, *A Modest Defence of Publick Stews* (London: 1724; the Augustan Reprint Society, introduction by Richard I. Cook; pub. no. 162, William Andrews Clark Memorial Library, University of California, Los Angeles); and Naomi Wolf, *Fire with Fire.*

271 "The gravest consequences": Mandeville, 3–4.

271 "All our late": Ibid., 41.

271 "All young Women": Ibid., 41–42.

272 "When he enters": Ibid., 37.

272 "The only way to": Ibid., 50–51.

272 "prefer the ready": Ibid., 59.

273 "all women suffer": Wolf, 111.

273 Outraged Women Demand Chaste Men: The sources for this section are Lucy Bland, *Banishing the Beast: Sexuality and the Early Feminists* (New York: New Press, 1995); Fraser Harrison, *The Dark Angel: Aspects of Victorian Sexuality* (London: Fontana, 1979); Sheila Jeffreys, *The Spinster and Her Enemies: Feminism and Sexuality, 1880–1930* (London: Pandora Press, 1985); Derrik Mercer, ed., *Chronicle of Britain* (London: Chronicle Publications, 1992); Mary Lynn Shanley, *Feminism, Marriage and the Law in Victorian England, 1850–1895* (London: Tauris, 1989); Keith Thomas, "The Double Standard," *Journal of the History of Ideas* 20 (April 1959): 195–216; and Richard Zacks, *History Laid Bare: Love, Sex and Perversity from the Etruscans to Warren G. Harding* (New York: HarperCollins, 1994).

273 "go a bad way": Harrison, 231.

273 "Why shouldn't we": Ibid., 247.

274 These Acts authorized: Shanley, 84.

274 Homeless girls were: Mercer, 927, 938.

274 "What think you of": Thomas, 205.

275 "a degraded life": Jeffreys, 12.

275 "Ay, I know that": Ibid., 14.

275 "Is it fair for": Ibid., 15.

276 What the Union members: Ibid., 19, 20.

276 The Contagious Diseases Acts: The campaign against the Acts was spearheaded by Mrs. Josephine Butler of the Ladies Association for the Repeal of the Contagious Diseases Acts.

276 "The man or woman": Jeffreys, 50. The author of these stirring lines wrote them to the *Freewoman* magazine.

276 The other myth: Other "symptoms" of too much celibacy were lunacy, spermatorrhea in males, and hysteria in women.

277 His grandstanding journalistic: Stead advertised his sensational, four-article series with the following: "WARNING: All you who are squeamish and all who are prudish, and . . . prefer to live in a fool's paradise of imaginary innocence and purity . . . will do *well not to read the* Pall Mall Gazette *of Monday and the following three days*." Bland, xv. Quotations from Stead's articles in the *Pall Mall Gazette,* July 6, 1885, are taken from Zacks, 399–404.

278 "An Earthquake has": Bland, xvi.

278 The legislators, secret clients: Thomas, 199; Zacks, 404.

279 White Women, Black Men: The main sources for this section are Catherine Clinton, *The Plantation Mistress: Women's World in the Old South* (New York: Pantheon Books, 1982); John D'Emilio and Estelle Freedman, *Intimate Matters: A History of Sexuality in America* (New York: Harper & Row, 1988); Elizabeth Fox Genovese, *Within the Plantation Household: Black and White Women of the Old South* (Chapel Hill: University of North Carolina Press, 1988); Eugene Genovese, *Roll, Jordan, Roll: The World the Slaves Made* (New York: Pantheon Books, 1974); H. Gutman and R. Sutch, "Victorians All? The Sexual Mores and Conduct of Slaves and Their Masters," in Paul A. David, Herbert G. Gutman, Richard Sutch, Peter Temin, and Gavin Wright, eds., *Reckoning with Slavery* (New York: Oxford University Press, 1976); James R. McGovern, *Anatomy of a Lynching: The Killing of Claud Neal* (Baton Rouge: Louisiana State University Press, 1982); Stewart E. Tolnay and E. M. Beck, *A Festival of Violence: An Analysis of Southern Lynchings, 1882–1930* (Urbana: University of Illinois Press, 1995); and Ronald G. Walters, "The Erotic South: Civilization and Sexuality in American Abolitionism," *American Quarterly* 25, no. 2 (May 1973): 177–201.

279 "In Georgia": D'Emilio and Freedman, 186.

280 "The men of the South": Clinton, 208, citing James Buckingham in 1840.

280 In fact, the mixed-race: This was truest during the seventeenth century and then Reconstruction. After the Civil War, with so many marriageable men dead, some white women married black men.

280 One Louisiana planter: Genovese notes that most miscegenation took place in urban areas, much less on plantations or even farms.

280 "scorn of secrecy": Clinton, 216–17.

280 "God forgive us": Genovese, 426.

280 Twentieth-century, Mississippi-born: Ibid., 427–28.

281 The high rate of miscegenation: Many of these unions were the result of deep love. Genovese cites several examples of freed mulatto slaves who spoke of their black mother's relationship with their white father as grounded in affection and respect.

281 "Slaveholders generally should": Walters, 181.

281 The abolitionists yearned: Some, of course, were not so ethical and wished emancipation so they could ship all blacks "back" to Africa where, by the mid–nineteenth century, virtually none had come from.

281 "irritable state of the testes": Genovese, 424–25.

282 "After taking the nigger": McGovern, 80.

282 Chastity Belts: The main sources for chastity belts are Lawrence A. Conrad, "An Early Eighteenth Century Reference to 'Putting a Woman on the Prairies among the Central Algonquians and Its Implications for Moore's Explanation of the Practice among the Cheyenne,'" *Plains Anthropologist* 28, no. 100 (1983): 141–42; E. J. Dingwall, *The Gir-*

Notes

dle of Chastity: A Medico-Historical Study (London: George Routledge and Sons, 1931); George Grinnell Bird, *The Cheyenne Indians: Their History and Ways of Life,* vol. 1 (New York: Cooper Square Publishers, 1962); K. N. Llewellyn and E. Adamson Hoebel, *The Cheyenne Way: Conflict and Case Law in Primitive Jurisprudence* (Norman: University of Oklahoma Press, 1941); John H. Moore, "Evolution and Historical Reductionism," *Plains Anthropologist: Journal of the Plains Conference* 26, no. 94 (pt. 1) (November 1981): 261–69; and Serena Nanda, *Cultural Anthropology,* 5th ed. (Belmont: Wadsworth Publishers Col., 1994).

284 Even after marriage: Cheyenne males also practiced rigorous sexual control. They could not court or marry until they had been in a war party, and they spaced their children ten to twelve years apart, with celibacy as birth control. Some even swore an oath that they would abide by this practice, which won them great respect in their camp.

285 "they post some thirty": Conrad, 142.

285 Female Genital Mutilation: The main sources for this section are Raqiya Haji Dualeh Abdalla, *Sisters in Affliction: Circumcision and Infibulation of Women in Africa* (London: Zed Press, 1982); Anne Cloudsley, *Women of Omdurman* (New York: St. Martin's Press, 1983); N. El Saadawi, *The Hidden Face of Eve* (trans. S. Hetata) (Boston: Beacon Press, 1981); Fran Hosken, *The Hosken Report* (London: Zed Press, 1980); Hanny Lightfoot-Klein, *Prisoners of Ritual: An Odyssey into Female Genital Circumcision in Africa* (Binghampton: Harrington Park Press, 1989); Awa Thiam, *Black Sisters Speak Out: Feminism and Oppression in Black Africa* (London: Pluto Press, 1986); and Alice Walker and Pratibha Parmar, *Warrior Marks: Female Genital Mutilation and the Sexual Blinding of Women* (New York: Harcourt Brace, 1993). "Men's Traditional Culture," *The Economist,* August 10, 1996, was also used.

285 It is usually called: It is also called clitoridectomy or female circumcision.

285 *"Excision or Clitoridectomy:"*: Walker, 367.

286 Old women with: Walker noted "black gunk" under the excisor's fingernails and blue cataracts, indicating the woman could barely see.

286 often dying "patients": When Walker asked a circumciser how she felt when the children cried and screamed as she mutilated them, the old woman replied she did not hear them.

286 P.K., a Malian woman: This story is told by Thiam, 62–63.

286 "Blood cannot be": Lightfoot-Klein, 130.

286 Even if a physician: Ibid., 128.

287 "There is nothing left": Ibid., 133.

287 "is virtually impossible": Ibid., 125.

287 "Pharaonic circumcision": Ibid., 150.

287 Though people elsewhere: Walker, 312–13.

288 "are like a watermelon": Cloudsley, 118.

288 widely practiced in forty: Until recently, FGM was also practiced in North America. In the nineteenth century, American physicians performed thousands of clitoridectomies to treat lesbianism, both suspected and real, and "mental disorders" such as hypersexuality, hysteria and nervousness, epilepsy, catalepsy, melancholy, even kleptomania. Until 1905, infibulation was used to stop masturbation. In England, however, Dr. Isaac Baker Brown was expelled from the Royal College of Surgeons for performing hundreds of clitoridectomies to cure masturbation as a cause of women's mental disorders.

288 "If you circumcise": El Saadawi, 39.

288 Bound Feet: The sources for the following section are Howard S. Levy, *Chinese Footbinding: The History of the Curious Erotic Custom* (New York: Walton Rawls, 1966); and Richard Zacks, *History Laid Bare: Love, Sex and Perversity from the Etruscans to Warren G. Harding* (New York: HarperCollins, 1994).

289 "Why must the feet": Levy, 41.

290 Conversely, lower-class girls: "Walking was an absolute necessity for the girl reared in poorer circumstances," recalled one woman. "I had many household tasks to do, so I had

to walk with my bound feet from the very start. . . . By the age of sixteen, I was completely used to walking." Levy, 260. Poorer girls usually had their feet bound much later and often removed the binding after marriage.

290 "If you care": Ibid., 49.

290 "I was used to freedom": Ibid., 222–23.

291 As chastity in women: Hobbling women's feet without actually mutilating them was a challenge that certain high-ranking Venetians of the sixteenth and seventeenth centuries solved by forcing them to wear impossibly high shoes. This footgear—*shoes* seems a misnomer—were wooden clogs, covered in leather and built up to at least twelve inches, so the woman so encumbered had to cling to servants to maintain her balance as she tottered along. A seventeenth-century British traveler reported that the explanation for this ludicrous fashion was "to keep the wives at home, or at least prevent them from going far, or going alone, or secretly." Zacks, 176–77.

Chapter 8: Abstaining in a Good Cause

293 No Loving, No Baby: The main sources for the following three sections are Kofi D. Benefo, May O. Tsui, and Joseph De Graft Johnson, "Ethnic Differentials in Child-Spacing Ideals and Practices in Ghana," *Journal of Biosocial Science* 26 (1994): 311–26; Pi-Chao Chen, "Birth Planning and Fertility Transition," *Annals of the American Academy of Political and Social Science* 476 (1984): 128–41; Germaine Greer, *Sex and Destiny: The Politics of Human Fertility* (New York: Harper & Row, 1984); K. N. Llewellyn and E. Adamson Hoebel, *The Cheyenne Way: Conflict and Case Law in Primitive Jurisprudence* (Norman: University of Oklahoma Press, 1941); William H. Masters, Virginia Johnson, and Robert Kolodny, *Heterosexuality* (New York: HarperCollins, 1994); Serena Nanda, *Cultural Anthropology,* 5th ed. (Belmont: Wadsworth Publishers Col., 1994); James L. Newman and Russell P. Lura, "Fertility Control in Africa," *Geographical Review* 73, no. 4 (1983): 396–406; and Robert J. Stoller and Gilbert H. Herdt, "The Development of Masculinity: A Cross-Cultural Contribution," *Journal of the American Psychoanalytic Association* 30, no. 1 (1982): 29–59.

294 "Sex is a mental": Greer, 98.

295 For these reasons: Ibid., 124.

296 The Grand Valley Dani: Historically, this distinction might go to the Cheyenne people, who aimed for ten-to-twelve-year gaps between children and achieved this by celibacy. Couples who pledged to abstain from sexual relations for these periods after childbirth were highly respected in their community. Nanda, 142.

296 Most intriguingly, Dani society: This information on the Dani people is taken from Greer, 102–3, who writes that "so extraordinary did Heider's observations seem to his colleagues that some of them believe to this day that he invented the whole story. . . . However . . . low energy systems may be commoner than used to be thought, especially in societies which have settled into a mutual accommodation with limited terrain and a circumscribed food supply, and are prevented from forcing their territories to support agriculture because of climate and soil conditions."

296 "If I were to have": Llewellyn and Hoebel, 261–62.

298 The benefits of this: Reality bears out this supposition. The West African Fulani, for example, one exception to the child-spacing rule, marry early, are constantly seeking to conceive, and continue sexual relations until menopause. They wean their children late, but practice only the Koran-recommended forty days of postpartum abstinence. Compared to societies with built-in mechanisms to control child spacing, the Fulani might be expected to be the most productive. To the contrary: at 4.9 people per family, they have the lowest fertility level of any tribe. However, other factors are at play: lean dry seasons, venereal disease, and a difficult marriage structure that leads to unending strife and insecurity. Newman and Lura, 403–5.

299 delayed marriage: The Kipsigis are an exception to the rule. Ibid., 400.

299 From the perspective: This does not stop them from genitally mutilating their daughters, however, in cruel, unhygienic, and barbaric fashion. It may be that the Kipsigis once practiced infanticide. Newman and Lura, 401, note that in 1924 a colonial official said that each year they killed "a considerable number" of infants. If so, the practice would have had nothing to do with birth control or child spacing but rather, controlling access to the rewards of age and status.

300 Voluntary Motherhood: The sources for the following are John Bartlett (ed. Justin Kaplan), *Bartlett's Familiar Quotations* (Boston, Toronto, London: Little, Brown, 1992); and Linda Gordon, *Woman's Body, Woman's Right: A Social History of Birth Control in America* (New York: Grossman Publishers, 1976).

301 "Our religion, laws": Elizabeth Cady Stanton to Susan B. Anthony, June 14, 1860, in Bartlett.

301 "Womanhood is the primal fact": Gordon, 14.

301 "I am nearly wrecked": Ibid., 15, citing an anonymous woman in Los Angeles.

Chapter 9: Coerced Celibacy

303 "Virtue is good": Peter Cominos, "Late-Victorian Respectability," *International Review of Social History* 8, nos. 1, 2 (1963): 232.

304 "regularly washing their": Pamela Horn, *The Rise and Fall of the Victorian Servant* (Great Britain: Alan Suttin Publishing, 1996), 155.

305 Doing Celibate Time: Most of my reflections on prison life stem from my experience as a part-time penitentiary teacher and as a former student and teacher of the history of criminology. I also used several quotations from Pete Earley, *The Hot House: Life Inside Leavenworth Prison* (New York: Bantam Books, 1992).

305 In the litany of: Others include loss of liberty, personal autonomy, access to goods and services, access to family and friends, privacy of mail and body and bodily functions, physical and emotional security.

305 The helplessness, the horrifying: His options are hopeless. If he complains to the authorities and is transferred into protective custody, he can never return to the general population—to do so would risk his very life. But in PC, he will have little exercise, worse food, no companionship, no chance to work and earn canteen money or to join activities that might reduce his sentence. As well, the authorities might reject him anyway, but the other men will know of his escape attempt and persecute him even more relentlessly.

306 Some have wives: Prison rape is staggeringly aberrant behavior. The same men who practice it in prison often pride themselves on their toughness and masculinity and, outside, would never sexually bother with other men.

307 Vestal Virgins of St. Petersburg: The source for the section is Christine Ruane, "The Vestal Virgins of St. Petersburg: Schoolteachers and the 1897 Marriage Ban," *Russian Review* 50 (April 1991): 163–82.

307 In 1897, the St. Petersburg Duma: A grandfather clause exempted married women already teaching before 1897 from this draconian legislation.

308 "This situation weighs": Ruane, 176.

309 "THEY DO NOT NEED": Ibid., 174.

309 "The Duma's vestal virgins!": Ibid., 175.

309 "Celibacy has a harmful": Ibid., 174.

309 "battle against the": Ibid., 178. The vote was 41–40.

309 Celibacy in Mao's Cultural Revolution: The source for this section is Anchee Min, "Red Fire Farm," *Granta* 39 (spring 1992): 193–211.

311 "He raped me": Ibid., 197–99.

311 Celibacy in a Crowded Marriage: The source for this section is Geraldine Brooks, *Nine Parts of Desire: The Hidden World of Islamic Women* (New York: Anchor Books, 1995).

312　Celibate Victims of Skewed Gender Ratios: The source for this section is Norman D. West, "Sex in Geriatrics: Myth or Miracle?" *Journal of the American Geriatrics Society* 23, no. 12 (December 1975): 551–52. Various newspaper articles were also used.

312　Female infanticide: "Obsession with Boys Skews China's Demographics," *Globe and Mail,* January 20, 1995. Baby girls are exposed in riverbeds, and 97.5 percent of abortions are performed on fetuses revealed by ultrasound machines to be female.

312　"the number of hopeless": Ibid.

312　They find such eroticism: West, 551.

313　Chaste Hindu Widowhood: The main sources for this section are Ray Bharati, *From the Seams of History* (Delhi: Oxford University Press, 1995); William W. Emilsen, *Violence and Atonement: The Missionary Experience of Mohandas Gandhi, Samuel Stokes and Verrier Elwin in India Before 1935* (Frankfurt, New York: P. Lang, 1994); Monica Felt, *A Child Widow's Story* (New York: Harcourt, Brace & World, 1967); Shakuntala Narasimhan, *Sati: A Story of Widow Burning in India* (New Delhi, New York: Viking, 1990); Arvind Sharma et al., *Sati: Historical and Phenomenological Essays* (Delhi: Motilal Banarsidass, 1988); and Dorothy Stein, "Burning Widows, Burning Brides: The Perils of Daughterhood in India," *Pacific Affairs* 61, no. 3 (1988–89): 465–85. Various newspaper articles were also used.

314　"Some say that child": Felt, 164.

314　Manu, the Hindu lawgiver: Narasimhan, 37.

314　"I shall be alone": Bharati, 46.

315　"Where," he demanded: Ibid., 153.

315　"The inhuman treatment": Emilsen, 75.

315　"A man with a hundred": Narasimhan, 28.

315　"falsehood, thoughtless action": Ibid., 28–29.

315　"Stealing grain or cattle": Ibid., 31.

316　"if there was no cremation": Ibid., 35.

317　As Roop's in-laws: Stein, 472–73.

317　"The Latin word": Ian McCormick, ed., *Secret Sexualities: A Sourcebook of 17th and 18th Century Writing* (London and New York: Routledge, 1997), 23.

318　"that he might have": Ibid.

319　Eunuchs in Greek Mythology: The main sources for this section are Sue Blundell, *Women in Ancient Greece* (London: British Museum Press, 1995); Catullus (trans. Guy Lee), *Poems of Catullus* (Oxford: Clarendon Press, 1990); Michael Grant and John Hazel, *Who's Who in Classical Mythology* (London: Weidenfeld & Nicolson, 1973); Robert Graves, *The Greek Myths,* vol. 1 (Harmondsworth: Penguin Books, 1955); Deborah Sawyer, *Women and Religion in the First Christian Centuries* (New York: Routledge, 1996); and Marteen J. Vermaseren (trans. A. M. H. Lemmers), *Cybele and Attis, the Myth and the Cult* (London: Thames and Hudson, 1977).

320　"They cut your cock": Sawyer, 122.

320　"that holy and inexpressible": Vermaseren, 97.

320　Chinese Eunuchism as a Career Opportunity: The main source for this section is Taisuke Mitamura (trans. Charles A. Pomeroy), *Chinese Eunuchs: The Structure of Intimate Politics* (Rutland: Charles E. Tuttle Company, 1970). All quotations are from Mitamura.

320　In December 1996: Ninety-two-year-old Sun Yaoting's father had castrated him at age eight so he could apply to serve in the bustling and lucrative imperial palace. Unfortunately for him, one month later, the Manchu dynasty fell and was replaced by the Republic.

321　From the Yin dynasty: The palace was three kilometers long and two and a half wide, with gates on each side. The palace building was 760 meters wide and one kilometer long and surrounded by a moat. The distance between emperor and subject, the Chinese say, is like that between heaven and man.

323　For forty years: His death in 1912 coincided with the death of the Manchu dynasty and the imperial system of eunuchism.

324 Byzantine Eunuch Paradise: The main sources for the section on Byzantine eunuchs and General Narses are Peter Brown, *The Body and Society: Men, Women and Sexual Renunciation in Early Christianity* (New York: Columbia University Press, 1988); Vern L. Bullough, *Sexual Variance in Society and History* (New York: John Wiley & Sons, 1976); J. A. S. Evans, *The Age of Justinian: The Circumstances of Imperial Power* (London: Routledge, 1996); Lawrence Fauber, *Narses Hammer of the Goth: The Life and Times of Narses the Eunuch* (New York: St. Martin's Press, 1990); André Guillou, *Studies on Byzantine Italy* (London: Variorum Reprints, 1970); and Ute Ranke-Heinemann, *Eunuchs for the Kingdom of Heaven: Women, Sexuality, and the Catholic Church* (New York: Doubleday, 1990).

324 By the tenth century: The great influence of the eunuchs ended only in the second half of the thirteenth century when the influence of Western thought deemed them inferior physical specimens. See Guillou.

325 "among the few": Edward Gibbon, cited by Fauber, 15.

326 Black African Eunuchs of the Ottoman Empire: The main sources for this section are Shaun Marmon, *Eunuchs and Sacred Boundaries in Islamic Society* (New York: Oxford University Press, 1995); Justin McCarthy, *The Ottoman Turks: An Introductory History to 1923* (New York: Longman, 1997); V. J. Parry et al., *A History of the Ottoman Empire to 1730: Chapters from the Cambridge History of Islam and the New Cambridge Modern History* (Cambridge, New York: Cambridge University Press, 1976); Ehud R. Toledano, "The Imperial Eunuchs of Istanbul: From Africa to the Heart of Islam," *Middle Eastern Studies* 20 (July 1984): 379–89; and Andrew Wheatcroft, *The Ottomans* (London: Viking, 1993).

326 "neutral emissaries in": Marmon, 5.

327 "to lock and unlock": Toledano, 382–83.

328 The nature and urgency: Wheatcroft, 35–36. "It was a warren of narrow passages, and blanked-off corridors; often it was impossible to gain direct access between adjacent rooms, except by a roundabout route under the watchful eyes of the black eunuchs, who superintended every aspect of the women's lives."

329 The *Hijras* of India: The main sources for this section are Arthur R. Kroeber, *Far Eastern Review,* March 2, 1989; and Serena Nanda, *Neither Man nor Woman: The Hijras of India* (Belmont: Wadsworth Publishing Co., 1990).

331 "God has made us": Nanda, 8.

331 Some simply conclude: Kroeber, 76, refers to a Delhi University study of eighty-nine *hijra*s in which sixteen claimed to have been conscripted rather than to have volunteered.

332 The Castrati of the Opera: The sources for this section are Angus Heriot, *The Castrati in Opera* (London: Secker & Warburg, 1956); and Ian McCormick, ed., *Secret Sexualities: A Sourcebook of 17th and 18th Century Writing* (London and New York: Routledge, 1997).

332 Imagine a voice: This is based on music historian Enrico Panzacchi's comments about a castrato in the Vatican choir, cited in Heriot, 36–37.

332 "One God, one Farinelli!": Ibid., 99.

333 Indeed, until the late: Only France resisted the allure, virtually banning both Italian opera and castrati.

333 "A pig attacked": Heriot, 21.

333 The last known castrato: This was despite Pope Pius X's 1903 interdiction of castrati in the papal chapel.

334 "In a well-made corset": Heriot, 54.

334 "One sees a stout": Ibid., 28, citing an English visitor to a Portuguese theater in 1787.

334 All this attention: The early-eighteenth-century writer Charles Ollican or Ancillon, in *Eunuchism Display'd, Describing All the Different Sorts of Eunuchs, Etc.,* cited in McCormick, 21, complained of eunuchs "puffed . . . up with a vanity which is ever peculiar to eunuchs, and some of them have got it into their heads that truly the ladies were in love with them, and fondly flattered themselves with mighty conquests. But alas! our ladies have not so little natural philosophy but they know how to make a just distinction, and have too fine a gout to be satisfied with mere shadow and outside."

334 "By the grace of God": Heriot, 224.

335 Castration to Punish Offenders: The main sources for this section are Gunnar Broberg and Nils Roll-Hansen, eds., *Eugenics and the Welfare State: Sterilization Policy in Denmark, Sweden, Norway, and Finland* (East Lansing: Michigan State University Press, 1996); Piero Colla, "Sterilization Policy in Sweden, 1934–75," in Broberg and Roll-Hansen, *Eugenics and the Welfare State;* Geoffrey J. Giles, "'The Most Unkindest Cut of All': Castration, Homosexuality and Nazi Justice," *Journal of Contemporary History* 27 (1992): 41–61; Mark H. Haller, *Eugenics: Hereditarian Attitudes in American Thought* (Rahway: Rutgers University Press, 1963); Nikolas Heim and Carolyn J. Hursch, "Castration for Sex Offenders: Treatment or Punishment? A Review and Critique of Recent European Literature," *Archives of Sexual Behavior* 8, no. 3 (May 1979): 281–304; Lincoln Kaye, "Quality Control: Eugenics Bills Defended against Western Critics," *Far Eastern Economic Review* 157, (1994): 22; Daniel J. Keules, *In the Name of Eugenics: Genetics and the Uses of Human Heredity* (New York: Alfred A. Knopf, 1985); Edward J. Larson, "The Rhetoric of Eugenics: Expert Authority and the Mental Deficiency Bill," *British Journal for the History of Science* 24, no. 1 (1991): 45–60; Walter J. Meyer and Collier M. Cole, "Physical and Chemical Castration of Sex Offenders: A Review," *Journal of Offender Rehabilitation* 25, no. 3/4 (1997): 1–18; and Peter Weingart, "German Eugenics between Science and Politics," *Osiris* 5 (1989): 260–82.

336 Other side effects: One study showed that psychologically, 31 percent felt more depressed and inadequate. Twenty-six percent were unhappy with their forced castration, and 22 percent were intensely bitter.

337 In Thailand, an amateur: The source for this section is *Penis Amputation in Thailand,* a documentary by Matt Fry shown on CBC television, August 2, 1998, on the *Sunday Morning Live* program.

Chapter 10: Celibacy to Repress Unconventional or Sorrowful Sexuality

339 Nonetheless, the following: The main sources for the following sections are Joan Abse, *John Ruskin: The Passionate Moralist* (London, New York: Quartet Books, 1980); Paula Blanchard, *Sarah Orne Jewett: Her World and Her Work* (Massachusetts: Addison-Wesley, 1994); Serge Bramly, *Leonardo: Discovering the Life of Leonardo da Vinci* (New York: Harper-Collins, 1991); Lillian Faderman, "Nineteenth-century Boston marriage as a possible lesson for today," in Esther D. Rothblum and Kathleen Brehony, eds., *Boston Marriages: Romantic but Asexual Relationships among Contemporary Lesbians* (Amherst: University of Massachusetts Press, 1993); Lillian Faderman, *Odd Girls and Twilight Lovers: A History of Lesbian Life in 20th Century America* (New York: Penguin, 1991); Michael Field, *Underneath the Bough: A Book of Verses* (Portland, Maine: T. B. Mosher, 1898); Sigmund Freud (trans., ed. John Strackey), *Art and Literature* (Middlesex: Penguin, 1987); Sigmund Freud (trans. A. A. Brill), *Leonardo da Vinci: A Psychosexual Study of an Infantile Reminiscence* (London: Kegan Paul, French, Trubner & Co., 1932); Phyllis Grosskurth, *Havelock Ellis: A Biography* (Toronto: McClelland and Stewart, 1980); Olwen Hufton, *The Prospect Before Her: A History of Women in Western Europe, 1500–1800* (New York: Alfred A. Knopf, 1996); Linda Lear, *Rachel Carson: Witness for Nature* (New York: Henry Holt, 1997); Phyllis Rose, *Parallel Lives: Five Victorian Marriages* (New York: Alfred A. Knopf, 1984); Ester D. Rothblum and Kathleen L. Brehony, eds., *Boston Marriages: Romantic but Asexual Relationships among Contemporary Lesbians* (Amherst: University of Massachusetts Press, 1993); and Irving Wallace, Amy Wallace, Sylvia Wallace, and David Wallechinsky, *The Intimate Sex Lives of Famous People* (New York: Delacorte Press, 1981).

340 "doubtful whether he": Freud, *Art and Literature,* 161.

340 Among his earliest: Bramly, 129.

340 "so disgusting that": Freud, *Leonardo da Vinci,* 14.

340 "appears to us as": Ibid., 67–68.

341 "I am fond": Wallace et al., 125.
341 "Would you kindly": Ibid., 127.
342 "He was as fond": Ibid., 126.
342 "if you limit your": Ibid., 127.
343 "I never could love": Rose, 75.
344 *"sinful* to enter": Ibid., 82.
344 "John Ruskin was": Ibid., 91.
344 "just in the very": Abse, 175–78.
346 Once upon a time: Sexologists invented the term *lesbian* in the 1870s. By the second decade of the twentieth century, it had infiltrated the popular consciousness, and intensely affectionate relationships between women were seen as suspicious.
347 In *The Bostonians,*: Rothblum and Brehony, 30–33.
348 "Out of the darkness": Faderman, *Odd Girls and Twilight Lovers,* 22.
348 A few even adopted: Field, 50.
348 "I urge eternal feud": Ibid., 17.
348 "as a sign of something": Blanchard, 123–24.
348 "the friend he would": Ibid., 134.
349 "To work in silence": Ibid., 359.
350 "white hyacinth": Referring to the story of a man who, with two pennies, would buy bread with one and with the other, a white hyacinth for the soul. Dorothy was, in other words, Rachel's white hyacinth for the soul.
350 "All I am certain": Lear, 254.
350 "The suddenness and intensity": Ibid., 252.
351 "Rachel's letter left": Ibid., 256.
351 "has a new and": Ibid., 265.
351 "I think that you": Ibid., 442.

Chapter 11: Impotent Celibacy

353 Limp as Yesterday's Lettuce: The main sources for this section are Ovid, "Amores," in Diane J. Rayor and William W. Batshaw, eds., *Latin Lyric and Elegiac Poetry: An Anthology of New Translations* (New York: Garland Publishing, 1995); Petronius (trans. several hands), *The Satyricon* (London: privately printed, 1899); and Albus Tibullus, "To Priapus by Albus Tibullus concerning the inertia of his privy member," in L. C. Smithers and Sir Richard Burton, *Priapeia* (London: Wordsworth, 1995).
354 "With dreadful Steel": Petronius, 206.
354 "He still continu'd": Ibid., 295.
354 "What's the matter?": Ovid, III 7.
355 Testing for Impotence in Prerevolutionary France: The main sources for this section are Marie-Véronique Clin, "Joan of Arc and Her Doctors," in Bonnie Wheeler and Charles T. Wood, eds., *Fresh Verdicts on Joan of Arc* (New York, London: Garland Publishing, 1996); and Pierre Damon, *Trial by Impotence: Virility and Marriage in Pre-Revolutionary France* (London: Chatto & Windus, 1985).
355 "an attack upon": Damon, 61.
356 "Of a certain young": Ibid., 83–84.
356 "Critical and superstitious": Ibid., 178–80.
357 "out of spite": Ibid., 152–53.
357 Celibacy in Response to Vaginismus: The source for the following section is William H. Masters, Virginia E. Johnson, and Robert C. Kolodny, *Heterosexuality* (New York: HarperCollins, 1994).
358 So may serious: A surgical excision of the perineum to enlarge the vulva during childbirth.
359 You *Can* Be Too Thin: Anorexic Celibacy: The main sources for this section are Rudolph M. Bell, *Holy Anorexia* (Chicago: University of Chicago Press, 1985); Carol Bloom et al.,

Eating Problems: A Feminist Psychoanalytic Treatment Model (New York: Basic Books, 1994); Hilde Bruch, *Conversations with Anorexics* (New York: Basic Books, 1988); Peggy Claude-Pierre, *The Secret Language of Eating Disorders* (New York: Times Books, 1997); Rosalyn M. Meadow and Lillie Weiss, *Women's Conflicts About Eating and Sexuality* (New York, London, Norwood: Haworth Press, 1992); C. Don Morgan, Michael W. Wiederman, and Tamara L. Pryor, "Sexual Functioning and Attitudes of Eating-Disordered Women," *Journal of Sex & Marital Therapy* 21, no. 2 (1995): 67–77; Susie Orbach, *Hunger Strike: The Anorectic's Struggle as a Metaphor for Our Age* (New York: Avon, 1986); Walter Vandereycken and Ron Van Deth, *From Fasting Saints to Anorexic Girls: The History of Self-Starvation* (London: Athlone Press, 1990); Michael W. Wiederman, "Women, Sex, and Food," *Journal of Sex Research* 33, no. 4 (1996): 301–11; and Michael R. Zales, *Eating, Sleeping, and Sexuality: Treatment of Disorders in Basic Life Functions* (New York: Brunner/Mazel Publishers, 1982).

360 "The main theme": This is one theme in Bruch.

360 So many medieval female: Bell's *Holy Anorexia* is the classic study.

360 "is a manifestation": Wiederman, 302.

360 Even today, anorexic women: Ibid. Wiederman, 301, outlines the state of the research on this issue and concludes that "the empirical research . . . has been unfocused and of relatively poor quality."

360 "the acute stage": Claude-Pierre, 108.

361 "is oddly desexualized": Orbach, 102.

361 "I am the thinnest": Vandereycken and Van Deth, 237.

361 The evidence of Kafka's: Ibid., 237–39.

361 It also fulfills: I am fully aware of anorexia's many other issues—excessive dieting to achieve fashionable thinness, for instance—but have mentioned only those directly relevant to the theme of celibacy, a major component of the disease.

Chapter 12: Celibacy in Literature

363 Courtly, Ennobling, and Unrequited Love: The main sources for this section are Anonymous, "The Ten Commandments of Love," in Russell H. Robbins, *Secular Lyrics of the 14th and 15th Centuries* (Oxford: Oxford Clarendon Press, 1941); Larry D. Benson, "Courtly Love and Chivalry in the Later Middle Ages," *Fifteenth-Century Studies* (Archon Books, 1984); Andreas Capellanus, "Rules of Courtly Love," in *The Art of Courtly Love* (trans. J. J. Parry) (New York: Columbia University Press, 1941); A. Kleinbach, "The Main Characteristics of Courtly Love" (on-line: http://www.millersv.edu/homepage/duncan/medfem/fact3.html [August 30, 1997]); Norman MacKenzie, ed., *Secret Societies* (New York: Collier Books, 1967); Herbert W. Richardson, *Nun, Witch, Playmate: The Americanization of Sex* (New York: Harper & Row, 1971); Denis de Rougement, *Love in the Western World* (Princeton, N.J.: Princeton University Press, 1983); Irving Singer, *The Nature of Love: Courtly and Romantic* (Chicago, London: University of Chicago Press, 1984); and Kay L. Stoner, "The Enduring Popularity of Courtly Love" (on-line: http://www.millersv.edu-english/homepage/duncan/medfem/court.html [August 28, 1997]).

364 "But I, my lyf": Benson, 240.

364 "Out of love": de Rougement, 76.

364 The Virgin Mary: This notion comes from Stoner and Richardson.

365 "never combed, rarely": MacKenzie, 97.

365 Milton and the Chaste Lady: The sources for this section are Hoffman Reynolds Hays, *The Dangerous Sex* (New York: Putnam, 1964), chap. 17, "The Bosom Snake"; John Milton, *Comus: A Mask* (London: Printer for the Proprietors, 1795); and John Milton, *Paradise Lost: A Poem in Twelve Books* (London: Union Printing Office, 1808).

365 "List, Lady; be not coy": Milton, *Comus*, 222, 225, 227.

366 "in the rites of nature": Hays, 171.
366 "Because the flush": Ibid., 170.
366 "It is not strange": Ibid., 171.
366 "For that fair female": Milton, *Paradise Lost,* 338.
367 "So rose the Danite": Ibid., 274.
367 ". . . and miserable it is": Ibid., 312.
367 *Pamela, Shamela*: The sources for this section, and for all quotations, are Henry Fielding, *The History of the Adventures of Joseph Andrews and His Friend Mr. Abraham Adams* (London: Smith, Elder, & Co., 1882); and Samuel Richardson, *Pamela,* 2 vols. (London: J. M. Dent & Sons, 1931).
369 Tolstoy's *Kreutzer Sonata*: The source for this section is Leo Tolstoy, *The Kreutzer Sonata and Family Happiness* (London: Walter Scott, 1888).
370 *"try to persuade"*: My italics.
371 Judith Shakespeare: The source for the following is Virginia Woolf's 1929 essay *A Room of One's Own* (New York: Harcourt, Brace & Co., 1929).
372 Garp's Mother: The source for the following section is John Irving, *The World According to Garp* (New York: Simon and Schuster, 1976).
373 Vampire Celibacy, Medium Rare: The main sources for this section are Matthew Bunson, *The Vampire Encyclopedia* (New York: Crown Trade Paperbacks, 1993); an unpublished essay by Meredith Burns-Simpson; Greg Cox (ed. Daryl F. Mallett), *The Transylvanian Library: A Consumer's Guide to Vampire Fiction* (San Bernardino: Borgo Press, 1993); and Chelsea Quinn Yarbro, *Cabin 33,* in Cox, *The Transylvanian Library.*

Chapter 13: The New Celibacy

376 "many of the neuroses": Cited by Patricia Wittberg, *The Rise and Fall of Catholic Religious Orders: A Social Movement Perspective* (New York: State University of New York Press, 1994), 250.
376 The Jesuit Rule 32: Neil McKenty, *The Inside Story* (Quebec: Shoreline Press, 1997), 62.
376 "the traditional way": Wittberg, 250.
376 Vatican Decrees Celibacy a Brilliant Jewel: The main sources for the following section are James F. Colaianni, ed., *Married Priests and Married Nuns* (New York: McGraw-Hill, 1968); Raymond Hickey, *Africa: The Case for an Auxiliary Priesthood* (London: Geoffrey Chapman, 1980); Timothy McCarthy, *The Catholic Tradition Before and After Vatican II, 1878–1993* (Chicago: Loyola University Press, 1994); Neil McKenty, *The Inside Story;* Cardinal John J. O'Connor, "The Wonder of Celibacy" (on-line: http://www.inter-path.com/nmdoyle/savannah/oconnor [August 27, 1997]); Pope Paul VI, *Sacerdotalis Caelibatus—24 June 1967* (on-line: http://listserv.american.edu/catholic/church/papal/paul.vi/sacerdot.caelibat [August 27, 1997]); W. F. Powers, *Free Priests: The Movement for Ministerial Reform in the American Catholic Church* (Chicago: Loyola University Press, 1992); Michele Price, *Mandatory Celibacy in the Catholic Church: A Handbook for the Laity* (Pasadena: New Paradigm Books, 1992); David Rice, *Shattered Vows: Exodus from the Priesthood* (London: Michael Joseph, 1990); A. W. Richard Sipe, *A Secret World: Sexuality and the Search for Celibacy* (New York: Brunner/Mazel, 1990); Patricia Wittberg, *The Rise and Fall of Catholic Religious Orders;* J. G. Wolf, ed., *Gay Priests* (San Francisco: Harper & Row, 1989); and Karol Wojtyla (Pope John Paul II) (trans. H. T. Willets), *Love and Responsibility* (New York: Farrar Straus Giroux, 1981). Newspaper and magazine articles were also used.
377 "Priestly celibacy has been": Pope Paul VI, *Sacerdotalis Caelibatus.*
377 "the sum of these": Ibid.
378 "the present law": Ibid.
378 "The law of priestly celibacy": Ibid.
378 "Virginity as a deliberately": Wojtyla, 258.

379 "To all three categories": Cardinal O'Connor.
379 "marriage is the focus": Anglican clergyman John Mbiti in Hickey, 133.
379 "In African culture": Rice, 164.
380 "Compulsory celibacy is": Ibid., 166.
380 Compelling logic: Rice documents countless other examples of overt clerical uncelibacy among priests the world over. "No place is virginal in this matter," he concludes, 167.
380 "there is the priest": Ibid.
381 A *Newsweek* poll: *Newsweek*, August 16, 1993; and *Maclean's*, December 19, 1994.
381 Sipe interprets data: Sipe, 107.
381 The priestly rebellion: Gay nuns are barred from ordination by their gender, so their issues are quite different from those of gay priests.
381 Yet it cannot be impervious: Rice, citing a bulletin from the group Advent, 165–66.
382 Misogynous Exceptions to the Papal Rule of Celibacy: The main sources for this section are "The Question of the Ordination of Lay Men and Women to the Priesthood in the Catholic Church" (on-line: http://christ-usrex.org/www/CDHN/kephas.html [August 30, 1996]); and A. W. Richard Sipe, *A Secret World: Sexuality and the Search for Celibacy* (New York: Brunner/Mazel, 1990).
382 "At the present time": "The Question of the Ordination of Lay Men and Women."
383 "The special permissions": Ibid.
383 It also prohibited: Pope John Paul II approved the statutes governing the admission of these new priests on June 2, 1995.
384 "It is hard to": Sipe, 51.
384 Catholic Priests Vote with Their Feet: The main sources for this section are Helen Rose Fuchs Ebaugh, *Women in the Vanishing Cloister: Organizational Decline in Catholic Religious Orders in the United States* (New Brunswick, N.J.: Rutgers University Press, 1993); Neil McKenty, *The Inside Story* (Quebec: Shoreline Press, 1997); David Rice, *Shattered Vows: Exodus from the Priesthood* (London: Michael Joseph, 1990); A. W. Richard Sipe, *A Secret World: Sexuality and the Search for Celibacy* (New York: Brunner/Mazel, 1990); and Gordon Thomas, *Desire and Denial: Celibacy and the Church* (Boston: Little, Brown, 1986). Newspaper and magazine articles were also used.
384 They may also: The rule of celibacy no longer condemns nocturnal emissions or even masturbation; most priests who are surveyed masturbate at least once yearly. Sipe, chap. 7, "The Masturbations."
385 At the same time: In 1965, U.S. seminaries had 48,000 students; in 1986, 10,300; in 1996, 6,200. Theologates have also declined 59 percent. Rice, 23.
385 Swiftly and steadily: The vow of chastity is also the main reason given by young people who decide not to join holy orders: *Halifax Chronicle-Herald*, June 14, 1997, reporting a survey by the Center for Applied Research in the Apostolate; Thomas, 23; Ebaugh, 128.
385 "It was mainly about": *Globe and Mail*, November 16, 1994. The priest, Dominic, who now spends half of each year in Ontario, was interviewed by columnist Michael Coren.
385 "the celibacy requirement": Rice, 226. A 1983 U.S. poll reported that 94 percent of nuns and priests who had defected identified their inability to maintain their vows of celibacy as the reason for their defection. Thomas, 11.
385 "solitary, shuffling pariahs": Rice, 197. However, Canadian ex-Jesuit Neil McKenty had a different experience when he announced his decision to leave in 1969. "There was no hint of blame, no mention of the enormous sums of money the Jesuits had invested in my education and my health through a period of twenty-five years. Quite the contrary— I was invited to stay in my old room . . . until I could find a job." McKenty, 115.
386 Sipe's study estimated: McKenty, for example, had an on-again, off-again, decade-long sexual liaison with Denise, a divorced Catholic woman (McKenty, 86–87). Overwhelming anecdotal evidence also supports Sipe's view, indeed suggests that it is conservative.
386 The Third Way of Sophistry and Cheating: The main sources for this section are Rosemary Curb and Nancy Manaham, eds., *Breaking Silence: Lesbian Nuns on Convent Sexu-*

ality (London: Columbus, 1985); Mary Griffin, *The Courage to Choose: An American Nun's Story* (Boston: Little, Brown, 1975); David Rice, *Shattered Vows: Exodus from the Priesthood* (London: Michael Joseph, 1990); A. W. Richard Sipe, *A Secret World: Sexuality and the Search for Celibacy* (New York: Brunner/Mazel, 1990); and Karol Wojtyla (trans. H. T. Willets), *Love and Responsibility* (New York: Farrar Straus Giroux, 1981). Newspaper articles were also used.

386 Decades later, nuns: Sipe, 99; Griffin, 167.

387 "devote themselves full-time": Griffin, 167.

387 Other priests with mistresses: "Clerical Liaisons: The Sins of the Fathers," *Globe and Mail,* June 24, 1995.

387 How, given the cross fire: *Globe and Mail,* October 22, 1993, reporting a June 1993 declaration by Pope John Paul II.

387 Surely it would be far more: *Globe and Mail,* April 2, 1994, reporting Pope John Paul II's statement during a public audience at the Vatican.

388 Divorce à la Catholic Church: The main sources for this section are William F. Powers, *Free Priests: The Movement for Ministerial Reform in the American Catholic Church* (Chicago: Loyola University Press, 1992); and David Rice, *Shattered Vows: Exodus from the Priesthood* (London: Michael Joseph, 1990). Newspaper and magazine articles were also used.

388 Corpus began in 1974: Worldwide, there are many such groups: the UK's MOMM—the Movement for the Ordination of Married Men—and Advent; Chile's Siete Sacramentos; and groups in dozens of other countries.

388 By 1996, We Are Church: "Reform Group Gathers in Rome," *Catholic New Times* 20, no. 22 (December 15, 1996): 2.

388 Canada's Catholics of Vision: "Catholic group calls for major change," CP Newswire, October 31, 1996; "Canadian Campaign in Planning Stage," *Catholic New Times* 20, no. 16 (September 22, 1996): 12; *Alberta Report* 24, no. 12 (March 3, 1997): 34–35.

388 Some of these act: Powers, 258.

388 "A relationship with God": *Globe and Mail,* November 16, 1994. Michael Coren's interview with ex-priest Dominic.

388 "counseling situations gone": "The Catholic Church: Wages of Sin," *Economist,* August 30, 1997.

389 The Bleeding: The main sources for this section are Helen Rose Fuchs Ebaugh, *Women in the Vanishing Cloister: Organizational Decline in Catholic Religious Orders in the United States* (New Brunswick, N.J.: Rutgers University Press, 1993); Gordon Thomas, *Desire and Denial: Celibacy and the Church* (Boston: Little, Brown, 1986); and Patricia Wittberg, *The Rise and Fall of Catholic Religious Orders: A Social Movement Perspective* (New York: State University of New York Press, 1994). Newspaper and magazine articles were also used.

389 "the most meaningful": Wittberg, 250.

389 By the twentieth century: Sister Rosalia Kane, a nun in Charlottetown, P.E.I.'s Sisters of St. Martha order, explains that then "the families were larger; the career opportunities were less. Families often saw religious life as a very positive option." *Toronto Star,* September 21, 1991.

390 "'to the fullness": Wittberg, 213.

390 "In one stroke": Ibid., 214.

390 The respect they: *Globe and Mail,* October 1, 1987.

391 "Celibacy was an": Ebaugh, 40.

391 "an intellectual attraction": Ibid., 41.

391 "started to have dreams": Ibid., 42.

391 "I began to want": Ibid., 46.

392 For a great many: There is a growing literature about lesbian nuns who remain cloistered, sometimes celibate and engaging in loving Boston-marriage–type relationships with other nuns, sometimes sexually active.

392 New Age Monasticism: The source for the following section is Charles A. Fracchia, *Liv-*

ing Together Alone: The New American Monasticism (San Francisco: Harper & Row, 1979).

392 "We are celibate": Ibid., 20.

392 "When you love God": Ibid., 81.

392 "The 'new monasticism'": Ibid., 21.

393 Celibacy as an Undivided Heart: All quotations in this section are from Kathleen Norris, *The Cloister Walk* (New York: Riverhead Books, 1996).

393 "The worst sin against": Ibid., 254.

393 "It is a daily choice": Ibid., 261.

394 "seeks to love": Ibid., 260.

394 "to love many people": Ibid., 262.

394 "an undivided heart": Ibid., 253.

394 By age sixteen and seventeen: Michele Ingrassia, "Virgin Cool," *Newsweek*, October 17, 1994, 61; Nancy Gibbs, "How Should We Teach Our Children About Sex?" *Time*, May 24, 1993, 53.

394 fully 72 percent: Gibbs, 53. Forty-two percent reported one partner, 29 percent reported two or three, 6 percent reported four, and 15 percent reported five or more.

394 Rates of sexually transmitted disease: "Teenage sex: Just say 'Wait,' " *U.S. News & World Report*, July 26, 1993, 61. The source is the Atlanta Centers for Disease Control.

394 Equally sobering is that: Ingrassia, 69.

394 Alarmingly, even more girls: Gibbs, 53.

395 For one thing: Michele Ingrassia reminds us that a century ago, girls reached puberty at about fifteen and married at twenty-two.

395 "the zipless fuck": It is decades since I read *Fear of Flying*, but Jong's single-minded quest for said "zipless fuck" still resonates in my memory.

396 It, too, has its youth wing: After marriage, however, the ex-virgin can look forward to a steamy sex life. She can be a Real Woman, for instance, and tease her husband by receiving him naked or in a fetching costume when he appears home each evening (from the outside world, where he has been hard at work earning their living), thus stimulating his sexual appetite for her, keeping him from straying, and also gently influencing him to reward her with tangible goods suitable for such a good wife and Real Woman.

396 True Love Waits: The main source for this section is True Love Waits literature. Wendy Kaminer, *True Love Waits: Essays and Criticism* (Reading: Addison-Wesley, 1996), and newspaper and magazine articles were also used, especially Nancy Gibbs, "How Should We Teach Our Children About Sex?" *Time*, May 24, 1993, 56; and Michele Ingrassia, "Virgin Cool," *Newsweek*, October 17, 1994.

396 It is an identifiable phenomenon: As one fundamentalist puts it, "It wasn't Adam and Steve, let's get this right." L. A. Kauffman, "Praise the Lord, and Mammon," *The Nation*, September 26, 1994, 308.

396 "We're the only virgins": Ingrassia, 62.

396 "Students who have failed": From True Love Waits literature.

397 But the truly spectacular: Erica Werner, "The Cult of Virginity," *Ms.*, April 1997, 41–42.

397 "the students should": From the True Love Waits/Goes Campus campaign literature.

398 True Love Waits has: Kelly E. Young, "True Love Waits helps Wilson launch his statewide parental responsibility program," *Stanford Daily*, April 28, 1997.

398 "Teachers tell me": Patrick Meagher, "Lining up to be virgins, teens let true love wait," *Toronto Star*, December 13, 1997.

398 "I have always wanted": "True Love Waits—South Africa," 1–2.

398 "a new way of sharing": John Zipperer, " 'True Love Waits' Now Worldwide Effort," *Christianity Today* 38 (July 18, 1994): 50.

399 "My Body is a Temple": L. A. Kauffman, "Praise the Lord, and Mammon," *The Nation*, September 26, 1994, 306.

399 Meanwhile, Waiters indulge: Kaminer, 15.

399   "It is my life": Two teenage True Love Waits Canadian converts quoted by Scott Steele, "Like a Virgin," *Maclean's*, March 14, 1994, 59.

399   The chastity movement: For example, in its March 1998 issue, *Jump* magazine for teenagers focused on virgin boys. In "Boys on Virginity: what it means to give it up" by Mia Byers, 49–51, five young men discussed their feelings about virginity. Two of the five are still virgins, Alex until he meets his future wife, Joe because he feels too emotionally vulnerable.

399   "the ultra geek": Ingrassia, 60.

399   "Sex is *never*": William Shaw, "Homme Alone 2: Lost in Los Angeles," *Details*, April 1994, 168.

400   In the movie *Clueless*: Personal communication from Kelly Thomas.

400   "I am still a virgin": David Whitman, *U.S. News & World Report*, May 19, 1997.

400   The sexual revolution's legacy: *U.S. News & World Report*, May 5, 1997, 30; *Globe and Mail*, January 17, 1998, citing a twenty-year examination of teen pregnancies in *Health Reports*, published by Statistics Canada.

401   "full-blown slutitis": BAVAM! newsletter (on-line).

402   "Children should not": Andres Tapia, "Radical Choice for Sex Ed," *Christianity Today*, February 8, 1993, 29. This is the most thoughtful and comprehensive article I encountered on the issue of sex education.

403   "petting [before] marriage": Ingrassia, 64.

403   "the only way to avoid": Philip Elmer-DeWitt, "Making the Case for Abstinence," *Time*, May 24, 1993, 54–55.

403   Like the Maryland ad campaign: Gibbs, 56.

403   "84 percent wanted": Joseph Shapiro, "Teenage Sex: Just say 'Wait,'" *U.S. News & World Report*, July 26, 1993, 58.

405   "I'm twenty-five years old": McCarthy, 211.

405   "whether it's really been": Ibid., 139.

405   "I am not a right-wing": Ibid., 3–4.

405   "the words *chaste*": Ibid., 87–88.

405   "Since it's the only": Ibid., 88.

406   Reborn Chastity: The main sources for this section are Judith E. Beckett, "Recollections of a Sexual Life, Revelations of a Celibate Time," *Lesbian Ethics* 3, no. 1 (spring 1988); Gabrielle Brown, *The New Celibacy: Why More Men and Women Are Abstaining from Sex* (New York: McGraw-Hill, 1989); Sally Cline, *Women, Passion and Celibacy* (New York: Carol Southern Books, 1993); Carolyn Gage, "Pressure to Heal," *Lesbian Ethics* 4, no. 3 (spring 1992); Tuula Gordon, *Single Women, on the Margins?* (London: Macmillan, 1994); Celia Haddon, *The Sensuous Lie* (New York: Stein and Day, 1982); Marny Hall, "Unsexing the Couple," *Women and Therapy* 19, no. 3 (1996): 2–10; Wendy Shalit, *A Return to Modesty: Discovering the Lost Virtue* (New York: Free Press, 1999); and Candace Watson, "Celibacy and Its Implications for Autonomy," *Hypatia* 2, no. 2 (summer 1987): 157. Newspaper and magazine articles were also used.

407   Statistics confirm this: Brown, 122–23.

408   Further, over half: Ibid., 15, citing Gary Hanauer, "Turning On to Turning Off," *Penthouse*, January 1986, 65–71.

408   Celibacy, too, is a form: Ibid., 1.

408   "Physical closeness without": Ibid., 117.

409   It "can help a man": Ibid., 100.

409   "celibacy has been": Ibid., 98, 99.

409   "Just as when you're": Ibid., 212.

410   "try to formulate": Haddon, 183.

410   "will lead us away": Ibid., 185.

410   "by the activities": Ibid., 188.

410   "Despite the functioning": Cline, 22.

410 "women in particular": Ibid., 1.

411 "kinky but safe": Gordon, 123–26.

411 "leaves celibates vulnerable": Norris, 259.

411 "*in some way*": Cline, 111. Cline's emphasis.

411 "a source of power": Ibid., 254.

412 "for the fifty-fifty arrangement": *Ms.* 4, no. 4 (October 1975): 69.

412 "I began to have": Ibid., 71.

412 "Friendships, with males": Francine Gagnon, "Vivre en solo," *La Gazette des femmes* 10, no. 5 (January–February 1989): 21.

413 "insisting on your right": Shalit, 212.

413 "While our culture": Candace Watson, "Celibacy and Its Implications for Autonomy," *Hypatia* 2, no. 2 (summer 1987): 157.

413 "purposeful, self-chosen": Cline, 151.

414 "Masturbation . . . is primarily": Brown, 199.

414 Lesbian Celibacy versus Lesbian "Bed Death": The main sources for this section are Judith E. Beckett, "Recollections of a Sexual Life, Revelations of a Celibate Time," *Lesbian Ethics* 3, no. 1 (spring 1988); Carolyn Gage, "Pressure to Heal," *Lesbian Ethics* 4, no. 3 (spring 1992); and Marny Hall, "Unsexing the Couple," *Women and Therapy* 19, no. 3 (1996): 2–10.

414 For a plethora: Hall, 2. In 1983, a major study by Richard Blumstein and Pepper Schwartz, *American Couples,* "documented" lesbian bed death. For example, lesbians reportedly have less sex after two years than heterosexual couples after ten years.

414 "lesbians, diagnosed as": Hall, 3.

414 "We just want to help": Gage, 129.

415 "nonsexual pair-bonding": Hall, 7.

415 "The relentless quantification": Ibid., 3.

417 "implicit in the idea": Katie Roiphe, *Last Night in Paradise: Sex and Morals at Century's End* (Boston: Little, Brown, 1997), 120.

417 Deep in the Judeo-Christian: Albert R. Johnson and Jeff Stryker, eds., *The Social Impact of AIDS in the United States* (Washington, D.C.: National Academy Press, 1993), 129.

417 Sex and AIDS: The main sources for this section are Dennis Altman, *AIDS and the New Puritanism* (London: Pluto Press, 1986); Philip Berger, "Ten Years of AIDS: The GP's Perspective," *Canadian Medical Association Journal* 146, no. 3 (1992): 378–80; Mark J. Blechner, ed., *Hope and Mortality: Psychodynamic Approaches to AIDS and HIV* (London: Analytic Press, 1997); Rhoda Estep et al., "Sexual Behavior of Male Prostitutes," in J. Huber and Beth E. Schneider, eds., *The Social Context of AIDS* (London: Sage Publications, 1992); Harvey L. Gochros, "Risks of Abstinence: Sexual Decision-Making in the AIDS Era," in *National Association of Social Workers, Inc.* (1988): 254–55; Robin Gorna, *Vamps, Virgins and Victims: How Can Women Fight AIDS* (London: Cassell, 1996); Mary E. Guinan, "Virginity and Celibacy as Health Issues," *Journal of American Medical Women's Association* 43, no. 2 (1988): 60; Albert R. Johnson and Jeff Stryker, eds., *The Social Impact of AIDS in the United States* (Washington, D.C.: National Academy Press, 1993); Ernest H. Johnson, *Risky Sexual Behaviors Among African-Americans* (Westport: Praeger, 1993); Jeffrey A. Kelly, *Changing HIV Risk Behavior: Practical Strategies* (New York: Guildford Press, 1995); Robert E. Lee, *AIDS in America, Our Chances, Our Choices: A Survival Guide* (Troy, N.Y.: Whitston Publishing Co., 1987); Deborah Lupton, *Moral Threats and Dangerous Desires: AIDS in the News Media* (London: Taylor & Francis, 1994); L. Stewart Massad et al., "Sexual Behaviors of Heterosexual Women Infected with HIV," *Journal of Women's Health* 4, no. 6 (1995): 681–84; William H. Masters and Virginia E. Johnson, *Crisis: Heterosexual Behavior in the Age of AIDS* (London: Weidenfeld and Nicolson, 1988); Joseph G. Pastorek, "Sexually Transmitted Diseases: Should physicians more strongly advocate abstinence and monogamy?" *Postgraduate Medicine* 91, no. 5 (April 1992): 297–302; Ira Reiss, *Solving America's Sexual Crises* (Amherst:

Notes

Prometheus, 1997); Tim Rhodes, "Safer Sex in Practice," *The Practitioner* 232 (December 1988): 1339–40; Katie Roiphe, *Last Night in Paradise: Sex and Morals at Century's End* (Boston: Little, Brown, 1997); Steven Schwartzberg, *A Crisis of Meaning: How Gay Men Are Making Sense of AIDS* (New York: Oxford University Press, 1996); and James Monroe Smith, *AIDS and Society* (Upper Saddle River, N.J.: Prentice Hall, 1996). Statistical information comes from "Report on the Global HIV/AIDS Epidemic (Sub-Saharan Africa), 1998" (on-line: http://hivsite.ucsf. edu/social/un/2098.3ce2.htmlH5 [July 30, 1998]); "AIDS in Canada: Quarterly surveillance update: August 1997," prepared by the Laboratory Center for Disease Control, Health Protection Branch, Health Canada, *HIV/AIDS Surveillance Report* 9, no. 2 (1997): 40 (on-line: http://www.cdc.gov [July 30, 1998]); "Commentary on Surveillance of HIV Positive Test Reports and AIDS Diagnoses," April 1998, from Laboratory Center for Disease Control, Health Protection Branch, Health Canada, *HIV/AIDS Surveillance Report* 9, no. 2 (1997): 40; "AIDS in Africa: A Brief Overview of the African HIV/AIDS Epidemics," by the Hollandia Life Reassurance Company Ltd. (on-line: http://hivinsite.ucsf.edu/international/africa/-2098.34a3.html#regional [July 30, 1998]); "International Epidemiology of HIV/AIDS," by the AIDS Knowledge Base editors; *HIV/AIDS Surveillance Report,* from Atlanta Center for Disease Control and Prevention, 1997 (2) (on-line); and "CDC AIDS Data All States" and "Statistics—Cumulative Cases," *HIV/AIDS Surveillance Report* 9, no. 2 (1997): 40. The movie *Jeffrey* and various newspaper articles were also consulted.

418   "Take responsibility": Johnson quoted in *The Gazette* (Montreal), June 15, 1992.

418   "I honestly believed": Quoted in *Kansas City Star,* February 16, 1996.

419   In a series of novels: I have read *How Town, Goldenboy, The Little Death,* and *The Death of Friends.*

420   "I'd rather be dead": Masters and Johnson, 127.

420   "the sexual revolution": Ibid., 141.

420   "the true cure": *The Winnipeg Free Press,* November 9, 1991.

420   "Condoms will help": *The Toronto Star,* May 14, 1987.

420   "condoms *break.*": Roiphe, 180.

421   "We should not forget": Kelly, 112.

421   Women are struck: HIV transmission begins in the early teens and peaks before age twenty-five. Thirty percent of breast-fed babies contract HIV from infected mothers.

422   "We need to teach": *Calgary Herald,* December 1, 1991.

422   When celibacy is expected: One 1992 study showed that 68 percent of men with celibate, lactating wives sought sex elsewhere. Ng'wshemi et al., *HIV Prevention and AIDS Care in Africa* (Netherlands: Royal Tropical Institute, 1997), 120.

423   "bombarded with terrifying": Edmond Kizito and Margaretta Gacheruwa, "Scared Celibate," *World Press Review,* September 1993, 46.

423   American AIDS statistics: The figures for reported AIDS cases to date are 288,541 whites, 230,029 blacks, 115,354 Hispanics, with other races totaling less than 7,000. Given the ratio of blacks and Hispanics to whites in the USA, these rates are staggeringly high.

423   "intellectual seductress": Sonja Kindley, "Emotional Promiscuity," *Elle,* March 1996, 256.

424   Some investigations have: The chances of contracting HIV from unprotected anal sex with an infected partner are one in fifty to a hundred, whereas unprotected vaginal sex carries a one in five hundred risk for a woman, one in seven hundred risk for a man. Gochros, 40.

INDEX

Index

Index

Index

Capellanus, Andreas, 364
Caracalla, Emperor of Rome, 42
Caribou Inuit, 184–85
Carlisle, Countess of, 304
Carpenter, Karen, 21
Carroll, Lewis, 16, 21, 341–42, 344
Carruthers, Bob, 212
Carson, Rachel, 350–51
Carthage, celibacy oath in (401), 110
Casanova, Giovanni, 334
Cassian, John, 85, 88
Castissima (Emerald), 75–78, 81
castrati, 15, 20, 317, 332–35
castration, 15, 20, 35, 63, 80, 99, 103, 156, 317–37
  description of, 321, 325, 329–30, 333
  lynching and, 282, 318
  to punish offenders, 335–37
  for violating nuns, 144, 145
  see also eunuchs
Cather, Willa, 349
Catherine of Alexandria, Saint, 231–32, 235
Catherine of Aragon, 240
Catherine of Siena, Saint, 18, 60, 119, 121–27, 133
  Kateri compared with, 129, 132, 133
  power and influence of, 132, 135
Catholic Church, *see* Roman Catholic Church
Catholics of Vision, 388
celibacy:
  defined, 15, 16–17
  see also specific topics
"Celibacy, Sexuality, and the Transformation of Gender into Nationalism in North India" (Alter), 227–28
cenobites, 100
Chamberlain, Joseph, 253
Changing HIV Risk Behavior (Kelly), 421
Charlemagne, 104
Charles II, King of England, 269
Charles VII, King of France, 231–32
chastity:
  defined, 17
  male, 15, 18, 296, 297
  see also virginity, virgins
chastity belts, 279, 282–85
Chaucer, Geoffrey, 363, 364
Cher, 399–400
Cherokees, 209, 212–14
Chestnut, Mary Boykin, 280
Cheyenne:
  chastity belts of, 279, 283, 284–85

male chastity and, 285
  postpartum abstinence of, 296, 297
Chih-Hsien, 178
childbirth, 26, 50, 60, 62, 96, 125
  emancipation from, 17, 19, 95, 134, 150
children:
  adoptive, 207
  crowded marriages and, 311–12
  death of, 149, 150, 254, 297
  forced into convents, 139, 140–41, 144–45
  Motherhood movement and, 254–55
  of priests and bishops, 107–10, 112, 113, 387
  sex observed by, 148
  of Shakers, 151, 153, 154
China, 92, 198
  Buddhism in, 177–78, 180
  eugenics in, 337
  eunuchs in, 110, 318, 320–25, 328
  foot-binding in, 260
  involuntary celibacy in, 20, 294, 303, 309–12
  Maoist, 20
  "one child per family" policy in, 20, 293–94
  skewed sex ratio in, 20, 294, 303, 312
  undervaluation of women in, 20, 257, 294
  virgins vs. disgraced maidens in, 259–60
Ching Shih Fang, 323
Chinn, Julia, 280
Cholenec, Father, 130, 132
Christian Brothers, 15
Christianitas, 100, 105
Christianity, Christians, 17–18, 21, 46–97
  Buddhism compared with, 163–64, 177
  clerical celibacy and, *see* clerical celibacy, Christian
  Desert Fathers and, 83–88, 100, 107
  Desert Mothers and, 17–18, 90–97
  early, 47–97, 313
  emancipation of women in, 17–18, 60–61, 72–76, 81, 91–96, 115–20, 126, 134–35, 150, 153, 163
  Encratites and, 61–62, 63
  Essene asceticism compared with, 46, 49, 54
  Gandhi influenced by, 222
  Gnosticism and, 61–64
  Greco-Roman deities and, 23
  Hinduism compared with, 163, 165–66, 168, 169, 172, 173, 313

Index

Index

Heider, Karl, 296
Helen (grandmother of Constantina), 68
Helen of Troy, 29
Helia, legend of, 73–76, 88, 109
Héloise, 103
Henry I, King of England, 104
Henry IV, King of Germany, 104
Henry VIII, King of England, 239–42, 245
Henry of York, Archbishop, 144, 145
Hephaestus (Vulcan), 24, 25
Hera (Juno), 24, 27, 34
Herbert, John, 305
Hermes (Mercury), 23–24
Herodotus, 263
Hestia (Vesta), 15–16, 23, 24, 27–28, 30
   virgins of, *see* vestal virgins
Heywood, Ezra, 301
Hidden Face of Eve, The (El Saadawi), 262
hierodules, 38
hijras, 20, 329–31
Hildegard of Bingen, 127–28, 135
Hinduism, 17, 20–21, 107, 163–74, 179
   Brahma Kumaris in, 164, 171–74
   Buddhism compared with, 175
   celibacy in stages in, 165–69; *see also* brahmacharya
   empowerment of women in, 163–64
   Jainism compared with, 180
   misogyny in, 163, 164, 170–71
   Shiva in, 164–65, 167
   widows and, 20–21, 250, 304, 313–15, 427
Hippocrates, 197–200
Hippolytus, 26, 30–32
Hippolytus (Euripides), 26, 30–32
Hoddle, Glenn, 215
Hoge, Dean R., 385
Holmes, Oliver Wendell, 347, 348
Holy Eucharist, 56, 62, 72, 137–38
Holy Spirit, 47, 56, 57, 61, 62
Homer, 27
homosexuality, 16, 21, 44, 87, 339–41
   AIDS and, 415–18, 420–21, 424
   castration and, 325, 329, 331, 334, 336
   of Catholic priests, 381, 388
   masturbation as cause of, 204
   of monks, 103
   in prisons, 305–7
   sports celibacy and, 210, 211
   "honor killings," 19, 261–62
Hopkins, Jane Ellice, 274–75

Hosmer, Harriet, 348
Hot Press, 405
Howard, Catherine, 240
Howard, Marion, 403
Hsi, Empress Dowager of China, 323
Hsui-Chen, Mrs., 290–91
Hudson, Rock, 418
Hundred Years' War, 231–35
hymen, and proof of virginity, 58, 262–64, 278, 356–57

Igjugarjuk, 184–85
Ikkos of Tarentum, 209, 210
Iltani, Princess, 190, 191
Immaculate Conception, 59
impotence, 21, 147, 197, 312, 353–61
   anorexia and, 353, 359–61
   hijras and, 329, 330
   testing for, 355–57
   vaginismus and, 353, 357–58
Incas, *acllas* of, 19, 43, 187–90
India, 19
   Buddhism in, 174–77, 179–80
   hijras in, 20, 329–31
   independence struggle in, 222, 225–26
   Jainism in, 180
   wrestlers in, 197, 209, 217–19
   see also Hinduism
Indonesia:
   clerical celibacy in, 379
   postpartum abstinence in, 296
infibulation (pharaonic circumcision), 285
Innocent VIII, Pope, 113
Inquisition, 233–35
Institute of the Blessed Virgin Mary, 120
Institution for the Care of Sick Gentle-women, 246
Interview, 399
Intimate Relations (Kakar), 223
Inti the Sun God, 188
involuntary celibacy, 303–13
   in crowded marriages, 311–12
   due to skewed gender ratios, 312–13
   in Mao's Cultural Revolution, 309–11
   in prisons, 305–7
   of St. Petersburg teachers, 307–9
Iphigenia, 27
Iroquois, 18, 128–33
Irving, John, 372–73
Isaiah, 48, 57
Isis, cult of, 36–37
Islam, *see* Muslims, Islam
Israel, honor killing in, 261

Index

Index

Index